"This is just great writing. Duncan really knows how to assemble a compelling story, and with Lafayette he has an amazing subject with which to work. Restores some of the well-deserved luster to the Frenchman's historical reputation."

—Dan Carlin, host of *Hardcore History*

"All listeners of *The History of Rome* and *Revolutions*—as well as readers of *The Storm Before the Storm*—know the joy of Mike Duncan guiding them through epic, operatic moments in Western history. Now Duncan has zeroed in on his perfect subject, a towering figure through whom Duncan can explore and even upend the birth of political liberalism. Duncan has reintroduced the Marquis de Lafayette for a whole new generation, bringing him to life with all his passions, contradictions, and hypocrisies. Never mind the Broadway musicals, here's the *Hero of Two Worlds*."

—Spencer Ackerman, Pulitzer Prize–winning journalist
and author of *Reign of Terror: How The 9/11 Era
Destabilized America and Produced Trump*

"Comprehensive and accessible....Duncan marshals a wealth of information into a crisp and readable narrative. This sympathetic portrait illuminates the complexities of Lafayette and his revolutionary era."

—*Publishers Weekly*

"Mike Duncan's ability to weave a rich and compelling story is on full display in *Hero of Two Worlds*. He takes the reader on a gripping roller-coaster ride that follows the Marquis de Lafayette's fortunes through decades of victory, defeat, and revolution on two continents....Duncan has an exceptional eye for both human potential and human fallibility, grasping the qualities that make figures like Lafayette real, three-dimensional people, simultaneously victims of circumstance and active participants driving forward the course of history. *Hero of Two Worlds* is biography and narrative at its best, an informative page-turner crafted by a master of historical storytelling."

—Patrick Wyman, creator of *Tides of History*
and author of *The Verge: Reformation, Renaissance,
and Forty Years that Shook the World*

"I first learned of Mike Duncan's work when a prominent politician told me he'd been addicted to his podcast on the French Revolution and found it startlingly relevant in 2021. Duncan's work is a reminder that history can also be a gripping yarn full of compelling characters, and in *Hero of Two Worlds* he brings alive one of the great characters of American history."

—Ben Smith, *New York Times* columnist

"Mike Duncan has dug deep into the world of revolutions, and the richness of detail in this book is beguiling. But Mike's superpower is his storytelling skill. *Hero of Two Worlds* hooks you from page one with humor, a sly perspective, and a page-turning narrative drive worthy of a life like Lafayette's."

—Rian Johnson, award-winning filmmaker

"Mike Duncan's excellent, well-researched book portrays Lafayette's extraordinary life as a fascinating, transatlantic drama with three great revolutions and transitional interludes that carry the reader through seven explosive decades of historical change. The hero of this drama plays starring public roles in the American Revolution and the French Revolutions of 1789 and 1830. But Duncan weaves the people, conflicts, and legacies of these vast public events into stories about a personal life that was always entangled with complex family networks and multi-generational friendships as well as a loving marriage and emotionally charged relationships with other women."

—Lloyd Kramer, University of North Carolina,
Chapel Hill, and author of *Lafayette in Two Worlds:
Public Cultures and Personal Identities in an Age of Revolutions*

HERO OF
TWO WORLDS

The Marquis de Lafayette
in the Age *of* Revolution

Mike Duncan

PUBLICAFFAIRS
NEW YORK

PublicAffairs
Hachette Book Group
1290 Avenue of the Americas, New York, NY 10104
www.publicaffairsbooks.com
@Public_Affairs

Printed in the United States of America
First Edition: August 2021

Published by PublicAffairs, an imprint of Perseus Books, LLC, a subsidiary of Hachette Book Group, Inc. The PublicAffairs name and logo is a trademark of the Hachette Book Group.

The publisher is not responsible for websites (or their content) that are not owned by the publisher.

Print book interior design by Linda Mark.

Library of Congress Cataloging-in-Publication Data
Names: Duncan, Mike, 1980– author.
Title: Hero of two worlds : the Marquis de Lafayette in the Age of Revolution / Mike Duncan.
Description: First edition. | New York : PublicAffairs, 2021. | Includes bibliographical references and index.
Identifiers: LCCN 2021005452 | ISBN 9781541730335 (hardcover) | ISBN 9781541730328 (ebook)
Subjects: LCSH: Lafayette, Marie Joseph Paul Yves Roch Gilbert Du Motier, marquis de, 1757–1834. | Generals—France—Biography. | Generals—United States—Biography. | Statesmen—France—Biography. | France. Armée—Biography. | United States—History—Revolution, 1775–1783—Biography. | United States—History—Revolution, 1775–1783—Participation, French. | France—History—Revolution, 1789–1799.
Classification: LCC E207.L2 D86 2021 | DDC 355.0092 [B]—dc23
LC record available at https://lccn.loc.gov/2021005452

ISBNs: 978-1-5417-3033-5 (hardcover), 978-1-5417-3032-8 (ebook)

LSC-C

Printing 3, 2021

For Mom and Dad,
who made everything possible

CONTENTS

PART I

CUR NON

CHAPTER ONE

THE ORPHAN MARQUIS

[1757–1772]

ESTLED IN THE HILLY COUNTRY OF PROVINCIAL AUVERGNE
sat an unremarkable château in the unremarkable village of
Chavaniac. Then, as now, Auvergne was rustic and sparsely
populated—far from the modern world. It was beautiful and natural,
with huge outcroppings of volcanic rock erupting from the rich soil.
Pastures, fields, and ancient primordial forests sprawled in all directions. Isolated in the vast empty space of south central France, Chavaniac was little more than a few dozen poor houses huddled together
around the château for protection.

Elsewhere in the Kingdom of France, noble families embraced the
Renaissance, the scientific revolution, and the Enlightenment. They re-
built their homes in the latest and most expensive styles. But the château
in Chavaniac was a product of its environment—simple and sturdy, be-
reft of adornment, splendor, or ornamentation. There was no need to
show off, for there was no one to show off to.

In the late summer of 1757, Château de Chavaniac was the home of
Gilbert du Motier, the marquis de Lafayette. The Lafayettes claimed an
ancient noble lineage stretching back to the year 1000, which included
a *maréchal de France* who fought alongside Joan of Arc; a knight who
participated in the Crusades; and most recently, the celebrated novelist

3

Madame de Lafayette. But despite these ancient claims, the Motier branch of the family descended from the younger sons of younger sons. It was only thanks to a cascade of sonless deaths in the main branch of the family a century earlier that the title "marquis de Lafayette" landed on the shoulders of their obscure Motier cousins.

Gilbert du Motier married up in the world. His wife, Julie de La Rivière, now styled the marquise de Lafayette, came from a family of Breton nobles who traced their lineage to the great medieval king Louis IX. Wealthier and more respectable than the Lafayettes, the Rivières made their home in the center of Paris rather the peripheral outskirts of the kingdom. Julie's grandfather was a legendary colonel once awarded the Cross of St. Louis, and who remained a fixture of the French military establishment. Her father, the comte de La Rivière, owned lucrative estates in Brittany. Rare among his noble brethren, he possessed a head for business and parlayed shrewd investments and modern agricultural techniques into an enviable fortune.

Gilbert and Julie married in May 1754. In the world of the French nobility, marriage was about dynastic alliances and the consolidation of property. Love was irrelevant. By these standards, their union was a huge success for both families. As an aspiring young soldier, Gilbert's new connection to the Rivières promised to advance to his career. In exchange, they gave their daughter's hand to a poor rustic noble willing to accept a modest dowry that wouldn't strain the family fortune. It was only by happy accident the newlyweds discovered they actually liked each other. Julie didn't even mind relocating from the heart of Paris to the rugged pastures and hills of Auvergne.

Thanks to his entrance into the Rivière family orbit, Gilbert du Motier secured a commission as a colonel on the eve of yet another European war of dynastic ambition. In the history books, this latest round of royal bickering and imperial maneuvering is called the Seven Years' War. It started in 1756 as a limited contest in central Europe between Prussia and Austria, but soon drew in all the great European powers and spread across the world from India to the Americas. After receiving orders to join his regiment along the Rhine river, Colonel Gilbert du Motier left Julie in the company of his widowed mother, Marie-Catherine de Chavaniac, his unmarried sister Madeleine, and a small host of servants and staff. Emerging from this little pocket of quiet timeless peace, he rode off to join the destructive thunder of a modern global war.

Colonel Lafayette remained stationed along the Rhine as Julie gave birth to the couple's first child on September 6, 1757. The next day, a priest baptized the baby boy Marie-Joseph Paul Yves Roch Gilbert du Motier. Despite this mouthful of an official title, the boy would be called Gilbert, like his father. Acutely aware his parents saddled him with an absurd procession of names, Lafayette later said, "I was baptized like a Spaniard. But it was not my fault. And without pretending to deny myself the protection of Marie, Paul, Joseph, Roch, and Yves, I more often called upon Saint Gilbert."[1] Which is to say he relied on himself.

⬦

AT THE TIME of little Gilbert's birth, the Kingdom of France was divided into three social and legal "estates." The First Estate comprised the clergy. The Second Estate comprised the nobility. And the Third Estate comprised . . . everyone else. The first two privileged estates numbered perhaps 5 percent of the population and enjoyed all the wealth, privileges, and power the kingdom had to offer. Of them little was asked and much was given. The Third Estate accounted for the remaining 95 percent of the population. Of them much was asked and little was given.

Gilbert was born into the Second Estate—the nobility. He joined the tiny elite of ducs, comtes, vicomtes, and marquises who ruled the kingdom and claimed a litany of special privileges, exemptions, powers, and responsibilities carried over from the ancient days of feudal society. Young Gilbert was destined to be the noble lord of Chavaniac—where the common peasants who lived around his family estates were obligated to pay certain rents and taxes while displaying social and legal subservience. The Lafayettes enjoyed a local reputation as honest and fair masters. But they were still masters, and they never failed to collect what their vassals owed.

Not all nobles were cut from the same cloth, and the Second Estate itself contained important legal, social, and economic stratifications. As the nobility originally derived from the warrior knights who supported the kings of medieval France, families who traced their lineage back to those armor-clad retainers were called the *noblesse d'épée*—the sword nobles. But in recent years, a new breed of noble rose up alongside them: the *noblesse de robe*, or robe nobles. Chronically short of cash, the Crown sold offices and titles to rich members of the Third Estate who ambitiously hoped to transcend their common origins and enjoy the privileges of nobility, particularly exemption from taxes. A one-time payment to the cash-starved Crown secured such titles and privileges. The old sword nobility scorned this upstart class of robe nobles. They were especially bitter because the economic fortunes of many of the sword nobles declined as those of the robe nobles improved. The sword nobility believed they deserved their rank and status because their ancestors once stood courageously by the king at Agincourt and Castillon, not because their father recently made a fortune selling barrels of salted fish.

At the very apex of French society were those who boasted ancient titles and still retained vast personal wealth. The kings of France called upon this innermost elite to make their homes at Versailles, where they were systematically domesticated, tamed, and transformed from independent lords of the realm into pampered courtiers maneuvering for the right to hand the king his stockings or watch him eat dinner. There was very little chance baby Gilbert would ever lay eyes on this world. The Lafayettes were poor provincial sword nobles. Their job was to make sons to inherit their modest family title, then go die in service to the king. This was the fate of many Lafayettes. It would be the fate of Lafayette's father. It was likely the fate Lafayette expected for himself.

⚏

THE NEXT TWO years passed happy and contented. Julie and baby Gilbert lived at Chavaniac under the care of the elderly Madame Chavaniac. Colonel Lafayette remained tied to his regiment on the frontier, only making brief visits home. There was little action on the front lines, though, and he wrote home in July 1759, "We are always in the greatest tranquility, I send this to you with as much pleasure as in the hope of calming your worries. The enemies are in the same position, and we in our unassailable camp. . . . As we are not in any of the sieges to be made, you can, my dear mother, be in the greatest security on my account." He closed with expressions of tender affection for his wife and his sister, but he reserved the final line at the bottom of the letter for his only child: "I kiss my son."[2] This was the last letter he ever wrote home.

After a long period of inactivity, the French army finally launched an offensive at the end of month. This advance swept Colonel Lafayette into the thick of the Battle of Minden, one of the largest battles of the war. On August 1, 1759, Colonel Lafayette's commander brazenly advanced onto an exposed ridge in an apparent show of reckless bravado. British artillery sighted this surprisingly exposed French regiment and pummeled it with shells. The reckless commander was killed immediately. Colonel Lafayette briefly took his place, before a shell blew him to pieces. He was just twenty-seven years old.

An older Lafayette noted ruefully his father's death fit into a long Lafayette family tradition. Historically the family produced "such a large proportion of people killed on the battlefields, from father to son, that it had become a kind of proverb in our province."[3] Colonel Lafayette left behind a young widow and a two-year-old son who now bore the auspicious and possibly cursed title "marquis de Lafayette."

Julie, pregnant with the couple's second child, was grief-stricken. She returned to live with her own family in Paris, where she would give birth to a baby girl a few months later. She left little Gilbert behind under the care of his grandmother Madame Chavaniac. Julie leaving her young child was no great scandal. It was common enough for tutors, nurses, or older relatives to raise the children of the aristocracy. Lafayette's contemporary Talleyrand, who would serve as foreign minister to multiple French governments, said in his own memoirs he did not enjoy "the sweetness of being under [my] parents' roof" for a single week of his childhood.[4]

Despite a dead father and an absent mother, little Gilbert enjoyed a happy childhood. As the little lord of Chavaniac, he stood at the exuberant center of a warm circle of caregivers. His grandmother was revered locally for her prudence, generosity, and judgment. Madame Chavaniac was also a canny estate manager who carefully supervised her grandson's inheritance. His dead father's two sisters also joined the household: Aunt Madeleine, who never married, and Aunt Charlotte, who was herself recently widowed. Charlotte came bearing a daughter, Marie, who was just a few years older than Gilbert. Marie became a beloved surrogate sister, for whom Lafayette bore nostalgic affection his entire life, saying, "Never did brother and sister love each other more tenaciously."[5] These women ran the household and watched over the little lord as he romped through the fields, hills, and forests surrounding Chavaniac.

Shortly after the death of his father, two more deaths shaped the course of the little lord's young life. In April 1760, his younger sister Marie-Louise Jacqueline died after just three months of life. Gilbert would forever after remain an only child—and thus the sole receptacle of all the family's titles, fortunes, and expectations. The following year his maternal uncle died. As the only heir to the Rivière fortune, his death meant Julie's three-year-old son Gilbert was now destined to inherit property and riches dwarfing the rustic Lafayette estates—however well they were managed by Madame Chavaniac. The little marquis now represented the future of the Rivières as much as the Lafayettes.

When Gilbert turned seven, Madame Chavaniac hired a young local priest, Abbé Fayon, to serve as a live-in tutor. Fayon taught young Gilbert reading, writing, and math. He introduced classics like *The Iliad*, *The Odyssey*, and Julius Caesar's *Commentaries on the Gallic War*, which was the story of the conquest of Lafayette's own homeland. The province of Auvergne derived its named from the Arverni, an ancient Gallic tribe that produced Vercingetorix, the last and greatest leader of the Gallic resistance to the Roman conquest. The Battle of Gergovia, one of Caesar's rare defeats in the war, occurred practically in Lafayette's backyard. The boy thrilled with these tales of daring, adventure, courage, rebellion, and glory. He said later, "I can recall no time in my life when I did not love stories of glorious deeds, or have dreams of traveling the world in search of fame."[6]

Under the guidance of Abbé Fayon, Gilbert blossomed. An older cousin, the marquis de Bouillé, visited Chavaniac and found the young lord of the house "singularly well-informed for his age . . . remarkable for his thinking, his wisdom, his discretion, his self-control, and his powers of judgement." But he also said he detected in the boy "the seed of self-esteem and even ambition."[7] In that time and place, this was not meant as a compliment, but a warning.

No biographer can resist illustrating Lafayette's emerging character with the story of the Beast of Gévaudan—especially as it is a story Lafayette himself used to illustrate such points. In the late 1760s, local shepherds attributed a string of mysterious attacks on their livestock to a half-mythical beast living in the dark forests. The story of the beast spread, drawing the best hunters in France hoping to win fame by killing the monster. Eight-year-old Gilbert convinced himself that as a local lord, he bore a special responsibility to find and kill the creature. But despite bold marches through the forest, he found no trace of the beast.

This vignette of boldly adventurous youth also shines a light on another side of Lafayette's personality. One day he was mortified by a notice he read in the newspaper. He later wrote, "I was furious that, by an error in name, they gave mine to another man who was said to have been unable to kill the beast because he was afraid."[8] Intuitively aware of the importance of projecting a heroic public image, this eight-year-old boy went so far as to write an angry letter to the journalist demanding a correction. His guardians possessed the good sense not to send it.

⚜

AFTER GILBERT TURNED ten, Julie called him to Paris. The change could not have been more drastic. Chavaniac was an isolated rural hamlet. Paris was one of the largest cities in the world. Gilbert moved from a tiny rural village to a sprawling world capital. Chavaniac was frozen in timeless feudal tradition. Paris was at the cutting edge of art, science, literature, architecture, and philosophy. The natural serenity of the forests, hills, and pastures were replaced by the cacophonous bustle of human civilization: porters, merchants, travelers, artisans, bankers, aristocrats, laborers, and students all sharing the same crowded, muddy, and noisy streets. In Chavaniac, the Lafayette family governed a small collection of peasants—humble and impoverished people led by humble and impoverished nobles. In Paris, the richest aristocrats in France indulged their pretensions to rule the whole world.

After a two-week carriage ride across bumpy roads, Gilbert entered Paris and joined his mother in family apartments at the Luxembourg

Palace, a sparkling and ornate monument to the high Renaissance surrounded by meticulously cultivated gardens. Here, the Rivière family
rented a cluster of apartments in one of the most opulent buildings
in the world. He was very far from the simple and sturdy Château de
Chavaniac.

For Gilbert, the move to Paris in 1768 also meant leaving behind
a world where he was the star of the show—where even the village
elders doffed their caps—to enter a world where he was a nobody. Just
some boy. Adults ignored him. Other children gawked at his provincial
accent and clumsy manners. But over time, Julie helped him adapt to
this new environment, and after years apart, they forged a special bond
as she guided him through this bizarre new world.

Though Abbé Fayon escorted Gilbert to Paris, the boy needed more
rigorous and formal education to prepare him for life as a Parisian noble.
Gilbert's grandfather enrolled him at the Collège du Plessis, a secondary school operating alongside the Sorbonne since 1322. His classmates
did not come from the highest rungs of the French nobility—those
types were all at Versailles. Gilbert's classmates were, instead, sword
nobles headed for a career in the military; recently elevated robe nobles
bound to become lawyers, civil servants, or clergymen; or particularly
bright young boys from the Third Estate attending school on scholar-
ship. This last group produced many future revolutionaries, including
Maximilien Robespierre and Camille Desmoulins, who were just a few
years younger than Lafayette and attended the Lycée Louis-le-Grand
around the corner.

The curriculum of these schools later became infamous for the
contradiction of ideals and reality planted in the generation raised in
the 1760s and 1770s—the generation who would tear down the world
they inherited in the 1780s and 1790s. On top of standard courses in
grammar, rhetoric, and mathematics, students learned the latest in natural science and philosophy. They read Newton, Voltaire, and Montesquieu, drinking from intellectual waters laced with science, skepticism,
and rational idealism. But the core of the destabilizing contradiction
was the heavy emphasis on the classics: Cicero, Virgil, Livy, Polybius,
and above all Plutarch's moralizing biographies of famous Greeks and
Romans.

It was not lost on observers, then or now, how crazy it was for this most absolutist of monarchies to require an entire generation of students to steep themselves in the literary, moral, and political virtues of the ancient heroes of Athenian democracy and the Roman Republic. Louis-Sébastien Mercier, a famous writer and dramatist slightly older than Lafayette, later wrote of his own education, "The name of Rome was the first to strike my ear. . . . The names Brutus, and Cato and Scipio pursued me in my sleep, the familiar epistles of Cicero are stuck in my memory."[9] He said when he read Livy, "I was a republican among republicans."[10] He further noted the difficulty of readjusting from a fantasy life as a citizen of republican Rome to the reality of being a subject in an absolute monarchy.

Others were less willing to make this readjustment. Desmoulins later wrote, "The first Republicans who appeared in 1789 were young people, who, fed on the reading of Cicero in the colleges, were passionate about freedom. We were raised in the schools of Rome and Athens and in the pride of the republic."[11] He thought the government insane for believing they could exalt the old Romans without naturally abhorring "the man-eaters of Versailles," or that young men like himself could "admire the past without condemning the present."[12] And condemn it they would.

Gilbert staked out his own unique position in this tense frontier between ancient freedom and modern oppression. Unlike his friends, who worshipped Cato, Brutus, and Cicero, Lafayette preferred to idolize the free, independent, and martyred glory of his ancient Gallic ancestor Vercingetorix. Vercingetorix was a great leader who lived and died fighting for liberty *from* the Romans his classmates worshipped. Lafayette even preferred the independent Gauls to their Frankish successors who founded what became the Kingdom of France: "I will not tell you if I am Gaul or Frank," he said. "I hope to be Gaul . . . I prefer Vercingétorix defending our mountains than Clovis and his successors."[13]

This early attachment to the spirit of freedom is further illustrated in a school assignment that gives us, like the Beast of Gévaudan, another animal avatar through which the young marquis channeled his identity. "I was given one task," he later wrote, "of composing the description of a perfect horse." But instead of following his classmates by highlighting ready obedience or an eagerness to please, Lafayette said,

"I painted this perfect horse throwing, on the main street, its rider on the ground."[14] Lafayette believed a truly perfect horse would live free of the whips and whims of mankind.

⚓

GILBERT'S HAPPY CHILDHOOD came to a startling and tragic end in the spring of 1770 when his mother came down with a sudden illness. She was young and healthy, however, so at first her illness was merely worrisome, not cataclysmic. After a week, her health improved, but without warning she took a sharp turn for the worse. On April 3, 1770, Julie de La Rivière de Lafayette died at the age of just thirty-two.

Twelve-year-old Gilbert was shattered. He was unmoored, left emotionally and psychologically alone in the world. His love for his mother, and hers for him, had become a solid foundation of his life. In our contemporary age of advanced medicine, there reigns a persistent myth that people in the past must have somehow been emotionally tougher and harder than us. More distant from each other. How else can one explain living in a world filled with so much death? But the truth is they were not harder and more distant. They loved each other and were loved by each other. The death of a small child was a deep tragedy. The sorrow, tears, grief, and rage were real. When a twelve-year-old boy is told his mother has died, the wretchedness of lonely depression haunts him no less in the eighteenth century than in the twenty-first century. Just a few weeks later, the family tragedy was compounded by the sudden death of his grandfather—widely considered the result of heartbreak over the death of his beloved daughter Julie.

After the death of his mother, loving guardians no longer protected Gilbert. Now detached agents supervised his development. To this new coterie of minders, he was not Gilbert, a twelve-year-old boy with hopes and dreams and feelings, but the marquis de Lafayette, a young nobleman with lands and estates to manage. And there were *lots* of lands and estates to manage. He inherited a fortune. After merging the Lafayette property and the Rivière property, the ledgers now bearing Lafayette's name showed the young marquis to be one of the richest people in the kingdom. He ultimately inherited land generating 100,000 *livres* annually, in an age where common laborers might make 1,000 livres over the course of their entire lives. In his grief, Gilbert hardly registered this increase in fortune. He said others were more impressed with the revelation than he was, while he "only thought of regretting my mother."[15]

This windfall of riches changed his life in ways he could not expect or anticipate. For example, it immediately made him one of the most eligible bachelors in France. Word circulated through society the young marquis de Lafayette just inherited a massive portfolio of estates. As both an orphan and an only child, the boy would not have to split his fortune with anyone. He was a rare unicorn and attracted suitors from the best noble families in the kingdom. Among the first to come calling were representatives from the *very best* noble family: the Noailles.

The Noailles were the highest of the high nobility, as ancient as they were rich. When John Adams arrived in Paris a few years later, he wrote, "I was very inquisitive concerning this great family of Noailles, and I was told by some of the most intelligent men in France . . . that there were no less than six marshals of France of this family; that they held so many offices, under the King, that they received eighteen millions of livres annually . . . this family was in short become more powerful than the house of Bourbon."[16] The most important family in France now aimed to make this orphan marquis from the provinces one of their own.

⛬

JEAN DE NOAILLES, duc d'Ayen, was the quintessential enlightened courtier. He was the eldest son of the aging duc de Noailles, the grand patriarch of the Noailles clan. Plump, intelligent, and confident, the duc d'Ayen was a patron of the arts, literature, and culture. He was also an amateur scientist who used every string, lever, and favor at his disposal to secure an appointment to the famous Académie de science. In those chambers he was respected for diligently respecting the scientific method. In the high society of Paris and Versailles, he was praised for his wit and casual ease in the grandest of settings.

But d'Ayen had a problem. His marriage to Henriette d'Aguesseau, now styled the duchesse d'Ayen, produced a happy brood of five young girls. But in patriarchal France, the social and legal ramifications posed by this happy brood were enormous. No sons meant an uncertain future for the great House of Noailles. On a strictly financial level, it meant carving out money and estates to pay the expected dowries of each of his five daughters. A practical man, and not one to avoid unpleasant puzzles, d'Ayen started hunting for husbands even before his eldest daughters reached puberty. For Louise, the oldest, a match had long since been made to her cousin Louis, who already bore the title vicomte de Noailles. This positioned the young man to play the role a natural son would have otherwise played. And as he already bore the name Noailles, the dynastic sleight-of-hand would hardly register in the all-important tables of genealogical lineage.

The problem of family inheritance settled, d'Ayen kept his ears open for his second daughter, Marie Adrienne Françoise—known to all as Adrienne. She was pretty and intelligent and gracefully balanced sincere innocence with honest practicality. She was just twelve years old in 1772 when tales of an obscure provincial orphan who inherited a fortune reached her father's ears. The marquis de Lafayette was perfect. His vast independent wealth meant the Noailles could lowball the dowry and, in lieu of estates, offer otherwise unattainable opportunities that came with marrying into such a great family. Even more enticing for d'Ayen was the absence of Lafayette's mother, father, and both grandfathers. If the young marquis de Lafayette married into the Noailles family, they could absorb him completely. D'Ayen would not have to bid farewell to a daughter, but instead welcome a new son. It was almost too good to be true.

The biggest obstacle to the union was his wife, the duchesse d'Ayen. A religiously devout, strong-willed woman, who preferred a quiet life at home to the busy life at court, she objected to the proposed marriage. Not because Lafayette was unsuitable, but because Adrienne was too young. Even in these days of arranged dynastic marriages, the typical bride was in her late teens or early twenties. Adrienne was closer to ten than she was to twenty. For months, the duchesse refused all the duc's arguments and protests. Adrienne and her sisters noticed their parents fighting, and it was not until much later Adrienne realized she herself was the cause of it. But Lafayette was ultimately too good an opportunity to pass up. After a few months, the duchesse relented—but only after it was agreed the engagement would last for two years *and* be kept a secret from both Lafayette and Adrienne.

It was thus in a state of complete ignorance Lafayette learned from his guardians the Noailles family had taken a benevolent interest in him and he was to go live at one of their homes in Versailles. It was also in a state of complete ignorance he made the acquaintance of his future wife. He found she possessed a loving disposition instilled in her by her mother. But the duchesse also raised her daughters to think for themselves. Adrienne did not have a hostile personality, but she didn't have a docile personality either. She quickly took a compassionate interest in this tragic boy come into the family's care. Adrienne later said her concern for this strange boy quickly turned from affection to love. It would take longer for Lafayette to see in her what she saw in him.

⁂

Most of life is out of our hands. Both the road ahead and the road behind set by accident, fate, or luck. Lafayette's ancestors elevated themselves to noble status in the deep mists of the medieval past. This allowed a boy born eight hundred years later to have opportunities, privileges, and comforts denied his closest neighbors, those peasants over whom he legally reigned thanks to a prevailing social ideology planted deep in the minds of everyone: rich and poor, strong and weak, old and young, man and women, lord and commoner, king and subject. In all cases, the former claimed superiority over the latter. Lafayette was blessed with a privileged place in this society thanks only to the fact of his birth.

But though he was a rich nobleman in a world built for rich noblemen, Lafayette was still a powerless object of forces beyond his control. He had no say in anything happening around him. He could not stop the deaths of his mother, father, aunts, uncles, or grandparents. Strange adults arranged a marriage they did not tell him about. He was sent off to live in the home of a family he did not know. By any objective measure, Lafayette's transfer to the Noailles family was a social promotion. But these arbitrary forces so generously shaping his material, social, and personal fortunes left him isolated and lonely. As all teenagers can and must do, Lafayette questioned his own lack of agency. When he realized the duc d'Ayen aimed to fit him for an uncomfortable saddle, Lafayette remembered his vision of the perfect horse, and would throw off his rider.

CHAPTER TWO

A BIRD IN A GILDED CAGE

[1773–1776]

I N FEBRUARY 1773, THE MARQUIS DE LAFAYETTE MOVED INTO the Noailles family home at Versailles—a grand *hôtel* abutting the great palace built by King Louis XIV to ensnare the perennially rebellious French nobility. His move necessitated a change in schools. Lafayette was now expected to travel in the most transcendent circles of the kingdom, and the duc d'Ayen wanted to make sure his future son-in-law received the necessary training for such a life. Lafayette was removed from the Collège du Plessis and transferred to the Académie de Versailles, the elite grooming school for the future leaders of France. The academy did not emphasize book learning. These boys would always have men of business to handle reading, writing, and calculations. Instead, they practiced riding, dancing, swordsmanship, and etiquette to perfect the manners and mannerisms of the high nobility. For their lives would be performance, and Versailles would be their stage.

Stepping out onto this stage for the first time, Lafayette faltered. The other boys were raised in high aristocratic society. As children they watched and copied the prescribed methods for bowing, nodding, eating, drinking, and laughing. One could not simply walk. One must *glide effortlessly*. Lafayette, in contrast, spent his childhood charging through the hilly forests of Auvergne without a care in the world.

The villagers doffed their hats whether he tiptoed, plodded, stomped, or skipped. Growing awkwardly into a tall and gangly frame, Lafayette found himself clumsy and deficient in nearly every way. He was not a naturally gifted rider. His earliest swordplay was waving sticks at imaginary Romans, not the meticulously choreographed dance of fencing. The comte de La Marck, one of the young court nobles who observed Lafayette's arrival at Versailles with disdainful bemusement, later recalled, "He was awkward in all his ways . . . he danced without grace, rode badly, and the young men with whom he lived were all more skillful than he in the various exercises of the body then at the fashion."[1] Lafayette also discovered he lacked a ready wit. The art of chattering conversation, meant to resemble in its spontaneity the scripted dialogue of theater, eluded him. He was never quick with the *bon mot* that would steal the scene. To his credit, he also did not excel at the malicious gossip driving many of these conversations. Lafayette had neither the ability nor the desire to join these games. Both he and those around him soon noticed.

At the other end of the spectrum was a boy who could do all Lafayette could not—his sixteen-year-old classmate Charles Philippe, comte d'Artois. Artois was the youngest of the three royal princes. His oldest brother, Louis-Auguste, was heir to throne, currently waiting with some trepidation for the death of their geriatric grandfather, Louis XV. His second brother, Louis Stanislas Xavier, comte de Provence, was coldly pedantic and lived solely on the obsequiousness of craven social climbers for his social victories. But Artois was vibrant, dashing, and certainly the best liked of the three brothers. Everything came easy to him: he was graceful, sharp, and refined, where Lafayette was clumsy, dull, and gauche. In time, each of the three royal brothers would become a king of France. Lafayette would undermine each of them in turn.

As he floundered among his new "friends," Lafayette was finally told why his guardians thrust him into a world where he did not belong. Near the end of 1773, both Lafayette and Adrienne were informed of their secret engagement. Adrienne was ecstatic. Lafayette was less passionately roused, but not displeased. He found his future wife pretty, kind, and affectionate. He considered himself lucky.

The couple wed on April 11, 1774, at the Noailles family chapel in Paris. The groom was sixteen, the bride fourteen. As this was a wedding for the great Noailles family, the archbishop of Paris himself presided, and the bride's guest list boasted some of the most important names in France. The groom, meanwhile, brought only nine guests, all of far lower rank. After a massive reception that wasted more food than some poor families consumed in their entire lives, the couple retreated for the night . . . to separate bedrooms. The duchesse d'Ayen's final condition for agreeing to the marriage was her fourteen-year-old daughter would not yet lose her virginity.

⁂

THE MARRIAGE OF the Lafayettes was a small blip in the larger social calendar of Paris and Versailles. And it was a blip soon banished to oblivion by the arrival of an all-consuming social supernova. On May 10, 1774, King Louis XV died. Having ascended to the throne in 1715 at the age of just five, Louis XV reigned for fifty-nine years. Plenty of his subjects born after his reign began died before it ended. But now it was time for a new king of France.

The newly crowned king, Louis XVI—still not twenty years old— would have liked nothing more than to remain in undisturbed seclusion. He enjoyed reading, hunting, and tinkering with clocks. He found solace in these precise, detailed, and delicate machines all working together to perform a single unified function. A well-built clock was a beautifully engineered design he found nowhere in the kingdom he now ruled—so full of contradictions, paradoxes, tensions, conflicts, egos, misunderstandings, miscommunications, hopes, fears, corruption, blindness, and dysfunction. Clocks he understood. People he did not.

Louis ascended to the throne alongside his already infamous wife, Marie Antoinette. It was not necessarily Marie's fault she was infamous. Her original sin was being born an Austrian archduchess. The Austrians had been the enemies of the French for centuries, and despite a recent treaty of alliance, old prejudices die hard. Her marriage to Louis in 1770 was meant to cement the unpopular Bourbon-Habsburg alliance, but in palace corridors, city streets, and village markets, the Austrians remained a bête noire for the French. The French public particularly blamed Austria for France's humiliating defeat to the up-start British and Prussians in the recent Seven Years' War. So when this fourteen-year-old Austrian girl was bundled up and presented to the French as their future queen, she was not exactly received with open arms. Nor was she received with open arms by her new husband, whose reticent diffidence was exacerbated by a physical defect making sex uncomfortable, which led to a quasi-estrangement for the young couple.

But if Marie Antoinette married into a difficult circumstance, she did little to ingratiate herself to her new people. She sought solace with a group of sympathetic friends who reveled in the carefree frivolity always bursting forth from teenagers of privilege. Witty critics in the press dubbed her "Madame Deficit," and her lifestyle became a living symbol of the systematic and grinding inequality of *ancien régime* France.

For Lafayette and his friends, the most immediate impact of the couple's elevation to the throne was a complete change in atmosphere at Versailles. Churlish stagnation and tedious sloth defined the last years of the reign of Louis XV. The king and his intimates neglected the balls, receptions, and parties that previously enlivened life at court. The palace had long since sunk into a stuffy, boring, lifeless malaise. That was all over now. Marie Antoinette reigned and anyone who wanted to keep up would have to indulge her penchant for drinking, gambling, and dancing. The young and irreverent rapturously embraced this radical change. Their taciturn elders furrowed their brows in disapproval.

⁂

LAFAYETTE WAS NOT present for the first summer under the new regime of frivolity. The duc d'Ayen pulled strings and got his son-in-law a commission as captain in the family regiment, the Noailles Dragoons. Neither his age nor experience merited Lafayette this commission. In fact, d'Ayen only secured it after agreeing Lafayette would not become active in the chain of command until his eighteenth birthday. But still, both d'Ayen and Lafayette were happy about the appointment. It was hopefully the start of a long military career. This career commenced in the summer of 1774 when Lafayette reported to the peacetime army permanently garrisoned in the frontier city of Metz. It was the last time, for a long time, d'Ayen and Lafayette shared anything resembling mutual satisfaction.

While in Metz, Lafayette finally secured two close friends. The first was his new brother-in-law Louis, vicomte de Noailles. Everything came as naturally to Noailles as it did awkwardly to Lafayette. Noailles was dashing, witty, graceful, and boasted a prodigious capacity for alcohol—a trait that never fails to impress young men. The other was Louis-Philippe, comte de Ségur. Cultivated and cultured, Ségur was eventually destined for the diplomatic service, where sly conversation and unflappable intellectual dexterity count for so much. The three began an earnest and lifelong friendship that finally gave Lafayette allies and protectors in the viper pit of his elite social life.

The three friends arrived in Metz as inexperienced officers in immaculate uniforms unsullied by parade ground dust, let alone the mud and blood of real battle. In this era of European peace, young officers treated summer maneuvers in Metz as an endless party, occasionally interrupted by practice drills. But Lafayette had an acute sense he must find *something* he was good at or he wasn't going to survive. In between the parties, he read manuals on strategy and tactics; during drills, he paid attention. Lafayette may have been young, clumsy, and inexperienced. But he refused to be ignorant and lazy.

When he returned home, he found an opportunity to finally bond with his new wife. While in Metz, Lafayette learned about the new theory of inoculation promising to free humanity of the myriad deadly diseases that so often turned loved ones into painful memories. Lafayette was determined to inoculate himself against smallpox, one of the deadliest and most frequent of these killer diseases—especially for those who lived their lives in army camps. The process required two weeks of seclusion, so he rented a house on the outskirts of Paris. Adrienne insisted on nursing him through the process, and the duchesse d'Ayen, who was herself immune to the disease after almost dying of smallpox years earlier, also insisted on helping—if only to keep an eye on the young couple. By the admission of everyone involved, Adrienne and Gilbert formed the first permanent emotional bonds of their long, mutually supportive, and relatively happy marriage during these two weeks. The duchesse, meanwhile, came away more affectionately protective of Lafayette, moving him decisively from well-liked ward to much-loved son.

⊷⊶

ONCE HE RECOVERED, the marquis and marquise de Lafayette rejoined the swirling milieu of Marie Antoinette's court. Adrienne attended the queen's weekly balls, but aside from these formal occasions, she tended to stay home. Lafayette, meanwhile, joined the unofficial escapades of the young nobility with his close friends Ségur and Noailles. They were joined by Noailles's older brother, the prince de Poix, and partied with those in the circle of Marie Antoinette and the comte d'Artois. Also in this set was the duc de Chartres, a royal cousin from the house of Orléans—the branch of the family that would inherit the throne if the Bourbon line went extinct. The longstanding rivalry between the two royal branches was shared by this younger generation. After Chartres inherited the title duc d'Orléans in 1785, he would use his money, power, and position to promote himself at the expense of the king and queen. Marie Antoinette *hated* Chartres. She eventually blamed him—not unjustly—for cynically bankrolling the men and women who staged the French Revolution.

For now, this young crowd drank, danced, and made cutting remarks at each other. They dubbed themselves *La Société de l'épée de la bois*—the Society of the Wooden Sword—named after a particular drinking establishment they frequented. The members of the *Société de l'épée* caroused the cafés of the Left Bank and slummed their way through the dance halls on the outskirts of the city. They spent the rest of their time playing cards and racing horses. Through benders and hangovers, they gossiped endlessly about who did what with whom the night before. Lafayette barely kept up. He was a clumsy dancer, earning himself a permanent place as the butt of jokes after stumbling his way through a dance with Marie Antoinette with a witness recalling, "He showed himself so awkward and so gauche the queen could not help laughing."[2] He was also a bad drinker and envied his brother-in-law Noailles, able to drink his weight in wine. Determined to keep up, Lafayette once got so drunk his companions were forced to carry him to the carriage, and on the ride home he kept muttering, "Don't forget to tell the vicomte de Noailles how much I drank."[3]

Lafayette recognized more and more he did not fit in and shifted his demeanor to compensate. He smothered his naturally outgoing nature under a blanket of silence—heavily weighted by self-conscious resentment. It was an understandable defense mechanism, but in a world that prized sparkling wit and free verbosity, Lafayette's descent into silence only further damaged his reputation. A contemporary referred to him as "pale, cold, and lifeless."[4] Word soon reached the Noailles family and they fretted over his behavior, at one point encouraging Ségur to do what he could to prod Lafayette back to life, "to rouse him from his indolence, and to add a little fire to his character."[5]

Lafayette later said he knew full well his silence was socially debilitating, but turned aloof because "I did not think about and hardly heard things that did not seem to me worth discussing."[6] While admitting this was probably the result of "disguised pride," he also said it was not "softened by the awkwardness of my manners, which, without being out of place on great occasions, never bowed to the graces of the court or to the enjoyment of a supper at the capital."[7] If court society disdained him, he was happy to dismiss them all as a flock of empty-headed pigeons. But Ségur remained an astute observer of his friend, and knew Lafayette was not what he appeared. He later said Lafayette's "cold and serious bearing . . . sometimes created a false impression of timidity and embarrassment," but it "concealed the most active spirit, and the most burning soul."[8]

Court society also looked at Lafayette sideways because he was a virile young man who had yet to take a mistress. In the French aristocracy, love was not meant to take place in the home. By *not* cheating on Adrienne, he was committing quite a *faux pas*. Aware of this (and being a virile young man), Lafayette made a few stabs at carrying on an affair. One attempt was with a mysterious woman unknown to history that "came to nothing."[9] Another was a futile attempt to woo Aglaé de Hunolstein, the object of many men's affections. She was well out of Lafayette's league, and presently the acknowledged mistress of the duc de Chartres. But Lafayette got so caught up in his infatuation, and was apparently so eager to practice the peculiar rituals of manly honor, he accused Ségur of being his rival. He spent a drunken evening challenging Ségur to a duel. Ségur said Lafayette tried to "persuade me to fight, sword in hand, over the heart of a beauty over whom I had not the least claim."[10] Ségur could only laugh, attempt to talk his friend down, and wait until all was forgotten in the morning.

The duc d'Ayen's increasing disillusionment with his clumsy son-in-law peaked when the duc pulled some strings to get Lafayette a permanent position in the entourage of the comte de Provence. Lafayette was horrified. He planned to be an army officer. A permanent attachment to Provence meant a life trapped in a world that despised him, and that he despised in return. Lafayette decided to spike the deal. At a masquerade ball, Lafayette found the unmistakably plump figure of the comte showing off his impressive memory. Lafayette worked his way into the circle surrounding Provence. At an opportune moment, he scoffed at the show-off, saying, "Memory is the intellect of fools."[11] Provence was left red-faced and seething beneath his mask.

The remark got back to d'Ayen, who could not believe how incompetently frustrating his son-in-law truly was. He arranged an opportunity for Lafayette to apologize and say he did not realize it was Provence under the mask—a convenient social lie allowing everyone to save face. At this arranged summit in a corridor at the palace, Provence asked Lafayette if he knew it was him behind the mask. Instead of playing along, Lafayette said yes. Furious at the insult, Provence turned on his heels and walked away. Lafayette would have no place in his entourage. Ever. D'Ayen raged at Lafayette for destroying this golden opportunity, thinking it the product of astonishing stupidity rather than calculated defiance. Lafayette later spoke for teenagers throughout history by saying of the incident, "I did not hesitate to be disagreeable to preserve my independence."[12]

Despite the growing divide between Lafayette and d'Ayen, he could still count on a few supporters inside the family. Unlike her husband, the duchesse d'Ayen defended her son-in-law. As did d'Ayen's sister, the comtesse de Tessé, who was an intelligent, witty, and iconoclastic fixture of Parisian society. Adrienne was also steadfastly in her husband's corner. Over the winter of 1774–1775, the couple began defying the ban on sleeping together. As she later recalled, Lafayette snuck into her room at night where they demonstrated their "tender and stable affections."[13] These liaisons were not hidden for long. Adrienne soon became pregnant. Her first pregnancy eventually miscarried, but in the spring of 1775, she was pregnant again. This time for good. Adrienne was only fifteen years old. By the time the second pregnancy was discovered, Lafayette had already departed for another round of summer maneuvers at Metz.

⚓

THE SUMMER OF 1775 was, without a doubt, the most consequential summer of Lafayette's life to date. The commander of the Metz garrison was the infamous Charles-François de Broglie. Broglie enjoyed a well-earned reputation for charismatic scheming. He was outwardly friendly, gregarious, and generous. But this was an invitation to sit at the table of a cutthroat pirate. Years later, Thomas Jefferson described Broglie as "a high flying aristocrat, cool and capable of everything."[14] For years, Broglie denied being the head of the never officially acknowledged *secret du roi*, the secret service of the late King Louis XV. Running a shadow agency of foreign operatives alongside the official channels of the Foreign Ministry, Broglie pursued every conceivable angle to restore French power and diminish the British. Broglie was not particularly well liked, and his service to the Crown was interrupted by two prolonged exiles from court. He had no connections whatsoever to the new king, Louis XVI, so instead of orchestrating a revival of French fortunes, he presided over a peacetime garrison in de facto exile. But he never stopped looking for opportunities.

Broglie welcomed Lafayette, Noailles, and Ségur into the ranks of his officer corps. All of them came from the best families in France and all of them ran in the same circles as the queen. They might provide Broglie a ticket back to the center of power. He was especially well disposed toward Lafayette. A lifetime ago, Broglie served as an officer at the Battle of Minden, where Lafayette's father was killed in action. He reminded Lafayette of the connection and made sure to lament the cause of it.

Broglie also happened to be a master Freemason and invited the young men to enroll in a lodge for military officers at some point during the summer. The Freemasons have a longstanding reputation as the hidden architects of every revolution in history. Though Masonic conspiracy theories are exaggerated, it's true many prominent intellectuals, politicians, and military officers throughout the European world were drawn into their ranks in the eighteenth century. There they left antiquated social classes and religious superstition at the door. Among their Masonic brethren, they discussed the progressive ideas with far more egalitarian freedom. They lauded the scientific method, and disdained the power-hungry hypocrisy of the Catholic Church; they lamented the oppression of subjects, and celebrated the rights of free citizens.

It is hard to pin down the precise moment Lafayette latched on to the great ideas that animated the rest of his life: liberty, equality, and the rights of man. But it seems reasonable to pinpoint this summer in Metz as the moment they first began coalescing in his mind. Whether plucked directly from a Masonic meeting, or picked up in adjacent conversations, Lafayette learned the language of freedom and liberty—though he did not yet have a clear idea what he was trying to say. For men like Broglie, these enlightened ideas were merely playthings to pass the time while waiting for an opportunity to continue his great game of realpolitik. But Lafayette took them seriously.

Of the adjacent conversations firing up his imagination, one in particular looms over the rest. On August 8, 1775, Broglie invited Lafayette to a dinner thrown in honor of the visiting Duke of Gloucester, younger brother of King George III. Gloucester and the king were not on the best of terms, and when the duke sat down to dinner with his French hosts, he had plenty to say about the extraordinary news from across the Atlantic. British colonists in North America had launched an armed rebellion against the Crown, and Gloucester, fortified by plenty of wine, was of the opinion the colonists had every right to revolt against his brother. It may have been in these discussions Lafayette first heard the name George Washington, the Virginia planter recently named commander in chief of the rebel army. Lafayette was inspired by the struggle between the brave Americans and the oppressive British and wrote later, "When I first learned of the quarrel, my heart was enlisted, and I thought of nothing but joining the colors."[15] His childhood ambition to win fame and glory now joined the romantic dream of fighting, and possibly dying, for a noble cause.

When Lafayette, Noailles, and Ségur returned home in the fall of 1775, they continued their moderately subversive education. In December, they attended meetings of the Saint-Jean de La Candeur Masonic Lodge in Paris. Probably thanks to his new social and intellectual connections, Lafayette became familiar with Abbé Raynal, a defrocked Jesuit intellectual who, with the assistance of a small army of researchers and uncredited coauthors, published the infamous *History of the Two Indies*. The book was billed as an innocuous history of the French colonial empire, but Raynal smuggled in extended tangents denouncing European colonial conduct in the Americas, including a devastating critique of African slavery. The thrust of these critiques would, in time, become meaningful to Lafayette. But many years would pass before he fully grappled with the incompatibility of liberty, equality, and slavery. The censors banned *History of the Two Indies*, turning it from obscure tome to celebrated masterpiece. The state deemed it dangerous, so now everyone had to read it.

In December 1775, Adrienne gave birth to a little baby girl named Henriette. Lafayette was now a father at the age of eighteen. Henriette's life—and Lafayette's relationship with her—would forever cast a sad shadow on his life. After following his ambitious heart to America he would write home, "Hug Henriette for me . . . those poor children have a father who is something of a rover, but who is basically a good and honorable man, a good father who truly loves his family."[16] But Henriette would barely know the sound of her father's voice. He would leave her as an infant and she would be dead before he came home.

⁂

MEANWHILE, FORCES OUTSIDE Lafayette's control once again conspired to alter his destiny. Upon turning eighteen, he was awarded the rank of full captain. He was proud of his commission. It was a bright spot of success amid a social life marked by awkward frustrations and silent resentment. Lafayette worked hard to turn himself into a model officer, but unfortunately too many young men of his breed did not. The army was positively infested with well-connected teenagers from important families holding ranks they did not deserve. The absurd social farces of Versailles had long since drained the high nobility of their military spirit. The greatest nobles of the realm were now masters of theater rather than war. They were actors, not soldiers. But unfortunately for the army, the kings of France continued to appoint them colonels, generals, and marshals as if they were still the warrior knights who fought alongside Joan of Arc.

After the humiliations of the Seven Years' War, it became obvious something must change. When King Louis XVI ascended to the throne in 1774, his new prime minister tasked a career soldier, the comte de Saint-Germain, with reforming the French military—ideally before they found themselves fighting another war. Saint-Germain was himself victim of an irrational and self-defeating system that promoted blood over merit. He considered himself a man of merit, experience, and talent unjustly passed over for promotion in favor of pompous buffoons who played at soldier while losing half the empire. His analysis of French society was scathing, and he denounced the "pernicious distinction between the nobility of the court, and that of the provinces . . . between the rich and the poor, in a way that one has everything without deserving anything and the other gets nothing no matter what they deserve."[17] Plenty of influential leaders appreciated Saint-Germain's ideas, and he was invited to clean up the army. He went through the officer rolls hunting for places to cut, economize, and discharge.

High on Saint-Germain's hit list were antiquated family regiments. In the days of medieval warfare, the kings of France relied on the ducs, comtes, and marquises of the realm to outfit their own regiments whenever the king declared war. But that was all in the past. Now they were breeding grounds for sloth, bloat, and unprofessional conduct. Most especially, Saint-Germain hunted for young officers from the best families who seemed to believe the army existed so they could put on a uniform and impress girls. Ironically, had Lafayette remained simply the marquis de Lafayette, a poor provincial noble working hard to make himself a dependable officer, he may have been saved. But now he was a Noailles, and a full captain at the age of eighteen—a rank secured only as a favor to his influential father-in-law. On paper, Lafayette was the personification of everything Saint-Germain hated. It was easy to strike

Lafayette's name from the active-duty roster. Though he did not know it, Lafayette's career in the French army ended before it began. His entrance into the Noailles family was not the breath of life, but a kiss of death. On June 11, 1776, the king signed the order radically altering the officer corps of the French army. Lafayette found his name on the reserve list.

It was a cruel blow. Lafayette's career path in the army evaporated. Glory, fame, and honor no longer lay ahead—not even garrison duty at Metz. No more drills or maneuvers. No more training and practice. No longer any hope of rising in the ranks and settling into an honorable career. At eighteen years old, the marquis de Lafayette saw his whole life flash before his eyes. He already burned his bridges at court. He had no head or heart for business. Expecting a public life of valor and accomplishment, he now faced an isolated existence of impotent obscurity. What on earth was he going to do?

CHAPTER THREE

WHY NOT?

[July 1776–April 1777]

ON JULY 6, 1776, A MIDDLE-AGED CONNECTICUT LAWYER named Silas Deane arrived in Paris. He claimed he was a commercial agent representing merchants in British North America on a mission to increase trade with the indigenous tribes of the interior. But this was just a cover story. Really Deane was on a secret mission from the Second Continental Congress, the colonial assembly leading the rebellion against the British Crown and Parliament. Deane's true purpose was soliciting aid from Britain's most implacable foe, the Kingdom of France.

At first glance, an alliance between the colonial rebels and the Kingdom of France was ludicrous. Why on earth would French Catholic monarchists help a bunch of Anglo-Protestant republicans? Why would those Anglo-Protestant republicans even ask French Catholic monarchists for help? For 150 years, the principal enemy of the British colonists in America were the French. In fact, one of the major complaints of these rebellious subjects was the British Crown *increasing* the presence of the regular army in the colonies despite the neutralization of the French in 1763. The French had always been the enemy. But the time had come for enemies of enemies to become friends.

For the French, helping the American rebels held obvious allure. It presented an opportunity to avenge their defeat in the Seven Years' War. True, the territorial loss of Canada could be exaggerated—Voltaire infamously dismissed Canada as "a few acres of snow."[1] It was also true the economic impact of the defeat could be exaggerated—France retained control over her Caribbean colonies, where enslaved Africans produced the sugar, coffee, and cotton generating the *real* wealth of the French colonial empire. But statecraft was not all hard economics: pride and prestige were important, too. Since the end of the last war, the French wallowed in national resentment. Any chance to knock the British down a peg was a chance worth taking. The public certainly seemed enthusiastic. When the rebellion in American broke out, the cause of *les insurgents* became all the rage in French society.

But there were risks. Lord Stormont, British ambassador to France and a seasoned diplomat, made it plain his government considered the conflict an internal affair. The consequences for a foreign power aiding the rebels would be dire. He was confident France would stay out of it, though. Despite the allure of humbling the British, the literal cost of getting involved appeared prohibitive. France's national treasury faced growing budget deficits each year thanks to an archaic tax system exempting anyone who actually possessed real wealth. The French monarchy floundered in dysfunctional debt for most of the eighteenth century and things were only getting worse. It did not appear France's dream of cleaving the British Empire in twain could survive the reality of her annual budget reports. King Louis XVI would be wise to focus on financial reform, not imperial war.

To fix the financial mess, the king's elderly prime minister, the comte de Maurepas, brought in a highly skilled economist named Anne-Robert-Jacques Turgot. Turgot's modern theories about trade, commerce, and markets led him to express in French the same liberal economic philosophy expressed in English by his contemporary Adam Smith. Turgot embarked on a program of reform to aggressively cut expenses and increase revenue. It was a difficult task threatening entrenched interests—as was true for Saint-Germain's military reforms. But if Turgot succeeded in overhauling how the Kingdom of France did business, he might set his country on a path to renewed glory.

Turgot's project quickly ran into an unforeseen obstacle, further indicating France's domestic problems would keep her out of expensive foreign entanglements. Just as the redcoats and minutemen traded gunfire at Lexington and Concord in the spring of 1775, France endured an acute grain shortage. Turgot's deregulation of the grain trade happened to coincide with a terrible harvest. Limited supply and high demand drove prices up—a problem exacerbated by hoarders and speculators eager to exploit the crisis for personal gain. A wave of protests and riots swept across France as families found themselves unable to put food on the table. Later dubbed the Flour War, the unrest only subsided when the government canceled the deregulatory reforms and more bountiful harvests restored prices to normal. With the benefit of hindsight, the Flour War is seen as a precursor of the national crisis set to explode spectacularly a decade later. At the time, it apparently precluded the Kingdom of France from meddling in British colonial affairs while their own house was in such disorder. So it seemed.

THERE WAS A small clique inside the French government undeterred by obstacles to backing the British colonists: people who continued to see the rebellion in America as *the* opportunity for France to avenge herself upon Britain. The leader of this clique was Charles Gravier, comte de Vergennes. A savvy old diplomat, Vergennes had recently been elevated to foreign minister by Louis XVI. Though not initially in the king's inner circle of advisers, Vergennes was well on his way to forging an influential bond with the young king. This was a bond that would endure until the tragically mistimed death of Vergennes in 1787, right at the beginning of the great financial crisis that would hurl France into revolution, and that Vergennes helped create here in 1775.

Vergennes developed plans to covertly help the rebellious Americans even before the shooting began. He paid close attention to mounting tensions built up in the 1760s and early 1770s by the Stamp Act, the Navigation Acts, and the Intolerable Acts. His agents in England and America reported the British government was poisoning relations with their American colonists. Already listening attentively, Vergennes heard the shot heard round the world loud and clear in April 1775. He is, in fact, the principal reason the Battle of Lexington and Concord became a shot heard *round the world*, rather than fading away into the historical silence of so many skirmishes in long forgotten local uprisings.

Without official approval, Vergennes sent an emissary to America in December 1775 to open a back channel with the rebel congress. While Lafayette became a father and read Abbé Raynal, Vergennes's emissary met a secret committee of American rebels led by the most famous American in the world, Benjamin Franklin. Silas Deane's arrival in Paris the following summer was a direct result of the vague understanding the two sides reached the previous winter. The French could not, as of yet, do anything in the open. Certainly, they could not join the fight. But there were plausibly deniable ways to help.

Vergennes's principal agent in this exercise in plausible deniability was Pierre-Augustin Caron de Beaumarchais, an adventurous polymath who was, at different stages in his life, an inventor, a musician, a watchmaker, a philanthropist, and a playwright. The last occupation earned him international fame as the author of deliciously subversive plays like *The Barber of Seville* and *The Marriage of Figaro*. But Beaumarchais was also, from time to time, a paid agent of the Crown. He entered government service after an unfavorable legal judgment stripped him of certain civil rights. To win back favor, Beaumarchais offered to perform delicate tasks for the government, beginning his shadow career as a secret agent and a spy. He was among those voices in London in the 1760s and 1770s eagerly reporting the latest bad news for Britain. Now Vergennes added another job to Beaumarchais's eclectic resume: arms dealer.

Silas Deane's official instructions from the Second Continental Congress were limited to seeking four qualified French military engineers along with "clothing and arms for twenty-five thousand men with a suitable quantity of ammunition, and one hundred field pieces."[2] Congress could not pay for these materials, and all Deane could offer was the vague observation that if the colonies broke away from Britain, their economy would, by necessity, orient toward France. But this was enough. Vergennes was more interested in international realpolitik than international trade. Beaumarchais was more interested in a fat commission than who was going to pay for it. To facilitate the transfer of French military surplus to the colonists, Beaumarchais established an allegedly Spanish trading company called Roderigue Hortalez et Cie and got to work shipping arms and supplies across the Atlantic.

The initial pipeline now opened, Vergennes and Beaumarchais led Silas Deane toward increasingly grandiose plans. Why stop at four engineers and a single ship's worth of supplies? Why not think bigger? In his defense, Deane worked blind for most of 1776. Thanks to the Royal Navy, he was entirely cut off from the Congress he served. Though the Declaration of Independence was proclaimed before Deane even arrived in Paris, the rumor of its existence was not officially confirmed until November. Working without guidance or instructions, Deane allowed his projects to balloon in size and scope. Beaumarchais financed millions of dollars' worth of artillery, gunpowder, uniforms, boots, bayonets, mortars, balls, tents, and muskets, ultimately resulting in ten fully loaded ships departing for America by the spring of 1777. To pay for it, Deane promised nearly twice the real cost of these supplies in colonial produce like tobacco. Beaumarchais eagerly agreed to the deal. One way or the other, he would make out like a bandit.

⊰⊱

THE BRITISH EVACUATION of Boston in the spring of 1776 raised high hopes for a quick and decisive victory. But this was the last good news from across the Atlantic. The British spent the rest of the year chasing George Washington and his Continental Army out of New York. These ignominious retreats led some in France to draw the conclusion it was necessary for professional European officers to lead the amateur Americans. Vergennes and Beaumarchais agreed with this assessment and encouraged Silas Deane to sign up experienced French officers for service in the Continental Army. The marquis de Lafayette was not the only young officer recently reformed out of the army, so Deane could draw from a deep well of potential recruits. Both because he thought it was a good idea, and because Vergennes hinted it was necessary to keep the supply ships sailing, Deane exceeded his original mandate and began commissioning officers.

When word got out Silas Deane was the head recruiter of the Continental Army, officers flocked to his doorstep. By November 1776, Deane was tearing his hair out, and griped of being "well-nigh harassed to death" by every reformed officer in France.[3] These officers came brandishing inflated résumés and even more inflated demands. It was thus something of a relief when a German officer in the French service showed up one day speaking excellent English and offering to help Deane separate the wheat from the chaff. This is how Baron Johan de Kalb joined the American cause.

De Kalb was born a middle-class commoner in a tiny German principality in the orbit of the great Kingdom of Prussia. His lack of nobility precluded advancement in the Prussian army, so de Kalb took a novel path to satisfying his military ambition. Fluent in French, he crossed the Rhine in 1743 and presented himself to the French army, falsely claiming he was actually the noble "Baron de Kalb." After securing a commission thanks to phony credentials, de Kalb invited his superiors to not ask too many questions by displaying an impressive talent for soldiering. Rising to the rank of lieutenant colonel, he served with distinction in both the War of the Austrian Succession and the Seven Years' War.

De Kalb provided welcome relief for the beleaguered Silas Deane. Having himself traveled to America in 1768, de Kalb offered to act as a well-informed collaborator—to help pick and choose who should get a commission and who should be rejected. He also told Deane that French captains demanding to be colonels, and French colonels demanding to be generals, was perfectly reasonable—it was necessary to offer inducements to entice good officers to "quit their native country and friends to hazard life and all in a cause which is not their own."[4] Taking the hint, Deane signed Lieutenant Colonel de Kalb to a commission as a major general in the Continental Army. With de Kalb's helpful guidance, Deane offered sixteen more men commissions in the Continental Army—not one of which Deane was actually authorized to offer.

But de Kalb was not all he seemed. During his years in the French service he attached himself to Charles-François de Broglie, Lafayette's old commander in Metz. After the Seven Years' War, de Kalb followed

Broglie into the king's secret service. His voyage to America, in reality, was a clandestine intelligence mission to report on conditions in the British colonies. Like Vergennes, Broglie was hardwired to look for ways to aggrandize France and undermine Britain. He was also hardwired to look for ways to aggrandize *himself*.

At some point in 1776, Broglie dreamed up a wildly implausible scheme: to replace George Washington as commander in chief of the Continental Army. Agreeing with the assessment that the backwoods rebels suffered from a want of real officers, Broglie imagined himself sailing to their rescue and becoming Stadtholder of America. He modeled this dream on the role played by the Prince of Orange in the Dutch United Provinces: a political sovereign and military commander in chief who presided over an oligarchy of powerful merchants. Had Broglie been in full possession of the facts, he would have realized this dream was ludicrous fantasy. The Anglo Protestants in America were never going to accept a French Catholic sovereign. Nor were the senior officers of the Continental Army going to replace Washington with some arrogant and condescending European interloper. But Broglie was not in full possession of the facts. All he saw was a ragtag insurgency that caught the British flat-footed in 1775, and now stood on the brink of defeat because they lacked a real leader. So he hatched a plan historians are pleased to call the "Broglie Intrigue."

Broglie sent de Kalb to Silas Deane to advance this project. As de Kalb steered Deane toward men loyal to Broglie, he observed the Continentals might do better if they added not just officers of middling rank, but a real European commander in chief. Like, for example, Charles-François de Broglie. Deane was removed enough from the political and emotional realities back home that he allowed himself to get swept up in this idea. He wrote excitedly to Congress, "I submit one thought to you: Whether if you could engage a great general of the highest character in Europe, such, for instance . . . Marshal Broglio [*sic*], or others of equal rank to take the lead of your armies, whether such a step would not be politic, as it would give a character and credit to your military and strike perhaps greater panic in our enemies."[5] When Deane's letters finally reached America, his colleagues were aghast at the alarming leaps made by their man in Paris. But back in

France in late 1776, it seemed like it might be the last best chance of winning the war.

⊰⊱

WHEN LAFAYETTE AND his two best friends, Noailles and Ségur, learned a recently arrived merchant from Connecticut was actually head of recruitment for the insurgent army in America, they hatched their own ludicrous plan. They would go fight for the Americans. With Lafayette reformed out of the army, and little promise of action in Europe anyway, the thought of a glorious campaign fighting for freedom was catnip to his stifled ambitions. Even better, he would get to fight their ancient enemy. Ségur later said the three friends resolved to go fight from a "desire to right the wrongs of the last war, to fight the English, to fly to the aid of the Americans."[6]

Achieving their goal would be a delicate matter. The three boys were inner-circle members of the French nobility. The British might deem their participation an act of war. Lafayette first approached Broglie for advice, knowing only the older general was sympathetic to the American cause. Lafayette knew nothing of Broglie's already unfolding plan to make himself Stadtholder of America. Broglie made a careful show of resisting Lafayette's enthusiasm. Reminding Lafayette he was at the Battle of Minden, Broglie initially refused to help Lafayette connect with Deane, saying, "I don't want to contribute to the ruin of the only remaining branch of the family."[7] But this was the calculated deterrence of an old Zen master testing a potential student. If Lafayette was serious, he would push through the resistance. If he was not, it was best to find out now before the boy disrupted Broglie's own plans.

Still being minors, Noailles and Ségur both believed they needed permission from their parents. Though Lafayette was technically the head of his own family, he too was a legal minor and unable to simply do whatever he wanted. They all expected their parents to look askance at this far-fetched idea, and Lafayette's own fraught relations with the duc d'Ayen led him to later recall, "Circumstances . . . had taught me to expect from my family only obstacles to the attainment of my goal."[8]

Lafayette's suspicions were confirmed when he and Noailles put the idea to their father-in-law. D'Ayen was surprisingly sympathetic—at least to *Noailles's* eager wishes. To Lafayette he said, "This sort of thing is all very well for the vicomte de Noailles, who is strong, energetic, and sufficiently determined to undertake anything, but what on earth would *you* find to do over there?"[9] D'Ayen agreed to sound out the government on behalf of Noailles, but not Lafayette. He was well past risking his reputation on the disappointing husband of his second daughter.

This rebuff only hardened Lafayette's resolve. He felt trapped. His life, career, and future all hinged on the support of d'Ayen, and d'Ayen now withheld that support. So Lafayette went back to Broglie. Now convinced the rich young marquis was a potential asset, Broglie switched tactics entirely. Instead of putting Lafayette off, he sympathized with the stymied young man dying under the oppressive shadow of his father-in-law. "Good!" Broglie said. "Get even! Be the first to go to America. I will take care of it."[10]

At Broglie's order, de Kalb met with Lafayette and opened negotiations with Silas Deane. Unlike most of the officers beating a path to Deane's door, Lafayette was a fabulously wealthy young man, so he required no great salary. But he *would* need a high rank to turn heads and quiet objections, so Lafayette insisted on a commission as a major general. What he lacked in experience, he made up with the publicity his participation would generate. Lafayette hinted to de Kalb permission from the Noailles family hinged on being appointed major general. De Kalb hinted to Deane future support from the French government hinged on Lafayette becoming a major general. So, after some hesitation, Deane agreed to make Lafayette a major general.

On December 7, 1776, Baron de Kalb escorted the marquis de Lafayette to a meeting with Silas Deane. Deane presented Lafayette a commission specifically highlighting "his high birth, his alliances, the great dignities which his family hold at court, his considerable estates in this realm" as the main reason for this extraordinary appointment of an untested teenager to the rank of major general.[11] Lafayette explicitly clarified, "I offer myself . . . to serve the United States with all possible zeal, without any pension or particular allowance."[12] After reading the contract over one last time, the two men signed the paperwork. And that is how the marquis de Lafayette joined the American Revolution.

⁂

THE SAME DAY Lafayette signed up for the Continental Army, Prime Minister Maurepas refused permission for vicomte de Noailles to join the Americans. The scion of one of the most important families in France fighting alongside rebellious British colonists? It was out of the question. It would be an act of war. Lord Stormont already groused about secret French support and was only kept at bay by Vergennes's steady stream of erudite lies. Maurepas did not want to risk a diplomatic incident. Or a war.

Stormont was actually better informed than Maurepas about French support for the colonists. As he sat through Vergennes's steady stream of erudite lies, he knew he was listening to lies. Stormont knew everything because Silas Deane's personal secretary, a thirty-one-year-old physician and natural scientist named Edward Bancroft, was a British spy. Trusted with the most sensitive paperwork, Bancroft used invisible ink to compose weekly letters for his British handlers and planted them in a certain tree in the Tuileries Garden. Stormont did not want to expose this valuable mole at the very heart of rebel plotting and never failed to listen with apparent credulousness as Vergennes lied his head off for hours on end.

The duc d'Ayen raising the subject of his son-in-law fighting in America was a gift to Stormont. The request became public knowledge, giving Stormont the excuse he needed to demand his French counterparts curb all meddling in internal British affairs. To satisfy the British, Maurepas issued a decree forbidding French officers to join the Continental Army. Port authorities would inspect passenger manifests of departing ships to seal off the leaks. Three ships arranged by Beaumarchais were already loaded in Le Havre when the order came down. One sailed away before the authorities got their act together, but two more were held in port, much to the frustration of de Kalb and the other officers loyal to Broglie scheduled to sail on those ships.

It was here Lafayette rendered his first real service to the American cause. Either at his own initiative, or at Broglie's manipulative suggestion, Lafayette salvaged the expedition by offering to purchase a new ship with his own money. Eager to demonstrate his commitment in such a material way, Lafayette said to Deane, "Before this you have only seen my enthusiasm; perhaps it will now become useful: I shall buy a ship to transport your officers. Be confident. I want to share your fortune in this time of danger."[13] Broglie dispatched an agent to Bordeaux to purchase a ship before Lafayette changed his mind. They soon found a suitable vessel, made the sale, and rechristened the ship *La Victoire*.

It was likely here in these winter days of late 1776 the restlessly defiant Lafayette changed the motto on his family coat of arms. For centuries the family was guided by the stolid and workmanlike *vis sat costa fatum*—"determination is enough to overcome adversity." Lafayette now altered it to the more whimsically adventurous *cur non*: "why not?"[14]

⁂

THERE IS A great deal of historical speculation about the breadth and depth of Lafayette's clandestine deceptions. He later claimed, "The secrecy of those negotiations and of my preparations was truly miraculous. Family, friends, ministers, French spies, English spies, all were blind to them."[15] It's not clear how much of this is true. Both the French and British governments monitored Deane like a hawk. Lafayette let de Kalb believe his family tacitly consented to everything, but probably told the Noailles family nothing. It remains a mystery what, if anything, he said to Adrienne. If she was a secret confidante and knew his plan to disappear on a grand adventure for the sake of his pride, position, and future status, so much the better. But far more likely, he concealed everything from his wife, now pregnant with a second child and holding their baby daughter in her arms.

Either to curtail Lafayette's plans, or console him for Maurepas's apparent final word that adventure in America was out of the question, the Noailles family sent Lafayette on a short vacation abroad in February 1777. Ironically, they sent him into the belly of the beast he set his heart on slaying: London. While in London, Lafayette stayed at the home of the French ambassador to the Court of St. James, who just so happened to be Lafayette's uncle-in-law. His traveling companion was the prince

de Poix, the vicomte de Noailles's older brother and himself something
of an irrepressible rake. The boys planned to have a fine time.

The two young French nobles drank, danced, and chatted their way
through London society. Now directly connected to the British colonial question, Lafayette quickly fell in with the opposition elements of
London society who criticized their government's antagonistic policy
in America. He also happened to run into General Henry Clinton at
the opera, neither suspecting they would soon face each other on opposite sides of a war. Lafayette also heard the first piece of good news from
America for quite some time. After a year of retreats, the Continentals finally scored a victory with a daring Christmas raid on Trenton,
New Jersey. Lafayette said that, while in London, he openly cheered
the cause of the colonial rebels. He was also presented to King George
III, and said later, "At nineteen, one may take too much pleasure in
mocking the tyrant whom he is about to fight."[16] Lafayette delighted in
the hidden knowledge that within a matter of days he would skip town
to go pry North America from the king's clutches.

Every day Lafayette awaited word *La Victoire* was ready to sail.
Knowing it was coming, he composed letters to Adrienne and the duc
d'Ayen explaining what he was about to do. To d'Ayen he wrote, "You
will be astonished dear papa by what I am about to tell you . . ."[17] And
indeed d'Ayen *was* astonished by what he read: Lafayette was not coming back—he had accepted a commission in the Continental Army, purchased a ship, and would soon set sail for America. When the news finally
arrived in London *La Victoire* was ready and waiting at the French port
of Bordeaux, Lafayette did not linger. He departed England without
telling anyone, skipping out on a ball meant to be held in his honor. For
the next few weeks, Lafayette's unknown whereabouts and intentions
caused frustration, embarrassment, anger, elation, laughter, toasts, and
denunciations in both England and France.

As he departed, Lafayette wrote joyfully to one of Deane's secretaries
that in one month's time, "I hope to be able to take to your country the
zeal that animates me for their happiness, their glory, and their liberty."[18]
One suspects Lafayette was also talking about his own happiness, glory,
and liberty.

BEFORE STRIKING OUT for Bordeaux, Lafayette first traveled to Paris undercover. He holed up with de Kalb at an apartment on the outskirts of the city and did not make contact with his family. He did, however, find time to drop in on Ségur and probably receive a clandestine visit from vicomte de Noailles. This afforded him the pleasure of watching his amazed friends burst with jealousy. "One morning, at seven o'clock," Ségur recalled, "he suddenly entered my room, closed the door tightly, and, sitting down near my bed, said to me: 'I am leaving for America' . . . I did not need to express to my friend the sorrow I had at not being able to accompany him."[19] Lafayette told de Kalb he avoided the Hôtel Noailles to avoid any final emotional entanglements with Adrienne. But the truth was, nobody in the family yet knew what he was about to do. On March 16, the pair departed for Bordeaux, where *La Victoire* and the other officers commissioned by Deane awaited.

According to de Kalb, Lafayette did not reveal his family knew nothing of his plans until they reached Bordeaux. De Kalb was stunned at this confession, and dashed off a letter to Deane saying Lafayette "surprised me when he first confessed it to me on his arrival here . . . for we were both confident that all was done in the matter by the advice and consent of his nearest relations."[20] Lafayette himself drafted a letter asserting he was the unmanipulated author of his own actions. It is impossible to gauge precisely how much in these letters was cover story and how much was genuine. Everyone connected to Vergennes, Deane, Beaumarchais, and Broglie spoke out of both sides of their mouth, with fingers crossed just to be safe. But in the flurry of letters generated by Lafayette's departure they all hammered the same note: Lafayette did everything of his own free will.

Just as Lafayette hoped, his departure caused a minor sensation. Secrets were impossible to keep at court, and the chattering gossip now revolved entirely around Lafayette's escape attempt. Lord Stormont angrily confronted Vergennes about Lafayette's insulting behavior in London—applauding rebellious colonists, then running off to join them. The British ambassador raged it was impossible to believe the duplicitous Vergennes was not the mastermind of the mission to send Lafayette to America. But, in truth, it is unlikely Vergennes orchestrated the plot. He did not believe France was ready to openly fight Britain, and now fretted Lafayette's reckless haste would ruin everything. Prime Minister Maurepas, meanwhile, groaned under the weight of this unwelcome baggage. He had been assured this was all settled. Now he found himself engulfed in an international imbroglio he wanted no part of.

Meanwhile, the Hôtel Noailles filled with anger and grief in equal measure. Adrienne cried while her mother and sisters consoled her. D'Ayen stormed through the halls, corridors, and salons of Paris and Versailles. His anger turned toward Broglie and Deane, the pied pipers of his son-in-law's demented behavior. Both men raced to disassociate themselves from Lafayette's impetuous shenanigans, swearing they believed the Noailles family consented to everything. Why else would they have gone ahead with it? Broglie swore it was a misunderstanding. Silas Deane agreed to forward letters from the family to de Kalb demanding the boy return.

Having kicked up all this dust, Lafayette wrote one of Deane's secretaries. "Do not worry," he said, "once I am victorious everyone will applaud my enterprise."[21] This is exactly the kind of thing one says to rationalize leaping off a particularly dangerous cliff right before drowning in the waters below. But in Lafayette's case, thanks to a mix of design, luck, courage, resilience—and what he would come to call "my good star"—events would, improbably, prove him right.

⁕

But there was still one final comedic act to play out in Lafayette's journey from clumsy adolescence to heroic maturity. Under diplomatic pressure from the British and the personal demands of the duc d'Ayen, King Louis XVI signed another proclamation forbidding French officers from serving in the Continental Army, singling out "notably Monsieur le marquis de La Fayette."[22] It was also strongly implied the king signed a *lettre de cachet* for Lafayette. The lettre de cachet was an infamous tool in the kit of royal absolutism allowing arbitrary detention of subjects who displeased the Crown. The lettre de cachet was a symbol of royal despotism later targeted for extinction by the French Revolution. But in practice, they were issued almost exclusively at the behest of noble families seeking to rein in embarrassing black sheep. Lafayette's own case fit squarely in this tradition, though there is no evidence such a letter was actually drafted. The threat was supposed to have been enough to alert him of the severity of the Crown's displeasure. It was further decided the duc d'Ayen and his sister, comtesse de Tessé, would take Lafayette on a six-month vacation to Italy. There, they could keep him under continuous watch until his spirit was properly broken. Lafayette was ordered to proceed directly to Marseilles to meet them.

If Lafayette did everything on the assumption his family would not resist a *fait accompli*, he found his bluff called. Rather than acceptance and best wishes, he faced thorough disapproval and a sentence of exile supervised by a terminally disappointed father-in-law. As he wrestled over what to do, *La Victoire* temporarily sailed from Bordeaux to a small Spanish port just over the border to escape the jurisdictional authority of French officials. After weighing anchor, Lafayette decided to return alone to Bordeaux to manage the situation. When the boy left, de Kalb did not expect to see him again. Though fond of Lafayette, his foolhardy deceptions frustrated de Kalb and risked the greater plan of putting Broglie in charge of the American army. But de Kalb would soon learn he was not playing a bit part in the story of Broglie, stadtholder of America, but a bit part in the story of Lafayette, Hero of Two Worlds.

La Victoire likely would have sailed away and left Lafayette to his miserable fate if not for one crucial detail: Lafayette owned the ship. So the officers and crew waited to see how things played out. Lafayette nearly gave up and went to Marseilles, but outside Bordeaux he was intercepted by the vicomte de Mauroy, who, like de Kalb, was one of Broglie's most trusted agents. Despite Broglie's protestations of wide-eyed innocence, he dispatched Mauroy to persuade Lafayette to get on *La Victoire* and sail away. This, Broglie calculated, was the only way his own plans stood any chance of success. And having very publicly disavowed Lafayette's actions, he would not suffer if the boy left of his own youthful impetuosity.

Mauroy came bearing a very different story for the vacillating young marquis. He said the duc d'Ayen was furious, but everyone else delighted in Lafayette's behavior. There was no real lettre de cachet, the threat was just for show. The king and his ministers secretly supported him. Most importantly, the chattering classes of Paris and Versailles cheered his name. He was told the ladies admired his daring and the men were jealous he was about to go serve a glorious cause. Lafayette believed all of this, and to be fair, it was only partly fabricated. The government did not, in fact, want him to leave, but society *was* impressed. They never knew he had it in him. Lafayette wrote again to Deane's secretary, "On the whole this affair has produced all the éclat I desired and now that everyone's eyes are on us, I shall try to be worthy of that celebrity."[23] He turned around again and headed back to *La Victoire*.

De Kalb also did not know Lafayette had it in him. Instead of meekly submitting to six months of verbal tongue-lashings from his father-in-law, Lafayette returned and said he was ready to set sail. He drafted a final letter to Adrienne. "My heart is broken," he said. "Tomorrow is the moment of cruel departure."[24] Adrienne herself was, at that moment, being consoled by her mother, who soothed her by saying Lafayette's bold stab at independent glory to avoid life as a disappointing nonentity was a *good* thing. Adrienne should take pride in her husband for showing such spirit. Adrienne would adopt this attitude later in life. At the time, one imagines, she was not so confident everything would work out for the best.

On April 20, 1777, *La Victoire* set sail for America. Against enormous obstacles, Lafayette achieved what his friends Noailles and Ségur had long since concluded was fantasy. Even though Lafayette changed his family motto from "determination is enough to overcome any obstacle" the old family motto continued to serve him well. Throughout Lafayette's life, determination, far more than cunning, guile, or raw intelligence, was his greatest strength. But as he struck out toward a new world, on a new adventure, as a new man, he was guided by a new motto: Why Not?

CHAPTER FOUR

BRILLIANT MADNESS

[1777]

L AFAYETTE HAD NEVER SAILED IN A SHIP ON OPEN WATERS. It turned out to be his worst nightmare. He was trapped in confined quarters with no possibility of escape, powerless over a vast ocean that could swallow him whole whenever it wished. But beyond the existential dread, he also suffered from terrible seasickness. During his first week on *La Victoire*, Lafayette departed his bunk only long enough to vomit.

Even after physically adjusting to life on board the ship, Lafayette still suffered mentally. He discovered more than anything else life at sea was tedious and boring. To pass the time he wrote to Adrienne, "One day follows another here, and, what is worse, they are all alike. Always the sea, always the water, and again the next day the same things."[1] A long stretch of calm winds only prolonged Lafayette's misery. "Since my last letter," he wrote, "I have been in that most tedious of regions; the sea is so dismal, and I believe we sadden each other, she and I."[2]

To pass the monotonous weeks of close confinement, Lafayette spent his time reading military manuals and books in English. His only military experience was two summers of maneuvers in Metz. He knew he needed to learn more to succeed in America. But his study of English was even more important to his success. The vast majority of French officers presenting themselves to Congress spoke only French. As French was the language of civilized peoples, they assumed this would not be an issue—much to the consternation of the English-speaking Americans. Lafayette, on the other hand, resolved to learn the language of the people one hoped to serve. If his wealth and title opened the door to America, Lafayette's earnest commitment to speaking English made him truly welcome.

Lafayette also became acquainted with his fellow passengers, especially vicomte de Mauroy, the one who convinced him the people of France were behind him. After fifteen years in the French army, Mauroy rose to the rank of lieutenant colonel, but then, like Lafayette, found himself abruptly reformed out of the service by Saint-Germain. His principal object in joining the expedition was clearing a path back to the French army by performing valorous service in America. Mauroy shared none of Lafayette's boundless enthusiasm for the Americans or "the cause of liberty," which the cynical veteran thought comically misguided. Mauroy took a shine to Lafayette, though, and so from a place of benevolent interest braced the boy for disappointment.

One day at sea, Lafayette said to Mauroy, "Don't you believe that the people are united by the love of virtue and liberty?" Mauroy replied the Americans were not some novel species, they were simply transplanted Europeans "who brought to a savage land the views and prejudices of their respective homelands." He proceeded to give Lafayette a brief moral history of European colonization: "Fanaticism, the insatiable desire to get rich, and misery—those are, unfortunately, the three sources from which flow that nearly uninterrupted stream of immigrants who, sword in hand, go to cut down, under an alien sky, forests more ancient than the world, watering a still virgin land with the blood of its savage inhabitants, and fertilizing with thousands of scattered cadavers the fields they conquered through crime."[3] This, Mauroy informed Lafayette, was the reality of the "new world" toward which they sailed.

Having departed Europe in April, *La Victoire* was still at sea in June. Uncooperative winds extended the long voyage, as did the decision to avoid Caribbean ports where arrest warrants might be waiting and head straight for Charleston, South Carolina. Eventually, the passengers saw birds—the unmistakable harbinger of land. As they approached civilization, their first encounter with another ship reminded them of their perilous situation: they were a pack of foreign soldiers of fortune attempting to insert themselves in the middle of a civil war. As the unidentified ship approached, the air was fraught with tension. What if it was British? But the ship turned out to American. But though they posed no threat, they bore a serious warning: two Royal Navy frigates blockaded Charleston harbor. A direct approach on the city was impossible. So *La Victoire* found an anchorage fifty miles north, off the coast of North Island. Lafayette, de Kalb, and a few others rowed ashore. On June 13, 1777, they set foot on dry land after fifty-four days at sea.

⌁

LAFAYETTE'S ARRIVAL IN this land of freedom and liberty could not have been richer with ironic hypocrisy. The first people he encountered were a small group of enslaved Africans crewing an oyster boat. In his youth, haste, and idealistic fantasizing, Lafayette did not yet register the insurmountable contradiction of American liberty and African slavery. As a nineteen-year-old French aristocrat with a head full of adventurous excitement, Lafayette recognized these African oystermen as merely servants of a master, not property of an owner. And servants were common everywhere. Lafayette would not remain in this blinkered state forever, but for now he remained blind to what he saw. The oystermen agreed to take the Frenchmen to their master—their *owner*—Major Isaac Huger, an officer in the South Carolina militia and operator of a lucrative rice plantation.

They did not arrive at Major Huger's house until midnight, and after a few tense minutes of interrogation to discern whether the strangers were dangerous, Major Huger invited them in to eat, drink, and sleep. Lafayette spent his first night in America on a slave plantation. The next morning, Huger arranged for a local pilot to navigate *La Victoire* to a safe harbor, but suggested Lafayette and his companions walk overland to Charleston. Warned that escaped slaves lived in secret settlements and survived by stealing from their former masters, the party of French officers loaded themselves with guns and ammunition rather than a change of clothes. Then they departed for Charleston.

After three days and two nights tromping southwest through blazing coastal sands, they finally made it back to civilization. One of Lafayette's companions said they arrived "looking very much like beggars and brigands."[4] They were greeted as such. De Kalb attempted to explain they were French officers come to serve in the Continental Army. The residents of Charleston scoffed. The city was full of French mercenaries spinning such tails, claiming impeccable credentials and legendary feats of strength, almost all of them liars and charlatans. Most of these adventurers were inferior officers who migrated up from colonial garrisons in Martinique, Guadeloupe, or Saint-Domingue. While it was true they carried letters of recommendation from their superiors, those superiors happily sung the praises of the most disreputable, drunken, and unreliable men in their units—eager, as they were, to be rid of them. These shiftless French officers laughed when Lafayette claimed he was a marquis. They heard that story a thousand times before.

The jeers ceased the next morning. A sharp wind blew the two Royal Navy frigates out to sea, leaving an opening through which *La Victoire* entered Charleston harbor. It turned out the bedraggled strangers told the truth. One of Lafayette's companions said the arrival of the ship caused "a complete reversal of opinion about us . . . we now received the warmest welcome possible, and the French officers, who had been the first to jeer at us, came in crowds to fawn upon the marquis de Lafayette and try to join his party."[5] Lafayette's group spent the next eight days in Charleston, dining and drinking with the best of local society. He toured the famous fortification that defended the city so admirably during a failed British siege the previous summer—one of the rare military triumphs in an otherwise dismal year of retreat and defeat. After this inspection, Lafayette grandly pledged enough cash to outfit a hundred men, a display of spontaneous generosity reported in newspapers as far away as Boston, who noted with interest the arrival of this rich and generous French marquis.

Lafayette and de Kalb believed they were going to sell both the cargo and *La Victoire* to earn the money they needed to live in America. But young Lafayette signed his purchase agreement without reading or understanding the fine print. He did not know the proceeds from the sale of *La Victoire*'s cargo were earmarked to repay the debt he contracted to buy the ship in the first place. Nor did he know *La Victoire* was required to load herself with American cargo and return to Bordeaux. Lafayette was forced to take out a high-interest loan to pay his expenses—cosigned by de Kalb since Lafayette was still a minor. They used the money from this loan to outfit themselves with supplies, clothes, horses, and carriages for the nearly seven-hundred-mile trip to Philadelphia. Lafayette envisioned a comfortable ride in a fine carriage through an American Arcadia. This would soon prove to be a pipe dream.

A few days after depositing his passengers, the captain of *La Victoire* commenced the return voyage to France. But as the ship sailed out of Charleston harbor, she struck a sand bar and sank. Having performed her one historical service of delivering the marquis de Lafayette safely to America, *La Victoire* was swallowed by the sea and never seen again.

⸙

To reach Philadelphia, the former passengers of *La Victoire* split into three groups. Lafayette and de Kalb led one group, vicomte de Mauroy led another, while a third elected to make the trip by sea. Though the nautical approach was more dangerous, it was certainly more comfortable. As it turned out, the carriages Lafayette purchased were unsuited for cross-country travel. Four days into the trip, the axles broke. Lafayette and his companions abandoned the carriages, along with the supplies they hauled—most of which were subsequently stolen. But the horses they now rode were also unsuited for such a long trip. One by one, they pulled up lame or collapsed from exhaustion. The party was forced to detour and purchase new ones.

Lafayette kept up a continuous letter-writing regimen during the trip, asking in every coastal town whether ships were leaving for France. Still guided by irrepressible enthusiasm, Lafayette remained upbeat and bore his trials with good humor. "You know that I departed most handsomely in a carriage," he wrote Adrienne, "we are all now on horseback after having broken the carriages . . . I expect to write you in a few days that we have arrived on foot."[6] Lafayette described America as a glorious land full of magnificent people. Wherever Lafayette looked he saw egalitarian republicans of simple homespun virtue. The Americans, he said, were defined by "a simplicity of manners, a desire to please, a love of country and liberty, and an easy equality prevails everywhere here."[7] In one letter, Lafayette marveled, "The richest man and poorest are on the same level," because "every individual has an adequate amount of property." In the original paper manuscript of this letter, someone later crossed out young Lafayette's observation Americans were equal because everyone owned "a considerable number of negroes."[8] This embarrassing remark did not fit with the beliefs of an older and wiser Lafayette, so someone crossed out the line when the family posthumously published his correspondence.

His companions were less thrilled by what they found in America. Where Lafayette saw simple goodness, they saw only backward simpletons. They felt acutely self-conscious of the deep anti-French, anti-Catholic sentiment of these Anglo settlers and detected latent hostility in people they encountered. Pierre du Rousseau de Fayolle, a member of Lafayette's party who later wrote a journal of his experiences, observed, "One thing is certain, we have not been flattered with attentions . . . I do not know whether the future will be better for us, but things are not at all as they were described to us in France."[9] But, then again, none of them were a young, rich marquis speaking delightfully broken English with rapturous delight.

Neither Lafayette, in his enchantment, nor his companions, in their misanthropy, told untruths. Their observations and experiences reflected their own perceptions, beliefs, and projections. But one thing was painfully clear to all of them: the war was going badly. Rousseau de Fayolle said, "The people are not united in a common cause, and I do not think they will ever do anything spectacular."[10] As they trudged wearily toward Philadelphia they learned the British captured Fort Ticonderoga, sentinel of the northern border with Canada. If they did not hurry, the war might be over before they even had a chance to fight.

❧❦

ON JULY 27, 1777, Lafayette's party arrived in Philadelphia, thirty-two days after leaving Charleston; forty days after landing in America;

ninety-four after departing Europe; and more than one hundred fifty days since Lafayette bid *adieu* to his family and left Paris for London. They said goodbye under the assumption he would return within a matter of weeks. Now, many months later, the time had finally come to justify the consternation, pain, disappointment, anger, and doubt he caused in the meantime. But Lafayette's reception in Philadelphia became an even greater farce than his reception in Charleston.

The Frenchmen arrived on a Sunday, so the Second Continental Congress was not in session. They first approached the residence of Mr. John Hancock, Boston merchant, ardent patriot, and current president of the Congress. But rather than greeting the officers with open arms and praises to God for arrival of saviors from France, Hancock informed them brusquely foreign officers were not his responsibility. Hancock told them to go see Robert Morris, the Philadelphia financier, banker, and speculator who sat on the foreign affairs committee under whose direction Silas Deane allegedly operated.

Not suspecting anything was wrong, the French officers walked over to Morris's house. Morris was no more accommodating than Hancock. He told them to return the next day to the Pennsylvania State House where their claims would be heard and addressed. Put off and put out, but not yet realizing the scope of congressional hostility, Lafayette, de Kalb, and their companions found lodgings for the night.

The next morning, Lafayette and thirteen other officers arrived at the State House, clutching commissions from Deane. All they needed was Congress's stamp of approval and directions to the nearest battlefield. But no one met them. So they waited. And waited. Eventually, Morris arrived alongside James Lovell, a stern New England schoolmaster fluent in French. Hardly even pausing to stop, Morris indicated the Frenchmen were Lovell's responsibility. Thoroughly confused, they introduced themselves, but Lovell cut them off and launched into an irritated diatribe denouncing Silas Deane for overstepping his authority. Lovell said Congress sent Deane to get four engineers, and instead he sent every French scoundrel with delusions of grandeur he could find—each more pompous, useless, and offensive than the last. Luckily, Lovell went on, Benjamin Franklin secured the needed engineers, who arrived back in April. As no further foreign officers were needed at this time, Lovell said goodbye and walked away. One of Lafayette's shocked companions later said Lovell "left us after calling us adventurers." But in quintessentially French fashion, the officer noted Lovell did so "in very good French."[11]

There was nothing they could do but return to their temporary lodgings in baffled confusion. Only later did they discover how much they did not know. First, Deane really *had* exceeded the bounds of his authority when signing their commissions. Then they learned more about the various French officers who preceded them. These lone mercenaries wore out their welcome, demanding rank and pay well above their station, and treating the colonials like inferior dullards. George Washington was among those sick to death of the influx of French officers. "I have often mentioned to you the distress I am in," Washington wrote John Hancock, "laid under by the application of French officers for commissions in our service . . . this evil, if I may call it so, is a growing one . . . they are coming in swarms from old France and the [Caribbean]."[12] In another letter to Hancock he pleaded, "You cannot conceive what a weight these kind of people are upon the service, and upon me in particular, few of them have any knowledge of the branches which they profess to understand, and those that have, are entirely useless as officers from their ignorance of the English language."[13] He further begged Major General Horatio Gates, "I shall be much obliged for you to stop the shoals of Frenchmen who are coming."[14] In the summer of 1777, he drafted his latest scathing opinion of French officers: "I have found by experience, that however modest they may seem to be at first, by proposing to serve as volunteers, they very soon extend their view and become importunate for offices they have no right to look for."[15] He wrote this last remark just days before the marquis de Lafayette arrived in Philadelphia.

As a result of all this, Congress created a new committee to handle applications from foreign officers. They named James Lovell chair of the committee because he was hostile to Silas Deane specifically, and the French generally. It seems Lovell believed his job was to use his very good French to tell arrogant European impostors to get lost, just as he did with the latest batch who came up from Charleston. Returning home after curtly dismissing the Frenchmen, Lovell wrote a fellow delegate about Deane, saying, "Ought not this weak or roguish man be recalled?"[16]

⊰⊱

IT TOOK A full day for Congress to finally read the letters from Deane accompanying the commissions, as well as letters from Charleston notables, confirming the story that the lanky and sandy-haired teenager was, in fact, a real marquis. He was a scion of one of the best families in France. He was an intimate of the queen. His uncle was the French ambassador to the Court of St. James. And best of all, he was rich. The boy could be a major asset in the dream of securing the support not just of penniless French rogues, but the full might of the Kingdom of France.

Lovell returned to Lafayette's lodgings accompanied by another French-speaking American named William Duer. Clearly there had been some misunderstanding. Lafayette confirmed everything said about him. As every previous French officer demanded exorbitant pay, they double- and triple-checked the bit about Lafayette serving without a salary. Lafayette reiterated his pledge to pay his own way. After more back-and-forth, Lafayette promised to serve under three simple conditions: he would serve without pay, he would serve as a volunteer, but he wanted to serve directly under George Washington. If Congress met those three conditions, he would happily lend his name, rank, and fortune to the American cause.

When Congress debated the matter, they concluded there was nothing to lose and everything to gain. Lafayette's commission cost them nothing, and he might serve as conduit to the inner circles of French power. They approved his commission. On July 31, 1777, Congress proclaimed the marquis de Lafayette a major general in the Continental Army. The proclamation made no mention of his military experience, but instead went out of its way to note the rank was bestowed "in consideration of his zeal, illustrious family and connections."[17]

In making this appointment, Congress believed they bestowed upon Lafayette an honorary rank for political reasons. Henry Laurens, a recently elected congressmen from South Carolina, wrote they expected Lafayette to "have a short campaign and then probably return to France

and secure to us the powerful interest of his high and extensive connections."[18] But Lafayette walked away under the impression he was now a
real general. George Washington—already sick to death of French officers and their grandiose demands—was left to sort out the confusion.

⊰⧉⊱

THE DAY LAFAYETTE received his commission, Congress held a dinner for Washington at City Tavern. Having just marched down with
his army from New Jersey, Washington was in Philadelphia to confer
with his civilian masters. Before he arrived, Washington was briefed
on the appointment of the curious young French marquis. No doubt
chagrined, Washington provisionally accepted the story this Frenchman was different. At the dinner, the two sat at opposite ends of the
table, but afterward Washington "took Lafayette aside, spoke to him
very kindly . . . and then told him he should be pleased if he would
make the quarters of the commander in chief his home . . . and consider
himself at all times one of the family."[19] Washington always referred to
his circle of aides and fellow officers as his "family." Lafayette took it to
mean he was being invited into Washington's personal household. He
was thrilled by this unexpected gesture.

For Lafayette, this was a seminal moment of his life. It was the beginning of a relationship that would define him long after Washington
was dead. Much has been made of the importance of the relationship,
especially given the emotional subtext of the childless Washington and
the fatherless Lafayette, each filling a hole in the other's heart. For Lafayette, there was a great deal of truth to this. His first would-be surrogate, the duc d'Ayen, did not exactly pan out. Lafayette still needed
a father. But Washington's emotional needs are harder to gauge. He
was surrounded by many young men in need of a father figure, and he
showed no great urge to be *their* adoptive father. In fact, Washington's
isolating reserve and lack of personal affection were legendary. Lafayette broke through Washington's reserve in a way those who knew the
general best considered unique and unprecedented. We know, however,
that on the night of July 31, 1777, George Washington had no idea how
much he would come to love this young French nobleman. Lafayette,
on the other hand, already anticipated a great friendship.

Washington became Lafayette's idol, mentor, and role model. A model promising to balance many of his own impetuous behaviors. Lafayette was naturally excited and excitable. He was passionate, bouncy, eager, intimate, and friendly. These qualities endeared Lafayette to everyone he met in America. They were also traits no one used to describe George Washington. And this is exactly what Lafayette was looking for. He was acutely aware of his own social defects: his clumsy lack of grace and happy effervescence led people to dismiss him and not take him seriously. Lafayette felt indulged and tolerated, when he wanted admiration and respect. When he looked at Washington, Lafayette saw a man projecting authority through calm, stoic dignity. It was not in Lafayette's nature to be calm, stoic, or dignified. But with Washington as his model, he would forever try.

Lafayette already emulated his new role model in one damning respect. George Washington espoused the cause of liberty while enslaving human beings. He was one of the largest slave-owners in North America. And though it is often passed over, we know during these early days in Philadelphia, Lafayette came to own a slave—a "negro boy"—purchased by one of the Americans who sailed with him on *La Victoire*.[20] The boy was purchased in Annapolis for 180 pounds and used by Lafayette to run errands in Philadelphia. No further reference is ever made of the boy after September 1777. His life after this brief period with Lafayette is a total mystery. For Lafayette, it became another inconvenient fact about his early life he never spoke of in later years.

Lafayette spent the next few weeks bouncing between Philadelphia and Washington's nearby headquarters. Invited to review the Continental Army, Lafayette could not help but find them poorly clothed, armed, and disciplined. The French troops stationed at Metz were the only soldiers he knew. And *these* men were not like *those* men. Self-consciously, Washington said, "We should be embarrassed to show ourselves to an officer who had just left the French army." To which Lafayette famously replied, "I am here to learn not to teach."[21] Lafayette said this with evident sincerity. It was probably the first moment Washington realized Lafayette might be more than a nuisance tolerated for diplomatic reasons.

But Lafayette also spent these early weeks peppering Washington with requests for a real division to command. Washington was under the impression Lafayette's commission was merely honorary and wrote Congress for clarification. They confirmed the appointment was honorary. They did not expect the marquis to actually command troops in battle. Washington called Lafayette into a meeting and said he would not assign him a real command, but Lafayette should still consider himself Washington's son and friend. The commander in chief continued to mean this metaphorically. Lafayette took it literally. The orphan marquis believed he finally found a real home.

⚜

GEORGE WASHINGTON'S MAIN preoccupation in the late summer of 1777 was trying to figure out what the hell the redcoats were up to. The movements of the British armies in North America baffled him. General John Burgoyne was presently marching down from Canada. After capturing Fort Ticonderoga, Burgoyne continued moving south from Lake Champlain through the wilderness of New York. Meanwhile, General William Howe, commander in chief of all British forces in America, was established in New York City after effortlessly expelling Washington from the city the previous year. It seemed logical, reasonable, and inevitable Howe would head north up the Hudson River to link with Burgoyne. This would detach New England from the rest of the colonies, and likely mark the beginning of the end of the rebellion. But instead, in July 1777, Howe ordered his men to board ships and sail away from New York City altogether. They had not been seen since. Washington could not make heads or tails of it.

Washington's great mistake, of course, was trying to make sense of the senseless. He did not realize he was witnessing one of the great instances of the British *losing* the War of Independence as much as the Americans winning it. The British minister of war somehow managed to approve two contradictory plans during the campaign of 1777: General Burgoyne marching down from Canada and General Howe capturing Philadelphia. The miscommunication among the senior command was so great that as Burgoyne continued his leisurely stroll through the forests north of Albany—which some have taken to calling Gentleman Johnny's Party Train—he remained under the incorrect assumption Howe's army would arrive to support him. Burgoyne had no inkling of Howe's plan to sail away to Philadelphia. Washington puzzled over a chessboard trying to grasp the hidden trap—little realizing his opponent was simply making a blunder.

On August 22, 1777, Howe's army was finally spotted in Chesapeake Bay. Washington rode out to personally reconnoiter the situation and invited Lafayette to come along. Lafayette enjoyed his first action in a uniform, on a horse, and serving a glorious cause. After investigating the British movements, the Continental officers determined Howe planned to capture Philadelphia. Congress begged Washington to fortify the city to withstand a siege, but Washington told them such a project was doomed to failure. The Continental Army would either stop the redcoats in an open battle or they would not stop them at all.

In the first week of September, it became clear Howe was leading his army on an oblique arc to approach and capture Philadelphia from the west. Washington and his war council decided the best place to halt this advance was at Brandywine Creek, roughly twenty miles southwest of Philadelphia. The Brandywine's swift current afforded only a limited number of crossing points, the most stable of which was Chadds Ford. Here, the banks of the river were enclosed by cliffs, and packed with large rocks and solid trees. It was the best possible place to make their stand.

❧

SEPTEMBER 11, 1777, dawned heavy with fog and anticipation. For Lafayette, this was all his dreams come true. Here he was in America—a major general in an army on the dawn of battle. From the time he was a boy, he planned to become a great soldier—winning glory and fame through courage and daring. Now the moment of truth was at hand. How would he respond? Would he shrink from the fight? Hesitate? Run? Would he trip and fall on his face? Would he die? This last question was the most important, but it was likely the furthest from his mind—not simply because all teenage boys are invincible, but because he told Adrienne being a major general was a great guarantee of living through battle. It's not like he was a colonel on the front line like his dearly departed father.

The Battle of Brandywine ultimately hinged on bad intelligence. In the morning, Hessian soldiers—German mercenaries in the king's employ— approached Chadds Ford as expected. But around noon, Washington was told a second British column wheeled around to the north. Realizing this meant the force in front of him at Chadds Ford was numerically inferior, Washington nearly ordered his men to charge down across the river. But then he was told the second British column was a mirage. So he held back. Unfortunately, the first report was true, the second mistaken. With the clarity of hindsight, it is easy to see Washington's missed opportunity. But in the confusion of approaching battle, nothing is clear at all. Besides, another crucial piece of bad intelligence already sealed the fate of the Continental Army. Despite reports to the contrary, there was another stable crossing farther up the river. Washington's army was about to be outflanked.

In the late afternoon, frantic word came that a British force previously unaccounted for bore down on the relatively weak Continental right flank. With the battle lines shifting, Lafayette requested permission to ride off and join the fray. Washington agreed—either too distracted to realize he was sending this invaluable marquis into the thick of battle, or because he knew the boy needed a real war story to brag about back home to help sell the French government on the merits of the American cause. Whichever it was, Lafayette raced off at top speed before Washington changed his mind.

Lafayette rode straight into blistering and noisy chaos. With unruffled nerves, he took stock of the situation and did what he could to bolster the Continental line, crumpling under heavy British fire. He dismounted and physically pushed men forward, calling in his best English to fix bayonets and prepare for close quarters combat. But the Continental soldiers wanted no part of bayonet duels with the stronger and better-trained British regulars, which would most likely leave them dying slowly on the forest floor from a punctured lung, pierced heart, or slashed throat. As Lafayette raced about, a musket ball shot clean through the fleshy muscle of his lower calf. His adrenaline pumping,

Lafayette did not even feel it. Only after looking down and noticing blood pouring from a hole in his boot did he realize he was wounded.

As dusk descended, the battle was lost. General Washington found the young marquis forced back onto his horse by an aide, lightheaded from a loss of blood, and unable to continue fighting. As Washington deployed reinforcements to cover the Continental retreat, he ordered Lafayette to quit the field. Despite his wound, Lafayette continued serving as best he could. With men retreating haphazardly toward the town of Chester, he posted himself at the bridge over a small creek to intercept men in flight. He re-formed them to hold the bridge and protect the retreat of their comrades. This is where Washington next found Lafayette: the potentially burdensome young French noble-man, wounded but imposing order amid so much disastrous confusion. Though Washington grappled with the grim embarrassment of defeat, he was impressed by Lafayette's dogged and selfless courage. The boy was *not* like the others.

⁂

THE BATTLE OF Brandywine was a crucial defeat for the Americans that led to the fall of Philadelphia. The Continental Army inflicted real casualties on its opponents, but absorbed as many losses as it inflicted. Probably more. They lost four hundred soldiers captured by the en-emy—to say nothing of the Pennsylvania militia forces, most of whom ran off never to return. It was another low point for Washington in what had become a war defined by low points.

For Lafayette, the Battle of Brandywine was a great success, a for-midable first step onto the stage of history. He accomplished every-thing he came to do. He passed his test with flying colors. He ran *toward* battle, not away from it. He stood his ground under heavy fire. He was shot and shrugged it off. His commander in chief found him wounded and bleeding, but still struggling to protect his comrades. Since joining the Noailles household, Lafayette seemed destined for inconsequential obscurity—occasionally mocked but usually ignored. Society even described his admirable decision to run away to Amer-ica as *brillante folie*—"brilliant madness." Yes, it was brilliant . . . but still madness.[22] The most likely result of these amusing dramatics was

Lafayette returning home a failure, proving he was indeed a fool. But instead . . . he succeeded. Brilliantly. At the Battle of Brandywine, Lafayette objectively and incontrovertibly proved himself.

The adroitly diplomatic George Washington, himself pleasantly surprised at Lafayette's bravery and sense of duty—welcome virtues in an army of soldiers known for running, hiding, and deserting—paid him public honor. In his brief dispatch to Congress announcing the unfortunate defeat at Brandywine, Washington did not fail to mention "the Marquis de Lafayette was wounded in the leg."[23] Washington knew newspapers would publish the dispatch, flattering Lafayette's vanity. It also spread the idea the interests of America and France were now joined in this dashing young hero, the marquis de Lafayette.

After his wound was bandaged, Lafayette headed back to Philadelphia to prepare for a general evacuation. When Lafayette reentered Philadelphia, he rejoined his erstwhile comrades from *La Victoire*. They were still put off by Congress and many prepared to return home. De Kalb was the only one who made any headway because he spoke English. The other French officers admired Lafayette's exploits. One joked Lafayette's wound would buy more advantages than his entire fortune. Now that he had what he came for—martial glory, a great adventure, and an honorable but non-life-threatening wound—they suggested he come home with them. But Lafayette refused. The blood he spilled at Brandywine was not the end of the story, but the beginning. He now considered himself not just a member of the Noailles, but of the Washingtons. He could not leave now. Not when there was so much left to do.

From this proving ground beside Brandywine Creek, the legend of Lafayette, "the Hero of Two Worlds," was born. Though tales of his exploits would grow, take on a life of their own, and culminate with enshrinement in the pantheon of American history, the legend was not grounded in fiction. It was not a literary invention. It sprang from real personal bravery, determination, and sacrifice. As he said before leaving France, "When I succeed everyone will applaud my efforts." For anyone else, these might have been famous last words. For Lafayette, they were his opening lines.

CHAPTER FIVE

A HELL OF BLUNDERS, MADNESS, AND DECEPTION

[1777–1778]

L AFAYETTE'S WOUND WAS NOT LIFE THREATENING, BUT IT did need time to heal. So as patriots in Philadelphia evacuated the city, Lafayette did not return to Continental Army head-quarters. Instead, he was directed to the town of Bethlehem, where a community of devout Moravians, who were opposed to the war on re-ligious grounds, cared for wounded. Shortly after he arrived, he was visited by George Washington's personal doctor, under orders to look after Lafayette "as though he were his son."[1] The doctor pronounced the marquis in no danger and Lafayette wrote playfully to Adrienne, "If a man wishes to be wounded for his own amusement, he should come and see my wound and have one just like it."[2]

Lafayette was delivered to Bethlehem in the carriage of Henry Laurens, a South Carolina plantation owner only recently elected to Congress. Laurens was a pillar of the Charleston community, owning extensive estates and more than three hundred slaves. A devout and industrious Christian with wide intellectual interests, Laurens was a fine specimen of the colonial planter aristocracy. He wistfully yearned for the demise of slavery, but not if it meant undermining the foundation of his wealth and social standing. Laurens also spoke good French, so as his congressional colleagues bustled about collecting papers, clothes, trunks, horses, and slaves, Henry Laurens made sure to pick up Lafayette and escort him out of Philadelphia. On the road, the fifty-three-year-old Laurens and the twenty-year-old Lafayette became friends. This turned out to be more light from Lafayette's good star. After depositing Lafayette in Bethlehem, Laurens joined the reconvened Congress in the interior town of York. Within a few weeks, his new colleagues elected Laurens president of Congress, replacing the outgoing John Hancock. This gave Lafayette a direct line to the center of civilian authority, just as his new relationship with George Washington gave him a direct line to the center of military authority.

Because he was wounded, Lafayette missed the Battle of Germantown, where the Continental Army suffered another frustrating setback on October 4. Washington's army once again retreated from the field. The disappointment of this latest defeat contrasted sharply with the spectacular news soon arriving from the north: General John Burgoyne's army had been defeated and captured. While preparing his invasion, Burgoyne spent as much time fretting over the supply of food, wine, rum, sugar, coffee, china, and silver as he did strategizing for the campaign itself. Meanwhile, the French supply ships organized by Beaumarchais finally arrived in Boston and the massive cache of weapons, ammunition, and supplies raced to the Continental forces in New York. Burgoyne subsequently stumbled into two shocking defeats in a row, collectively known as the Battle of Saratoga. On October 17, he surrendered his sword to Continental general Horatio Gates. The victory at Saratoga made for a sensational contrast to Washington's defeats at Brandywine and Germantown. It also meant, in the future, historians would identify Saratoga as the major turning point of the war. At the time, it led more than a few to wonder whether they ought to replace Washington as commander in chief.

Among those disillusioned with Washington was Brigadier General Thomas Conway. The Irish-born Conway spent his early military career in the French army and was among the first European officers to sign a contract with Silas Deane. Though a respected soldier, Conway's arrogant demeanor grated on superiors and subordinates alike. But despite his egotistical pomposity, Conway was an efficient officer and his men were always well disciplined. While the marquis de Lafayette was riding into the crumpling right flank of the Continental Army at Brandywine, Conway's brigade was one of the few holding the line. After the battle, Conway sought out Lafayette. Well versed in French etiquette, Conway presented a different face to Lafayette. No longer rude and overbearing, but deferential and flattering. Conway knew an opportunity for advancement when he saw one.

Despite enjoying the thrill of battle, Lafayette remained upset he had not been given a real divisional command. Conway stoked this resentment and hinted Lafayette should redirect his energies toward a new adventure—otherwise he risked becoming simply a valuable ornament to a bunch of rebellious farmers. With nothing better to do, Lafayette and Conway actively collaborated on a bold proposal: a naval campaign against the British. The plan called for Lafayette and Conway to secure an American warship, sail down to the Caribbean, recruit French privateers, and raid Britain's colonial possessions. After wreaking havoc in the Caribbean they would sail away to India. The limited object was disrupting British commerce, but the larger object was provoking a war between Britain and France. Once it became known a couple of French generals were raiding British colonies under an American flag, it might break the peace. And of course, this would all result in Lafayette winning international fame as a daring and patriotic corsair.

Lafayette was serious enough about this plan that he drafted a detailed memo to Prime Minister Maurepas extolling its virtues. When he read this memo, Maurepas allegedly said, "Someday he will end up selling all the furniture in Versailles to support the American cause . . . once he gets something in his head, it is impossible to resist him."[3] Lafayette was not planning to sell furniture to fund this expedition, though. Carried away by his enthusiasm for the project, young Lafayette wandered into another moral embarrassment for an older and wiser Lafayette. Eager to promote the plan, Lafayette argued if they rounded up and sold English slaves, "the Negroes would cover the cost of the enterprise."[4] Ultimately Maurepas rejected the whole scheme, but if the expedition had launched, the marquis de Lafayette might have gone down in history as a slave-trading pirate.

⊰⊱

MEANWHILE, BACK IN France, Lafayette's friends and family followed along as best they could. The British navy routinely disrupted the flow of direct correspondence across the Atlantic, so American news reaching Paris was generally a mix of gossip and rumors amplified by the sensationalist British press. In the fall of 1777, rumors swirled through Paris Lafayette had been shot and killed. Another story said he drowned. It was also said he ran away to America to impress Aglaé de Hunolstein, whom he was supposedly in love with. The unconfirmed tales of her husband's death and infidelity distressed Adrienne, who recently gave birth to the couple's second child, a girl named Anastasie. To get away from the malicious gossip, her mother took Adrienne to live in the country. But the family soon endured a tragedy that eclipsed worries about her husband. In October 1777, little Henriette died just shy of her second birthday. Lafayette would not find out for another seven months that when he left Henriette behind in February, he left her behind forever.

But life was not all tragedy and scurrilous rumors. Lafayette's reputation soared after his departure the previous spring. His friends wallowed in agonized envy. Ségur noted the change in society after his friend's escape to America: "The court almost seemed proud of him and all the young men envied him." Ségur also said, "The very persons who blamed him most for his bold enterprise now applauded him."[5] The comte de Vergennes seized on the stories of Lafayette's intimacy with George Washington to push the king to do more to help the Americans. They now had a direct line to the American commander in chief.

But as every history textbook shows, it was not Lafayette who moved the king, but the Battle of Saratoga. Vergennes seized on this miraculous American victory to bring his heretofore covert support for the Americans into the open. On December 6, he invited the American commissioners, now led by Benjamin Franklin, to emerge from behind their implausibly thin cover stories and speak directly with the Crown. To soothe fears of the financial costs, Vergennes trumpeted the commercial boon of a victorious alliance with the Americans. "The power that will first recognize the independence of these Americans," he said, "will be the first to reap the fruits of this war."[6] While France would be the *kingdom* benefiting most from being first to join the Americans, no one would reap greater fruits *personally* than the marquis de Lafayette.

One man who would *not* enjoy any American fruits was Charles-François de Broglie. Congress eventually honored Baron de Kalb's commission after he threatened to sue them for fraud back in France—thus threatening to discredit Congress in the eyes of the people they were trying to woo. But by then, de Kalb concluded his farfetched plan to make Broglie "Stadtholder of America" never had a chance. When de Kalb asked around, he received only incredulous laughter at the thought of replacing Washington with a Frenchman. So despite accepting service in the Continental Army, de Kalb wrote Broglie, "It is impossible to execute the great design I have so gladly come to subserve . . . it would be regarded as no less as an act of crying injustice against Washington, than as an outrage on the honor of the whole country."[7] This letter marks the end of the so-called Broglie Intrigue—a half-baked conspiracy that swept the marquis de Lafayette up and deposited him on the shores of America. As the plot receded into obscurity, Lafayette picked himself up and continued walking toward his historical destiny.

⊰⊱

WHEN LAFAYETTE'S LEG healed enough to walk, he left the Moravians and their pleasant, but futile, sermons against war to rejoin the Continental Army outside Philadelphia. Upon arrival, he found Washington and Congress engaged in an argument about whether to mount a winter assault on the occupied capital. Congress thought it essential. Washington thought it hopeless. After assessing the situation, Lafayette concurred an attack on Philadelphia was madness. The marquis could be impetuous, audacious, and succumb too easily to reckless optimism, but he always tried to temper these instincts with a realistic assessment of the odds. He was happy to dare what he thought improbable. But he dared not pursue what he thought impossible.

Washington selected the strategic heights of Valley Forge as the best place to make winter quarters. As late as November, British units under

Lord Cornwallis continued striking at Continental forts in New Jersey. So Washington ordered General Nathanael Greene to deflect these probes. Greene was a thirty-five-year-old lapsed Quaker from Rhode Island who walked away from his pacifist brethren to become an armed patriot. A self-taught general, he was now one of Washington's most trusted officers. Eager for something to do, Lafayette volunteered for the mission. Washington's approval came with a joyous bonus: Lafayette would personally command a unit composed of Continental soldiers, militiamen, and a cohort of Daniel Morgan's increasingly legendary Virginia riflemen. Near the town of Gloucester, New Jersey, Lafayette ran into an outpost of Hessians. He opened a withering attack, driving back not just the Hessians, but British attempts to reinforce the outpost. Like everyone else, Greene took a shine to Lafayette, and was now more impressed than ever. He told Washington the marquis's bravery and instinct for battle did him great credit. He noted with a mix of approbation and trepidation: "The Marquis seems determined to put himself in danger."[8]

After Gloucester, the ongoing confusion about the nature of Lafayette's role in the army dissolved. Washington finally relented to Lafayette's request to command a division as a full-fledged major general. The boy had proven himself. He had earned it. On November 30, 1777, Washington told Lafayette he could lead a division of his choosing. Lafayette was ecstatic, and the news gave him the courage to write a letter he had been putting off to the duc d'Ayen. Though assured his father-in-law's initial fury had long since abated, Lafayette still needed to assuage d'Ayen's deeper concerns about his wayward son-in-law. Lafayette could now write truthfully he was a real major general, as well as a confidant of General Washington. He spoke of Washington's "warm friendship and complete confidence in me regarding all matters great and small."[9] He said he lived with Washington, "as though in the household of a friend of twenty years."[10] Lafayette had once before been adopted by a great household, where he subsequently found himself barely tolerated. One assumes this was not lost on d'Ayen as he read Lafayette boast of his new family.

THE LONGER LAFAYETTE stayed in America, the more scales fell from his eyes. His fantasy of every American as a liberty-loving republican gave way to the reality many were hostile to the glorious cause. Lafayette wrote Adrienne he walked into "a kind of civil war."[11] He later recalled Philadelphia awaited the outcome of Brandywine "separated in two groups in all the squares and public places."[12] One group cheering for Washington, the other group cheering Howe. This second group felt their lives, liberty, and property threatened not by king and Parliament, but hysterical rebels gone mad. The longer he stayed in America, the more internal acrimony he witnessed. "The violence of party spirit divided provinces, cities, and families," he remembered. "One saw brothers, officers in opposing armies, meet by chance in their father's house and seize their arms to fight each other."[13] Every revolution is ultimately a civil war, a lesson Lafayette first learned in America.

He also learned there were hostile factions *inside* the patriot camp. His first encounter with such a faction was the collection of anti-Washington grumblers melodramatically dubbed by history the "Conway Cabal." The cabal was named after Lafayette's new friend, Thomas Conway, who was thoroughly disillusioned with Washington. The list of participants includes former quartermaster general Thomas Mifflin, Colonel Richard Henry Lee, and Congressman Benjamin Harrison. These men shared little in common but a desire to replace the eternally retreating George Washington with the recently triumphant Horatio Gates. To advance this loosely defined project, they induced Congress to create an oversight committee called the Board of War. The new board was staffed with critics of Washington who promptly invited Horatio Gates to become its president.

Another potential ally the Conway Cabal hoped to enlist was the marquis de Lafayette. Since Lafayette already secured his divisional command, the Board of War determined to do him one better—they offered an *independent* command in a theater where a French commander would be of enormous value: Canada. Since the beginning of hostilities with the mother country, the rebels of the southern states attempted to win their northern cousins to the cause. When Canada remained aloof, the rebels attempted to capture Quebec over the winter of 1775–1776. The campaign was a failure; the only notable result was

General Benedict Arnold emerging as patriotic hero. The Board of War resurrected the dream of an "irruption into Canada."[14] Even if the British settlements along the coast resisted, surely the French Canadians of the interior would flock to the banner of an army led by one of their countrymen. It was a mission perfectly designed to satisfy Lafayette's ambition and vanity.

But before Lafayette departed for the liberation of Canada, Washington revealed the possible machinations behind the offer. Conway had apparently written a letter to Gates disparaging Washington—remarks subsequently repeated by a drunken aide-de-camp. Washington told Lafayette there was a loose plot to remove him from command and sending Lafayette to Canada was likely part of that plot. Lafayette was incensed. He was already so thoroughly comingling the ideas of America, liberty, and George Washington he could not imagine separating them. Lafayette returned to his tent and composed a long letter declaring unequivocal loyalty to Washington. If Washington was removed, Lafayette said he would resign and go home—taking his wealth and connections with him.

Washington was touched. In truth, they barely knew each other. Lafayette had only been in the army a few months. Washington spoke no French. Lafayette spoke only broken English. Washington's offer for Lafayette to join his family was a diplomatic gesture to flatter a politically valuable resource. But after Lafayette's conduct at Brandywine, his further bravery at Gloucester, and now this declaration of undying loyalty, Washington came to really like the French marquis. Lafayette fell in love with Washington at first sight. But it was probably here in the frigid cold of the infamous winter at Valley Forge Washington started returning his affection.

⚏

LAFAYETTE'S RELATIONSHIP WITH Washington was important, but it was not the only important relationship he developed. When he looked around at his fellow generals he saw a collection of men much older than him. De Kalb was over fifty. Washington was in his midforties. Only the former bookseller turned artillery commander Henry Knox was under thirty. These men may have been Lafayette's peers on the table of ranks, but they were not his emotional or psychological peers. For that he needed to look lower in the chain of command where ambitious young men like Lafayette are usually found. It was here he found lasting friendship with several of Washington's aides-de-camp.

Lafayette first met Colonel Alexander Hamilton shortly after arriving at headquarters in August 1777. Born and raised in the tiny Caribbean colony of Nevis, Hamilton was the illegitimate son of a dead mother and an absentee father. He first apprenticed at a merchant house, where the precocious teenager was so promising, benefactors took up a subscription to enroll him at King's College in New York City (now Columbia University). When the war came, young Hamilton sided with the patriots and volunteered for service in a Continental artillery company. He displayed intelligent courage throughout the disastrous campaign of 1776, and was soon recommended to George Washington. Transferred to headquarters in the spring of 1777, Hamilton quickly became Washington's de facto chief of staff. When Lafayette arrived, Washington assigned Colonel Hamilton to be his liaison officer, because among his many other talents, Hamilton spoke French.

Lafayette and Hamilton hit it off immediately and discovered they traveled divergent, yet eerily similar paths. On his father's side, Hamilton claimed noble Scottish lineage rivaling Lafayette's own distinguished family tree. Hamilton later commented, "The truth is that, on the question of who my parents were, I have better pretentions than most of those who in this country plume themselves on ancestry."[15] But he said this with a hefty dose of irony. His father was the black sheep of his family—an indolent paragon of downward mobility who walked out on his family when Hamilton was just a boy. Like Lafayette, Hamilton grew up without a father. He also lost his mother to a fatal illness at almost the same age Lafayette lost his. But where the tragedies of Lafayette's childhood made him the heir of a fabulous fortune, the tragedies of Hamilton's illegitimate childhood left him systematically cut out of his family's inheritance. So where the dark clouds of Lafayette's life were lined with silver, the dark clouds of Hamilton's life were simply dark. Lafayette emerged from childhood buoyant and effusive, Hamilton cynical and reticent. But even though Hamilton started life a penniless bastard on the periphery of European civilization, and Lafayette started life an insanely wealthy heir in the heart of a great kingdom, they fell into an easy friendship. French was not the only language the two young men shared. The also shared a code of personal honor and a desire to prove themselves to the world.

Joining these budding young friends was twenty-three-year-old Colonel John Laurens, the son of president of Congress Henry Laurens. The younger Laurens was studying law in London when the relationship between mother country and colonies broke down in 1774, 1775, and 1776. And though Henry would have liked his son to stay in England, John burned to join his countrymen. Though he was the scion of Charleston slave society, John underwent an emotional and moral education in Europe. He attended school in the Republic of Geneva, home of Rousseau and the refuge of Voltaire. John devoured humanist philosophy and picked up radical ideas. Then he radicalized still further after moving to London to study law. John Laurens was a politically obsessed law student when crusading abolitionists rescued an enslaved African man, James Somerset, from the hold of a ship in the Thames in 1772. The abolitionists successfully sued for his freedom and "Somerset's Case" set John Laurens on the road to abolitionism. His conversations with Lafayette in Valley Forge almost certainly directed Lafayette to the same path.

When the colonies declared independence, John Laurens quit school and returned home to fight. His English friends could not understand his support for the cause. They echoed the famous quip from Samuel Johnson: "How is it that we hear the loudest yelps for liberty among the drivers of negroes?"[16] But Laurens believed in the cause of liberty. When America was victorious, he did not plan to sweep the hypocrisy of slavery under the rug; he planned to abolish it completely. After arriving in camp, the newly minted Colonel Laurens was assigned to Washington's staff and fell in with Hamilton and Lafayette. Hamilton's son would later call them the Three Musketeers of the American Revolution. All three were young and eager for battlefield glory, Laurens somehow even more than Lafayette or Hamilton—and his battlefield courage swerved dangerously toward suicidal recklessness. Though they were all close, Hamilton and Laurens developed a special bond, leading to professions of intimate affection that may or may not have been consummated.

-⚏-

THOUGH WASHINGTON WAS skeptical of the "irruption into Canada," he gave Lafayette his blessing to accept the command. In late January 1778, Lafayette departed Valley Forge. He first went to York, Pennsylvania, to clarify his position with Congress. At a meeting with General Gates and other members of the Board of War, Lafayette first ensured the mission would not be considered independent of Washington's overall command. Next, he tried to have Conway—whom he no longer liked or trusted—removed from the expedition. When that didn't work, he successfully got General de Kalb appointed second in command. These arrangements made, Lafayette later said he "embarrassed them by making them drink to the health of their commander-in-chief."[17]

Lafayette departed north with high hopes. He expected to find "2500 men assembled at Albany, a large body of militia at Coos, 2 millions of paper money, some silver money, and the means of crossing the ice of Lake Champlain."[18] Lafayette wanted to reach this assembled army and get moving before the ice melted. He further expected to find thousands of willing French-Canadian volunteers who would leap at the chance to expel the hated British, presumed to be in demoralized disarray following Burgoyne's surrender. Lafayette believed all of this right up until the moment he pulled into Albany.

Lafayette discovered upon arrival the "irruption into Canada" was premised on wishful thinking. For starters, he found less than half the promised number of troops—none of them ready or eager to fight. The militia forces were also nowhere to be found. Apparently, no one told the regional commander of the New York militia to muster them. At least that's what he later claimed. But given how hostile everyone was to a winter march into Quebec, it's unclear what was uncommunicated and what went deliberately unheard. Lafayette sounded out veteran Continental officers in the city, including the legendary Benedict Arnold, presently convalescing from wounds suffered at Saratoga. Arnold ridiculed the plan and bluntly told Lafayette it was an impossible suicide mission. Arnold said the British in Canada were not demoralized.

As for the French Canadians, they hated the Anglo-Americans even more than they hated the British.

After a few days of depressingly realistic advice, Lafayette reported to Congress the expedition was impossible. It couldn't be done. In a separate letter, he angrily told Henry Laurens when he arrived in Albany all he found was a "hell of blunders, madness, and deception."[19] Lafayette felt his honor besmirched. Upon receiving the command, he wrote proudly back to France of his mission to liberate Canada. Now he would look like a fool. In high dudgeon, Lafayette threatened to resign from the army if this was how they planned to treat him. Laurens and Washington talked Lafayette down, both assuring him it was not as bad as all that. Washington said, if anything, Lafayette would come off looking good. "It will be no disadvantage to have it known in Europe," he said, "that you had received so manifest a proof of the good opinion and confidence of Congress as an important and detached command—and I am persuaded that everyone will applaud your prudence in renouncing a project, in pursing which you would vainly have attempted physical impossibilities."[20] Lafayette calmed down. He would not quit and go home. But neither would he enjoy the glory he so recently thought in his grasp.

⚍⚎

BEFORE HE LEFT Albany to return to headquarters, local leaders called Lafayette to perform a service that brought him into contact with the other dark shadow sprawling across the history of the United States: the Native Americans. It was time for Lafayette to meet the people whose blood, vicomte de Mauroy once told Lafayette, fertilized the fields the American pioneers plowed as they expanded their utopia of liberty and equality.

In northern New York, massacres and counter-massacres defined the conflict between the Six Nations of the Iroquois and the Americans. When the war began, the Iroquois almost uniformly sided with the British. The Anglo-American settlers moving west were, by far, the greater threat. They knew one of the proximate causes of the rebellion was the Quebec Act, a decree expanding the province of Quebec to include almost all the territory on the far side of the Appalachians. It was interpreted by everyone as a move to hinder further migration west by the coastal colonists. It also threatened the lucrative land speculation so beloved by colonial leaders like George Washington and Thomas Jefferson. A string of forts erected by the British to maintain a permanent military presence on the frontier were clearly not just to defend British subjects from hostile indigenous tribes, but also bottle up the settlers moving west with violent impunity. It was not a difficult choice for the Iroquois to side with the British when the colonists went into revolt.

Those rebellious colonists now hoped to neutralize the threat posed by the Iroquois. As the Iroquois were known to be better disposed toward the French, local patriot officials invited Lafayette to participate in a summit arranged with leaders of the Six Nations. In late February 1778, Lafayette traveled to Johnstown for the rendezvous. Even later in life, Lafayette maintained the Iroquois were only ever hostile to the Americans because of English bribes, never quite imagining they might have a real motivation for joining the British. That they too were fighting for freedom, liberty, and self-determination from encroaching foreigners who seized by force what they did not simply take.

When Lafayette arrived, he found "five hundred men, women, and children, gaudily painted and bedecked in feathers, their ears pierced, their noses ornamented with jewels." He noted, "As the old men smoked, they discoursed very well on politics," but he also said they might succeed in their desire to secure a balance of power between all the foreigners "if their drunkenness with rum, like drunkenness with ambition in Europe, did not divert them."[21] After a few days of eating, drinking, and talking, the Iroquois adopted Lafayette into a tribe under the name Kayewla, the name of a legendary warrior. But little came of the summit. The Seneca refused to even send representatives. Most of the others remained aloof. Only the Oneida showed any interest at all—and fifty warriors promised to come fight with Kayewla in the spring. Lafayette then returned to Valley Forge. The whole mission had been a fiasco, but Washington was right: Lafayette's reputation did not suffer for it.

WHEN LAFAYETTE RETURNED to Valley Forge in March 1778, he was pleased to discover the army transformed. Though the men still suffered through their famously grueling winter—desperately short of food, boots, blankets, jackets—the feeling in camp was different. This change was largely thanks to the arrival of the rotund and volatile Friedrich Wilhelm von Steuben. He arrived in camp calling himself "Baron von Steuben" and carrying letters of recommendation from Benjamin Franklin. Franklin confirmed Steuben's story that he was a Prussian general who had served directly under the legendary Frederick the Great. Steuben's tale was mostly fiction and, at first blush, the same kind of lie told by practically every other European officer hunting for cash and prizes in America. Technically, Steuben *had* served under Frederick the Great, but only as a young aide-de-camp, not as a general. But like Lafayette, Steuben was different. Benjamin Franklin recognized his talents and helped the penniless "Baron" secure a loan and letters of recommendation to take to America.

As the self-declared patrons of European officers, Lafayette and Steuben corresponded before Lafayette returned to Valley Forge, and upon the marquis's return they became friends. Because Steuben spoke French and German but not English, he required translators to speak to the men, and Lafayette was among those who pitched in. Taking over as inspector general of the Continental Army, Steuben undertook an improvised reorganization of tactical training. The Continentals were deficient in everything, from marching, to shooting, to close quarters fighting. The only thing they seemed to do well was retreat. As he drilled the soldiers, Steuben's comically over-the-top exhortations became the stuff of instant legend. Steuben would yell orders in French while an aide translated the commands into English. When the men made mistakes, Steuben blustered barely comprehensible strings of *goddammits* before asking his interpreter to take over swearing at the men in English.

The men found Steuben's antics endearing rather than frightening because his concern for the well-being of the common soldiers was obvious. Knowing they were not professionals, Steuben took time to explain not just *what* they must do, but *why* they should do it. As he later wrote to the French minister of war, "In France you tell a soldier to do something and he does it. In America, you have to explain *why* and then they will do it."[22] Above all, Steuben's message was: if you don't do this properly you will die in battle. Lafayette was among those who helped Steuben translate a simplified training manual, which subsequently became the basis of American military drill for the next fifty years. It was full of reminders that a republican army could not function like a royal army. Officers must show care and love for the common soldiers. It was essential for good discipline. Steuben loved his boys and they loved him back.

But nothing changed the mood in Valley Forge more than the arrival of miraculous news on May 1, 1778: the Kingdom of France had signed an alliance with the "United Provinces of America." On February 6, 1778, the two sides signed what appeared to be primarily a commercial treaty. But the agreement was premised on France recognizing the sovereign independence of the former British colonies. When Benjamin Franklin was presented to the king to celebrate the new accord, he mustered the full depths of his ingratiating charms and said, "If all monarchies were governed by the principles which are in your heart, sire, republics would never be formed."[23] He spoke these words almost exactly fifteen years before the First French Republic chopped off Louis's head.

While the initial treaty was strictly commercial, the parties agreed to a separate alliance of mutual defense should France find itself at war with Britain. With France recognizing American independence, war was a foregone conclusion. Two weeks later, Lafayette's uncle presented this treaty to the Crown of England. The two kingdoms broke off diplomatic relations and declared war on each other.

At Valley Forge, news of the alliance led to singing, dancing, parades, and banquets. The combined force of France and America could not lose. Lafayette's personal ecstasy was predictable. He was so excited, he seized George Washington and kissed him on both cheeks. This was a shocking display as even those closest to Washington hardly dared to touch him. But Lafayette found a place in Washington's heart reserved for few others.

The news from France was not all rapturous. In the same bundle of mail, Lafayette finally learned his daughter Henriette died the previous fall. For seven months he had written letters to Adrienne asking her to kiss Henriette, imagining the wonderful time their family would have when they were all reunited. For seven months, Adrienne read these letters and was reminded her little girl was dead, and her husband never even knew her. Fame and glory demand sacrifice. And though this is terrible for those doing the sacrificing, it is more terrible still for the sacrificed.

CHAPTER SIX

THE ALLIANCE

[1778–1779]

FRANCE'S ENTRY INTO THE WAR TRIGGERED A SHAKE-UP IN the British high command. King George recalled commander in chief William Howe to London. The capture of Philadelphia was supposed to be the capstone of two years' uninterrupted success. Howe beat Washington in every battle, drove the Continentals from every field, and now occupied the rebel capital. By all rights he ought to be raising a glass of champagne to final victory. Instead, the Continentals stubbornly hung together long enough for the French to bail them out.

General Henry Clinton succeeded Howe as commander in chief. Clinton was a forty-eight-year-old veteran officer who had been fighting in America since the Battle of Bunker Hill (and who once made the acquaintance of a young French marquis while home on leave in the winter of January 1777). Clinton inherited a precarious situation. With the French preparing to sail a navy across the Atlantic, it was not safe for the British to remain in Philadelphia. Clinton's first mission was to lead the army back to the more defensible New York City. As Clinton prepared the evacuation, General Howe enjoyed a running series of farewell banquets and all-night parties.

Seeking the details of Clinton's plans, Washington turned to La-fayette. He assigned Lafayette 2,200 Continental soldiers, 600 Penn-sylvania militiamen, and the attachment of 50 Oneida warriors who had come down to serve under Kayewla. Lafayette's orders were to re-connoiter the environs of Philadelphia while suborning as many spies and informants as he could. The debacle in Albany notwithstanding, it would be Lafayette's first independent command. Washington gave Lafayette unusually detailed instructions for the mission. Above all, Lafayette must not give the enemy any opportunity to kill or capture him. That would be a disastrous beginning to the Franco-American alliance. Washington instructed Lafayette to stay on the move, and never make camp in the same place twice.

On May 18, 1778, Lafayette rode out of camp with his friend Col-onel John Laurens at his side. They crossed the Schuylkill River and advanced to Barren Hill, a well-situated bluff midway between Valley Forge and Philadelphia. There, they spent the night in camp. Then, either from overconfident complacency or youthful idiocy, Lafayette ignored the instruction to keep moving. Instead, he stayed on Barren Hill a second night. This decision nearly cost him everything.

A deserter from the Continental army slipped away to Philadelphia and told General Howe the marquis de Lafayette was a sitting duck perched atop Barren Hill. Howe could not believe his good fortune. His critics back home delighted in Howe's recent disgrace. But what if he disembarked in London with a lovely present for the king? What if he bagged the marquis de Lafayette? Howe suspended the rolling fare-well party and roused his soldiers for one last campaign. In the small hours of May 20, Howe ordered a vanguard of five thousand men to get moving. He and Henry Clinton followed a few hours later with another seven thousand. This was not some little snatch-and-grab operation—the whole British army was on a manhunt.

Only a stroke of luck saved Lafayette. He was alerted to danger when a local doctor heard the British vanguard marching past his house and raced to warn the soldiers camped on Barren Hill. By his own admission, Lafayette received this alarming news after retiring to his tent for the evening where he was "chatting with a young lady."[1] Lafayette claimed he was recruiting her to be a spy, but this was the middle of the night, everyone else was asleep, and some conclusions naturally draw themselves.

Lafayette sprang out of his tent and ordered his men to ditch Barren Hill. He sent one unit to fan out and pretend to be a much larger force in an effort to spook and confuse the British vanguard. He ordered snipers to pin down Howe's central column coming up the main road. Lafayette led the rest of his men down the only other open road available. Lafayette threaded an incredibly tight needle, but he threaded it successfully. When Howe reached Barren Hill, the bluff was deserted.

Had Lafayette been captured, there would have been no worse end to his story. The humiliation would have been intolerable. He would have returned to Europe not a conquering hero but a pathetic prisoner—his hands not raised in triumph but clapped in irons. All because he couldn't so much as lead a simple scouting expedition without messing everything up. But he was *not* captured. He merely returned to Valley Forge somewhat sheepish and out of breath. Sensitive to the young man's feelings, Washington only mildly damned Lafayette with faint praise. "The Marquis," Washington reported, "had very near been caught in a snare—in fact he was in it—but by his own dexterity, or the enemy's want of it, he disengaged himself . . . by an orderly, and well conducted retreat—upon the whole, the Marquis came handsomely off."[2] George Washington knew sometimes the key to victory was a handsome retreat.

⁓

After General Howe sailed home empty-handed to begin a comfortable retirement defending his reputation, General Henry Clinton evacuated of Philadelphia. He ordered as much as possible loaded onto ships, but ten thousand men and a huge baggage train needed to travel overland to New York City up through New Jersey. This procession would be further encumbered by thousands of Loyalists desperate to get out of Philadelphia. Those who celebrated Howe's victory at Brandywine justifiably dreaded reprisals when the British departed. On the morning of June 18, 1778, Clinton ordered this slow train out of Philadelphia.

After watching British movements for weeks with nervous anticipation, Washington and his army broke camp the next morning. It had been a terrible winter, but the men were stepping livelier than ever thanks to Steuben's colorful drills. Lafayette rode at the head of a division of Virginians and North Carolinians. Hamilton and Laurens rode alongside Washington. All were eager for action. The promise of glory lay ahead. They left behind the hills of Valley Forge to be consecrated by high priests of American mythology.

Not everyone in the Continental Army was eager for battle. Just before the departure from Valley Forge, General Charles Lee rejoined Washington's war council. As thin and unpleasant as a hickory switch, Lee was an old English veteran of European warfare. His irascible and idiosyncratic beliefs carried him to America in 1775, and Congress happily appointed him major general. This was before they realized how obnoxiously arrogant European officers could be. Washington considered Lee to be a master of tactics and strategy, despite his personality. Lee did not hold Washington in the same high regard. Despite efforts to placate the grouchy Englishman, Lee became a thorn in Washington's side throughout the disastrous campaigns in New York. This thorn was temporarily removed by British soldiers who captured General Lee leaping naked from a tavern window in December 1776.

Held prisoner in New York City, Lee's captors flattered and indulged him. It was not hard for General Howe to lure Lee into treasonous correspondence. Lee willingly named the Continental Army's weaknesses—especially George Washington's weaknesses, of which he thought there were many. Lee's treason passed unnoticed during the lifetimes of all the men he betrayed. The truth was not revealed until archivists discovered incriminating letters among General Howe's papers in 1857.

In the spring of 1778, a prisoner exchange returned Lee to active duty. When he rejoined the army, he advised avoiding contact with the redcoats at all costs. The French were on the way. There was no reason to risk defeat before *real* reinforcements arrived. Lee said the Americans should build the British "a bridge of gold" to New York City. Washington initially heeded this advice. His army marched parallel to Clinton's procession, but always hung back.[3]

Others on Washington's staff argued the time was ripe for a bold strike. Clinton would never be more exposed. Among those making this argument were Greene, Hamilton, Steuben, Laurens, and the marquis de Lafayette. They encouraged Washington's own instincts to attack. Washington tentatively agreed and sent a few units forward to harass the British march. They reported the enticing news Clinton had divided his forces. The large baggage train lay between a vanguard and a rearguard—each isolated and vulnerable. Now convinced there was a chance to maul Clinton's hindquarters, Washington ordered more brigades forward. He offered command of this attack force to Lee, but Lee declined, believing it foolhardy and beneath his dignity. So Washington offered it to the ever-hungry and energetic Lafayette, who rushed to saddle his horse before anyone changed their minds.

After Lafayette departed, Lee discovered Washington issued the marquis further instructions to bring all the scattered forward detachments under a single unified command. Before night fell, Lafayette would be in command of a whole second army. Lee's military honor kicked in. As the senior major general, he *must* command this second army or be degraded professionally. Washington could not deny this logic of military protocol. Washington ordered Lee to catch up with Lafayette and take over—though he made sure to send him with another thousand men, specifically to make it appear Lafayette was not being relieved of command. Lafayette got within five miles of the enemy—currently encamped at Monmouth Court House—before breaking off and rendezvousing with Lee. The next morning, they would attack.

If the Battle of Brandywine hinged on bad intelligence, the Battle of Monmouth Court House hinged on miscommunication. More to the point: the absence of communication. On the blazing hot morning of June 28, 1778, the British broke camp. Aware the Continental Army stood poised to attack, General Clinton and Lord Cornwallis both stayed behind with a rearguard composed of their best troops. As the Americans advanced, Lafayette commanded the right wing. Unfortunately he had no idea what he was supposed to do. That morning, Lee improvised a plan of attack in his head—but did not communicate it to his subordinates. Nor did he communicate anything to Washington, now prodding the main army forward as fast as he could. As Lee's brigades approached the British line, there was no coordination or communication between them. This left individual units exposed, forcing them to fall back to a more protected position, leading detachments elsewhere to stall the advance and fall back. Each tactical retreat forced further tactical retreats. They were there to attack, and instead fell back before making contact with the enemy.

When Washington rode in to confirm the unbelievable stories of retreat, he located General Lee and berated him. This encounter became an oft-told tale in the legend of George Washington. The stoic warrior who never uttered a curse allegedly let fly like a drunken sailor. A version of the story has Lee sputtering the Continentals could not withstand British bayonets and Washington shouting, "You damned poltroon you never tried them!"[4] One entertained officer later said Washington cursed "till the leaves shook on the trees."[5] Unfortunately, this beloved anecdote has been exaggerated to the point of fiction. None of the stories trace back to men who actually witnessed the dressing-down. Lafayette himself loved to tell the story and recounted years later, "This was the only time I heard General Washington swear."[6] But he wasn't there either.

Washington took over, halted the retreat, and launched a new offensive. With the main army joining the fray, the Continentals pressed forward and battle raged for the rest of the day. Neither side seized the advantage and only darkness ended the fighting. Laurens and Hamilton both earned plaudits for their actions that day, but Washington relegated Lafayette to a position in the back lines. In the future, Lafayette and his admirers passed over Monmouth Court House when listing his heroic deeds in America. Washington did not hold Lafayette personally responsible for the fiasco, however, and when the fighting ended, Washington spread out a cloak and invited the marquis to sleep beside him in the open air. When they awoke they discovered the tactical draw had become a technical victory. During the night, Clinton ordered a midnight retreat. The enemy was gone. For the first time in a long time, George Washington found himself master of the field.

More than a strategic victory, the Battle of Monmouth Court House was a moral triumph. The retrained Continentals emerged from Valley Forge and went toe-to-toe with the allegedly invincible British army.

With their new French allies on the way, it was a perfectly timed display of professional soldiering. Blame for any deficiencies was laid squarely at the feet of General Charles Lee. Accusations of cowardice, incompetence, and disobedience culminated in a court-martial suspending Lee from the service for one year. Lee quit the army in disgust. He spent the next few months publicly disparaging Washington, until the general's family finally heard enough. John Laurens challenged Lee to a duel, with Alexander Hamilton acting as his second. It was Hamilton's first duel.

It would not be his last.

⊞

ON JULY 5, 1778, a fleet was sighted off the Maryland coast. To great excitement it turned out to be the long-expected French reinforcements. The fleet was commanded by Charles Henri Hector, the comte d'Estaing. Though a career army officer, for this expedition he carried the additional rank of admiral—a rank the naval captains under his command respected so much they only ever addressed him as "general." D'Estaing brought with him twelve ships of the line, four frigates, and four thousand French marines. Also on board d'Estaing's flagship was Conrad Alexandre Gérard—set to serve as the first official French envoy to the "United Provinces of America"—and Silas Deane, the commissioner in Paris who sent Lafayette and dozens of other French officers across the Atlantic. Deane had been recalled by Congress, unaware they meant to accuse him of scandalous impropriety. D'Estaing dropped Gérard and Deane in Philadelphia before sailing to a rendezvous with the Continental Army at Sandy Hook, New Jersey.

For Lafayette, the arrival of the French fleet was a dream come true. He immediately cast himself in the role he would play for the rest of his life: the indispensable *doyen* of Franco-American relations. He wrote a flurry of letters and memorandums to d'Estaing, Washington, Henry Laurens to ensure the historic Franco-American union got off on the right foot. These letters crystalize our understanding of Lafayette's original motivation for joining the American War of Independence. Though he was more honest, sincere, and idealistic than his fellow passengers aboard *La Victoire*, extolling the cause of freedom and liberty even before he left France, Lafayette always saw service in America as a stepping stone back into the French army. He was personally loyal to his fellow American officers—Washington, Hamilton, Laurens, Greene, and Knox—but Lafayette never forgot he was a Frenchman. After the alliance was announced, he wrote to a French financial agent in Boston saying that as soon as the French navy arrived he would "fly to their colors."[7]

The French anchored off Sandy Hook on July 11. Though their overly long eighty-seven-day voyage meant they missed the chance to bottle up Clinton in Philadelphia, attention now turned to New York City. The obvious plan called for a coordinated assault—the Americans attacking by land, the French by sea. But there was a problem. The sea lanes approaching Manhattan Island proved too shallow for the French ships. Despite a massive bounty offered to any American pilot capable of navigating an approach, no one took the job, because the job was impossible. They would have to look elsewhere for the first target of the Franco-American alliance. Luckily, just such a target existed: Newport, Rhode Island.

⚏

LOCATED ON THE tip of the eponymous island giving the colony Rhode Island its name, Newport was occupied by the British early in the war. It was not quite the prize New York City might have been, but garrisoned by six thousand British regulars obstructing the entrance to Narragansett Bay, it was a prize nonetheless. A small army of Continentals commanded by General John Sullivan kept watch on Newport. A proud and tempestuous Irishman, Sullivan relished the opportunity to transition from idle watch to active duty. Unfortunately, Sullivan was no Francophile. Where Lafayette saw the dawning of a beautiful friendship, Sullivan saw the French alliance as a military and political necessity, nothing more. He would be on high alert for displays of French arrogance or dismissive superiority. Sullivan believed the French were there to help the Continental Army win the war—not push them out of the way and take over. Sullivan was a good officer and could not rationally be removed from command in Newport—but he was not a great choice to be spearheading the first exercise in Franco-American cooperation.

To help smooth the union of the two armies at Newport, Washington dispatched Lafayette with two thousand men to reinforce Sullivan. Though Colonel John Laurens served as Washington's official liaison to d'Estaing, the presence of Lafayette would surely guarantee a good working relationship between the two forces. But when Lafayette arrived in Rhode Island and paid a call on d'Estaing's flagship, the gaze of his countrymen exposed his awkward position. Technically, Lafayette was still a runaway fugitive who ignored a direct order from the king not to leave France. For d'Estaing, hosting a man still under the shadow of the Crown's official displeasure was fraught with complications. Had the boy turned into a republican freedom fighter? Was he a traitor to France? To d'Estaing's relief, Lafayette made it plain nothing could be further from the truth. He said his first loyalty was to France, and his only real crime was an overzealous desire to serve his country by killing Englishmen. "I have always thought, and I have written and said everywhere here," he told d'Estaing, "that I would rather be a soldier in the French service than a general officer anywhere else."[8]

Satisfied Lafayette was sound, d'Estaing offered a thrilling opportunity to the young marquis: commanding French troops in battle. D'Estaing proposed Lafayette lead a joint force of American and French soldiers to attack Newport from the northwest while Sullivan led the main American army down from the northeast. Lafayette joyfully presented this idea to John Sullivan and Nathanael Greene, but was disappointed they did not share his enthusiasm. Though the American forces swelled with the influx of Massachusetts militia under John Hancock—now playing soldier after his service in the Continental Congress ended—the regular Continentals would need to be at full strength and led by their best officers. Sullivan would *not* allow Lafayette to detach himself and join the French. Undeterred (his natural response to not getting what he wanted), Lafayette pushed his American comrades to change their minds. Lafayette's determination soon ran him afoul of even his best American friends. John Laurens wrote his father, "His private views withdrew his attention sorely from the general interest."[9] Nathanael

Greene wrote Washington, saying, "The Marquis's great thirst for glory and national attachment often run him into errors."[10] Greene said this in defense of Lafayette, however, rather than condemnation.

Lafayette nearly got what he wanted. On August 9, the French and Americans settled on a plan to attack the following day. This plan included Lafayette leading his desired Franco-American detachment. With an attack imminent, British forces abandoned fortifications on the north end of the island to consolidate in Newport itself. Not wanting to miss an opportunity to seize these abandoned positions, Sullivan launched his part of the offensive hours ahead of schedule. The French officers took this as an insult. As a matter of honor, the French expected to land first, *then* the Americans would cross over. If this seems like a silly quibble in retrospect . . . it seemed so at the time, too. On board d'Estaing's flagship, John Laurens watched in exasperation as the French officers obsessed over their wounded pride. He said, "They conceived of their troops injured by our landing first," and then proceeded "to talk like women disputing precedence at a country dance."[11] Despite this aggrieved clucking, d'Estaing himself remained focused on the mission. He ordered his four thousand marines to land on schedule. Matters of honor could be settled later.

As the Americans moved into position, and the French groused about their honor, thirty-six British sails appeared on the horizon. D'Estaing had two options—stay parked beside Newport and risk being trapped, or confront the Royal Navy on the high seas. He chose the latter, even though it meant delaying the assault on Newport. Leaving behind a few frigates to cover a fuming General Sullivan, d'Estaing sailed out to face the incoming British. At first, Lafayette's heart swelled as he spied the Royal Navy running away. He knew once d'Estaing chased off the British, he would return to commence the liberation of Newport.

Mother Nature wrecked this plan. On August 11, a storm erupted from the firmament, battering land and sea. The Continental camp became a morass of sinking mud as torrential rain bombarded New England for three successive days. They lost all contact with the French fleet. Even after the storm cleared, they were nowhere to be seen. Grimly determined, Sullivan ordered a creeping advance through the mud to put his army within two miles of Newport by August 20. That was the day the French fleet finally came limping back into view.

The news was all bad. D'Estaing's now rudderless and de-masted flagship was being towed. The rest of the fleet were in various states of disrepair. One ship was lost completely. None of the ships were fit for service. In fact, d'Estaing came back to Newport only to fulfill a promise to Sullivan he would return. An assault was out of the question. The French fleet must go to Boston for repairs. All d'Estaing could do was offer to ferry Sullivan's army back to the safety of the mainland.

Sullivan was furious. He believed he was being denied a glorious feather in his cap due to the perfidy and unreliability of the French. He believed they were just making excuses not to fight. Lafayette and Greene hurried to d'Estaing's ship to implore him to stay for forty-eight more hours. He could disembark his marines and provide artillery cover, even if his ships couldn't maneuver. D'Estaing wanted to stay but long since resolved to leave naval matters to the navy. If his captains said they needed to go to Boston, they needed to go to Boston. And so they sailed away.

Sullivan's passions then got the better of him. He drafted a nine-point complaint addressed to d'Estaing that read like a manifesto. Sullivan denounced "the ruinous consequences which would result to this army from his abandoning the harbor of Newport," and lodged a solemn protest "against the measure as derogatory to the honor of France . . . destructive in the highest degree to the welfare of the United States of America and . . . highly injurious to the alliance between the two nations."[12] Now it was Lafayette's turn to rage. He believed Sullivan was being unfair. He would not hear of any more attacks on his countrymen. "I told those gentlemen that my country was more dear to me than America," he said, "that whatever France did was always right."[13] Lafayette implied he would be happy to settle matters on the field of honor with anyone who cared to accept the challenge. Here Lafayette carried himself well beyond reason—anyone who believes their country can do no wrong has moved from healthy patriotism to cultish nationalism. But despite his passionate excesses, Lafayette had a point. Sullivan should not have publicly aired his grievances. When his temper cooled in the morning, Sullivan agreed and promised to make amends. He granted Lafayette leave to ride to Boston and do what he could to make sure the Franco-American alliance did not break before it was able to properly whack the British in the side of the head.

The trip to Boston was Lafayette's first time in the cradle of American liberty. He found the city extremely tense. Though a furious ride got him to Boston just hours after the French fleet arrived, Sullivan's nine-point anti-French manifesto beat them both. New England had long been on the front lines of colonial wars against the French. Now Sullivan told them this most uncomfortable bedfellow shamefully ran out on them at the first opportunity. Many of their friends and relatives served in the American forces the French just left behind. The Bostonians were angry.

Lafayette interceded along with Boston luminaries like John Hancock to cool temperatures. In navigating the terrain between his mother country and his adopted country, Lafayette showed he too could talk out of both sides of his mouth. He wrote John Hancock a glowing letter of introduction to present to d'Estaing, calling Hancock "Brutus in the flesh."[14] But he also sent a personal letter informing d'Estaing candidly Hancock "has only wit necessary to get him out of difficulty . . . his vanity equals his reputation." And while the French stood accused of cowardice, Lafayette said Hancock returned to Boston because of the "lack of eagerness he displays for English bullets."[15] Luckily for the alliance, neither d'Estaing nor the American leaders actively sought a breach. Washington and Congress both agreed it was Mother Nature who was to blame for this whole mess.

Lafayette was still in Boston when he got word Sullivan was pulling out of Newport. Between the storm and the departure of the French, the local militia forces were dissolving. The Continental regulars would soon be outnumbered four-to-one. The British were likely to attack at any moment. Lafayette mounted a horse on August 29 and rode as fast as he could, covering eighty miles in just eight hours. He did not know the battle he raced to join was already over. The Continentals withstood multiple charges and eventually forced the British to give up and retreat back into the city. Lafayette arrived the evening after the Battle of Newport. All he could do was insist on taking command of the last remaining rearguard. Sullivan praised Lafayette's leadership of the final evacuation: "He did it in excellent order, not a man was left behind, not the smallest article lost."[16] It was another handsome retreat in a war of handsome retreats.

The Continentals pulled out just in time. The very next morning, a hundred British sails were spotted on the horizon. It was another Royal Navy fleet with five thousand reinforcements from New York City. Had d'Estaing and the fleet stayed behind, they likely would have been destroyed. Had Sullivan waited one more day to leave Newport, he would have been trapped. Instead, General Clinton found no prizes to capture, and no battle to wage, so he returned to New York City. The first joint Franco-American operation in history could have gone better. It also could have gone much worse.

⚌

As became Lafayette's lifelong habit when faced with downtime and disappointment, he devised bigger and grander plans. In the idleness after the Battle of Newport, Lafayette began pitching a variety of possible campaigns to d'Estaing. He attempted to revive both the "irruption into Canada" and the naval campaign in the Caribbean, encouraging d'Estaing to present these various schemes as if they were his own. Meanwhile, he wrote Washington, Henry Laurens, and others saying d'Estaing was brimming over with possible campaign plans.

The boredom of the fall of 1778 also led Lafayette down the ridiculous path to the field of honor. At the end of August, the Earl of Carlisle, head of a rejected British peace commission, published a broadsheet warning Americans not to trust their new French ally. He called upon the colonists to avoid aligning with the hated French, "the enemy of all civil and religious liberty" with "a perfidy so well known to require any new proof."[17] When Lafayette read this, he resolved to challenge Carlisle to a duel. According to the byzantine moral logic of duels, they were meant to be affairs of *personal* honor. Carlisle's manifesto was simply wartime politics. But Lafayette said, "I have nothing very interesting to do here," so he may as well kill Carlisle.[18] Lafayette sent a challenge, saying of Carlisle's insults, "I do not deign to deny it my Lord, but to chastise you for it."[19] Carlisle simply laughed at the impetuous marquis. He replied, "I confess I find it difficult to make a serious answer," and informed Lafayette that in matters of official business he answered only to king and country.[20] The challenge went unaccepted.

Lafayette's hopes for another campaign or battle in 1778 faded. As winter approached, all sides remained idle. With Washington preparing to lead his army into winter quarters in Morristown, Pennsylvania, Lafayette concluded the time had finally come to go home. Many expected him to leave after Brandywine—an adventure enjoyed and battle scar earned. But he convinced himself—not entirely without justification—he was needed in America: first as a loyal officer supporting George Washington, then as facilitator of the newly forged Franco-American alliance. But the onset of winter promised no new adventures. Lafayette concluded he would best serve his new comrades—and himself—by returning home to champion the American cause in France.

Lafayette was also eager to return because he heard rumors the French government planned an invasion of England. This triggered Lafayette's restless yearning for glory and fame. Still seeking service with his own countrymen, he longed to march triumphantly through England and enjoy "the pleasure of seeing a glorious fire in London." In not-at-all melodramatic fashion he said, "If they were to go off without me, I would hang myself."[21]

Lafayette was originally supposed to depart back to France on board d'Estaing's flagship. The repaired fleet planned to winter in the Caribbean, and Lafayette could catch a ride home to Europe from there. But news of his departure led Congress to swarm all over him. Delayed in Philadelphia by meetings, interviews, and petty personal dramas, Lafayette missed his chance to sail with d'Estaing and could only lament Philadelphia had become "a tiresome prison."[22]

Lafayette made new plans to go to Boston to take passage on a brand-new American naval ship auspiciously christened USS *Alliance*. But while en route a terrible fever struck him down. After attempting to survive on a regimen of nothing but "wine, tea, and rum," Lafayette finally collapsed into bed.[23] He entertained some feverish fear he was dying—agonizing over the "cruel disappointment" of dying in bed rather than the battlefield.[24] Washington's personal physician again attended to Lafayette and announced the boy would live. Washington himself came to check on Lafayette personally. They had been close friends for over a year. Their bond was real. Neither wanted it to be the last time they ever saw each other.

After recovering, Lafayette lingered in Boston for a few weeks while the newly built *Alliance* found a crew for her maiden voyage. His baggage was loaded with correspondence to Americans in France, including official credentials and instructions to Dr. Franklin, who had just become the first fully accredited diplomat in American history. He also bore complimentary letters of recommendation from George Washington, Henry Laurens, comte d'Estaing, Conrad Gérard, and other notables all attesting to Lafayette's honor, valor, honesty, courage, and fidelity. All of which would be very helpful in smoothing the fugitive's return to court. Just as his departure caused a sensation, he hoped his return would have the same effect. On January 11, 1779, the *Alliance* set sail. Lafayette was going home.

CHAPTER SEVEN

PURCHASING GLORY

[1779–1780]

ONOTONY AND BOREDOM DEFINED LAFAYETTE'S FIRST trip across the Atlantic, but his return trip was entirely different. Departing in the dead of winter, the *Alliance* cut her way through the ice of Boston Harbor. Then, as the ship crept up the Newfoundland coast, she found herself not in excruciating calm, but a furious storm. For days, the *Alliance* bobbed perilously amid angry waves. Seized once again by the thought he might die, a horrendously seasick Lafayette groaned "at my time of life—barely twenty years of age—with my name, my rank, my fortune and having married Mlle. Noailles, to leave everything and serve as breakfast for codfish!"[1] But the storm passed, denying the codfish their chance to dine on a famous French marquis.

Surviving the storm was not the end of dangerous excitement, though. In order to fill the crew complement for the *Alliance*, the captain drafted sailors from the stockades of Boston. At least a third of the crew were former prisoners of war—mostly English, Irish, and Scots. These sailors knew King George offered lucrative bounties to any crew who sailed an enemy ship into a British port. As the *Alliance* approached Europe, they plotted mutiny. But they made a mistake. They let into their group a sailor with an Irish accent who was in fact a loyal American patriot. He informed Lafayette of the plot, and Lafayette and the captain led an armed party to surprise the ringleaders while they slept in their bunks. Interrogations led to further arrests. The mutiny was suppressed. When the *Alliance* sailed into Brest on February 6, 1779, thirty-eight members of its crew were clapped in irons.

⎯⎯⎯

AFTER ALMOST EXACTLY two years, Lafayette was home. But he could not make straight for the Hôtel Noailles because he remained in awkward legal limbo. He was still technically a fugitive who disobeyed his king. As a matter of protocol, Lafayette must first present himself to the authorities at Versailles and accept the consequences of his actions.

This initial stop in Versailles gave Lafayette the first taste of the bountiful harvest he stood to reap for his success: No longer the awkward punchline but a celebrated hero. Not a clueless dunce, but a prescient speculator of political fortune. Where he went, France had followed. Lafayette strode into Versailles at two o'clock in the morning on February 11, which happened to be *carnival*. He learned a wild party was in full swing at the home of the prince de Poix, the Noailles cousin with who Lafayette went to London in 1777—just before Lafayette skipped town to America. Lafayette walked into this party in full uniform, instantly becoming the center of attention. He basked in the glow of celebrity, and noted with satisfaction the envy he aroused. He successfully escaped his old life. A new life was set to begin.

Though they cheered his success, the young men and women who fawned over Lafayette were disconnected from the war he returned from. The Franco-American treaty of alliance was signed over a year ago. France was at war. But you could hardly tell in Versailles. In these days before democratic levies and mass conscription, wars were fought by professional soldiers who served wherever it pleased the king to send them. Those campaigns had little direct impact on life at home. Other than a vague awareness a conflict was happening *somewhere*, the war did not interrupt the young aristocrats' swirling lives of love, gossip, and scandal. Plenty of them could not find Philadelphia or Boston on a map.

The next day, the prince de Poix escorted Lafayette to the palace to face the music. Prime Minister Maurepas welcomed Lafayette into his office and spent hours debriefing him. Though a great deal had changed since Lafayette left, Maurepas told Lafayette he could not yet see the king. Protocol would not allow an audience with a subject still living under the official disfavor. Maurepas ordered Lafayette to proceed directly to the Hôtel Noailles, where he would remain under house arrest until the government figured out what to do with him. Lafayette counted himself lucky he did not have to spend any time in the Bastille.

-⊟⊠-

LATER THAT DAY, Lafayette returned to his gilded cage. His arrival caused great excitement. Alerted their wayward son was on the way, the duchesse d'Ayen broke the news to Adrienne as gently as possible—fearing the consequences not of crippling sorrow but manic joy. When Lafayette strode through the door, she ran to embrace him. Writing to Lafayette's aunts in Chavaniac, she gushed, "There is no need for me to tell you of my happiness . . . it is easy to believe and hard to express." She also expressed feelings of awestruck inadequacy: "I am distressed at being so much less gracious than he is, and I hope that my affection may make up for what I lack in charm."[2] But Adrienne did herself a disservice. The last two years were hard and unhappy. Her husband abandoned her while pregnant and caring for their small child. The transatlantic separation was defined by malicious rumors he was dead or had done it to impress another woman. He missed the birth of Anastasie. He missed the death of Henriette. He filled his occasionally delivered letters with regrets over his absence, just before telling her he must stay awhile longer. Lafayette was not perfect. While striving to be a great man he behaved like a clueless child. It would be some time before Lafayette understood the pain he caused, what he meant to Adrienne, and what Adrienne meant to him.

Though under house arrest, the door to Lafayette's gilded cage was unlocked. Maurepas limited him to visits from members of his family, but as the Noailles were related to *everyone*, this restriction was no restriction at all. Lafayette was even now related to his best friend, the comte de Ségur, who recently married Antoinette d'Aguesseau, the duchesse d'Ayen's much younger sister—technically making him Lafayette's uncle. Lafayette reveled in the attention as a procession of important men and women paid call. He was the talk of Paris and Versailles. He loved it. And Adrienne loved having him all to herself for a change. She was soon pregnant.

The biggest coup of Lafayette's return was the change in the duc d'Ayen. Recognizing his son-in-law's transformation from black sheep to white knight, d'Ayen became Lafayette's biggest booster. The Noailles so thoroughly embraced Lafayette that when American envoy John Adams dined with the family a few months earlier, d'Ayen changed the story a bit, saying he backed Lafayette from the beginning. Adams recorded in his diary, "When the American revolution commenced, a family council had been called to deliberate upon this great event . . . that it was expedient to send one of their sons over to America to serve in her army, under General Washington. . . . The Marquis, who was represented as a youth of the finest accomplishments, and most amiable disposition, panting for glory, and ardent to distinguish himself in military service, most joyfully consented to embark in the enterprise."[3] This is of course not how it happened. But when times change, history must change to keep up.

D'Ayen helped Lafayette draft a suitably ingratiating apology letter to King Louis, claiming his defiance was accidental, the result of miscommunication and excessive patriotism. This letter won him a personal audience with the king. After some performative chiding, Louis commended Lafayette for his heroic adventures and invited the marquis to go hunting—one of Louis's great pleasures. To join his hunt was a mark of royal favor. Fully rehabilitated, Lafayette was free to return to society.

Lafayette could not have been happier. Everyone loved him. He came home victorious and everyone applauded his efforts. Literally. When he and Adrienne attended a show at the Comédie-Française, the crowd cheered as he waved from his box. After his return to France, Lafayette recollected, "I enjoyed the honor of being consulted by all the ministers, and what was far better, being kissed by all ladies."[4] Aglaé de Hunolstein, long an object of unrequited love, now returned the attention. While denying the silly rumor Lafayette did it all for her, Hunolstein wrote a friend, "He has won universal approval and his vanity is greatly pleased . . . I see him frequently, and consider myself happy to have earned part of his esteem."[5]

The only people who remained aloof from such universal approval were the rivals for the affection of Hunolstein. Another of her suitors, the prince de Ligne, could not believe everyone was embracing "so wishy-washy a creature as Lafayette, null in mind, body, and face and disposition." Through a mouthful of sour grapes he complained, "An excessive amount of noise has been made over a few wretched little skirmishes in America."[6] Also unimpressed was Hunolstein's official lover, the duc de Chartres. Chartres was said to be steaming mad she spent so much time with Lafayette. He was convinced Lafayette was trying to steal his girlfriend.

Everyone else loved him. Even those who once dismissed him. Queen Marie Antoinette, who previously mocked him, accelerated his return to favor. When an old colonel retired from the King's Dragoons, the queen steered the vacancy to Lafayette. He was given the privilege of spending 80,000 *livres* to purchase the commission. Lafayette did not hesitate. He was now officially off the reform list and back on active duty in the French army. Meanwhile, his beleaguered financial manager cringed at the arrival of yet another bill. Bills of exchange, receipts, and IOUs proliferated wildly ever since his young client departed for America. "I am in an acute sense of embarrassment," the manager said. "The more I take these in hand, the more they grow."[7] But Lafayette didn't care. He was the Hero of Two Worlds, not an accountant.

꧁꧂

NEITHER LAFAYETTE'S RETURN to French society nor his return to the French army conflicted with the duties his American comrades entrusted to him. He remained a major general in the Continental Army. He conveyed to the French government all Congress asked him to convey. Whether in the halls of power or salons of society, the American cause was a relentless topic of conversation. In America, Lafayette promoted France. Now back in France, he promoted America.

This promotional tour brought him into active collaboration with Benjamin Franklin. The old American republican and young French nobleman were two ships passing in the night over the winter of 1776–1777—with Franklin arriving and Lafayette departing almost simultaneously. After settling into his home in Passy, just outside Paris, Franklin conquered French society. The self-made entrepreneur, turned natural scientist, turned Enlightenment philosopher, turned rebel leader, now played the part of the rustic sage. He donned a beaver pelt hat to encourage the perception he was a virtuous savage from Rousseau's state of nature who loved only freedom and liberty. In reality, Franklin was a cunning man of the world. He was also, thanks to the credentials presented to him by Lafayette, now the American plenipotentiary to the king of France.

Franklin took an immediate liking to Lafayette. He reported to Washington with genuine affection Lafayette showed "zeal for the honor of our country, his activity in our affairs here, and his firm attachment to our cause, impressed me with the same regard and esteem."[8] Franklin and Lafayette teamed up to extract as much as possible from the alliance. Lafayette reported firsthand the Americans were in want of everything: supplies, uniforms, powder, guns, pistols, ships, sailors, soldiers, and most of all money. With Lafayette providing enthusiastic entreaties from a popular hero, Franklin provided the sober voice of an elder statesman—a welcome tonic for veteran ministers not used to grappling with bouncing youths. But they both delivered the same message: America needed everything France had to give.

Their mutual ally inside the ministry was the comte de Vergennes, now happy to be working on the American project out in the open rather than furtively in the shadows. Vergennes also took an affectionate interest in the sincere patriotism and enthusiastic energy of Lafayette. His letters to the marquis were full of guidance, advice, and concern. It would be easy to say Franklin and Vergennes, cynically sophisticated old men, *used* the young and naive Lafayette. But their friendly professions are nowhere contradicted by mean-spirited guffaws behind his back. Nor did they induce Lafayette to do anything he would not have done otherwise. They wanted the same things. If this means they were using each other, then every friendship, attachment, and association in human history can be reduced to raw calculation of self-interest. But that's not how humans work. Divining cynical motives in others often makes us feel we are revealing hard truth. But, as often as not, the bleak reductivism distorts as much as it clarifies.

⊰⊱

ASIDE FROM LOBBYING for cash and prizes from the French, Lafayette and Franklin dreamed up another grand adventure for the ever-eager marquis. When Lafayette returned to France in February 1779, it did not appear the rumored invasion of England he'd heard about was actually in the offing. So he and Franklin planned one themselves. For this project, they brought in the American naval hero John Paul Jones, residing in France for the winter. The trio of collaborators proposed a squadron of American ships under Jones, carrying two thousand French soldiers under Lafayette, raid through the British Isles— attacking in turn Liverpool, Whitehaven, Lancaster, and Cork. The mischief-making expedition would force the British to hold back forces that might otherwise be used to prosecute the war on the far side of the Atlantic. The plunder and ransom seized from the terrified British towns would make the venture not just fun, but profitable. Lafayette and Franklin sold the idea to Vergennes, who encouraged them to get started at once.

Lafayette and Jones spent all of March and April 1779 arranging ships, supplies, and ammunition. The vessels were in the middle of being loaded in Le Havre when the French government suddenly backed out of the plan. They ordered Lafayette to take his regiment to the garrison at Saintes, a town in southwestern France set back from the coast between Rochefort and Bordeaux. The abrupt and unexplained cancellation set Lafayette bursting with indignation. Prone to theatrical denunciations when he didn't get his way, he wrote Franklin in angry and broken English the ministers were "unhappily of the same nature (whatever corrupted it might be) as the rest of mankind."[9]

But Lafayette's peevish impatience faded once Vergennes called him to Versailles to reveal amazing news. After careful consideration, the kingdom of Spain had elected to honor "the family pact" with their royal cousins in France and declare war on Britain. With the British committing so many resources across the Atlantic, a combined Franco-Spanish armada could seize control of the English Channel. Lafayette's planned raids were canceled not because of French cowardice or cold feet, but because they would be superseded by a full-blown invasion of England.

Told he would serve in the vanguard, Lafayette relocated to Le Havre to make ready. He would get to see London burn after all. But the brief burst of expectant joy gave way to idleness and frustration as the Franco-Spanish armada failed to arrive. As the summer days in Le Havre grew shorter, Lafayette could only sigh wistfully as his friend vicomte de Noailles pole-vaulted over him. In the early summer of 1779, Noailles was assigned to join d'Estaing's fleet in the Caribbean. Upon arrival, he served with glorious distinction in the invasion of Grenada and would soon accompany d'Estaing to Georgia. While Lafayette twiddled his thumbs, Noailles snatched the laurels of the battlefield.

Lafayette spent the rest of June and July waiting for the increasingly mythical armada. He did not know bureaucratic snafus, bad weather, and an epidemic of scurvy and smallpox turned the expedition into a *cursed* expedition. He passed the time writing letters to his American friends filled with regret for having ever come back. He mentioned trying to start a revolution in Ireland, but mostly he wanted to lead a grand French army back to America where he belonged. Lafayette hoped to use this army to hunt Canada, his great white whale.

In the first week of August 1779, that hunt was called in favor of the greatest trophy of all: England. The sixty-six ships of the Franco-Spanish armada finally arrived. But raised hopes were dashed again. The crew was in bad shape. They were sick and running low on provisions. The French admiral in charge of the expedition was deeply skeptical of invasion and personally reeling from the recent suicide of his son. Not trusting his ships, his crew, or himself, the admiral led the fleet back to La Rochelle, where it would remain idle as August turned to September. No further orders came. The potential invasion of England was a mirage.

DURING LAFAYETTE'S IDLE summer in France, he began to seriously ponder the meaning of the words *liberty* and *equality*. What did he hate about the Old World? What did he hope for the New World? It took several years of study and reflection to fully develop his own personal definition of these words, but by the summer of 1779, one pillar was already in place: Lafayette believed aristocratic feudal hierarchies and nobility of the blood were pure nonsense.

Lafayette witnessed very little in his short life to suggest the nobles who ruled Versailles and Paris were superior beings. Quit the opposite. After his arrival in the Hôtel Noailles, he encountered either old stodgy imbeciles or young frivolous imbeciles. It did not take Lafayette long to develop a deep suspicion that bloodlines and genealogical tables bore little relation to intelligence, merit, or talent. The suspicion deepened further in America. Everywhere he looked, the best people were drawn from the lowest station. Hamilton was a disinherited orphan from a cluster of rocks in the Caribbean. Henry Knox was a bookseller; Benedict Arnold a druggist; Nathanael Greene, the son of a merchant farmer. The worth of these men derived from their intelligence, hard work, and energy, not their family trees. Writing to Franklin about the possibility of fomenting revolution in Ireland, Lafayette said, "I am not so fond of seeing Dukes and Lords of the head of such business . . . I prefer the yeoman and farmers."[10] To compare Alexander Hamilton to some *vicomte* drunkenly carousing the streets of Paris was no comparison at all: Hamilton was superior in every way.

Lafayette also displayed the soldier's contempt for effete civilian aristocrats who risked nothing yet enjoyed all the rewards thanks to a well-placed friend or walk in the garden with the king. If he was ever up for promotion, Lafayette asked Vergennes to remember, "I am not of the court and still less a courtier. When you consider me please consider me a man of the barracks."[11] This was only partially true. Lafayette may have hated life at court, and loved life at camp, but he was not above parlaying the queen's favor into a commission in the King's Dragoons. In Lafayette's mind, however, it was always *what you did*, not *who you were*, that mattered. In retrospect, he was making all the same arguments the comte de Saint-Germain made when he reformed Captain Lafayette out of the service back in 1776.

Lafayette ceased believing in the self-justifications offered by his noble brethren—that they ruled because they were born to rule. He didn't realize it yet, but a few years later, Lafayette would be at the forefront of a revolutionary movement dismantling the old feudal social order built on such obviously unsubstantiated foundations. But Lafayette also believed not everything possible in America was possible in France. A true republic might sprout from the free soil of America, but not in the ancient rot of France. During his downtime in the summer of 1779, Lafayette wrote a letter of recommendation on behalf of "Doctor Noemer," a Dutch natural scientist interested in emigrating to America. Lafayette said, "He has, by his calculations, found that men were born to be free, and that freedom was to be perfectly enjoyed but upon American shores."[12] This is a sentence Lafayette could have written at any point during the remaining sixty years of life.

But Lafayette always beheld those American shores through rose-colored glasses. And as he marveled at the egalitarian freedom of America, he again passed over the enslavement of Africans and the genocide of Native tribes. He celebrated his friends George Washington and Henry Laurens for becoming leaders thanks to their good works, not their good genes, but failed to acknowledge their social standing was founded on aggressive land theft and the ownership of human beings. The most precious parts of George Washington's financial portfolio— about which he wrote volumes of correspondence—were his slaves in Mount Vernon and the speculative titles to tracts of land in Ohio. Titles that would only pay off if white settlers pushed aside the Native inhabitants. If we are to judge people by *what they do* rather than *who they are*, we must look at *all* they do. Lafayette easily expressed disgust with the absurd hypocrisies of the Old World, but he still struggled to see the absurd hypocrisies of the New World.

※

As the fall of 1779 settled in and no action in Europe appeared imminent, Lafayette itched to return to America. The situation there only deteriorated after he left. As the fourth year of the war crawled along, the conflict became forgotten background noise for most of the population. Just like the young French nobles partying in Versailles, the good republican citizens of America often took little notice of the army fighting for their freedom. Farmers and merchants were happy to trade with British commissars for hard dependable cash, not worthless Continental scrip—of which de Kalb complained, "Money scatters like chaff before the wind, and expenses almost double from one day to the next, while income, of course, remains stationary."[13] Corrupt merchants saw the Continental Army as a lucrative dumping ground for shoddy tools, defective weapons, and rotten food. Washington and his officers grumbled bitterly. Their ranks thinned with desertions and resignations. Few new recruits volunteered to replace them.

Meanwhile, there was little for Washington's dwindling army to do. Led to believe the southern colonies were far more loyal than the rebellious northern colonies, the British changed strategy again. Henry Clinton directed an army to Georgia but Washington could not safely abandon his vigil over New York City, so the southern armies had to fend for themselves. And they were faring poorly. The British quickly captured Savannah and Augusta.

John Laurens departed Washington's staff to fight for his southern homeland shortly after Lafayette sailed back to France. Laurens was less blind to the absurd hypocrisies of the New World and carried to South Carolina a plan to win the war and solve the great moral contradiction of America in one audacious swoop: promise the enslaved African population liberty in exchange for military service. Laurens believed this a perfect solution to the problem of recruiting an army from a majority enslaved population. It would also resolve the problem of the British promising the slaves freedom if they rebelled against their owners. This threat would be neutralized if the owners freed their slaves themselves. But when Laurens presented his plan to the South Carolina legislature, they laughed him out of the room. If the choice was between freeing their slaves and losing the war, the South Carolina planters said, "God Save the King."

Lafayette could only follow the resulting disasters from afar. The French and Americans teamed up to retake Savannah, but poor planning, bad luck, and a few crucial mistakes turned the Battle of Savannah into a bloody debacle for both the Americans and the French. D'Estaing himself was badly wounded. Though vicomte de Noailles fought well, and was now returning home for the winter, John Laurens only lived through the battle by luck. His reckless valor now morphed into something closer to suicidal self-destruction. Stories circulated saying he literally bared his chest to the enemy in the midst of defeat in the vain hope they would make him a martyr to liberty with one well-placed shot. But the British did not oblige and Laurens retreated with the rest of the Continental forces.

These setbacks led Lafayette and Franklin to badger Vergennes, Maurepas, and other government ministers for more aid and support. They especially lobbied for a new French expeditionary force to augment and supersede the original force sailing under d'Estaing. Persuaded by Lafayette's unminced words describing the imminent disintegration of the Continental Army, Vergennes supported the idea. French honor—to say nothing of Vergennes's own reputation—were now on the line. To let the Americans fail so soon after the French joined was unthinkable. Other ministers hesitated at the expenditure, including the new controller of finances Jacques Necker, a Swiss Protestant banker well aware of the king's financial problems. Necker tried to halt the plan to deepen French involvement in America. But Maurepas was growing old and weak, and Vergennes took over as the king's most trusted adviser. The new expedition was approved.

Lafayette's frequent meetings and official business were only briefly interrupted on Christmas Eve 1779 when he received a note from Adrienne announcing the birth of a healthy and happy baby boy. Lafayette was thrilled he now had a son and heir, as was the whole Noailles clan. The family did not even fight when Lafayette insisted on naming the boy Georges Washington Lafayette. Adrienne implored Lafayette to come be with his family. "The occupations of paternity are so sweet," she wrote. "Give in to them. They can only be good."[14] Lafayette would not come to appreciate her words until many regretful years later. He spent a few days with Adrienne, Anastasie, and baby Georges. Then he went back to plotting his triumphant return to America.

⚌

THE DETAILS OF the new expedition fell into place in February 1780. Six or seven ships of the line, plus a handful of frigates, and a convoy of supply and transport ships to carry ammunition, weapons, and supplies. Most important, the minister of war approved six thousand regular army troops to reinforce the Continentals on land. When word leaked another expedition was about to be approved, every young officer in France rushed to sign up. Vicomte de Noailles received a spot, as did Ségur, the last of the three friends to make it to America. The three of them would form the center of a progressive young corps of French officers who served in America and returned home eager to reform the myriad problems of their own kingdom.

Lafayette wanted more than just a place in the army. He wanted to command the whole expedition. Personally leading six thousand troops to Washington's rescue was an enticing vision—one that could only be seriously entertained while in a state of intoxication. Lafayette was only twenty-two. In the French table of ranks, Lafayette was only a colonel. Expecting to lead an entire expedition was a dream inspired by foolish cupidity. But there were just enough arguments in his favor for Lafayette to hold out hope. Vergennes said at least *he* thought it would be advantageous to have a man the Americans trusted inside the French command tent after so many mutual recriminations and misunderstandings at the Battle of Newport.

But the French minister of war was one of the few men on Earth unmoved by Lafayette's charms. He let Lafayette make his case, then assigned the command to the comte de Rochambeau. Rochambeau was a cultured, smooth, and diplomatic officer who was a general before Lafayette was born. Though a forty-year veteran of numerous continental campaigns—with plenty of scars to prove he was a real soldier and not a soft aristocrat—this would be Rochambeau's first truly independent command. This was a mission he was more than ready for.

Lafayette was disappointed to be denied the command, but he could hardly dwell on losing something he had so little rational reason to expect. Meanwhile, the French government ordered him to resume his place as a major general in the Continental Army. The French lodged as many complaints about the Americans as the Americans lodged about the French, and Vergennes liked the idea of placing a man *he* trusted at Washington's side. For Lafayette this was not an unpleasant consolation prize—though he insisted it be circulated *he* requested this return to the Continental Army, lest the Americans wonder why he had been passed over.

Before Lafayette left, he arranged a loan of 120,000 *livres* to cover his expenses in America. This left his financial manager tearing his hair out. He wrote Lafayette's aunts in Chavaniac, warning them their nephew was "purchasing his glory at the expense of his fortune."[15] Lafayette did not concern himself with such trivialities. He was young and rich. The pool of money bottomless. What did the price of glory matter when the money never ran out? His financial manager was left to juggle the bills Lafayette left in his wake.

Adrienne was inconsolable. Her husband had been home for less than a year. He spent most of his time stationed with his garrison or meeting with government officials. Now he was sailing away again. He left her in virtually the same condition as three years earlier—the only difference was this time she held a baby in her arms rather than in her womb. Adrienne would eventually forgive him. She loved him. She supported him. She accepted he had to do what he had to do. He was a young man chasing fame and glory and position—utterly typical behavior for most of the men who surrounded her. He was hardly putting her in a unique position relative to other wives. The only difference was she loved her husband in a way most of those other wives did not. After he departed she took to her bed for two weeks.

Leaving Paris, Lafayette made one last trip to the palace at Versailles. A year ago he returned to the palace with his head bowed submissively; now he departed with his head held high. Donning the uniform of a Continental major general, he presented himself to the king and queen. They bid him good luck and good fortune. Then Lafayette left to rejoin a revolution aimed at overthrowing kings and queens forever.

CHAPTER EIGHT

RED AND BLACK FEATHERS

[1780–1781]

L AFAYETTE'S THIRD TRIP ACROSS THE ATLANTIC WAS BLESS-
edly uneventful. No torturous calm, no terrifying storms,
nor bloody mutiny. No encounters with the Royal Navy. No
plagues, starvation, or dehydration. Only one crew member died of
a fever—which for transatlantic travel in the eighteenth century was
pretty standard. After thirty-eight days at sea the *Hermione* pulled into
Massachusetts on April 27, 1780.

Lafayette's return to Boston sparked enthusiastic celebration. As
soon as word spread the ship that had just pulled into the harbor carried
the marquis—*our* marquis—Bostonians flocked to the wharf to greet
him. Lafayette spent the next few days toasted by elite leaders like John
Hancock and Sam Adams, as well as the common people who lit bonfires and fireworks in his honor. One of Lafayette's fellow passengers on
the *Hermione* happened to be Pierre du Rousseau de Fayolle, a companion from the first trip aboard *La Victoire*. In 1777, Rousseau de Fayolle
found the Americans suspicious and hostile. Landing in Boston three
years later, he could not help but notice the pleasantly stark contrast to
those first inhospitable encounters.

Lafayette performed his public merrymaking in Boston with good
humor but was eager to return to his true home in America: George

Washington's headquarters. He dispatched a letter to Washington the minute he touched solid ground, saying, "Here I am, my dear General."[1] The news of his return electrified the Continental camp. The eternally stoic Washington could hardly contain his elation. Hamilton, Greene, Knox, and the others couldn't wait to see their friend again. The rank and file also had reason to cheer. Lafayette's youthful courage and eager generosity long made him a favorite among the common soldiers. Lafayette rode into camp on May 10, 1780, to general rejoicing. As the camp gathered round, he and Washington embraced. Beloved by two families—one in France, the other in America—Lafayette found that whenever he crossed the Atlantic, he was always coming home.

<hr>

WASHINGTON'S PLEASURE AT Lafayette's return only increased when Lafayette revealed another French expeditionary force was on the way. Washington told Lafayette, if anything, he *undersold* the dire situation of the Continental Army. While the winter at Valley Forge has become the proverbial dark night of the patriot soul, this most recent winter in Morristown was even worse. Ceaseless blizzards pounded the countryside. Rivers and harbors iced over with sheets thicker than anyone could remember seeing. Private Joseph Plumb Martin, who maintained a daily journal during his years in the Continental Army, said, "We are absolutely literally starved—I do solemnly declare that I did not put a single morsel of victuals into my mouth for four days and as many nights."[2] De Kalb wrote home, "Those who have only been in Valley Forge . . . the past two winters, but have not tasted the cruelties of this one, know not what it is to suffer."[3] Everyone was miserable.

That the horrendous winter in Morristown imprinted itself less on America's cultural memory is fitting. American citizens at the time were letting the war fade into the background. State and local governments neglected to pay and supply their soldiers. The powerless national Congress lacked the authority to impose direct national taxes. The paper money they printed was worthless, the decrees they issued ignored. Five years after Lexington and Concord, the credit, goodwill, and attention of the people were exhausted. The handful of stubborn true believers tasked with maintaining the flame of liberty froze to death in its dying light. Many resigned. Many deserted. Few took their place.

Even the senior leadership of the army felt abandoned. Greene wrote, "A country overflowing with plenty are now suffering an army, employed in defense of everything that is dear and valuable, to perish for want of food."[4] Colonel Ebenezer Huntington wrote, "The rascally stupidity which now prevails in the country is beyond all description . . . I despise my cowardly countrymen who flinch at the very time when their exertions are wanted and hold their purse strings as though they would damn the world rather than part with a dollar to their army."[5] Hamilton wrote Laurens, "I am disgusted with everything in this world but yourself and *very* few more honest fellows."[6] The growing abscess of resentment was a dangerous development. Soldiers mistreated by civilian authorities often cease guarding the flame of liberty, and instead use its last embers to heat the branding iron of military dictatorship.

In these conditions, Lafayette's revelation France was sending more money, supplies, guns, and men was manna from heaven. But there was more. Well briefed by Lafayette on the political importance of George Washington, the French government ordered General Rochambeau to consider himself serving under Washington's ultimate authority. Lafayette told them anything less would be an intolerable insult to American honor. But when the French government clarified the hierarchy of ranks, they made no mention of the authority of Congress. Washington was bound by law to consult Congress on the organization, movements, and strategies of the Continental Army. Lafayette informed Washington he would be bound by no similar constraints with the incoming French Army. According to the French government, Rochambeau and his men would answer to Washington alone. Personally commanding six thousand foreign soldiers who would go wherever he ordered, whenever he ordered, might prove a tempting solution to the problem of flagging civilian attention. A state assembly could ignore dispatches and memos no matter how urgent. They could *not* ignore the guns and bayonets of soldiers sent by an angry general to collect what he was owed.

There were some in Congress who would have welcomed a brief period of military rule. Cautious whispers gave way to open debate on the merits of temporarily appointing George Washington dictator. After all, the Roman Republic frequently invoked temporary dictators to see them through a crisis. And if there was any man they could trust to hand back absolute power it was Washington. Lafayette himself admitted how conflicted he was about the idea: "I do not know whether as his friend I ought to desire it for him, but know very certainly that I must neither speak of it nor ever appear to wish for this measure, which nevertheless seems immensely important to me."[7] Though reticent to discuss the idea, Lafayette certainly saw its merits.

Washington's response to these suggestions imprinted deeply on Lafayette. The commander in chief categorically rejected becoming a dictator, staging a coup, or ruling by force. This powerful example of political self-abnegation was one of the most important virtues Washington modeled for Lafayette. After being exiled to Saint Helena in 1815, Napoleon Bonaparte attempted to argue, "Had I been in America, I would willingly have been a Washington . . . but had Washington been in France, exposed to discord within, and invasion from without, I would have defied him to have been what he was in America; at least, he would have been a fool to attempt it."[8] Setting aside Napoleon's laughably ignorant mischaracterization of the American War of Independence—as if it were not rampant with internal discord and external invasion—one cannot help but wonder what Napoleon would have done in the spring of 1780. Frustrated by civilian mismanagement, angry over the unnecessary suffering of his men, and informed a foreign army would do his bidding, one wonders exactly how many hours would have passed before Napoleon marched on Philadelphia; used that army to requisition what he needed; conscripted at bayonet point more soldiers and sailors necessary to win the war; brushed aside the state legislatures and declared himself dictator. How many hours? Twelve? Twenty-four? Would he have hesitated at all? Washington did none of these things. There is no evidence he even considered it. The indefatigable republican commitment to civilian authority displayed by Washington stuck with Lafayette the rest of his life. It certainly fueled his later antipathy to Napoleon's dictatorship.

It all came to nothing. The brief debate in Congress over whether to make Washington a dictator ended. He wouldn't have accepted anyway.

Nor, as it turned out, would he actually enjoy the power delegated to him on paper by the French government. His authority over Rochambeau was a pleasant diplomatic formality—Rochambeau was not there to blindly take orders from Washington. Besides, news of the French expedition was exactly the jolt of electricity necessary to prod the lethargic American politicians to life. Lafayette threw himself into the task of lobbying Congress, state legislatures, and local militias to give everything they had to give. The war *had* been going on too long. If they all threw their shoulders into one last great push . . . there was no reason the summer of 1780 could not be the last summer of the war.

⚏

THE WAR IN 1780 was really two wars. One in the North defined by stalemate, the other in the South defined by defeat. New York City remained the main base of Loyalist operations, and retaking the city remained George Washington's central preoccupation. But he made no progress toward this goal after Lafayette's departure a year and a half earlier. His army was neither big enough nor strong enough. He had no navy to speak of. But neither could Henry Clinton do anything to break Washington's northern army, because in 1779, the British again changed strategy. Most of Clinton's forces went south to focus on the reconquest of Georgia and South Carolina. There, the Americans suffered a string of demoralizing defeats. In early 1780, Henry Clinton personally led an armada to besiege Charleston. Well briefed on the state of Washington's army, Clinton knew he could leave a token force behind in New York City without fear of losing the city.

The promise of French reinforcements changed the strategic calculations in the North. If the French arrived soon, they would break the stalemate. The Americans and French could pluck New York City out of Clinton's back pocket. As they scanned the horizon for French ships, the Continentals received ever-worsening news from the South. The British siege of Charleston methodically advanced. No relief army could be raised. Even Washington could only send a small detachment under General de Kalb to help. The rest of his men were not fit for service. After de Kalb left, the news got worse: Charleston was in dire straits. Charleston was about to fall. Then the final blow: Charleston has fallen. The Continental Army soldiers defending the city were captured and humiliated by Clinton. He forced them to march out with their colors locked away, rather than unfurled in honorable surrender. Lafayette and his friends were hit hard by the additional news their friend John Laurens—who had argued futilely that the people of Charleston should arm their slaves and fight to the last man—was now a prisoner of war.

Scanning of the eastern horizon for the French fleet became an act of nervous impatience. After the fall of Charleston, Clinton was sure to return to New York City with a significant bulk of his army and navy. If the French did not arrive soon, the plan to capture New York City might have to be called off. The war would never end. Finally on July 11, 1780, French sails were sighted off Newport. Miraculously, Clinton was still not back in New York City. They might just be able to take the city. But they would have to move fast.

Lafayette's role in coordinating the attack on New York City was obvious. He would serve as the principal liaison between the two armies. Washington dispatched Lafayette to Newport to confer with Rochambeau, lay out the American plan for attack, and gauge precisely when the campaign could begin. Lafayette rushed to Newport, and though vicomte de Noailles and many of his other friends from France were aboard French ships, he could only spare them a fleeting reunion. He was on his way to important business with the high command.

General Rochambeau and the ranking naval commander, Admiral Ternay, delivered sobering news. Rochambeau brought only about four thousand men, not the expected six thousand, and most of them were presently sick and malnourished. Rochambeau estimated they would not be ready to fight for at least two months. Worst of all, disruptions in the supply chain back in France meant the cargo ships were left behind to sail at a later date. All the uniforms, boots, weapons, and ammunition expected to outfit the Continentals in 1780 were still back in France. No part of Rochambeau's report so much as hinted at the possibility of quick action. If time was of the essence, then time was going to run out.

Dejected, Lafayette returned to Continental headquarters to give a full account of his meeting to Washington. But his lust for action overwhelmed his good sense. Despite everything he heard, Lafayette suspected Rochambeau was overstating the risks and understating the rewards of a lightning strike on New York City. He drafted a memo for Washington detailing the minutes of the meeting and, wanting to make sure he got everything right, Lafayette sent a copy to Rochambeau for his comments. While this was an admirable enough instinct, what Lafayette wrote was hardly a dispassionate recitation of the facts. His summary drifted into personal editorializing, then lurched into a final paragraph easily read as direct criticism of Rochambeau and Ternay: "From an intimate knowledge of our situation, Sirs . . . it is important for us to act during the present campaign, and that all the troops which you may expect from France next year, as well as all plans with which you may fondly foster, will not repair the fatal consequences of inaction now."[9] This was tantamount to questioning both the judgment and the courage of the French commanders. Oblivious to the dangerous waters he paddled into, Lafayette sent his provocative twelve-page memo to Rochambeau for review.

Rochambeau responded to Lafayette with a curt response saying he looked forward to a personal meeting with General Washington, where he would express his own opinions directly to the commander in chief. Rochambeau criticized Lafayette's understanding of strategy, tactics, and logistics—hinting Lafayette's opinions were based on youthful fantasy, while Rochambeau's were based on "events of which I have seen so often in my life."[10] Rochambeau wrote another letter to the new French envoy in Philadelphia, chevalier de La Luzerne, implying Lafayette must be speaking on behalf of some secret cabal of impatient hotheads. "He proposes extravagant things to us like taking Long Island and New York City without a navy," Rochambeau said with amazed incredulity.[11] But the only member of this cabal of hotheads was Lafayette's own hot head.

Lafayette recognized instantly he screwed up. The brevity of Rochambeau's reply said it all. He was an inexperienced twenty-two-year-old kid foolishly running his mouth to a superior officer. He immediately wrote an explanatory, and suitably prostrate, letter of apology. Lafayette's groveling in hand, Rochambeau let him off easy. He had known Lafayette for many years—Rochambeau was an old family friend of the Rivières. He now changed his tone: "Allow an old father, my dear marquis, to reply to you as a cherished son whom he loves and esteems immensely." He then offered advice all eager young officers should hear: "I'm going to tell you a big secret derived from forty years experience. There are no troops more easily beaten [than] when they have lost the confidence in their commander, and they lose that confidence immediately when they are exposed to danger through private and personal ambition." He went on to say, "If I have been fortunate enough to retain their confidence until now, I owe it to the most scrupulous examination of my conscience that, of all the nearly 15,000 men who have been killed or wounded under my command, in the various rank, and in the most murderous actions, I need not reproach myself that a single one was killed for my own personal advantage."[12] The men who die on the battlefield are real. Rochambeau warned Lafayette their bodies ought not be piled up so one man may scale the heights of personal ambition.

⧉

LAFAYETTE BOUNCED BACK from this face-plant, as he always did. With the campaign against New York City delayed, the Continental Army could only lightly skirmish around New Jersey. For Lafayette, this might have proven so much empty maneuvering, but Washington conceived of an elite brigade of light infantry able to travel fast in the vanguard position to the main army. Washington offered command of this elite brigade to Lafayette—which brightened his mood considerably.

Lafayette relished his new role—even knowing he wasn't Washington's first choice. The command was first offered to Major General Benedict Arnold, who was wrapping up a tumultuous tenure as military governor of Philadelphia. During the past year, the vain, tempestuous, but undeniably brilliant Arnold fended off civil litigation and a court-martial leaving resentments embedded in his heart like shrapnel. Not wanting to lose Arnold's virtues on account of his vices—real or imagined—the commander in chief blunted Arnold's growing belief *everyone* was out to get him. Barely acknowledging the drama swirling around Arnold, Washington offered him command of the elite light infantry. But Arnold turned it down, citing ongoing complications from the leg injury he suffered during the campaigns of 1777. So Washington offered Arnold another job, still signaling Washington's deep and abiding faith: command of West Point—the defensive fortifications guarding the Hudson River and possibly the linchpin of the entire war effort. Were it lost, the colonies would be fatally divided.

Lafayette was thrilled to learn Arnold passed on the light infantry command. He now got to run around at the head of a division composed of picked companies from New Hampshire, New York, Connecticut, Massachusetts, and Pennsylvania. They came together under a single elite banner, breaking down longstanding regional outlooks and forging a new national *esprit de corps*. Lafayette wanted to symbolize his men's elite status with a distinguishing mark. Though he would, as he wrote to Noailles, "prefer that it were distinguished by a uniform or a good pair of shoes," he settled for a pair of black and red feathers pinned to the breast or fixed to a cap.[13] This was Lafayette's first flirtation with the power of visual symbols to express solidarity and identity. It triggered a brief fad of *everyone* donning red and black feathers until Washington issued general orders in late August that *only* Major General Lafayette's light infantry division was allowed to wear them. The point was for the feathers to be a special distinction and it hardly worked if *everyone* sported them. Lafayette spent the rest of summer 1780 training, camping, and campaigning with his division. Though action was slight, spirits were high. A surgeon in the army said Lafayette's men displayed the best morale of any in the Continental Army: "A noble spirit of emulation universally prevailed among them. . . . They were the pride of his heart, and he was the idol of their regard."[14]

Such high morale was atypical in the North. In the South, it was nonexistent. The reinforcements under de Kalb never made it to Charleston before the city fell, and they found themselves facing the apparently unstoppable British envelopment of the southern colonies—now under the direction of the formidable Lord Cornwallis. Hoping to draw the line somewhere in South Carolina, Congress dispatched Horatio Gates to take command. Surely he would defeat Cornwallis as he once defeated Burgoyne. Instead, the victor of Saratoga led his men into one of the worst defeats of the war. Colonel Richard Henry Lee, who was present for Gates's disastrous tenure as commander of the South, said Gates was "calculating probably on the weight of his name," and "if good fortune invites hubris, it is the sure precursor of deep and bitter adversity."[15]

Deep and bitter adversity is what they got. Ignoring sound advice from de Kalb, Gates marched an army of underfed, undersupplied, and acutely sick soldiers directly at Cornwallis's base in Camden, South Carolina. In the ensuing Battle of Camden on August 16, 1780, the British charged and the Americans broke and fled. Gates himself sped away from the battle on horseback, claiming he was going to turn around those in retreat. His men never saw him again. Battlefield command fell to General de Kalb, who led a valiant last stand on the American right wing before succumbing to eight musket balls and three bayonet plunges. Cornwallis found him dying on the field and said, "I regret to see you so badly wounded, but am glad to have defeated you."[16] He ordered his personal physician to tend to his fallen counterpart. Meanwhile, Gates did not stop running until he was back in Philadelphia. Of Gates's cowardly flight, Hamilton wrote in caustic disgust, "Was there ever so precipitous a flight? One hundred and eighty miles in three days and a half. It does admirable credit to the activity of a man at this time of life."[17] Gates never commanded troops in battle again.

As Gates slept peacefully in Philadelphia, Baron Johan de Kalb lay dying in Camden. De Kalb was an instrumental midwife of the Franco-American alliance. His original object was making Broglie stadtholder of America, but de Kalb's most famous contribution turned out to be ushering Lafayette onto the stage of history. When he took up his own commission in the Continental Army, de Kalb acted as a friendly uncle and willing mentor to the young French marquis who was unfailingly endearing, if occasionally exasperating. They missed the chance for one last meeting by a matter of days the previous May. Lafayette was riding to Philadelphia on business just as de Kalb departed for the South. In one of his last letters home, de Kalb wrote his wife, "How gladly I would have tarried a few days in Philadelphia, to await the arrival of the Marquis de Lafayette . . . I had hundreds and hundreds of questions to ask him, and would have been glad to have chatted with him for some hours."[18] But they never saw each other again.

⫘

As DEFEATS IN the South mounted, the stalemate in the North continued. In September 1780, Washington finally felt comfortable enough with the state of his army—ever on the verge of mutiny and desertion—to finally depart for an in-person meeting with General Rochambeau and Admiral Ternay. Accompanied by an entourage including Knox, Hamilton, and Lafayette, Washington set out for a rendezvous at Hartford, Connecticut. Along the way, Benedict Arnold came down from West Point to host them for lunch and escort them across the Hudson River. On the ferry, Lafayette made an offhand remark about Arnold's "communication with the enemy," because maintaining contact with his counterparts in the British army was a routine part of Arnold's duties. Arnold was flustered and cried, "What do you mean?"[19] Lafayette did not think anything of it at the time. Certainly not that Arnold's startled jump would be used by future historians as ominous foreshadowing.

The Franco-American summit in Hartford was a success of limited consequence. All the young French officers registered their awe-struck admiration of Washington. All of them were raised on Livy, Polybius, and Plutarch, and they marveled at the Cincinnatus of America—the man who set down his plow to defend his people. Rochambeau and Ternay were less awestruck, but on their best behavior. The pleasant diplomatic fiction of Washington's seniority was maintained—even as Washington himself correctly surmised it was, in fact, a pleasant diplomatic fiction. They agreed on the shared desire to take New York City, but further agreed this would only be possible after the second half of the French expedition arrived. For now, there was nothing to be done. Lafayette acted as principal interpreter for these discussions. When he wrote up minutes this time, he kept his personal opinions to himself. Everyone signed the report without complaint.

On their way back to headquarters, Washington and his entourage swung through West Point. They planned to have breakfast with Benedict Arnold and his young wife, Peggy, who were living in a mansion across the river from the main fortifications. But when they arrived, they found Arnold called to urgent business at West Point, and Mrs. Arnold indisposed in her room. For most of the officers, this last bit was the only distressing news. Peggy Arnold was a young, pretty, and charming fixture of Philadelphia society who relished flirtation as a sport. After a far less entertaining breakfast than expected, Washington, Lafayette, and company went to tour the network of fortresses and redoubts on the bluffs overlooking the Hudson. Expecting Arnold to greet him, Washington was perturbed when the officers on duty said they had not seen the general all day. Nor were they aware of any urgent business. When Washington toured the fort, his annoyance grew. He found walls crumbling, repairs abandoned, and planned new construction never begun.

With the mood thoroughly soured, Washington and his officers returned to the Arnolds' house for dinner. As Lafayette dressed in his room, a young aide named Major McHenry burst into the room, searched frantically for his pistols, then raced out without a word of explanation. When Lafayette came out of his room, he discovered McHenry and Hamilton had dashed from the house in a mad rush. He came across Washington in the parlor. Tears in his eyes and clutching some papers, Washington said, "Arnold has betrayed us." Lafayette later said, "I have never seen General Washington so affected by any circumstances."[20]

The truth soon came out. The day before, a militia patrol apprehended a British officer in civilian clothes. This captive was revealed to be British Major John André carrying a satchel of papers. When Washington reviewed the contents, he discovered to his horror a copy of minutes of a recent council of war Washington had forwarded to Benedict Arnold. More terrifying, there was also a detailed description outlining the best way to capture West Point written in Benedict Arnold's hand. The captured Major André turned out to be a spy acting as Arnold's contact and courier. Benedict Arnold was a traitor.

This revelation stunned Lafayette. It stunned everyone. Benedict Arnold was a hero. One of the earliest and most courageous patriot officers of them all. He had almost single-handedly undertaken the invasion of Canada in 1775. Everyone knew he was the *real* hero of Saratoga. Today Benedict Arnold's name is synonymous with treason, but until his treason was discovered, his name was synonymous with patriotic heroism. Washington summed up the mood: "Whom can we trust now?"[21]

They learned later Arnold fled to a British ship anchored in the Hudson after learning of André's capture. Washington sent Hamilton and McHenry to catch him—but they were too late. Safely on the other side of the lines, Arnold wrote a note to Washington showing no remorse, but absolving his poor wife, Peggy, of blame. Arnold swore she was innocent and must not be maltreated in any way. Washington and the other officers believed this story. Peggy put on a fine display of demented hysterics all day—hysterics they assumed triggered by her husband's betrayal. But Peggy was herself a staunch Loyalist who helped facilitate her husband's treason. She was now simply putting on a show until she too could cross the lines and rejoin her husband. Lafayette and the others never suspected a thing. Telling Washington she wished to return to her father in Philadelphia, Peggy was allowed to leave. Instead, she went to her husband in New York. They expected to be handsomely rewarded once the rebellious colonies returned to the bosom of the mother country.

The final coda of the Arnold affair was the fate of Major André. André was twenty-seven years old, handsome, intelligent, and sophisticated. He enjoyed writing poetry and sketching pictures. He was as comfortable in the salon as he was the battlefield. He was the model of the debonair officer men on both sides of the lines admired. On September 29, 1780, a court-martial unanimously sentenced André to death. Gentlemen prisoners of war typically enjoyed the honor of being shot, but André was caught out of uniform and bearing false papers, so the court-martial sentenced him to be hanged as a spy. During his final days of captivity, André chatted amiably with Hamilton and Lafayette, who both came to like him a great deal. Lafayette wrote home to Adrienne, "I had the foolishness to let myself acquire a true affection for him."[22] Washington was unmoved by their entreaties to give André the benefit of the firing squad. Spies were hanged—and this spy in particular nearly cost them everything. On October 2, 1778, Major John André was hanged in front of the whole army.

After this brush with treasonous disaster, Lafayette and Washington were preoccupied with ensuring it did not impact their relationship with the French. Rochambeau wisely and magnanimously agreed it was *great* the treason was uncovered rather than *terrible* it happened at all. Reflecting on the near misses and chance events allowing Arnold's treason to be uncovered just moments before its fatal execution, Washington invoked "a most providential interposition."[23] In slightly less mystical terms, Lafayette simply marveled it was all revealed by "an almost unbelievable combination of accidents."[24]

⚜

THE ADRENALINE OF the Arnold Affair soon gave way to the tedium of inaction. There was nothing to do. Always the eager soldier, Lafayette now learned what a life in arms was really like: supreme patience and endless waiting. He wrote home to Madame de Tessé things were now "dull as a European war."[25] Then came more distressing news: the Royal Navy successfully placed the second French fleet under a tight blockade. It would not be sailing anytime soon. Only a planned raid on Staten Island with his light division promised to break up the monotony. But even that operation was called off at the last minute because the quartermaster failed to provide enough boats to get Lafayette and his men across the Hudson River. Lafayette was deeply put out when the campaign season of 1780 was declared irretrievably lost. His beloved light infantry division disbanded as the army headed into winter quarters.

These months were not a total loss, though. With the French, British, and Americans all inert, requests by the younger French officers to visit the Continental Army were approved. Lafayette found himself hosting some of the old gang from back home—most importantly his brother-in-law Noailles. Four years ago they dreamed of being in America together. And though they took different paths, they all finally achieved that dream. Noailles arrived at the Continental camp with a small group of officers Lafayette knew from home; the eldest, the comte de Chastellux, a *bon vivant* soldier and sometimes philosopher, left for posterity a long and fruitful account of his travels in America.

On a variety of official and personal pretexts, Lafayette and his friends were given further leave to visit Philadelphia. There, they enjoyed the charming, if limited, pursuits of the American capital. The dashing French officers were a hit. Invitations flooded in for teas, suppers, and balls. During the day, Lafayette and his friends took excursions to visit the battlefields of Brandywine, Germantown, and Barren Hill. At night they drank and danced. Lafayette and Chastellux received invitations to join the famous American Philosophical Society: Chastellux on the basis of his renowned intellectual credentials, Lafayette on the basis of . . . being Lafayette. The French enjoyed themselves immensely.

In Philadelphia, they also reunited with John Laurens. Taken prisoner in Charleston, Laurens traveled to Philadelphia under a loose house arrest. As a senior officer, Laurens was ordered, on his word of honor, not to leave Pennsylvania. Otherwise he was free to come and go as he pleased. This was a stark contrast to rank-and-file soldiers herded onto notorious prison barges in the harbor of New York City. As the son of Henry Laurens, and a member of General Washington's military family, Laurens secured further special treatment. His name advanced to the top of the prisoner exchange list and he was soon released. Laurens briefly fretted over this special treatment but was so eager to return to the war he did not dwell long on the matter.

Laurens would not be going back to war, however. Congress concluded they needed another voice in France to lobby for men, money, and supplies. What they had received thus far was disappointing and inadequate. Some in Congress suspected Benjamin Franklin's avowedly pro-French sentiments led him to accept from his hosts far less than he should. When nominations for a new diplomatic position opened up, both Lafayette and Laurens submitted Alexander Hamilton's name for the post. He was after all fluent in French and especially brilliant on financial matters. They also knew he was unhappy as Washington's deskbound chief of staff. Hamilton made it clear to his friends he believed his time with Washington had run its course. But Congress passed over the still relatively unknown Hamilton in favor of Laurens, who boasted better credentials and a better pedigree. He too spoke fluent French, but had also been educated in Europe, and was the son of southern planter aristocracy. Plus Laurens's ardent, bordering on pathological, patriotism would make him an inflexible iron rod next to Franklin's gently bending willow. That was the idea, anyway.

Laurens tried to beg off this mission. He knew, as much as anyone, he was probably too hotheaded for diplomacy. But out of a sense of duty, he ultimately accepted the post. Lafayette and Laurens departed

Philadelphia together in the first week of January 1781 to meet with Washington and discuss the expectations for Laurens's mission. They said goodbye to their French friends. The party was over. It was time to get back to work.

⚜

As THEY RODE back to headquarters, they witnessed firsthand the precarious state of the American cause—increasingly as perilous as it was glorious. Lafayette, Laurens, and Hamilton typically complained about lack of action. The late Baron de Kalb had complained of exorbitant prices and frozen ink. But the common soldiers suffered still more. They often served for months without pay. Even when finally given wages it was usually worthless paper money or promises of discharge bonuses they were unlikely to ever see. They had no meat for their bellies. No fuel for their fires. No shoes for their feet. No blankets while they slept. No coats while they stood guard. The breaking point finally came for soldiers of the Pennsylvania line on New Year's Day 1781. Their terms of service, set to expire with the new year, were arbitrarily extended another year. A group of soldiers mutinied. They killed a few officers and marched for Philadelphia to demand a full redress of all their grievances. But they were sensitive to accusations of treason and marched under the plaintive but angry cry, "We are not Arnolds!"[26]

Lafayette and Laurens happened to be in the path of this mutinous procession and did what they could to defuse the crisis. As Lafayette in particular was popular with the rank and file, he met with the leader of the mutiny but failed to talk him down. Before Washington could take sterner measures, the Pennsylvania assembly—perhaps aware of their own culpability—hastily awarded back pay and promised to discharge those who wished to be discharged.

But this was not the end of it. The dangerous contagion of mutiny spread to the New Jersey line. They too were fed up. They refused orders, killed a few officers, and issued a list of demands. This time Washington sent General Anthony Wayne with an overwhelming force to surround the mutineers and accept only unconditional submission. Mutiny could not be tolerated, no matter how righteous the causes. Once Wayne secured their surrender, he ordered the newly pacified soldiers to execute the ringleaders of the mutiny. A tragic end for men who sacrificed so much only to be treated so poorly. But mutiny was mutiny and could not be tolerated.

In between the two mutinies, Lafayette and Laurens and Washington agreed to a list of necessities to present to the government in France—most especially money. Real money. Hard money. They were not deaf to the complaints of the mutineers. They desperately hoped France could bail them out before the whole army quit and went home.

⚞⚟

THE EARLY WINTER of 1781 marked the end of Lafayette, Hamilton, and Laurens as the three musketeers of Washington's family. Laurens departed for Boston along with the crabby polemicist Thomas Paine, who would serve as an unofficial secretary. Laurens carried a massive satchel of letters Lafayette had written to every person in France who might make Laurens's job easier and his stay more pleasant. To Adrienne in particular he wrote, "If I were home he would dine with me every night," and implored her to treat him as a part of the family.[27] Just as Laurens was set to depart, he received welcome news making his stay in France even easier. Vicomte de Noailles was reassigned to help the young American envoy navigate the byzantine world of Versailles. As a reminder of how disconnected communication in the past truly was, Lafayette spent months unaware two of his best friends departed on the same ship. He spent months writing to Noailles as if he were still in Newport.

The next to leave was Hamilton. For months he lobbied for reassignment, hoping to go *anywhere* but back to work drafting Washington's correspondence. But Washington insisted Hamilton was an indispensable cog of the commander in chief's machine. Lafayette played an unwitting part in a long-coming breach between his adoptive brother and adoptive father. On February 16, Washington and Hamilton passed each other at the head of a flight of stairs. Washington told Hamilton they needed to speak. Hamilton—on his way to hand off some papers—said he would return immediately. On his way back, he bumped into Lafayette, who detained Hamilton for a quick chat. In Hamilton's later estimation all of this "did not last two minutes."[28]

After leaving Lafayette, Hamilton returned to the stairs and found Washington waiting in a state of cold fury. He accused Hamilton of disrespect. Offended, Hamilton threatened to resign. Washington said fine, and turned on his heels. Just as marriages can dissolve over an unwashed stack of dirty dishes piled high on a mountain of accumulated resentment, so it was for Hamilton and Washington. Regretting his peevishness, Washington tried to heal the breach. But Hamilton already had both feet out the door. He resigned from Washington's staff.

Finally, it was Lafayette's turn to leave. He wrestled for months with the question of whether to accept a command in the southern theater of the war. It was where all the action was, but Lafayette had difficulty imagining not serving at Washington's side. "I don't like the idea of abandoning him," he wrote to Hamilton over the winter.[29] Hamilton understood Lafayette's feelings even as he himself pulled away from the man Lafayette clung to. But things now changed. As a reward for his meritorious service to the Crown, Benedict Arnold was made a general in the British army. Shortly after New Year's 1781, Arnold landed with a force in Virginia and raided with impunity. Washington decided to reassemble a version of the light infantry division and dispatch Lafayette south. Once in Virginia, Lafayette was to link up with the forces in the area under the command of General Steuben to put a stop to Arnold's insulting campaign.

This was a mission of the highest importance. It might see Lafayette deliver honorable vengeance for his adoptive father. Washington, for his part, was only too happy to define this mission in terms of personal vengeance. In his official orders to Lafayette, he wrote, "You are to do no act whatever with Arnold that directly or by implication screens him from the punishment due to his treason and desertion, which if he should fall into your hands, you will execute in the most summary way."[30] In the last week of February 1781, Lafayette rode south astride a great white horse, in search of a rope, a tree, and Benedict Arnold.

CHAPTER NINE

THE PLAY IS OVER

[1781]

WAR IS A CONTEST OF WILLS. WEAPONS, ARMIES, FLEETS, and fortresses are simply the means by which one breaks the will of their enemy. A generation hence, Clausewitz would write war has three broad objectives: "Destroying the enemy's armed forces; occupying their country; and breaking their will to continue the struggle."[1] But the first two are merely the means by which one achieves the third, the only true goal of war—breaking the enemy's will to continue the struggle. Victory and defeat are subjective psychological events, not objective material conditions. If the enemy's will is broken, a million cannons will sit idle. But if their will is *not* broken, it does not matter if they are disarmed or occupied. It does not matter how naked and defenseless they stand. They will simply kneel down, pick up a rock, and throw it.

Clausewitz goes on to say that though peace usually comes after one side concludes it is unable to carry on the struggle, there are two other grounds for making peace: "The first is the improbability of victory; the second is its unacceptable cost."[2] Though no one knew it, the British were moving toward these latter grounds in the summer of 1781. Voices in Britain opposing the war in America grew into a chorus—then a consensus—that the conflict was an endless quagmire costing too much blood and too much treasure. After five inconclusive years, British public opinion suspected the Americans would never stop fighting. Even if they were defeated, disarmed, and re-occupied, the Americans would kneel down, pick up a rock, and throw it.

The latest British war strategy only confirmed this suspicion. After capturing Charleston in May 1780, General Henry Clinton returned to New York City and left Lord Cornwallis to complete the conquest of the South. But Cornwallis found the alleged loyalism in the South overstated; so too the belief the American rebellion was on the verge of collapse. Cornwallis found himself isolated and alone, his campaign turning into an exercise in exhausting frustration. Up in New York, Clinton spent his days petitioning the government to be recalled. Back home, Parliament resisted sending additional men and money. In the Carolinas, much of the local population treated the British with hostile resentment. Unsupported and un-reinforced, every man Cornwallis lost became a man he could not replace.

In January 1781, American general Daniel Morgan lured a detachment of Cornwallis's army into a trap at Cowpens, South Carolina, and beat them soundly. In March, Cornwallis advanced into North Carolina, where General Nathanael Greene met him at Guildford Court House. Though Cornwallis forced Greene to retreat, the Continentals inflicted so many casualties one must turn to a quote from Plutarch's *Life of Pyrrhus* to understand the British situation: "If we are victorious in one more battle . . . we shall be utterly ruined."[3] Cornwallis gave up the idea of conquering the Carolinas. He decided to head to Virginia to start the British reconquest of America all over again, not realizing it would soon simply be *all over*. Despite their massive superiority in wealth, manpower, resources, technology, and experience, Britain's will was broken.

⚎

As HE MARCHED south in the spring of 1781, Lafayette did not know he marched toward the end of the American War of Independence. His principal object was hunting down and hanging Benedict Arnold. After landing with a thousand men in Virginia in January 1781, Arnold spent months ransacking the countryside. The local response to the emergency was distressingly ineffectual. Though Virginia was one of the centers of colonial rebelliousness—producing the grandees of Congress and the Continental Army like George Washington, Thomas Jefferson, Patrick Henry, George Mason, and the Lee family—Virginia had not seen shots fired in anger since the early days of the war. They struggled to respond to military invasion. General Steuben, dispatched to take over command of local militia forces, reported back to headquarters the Virginians were hopelessly flailing: "It is impossible to describe the situation I am in. . . . Nothing can be done in the state rather for want of arrangements than anything else."[4]

Lafayette's division was supposed to reinforce Steuben and give the defense of Virginia a professional backbone. Hoping to mask their intentions, Lafayette told his men to pack light for a short mission. Then they marched south and never stopped. In a week, they were in Trenton, a hundred miles away. Even then, most of the men did not know the ultimate plan. Lafayette's orders were to go to Head of Elk, Maryland. There he would rendezvous with a French naval squadron that would ferry him down Chesapeake Bay to Virginia. But when he arrived at his destination in the first week of March, Lafayette found no sign of his naval escorts. Annoyed and impatient, Lafayette suspected the French high command avoided the rendezvous so "they alone may display their zeal" and defeat the British unencumbered by Continentals.[5] Lafayette decided not to wait for a fleet that may not be coming. After inducing industrious patriots to round up "every vessel that may be collected," Lafayette shipped the bulk of his army to Annapolis.[6] He himself boarded a small fishing boat accompanied by thirty picked men to press on to Virginia and survey the situation.

As Lafayette approached Virginia, he began what turned out to be a lifelong relationship with Thomas Jefferson. After authoring the Declaration of Independence in 1776, Jefferson returned to Virginia and thus never made the marquis's acquaintance. At present, Jefferson was governor of Virginia, and his theories about the virtue of non-coercive self-government were failing to meet the practical challenge of defending Virginia from military invasion. Lafayette wrote Governor Jefferson from his fishing boat, reporting the urgent need to feed, clothe, and outfit his soldiers. Jefferson apologetically lamented Virginia's lackadaisical response, saying, "Mild laws, a people not used to war, and prompt obedience, the want of provisions of war and means of providing them render our service often ineffectual."[7] The response of a father who orders his children to clean their room, then shrugs when they do not comply.

And it is not like the military crisis was subsiding. As Lafayette approached, Clinton sent an additional two thousand men under General William Phillips to reinforce and expand the campaign in Virginia. Phillips was a career soldier and veteran of the Seven Years' War who started his career in the artillery. He had, in fact, been in command of an artillery company at the Battle of Minden in 1759 that spotted a curiously exposed French regiment, which he proceeded to pummel with merciless ease. Lafayette did not know it at the time, but the man who killed his father stood across from him in Virginia.

Outnumbered and with limited resources, Lafayette concluded there was no realistic chance of capturing Arnold. He was unsure how to respond to the change in circumstance and sent a flurry of dispatches back to headquarters. Should he stay in Virginia? Return to New York? Head farther south to reinforce Greene? After news of Guildford Court House, both Lafayette and Steuben wanted to lead their men to the Carolinas, but the Virginia legislature refused to let them take the Virginia militia across state lines. The militiamen were not only needed to fight British invaders, but also to prevent slave uprisings, which frightened the Virginians at least as much as the British army did.

WHILE LAFAYETTE LANGUISHED in Virginia, trying to decide what to do, he received mixed news from home. John Laurens reached France, linked with Benjamin Franklin, and did everything he could to secure badly needed money and supplies, but even the sympathetic Vergennes was at a loss. When presented with the grand total, Vergennes replied, "It would not be possible for the King to accede . . . and if he did it would surely ruin France!"[8] Vergennes wrote Lafayette to say the demands of the Americans were becoming a problem: "France is not inexhaustible."[9] The worst news of all was regarding the second half of Rochambeau's expedition—all those supply ships were *never* going to sail. Thanks to logistical foul-ups and the ongoing British blockade, the French government simply canceled the mission.

But then Jacques Necker stepped in to stop the run of bad news. The controller-general of the king's finances initially opposed the costly adventure in America. But unable to stop France from following Lafayette's lead and purchasing glory at the cost of her fortune, Necker changed his tune. After taking out high-interest loans to finance the war, he embarked on an unprecedented project of governmental transparency. On February 19, 1781, Necker published the *Compte rendu*—a massive volume of charts, tables, and commentaries describing in detail the Crown's revenue, expenses, payments, debts, and balances. For the first time, the public was allowed to peak behind the gilded opacity of the royal finances. The *Compte rendu* seemed to prove the annual revenue and expenditure of the government not only balanced, but showed a slight annual surplus. This demonstration reassured the king's subjects, the king's creditors, and the king himself everything was fine.

Based largely on the reassuring conclusion of the *Compte rendu*, the king agreed to cosign another loan of 10 million *livres* from Dutch bankers on behalf of the Americans. It was not everything Laurens and Franklin asked for, but it was more than they believed they were going to get. Then came more good news. Though the French government canceled the second half of Rochambeau's expedition, they ordered Admiral François Joseph Paul de Grasse, commander of the French fleet in the Caribbean, to sail up the coast in the late summer of 1781. Laurens returned to America with cash, supplies, and expectations that another French fleet was on the way.

But what was good news for America was bad news for France. As would soon be revealed, the *Compte rendu* painted a dangerously misleading picture of the situation. Necker took all the debts, bills, and interest payments sinking the monarchy like a stone and labeled them "extraordinary" expenses—temporary expenditures that would soon be off the books. Necker led everyone to believe they were nothing to worry about, when, in fact, they were all sitting on a pile of gunpowder ready to blow the Kingdom of France to kingdom come.

MEANWHILE, LAFAYETTE REMAINED stuck in Virginia where he could not effectively attack Phillips and Arnold, nor press on the Carolinas. By April 1781, the marquis fretted he had been banished to exile. He knew if Washington had his way, New York City would be the site of the final battle. He asked the commander in chief to recall him to headquarters, but lamented to Hamilton, "It is probable I will be in the southern wilderness until the end of the war."[10]

Still lacking clear instructions, Lafayette ordered his men farther south to stand between Cornwallis's incoming army and the forces under Phillips and Arnold. But Lafayette's men balked. They departed New York thinking they would be gone a few days, and now they had been gone close to a month. The New Englanders, in particular, feared the southern air was full of toxic diseases. Soldiers started deserting. Lafayette woke up each morning with fewer men than when he went to sleep. Though he pushed them forward, he wrote La Luzerne in Philadelphia, "Our officers and soldiers are not too happy about it. We have no money, clothing, shoes, nor shirts . . . our feet are torn for lack of shoes and our hands itchy for lack of linen."[11] Finally the desertions became so bad, Lafayette resorted to drastic measures. He ordered a captured deserter hanged in front of the whole division. Then he offered passes home to anyone who wanted one. The shaming worked and desertions stopped.

On April 25, Lafayette learned General Phillips was marching on Richmond, the capital of Virginia. Arnold already raided and burned the capital once, much to Governor Jefferson's acute embarrassment, but Lafayette hoped to prevent a repeat performance. Ditching his artillery and heavy baggage, Lafayette and eight hundred healthy soldiers raced to Richmond, reaching the city one day ahead of the British. When Phillips pulled into the environs, he found Lafayette already occupied the strategic high ground overlooking the town. Not realizing Lafayette did not have any way of exploiting the advantage, Phillips turned around and departed. "It is lucky he did," Lafayette reported, because "my cannon and my baggage" were all left behind.[12] Lafayette took further pleasure in later hearing, "Mr. Osborne, who was with [Phillips], says that he flew into a violent passion and swore vengeance against me."[13] One cannot always have what one wants, but a fine consolation prize is denying an enemy what *they* want.

Despite this small success, Lafayette faced insurmountable odds. He only commanded about one thousand men. The British forces now approached seven thousand. When he heard a false rumor Clinton was personally sailing down from New York City, Lafayette wrote to La Luzerne, "I hear from all sides General Clinton is coming to join the party, thus I am proscribed by this triumvirate. But not being so eloquent as Cicero it is not my tongue these gentlemen will cut off."[14] Lafayette's gallant but pessimistic assessment was that he could neither attack nor defend anything. Writing Washington, he said, "I am not even strong enough to be defeated."[15] Even the news General Anthony Wayne had been ordered to reinforce him brought little real hope. As Lafayette put it, Wayne's arrival would simply mean "we shall be in a position to be beaten more decently."[16] Meanwhile, he lost contact entirely with Steuben thanks to a smothering blanket of British cavalry patrols intercepting letters and dispatches. Steuben was only fifty miles west guarding the arsenal at Point of Fork, but found himself cut off and isolated. "I send express messengers everywhere, but I get nothing," he wrote. "I beg you to send me news . . . it is as though I am in Kamchatka."[17]

As history has no interest in providing satisfying climaxes to obvious narrative arcs, the Virginia campaign did *not* ultimately pit General Phillips against the marquis de Lafayette, ending with a dramatic showdown between a son and his father's killer. Instead General Phillips anticlimactically dropped dead of a fever on May 13, 1781. Lafayette never even knew their connection. He later came to believe the British officer responsible for his father's death died at Yorktown. And though he delighted in this erroneous belief, Lafayette never knew the identity of the man who *really* killed his father.

⧜

A WEEK AFTER Phillips died, General Cornwallis and his beleaguered forces arrived. Cornwallis planned to raid, plunder, and wreak havoc in Virginia, and hopefully draw renewed interest, money, and reinforcements from back home. As he prepared to launch this campaign,

Cornwallis discovered a delightful secondary objective. Informed that Lafayette commanded the massively outnumbered American forces, Cornwallis might be able do what General Howe was unable to do at Barren Hill three years earlier: capture the marquis de Lafayette. When Cornwallis ordered his forces to fan out across Virginia, all Lafayette could do was retreat into the tangled hill country of the Virginia interior. Cornwallis allegedly crowed to his superiors, "The boy cannot escape me!"[18]

The only good news for Lafayette was the end of Jefferson's term as governor. He was succeeded by a former Continental general named Thomas Nelson. As a military man, the incoming governor would at least have some understanding of supply and logistics. Though Lafayette and Jefferson enjoyed a budding personal friendship, the marquis was happy to learn dispatches to the governor's office were now read by a fellow soldier.

Lafayette got more good news on June 10, when General Wayne finally arrived—giving Lafayette a thousand more men, and the opportunity to be beaten more decently. But Lafayette's jaunty fatalism should not be taken for flippancy. This was his first real independent command and he took it very seriously. "To speak the truth," he wrote Greene, "I've become timid in the same proportion as I become independent. Had a superior officer been here I could have proposed a half-dozen schemes."[19] Lafayette previously enjoyed the safety of suggesting plans that, if judged foolhardy, would be set aside by wiser and cooler heads. Now he must *be* the wiser and cooler head. To think as Washington would think. To take Rochambeau's sage advice about not risking his men for his own personal glory. Greene echoed these thoughts. He warned Lafayette "in the voice of a friend . . . not to let the love of fame get the better of your prudence and plunge you into misfortune in eager pursuit after glory."[20] Lafayette knew his own natural instincts and took the advice to heart.

In his first real test as a mature commander, Lafayette acquitted himself brilliantly. While retreating in the face of a far superior force, he burned bridges, tossed felled trees across roads, and dispatched snipers to harass British regiments. He managed to stay one step ahead of his pursuers, proudly recalling later (in the habitual third person of his memoirs), "The Americans withdrew so that the enemy's vanguard arrived on the ground just as they had left it, and without compromising themselves, they delayed its progress as much as possible."[21] Lafayette also encouraged his men to smear charcoal on their faces and keep up a continuous string of surprise attacks—firing sudden volleys, then disappearing into the forest. "I have made an army of devils," Lafayette said, "and have given them plenty of absolution."[22] As the days stretched into weeks, the morale of Lafayette's men improved, while British morale inversely deteriorated. The British soldiers suffered from the heat, mosquitoes, and diseases of backwoods Virginia. They became more exhausted and disgruntled with each passing day.

By the last week of June 1781, the boy had successfully escaped Cornwallis. The British lines were too far extended, so they broke off pursuit and fell back toward the coast. Lafayette responded with a clever strategic decision. Rather than remaining in the safety of the interior, he followed Cornwallis's forces as they retreated. From the outside, it looked like Lafayette was chasing the British back to the sea. He told Greene when the British started retreating, "I follow and one would think I pursue him."[23] This had the intended effect on the local population. Militiamen suddenly appeared, guns in hand, hoping for an opportunity to join the chase. Food, provisions, and horses previously withheld were now offered up freely. No one likes to join a lost cause, but everyone loves to hop on the bandwagon. And Lafayette built himself a mighty bandwagon. An observer said Lafayette displayed "sorcery and magic . . . a very necessary science for an American general at this moment."[24]

During this phase of the campaign, Lafayette also faced the dilemma of what to do about African slaves. The British encouraged slaves to flee their American masters and promised freedom lay on the other side of the lines. Some of Washington's own slaves recently fled Mount Vernon to take the British up on the offer. Lafayette often encountered such runaways. Governor Nelson informed Lafayette official policy was to return all slaves to their former owners because "the principle on which it is supposed men fight at present is to protect and secure to themselves and fellow citizens their liberties and properties."[25] Lafayette's objection to this policy was not that "liberties" and "properties" were presented in nakedly hypocritical terms, but that the owners ought to at least pay the army "half the value in hard money," as a practical means of raising badly needed money.[26] Lafayette's response demonstrates that whatever abolitionist seeds John Laurens planted had yet to bear fruit. It is also clear from Lafayette's reports of the period he still viewed the slaves as property, not people. When he mentions slaves in his dispatches, it is invariably in sections concerning the baggage, horses, or supplies found in a town or enemy encampment, as when he described Cornwallis's difficult position: "He must give up ships, artillery, baggage, part of the horses, [and] all the negroes."[27] But though he had not yet made the mental turn to abolitionism in the summer of 1781, it is the last time one finds Lafayette thinking this way.

⚜

THOUGH HE WAS in high spirits as he chased the British back to the sea, Lafayette remained acutely aware of the contrast between himself and his adversary. Lord Cornwallis was easily the best British general of the war. Lafayette knew he squared off against a savvy, experienced, and deadly opponent who could turn the tables at any moment. He wrote, "The devil Cornwallis is much wiser than the other generals with whom I have dealt. He inspires me with a sincere fear and his name greatly troubles my sleep."[28] To the French ambassador he wrote, "In the end he will give me a good thrashing."[29] To Henry Knox he confessed, "To speak plain English I am devilishly afraid of him."[30]

Lafayette was not wrong to be afraid. Cornwallis nearly did give him a good thrashing. By the first week of July 1781, the line of British retreat necessitated they cross the James River. Lafayette and Wayne spied an opportunity to catch the British in mid-embarkation, exposed and vulnerable to attack. They made base at Green Spring Plantation and planned to use it as the staging ground for an attack on the British, presumed to be just up around the bend loading themselves onto ferries.

On the morning of July 6, General Wayne led a vanguard of about nine hundred men, while Lafayette brought up the rest of the army through open marshland. Wayne engaged in light skirmishes with a detachment of British cavalry, which was not unexpected and no cause for deeper alarm. What neither Lafayette nor Wayne realized was the

British forces were *not* up around the bend loading themselves onto ferries. They were, in fact, tucked back behind a screen of trees ready to spring a trap carefully laid by Cornwallis. *The boy would not escape him.*

As the American forces advanced, Lafayette rode out around his right flank to assess how far along the British were—and discovered to his horror they were not where they were supposed to be. It was too late to warn Wayne, and Cornwallis sprang the trap. The British charged out of the forest en masse. Badly exposed, Wayne had two options. He could cry retreat, most likely triggering a panicked flight and ultimate defeat; or he could stand his ground and fight. But apprehending immediately how much wider the advancing British line was, Wayne concluded standing his ground meant encirclement. So Wayne thought quickly and went with option three: he ordered his men to charge directly at the oncoming British. The British were shocked to see Wayne's men rushing headlong through heavy fire and had to halt their own charge in response. This pause provided just enough time for Lafayette to bring more men up to support Wayne and secure a disciplined retreat in good order. The trap failed. Cornwallis did not want to waste men and ammunition turning Green Spring into another Guildford Court House. The boy escaped him. Again.

Lafayette praised Wayne's quick and courageous decision to charge. It became one of the key moments in the romantic legend of "Mad Anthony" Wayne, who took impossibly daring risks and always came out on top. Wayne himself modestly said his charge was "one of those prudent, though daring maneuvers, which seldom fail of producing the desired effect; the result in this instance fully justified it."[31] One of those results being Lafayette would end the war a celebrated hero rather than a humiliated prisoner.

⸎

OTHER THAN THIS harrowing brush with defeat, Lafayette was mostly having a grand time in Virginia. But he still worried he was going to be left out of the main event. Washington and Rochambeau had recently conducted a second meeting at the end of May 1781 and agreed the centerpiece of strategic planning would be New York City. Rochambeau even agreed to leave Newport for the first time since arriving in America to demonstrate his commitment to the project. Lafayette subsequently received contradictory orders—with plenty of hints from Washington that whenever de Grasse's fleet arrived, they would finally be able to crack Manhattan.

The question of when exactly Washington relinquished his fixation on New York City remains a matter of debate. Shortly before he was sworn in as the first president of the United States, Washington wrote a letter to Noah Webster recollecting events from the last stages of the war, saying "that it was determined by me (nearly twelve months before hand) . . . to give out and cause it to be believed . . . New York was the destined place of attack." Washington said he always knew Virginia would be "the definitive and certain object of the Campaign . . . it never was in contemplation to attack New York."[32] When the story was published, General Timothy Pickering, who was quartermaster general at the time, told Benjamin Rush, "It is false, I know it is false, and it doesn't reflect well on him to say it."[33] Meanwhile, Rochambeau wrote dispatches to de Grasse in the early summer of 1781 reporting Washington was still fixated on New York City. By that point, both Rochambeau and de Grasse believed Cornwallis's army in Virginia made the far juicier target. So while Rochambeau told Washington he was doing everything he could to get the French fleet to come to New York City, he simultaneously told de Grasse to go to the Chesapeake Bay while Rochambeau persuaded Washington to move south.

George Washington probably clung fast to the dream of New York City until August 14, 1781, when he was given three pieces of news. First, the French fleet was on its way up the coast. Second, Admiral de Grasse's destination was not New York but the Chesapeake Bay. Third, de Grasse was not leading a mere squadron from his fleet. He was leading his *entire fleet* up the mainland coast: 26 ships of the line, 8 frigates, and 150 transport ships, bearing close to twenty thousand soldiers and sailors. Even with his longstanding and justifiable obsession with New York City, Washington could not ignore the opportunity this presented. If he and Rochambeau raced their forces to Virginia, they could capture Cornwallis's entire army.

Washington threw himself into this project with the fervor of a convert. He tirelessly organized and directed the combined redeployment of the French and Continental armies from New York to Virginia—a redeployment that needed to be hidden from General Clinton for as long as possible. In total, Washington and his officers organized nearly seven thousand men, plus support personnel, weapons, baggage, and supplies for a race south to bottle up Cornwallis. This scramble would only be possible if Cornwallis remained in place. It was left to Lafayette to ensure Cornwallis did not get away from the boy.

Luckily for the young marquis, Cornwallis did not know about the French fleet coming up from the Caribbean, nor about Washington and Rochambeau coming down from New York. He only knew Clinton ordered him to find a deepwater port to hold until reinforcements could be delivered. Cornwallis made a quick survey of the area and selected Yorktown, a small town on a hill overlooking the mouth of the York River, as the best spot to dig in. Lafayette made camp on the neck between the York and James Rivers with about 4,500 Continentals and Virginia militia to prevent his escape. Had Cornwallis gotten it in his head to make a run for it with all his forces—now numbering about ten thousand—he could have easily punched through Lafayette's line. But he never did.

The French and American armies linked south of Philadelphia to continue their march in tandem. Rochambeau was amazed when he first spotted Washington, "waving his hat at me with demonstrative gestures of the greatest joy."[34] Rochambeau soon learned why. De Grasse's massive armada had arrived at the Chesapeake and was hovering off the coast. Cornwallis was cut off from any relief by sea. Another said of Washington, "Never have I seen a man overcome with such great and sincere joy."[35] Another French officer said he was like a child "whose every wish had been gratified."[36] After years of stoic resolve, George Washington was beginning to get light-headed with the giddy thought of victory.

The joy increased on September 5, when the Royal Navy squadron sent to reinforce Cornwallis's position ran into de Grasse's recently arrived fleet. The subsequent battle off the Virginia Capes was a tactical draw leaving both fleets damaged, but it forced the British to withdraw, making it a major strategic triumph for the Americans and French. By

September 14, de Grasse's fleet was back in place at the opening of the Chesapeake. Cornwallis was isolated and his end was nigh.

Washington and Rochambeau arrived in Williamsburg after clearing nearly seven hundred miles in just under four weeks. It was Washington's first trip home since donning his uniform in 1775 to take his place in the Second Continental Congress, not too subtly hinting to his fellow delegates he had come to fight a war, not beg for mercy from the Crown. Though Lafayette was stricken with a fever, he rushed out of bed and dashed to Williamsburg. When they met, Lafayette "caught the general round his body, hugged him as close as possible and absolutely kissed him from ear to ear once or twice . . . with an ardor not easily described."[37]

On September 17, the host of officers around Washington and Rochambeau traveled out to meet with de Grasse on his flagship. De Grasse jokingly referred to Washington, who towered over the crew, as "*mon petit general.*"[38] And though Washington took great pride in his statuesque bearing, he was not amused by the tone of condescension he picked up from the French admiral. De Grasse said he would have to return to the Caribbean by the middle of October. Until then, he could support a siege of Yorktown—a slower but safer option. If Cornwallis did not surrender by then, it would have to be a direct assault—quick and bloody—or nothing at all.

⚜

ON SEPTEMBER 28, 1781, Washington and Rochambeau led their armies out of Williamsburg to begin the siege of Yorktown. Joined by additional reinforcements who arrived by transport, and marines who disembarked from de Grasse's fleet, they numbered close to twenty thousand men. This mass congregation of forces led to more happy reunions for Lafayette. Colonel John Laurens was back from his stint in Europe. Colonel Alexander Hamilton returned to active duty, hoping for a chance at real action. Vicomte de Noailles commanded a French regiment. All of Lafayette's best friends from both sides of the Atlantic were coming together in Yorktown, Virginia, to live out their fantasies of battlefield glory.

Upon arrival, they found Cornwallis had built a fortified ring around the town. Behind these fortifications sat about ten thousand soldiers, along with two civilian groups desperate for Cornwallis to hold out or find an escape hatch: Tory Loyalists and African slaves. The consequences of defeat would be dire for both groups. The former faced dispossession, expulsion, and life as exiles at a minimum. At maximum, a speedy trial and a noose. For the Africans, it would be even worse. Encouraged to run away and join the British, they faced the prospect not just of reenslavement, but torturous punishment for running away: beatings, whippings, shackles, chains, amputated limbs. Some might be declared so incorrigible they would be sold to the sugar colonies in the Caribbean, a de facto death sentence where half of new arrivals died within eighteen months.

On October 5, sappers, miners, and engineers got to work digging parallel trenches to the British line. At least a third of the army was occupied cutting down trees. Lafayette marveled, "The engineers troll about like sorcerers making circles around poor Cornwallis."[39] On October 9, the artillery was in place and bombardment began. They kept up a thunderous and constant assault, filling the air with whistles, crashes, explosions, cries, dust, clouds, smoke, maiming, death, and destruction. In short order, the British ceased bothering to respond. Most of the men, hunkered behind the main bluff of Yorktown overlooking the river, only ventured out to do their shift on futile guard duty, which only staved off the inevitable for one more day. To make matters worse, an outbreak of smallpox raced through the closely confined population. Cornwallis himself ordered a grotto carved out of the side of the hill where he could sit and wait. There was no battle to plan. All he could do was hope Clinton would deliver his promised reinforcements.

Back in a subordinate role, Lafayette returned to his natural state of excitable daring. Sieges are tedious affairs, and Lafayette reported the men "chafe at the slowness of the approach and ask permission to shorten the time by taking this point or that with drawn swords."[40] Washington would not allow it. Lafayette said Washington was "determined to conserve the blood of his troops."[41] But eventually, drawn swords became necessary. On the far right of the American lines, two fortified British redoubts needed to be captured before a second line of trenches could be finished. The French were assigned to capture one, the Americans the other. Lafayette was thrilled when ordered to oversee the mission, especially as it reunited the three musketeers one last time: Colonel Laurens and Colonel Hamilton each led regiments under Lafayette's overall command.

Hamilton was especially desperate for action after so much time spent confined to a desk, and if history were not so resistant to following obvious narrative beats, Lafayette would have immediately given his oldest American friend command of the attack. But instead, Lafayette gave the honor to a fellow Frenchman, Colonel Jean-Joseph de Gimat. Gimat first came to America with Lafayette aboard *La Victoire*, served as Lafayette's first aide-de-camp, and then climbed the ranks of the Continental Army in his own right. Hamilton was furious when Lafayette passed him over and went straight to the commander in chief. Washington, who bore Hamilton no permanent ill will over their breakup the previous winter, helpfully pointed out the night of the attack *was* Hamilton's turn in the regular rotation and he should get the command. Lafayette acquiesced without further resistance.

On October 14, Hamilton led the assault with Laurens right behind him. They silently charged the redoubt with only fixed bayonets. After ten minutes of close quarters combat, the British guards surrendered. Over in the other redoubt, vicomte de Noailles commanded a French regiment in a similarly successful mission. As a major general, Lafayette himself did not take part in the actual fighting and settled for the honor of the skirmish happening under his overall command. Mostly he was relieved all his friends came back alive.

After the redoubts were captured, Cornwallis all but abandoned hope. As a cruel last-ditch maneuver he expelled a group of slaves stricken with smallpox as a form of biological warfare. Refused permission to cross the line, these poor souls were forced to simply lie down and die in the no-man's-land between the two armies. Cornwallis then decided his only hope was a risky escape across the York River to the city of Gloucester. He scheduled the escape attempt for the early hours of October 16, but a storm arrived, making the river impassable and escape impossible. Trapped, hungry, tired, wounded, and sick, Cornwallis and his officers concluded it was all over. They were defeated.

※

ON OCTOBER 17, 1781, a drummer boy appeared on the wall waving the white flag. Blindfolded and led to Washington and Rochambeau, the boy passed along a request from Cornwallis for a twenty-four-hour truce to arrange terms of surrender. Washington told the boy two hours would be sufficient. Commissioners were appointed to do the practical negotiations. Representing the French and Americans were two of Lafayette's best friends: vicomte de Noailles and John Laurens. They were sent to present extremely generous terms. The only hard sticking point was Washington's insistence the British surrender under the same terms Clinton demanded at Charleston: regimental colors locked up in a box rather than waving proudly. Cornwallis attempted to fight the demand, but in the end agreed.

On October 19, 1781, the French and American forces lined on opposite sides of Hampton Road to ceremonially supervise as Cornwallis's army filed out of the city to deposit their arms in a field. It was the first time in his long military career George Washington presided over such a surrender. It doesn't really matter how long it takes to oversee one's *first* surrender if that surrender is the *last* surrender of the war. In a not very subtle insult to the Americans, the British kept their eyes fixed squarely on the French army as they filed past. Well attuned to such insults, Lafayette prodded Continental musicians to play "Yankee Doodle Dandy" as loud as they could to force the British to turn and acknowledge their presence.

With the surrender complete, the mingling began. For career soldiers, social class was at least as important as national attachment. So as the rank and file remained herded together as prisoners of war, the British officers and their French and American counterparts drank, dined, and shared stories. Loosening up, Cornwallis joined this milieu. He put on a brave and genial face and invited Lafayette to a meeting. Lafayette took along maps of Virginia so the two generals could retrace the campaign of the summer, which saw Lafayette escape Cornwallis again and again. Each acknowledged the other's skill and fortune. Lafayette wrote home to Adrienne, "I pity Cornwallis for whom I have a high regard."[42]

There was much uncertainty about what victory at Yorktown meant. There was no doubt it was a *major* victory, but New York City remained in Clinton's hands. The British also continued to hold Charleston, Savannah, and Augusta. This did not *have* to be the end of the war. The British could press more soldiers into service, take out new loans, build more ships. Even if there were peace talks, those talks could easily break down. But Yorktown *did* turn out to mark the end of the American War of Independence, because there was no will to fight left in Britain. The costs of continuing the war were unacceptable. The likelihood of future victory improbable. When informed of Cornwallis's capture, British prime minister Lord North exclaimed, "Oh god! It's all over."[43] The British were defeated. Lafayette wrote home joyfully to Maurepas, "The play is over, Monsieur le comte, the fifth act is just ended."[44]

⚜

AT TWENTY-FOUR YEARS old, Lafayette could not have hoped for greater success. His life had not been perfect. He never knew his father, his beloved mother died far too young, his cousin and surrogate sister died in childbirth while he was in America. His entrance into the Noailles family seemed destined to be a story of expectations dashed by awkward adolescent embarrassments. Never crude enough to become a scandalous black sheep, he would most likely be treated as an ugly bird kept hidden in a cage under a blanket. Most of French society expected his brilliant madness in America to be a hilarious failure. Instead, Lafayette trusted himself, took a bold risk, and it paid off magnificently. Sure, his title, wealth, and connections opened doors in America but his courage, loyalty, and talent won him acclaim.

The late Baron de Kalb once said of his young protégé: "No one deserves more than he the esteem which he enjoys here . . . he is a prodigy for his age, full of courage, spirit, judgment, good manners, feelings of generosity, and of zeal for the cause of liberty on this continent."[45] Hamilton said of his friend: "The United States are under infinite obligations to him beyond what is known. Not only for his valor and good conduct as a Major General of our army, but for his good offices and influence on our behalf with the court of France. The French army now here . . . would not have been in this country but through his means."[46] Even the common soldiers held their young French leader in high regard, with Private Joseph Plumb Martin writing, "The general well knew what he was about; he was not deficient in either courage or conduct, and that is well known to all the revolutionary army."[47] Washington's feelings stemmed from true regard for Lafayette's character: "He possesses un- common military talents, is of quick and sound judgment, persevering, and besides these, is of a very conciliating temper and perfectly sober— which are qualities that rarely combine in the same person."[48]

And it was not just his new American friends who loved and re- spected him. On the French side, the comte d'Estaing said, "No one is in a better position than this young general officer to serve as an addi- tional link between France and America. He enjoys here a very desired esteem which is due to his zeal, valor and wisdom."[49] Conrad Alexandre Gérard, France's first diplomatic representative to America, said Lafa- yette displayed "wisdom and dexterity." He reported to Vergennes, "The prudent, courageous and amiable conduct of M. de Lafayette has made him the idol of the Congress, the army, and the people of America. We have a high opinion of his military talents. You know, Monsignor, how far I am from adulation, but I would be lacking in equity if I did not send you testimonies which are here in the mouths of everyone without any exception."[50] The marquis de Chastellux gave perhaps the most fitting and prescient description of Lafayette: "Fortunate is the coun- try who knows how to avail herself of his talents. More fortunate still should she stand in no need of them."[51]

There were many dreams Lafayette yet dared to dream. With so much success at such a young age, there was no reason to believe there were not even greater successes to come. The play in American might be over, but it was time to begin a new one in France. Lafayette bid tearful farewell to his men, embraced his friends and fellow officers, and prepared to sail for home. He hoped his country would be ready to avail herself of his talents. Though it might have been better if she had not stood in need of them at all.

The Liberties of All Mankind

[1782–1786]

O N January 21, 1782, Lafayette burst through the door of the Hôtel Noailles in Paris. He expected to be greeted by enthusiastic cheers, hugs, and applause. Instead, the house was empty. By sheer coincidence the entire family, and almost everyone in high society, was down the street at the Hôtel de Ville—Paris City Hall—attending a banquet thrown by the city leaders to celebrate the infant *dauphin*—the firstborn son of Louis XVI and Marie Antoinette. Born the previous October, the little baby boy secured the royal succession after eight years of uncertainty and malicious gossip. The kingdom was on firm footing for another generation.

Lafayette was recognized in the street and word spread to the party . . . Lafayette was back! Adrienne wanted to race home, but society protocol prohibited her from leaving before the queen. Apprehending this difficulty, Marie Antoinette graciously announced she was ready to go home. As the royal entourage prepared to depart, the queen offered to drive Adrienne home and drop her off. Lafayette emerged from the front door of the empty Hôtel Noailles to find the entire royal retinue pulling up, trailed by a crowd of spectators. When Adrienne climbed out of the queen's coach and laid eyes on her husband, safe and home at last, she fainted dead into his arms. Lafayette carried her diminutive figure back into the house as the royal family bid him a welcoming *adieu* and the crowd cheered. That was more like it.

Lafayette was further gratified as he made his social rounds in the weeks to come. "The reception I have met with from the nation at large, from the king and from my friends," he wrote Washington, "has surpassed my greatest expectations."[1] This was not just in his head. Benjamin Franklin wrote Lafayette "daily gains in the general esteem and affection and promises to be a great man here."[2] As a reward for his glorious military exploits, Lafayette was promoted to the prestigious rank of *mastre de camp*. One observer said Lafayette "planted his tree in America and sits under it at Versailles."[3]

⚔

EVEN THOUGH LAFAYETTE started his adventures less than five years ago, five years is an eternity in the life of a young family. He missed the early childhoods of both Anastasie and Georges. He barely knew them as babies, now they were walking and talking. Lafayette reflected to Washington: "My daughter and your Georges, are grown up so much that I find myself a great deal older than I apprehended."[4] Adrienne hoped her husband was home for good, if only to escape a life spent under a cloud of constant worry. "For several months she was on the point of feeling ill when he left the room," wrote their daughter years later. Adrienne knew her emotional attachment was uncommon among their social set. "She was terrified of such a strong passion," their daughter continued, "at the idea she could not always hide it from my father and that it would become embarrassing."[5] Not all passion was bad though and she was soon pregnant with the couple's next child. But as Lafayette returned to his family and marriage bed, he also rekindled his blossoming affair with Aglaé de Hunolstein. Much to his delight and Adrienne's chagrin.

In the summer of 1782, Lafayette approached his twenty-fifth birthday—the age of legal majority in France. The Lafayettes purchased a home on rue de Bourbon, just across the Seine from the Tuileries Garden. This was no time for penny-pinching, and Lafayette, ever believing he lived atop an infinite pile of money, signed notes giving his financial managers heartburn: 150,000 *livres* for the house and land, 100,000 for renovations, and 50,000 for furnishings. This bill necessitated selling productive land from Lafayette's portfolio and tipped his ledgers into permanent distress. After years of buying ships, outfitting regiments, signing IOUs, and taking out high-interest loans, the young marquis's income could no longer keep pace with his expenses. He never understood how money and finances worked. In this way, Lafayette was a microcosm of the whole rotten core of the *ancien régime*, blithely bankrupting itself without believing the bill would ever come due.

As the Lafayettes prepared their new home, Adrienne gave birth to Marie Antoinette Virginie Lafayette on September 17, 1782. Though officially named "Marie Antoinette" to flatter the royal family, there was no question the baby girl would be called Virginie. Writing to congratulate the happy couple, Benjamin Franklin said, "In naming your children, I think you do well to begin with the most ancient state . . . I hope you and Mme. de Lafayette will go through the thirteen . . . Miss Virginia, Miss Carolina, Miss Georgia will sound prettily enough for the girls, but Massachusetts and Connecticut are too harsh even for the boys."[6] Virginie would be the couple's last child, however. Their family was complete. There would be no monsieur Connecticut Lafayette.

Shortly after this joyful arrival, Lafayette received heartbreaking news. In October, he read a letter from Washington saying, "Poor Laurens is no more." Though major campaigning in America ended with Yorktown, light skirmishes continued to flare up in zones still occupied by the British. Ever eager to rush into battle, Colonel John Laurens volunteered to lead patrols in his native South Carolina. In an otherwise insignificant exchange of fire with British foragers at the Combahee River in August 1782—what Washington called "a trifling skirmish"—Laurens led a cavalry charge and was shot clean off his horse.[7] Having courted death his entire life, John Laurens was finally granted his wish to die in battle. He died at the age of twenty-seven. Lafayette would do his best to live up to his dead friend's memory—to completely fulfill the revolutionary ideals of liberty and equality or be damned by posterity as hypocritical opportunists. Even if his best was not always good enough.

IN 1782, NO one knew if the American War of Independence was truly over. Whether the paltry little skirmishes would prove a prelude to more war or lasting peace. Washington kept the Continental Army intact and alert. The British continued to occupy New York, Charleston, Savannah, and various points in between. In France, British diplomats dragged their feet and tried to break the Franco-American alliance. Lafayette had a front-row seat for the coming negotiations to potentially end the war. The comte de Ségur's father, now serving as minister of war, told Lafayette in the world of diplomacy, "you will see that there are as many absurdities in negotiations as in campaigns. You are going to be more than ever revolted by English pride, absurd Spanish vanity, French inconsistency and despotic ignorance."[8]

Though Lafayette played no formal part in the negotiations, he carried with him instructions from the American Congress ordering all their diplomatic officers in Europe "to confer with the Marquis de Lafayette and avail themselves of his information relative to the situation of public policy in the United States."[9] Lafayette was ecstatic at the official proof he was more to America than just a friend or ally—he was one of them. This appointment was not universally embraced. If French and American interests ever conflicted, many assumed Lafayette would side with his countrymen. John Adams grumbled of Lafayette's dual loyalties: "This mongrel character of French patriot and American patriot cannot last long."[10] Adams's fellow peace commissioner John Jay also worried about being assigned a French minder. The French, he replied to Adams, "are interested in separating us from Great Britain . . . but it is not in their interest that we should become a great and formidable people."[11] Whatever their personal regard for Lafayette, statecraft left only room for interests, not sentimentality. America needed to chart its own course in world affairs, and Adams and Jay feared Lafayette would steer them from humiliating dependence on Britain to humiliating dependence on France. Their cynicism was understandable but unjustified. In all his dealings with the French government on American affairs, the general complaint about young Lafayette was he tended to advocate positions far more favorable to the United States than France.

Lafayette remained highly skeptical of Britain's desire for peace. He approved keeping the Continental Army in the field, writing to Washington, "I think the evacuation of New York and Charleston is as far from their ideas for the next campaign, as the very evacuation of London."[12] He also said to the American secretary of foreign affairs, Robert Livingston, "The king is more irritated than humiliated," and it will be "necessary to convince him firmly of the impossibility of conquering us."[13]

Vergennes agreed with this assessment. As he parlayed with British negotiators, he simultaneously planned new military operations. While France could hardly afford to continue the war, they could also hardly afford *not* to continue the war. French prestige, honor, and prosperity were all tied to victory over the British. So planning commenced for a joint Franco-Spanish armada to sail to the Caribbean if Britain proved insufficiently committed to peace. The armada assembling in Cádiz, Spain, would be led by a fully recuperated comte d'Estaing. In a signal mark of faith, Lafayette was selected to command France's forces on the ground. He was only twenty-five and his dream of commanding a French army in battle was finally coming true. This appointment, however, was also not universally embraced. Informed Lafayette would be leading a potential invasion of Jamaica, the king of Spain reportedly exclaimed, "No, no . . . I don't want that. He will turn it into a republic!"[14] But Lafayette got the command. Before the year was out, he was packing his bags to return to war. Adrienne could only bid him *bon courage* while the cloud of constant worry re-formed above her head.

But the war ended before the armada was even ready to sail. The terms of the Franco-American alliance stipulated the two countries would not sign separate treaties, and both partners rebuffed overtures from the British to separate them. John Adams refused one attempt by saying, "Nothing could be done but in common with France."[15] When Vergennes was approached he insisted, "France would never treat without her allies."[16] But by the end of 1783, the British successfully exploited a difference of opinion between France and the United States about rights to the Mississippi River—the Americans wanted clear legal claim to westward expansion, while the French wanted to keep the young country confined to the eastern seaboard. When the

British offered a favorable bilateral treaty of peace to the American commissioners recognizing their right to the Mississippi, the Americans could not turn it down. Lafayette was moderately embarrassed by the conduct of his American friends, but the deed was done.

The American War of Independence was over. The United States was a free and independent nation. The other European powers signed their own separate treaties and peace returned to the Atlantic world. The armada in Spain never sailed. Lafayette's life as a soldier receded into the past. It was time to embark on a new phase of his life. He had made his mark on the world. Now he wanted to change it for the better.

⚞⚟

WHILE IN CÁDIZ in February 1783, Lafayette wrote George Washington a letter reflecting his desire to grow, change, and improve. He may have begun his adventures without a clear idea what the words *liberty* and *equality* meant, but if they were going to define his life, he needed to give them precise definition. One thought in particular took hold of his imagination, possibly driven by reflections on the recent death of John Laurens. Lafayette decided to become an abolitionist.

"Permit me to propose a plan to you," he wrote Washington on February 5, 1783, "which might be greatly beneficial to the black part of mankind. Let us unite in purchasing a small estate where we may try the experiment to free the negroes, and use them only as tenants." Lafayette knew Washington prized leadership by example and played on that virtue by emphasizing, "Such an example as yours might render it general practice. If we succeed in America, I will cheerfully devote a part of my time to render the method fashionable in the West Indies."[17]

For Lafayette, the proposal to purchase a plantation and set the slaves free was an extension of the courageous idealism that carried America into rebellion, revolution, and independence. Specifically, the ideals proclaimed in the Declaration of Independence: "That all men are created equal, that they are endowed by their Creator with certain unalienable Rights, that among these are Life, Liberty and the pursuit of Happiness."[18] Lafayette took these words seriously. He believed them. And he believed he and his revolutionary comrades needed to find new wellsprings of courageous idealism to make the words come true. "If it be a wild scheme," he said, "I had rather be mad that way, than to be thought wise on the other track."[19] For Lafayette, the American revolution remained a deed only half done. He hoped Washington would feel the same way.

As the richest and largest slave owner in America, Washington was more cautious about following the logic of the American Revolution to its obvious conclusion—as that conclusion would mean taking a sledge-hammer to the foundations of his own wealth and status. Washington did not completely dissuade Lafayette, but he also did not embrace the idea. On April 5, 1783, he replied to Lafayette: "The scheme, my dear Marquis, which you propose as a precedent, to encourage the emancipation of the black people of this country from that state of bondage in which they are held, is striking evidence of the benevolence of your heart. I shall be happy to join you in so laudable a work; but will defer going into detail of the business, until I have the pleasure of seeing you."[20] Lafayette took the general at his word. When they next met, the young marquis would eagerly pitch his wild scheme to fully deliver on the promise of the American Revolution: life, liberty, and the pursuit of happiness. For *all* mankind.

※

WITH THE ARMADA breaking up and peace at hand, Lafayette left Spain in March 1783. On his way back to Paris, he took the opportunity to return home to Auvergne for the first time in over a decade. When he arrived at Château de Chavaniac a few weeks later, he was greeted by his widowed and lonely Aunt Charlotte. She was the only one of the happy household of women who raised him still alive. His old grandmother and Aunt Madeleine were dead. His beloved surrogate sister Marie died in childbirth in 1778. Lafayette wrote to Adrienne his aunt was overwhelmed by his safe return, but "she gradually recovered . . . despite the abundance of her tears."[21]

When he arrived in March 1784, Lafayette discovered Auvergne suffering from a poor harvest the previous fall and unusually freezing temperatures over the winter. The residents of Chavaniac, whom Lafayette knew as former playmates, neighbors, and friends, were all hungry and freezing. After meetings with local officials, businessmen, and estate agents, Lafayette developed a good picture of the situation. With food supplies already tight, a government-licensed corporation controlling distribution of grain held back supply to drive the prices up even higher. Lafayette was incensed. "He seemed to me deeply touched by the general alarm," one local official recollected.[22]

Lafayette's agents told him now was a good time to sell his grain and make a tidy profit. But in an apocryphal anecdote commonly recounted in Auvergne, Lafayette retorted, "No! Now is the time to give it away!"[23] Though almost certainly a fanciful invention, the quote captures the essential truth of Lafayette's actions. The marquis ordered three hundred bushels of grain be distributed to the local community free of charge, then used the rest of his reserves to protect against future deprivations. He wrote Adrienne, "I would like the government to allow me to construct public granaries, to which I would add some of my grain, which would provide a bank of grain for seed."[24] His financial managers groaned at the missed opportunity, but Lafayette could not possibly care less. He would not exploit starvation. An official reported back to Versailles the people of Auvergne "avoided the horrors of famine only by the extraordinary aid provided to them by M. de La Fayette."[25]

Lafayette departed Chavaniac with his reputation as a popular hero sprouting new shoots from the seeds he distributed free of charge to his people. Adrienne went further and took it upon herself to organize a school and workshop for weaving so the local people might profit better from manufacturing their own thread and fabric rather than simply selling the wool from their flocks wholesale. At the simple tables of rustic Auvergne, the people raised glasses to the Lafayettes.

But Lafayette's brief sojourn in Chavaniac was also about closing the door on his relationship with Aglaé de Hunolstein, the object of youthful infatuation, then his mistress after his rise to fame. While noblemen were expected to carry on a string of love affairs, the same was not true for noblewomen. The double standard put women like Hunolstein in the crosshairs of a hypocritical society. Having been linked to several high-profile men—Lafayette only the most recent—Hunolstein's in-laws poisoned the wells of high society against her. Hoping to salvage her reputation, Hunolstein told Lafayette it was over and asked him to acknowledge the breakup before he returned to Paris. Lafayette's side trip to Auvergne gave him an opportunity to process the end of the relationship. He finally wrote Hunolstein a long letter: "You are too cruel my dear Aglaé. You know the torments of my heart." But he acknowledged in affairs like this, "it is you who risk everything while I get nearly all the pleasure." Despite his feelings, though, "you have placed your peace of mind and your safety in my hands," so he would not cause her further trouble. He acknowledged it was over.[26]

But it was too late for Hunolstein. Even as Lafayette broke it off, she found herself blacklisted by high society thanks to her furious in-laws. Shortly thereafter, Aglaé de Hunolstein withdrew from public life and entered a convent. Her husband, who himself never begrudged her conduct, provided a generous annual pension. She lived in the convent for the rest of her life, giving nearly all her money away to alleviate the suffering of the sick, disabled, and impoverished. So though she was disgraced by the high and mighty, she was revered by the poor and needy.

⊰⊱

LAFAYETTE RETURNED TO Paris and the family officially moved into their new home in May 1783. They settled into life as a happy and prosperous couple with three children and a stream of visitors. On Monday nights, the Lafayettes hosted a regular dinner frequently featuring American notables and visitors. After Abigail Adams arrived in Paris to join her husband, she found she did not much care for Paris, but enjoyed the Lafayettes very much—particularly Adrienne: "I should always take pleasure in her company. She is a good and amiable Lady, exceedingly fond of her children and attentive to their education." She could also not help but marvel at something not usually seen in Paris: Abigail exclaimed in a letter home Adrienne was "passionately attached to her Husband!!! A French Lady and fond of her Husband!!!"[27] Mrs. Adams could hardly believe her eyes.

Though he loved Adrienne and made a happy family, Lafayette maintained an active social life, including a new mistress: Diane Adélaïde, comtesse de Simiane. A lady-in-waiting to the comtesse de Provence, Diane de Simiane was described as a "beautiful and pretty woman, who showed the noblest and most tender sentiments."[28] Thoughtful, compassionate, and intelligent, it was said "the beauty of Mme. de Simiane did not harm her kindness: both produced a magical effect in her."[29] A salon hostess who often saw Lafayette and Simiane together said, "She passed for the prettiest woman in France, but had never had an affair. Everyone threw her into the arms of M. de Lafayette."[30] For Lafayette, Simiane became more than just a mistress. She was a friend and confidante, and he wrote to her frequently not just on personal but political affairs. Lafayette's relationship with Simiane would last for decades to come, even after they drifted apart sexually and politically.

In his role as quasi-official American attaché, Lafayette also hosted American merchants trying to enter French markets. They complained French customs authorities demanded an array of taxes, duties, and fees rendering their cargo terminally uncompetitive. Lafayette took up their cause. "I cannot too often repeat that after a great war and the beautiful peace, it would be ridiculous to lose the fruits of so much blood and treasure," he fumed to Vergennes, "and to lose this fruit only to one class of people who please no one."[31] To make a public appeal on behalf of the Americans, Lafayette drafted a pamphlet called *Observations on Commerce Between France and the United States*, which advocated tearing down trade barriers between the two countries. Lafayette would never be mistaken for a philosophical giant, and there was nothing groundbreaking in the pamphlet, but his first entry into the wider intellectual discourse was well received and showed Lafayette a progressive adherent of modern political economy.

One of the few novelties in the pamphlet was a rarely voiced concern about the misery of the enslaved Africans in French colonies. Lafayette argued that the French should eliminate tariffs on American foodstuffs arriving in French Caribbean ports. The French colonial authorities should listen to "the double voice of self-interest and humanity," and that, "as long as feeding the slaves depends on laws prohibiting the importation of foreign food produced into the colonies, the slaves will be few and poorly nourished, they will work little and die sooner."[32] This was an argument designed to appeal to the leaders of a slave economy, but Lafayette did not ultimately want well-fed and productive *slaves*. He wanted well-fed and more productive *free people*. He continued to think how he could advance this larger project.

Lafayette's deep involvement with the new United States always meant, in his mind, he would return often to his adopted country for regular visits. Having been away for more than two years, it was time to go back. Lafayette looked forward to seeing what the country was like free of the scourge of war. Adrienne, meanwhile, braced for another long separation. But at least this time her husband did not pack weapons and a uniform.

⁂

SAILING FROM BREST in June 1784, Lafayette traveled aboard the *Courrier de New York*, the first vessel regularly carrying commercial passengers between France and America. When he arrived in New York City on August 4, 1784, it was the first time Lafayette actually set foot in the city. Despite so many years assuming the final battle for America would be fought in New York, Lafayette never made it to the island of Manhattan.

After several days in New York, feted by the people and reminiscing with old comrades like Alexander Hamilton, Lafayette spent the next week slowly moving south. Every city he passed threw him a party or parade in his honor. He spent a week in Philadelphia reuniting with other veterans of the war and making new acquaintances among the intellectual, economic, and political elite of the new nation. But though perpetual celebrations slowed his progress, Lafayette kept moving steadily toward his intended destination: Mount Vernon.

Lafayette arrived at the plantation on August 18 to the warm and happy embrace of General Washington. They had not seen each other since Yorktown nearly three years earlier. In the meantime, Washington fulfilled his ambition to be the American Cincinnatus—returning to his plow after saving his people. When it became clear the British planned to abide by the peace, Washington resigned as commander in chief of the Continental Army. He handed over his sword to Congress in a formal ceremony on December 23, 1783, to the wonder and astonishment of friend and foe alike.

But Washington returning to Mount Vernon was hardly Cincinnatus returning to his plow. George Washington was no simple, salt of the earth farmer. Mount Vernon was the center of a network of commercial estates focused on productivity and profit—profit generated by the labor of the nearly three hundred slaves George and Martha Washington owned. For the next week, Lafayette followed Washington on his rounds and observed the general managing hundreds of details as he attempted to rebuild years of unintended decay and neglect. In between rounds, they talked about old times and future plans, hosted a stream of visitors, and enjoyed a life free of the emergencies of war.

We know from later references that at some point during the visit Lafayette broached the subject Washington invited him to broach: the experiment in emancipation. Though there is no direct account of the conversation, Washington probably said in person what he later echoed in letters: the political, economic, and social situation in the United States was too precarious for him to join such a venture at the present time. Emancipation and abolition were nice dreams, but the time was not right. Lafayette let the matter drop, though it would not stop him from pursuing the scheme.

⚜

AFTER A WEEK with Washington, it was time to move on again. They made arrangements for a second visit before Lafayette quit the continent for good, so though it was goodbye—it was not *goodbye*. Lafayette returned north, passing through Philadelphia on his way back to New York City. When he arrived, he learned the city leaders decided to confer upon him the civic status "Freeman and Citizen of the city of New York."[33] This was the first of many such awards of citizenship Lafayette would be granted by various states and municipalities in the United States over the years. The deepest and most all-encompassing was awarded by the Maryland Assembly a few months later. On December 28, 1784, they proclaimed Lafayette "and his male heirs shall forever be, and each of them hereby deemed, and judged, and taken to be, natural born citizens of the state and shall henceforth be entitled to all communities, rights, privileges of a natural born citizen thereof."[34] When the Constitution was ratified in 1788, natural-born citizens of each state were automatically granted reciprocal citizenship status in all the other states, beginning a decades-long process of forming a legal concept of national citizenship culminating with the Fourteenth

Amendment in 1868. Lafayette, having been deemed, judged, and taken to be a natural-born citizen of the state of Maryland as of December 1784, must therefore be deemed, judged, and taken to be a citizen of United States.

Ever eager to serve his adopted country, Lafayette accepted a request to undertake another diplomatic mission to the Iroquois. Those Iroquois who did not emigrate to Canada after the defeat of their British allies needed to come to terms with the new United States. Aware of his previous success among the Iroquois, Congress asked Lafayette to go along with their emissaries to help clear the path to permanent peaceful relations.

Two new companions joined him for this trip. The first was François Barbé-Marbois, a French *chargé d'affaires* who left a detailed account of journeys in America and whose solicitation for detailed information on the thirteen states served as the intellectual prompt for a monumental reply from Thomas Jefferson that became *Notes on the State of Virginia*. The other was Jefferson's friend and protégé James Madison. The thirty-three-year-old Madison was a civilian leader during the war, elected to both the Virginia House of Delegates and the Second Continental Congress. Madison and Lafayette spent no time together during the war, but they hit it off in Philadelphia and Madison joined the excursion north at the last minute.

Madison was fluent in French, and the three men enjoyed long discussions on the road from Philadelphia to Albany. Madison reported to Jefferson Lafayette had "three hobby-horses." The first was "the alliance between France and the United States," as evidenced by Lafayette's ongoing advocacy for American merchants as well as the recently published *Observations*. The second was "the union of the latter," which is to say, the unification of the United States. From his experiences in the Continental Army, Lafayette could attest firsthand the drawbacks of a national government with no power to compel states to act. Lafayette agreed with Madison's belief that the Articles of Confederation—the first constitution under which the United States lived—needed to be reformed to create a better, stronger, and more perfect union.

According to Madison, Lafayette's third hobbyhorse was "the manumission of the slaves." Lafayette exhibited no qualms about telling his major slave-owning friends like Washington, Jefferson, and now Madison they needed to take the ultimate step to fulfill the promise of the American Revolution. All agreed this third hobbyhorse was a sign of Lafayette's idealistic good nature, Madison himself commenting Lafayette's budding abolitionism "does him real honor as it is proof of his humanity."[35] But Lafayette's Virginian friends stubbornly concluded— as they always would—that while it was a nice thought, now was simply not the right time. As if there would *ever* be a right time.

Reaching upstate New York in late September 1784, the party tramped through roads in dismal, wet, freezing weather. Barbé-Marbois reported while they traveled that Lafayette "seemed immune to the extremes of the season."[36] Lafayette was not, at heart, a pampered court dandy and was well used to enduring miserable conditions. While his companions shrank and shuddered, Lafayette remained tall in his saddle. But Barbé-Marbois also reported this was because "he had taken, to protect him from the rain, a cloak of gummed taffeta, which had been sent him from France wrapped up in newspapers. The papers had stuck to the gum . . . so the curious could read, on his chest and back, the *Journal of Paris* or *Courier de l'Europe*."[37] He might look slightly ridiculous, but at least he was warm and dry.

The company survived the journey and the conference began on October 3. Lafayette wrote home, "Here I am in the country of the savages, surrounded by Hurons and Iroquois."[38] He managed to make an off-color joke that has not aged well but was meant to be a self-deprecating crack about his prematurely balding head: "I couldn't lose my scalp, because one doesn't lose, says the proverb, what one doesn't have."[39] When the conference began, Madison reported, "Lafayette was the only conspicuous figure."[40] Barbé-Marbois concurred: "M. De La Fayette has their confidence and devotion to an extraordinary degree. Those who had seen him before had a great urge to see him again."[41] Lafayette used his influence to urge peace and good terms with the United States. "If you remember the voice of Kayewla," he said, "I say to you now, the American cause is just, it is your cause."[42] Lafayette was proud to share this good news with the assembled tribes and sincerely believed it for the rest of his life. But the future history of relations between the Iroquois and United

States proved Lafayette wrong. The American cause was *not* their cause. Nor, with regard to their lands, interests, or families, was it particularly just.

Lafayette's paternalistic benevolence toward the Iroquois then took on a more direct form. A half-French, half-Iroquois teenager named Peter Otsiquette was present at the conference and, at Lafayette's interested urging, arrangements were made to send Peter to live with Lafayette in Paris. This was not an unheard of arrangement. In France, Otsiquette would receive a European education in the hopes he would return well equipped to act as a point of contact, negotiation, and translation between their two worlds. As Otsiquette's family took time to deliberate, Lafayette also took in hand an orphaned adolescent—a younger boy named Kayenlaha. He too would live with Lafayette in Paris and learn the language and customs of the Europeans to better serve his people when he grew up.[43]

After the conference wrapped up on October 6, Lafayette traveled back to Albany and then over to New England, where Lafayette picked up an honorary doctorate from Harvard. After the party went their separate ways, Madison wrote Jefferson his final assessment of Lafayette: "I take him to be as amiable a man as his vanity will admit and as sincere an American as any Frenchman can be."[44] Lafayette and Madison would remain friends and correspondents for the rest of their lives.

⌖

IN THE FIRST week of November 1784, Lafayette sailed from Boston back to Virginia. After proudly surveying the old battleground of Yorktown, still pockmarked with craters and trenches, he was invited to address the Virginia Assembly in Richmond. When he arrived, the assembly was in the midst of a heated debate. Two years earlier, the state authorized manumission, reasoning if the right of property meant anything, it meant the right to do with one's own property as one saw fit. But the law triggered a backlash. More than a few Virginians believed if slaves could be freed anywhere, it would threaten the institution everywhere. Petitions circulated demanding this thin end of the emancipation wedge be stricken from the books. When Lafayette addressed the Virginia Assembly on November 19, 1784, it was noteworthy he included a line hoping Virginia and America would "continue to give the world unquestionable proofs of her philanthropy and her regard to the liberties of *all mankind*."[45] The line was subtle and indirect, but in the context of the ongoing debate about manumission, his meaning was clear.

Before leaving Richmond, Lafayette reunited with another comrade of the War of Independence: James Armistead. Armistead was an enslaved African man in Cornwallis's entourage during the Virginia campaign, and doubled as one of Lafayette's best and most reliable spies. Armistead now petitioned for freedom as a reward for his service. Lafayette gladly drafted a personal testimonial confirming Armistead's invaluable wartime service. He said Armistead "perfectly acquitted himself with some important commissions I gave him and appears to me entitled to every reward the situation can admit of."[46] If Lafayette had been in charge, Armistead would have been freed on the spot. Instead, it took two more years of wrangling, petitions, and arbitration before Armistead finally won his freedom. The amount of kicking and screaming it took to liberate a single heroic veteran of the War of Independence did not bode well for Lafayette's hopes of emancipation catching on anytime soon. Armistead himself never forgot Lafayette's support, and when legally freed, he adopted the name James Armistead Lafayette.

Back again in Mount Vernon, Lafayette's final week with Washington was spent in nostalgic repose. But these idyllic days could not last forever. On November 28, Lafayette had to leave. To prolong their visit, Washington mounted a horse to escort the marquis in the direction of Philadelphia. But on December 1, 1784, they finally parted ways. They did not know when they were going to see each other again. They did not know *if* they were going to see each other again. Washington descended from a long line of short-lived men, and days after their tearful departure, he wrote Lafayette, "I often ask myself as our carriages distended whether that was the last sight I ever should have of you. And though I wish to say no, my fears answered yes."[47] Lafayette received this letter before he returned to France and quickly replied: "No, my beloved general, our late parting was not by any means a last interview—my whole soul revolts at the idea—and could I harbor it an instant, indeed, my dear General, it would make me miserable."[48] Lafayette was young and healthy and envisioned regular voyages to America. Surely this was not the end.

Washington was right and Lafayette was wrong. They never saw each other again. The friendship and bond formed at Valley Forge in the winter of 1777 would live on in transatlantic letters until Washington's death in 1799. But they already embraced for the last time. When Lafayette sailed from New York City on December 21, 1784, he expected to return to his adopted country shortly. Instead, he would not set foot in America for forty long years. When he finally returned, all that remained of his mentor, friend, and surrogate father was a tomb.

⸙

WHEN LAFAYETTE BOARDED the ship back to France, he was accompanied by two young wards: the young Iroquois Kayenlaha, and John Edwards Caldwell, the orphan son of a Protestant chaplain killed during the war. Lafayette pledged to look out for both boys and see to their educations. He started at once, spending the long weeks at sea tutoring the boys in French, English, literature, and history.

Returning home to Paris, Lafayette added the two boys to the household. Kayenlaha remained at *chez Lafayette* serving as a page, errand boy, and household servant. In between chores, Lafayette ensured the boy was safe, protected, and tutored in literature, history, math, and languages. Though Lafayette did not act from cruel motives, he treated Kayenlaha like a curiosity—a souvenir from America. The marquis was known to liven up *soirées* by inviting Kayenlaha to dance in Native costume for the delight of friends and guests. One young attendee later remembered Lafayette "has a savage dressed in his native costume . . . with a ring in his nose, a feathered headdress on his head . . . the entire costume consisted of a belt and feathers over flesh colored tunic."[49] As a mark of paternalistic benevolence it was also reported "the savage always calls him father."[50]

As for young John Edwards Caldwell, Lafayette used the boy's placement in a Paris boarding school as an opportunity to open another front in his crusade for social justice. Naturally the school was Catholic, but Lafayette insisted the American boy be allowed to follow his own Protestant practices. Lafayette was a nonbelieving, nonpracticing Catholic who made lots of Protestant friends in America and found the treatment of their brethren in France unacceptable. Protestants had not enjoyed legal rights in France since Louis XIV revoked the Edict of Nantes in 1685, driving a Huguenot diaspora toward the Americas, including the ancestors of both John Laurens and Alexander Hamilton. "Protestants live under intolerable despotism," Lafayette wrote. "Their children are bastards, their parsons hanged." As he built his new peace-time identity as a social reformer, wherever Lafayette perceived an injustice, he wanted to help. He would never sit back and wait for the vague and abstract force of "progress" to take care of things. "I have put it in my head to be a leader in the affair," he said, and made overtures to prominent members of the French Protestant community to ask what he could do to help them.[51]

Adrienne was herself a devout Catholic but supported her husband's call for religious tolerance. "My mother shared his beliefs," Virginie later wrote, "and received with keen interest the Protestant ministers who were attracted to our home." She also said, "My mother's tolerance was based on the first principles of religion. She considered it a great crime to interfere with the freedom that God granted to men."[52] En-lightened critics of the Catholic Church's persecutorial lust for power may have found Adrienne's take on her faith naive, but it was honest and sincere. Her Catholicism never conflicted with her belief in everyone's right to worship as they saw fit.

Nineteen-year-old Peter Otsiquette probably joined the family later in the year. Very little is known about his time in Paris, but it was not a quick visit. Otsiquette remained with the Lafayettes until at least 1788, and, like the young Kayenlaha, seems to have received a full education and been utilized by the family as a favored servant. Lafayette outfitted Peter in sartorial mix of European fashion and "In-dian dresses" depending on the occasion. Upon returning to America, Otsiquette was described as "highly cultivated and master of the French language and politeness," and took his place as a point of diplomatic contact between Iroquois and European civilizations.[53] In March 1792, Otsiquette joined a delegation to President George Washington and it is hard to believe their mutual connection to Lafayette did not come up. But Otsiquette's fate was ultimately unhappy. He died on that same trip to Philadelphia—some sources reporting natural causes, others that he fell victim to alcoholism. A Dutch immigrant living in upstate New York who knew Otsiquette commented after his death, "It may be justly questioned, if the vicinity of their white neighbors is to them not rather a curse than a blessing."[54]

⊰⊱

THE LAFAYETTES' MOST ambitious and audacious reform project was, by far, their abolitionism. Though Washington declined to participate, Lafayette was determined to prove emancipation was safe, beneficial, and lucrative. As with Lafayette's efforts on behalf of Protestants, Adrienne happily supported the venture. Virginie remembered, "The ardent desire to contribute to good, the horror of all injustices, was very keen in my mother's heart. She felt a real pleasure when my father worked for the abolition of the slave trade."[55]

It was thanks to his interest in emancipation Lafayette first met the marquis de Condorcet. Condorcet was, as much as any single person, the embodiment of the Enlightenment's greatest hopes and ambitions—armed with reason, science, and rationality, there was nothing humans could not improve. In 1781, under a pseudonym Condorcet wrote an antislavery pamphlet called *Reflections on the Slavery of Negroes*. Lafayette read the pamphlet in 1783 and mentioned to his friend Louis Alexandre de La Rochefoucauld—another noble social reformer—how much he admired it. Rochefoucauld introduced Lafayette to Condorcet, which led to further meetings, dinners, and discussions. Lafayette, Condorcet, and Rochefoucauld were all part of a growing collaborative milieu of idealistic reformers looking to change the world for the better. When Condorcet wrote *The Influence of the American Revolution on Europe*, he dedicated it to Lafayette.

To deepen his understanding of abolitionism, Lafayette wrote John Adams—then serving as ambassador to the Court of St. James—asking Adams to send "everything that has been written in England about the means to discourage [slavery]."[56] Lafayette planned to make himself a leading expert on the subject. But as his reform-mindedness was vast, rather than narrowly focused on a single issue, Lafayette also asked

Adams in this same letter for everything written on the subject of prison reform. He and Adrienne also agreed state prisons, jails, and various other kinds of punitive confinement were cruel and unjust.

Finally, in February 1786, Lafayette wrote Washington to tell him the big news: "I have purchased for 125,000 French livre a plantation in the colony of Cayenne and I'm going to free my negroes in order to make the experiment which you know is my hobbyhorse."[57] He wrote Henry Knox, "I confidentially entrust to you . . . that I am purchasing a fine plantation in a French colony, to make for the enfranchising our Negro brethren, god grant that it maybe propagated!"[58]

Lafayette's plan was a program of gradual emancipation. Having purchased an estate, the Lafayettes would take over management, pay the slaves wages, forbid them being sold, eliminate corporal punishment, and educate the children. Condorcet pointed Lafayette to a young natural scientist, Henri de Richeprey, eager to participate in the idealistic venture. Richeprey sailed to Cayenne to act as Lafayette's on-site estate manager. After finding aspects of the first plantation unsatisfactory, Richeprey recommended additional purchases to make the plan feasible. Later that year, Lafayette persuaded the French government to award him funds to make another purchase, making them profit-sharing partners in the scheme. Because who knew . . . it might even work. In Paris, Adrienne gradually took over management of the estates, which came to be referred to collectively as La Belle Gabrielle, after the largest plantation in their colonial portfolio. A ledger compiled in March 1789 showed the Lafayettes eventually owning seventy slaves—the youngest a newborn, the eldest a blind old man.[59]

Washington replied to Lafayette's big announcement, saying the experiment in Cayenne "is a generous and noble proof of your humanity." But he also lamented, "I wish to God a like spirit would diffuse itself generally in the minds of the people of this country, but I despair seeing it." He also worried "sudden emancipation would bring many evils."[60] Though he wished Lafayette well, Washington would not participate, nor push for emancipation in America anytime soon. One wonders how much Washington might have helped that like spirit diffuse generally in the minds of the people, if he himself, a massively influential Virginia plantation owner beloved from New Hampshire to Georgia, actively pushed for it rather than passively despairing of seeing it. Lafayette revered George Washington for the rest of his life; considered him a great man who could do no wrong, who always chose the true and virtuous path. But here it is Washington who should be idolizing Lafayette—for having the guts to actually believe all human beings enjoyed the unalienable right to life, liberty, and the pursuit of happiness.

Meanwhile, a literal crate of books soon arrived from London. This was the response to Lafayette's request for everything ever written on the suppression of Negro slavery. John Adams asked abolitionist Granville Sharp to take up the task, and Sharp jumped at the opportunity to cultivate Lafayette's interest. Lafayette wrote to Adams:

> Thank you for the valuable books you took the trouble to find for me. In the cause of my black brethren I feel myself warmly interested, and most decidedly side, so far as respects them, against the white part of mankind. Whatever be the complexion of the enslaved, it does not, in my opinion, alter the complexion of the crime which the enslaver commits, a crime much blacker than any African face, it is to me a matter of great anxiety and concern, to find this trend is sometimes perpetrated under the flag of liberty—our dear and noble stripes.[61]

This was quite a profound statement of how far his thinking advanced in just a few short years. It was also quite an understatement of the amount of slavery perpetrated under his dear and noble stripes.

In the five years since the end of the American War of Independence, Lafayette fully transitioned from adventurous soldier to liberal benefactor of humanity. Starving peasants, oppressed Protestants, enslaved Africans all deserved his time, attention, and resources. Lafayette believed all the evils of the world could be ameliorated, overcome, and eventually abolished by strength of will, vision, and an unerring sense of justice. He was not alone in this belief. Lafayette's own efforts combined with other currents of social reform in France to form a rushing river of progress swollen by centuries of distress, mismanagement, cruelty, superstition, resentment, anger, fear, and contradiction. In the summer of 1786, the dam holding them back finally burst and flooded the kingdom. We call this flood the French Revolution.

PART II

La Revolution

CHAPTER TEN

THE NOT ABLES

[1786–1787]

I N December 1786, the marquis de Lafayette made arrangements for a trip to Russia. His old friend, the comte de Ségur, entered the diplomatic corps after the American war and now served as ambassador to Empress Catherine the Great. The quintessential enlightened despot, Catherine enjoyed playing host to European luminaries and was curious to meet the famous marquis de Lafayette. Ségur arranged for Lafayette to join Catherine's imperial entourage on a tour of Crimea. But on December 27, 1786, Lafayette received a royal summons preempting the trip. The finances of the Kingdom of France had collapsed into a state of exhausted disarray. The king was summoning a group of prominent leaders to help sort it out, and Lafayette's name was on the list. Lafayette begged apologies to the empress of Russia and prepared instead to attend to his own king at Versailles. His country stood in need of his talents.

The financial crisis was hardly an unforeseen event. Anyone with even a passing familiarity with the Crown's accounts knew the problem: too much spending, not enough revenue. The royal family treated money as an infinite resource supplied to the Bourbons by God. But the money was not infinite; it came from taxes. And with a tax system exempting the richest families in France from contributing in proportion to their wealth, the Crown balanced its books on the backs of the king's poorest subjects. It was an absurd and unsustainable contradiction that could not last forever.

The king's ministers were not blind to the problem. They attempted financial restructuring multiple times after Louis XVI ascended the throne, but found themselves perpetually stymied, delayed, or ignored. The modernizing reformer Turgot was invited to completely overhaul the kingdom's economy in 1774, and for his trouble was driven out of office in 1776. Turgot's successor, Jacques Necker, believed if the French adopted a British-style national debt, they could finance their way to power and prosperity. But Necker fell afoul of enemies at court who did not want a Swiss-born Protestant commoner in charge of the king's finances. He was dismissed from service in 1781. Necker's lasting legacy was a mountain of debt and the *Compte rendu*, which misleadingly demonstrated there was nothing to worry about.

Necker was succeeded by the refined courtier Charles Alexandre de Calonne. Calonne took over the Ministry of Finance, scrutinized the books, and realized the *Compte rendu* was a massive bluff. In truth, the Crown faced ballooning obligations to service high-interest loans—many of which were taken out to finance France's participation in the American War of Independence. By the mid-1780s, fully 50 percent of the king's annual expenses were interest payments. Calonne concluded the only feasible approach was to pay off the high-interest loans by taking out new lower-interest loans. If managed with careful diligence, the balloon could be deflated. But to secure those new loans, Calonne needed the confidence of the financial community, so he introduced the novel policy of "useful splendor." He approved lavish royal expenditures to give the outward appearance of a healthy monarchy. Surely the Bourbons could not be in financial trouble if they spent money so wantonly and frivolously. Calonne himself enjoyed a taste for the finer things in life, decked himself in silken finery, and entertained guests in glorious luxury.

Useful splendor was a risky gambit that did not pay off. Literally. What finally brought everything crashing was the looming expiration of the *vingtième*—a universal 5 percent tax on income, originally imposed as a temporary expedient to pay for the Seven Years' War. Though never designed to be permanent, the vingtième was renewed several times over the past two decades and became a vital source of royal revenue. But now, the vingtième was set to expire once and for all at the end of 1786. Without this badly needed revenue, the Crown could not pay its debts. On August 8, 1786, Calonne revealed to the king that His Majesty was on the verge of bankruptcy. It would not be unreasonable to date the beginning of the French Revolution from this conversation.

※

IF THE PROBLEM was looming bankruptcy, what was the solution? There were several available options, none of them appealing. The king could attempt to impose new taxes by arbitrary fiat—after all, France *was* an absolute monarchy. But for all the theoretical pretensions of royal absolutism, the Kingdom of France was, in fact, a patchwork of estates, fiefdoms, duchies, free cities, provinces, and parishes. All of them connected through myriad feudal arrangements, each stipulating their own array of reciprocal rights, privileges, and jurisdictional limitations. Over the past two hundred years, the Bourbons eroded those feudal arrangements and replaced them with centralized royal authority, but they were not likely to withstand the inevitable pushback if King Louis attempted to tax his subjects by unilateral royal decree.

The most formidable resistance would likely be found in the thirteen *parlements* of France. The French parlements were not "Parliaments" in the English sense of the word, but rather high courts of justice located in major provincial capitals. The parlements had existed since time immemorial and their councilors expressed, defended, and defined the laws of the kingdom. Of late, they became the operational home base of the rising robe nobility. The robe nobles of the parlements formed a powerful counterweight to the Crown and articulated their own theories of government in opposition to royal absolutism. These theories were best expressed by Montesquieu, a councilor of the parlement in Bordeaux. In 1748, Montesquieu published his great work of political philosophy, *The Spirit of Law*, a massively influential defense of separating political power to limit the arbitrary authority of despotic executives.

The largest and most important parlement sat in Paris and wielded a unique political weapon. Technically, any new law must be registered with the Paris parlement before it took effect. Prior to registration, the councilors had the right to demand changes or clarifications from the king. They were, in fact, the *only* independent entity in the kingdom with the right to openly challenge the Crown's authority. Thanks to their special place in the political system, many viewed the parlements as the one thing preventing the kingdom from collapsing into abject tyranny.

Calonne desperately wanted to avoid direct entanglement with the parlements, as they would surely exploit the king's financial distress to their own advantage. But the other obvious solution was even worse: calling the Estates-General. The Estates-General was an assembly of the whole kingdom, organized into the three estates of clergy, nobles, and commons. The Estates-General had once been a semiregular feature of governance during the Middle Ages, but as the Bourbons embraced the theory of royal absolutism, they studiously ignored the Estates-General. In fact, they had not called them to convene since 1614. If Calonne dreaded tangling with the parlements, he was positively allergic to calling the Estates-General. Who knows what uncontrollable spirits lurked in *that* Pandora's Box.

Calonne's solution, after months of deliberation, was to resurrect another archaic institution of the past: the Assembly of Notables. This would be a convocation of a select group of high-ranking nobles, clergymen, and councilors. Calonne would present this assembly with the details of the financial crisis and ask for help conceiving a solution. The beauty of the plan was the king would handpick which Notables to invite. They were not an independent body with its own agenda like the parlements, nor a potentially uncontrollable assembly like the Estates-General. And when they approved new taxes, the king would not proclaim them alone, but in concert with an array of powerful and influential voices. It was the perfect solution. Calonne set to work drawing up a list of men he believed would approve his reform package without much fuss—among them the young, and hopefully pliable, marquis de Lafayette.

AFTER LAFAYETTE RECEIVED the king's invitation to participate in the Assembly of Notables, he wrote Washington, bringing the general up to speed. "There will be one hundred and forty-four members, archbishops, bishops, nobles, presidents of various parlements, mayors of towns," he wrote. "Your only acquaintances in this assembly are: the Count d'Estaing, the Duke of Laval and your servant, named among the thirty-six members of the nobility." He also described the seemingly innocuous and mundane purpose of the assembly: "the King's letter announces an examination of the finances to be adjusted, of the means to alleviate the taxes of the people, and of many abuses to be redressed. You easily conceive that there is at bottom a desire to make money somehow or other, in order to put the receipt on a level with the expenses, which in this country is become enormous on account of the sums squandered on courtiers and superfluities."[1] Though he did not know it, Lafayette, in this handful of banal words, perfectly described the trigger of the French Revolution.

Lafayette also revealed he almost did not make the final cut to participate. "I had been on the first list," he told Washington, "on the last one I was not; but before I could enquire which was the motive of exclusion, the matter had been set to rights."[2] The most obvious explanation is Lafayette was still a young man in his late-twenties. Most of the other names on the list belonged to gray-haired eminences well past middle age. There would have been nothing remarkable about dropping the youngest person on the list to make room for an older and wiser head. But Thomas Jefferson, now serving as ambassador to France, believed there was more to it—that the marquis's potentially dangerous radicalism nearly cost him his place: "His education in our school has drawn on him a very jealous eye from a court whose principles are the most absolute despotism."[3] Jefferson believed the court feared Lafayette would be a progressive loose cannon.

On the other hand, plenty of people inside France believed Lafayette's name was restored for the opposite reason—Lafayette's principal defect was not defiance but malleability. He was seen as an inner-circle member of the court: he was a Noailles; an old classmate of the comte d'Artois; a personal friend of the queen; an intimate of the king. They all dined, hunted, and played cards together. The gossipy and anonymously authored *Mémoires secrets* expressed this attitude in a rundown of the Notables as the first session of the assembly approached. They dismissed young Lafayette: "Coached by the Noailles, he will be counseled to be on the side of the court and not compromise." They asserted Lafayette won back his place on the list after promising the royal family "zeal and submission." In all, they rendered a final verdict on Lafayette: "Having a mild and timid character, uneducated, not much is to be expected."[4]

This portrait bears no resemblance to Lafayette whatsoever. It was an early instance of the kind of insinuation, rumor, and hearsay that would be a defining hallmark of the French Revolution. Knowing only a few publicly available facts—Lafayette was rich, a friend of the king and queen, and a Noailles—one could be forgiven for believing what the *Mémoires secrets* said about him. Their conclusion was, nonetheless, entirely off the mark. During the next several years, Lafayette's character, intentions, and plans would be the source of endless speculation—often leading to such gross mischaracterizations. Here in 1787, it was simply a matter of portraying Lafayette as a weak-willed puppet. In the future, he would be the subject of far more sinister portrayals. Almost none of the outwardly plausible caricatures were true. But truth is rarely a defense in the court of public opinion.

Lafayette himself was not entirely sure what role he would play among the Notables. He knew the kingdom's finances needed to be reformed, and knew privileged interests stood in the way. But he was also aware the royal family *had* behaved badly. He told Washington the greatest problem was almost certainly spendthrift aristocrats wasting money on pointless luxuries. In early February, Lafayette sketched a rough outline of his hopes to Washington, which show him focused on economic modernization and the decentralization of political power: "I flatter myself we may get a kind of House of Representatives in each province, not to fix, it is true, but to divide the taxes, and an abolition of several duties on the commercial intercourse within the Kingdom." He would also keep an eye out for opportunities to sneak in social reforms of interest to his American friends. But he was not optimistic: "It is not probable that the Protestant affair will be submitted to the Notables; it could fail there by the demands of the clergy and of a bigoted party. We will get to our goal somehow, I hope, before long."[5]

⫘

THE ASSEMBLY OF Notables might have been the end of it all. An obscure and terribly boring footnote in the economic history of France—of interest to a few specialists in eighteenth-century tax law, but hardly the beginning of an epochal transformation of the entire world. Were it not for a virus that swept through Paris and Versailles over the winter of 1786–1787, it might have gone according to plan. But instead the king's two most important ministers, Vergennes and Calonne, were both driven to their beds by debilitating illnesses.

For most of the past decade, the comte de Vergennes was the king's most trusted adviser. Neither an overeager radical nor a stubbornly blind conservative, Vergennes provided Louis a steady hand, realistic vision, and intimate understanding of the levers of power. The often indecisive king relied heavily on Vergennes's voice, counsel, and confidence. But on February 13, 1787, Vergennes succumbed to his illness and died at the age of sixty-seven. Vergennes's death came so close to the scheduled beginning of the Assembly of Notables, the opening session was pushed back to allow time for the funeral. Lafayette joined Louis's grief at losing not just an indispensable minister, but a valued mentor and personal friend. When the Notables finally convened, the uncertain king—terrified of making a mistake—was deprived of the man he trusted most.

But the death of Vergennes was only half the story. Calonne was also sick in January and February 1787. Though he recovered, the effects of his illness are plain in hindsight. He should have spent the final weeks leading up to the Assembly of Notables finalizing, tightening, and polishing his reform package. Instead, preparations stalled and drifted. Somewhat recovered by mid-February, Calonne called a cohort of capable young secretaries to rush the job to completion. Talleyrand was among those invited, and was shocked by the lethargic lack of focus he encountered. What he found in Calonne's office was a pile of disconnected proposals—some old, some new, some incredibly detailed, others barely outlined. "Thus, on February 14, there was no drafting done," Talleyrand later recalled. "We shared this immense work . . . we did so in a week, in a fairly bearable way, a job that the presumption and the carelessness of M. de Calonne had made him neglect for five months."[6] Calonne himself entered the Assembly of Notables tired, peevish, and blithely overconfident. He did not have a plan if they started asking tough questions. If indeed he had answers at all.

In Calonne's defense, most outside observers shared his assumptions about the Notables. They appeared to be a very fancy rubber stamp. A contemporaneous political cartoon shows a monkey dressed as a chef saying to an assembly of birds, "My dear creatures, I have assembled you here to deliberate on the sauce in which you will be served."[7] Thomas Jefferson wrote Abigail Adams, "The most remarkable effect of this convention as yet is the number of puns and *bon mots* it has produced . . . enough to make a larger volume than the Encyclopedia."[8] Lafayette himself reported to Washington some jokesters took to hilarious puns. "I have given you an account of the Assembly of Notables," he said, "wicked people say the *not ables*."[9] When the Assembly of Notables convened, it was treated as a source of jokes. Certainly no one expected them to conduct serious business, nor display resistance to the king, nor mark the beginning of a revolution. And yet.

⁂

ON FEBRUARY 22, 1787, the 144 "not ables" sat down for their opening session. The setting could not have been a more perfect metaphor for perceptions of their assembly. They gathered in the Hôtel des Menus-Plaisirs du Roi, a large building just down the street from the royal palace, principally used as a storage warehouse for backdrops, scenery, and props used in royal festivities. If the Notables hoped to avoid the perception they were mere props for the king, they were meeting in the wrong place.

After the king made a short opening speech laying out his expectations, he handed the proceedings to Calonne. Calonne minced no words. The annual budget deficit was out of control and unsustainable. Over the past decade the deficit doubled to 18 million *livres*, thanks largely to the 1.25 *billion* livres they borrowed to cover the cost of the American war. The king was drowning in red ink. New loans were neither sufficient nor forthcoming. Calonne said the Notables were there to identify and fix "whatever interferes with production, whatever weakens the sources of credit, whatever makes income insufficient, and all the unnecessary expenditures that destroy them."[10] The Notables were deeply disturbed by the reported deficits, a closely held secret many learned about for the first time. Most of them owned the *Compte rendu*, which clearly demonstrated everything was fine back in 1781. What the hell had the king and his ministers been doing these past five years?

After the opening session, the members divided into seven bureaus—each chaired by a royal prince. This was to keep the Notables under a further level of control. If malcontents started making trouble in one bureau, their ideas could be quarantined before spreading to the others. Lafayette was placed in the second bureau, chaired by the comte d'Artois, who was happy to keep an eye on his old classmate.

The first order of business was an olive branch from the king. In exchange for agreeing to financial and economic reform, local leaders would be invited to participate in provincial assemblies. These assemblies would be responsible for certain aspects of local administration, including public infrastructure and tax collection. They would not wield *real* power—no actual legislative authority and certainly no power to contradict or overrule the king's agents—but still, it was something.

The Notables approved the creation of the new assemblies, but debated how exactly the provincial assemblies would be organized. Would they meet along the traditional lines of the three estates, with each estate receiving one collective vote? Or would they convene as a single body with each delegate voting as an individual? Given Lafayette's later support of voting by head, it is curious he supported meeting along the traditional lines in the Assembly of Notables. Suspicious of the ultimate intentions of the king, Lafayette presently believed the independent provincial aristocracy could serve as a check on the threat of royal despotism. Clearly, he had been reading his Montesquieu. But within a few months Lafayette changed his mind and supported voting by head as a means of diminishing the power of the intransigent nobility.

＝⊫＝

WITH NEW PROVINCIAL assemblies approved, the Notables proceeded to the matter they were *really* there to address: taxes. Specifically, Calonne asked them to approve a new universal land tax, applied to everyone without exception. Further, this new tax would be permanent rather than another temporary expedient. Calonne premised the discussion by admitting his opening address understated the problems facing France. The annual deficit was not 18 million livres, but more like *114 million* livres. There could be no more delays. New taxes needed to be approved at once.

The Notables were shocked, and their shock quickly turned to hostile skepticism. It would be easy to explain the supposed explosion of the deficit if Calonne was simply lying. What if the Assembly of Notables was a charade? What if Calonne invented an emergency to force them to accept permanent new taxes? On the off chance there really *was* an emergency, the Notables demanded to know the precise cause. What had Madame Deficit been spending the kingdom's money on? Why was Calonne himself decked out in expensive clothes while crying poverty? Calonne only heightened their suspicions by invoking privilege over the royal ledgers. Calonne did not want the embarrassing details to leak out, but by playing coy, he invited the Notables to suspect the worst.

Calonne compounded the problem on March 12. He called the Notables together to thank them for their hard work. He expressed relief "the objections you have raised and which mainly relate to matters of form, do not contradict essential points of the goal that his Majesty has proposed to improve his finances."[11] When the Notables heard this they went ballistic. They were not going to let Calonne act like they did not have real substantive concerns. Over the next few days, they compiled lists of complaints, grievances, and objections. Lafayette's second bureau drew up minutes of their deliberations and asked they be entered into the record, so their views—their objective and unedited views—would not be buried under Calonne's self-serving characterizations. Far from being on the verge of deciding what sauce they wanted to be served in, the Notables decided maybe Calonne was the one who needed to be cooked for dinner.

Caught flat-footed and unprepared, Calonne improvised a counterattack to regain the upper hand: he appealed to public opinion. He knew the popular presses blamed Madame Deficit for everything. Calonne wanted people to understand who the *real* villains were. He ordered his speech published alongside an anonymously authored defense of his tax plan. This defense attacked the Notables as driven entirely by selfish greed. After pointing out the elimination of certain unpopular consumption taxes would actually *lower* the tax burden for most French families, it said: "What could be among the pretexts of concerns? Will we pay more? No doubt: but who? Only those who did not pay enough, they will pay what they owe in proportion, & no one will be burdened. Privileges will be sacrificed! Yes: justice wants it, need demands it. Would it be better to still overburden the non-privileged, the people?"[12]

Calonne thought the popular appeal would outflank the resistant Notables. But though the gambit made an impression on public opinion, mostly it backfired. When the Notables returned to work, they were furious. They said they did not resist Calonne because they were selfish or greedy. They resisted Calonne because he refused to show them the real books. Looking back a few years later, Lafayette said, "With what fury and by how many intrigues these notables, and especially the bishops, did defend themselves against the king's proposals, presented by M. de Calonne."[13] Talleyrand, watching from the wings, said the Notables "found glory in objecting."[14] The Notables prepared to fight Calonne over everything he put in front of them.

❧

FOR THE FIRST month of the Assembly of Notables, Lafayette was mostly quiet. The press noted his lack of participation in the early dramas, and the *Mémoires secrets* confirmed their earlier assessment, saying the young marquis, "so useful to the nation during the last war," now "made a very poor showing in the Assembly of Notables."[15] Lafayette's poor showing was partly because he was himself a very sick man. He suffered a debilitating chest infection, sapping his energy and causing his friends to worry he overexerted himself. Were it not for the Assembly of Notables, Lafayette would probably be confined to a bed.

Compounding his illness, Lafayette also received startling and embarrassing news just before the Notables convened. The husband of the comtesse de Simiane, his new mistress, committed suicide in January 1787. Lafayette became a target not just of the press's disappointment, but also their disapproval. One accusatory attack deplored "the despair of the gentleman, your equal, who has taken his own life because you have taken his wife's heart."[16] Lafayette was not the sole cause of the comte de Simiane's unhappiness, nor was he likely even the principal cause for the suicide, but it was a serious matter Lafayette could not easily move on from. His fun and games had real world consequences. Adrienne, as usual, endured the rumors about her husband with silent but pained forbearance.

In mid-April 1787, Lafayette came back to life as the Notables set aside the explosive tax issue and moved on to the issue of unprofitable royal estates. Calonne said the king's property should be put in the hands of more commercially oriented managers. But the Notables sidestepped this suggestion and demanded to know why the king's estates were so badly mismanaged in the first place. This opened the door for further accusations about corrupt real estate deals. Evidence recently surfaced of a scheme where favorites of the royal family bought property at low prices, then sold it to the Crown above market rate. Buyers, sellers, and middlemen all profited individually, while the kingdom's taxpayers footed the bill. These charges hit close to home as Marie Antoinette, the comte d'Artois, and Calonne himself were all implicated in these corrupt deals. Lafayette inserted himself in the middle of the controversy by demanding a full inquiry. Calonne was furious and Lafayette reported to Washington, "M. de Calonne went up to the King to ask I should be confined to the Bastille."[17]

But Calonne's days of making demands were numbered. The Assembly of Notables became a humiliating debacle for the royal family. There was only one thing to do: find a scapegoat. One of the leading opposition voices in the Notables, the respected Archbishop Loménie de Brienne, conveyed to the king and queen the Notables were far more hostile to Calonne personally than the reforms he presented. If the king removed Calonne, the reforms might be saved. So over the Easter recess, the king abruptly dismissed Calonne from service and exiled him from Versailles. He had asked Calonne to manage the Assembly of Notables the way a director arranges props on a stage. Instead Calonne set fire to the theater.

WITH CALONNE OUT of the picture, the Notables went back to work with renewed purpose. They met six days a week, from sunup to sundown, addressing a variety of issues. They agreed to dismantle most of the internal customs barriers disrupting the kingdom's economic activity. They voted to eliminate several consumption taxes hitting the poor hardest. They reformed the much despised *gabelle*, a tax on salt arbitrarily set at different rates in different provinces, which produced far more misery than revenue. They also agreed to reform the *corvée*, an archaic feudal obligation requiring peasants to provide a certain number of days of free labor for local lords.

But this did not mean the Notables became quiescent. Despite Brienne's promises, they did not cease hostilities just because Calonne was gone. Lafayette returned from Easter recess increasingly recovered from his illness and ready to join the fray. In his first major public address on domestic affairs, Lafayette renewed his call for an inquiry into the corrupt real estate deals. He used it as an opportunity to frame the issue as one facet of a larger system of injustice. "My sense of patriotism is alarmed and I demand full inquiry," he said. "The millions being disbursed come from taxes, which cannot be justified except to meet the real needs of the state. The millions abandoned to plunder and greed are the fruit of sweat, tears, and blood and the number of people sacrificed to misery of the sums so carelessly wasted shames the sense of justice and goodness we know to be the natural sentiments of his majesty."[18] Lafayette was not here to defend the privileged, but champion the people.

Lafayette then delivered two further addresses. In the first, he argued against imposing new taxes. There was nothing about the crisis that could not be solved with "virtuous and enlightened administration." Increasing taxes on the people of France would be "a cruel harvest" squeezing minuscule amounts from individual families, which were drops in the bucket compared with "the profligacy and luxury of the court and upper classes." He told his colleagues, "Let us follow those millions into the country cottages, and we will see the last hope of sustenance for widows and orphans, the final burden that forces the farmer to abandon his plow and a family of honest artisans to begging."[19] More taxes were not the answer.

In his second address, Lafayette laid out a litany of austerity measures the court could adopt—*must* adopt—before he could consider new taxes: eliminate gifts or sinecures for favorites, sell or rent unused property, allow for private commercial management of Crown lands, bring in expert bookkeepers to produce regular public audits. True to his new role as social reformer and public benefactor, Lafayette also suggested closing state jails. This would not only save money, but restore balance to the scales of justice. The jails were mostly filled with prisoners whose only crime was circumventing the very customs, duties, and tariffs the Assembly of Notables now slated for elimination. He said, "The King's heart would disavow these prisons as well as the laws of the kingdom that sent prisoners there, if he fully understood their uselessness and danger."[20]

These addresses show Lafayette unwilling to tax the poor to pay the bills of the rich. But whether he knew it or not, Lafayette pushed precisely the narrative his tax-exempt brethren wanted to push—that "new taxes" would be an unjust burden on the poor, and the "financial crisis" was caused solely by royal profligacy. Though Calonne's appeal to public opinion was a tactical mistake, it far better described reality than Lafayette's impassioned defense of the common people. The proposed universal land tax would land principally on *rich* families who had *not* been paying their fair share. The currently tax-exempt nobility eagerly confused, conflated, and equivocated the issue—making it appear they protected an overburdened population from oppressive new taxes, when in reality they only protected their own pocketbooks. By focusing on the plight of the poor, Lafayette encouraged this equivocation.

The most immediate effect of Lafayette's speeches was a permanent falling out with the royal family. The queen was especially angry, and Lafayette reported to Washington, "They don't forgive me the liberties I've taken."[21] His relationship with the royal family had always been complicated. They first treated him as an awkward teenage buffoon; then as a national hero welcomed into the inner sanctums of the palace; now they regarded him as a disloyal backstabber. The royal family started speaking Lafayette's name with derision and contempt. The invitations to dinner, cards, and hunts ceased. Henceforth, Lafayette and the Bourbons would be antagonists, even as Lafayette professed undying loyalty to the Crown.

❧

IN AN EFFORT to blunt continuing attacks from the Notables, the king invited Archbishop Brienne into his government. The hope was, as leader of the opposition, Brienne could coax his allies into approving the universal land tax. But as soon as he donned the robes of state and looked at the *real* books, Brienne realized the astonishing truth. The Assembly of Notables generally assumed Calonne refused to produce the king's ledgers so he could exaggerate the crisis and justify unpopular taxes. When Brienne opened the books, he discovered Calonne had been cagey not because the financial situation was better than he claimed, but because it was *much worse*. The king's finances were an appalling disaster.

Brienne came back to the assembly on May 10 and said it's all true, we have to do something. This revelation, however, did not provoke the intended response. Roused to a state of heightened suspicion, some believed the royal family bribed Brienne into continuing the charade of a financial crisis because Madame Deficit did not want to economize. But others took a step back and assessed the bigger picture. If the kingdom really did need new permanent taxes, was the Assembly of Notables the proper body to impose them?

Lafayette fell into the latter category. He rose and delivered another address echoing all his previous themes, but adopting a new and stunning conclusion. Lafayette told his colleagues that in his home province of Auvergne, "the farmers were leaving their plows, and the workers their shops, and the most industrious citizens, deprived of their earnings at home and abroad, will soon have no other alternative than poverty or emigration." He warned, "No matter how great the love of the people may be for their majesty, it will be dangerous to believe their resources are inexhaustible . . . let us hope this disastrous crisis, presenting as it does an inescapable contrast with the wasteful luxury and thoughtless squandering of the court, may make as deep an impression on those who can prevent this evil, as on those who are its innocent victims!" Then he pivoted to his dramatic finale: "The imprescriptible right of determining the public taxes belongs to the representatives of the nation alone . . . it seems to me that we have reached the point where we are to beseech His Majesty once more to assume responsibility for all measures and to assure their happy outcome forever by convoking a *national assembly*."[22]

Lafayette's colleagues greeted this call with stunned silence. "Seeing the effect produced by these two words uttered for the first time," he later recollected, "it would not have been judged that about two years later, they should reappear with a brilliance and a power which would fill France and the world."[23] He then went on to describe how the comte d'Artois broke the silence by leaping incredulously to his feet.

"What, sir!" said the comte d'Artois, "you are asking for the convocation of the Estates-General!"

"Yes, Monsignor, and even more than that."

"So you want me to write, and carry to the king: 'M. de Lafayette, making a motion to convene the Estates-General?'"

"Yes, my Lord."[24]

Lafayette went on to recall, "The idea which had just been thrown forward, the expression of 'more than the Estates-General,' that is to say of a *national assembly*, did not appear then, in the offices as in the society, [other] than the vain expression of thoughtless desire. This denomination of *national assembly* was adopted, as we know, at Versailles, in the first sessions of the constituent assembly."[25]

In early 1787, Lafayette remained on the leading edge of history. He continued to anticipate and move in directions the rest of France would later follow. The Estates-General *would* be called. It *would* become "more than the Estates-General" and declare itself a national assembly. Lafayette's ability to foresee the direction of events and position himself as a leader well ahead of the herd was a hallmark of his early career. His prescience and foresight were unerring. Right up until the moment they weren't.

‐☰‐

ARCHBISHOP BRIENNE CONCLUDED the Assembly of Notables was a dead end. They were never going to do what they were called to do. He asked the bureaus to submit final reports and scheduled a closing ceremony for May 25, 1787. Realizing this was not the end of the line, but the beginning of a much greater political movement, Lafayette recommended the second bureau insert into their final report a formal request for Protestant toleration and general reform of the criminal code. Artois cut him off, and said Lafayette was out of order, but the other members, also sensing a chance to go on record about more than just taxes, supported Lafayette's motion. The lines were inserted into the final minutes.

Measured on its own terms, the Assembly of Notables was a failure. Their job was to resolve a financial crisis, and they departed with the financial crisis unresolved. But this didn't mean they accomplished *nothing*. On many issues they showed an admirable willingness to dispense with burdensome and archaic institutions of feudalism. Times changed and the kingdom ought to change with them. But the greatest legacy of the Assembly of Notables was, by far, their surprising willingness to stand up to the king. Their defiance set a new tone, as the narrow financial crisis gave way to a wider political conflict that was then swallowed by an all-encompassing social apocalypse. Defiance and resistance would be the defining mood of the next few years—and the Assembly of Notables was the first to embody this new and intoxicating attitude.

Lafayette departed in high spirits, convinced the Assembly of Notables was the first step in the complete transformation of the Kingdom of France. Taxes and budgets were only the beginning. To a friend recently hired to become a royal tutor to the *dauphin*, Lafayette wrote, "You will do well to begin his history of France with the year 1787."[26] Though most histories actually don't begin the history of modern France for another two years, Lafayette correctly suspected a revolution had already begun.

CHAPTER ELEVEN

A CONSPIRACY OF HONEST PEOPLE

[1787–1789]

L AFAYETTE ENTERED THE SUMMER OF 1787 FULL OF BOUND-
less optimism. He hoped to capitalize on the defiance of the
Assembly of Notables and push toward a bright future full of
constitutional rights, rather than falling back into the dark past of feudal privilege. He wrote happily to George Washington, "The spirit of
liberty is prevailing in this country at a great rate—liberal ideas are can-
tering about from one end of the kingdom to the other."[1] Six months
later he looked back on the distinct change in tone of politics in France:
"Combustible materials have been kindled by the Assembly of Notables . . . a paper war ensued . . . some ministers have been burnt in
effigy." People now openly agreed the king did not have the right to
impose taxes, and that "nothing in that way can be stipulated but by an
Assembly of the Nation."[2] The need for financial reform opened the
door to political reform. Lafayette was thrilled.

This change of tone was not appreciated by the royal family. Nor
was Lafayette's eager embrace of it. At a dinner hosted by the comte
de Provence, the prince singled out Lafayette. "You're a republican,"
Provence said, "does that mean you approve of the execution of King
Charles I?"[3] Charles I was king of England, Scotland, and Ireland until

Oliver Cromwell and English Parliamentary leaders sentenced him to death more than a century earlier—an execution considered an abominable crime by conservative royalists. Put on the spot, Lafayette said he did *not* approve of the execution of Charles I, because he was opposed to arbitrary justice in all forms. Which was true, but hardly a ringing denunciation of the special crime of regicide. Lafayette became more estranged from his noble brethren with each passing day.

But Lafayette was not a lone liberal voice in the nobility. Far from it. Many friends from his own generation shared his excitement for the possibility of renewing, reforming, and rebuilding France. Some were veterans of American service like his old friends vicomte de Noailles, comte de Ségur, or the Lameth brothers, Charles and Alexandre, who served under Rochambeau and came home from America with distinctly liberal ideas. Others were idealist social reformers like Condorcet and Rochefoucauld who believed in the power of science and reason to end human misery. Still others were cynical opportunists like Talleyrand, who saw which way the winds blew and hoped to ride them to wealth, power, and prestige.

In this liberal milieu Lafayette first met Honoré-Gabriel Riqueti, comte de Mirabeau. Though Lafayette and Mirabeau traveled in the same political circles, they were very different men. Lafayette considered himself virtuous and moral, and projected an image of impeccable righteousness. Mirabeau on the other hand was cynical, hedonistic, and relished his own lack of scruples. Where Lafayette was thin, neat, and sharply dressed, Mirabeau was a gargantuan presence, conspicuous for his garish tastes as much as his girth. The wealthy Lafayette spent his riches to win popular acclaim; the terminally indebted Mirabeau used his popular acclaim to get rich. Lafayette frankly did not like or trust Mirabeau, and wrote in his memoirs (in the habitual third person), that Mirabeau's "immorality shocked him. Though he found much pleasure in his conversation and felt great admiration for his outstanding gifts, he could not help but adopting towards him an attitude of wounding contempt."[4]

Along with dozens of others, they formed the core of liberal nobles eager to participate in the great project of reforming the kingdom. And it wasn't just the young. Even the old duc d'Ayen, who always considered himself an enlightened modern gentleman, knew the time for reform had come.

⧈

AFTER THE FAILURE of the Assembly of Notables, the king did what he originally hoped to avoid: directly register the necessary tax reforms in the *parlement* of Paris. This meant the councilors of the parlement would have the opportunity to voice their own complaints, grievances, and objections. Thomas Jefferson believed if Brienne moved quickly, he might be able to keep attention narrowly focused on the financial matters. But Brienne moved slowly, which, as Jefferson later recalled, "gave time for the feelings excited by the proceedings of the Notables to cool off, new claims to be advanced, and a pressure to arise for a fixed constitution, not subject to changes at the will of the king."[5] The question was now moving decisively to the broader political question. And events advanced from financial crisis to political conflict.

Two months of negotiations left Brienne under the distinct impression the Paris parlement would never voluntarily register new taxes not approved by a national assembly. So he decided to play the king's final trump card. While the parlement could delay registration by demanding changes and clarifications, in the end, the king could simply order them to register his edicts. This was a rarely invoked right, as the lawyers in the parlement knew a thousand ways to make life miserable for any king who ordered them to do what they did not want to do. But Brienne decided to take the risk. On August 8, 1787, he convened a *lit de justice*—a "bed of justice"—an official ceremony where the parlement gathered under the auspices of the king, who lay in a literal bed of pillows. According to the rules of this absurdly anachronistic ritual, from his bed of justice, the king may order the parlement to register his laws. But this particular lit de justice turned out to be the perfect encapsulation of the despotic sloth and arbitrary indifference of the *ancien régime*. Laying on a comfortable pile of pillows in stuffy chambers thick with summer heat, Louis fell asleep. The king came to prove he deserved the sole divine right to rule France, and now his snores filled the hall.

The next day, the Paris parlement reconvened under their own auspices and refused to register the king's laws. Faced with direct defiance, Brienne drew up individual *lettres de cachet* for each member of the Paris parlement, ordering them to depart for the sleepy provincial town of Troyes—far from the streets, cafés, and salons of Paris providing the parlement moral and material support. Lafayette reported the troubling news to Washington: "Government has employed the force of arms against our magistrates and expelled them."[6] It was an ominous development not expected to bring the crisis to an end.

The crisis had now been going on for a full year, and nothing was fixed. Lafayette reported, "The affairs of France are still in an unsettled situation—a large deficit is to be filled up with taxes, and the nation are wary of paying what they have not voted."[7] Brienne hoped, while he negotiated an end to the standoff with the parlement, the provincial assemblies approved by the Assembly of Notables would deliver the kingdom from its financial troubles.

Though out of favor, Lafayette could not be left off the list of appointees to the provincial assembly of Auvergne. When he went home for a preliminary session over the summer of 1787, he made a tour of the province and found himself cheered and celebrated wherever he went. This was much to the scoffing disgust of his more conservative neighbors in the local nobility, one of whom said, "He was careful to let it be known well in advance when he planned to visit those towns . . . in which he knew that he would be received with honor, and . . . with a degree of pomp which was as ridiculous as it was extraordinary. He thought of nothing for making impression and being talked about."[8] Lafayette would always believe in the power of popular support, and was always eager to promote himself to cheering crowds. Even his friends knew this was one of Lafayette's weaknesses. Jefferson wrote to Madison, "His foible was a canine appetite for popularity and fame."[9] For now, the people loved him. But what would Lafayette do if that ever changed? Would he stick to his principles or chase the applause of notoriously fickle crowds?

By the fall of 1787, Brienne and the exiled councilors of the Paris parlement agreed to a compromise. The parlement agreed to a temporary extension of the *vingtième* and approved a new slate of five-year loans. In exchange, Brienne canceled the *lettres de cachet* and allowed the exiled councilors of the parlement to return to Paris. But his most stunning concession was an agreement to call the Estates-General before this new round of loans expired. Though the government was clearly kicking the can down the road—again—Lafayette observed with satisfaction, "From the proceedings that have taken place these six months past, we shall at least obtain the infusion of this idea into every body's head . . . that the King has no right to tax the Nation."[10] Archbishop Brienne prayed the whole crisis would be resolved before he had to keep his end of the bargain.

In October and November 1787, the provincial assemblies convened for full sessions across France. If they delivered the tax revenue the king needed, the problem might yet be solved. But the provincial assemblies turned out to be no more interested in bailing the king out than anyone else. Royal instructions informed Lafayette's assembly in Auvergne they must come up with 2 million *livres*. But applying current tax rates to their own assessment of Auvergne's productive wealth, they calculated they could only raise 1.3 million. When an emissary of the Crown came in person to order them to come up with the full amount, the assembly simply restated their conclusion. With Lafayette sitting in the key steering committees, the Auvergne assembly officially concluded if the king wanted them to send more money, new taxes would have to be raised. And those taxes could only be approved by an assembly of the whole nation. This meant the Estates-General.

Pleased with his efforts, Lafayette was further gratified to learn he scored another victory on a completely different front. Brienne persuaded the king to extend legal toleration to Protestants—a cause Lafayette championed after his return from America. Since the revocation of the Edict of Nantes in 1685, the Catholic Church had been the sole legal repository of birth, marriage, and death records. This forced devout French Protestants to either compromise their faith, emigrate abroad, or live in legal limbo. In November 1787, the king signed a

decree recognizing the legality of Protestant unions, baptisms, and fu-
nerals. It was a major step toward general religious toleration. Lafayette
was proud his efforts paid off, and it encouraged him to believe all his
other projects would meet with similarly happy success.

While the provincial assemblies met, the king and the Paris parlement met on November 19, 1787, to seal the terms of the compromise
Brienne brokered a few months earlier. But on the eve of this session,
the king received bad advice from hard-line conservatives warning the
compromise fatally undermined his divine right to rule. They said he was
on the road to becoming like the king of England, who presided over a
kingdom he did not govern. Heeding this advice, Louis veered off the
carefully arranged script at the last minute. He bluntly declared the parlement was not there to *agree* or *consent* to anything. They did not enjoy
that right. They would register his acts because he was ordering them to.
After a few moments of stunned silence, the duc d'Orléans rose and said,
"Your majesty, I consider this is illegal." To which Louis replied, "The
registration is legal because I have heard everyone's opinions."[11] Then he
walked out the door. This high-handed declaration of royal absolutism
struck precisely the wrong note of autocratic bluster. King Louis's knack
for doing the wrong thing at the wrong moment was a powerful force
keeping France on course for its looming date with revolution.

But the king wasn't done. The next day, he issued a *lettre de cachet* ex-
iling Orléans from Paris. This was a petulant blunder, as Louis's cousin
was far more popular than he was. After inheriting titles and property
in 1785, Orléans turned his Paris residence—a massive complex adjacent to the Louvre called the Palais-Royal—into the hottest spot in the
city. Orléans invited proprietors to open cafés, shops, and newsstands
in his arcades. As the Palais-Royal was private property, state agents
were not allowed inside, and it quickly became a popular haven for
Parisians, where they could buy, sell, and do anything. It made Orléans
enormously popular. It also made him dangerous. He turned a blind
eye to the production and distribution of scandalous, pornographic,
and treasonous material. Many of the radical journals, pamphlets, and
broadsheets stoking the seditious discontentment of prerevolutionary France emanated from the Palais-Royal. Now the king directly

attacked the people's hero. The court of public opinion rendered a scathing verdict on the king's conduct.

The king and queen were never in line to win a popularity contest, and by the end of 1787 their standing was at an all-time low. Marie Antoinette was herself a major reason the financial crisis became a political conflict. Not just because she was Madame Deficit—the living symbol of frivolous waste—but because she always encouraged her husband to do the wrong thing at the wrong moment. Whenever Louis was tempted to compromise, she faithfully reminded him wearing a crown requires a stiff backbone. She hated Orléans more than Louis did, and was among those urging him to sign the lettre de cachet. The queen was never merely a passive object of prerevolutionary fury, she was an active agent in keeping the fury roiling. "So great is the discontent," Lafayette wrote, "that the Queen dares not come to Paris for fear of being ill received."[12] Meanwhile, Marie Antoinette could only wonder in oblivious, resentful, and self-pitying myopia: "What harm have I done them?"[13]

They were still a long way from revolution, but Lafayette was pleased with the defiance of his fellow elites. "The general freedom of thinking, speaking, and writing . . . the spirit of criticism" prevailed everywhere, he reported. "The genius of the French is lively, enterprising, and inclined to contempt of their rulers. Their minds are getting enlightened by the works of philosophers, and the example of other Nations."[14] However, he still fretted the common people remained ignorant, hesitant, and docile. "And the people?" he wrote Washington. "The people, my dear General, have been so dull that it has made me sick."[15] Lafayette found them weak, frightened, and "ever ready to give way to a detachment of the guards."[16] Still, on the whole, things were moving in the right direction. "This country will, within twelve or fifteen years," he predicted to John Adams, "come to a pretty good constitution."[17] Whether one considers the French Constitution of 1799—the *fourth* constitution promulgated in the midst of a decade of war, chaos, and revolution—to be "pretty good," depends on one's political leanings. But it is certainly not what Lafayette imagined in 1787.

ALONGSIDE HIS EFFORTS at political reform, Lafayette continued his work as an enlightened social activist and blossoming abolitionist. In early 1788, he learned an abolitionist society had been formed in England. Thomas Clarkson later wrote:

> The marquis signified the singular pleasure he had received on hearing of the formation of a committee in England for the abolition of the Slave-trade, and the earnest desire he had to promote the object of it. With this view, he informed the committee that he should attempt the formation of a similar society in France. This he conceived to be one of the most effectual measures he could devise for securing the object in question; for he was of opinion, that if the two great nations of France and England were to unite in this humane and Christian work, the other European nations might be induced to follow the example.[18]

The English manumission society promptly enrolled Lafayette as an honorary member.

Lafayette never undertook the organization of a similar society, because other French abolitionists were well ahead of him. This society was the brainchild of Étienne Clavière, an enlightened Genevan financier, and his friend Jacques-Pierre Brissot. Brissot was a radical journalist who already earned notoriety for writing a libelously pornographic tract starring Marie Antoinette that earned him a stint in the Bastille in 1784. But scandalous muckraking was just a way to earn money. At heart, Brissot was a zealous social reformer and radical democrat who dreamed far greater revolutionary dreams than most of his contemporaries. Clavière and Brissot called their group the Société des amis des noirs—the Society of the Friends of the Blacks. It would be the first abolitionist society on the European continent.

Not wanting to mix their new group with the rancorous personality conflicts of the high nobility, Brissot and Clavière at first avoided inviting nobles to join. But thanks to his well-known emancipation experiment in Cayenne, they considered Lafayette a special case. Brissot and Clavière paid the marquis a visit in early February 1788 and invited him to their inaugural meeting. Though Lafayette was not technically enrolled as a "charter member" of the Société des amis des noirs, he was nonetheless intimately involved in the project by the time they held their first meeting on February 19, 1788.

After the inaugural meeting, Brissot and Clavière followed up with Lafayette. "When I saw him a few days later at my house," Brissot said, "he did not hesitate to tell me that, although I did not directly engage him, because I wanted to avoid the great lords as much as possible, he regarded himself from the birth of the company as one of its members; for a very long time he had been occupied with the means of alleviating the lot of the negroes in our colonies . . . so he saw with joy the formation of our society."[19] They soon recruited other members of the liberal nobility, including Condorcet, Rochefoucauld, Mirabeau, and two progressive clergymen: Abbé Henri Grégoire and Abbé Emmanuel Joseph Sieyès. Clarkson later wrote, "Women also were not thought unworthy of being honorary and assistant members of this humane institution; and among these were found the amiable Marquise de la Fayette."[20]

Following the same practical logic premising his experiment in Cayenne, Lafayette recommended his new abolitionist comrades "not to take refuge only in philosophical reflections but to seek to reconcile the interests of humanity with those of commerce . . . which is not impossible." They must not settle for the abstract ideal of emancipation but further encourage "not only the prosperity of the colonist but also the income of the actual landlords."[21] Lafayette was a gradual abolitionist who believed the most practicable path to emancipation was addressing, assuaging, and overcoming the objections of slave owners. If they could prove, for example, emancipation would not be an economic disaster, they would disarm a powerful weapon in the arsenal of slavery's defenders.

In the summer of 1787, Brissot planned to leave for a tour of America to study the cradle of liberty and slavery. Lafayette wrote letters of introduction for him, including one to Alexander Hamilton. He closed the letter with a note on his involvement with the emancipation movement: "[Brissot] will explain to you what has been done in this country respecting the negro trade, and slavery. I don't know whether you had me enlisted in the societies at New York and elsewhere; if not, I beg you will do it."[22] When Hamilton and John Jay subsequently enrolled La-fayette as an honorary member of the New York Manumission Society, he became the first person to boast membership in the emancipation movements of three different countries.

As the political situation in France continued to build toward the convening of some kind of national assembly, Condorcet wrote Lafay-ette reminding him they must seize the moment. "It is in the Estates-General that the cause of the Negro should be pleaded," he wrote. "And it is to you, the hero of American liberty, the wise and zealous advocate for the noble resolution on behalf of the Negroes . . . the generous man who has devoted part of his fortune and some of his brilliant youth to the search for ways to break the chains his eyes ought never to see—it is to you that belongs the defense there of liberty and the rights of man, which are all the same, no matter what their color or their country may be."[23]

Despite these hopes, Condorcet would be disappointed. Lafayette may have been a sincere abolitionist, but he was not a perfect abolition-ist. When the Revolution exploded in 1789, Lafayette accepted respon-sibility for maintaining order in Paris—a job leading him away from life as idealistic social reformer and back to the daily emergencies of soldier on campaign. He all but forgot about his centerpiece experiment in Cayenne. He left the project in the hands of Adrienne, who kept in regular contact with the on-site managers, but unfortunately, the La-fayettes never followed through on the plan to free their slaves before momentous events overtook them both.

⁂

As the political conflicts triggered by the financial crisis tumbled headlong into the opening maw of environmental and social disaster in the summer of 1788, revolution was fast becoming unavoidable. Still trying to salvage the Crown's authority, Archbishop Brienne attempted a final desperate gambit. In May 1788, he induced the king to issue six edicts that, taken together, would resolve the economic and political deadlock. But one of these edicts called for the abolition of the par-lements and the complete reorganization of France's judicial system. These edicts kicked off a wave of popular protest, as the parlement successfully framed the edicts as a tyrannical power grab by a despotic monarch. When the parlement of Grenoble—a provincial capital in the foothills of the Alps—was forcibly dispersed on June 7, 1788, the people rose to their defense. Angry crowds attacked and overwhelmed soldiers with bricks, paving stones, and roof tiles. The incident, dubbed the Day of the Tiles, was stark proof the political conflict no longer confined itself to the corridors of power. It was now in the street.

On the other side of the kingdom, the nobility of Brittany protested vigorously the king could not unilaterally dissolve their sacred provincial institutions. They drafted a formal petition and held a meeting in Paris in July 1788. Thanks to Lafayette's inherited property in Brittany, he was technically a "Breton noble" and both signed the petition and participated in the meeting. When a small delegation presented their collective protest to the king, Louis promptly ordered the delegation thrown in the Bastille. Lafayette joined the further protest against their imprisonment. Marie Antoinette raged over Lafayette's involvement. She demanded to know what business it was of his; he was not from Brittany. To which Lafayette replied, "I am Breton, just as your majesty is a Hapsburg."[24] As punishment, the king stripped Lafayette of his prestigious rank *mastre de camp*, awarded in the happier days after Yorktown. The demotion precipitated Lafayette's formal resignation from the army. The boy who dreamed of becoming a heroic soldier now chose to wage his campaigns for fame and glory in the battlefield of politics.

Some of Lafayette's friends worried the marquis's involvement in these affairs did not signal radicalism but conservatism. Though many defiant nobles spoke the language of rights and liberty, they were in fact fighting to maintain ancient privileges. "If you go to Lafayette's house," Condorcet wrote a mutual friend, "try to exercise the devil of aristocracy that will be there to tempt him in the guise of a counselor of parlement or of a Breton noble. For that purpose take along in your pocket a little vial of Potomac water and the sprinkler made from the wood of the Continental Army rifle and make your prayer in the name of liberty, equality, and reason, which are but a single divinity in three persons."[25] But after the meeting the mutual friend reported Lafayette was not deceived and appeared sound of mind, body, and soul.

It is doubtful the ongoing fight over taxes between king, nobles, and parlements would have resulted in the French Revolution had it not broken out in the middle of an ongoing environmental disaster. Europe was living through a period of prolonged cooling retrospectively dubbed the Little Ice Age—a climatic era that opened a new interval of dropping temperatures around 1770. In the midst of this cooling, a volcanic fissure in Iceland erupted continuously over the span of eight months between 1783 and 1784, which blanketed European skies in sulfurous ash. The eruption wreaked havoc on the climate. Weather patterns swung unpredictably between torrential rains and extended droughts, bracketed by winters of unprecedented severity.

All of these factors devastated agricultural production—and the harvests of 1787 were particularly bad. So while the elites of France fought over taxes, the common people faced starvation. The problem was not just lack of food, but lack of money. The economic reforms approved by the Assembly of Notables to liberate the grain trade from their allegedly oppressive controls happened to be rolled out at a moment of an acute supply shortage. Speculators and merchants did not miss the opportunity to make a fortune jacking up the price of precious grain as high as possible. These rising prices affected all segments of society. Thomas Jefferson later recalled, "The slender stock of bread-stuff had for some time threatened famine, and had raised that article to an enormous price. So great indeed was the scarcity of bread that from the highest to the lowest citizen, the bakers were permitted to deal but a scanty allowance per head."[26] With the price of food consuming so much of the household budget, the contraction of consumer spending of the middle and upper class triggered a recessionary collapse of France's nascent manufacturing sector. A steep decline in orders left the silk workers in Lyon, for example, in penniless limbo.

The harvest of 1788 was shaping up to ease the burden when Mother Nature struck again. On July 13, 1788, a massive hailstorm devastated most of northwestern France. Mind-bogglingly huge hailstones beat crops into crumpled and useless heaps. The harvest of 1788 now looked to be one of the worst in recorded history. Prices skyrocketed further. Pantries lay distressingly bare. Fear, anger, and dread took hold at all levels of society. Collective anxiety having nothing to do with the ongoing political battles gripped the Kingdom of France. But it gave those ongoing political battles a grave and desperate energy. *That* is how revolutions are born.

⚌

THE FINANCIAL CRISIS took on an urgent new dimension in August 1788. Brienne told the king the treasury was literally empty. The temporary loans were exhausted. There was not enough money in the royal vaults to even pay daily expenses. Two years after Calonne first announced the monarchy was *on the verge* of bankruptcy, the monarchy was now *actually* bankrupt. The king's creditors forced him to meet two nonnegotiable demands before they offered the Crown bridge loans to see them through the end of the year. First, Jacques Necker must be recalled to service. He was the only man carrying their personal confidence. Second, the king must convene the Estates-General. At once. It was the only way to overhaul, modernize, and secure the kingdom's finances. Archbishop Brienne announced the Estates-General would meet in the spring of 1789. Then he resigned from office.

Lafayette felt "keen pleasure" at the announcement.[27] Now that the king finally heeded the call of the nation, it was time for "promoting a spirit of wisdom, tranquility, disinterestedness, and forgiveness."[28] But Lafayette was not going to settle for the approval of a few new taxes. He wanted this new spirit to prevail, "in order that the national assembly may quietly attend to the plans of government, and the framing of a proper constitution."[29] Thomas Jefferson looked at the announcement in the context of the immediate disturbances of the summer of 1788. "Their convocation," he wrote a friend, "will tranquillize the public mind in a great degree."[30] On the same day, he wrote James Monroe, "They may yet have a constitution without spilling a drop of blood."[31]

The announcement did not end the march to revolution, however; it only changed the battle lines. The Estates-General last convened in 1614. There had been, to put it mildly, considerable political, intellectual, social, and scientific advancements in the intervening 175 years. Given those advancements, should they convene the estates according to an archaic feudal model or adopt a new principle of organization? Should each estate still receive one collective vote—allowing the nobility and the clergy to control the affairs of the kingdom even though they only represented 5 percent of the population? Was the other 95 percent to have no voice at all? Even though it included the entirety of the kingdom's productive labor and economic capacity?

Almost overnight, a new rallying cry filled the pamphlets, broadsheets, and impromptu speeches bursting out of the Palais-Royal: "Double the Third, Vote by Head." It expressed the simple demand that the delegation of the Third Estate be at least equal in size to the delegations of the clergy and nobility combined. Though they would still be grossly underrepresented, at least the playing field would be level. But it wouldn't matter if the delegation of the Third Estate was doubled, tripled, or quadrupled if they still only received one collective vote. Thus the critical demand for "vote by head," with each delegate casting one individual vote in a single communal assembly. A true national assembly.

The debate over how to organize the Estates-General forced many of those on the front lines of the political battles of the past two years to reveal their true loyalties. The Paris parlement, previously regarded as popular heroes for their steadfast defense of political liberty, issued a proclamation in late September 1788 declaring the Estates-General must convene in its traditional medieval form: three estates, with equal delegations, voting by order. With this declaration the parlement revealed they were never champions of liberty, equality, or justice. They were only jealously guarding their own privileges. All popular support evaporated in an instant. With the parlements fatally discredited, the people needed new leadership. The marquis de Lafayette and his friends hoped to provide it.

⊰⊱

To GUIDE THE nation through the next phase of the crisis, a group of liberal nobles met regularly in the home of Adrien Duport. Duport was a brilliant young leader of the Paris parlement. But unlike most of his fellow councilors, Duport fought to move France toward a new future, not re-entrench the past. An acolyte of Montesquieu and admirer of the British constitution, Duport invited like-minded people to join a collective effort to bring a modern constitution to France.

The press dubbed Duport's informal group the Society of Thirty, though in fact there were more than fifty regular attendees. Lafayette was a fixture at the meetings, along with many of his fellow members of the Société des amis des noirs, including Condorcet, Rochefoucauld, Abbé Sieyès, and Mirabeau. The wily and mercurial Talleyrand participated, believing a liberal constitution represented the best possible future for France. So too did Lafayette's oldest friend, vicomte de Noailles. A decade ago they were teenagers dreaming of battlefield glory. Now they were grown men ready to take over a kingdom. Jefferson said of the group: "This party comprehended all the honesty of the kingdom, sufficiently at its leisure to think: the men of letters, the easy bourgeois, the young nobility."[32] Mirabeau said they were simply "a conspiracy of well-intentioned people."[33]

Lafayette himself summed up the program of the Society of Thirty in a revealing letter to his favorite aunt-in-law, Madame de Tessé, who often hosted Lafayette and his friends at her Paris salon. Lafayette said they hoped to create "a sufficient degree of fermentation to produce a threat of civil war, though without letting it materialize: in the army, enough of patriotism to worry the government, without causing actual disobedience: in the collection of taxes, a sufficient number of obstacles to lead to capitulation, though not to bankruptcy. The general effect of all this will lead us, by the shortest possible road, to the winning of that constitutional liberty for the attainment of which other countries have not thought torrents of blood in 100 years of wars and misfortunes too high price to pay."[34] Lafayette and his friends believed they could pull off this delicate high-wire act. For a while they were right. Then they fell to earth.

In November 1788, the king convened a second Assembly of Notables to resolve the debate over the organization of the Estates-General. Lafayette was again invited to participate, but despite his best efforts, found the Notables uniformly opposed to any deviation from the traditional rules. The first Assembly of Notables defied the king to secure a strong voice for nobility in the kingdom's affairs; they were not about to let the rabble drown them out. The Notables met for a few weeks and issued their nearly unanimous recommendation to the king: three estates, equal delegations, vote by order. Upon later reflection, Lafayette believed the end of the second Assembly of Notables marked the beginning of "the fatal contest of the immovable prejudices of a small section of the privileged with the gradual development of public enlightenment."[35]

Lafayette and the Society of Thirty hoped to further that public enlightenment. After calling the Estates-General, the king relaxed censorship laws and invited his subjects to draw up *Cahiers de doléances*—lists of grievances and concerns for the Estates-General to consider. The Society of Thirty wrote, funded, and published explanatory pamphlets to help the people of France understand the process. They also published model cahiers with prefabricated grievances. If the village assemblies were so inclined, they could simply cut and paste from the list of examples provided.

Members of the Society of Thirty also wrote, funded, and published editorials over the winter of 1788–1789 to guide the nation's discourse. Abbé Sieyès wrote the most famous of these pamphlets: *What Is the Third Estate?* It was a brief polemic explaining why the conflict over the composition of the Estates-General mattered. It famously opened: "What is the Third Estate? Everything. What has it been in the political order? Nothing. What does it ask to be? To become something."[36] The pamphlet was a smashing success and made Sieyès one of the few nationally recognized figures heading into the Estates-General of 1789.

Thanks partly to the work of the Society of Thirty, Jacques Necker convinced the king to set aside the recommendations of the second Assembly of Notables. In December, Necker announced a partial victory for the nascent liberal leadership. Elections were set for early spring, and the delegations of the Third Estate would be doubled. But Necker pointedly *did not* address the more crucial matter of whether the Estates-General would vote by order or by head. That question would be left unanswered until the Estates-General assembled.

In March 1789, Lafayette went home to Auvergne to face his fellow nobles and ask for their vote. Lafayette found this assembly of provincial nobles bore little resemblance to the liberal salons of Paris. When he arrived he reported, "Division and jealousy exist here . . . I have the disadvantage of an audience warned and prepared against my opinions."[37] At risk of missing out on the single most important political event of his lifetime, Lafayette made a regrettable promise to secure election. He pledged not to support voting by head unless the king decreed it. Lafayette would not have been elected without making this pledge—even with it, he only secured a plurality of votes: 189 out of 393. But having made the promise, he bound himself to act against his own beliefs. Jefferson did not like it. "I've become uneasy for you," he wrote Lafayette. "Your principles are decidedly with *Tiers Estate*, and your instructions against them."[38]

But as he departed for Versailles, Lafayette was convinced a new day was dawning for France. His optimism was only slightly tempered by a cautionary letter he received from Washington. "I like not much the situation of affairs in France," Washington said. "Little more irritation would be necessary to blow up the spark of discontent into a flame that might not easily be quenched."[39] But Lafayette believed he and his friends could keep the flame of liberty burning just hot enough to melt the ancient chains of feudal despotism, without accidentally burning the whole kingdom down.

CHAPTER TWELVE

THE CATECHISM OF FRANCE

[1789]

T HE ESTATES-GENERAL OF 1789 WAS MEANT TO BE THE END of it all. The finale. What began in August 1786 as a financial crisis turned into nearly three years of political combat. This conflict then folded into an ongoing social crisis caused by climatic disaster and paltry harvests. To compound things, the winter of 1788–1789 turned out to be the worst on record. Food supplies dwindled. Families struggled to afford fuel for their hearths. Sources of public water froze solid. In this atmosphere, the Estates-General took on an aura of salvation. Starving peasants and refined nobles alike believed the Estates-General would be the panacea to cure all ills and end all conflicts. But it was only the beginning.

The events of the past few years generated two new revolutionary forces destined to merge in the cataclysmic summer of 1789: one formed in the salons, the other in the streets. In the salons, liberal nobles, lawyers, bankers, journalists, doctors, and businessmen gathered to think, plot, and discuss—often under the auspices of influential women in society like Lafayette's aunt Madame de Tessé. Their ultimate goal was taking the exciting intellectual theories of the past century and applying them to the real world. They wanted constitutional government, individual rights, the rule of law, accountable administration, and an elected legislature. Lafayette and his friends in the Society of Thirty were salon revolutionaries *par excellence*. Lafayette summed himself up: "At the age of nineteen, I dedicated myself to liberty of mankind and the destruction of despotism so far as an individual as weak as I am can venture upon such a task."[1]

Meanwhile out in the street, a different revolutionary force stirred, composed of workers, shopkeepers, porters, servants, stewards, apprentices, clerks, and students. Collectively they would be called the masses, the crowds, or the mob. Lacking access to the corridors of power, their only recourse was direct action. Their weapons were not pamphlets or speeches but pitchforks, pikes, and torches. They did all the things the salon revolutionaries could not or would not do: gather, chant, march, smash windows, light fires, verbally and physically menace defenders of the old order. In 1789 and beyond, the actions of the street revolutionaries gave their counterparts in the salons crucial leverage, even as the salon revolutionaries condemned and deplored the revolution in the streets.

These two revolutionary forces were driven by different motivations. Thwarted ambition or idealistic visions in the salons. Empty cupboards and icy hearths in the streets. They combined in the spring of 1789 because an intolerable situation drove them both in the same direction, fueled by centuries of aspirations, grievances, expectations, resentments, disappointments, and hopes. Fundamentally they both wanted dignity and respect. Liberty and equality. When these two forces merged, the Kingdom of France would never be the same. The world would never be the same.

❧❧

ON MAY 5, 1789, the delegates of the Estates-General assembled for the opening session. Like the Assembly of Notables, they met in the Hôtel des Menus-Plaisirs du Roi. Workers renovated the great hall to give the appearance of impressive splendor, but beneath the gold paint and heavy curtains lay flimsy wood platforms, not solid stone and marble. It was another too-on-the-nose metaphor for the *ancien régime*. The king presided over the opening ceremony from a hastily constructed throne flanked on either side by six hundred delegates from the first two estates. Lafayette and most friends from the Society of Thirty sat among the delegates of the Second Estate, including vicomte de Noailles, Talleyrand, and Rochefoucauld. Facing the king sat the six hundred delegates from the Third Estate. Only a few of them were known outside their hometowns. The most famous was the comte de Mirabeau, elected to represent the Third Estate of Marseilles after his noble brethren refused to elect him to a seat in the Second Estate. Mirabeau's enormous head was one of the few to stick out in the crowd. The rest of the delegates were unknown provincials called to national service for the first time, for example, an obscure Arras lawyer named Maximilien Robespierre.

The hall accommodated not only delegates but also thousands of observers filling wooden bleachers. Sitting in the audience were family members like Adrienne; journalists like Jacques-Pierre Brissot and the even more radical populist Camille Desmoulins; and foreign observers from around the world, like Americans Thomas Jefferson and Gouverneur Morris, the latter recently arrived in Paris hoping to replace Jefferson as ambassador to France and whose daily diary provides an invaluable chronicle of the French Revolution. After the king fumbled his way through the opening ceremony, Jacques Necker presented the details of the financial crisis in extensive and excruciating detail. Everyone strained to follow along. The acoustics of the hall were terrible and people mostly heard shuffling, coughing, and background conversation.

The next day, the delegates reassembled for their first sessions of real business. The three estates were ordered to break out into separate meeting halls to verify the credentials of their members. But this utterly routine request brought the Estates-General to a screeching halt. The issue of whether the delegates would vote by head or vote by estate was *still* unanswered. A majority of the Third Estate delegates, new to national politics, would have followed the order to break apart. But a few prepared activists stepped forward and said they must not accept, even in principle, that the estates were separate bodies. The Estates-General of 1789 must act, from the beginning, as a single national assembly. Swayed by these passionate arguments, the Third Estate announced their refusal to consider any business until all delegates verified every credential collectively.

This immediately placed Lafayette on the horns of his great dilemma. He personally believed they should meet as a single national assembly, but pledged to the electors of Auvergne he would not support voting-by-head in a single chamber. Lafayette and the handful of other liberal nobles in the Second Estate attempted to persuade their colleagues to join the Third Estate, but lost the vote by a crushing 46 to 334.

Jefferson believed Lafayette placed himself in a terrible position. He told Lafayette that believing the principles of the Third Estate, while remaining attached to the Second Estate, "may give an appearance of trimming between two parties, which will lose you both." If Lafayette waited until the king ordered the estates to combine, he "would be received by the *Tiers Estate* . . . coldly and without confidence." In this conflict between political principle and personal honor, Jefferson clearly believed political principle must win. He recommended Lafayette break his oath and lead a breakaway party of nobles to join the Third Estate. If he moved early, Lafayette would "win their hearts forever, be approved by the world, which marks and honors the man of the people, and will be an eternal consolation to yourself."[2] Lafayette never feared making historical leaps of faith. But in the early days of the Estates-General, he froze in place.

It wasn't just Lafayette who froze, though. The deadlock of the Estates-General went on for days, then weeks, with no resolution in sight. The Third Estate remained on strike. The other two orders refused to rejoin them. What France needed more than anything was King Louis XVI to step up and be a king. To *lead* his people. But at this critical hour, fate dealt Louis the most devastating blow imaginable. On June 4, 1789, his seven-year-old son died. The infant boy celebrated the night Lafayette returned from America was always a sickly child and finally succumbed to a prolonged battle with tuberculosis. His four-year-old brother became heir to the throne while Louis and Marie Antoinette plunged into a deep personal mourning. At the precise moment when his subjects stood most in need of the king's leadership, he disappeared behind a veil of tears.

In the king's absence, events lurched forward. On June 12, three priests from the First Estate crossed the line and joined the members of the Third. Thunderous applause greeted their arrival. One can only wonder how much Lafayette regretted missing out on such rapturous acclaim. The next day, six more clergymen, including the Abbé Grégoire, crossed over. Now, with at least a nominal claim to representing more than just the Third Estate, the delegates voted to rename themselves the National Assembly. This was the very combination of words Lafayette suggested at the Assembly of Notables in 1787. It was all happening. Just as he hoped. Just as he planned. Still he did not move.

On June 19, the delegates of the First Estate voted by a slim majority to join the National Assembly as a group. That night, Necker prevailed upon the withdrawn king to finally intervene in the interest of conciliation. To prepare for a royal session, the great meeting hall closed for renovations. But this was handled in the most provocatively clumsy way possible. With the First Estate scheduled to join the National Assembly on the morning of June 20, 1789, the delegates arrived to discover the doors locked and guarded by soldiers. It was impossible to believe it was anything but an attempt to prevent the merging of the estates. Filled with exhilarated panic, the delegates reconvened down the street at the royal tennis court where, under the presidency of astronomer-turned-politician Jean-Sylvain Bailly, they swore to continue meeting until they drafted a new constitution for France. This was all of Lafayette's dreams come true. The Oath of the Tennis Court meant the limited financial crisis had given way to a full-blown political revolution. But Lafayette was nowhere to be seen.

After five more days of tension, resistance, and recriminations, the duc d'Orléans helped bring the matter to a close. On June 25, he led a delegation of forty-seven nobles to join the National Assembly. Incredibly, Lafayette was *not* one of the forty-seven nobles led by Orléans. Still bound by his personal oath, he remained frozen in place. Gouverneur Morris reported after a conversation with Lafayette at the dinner table of Madame de Tessé: "He says he is determined to resign his seat."[3] It was all Lafayette could think to do.

Finally, the king released Lafayette from the anguish of self-imposed suspended animation. The dramatic defection of the Second Estate nobles ended royal resistance to the three estates meeting as a single body. On June 27, the Crown issued a declaration ordering all delegates to join the National Assembly. The Second Estate dissolved and Lafayette was finally free. The king's order signaled the Estates-General would not be the *end* of the financial crisis, but the *beginning* of a political revolution to replace royal absolutism with a constitutional monarchy. The last eight weeks marked a momentous shift in the history of France. To his chagrin, Lafayette ultimately played no part in any of it.

THE KING SANCTIONING the National Assembly did not mean reactionary ultraroyalist forces would not plot a counterattack. In the first week of July 1789, just such a counterattack seemed imminent. With the king still withdrawn, Marie Antoinette, the comte d'Artois, and the minister of war covertly transferred soldiers into the environs of Paris and Versailles. After weeks of backing down, it seemed likely the Bourbons planned to retake the initiative by employing the only instrument of political legitimacy that has ever truly mattered: violent force.

Now a member of the National Assembly, Lafayette finally made his voice heard for the first time on July 8. He rose to support a motion protesting the troop deployments. He advised his colleagues to regard the moves with justified alarm: "The presence of troops brought up around this assembly is a fact, clear to everyone of us . . . as for the course to follow in such a case, I will not insult the assembly by supposing any of us can hesitate."[4] Lafayette, Mirabeau, and a handful of others delivered a petition of protest directly to the king. When they handed the petition over, Mirabeau said, "The danger, sire, threatens the tasks which are our primary duty, and that can have full success, real permanent success, only in so far as the people regard them as entirely free."[5] The king did not receive this delegation warmly. He said, "If you don't feel safe in Versailles, I invite you to retire to Soissons or Noyen."[6] Which is to say, exile in provincial backwaters.

Lafayette left the meeting feeling particularly sure the king and court planned to dissolve the National Assembly by force. He also believed he was now personally in danger. Believable rumors swirled that a conservative faction in the palace drafted proscription lists, with Lafayette's name at the top. Fearing arrest, Lafayette wrote urgently to Jefferson, saying the royal family "are very angry with me. . . . If they take me up you must claim me as an American citizen."[7]

In these uncertain and tense days, agents of the duc d'Orléans approached Lafayette. Just as there were believable rumors of a reactionary coup, there were believable rumors that behind *all* the turmoil and conflicts lay a plot by Orléans to force the abdication of his cousin Louis XVI, elevate the four-year-old *dauphin* to the throne, and make Orléans an all-powerful regent. Orléans would gladly accept a British-style constitutional monarchy for France, and by the time the child king came of age, the constitution would have been entrenched for twenty years.

One of Orléans's most influential agents was Mirabeau, who approached Lafayette and advised the need to join forces. "They tell me that the head of M. le duc d'Orléans and mine have been marked," Lafayette wrote Madame de Simiane. "That sinister plots have been set in motion against me, as the only one capable of commanding an army; that M. le duc d'Orléans and I should coordinate our efforts; that he should be the captain of my guard, and I of his." But Lafayette refused to be drawn into Orléans's web. "Orléans is in my eyes only a private individual, richer than I, whose future is no more important than that of other members of the minority." Lafayette, in fact, settled into a more fatalistic belief they would all soon be martyrs: "We must move ahead without bothering ourselves about the consequences and either build edifices or leave the materials behind us."[8]

If it was indeed the destiny of the National Assembly of 1789 to live a short life and die a quick death, Lafayette wanted to leave behind a statement of who they were and what they tried to do—a proclamation of the tragically martyred idealists of 1789 to ring throughout the ages. Mostly, Lafayette felt rotten about his lack of impact on the Estates-General so far. "It is natural that when twelve hundred Frenchmen are at work trying to write a constitution I should wish to be one of them," he wrote Simiane, "no matter how anxious I may be to do my duty, that duty must be in the forefront of the political battle."[9] He was desperate to make his mark. "I have prepared a declaration of rights," he told Simiane. "This declaration, or something very like it, will be the catechism of France."[10] Expecting arrest at practically any moment, Lafayette rushed to give France her first bill of rights.

LAFAYETTE HAD BEEN dreaming of a declaration of rights for years. At his home on rue de Bourbon he liked to show off a custom-made display case. On one side sat a copy of the American Declaration of Independence, on the other side a blank space. Lafayette told visitors it was where he would place the French constitution. Around January 1789 Lafayette began composing an enumerated list of rights in anticipation of the coming Estates-General. Now, in July 1789, when a committee tasked with drafting the constitution voted to include a preamble laying out the rights of the nation, Lafayette jumped at the chance to present his list. He relied on Jefferson to serve as a more sophisticated editor of his efforts, and on July 10 wrote his American friend, "Tomorrow I present my bill of rights about the middle of the sitting. Be pleased to consider it again, and make your observations . . . I beg you to answer as soon as you get up and wish to hear from you about eight or nine."[11]

On July 11, 1789, Lafayette stood up before the National Assembly to give them their first look at a declaration of rights. His object was not to deliver a novel work of political philosophy, but to capture and distill essential points bubbling in enlightened discourse. He later pointed to examples in England and the Netherlands as presaging his own efforts but, Lafayette being Lafayette, mostly credited America predecessors. He cited the Virginia Declaration of Rights, the Declaration of Independence, and the forthcoming Bill of Rights as his most immediate source of material. To say nothing of Jefferson's own thoughts and revisions, which Lafayette was happy to brag about.

Lafayette's final draft consisted of nine points that, taken together, explain what he meant when he said *liberty* and *equality*. He embarked for America using these words as abstract slogans devoid of deeper meaning. But after returning from the war, Lafayette turned his attention to intellectual reflection and social reform. He took seriously the question of how to define the abstract slogans in real world terms. Here, he gave the fullest and most detailed expression of what he meant. It reflected the core of the liberal revolutionary program Lafayette embodied. For the rest of his life, when asked to define his political philosophy, he said it was all there in the Declaration of the Rights of Man.[12]

Lafayette's draft opened: "*Nature made men free and equal.*" This simple statement was the heart of everything. It captured the spirit of the age. It was the intersection of the most advanced conclusions of science, philosophy, art, and literature. In politics it meant the old medieval order—of kings and subjects, lords and peasants, superiors and inferiors—must bow to the reality that, in the eyes of God, and laws of nature, all humans were born free and equal. But as Lafayette, the National Assembly, the Kingdom of France, and the entire world would discover soon enough, this declaration might be the concise distillation of the spirit of enlightened progress, but the meaning of each and every word was subject to a massive range of interpretation. Lafayette himself was already acknowledging the realities of France in 1789 by immediately qualifying his sweeping statement: "*The distinctions necessary for social order are based only on general utility.*" As was common for Lafayette, his abstract ideals were always to be fulfilled in the real world.

Lafayette then moved to the concrete parameters of those abstract ideals of liberty and equality: "*Every man is born with inalienable and imprescriptible rights . . . the freedom of his opinions, the care of his honor and his life, the right of property, the entire disposition of his person, of his industry, of all his faculties, the communication of his thoughts by any means possible, the pursuit of well-being, and resistance to oppression.*" This list summarized the basic features of political liberalism to this very day: freedom of speech, religion, press, and assembly. Individuals have the right to search for their own definition of happiness and use their intelligence and labor to achieve it free of hindrance or obstacles. At the end of this list, Lafayette included the provocative right to resist oppression if the state threatened these inalienable and imprescriptible rights.

But, of course, the exercise of liberty cannot be truly unchecked. Even the most zealous defender of individual rights acknowledges other people exist who *also* have individual rights. So Lafayette's third article stated: "*The exercise of natural rights has only those limits which ensure their enjoyment to other members of society.*" In the colloquial, we render this as "my right to swing my fist ends where your face begins." Here too, however, we find a source for infinite interpretation. When and where do these limits exist? When is the enjoyment of another person threatened? Who decides? How can a society define behavioral expectations and determine the punishment for transgressions?

Lafayette believed the partial answer lay in his fourth article: "*No man can be subject to laws except those agreed to by him or his representatives, previously promulgated and legally applied.*" A legislative assembly composed of the people's representatives is the only legitimate method of crafting and promulgating laws limiting freedom. But as with other basic concepts embedded in Lafayette's declaration of rights, words like "consent" and "representatives" are extremely problematic. For example, in just a few months the National Assembly would declare those who do not earn a certain amount of money were ineligible to participate in elections, assemblies, and lawmaking. Where were *their* representatives? Where was *their* consent? To say nothing of women, excluded entirely from everything. Did their lack of consent and representation mean they were free to invoke their inalienable and imprescriptible right to resist oppression?

Lafayette's declaration avoids these questions and moves on to a great redefinition of political sovereignty: "*All sovereignty resides in the nation. No body, no individual can have an authority that does not expressly emanate from it.*" This is one of the permanent political legacies of the Revolution: political sovereignty does not come from God, or genetic inheritance, or the individual contractual clauses of feudal lords woven together to form a crown. The nation is collectively sovereign and all authority springs from it. Those who wield power do so in the name of the nation, but they merely *wield* power, they do not *possess* it. Only the nation does.

Extrapolating from this point, Lafayette opens his sixth article by saying, "*All government has as its sole goal the common welfare.*" This too was in keeping with the latest in political philosophy and posed a direct challenge to prevailing ideology of royal absolutism. Government did not exist to exalt one family, or serve the commands of the Crown, but to broadly ensure collective welfare of the whole community. This was among the most basic tests of the social contract: is the government serving the common welfare or the interests of a privileged few?

To ensure the common good remained the object, Lafayette drew straight from Montesquieu to finish his point: "*This interest requires that the legislative, executive, and judicial powers be distinct and defined, and that their organization ensures the free representation of citizens, the accountability of the people, and the impartiality of judges.*" This is exactly the theory underpinning the recently ratified American Constitution, as Lafayette well knew from correspondence with his personal friends Hamilton, Madison, Jefferson, and Washington. They believed the best way to ensure the government did not become a tool of selfish despotism was to delineate different aspects of power and assign them to different institutions so they could never all be wielded by a single tyrant.

As to what those separated powers legislated, executed, and adjudicated, Lafayette's seventh article states: "*Laws must be clear, precise, uniform for all citizens.*" This is one of the key practical expressions of *equality*: equality before the law. Nobles and peasants, Catholics and Protestants, men and women, rich and poor, all must live under a single, uniform system of laws. This was a particularly necessary reform for France. Historically, different authorities in the kingdom claimed different jurisdictional powers. They often overlapped and contradicted each other. Laws and regulations were opaque and often unpublished. And they could always be overturned, extended, or invented out of thin air by the whims of the monarch. The law must be made clear, uniform, and equal for all.

One of the most important subsets of the law, and indeed, the cause of the rolling political crisis, was taxes. Lafayette believed taxes must be levied by a representative assembly and fall equally on all citizens: "*Taxes must be freely granted and proportionally distributed.*" Lafayette believed in the American principle of "no taxation without representation" and also sought to end, as a matter of justice and rationality, the insane policy of the rich paying almost nothing while the poor were squeezed to the last drop. This was another practical expression of *equality*. Not just equality before the judge, but also the tax collector.

Finally, Lafayette ended his list by declaring what he and his colleagues did in 1789 must never be considered the final word—fixed for all time and not subject to revision: "*As the introduction of abuses, and the rights of the generations which follow, may require the revision of any human establishment, it must be possible for the nation to have, in certain cases, an extraordinary convocation of deputies, the sole purpose of which is to examine and correct, if necessary, the defects of the constitution."* This last article admitted nothing humans did was perfect. Lafayette and the National Assembly were not flawless sages or legislative gods. Lafayette fully expected future generations would uncover plenty of mistakes, abuses, and insufficiencies in their work. Believing one of the most fundamental rights of the nation was the right to self-government, Lafayette believed the living must not be ruled by the tyrannical hand of the dead.

Lafayette did not flatter himself that what he presented to the National Assembly on July 11, 1789, was anything but a starting point to be revised, extended, or corrected. He said explicitly he hoped this "first attempt of mine will induce other members to present other projects."[13] And that's exactly what happened. Lafayette's draft would *not* be the final version of the famous Declaration of the Rights of Man and of the Citizen. But most of his articles found their way into the final version. In the future, he called them nothing less than "the profession of my faith, fruit of my past, pledge of my future."[14] And it was true. Despite barbs from detractors who claimed Lafayette was an empty-headed fool, he *did* have a political philosophy guiding his actions—a philosophy neatly summarized in his declaration of rights. But one cannot remove his work from the immediate political crisis. Reflecting back on events a decade later, he also called his declaration of rights "at the same time a manifesto and an ultimatum."[15] If the National Assembly was about to fall to the forces of a despotic king, the ideals they represented—now specifically spelled out by Lafayette—would stand for eternity.

⊣⊢

LAFAYETTE AND HIS declaration of rights enjoyed center stage for less than twenty-four hours. His speech and list of enumerated rights were printed and distributed in Paris. It appeared like they would define political conversations for weeks to come. But instead, shocking news hit Paris the next day, pushing Lafayette out of the spotlight: Jacques Necker had been fired.

Ever since the financial crisis erupted in 1786, Necker stood as an icon of popular reform, the financial wonder boy who could save the king from himself. When the king ran out of money in 1788, the bankers of Paris made Necker's return to the ministry a nonnegotiable condition of bailing the king out. Over the past year, Necker always counseled reform and conciliation in opposition to conservative voices in the royal family. His abrupt dismissal was concrete proof reactionary conservatives had taken firm hold of the king's ear. The rumors of a coup must be true. The king was removing Necker to make way for counterrevolution.

The news electrified Paris. Over the past few months the emotional temperature of the city rose with the summer heat. There had already been a riot in April at the Réveillon wallpaper factory in the working class Faubourg Saint-Antoine. To stop the destructive looting, soldiers fired on the crowd, leaving at least fifty dead. Arthur Young, an English agriculturalist making a tour of France, was in Paris in early 1789 and described the packed cafés of the Palais-Royal:

> The coffee-houses in the Palais Royal present yet more singular and astonishing spectacles; they are not only crowded within, but other expectant crowds are at the doors and windows, listening . . . to certain orators, who from chairs or tables harangue each his little audience: the eagerness with which they are heard, and the thunder of applause they receive for every sentiment of more than common hardiness or violence against the present government, cannot easily be imagined. I am all amazement at the ministry permitting such nests and hotbeds of sedition and revolt, which disseminate amongst the people, every hour, principles that by and by must be opposed with vigor, and therefore it seems little short of madness to allow the propagation at present.[16]

Young leaves no doubt the Revolution in the street was already gaining momentum.

For months, the Parisians cheered the daily updates from Versailles: the strike of the Third Estate, the Tennis Court Oath, the formation of the National Assembly. The rumors of counterrevolution ran as hot in Paris as they did in Versailles. Necker's dismissal was taken as the opening shot of that conservative counterattack. On the night of July 12, 1789, Camille Desmoulins mounted a table at a café in the Palais-Royal and, with passionate conviction and exaggerated poetic license, told a

fast-gathering audience the king already made his move. As Desmoulins waved a pistol for effect, he said soldiers were coming to crush the
people—he could see them even now lurking outside the Palais-Royal.
"To arms!" came the cry, as the people poured out into the streets to
defend themselves. The political revolution pushed by salon revolutionaries in Versailles was now backed by an armed uprising of street
revolutionaries in Paris.

Gouverneur Morris happened to be in a carriage nearby and witnessed the confrontation at the Tuileries Garden between the Parisians
and soldiers. "All at once the carriages and horses and foot passengers
turn about and pass rapidly," he recorded in his diary.

> Presently after we meet a body of cavalry, with their sabers drawn
> and coming half speed. . . . The people take post among the stones
> which lie scattered about the whole place, being then hewn for the
> bridge now building. The officer at the head of the party is saluted
> by a stone, and immediately turns his horse in a menacing man-
> ner toward the assailant. . . . He pursues his route, and the pace is
> soon increased to a gallop, amid a shower of stones. . . . They fired
> several pistols, but without effect; probably they were not even
> charged with ball. A party of the Swiss Guards are posted in the
> Champs-Élysées with cannon.[17]

Things only got worse as the days progressed. Morris witnessed the
Parisians preparing for war: "The little city of Paris is in as fine a tumult as anyone could wish. They are getting arms wherever they can
find any; seize 600 barrels of powder in a boat on the Seine; break into
the Monastery of St. Lazare, and find a store of grain which the holy
brotherhood has laid in. Immediately it is put into carts and sent to the
market, and in every cart a friar. The *Garde-Meuble du Roi* is attacked,
and the arms are delivered up to prevent worse consequences."[18]

In the midst of the uprising, the Third Estate electoral assembly,
who selected the city's delegates for the Estates-General, reconvened in
the Hôtel de Ville and declared themselves an emergency government.
They called for citizens to arm themselves and form militia companies
to defend Paris against attack, maintain law and order, and protect grain

supplies. There was already talk the only man capable of leading this citizen militia was the marquis de Lafayette, the Hero of Two Worlds, who combined military experience with unimpeachable popular credentials. Sitting with his fellow Parisians electors, Condorcet praised Lafayette as "a character from a novel who, by the brilliance of his adventures, his youth, his figure and his fame, can enchant, so to speak, the imaginations, and rally all popular interests to it."[19]

⊰⊱

IN VERSAILLES, THE delegates of the National Assembly were forced to continuously respond to news from Paris at least twelve hours old. On July 13, Lafayette supported sending another deputation to beg His Majesty to withdraw the troops from Paris. This deputation returned with ominous news. The king told them curtly, "I have already made known my intentions regarding the measures the disorders of Paris have forced me to take. . . . It is for me alone to judge their necessity." When the delegation tried to press the matter, Louis dismissed them: "I have nothing to add."[20] Clearly the king did not consider the National Assembly partners in government. They should probably, in fact, consider themselves as much in the crosshairs as the mobs in Paris.

Now believing if they adjourned on the night of July 13 they would wake up on July 14 to find the doors of the assembly hall locked and guarded by soldiers, the National Assembly voted to remain in emergency session. Unfortunately, the presiding officer was an elderly archbishop not prepared to oversee an all-night vigil. So the delegates hastily elected a vice president for this critical midnight emergency: the marquis de Lafayette. Accepting the appointment to thunderous applause, Lafayette said: "My chief duty is never to separate myself from your efforts to maintain peace and confirm public liberty."[21] He braced himself with fatalistic purpose: "The constitution will be, even if we shall no longer be."[22] He was more convinced than ever he had turned in his declaration of rights just under the wire.

When dawn arrived on July 14, 1789, without any dramatic confrontations, Lafayette scribbled a note to Simiane: "The vice-presidency has earned me a sleepless night. I asked whether it was not appropriate to end the session; we proved that we would not separate. The majority shouted that it was necessary to stay. Many members of the municipalities, several members of the nobility and clergy paced the room while I dozed on a bench." This note continued with his assessment of what lay ahead, which, in retrospect, is hilariously incongruous with historical reality: "We are told from Paris that everything is quiet . . . I imagine we will have a deputation from the city this morning . . . I hope we will go to bed, because we only have rumors from Paris and those are appeased now."[23]

Paris was *not* free of the possibility of further disturbances. They were, in fact, in the throes of one of the most famous popular disturbances in world history. At six o'clock in the evening, Lafayette received the first inkling of the momentous events unfolding in Paris. A messenger told Lafayette and the other delegates a crowd was gathering in front of the Bastille, demanding the governor of the fortress surrender to the people. The delegates received this update knowing the information was at least twelve hours old. What on earth had already happened in the meantime? After midnight, they received their answer: the mob stormed the Bastille, the guards opened fire, and at least a hundred lay dead. In retaliation, the people breached the gates, seized the governor, and summarily executed him. They stabbed and shot him, then mounted his severed head on a pike. Paris remained in a state of lawless chaos. It was unfathomable.

The king himself was awoken at two o'clock in the morning. In an apocryphal but widely repeated account, Louis asked the messenger, "Is it a revolt?" To which the reply came, "No sire, it is a revolution."[24]

CHAPTER THIRTEEN

I REIGN IN PARIS

[1789]

A T ELEVEN O'CLOCK IN THE MORNING ON JULY 15, 1789, King Louis XVI appeared in the main assembly hall of the Hôtel des Menus-Plaisirs du Roi to address the National Assembly. There was no pomp or ceremony. No entourage. No protocol. No haughty reminders of his divine authority. He was flanked only by his two brothers, the comte de Provence and the comte d'Artois. He wore neither robe nor crown. He did not sit to address his subjects, and certainly did not lie in a bed and fall asleep.

When he spoke, the king addressed the delegates for the first time as "the National Assembly," a phrase he usually avoided. Then he read a list of peace offerings. To end the immediate crisis, he announced the withdrawal of all troops from Paris. He also promised to recall Jacques Necker to the ministry, reform the criminal code, abolish *corvée* labor, and ban judicial torture. These were all popular measures designed to soothe the people of Paris. To win over the National Assembly, Louis promised to recognize the nation's right to send delegates to a regularly convening assembly that would share responsibility for government, with specific power over taxation and state budgets. These were all measures the king previously resisted. Obviously things had changed.

Lafayette knew exactly what changed. "The cause of the people triumphed when the Bastille was taken," he said.[1] And though the king addressed himself to the National Assembly delegates, it is clear the people were the authors of their own triumph. Lafayette and his friends tried for years to extract the reforms the king now promised. But the king did not meet their demands until the people of Paris rose in uncontainable revolt. It was an early example of a recurring revolutionary dynamic: the salon revolutionaries only achieved their objectives by leveraging the danger posed by the street revolutionaries. Would the king have offered his list of concessions on July 15 absent the fall of the Bastille? No. But when faced with the loss of *all* his authority, the demands of liberal reformers in the National Assembly seemed tame by comparison.

To transmit the wonderful news, a procession of assembly delegates filling forty carriages departed for Paris. At their head rode the two most popular and well-known leaders: the astronomer turned president of the National Assembly, Jean-Sylvain Bailly, and the Hero of Two Worlds, the marquis de Lafayette. Upon arriving in Paris, they proceeded to the Hôtel de Ville, where Bailly read the king's concessions to a hall packed with Paris electors, National Assembly delegates, and other observers. Bailly's speech concluded to shouts of "Vive le roi!" and "Vive la nation!"

The Paris electors, now declaring themselves the legitimate municipal council of Paris, elected Bailly the first ever mayor of Paris. Then they turned to Lafayette and appointed him leader of their improvised citizen militia. The record of the meeting reported: "All voices joined together to proclaim Monsieur le marquis de Lafayette commander-general of the Paris militia."[2] The report continued, "M. le marquis de la Fayette, accepting this honor with all the signs of respect and gratitude, drew his sword and took an oath to sacrifice his life for the preservation of precious liberty."[3] One of the leaders of the Paris council, Médéric-Louis-Élie Moreau de Saint-Méry, rose and said he was thrilled. "The defense of French freedom could be entrusted to the illustrious defender of the freedom of the new world."[4] Moreau de Saint-Méry would know, as he himself came from that new world. Born and raised in the Caribbean colony of Martinique, he was leader of an influential lobby defending the rights of French Caribbean plantation owners—most especially blocking all efforts to abolish slavery for the next four years. He proved it was not just Anglo-Americans who overlooked the hypocrisy of liberty and slavery when it suited their interests.

Lafayette's appointment to lead the Paris militia marked a major transformation in his life, career, and role in the French Revolution. Though he never resigned his seat in the National Assembly, Lafayette's time would now be spent serving as commander general of the National Guard. This job demanded he simultaneously defend liberty and preserve order. Walking the line between liberty and order became the defining challenge of Lafayette's life. It was a treacherous path taking him first to the peak of glory, then leading him off a cliff to his doom.

⊰⊱

LAFAYETTE WAS NOT blind to the difficulties posed by his new assignment. That very afternoon he faced an opening test. A self-proclaimed militia captain from the Cordeliers district—a particularly radical neighborhood on the Left Bank—led a company of armed volunteers to inspect the Bastille to ensure it was properly secured for the people. Upon arrival, the militia captain challenged the credentials of the official appointed by the Paris council to supervise the fortress. After an unsatisfactory exchange, the militia company arrested the official and hauled him back to the Hôtel de Ville to see if his story checked out. Lafayette set the official free, chastised the self-appointed militia captain, and ordered him to return to his district. This was Lafayette's first encounter with future revolutionary leader and persistent nemesis Georges Danton. It would not be his last.

Things only got harder as an insane whirlwind of activity consumed Lafayette. Crowds, mobs, and gangs paraded through the streets while Lafayette rushed from emergency to emergency. He mostly defused the crowds and wrote Madame de Simiane on July 16, "The people, in their enthusiastic delirium, can only be moderated by me. Forty thousand souls assemble, then, when the fermentation is at its height, I appear, and a word from me disperses them. I have already saved the lives of six people who were to be hanged in different quarters." But he was aware of how precarious the situation was. "This frenzied, drunken people will not always listen to me," he said. "At the moment I write this, eighty thousand people surround the Hôtel-de-Ville and say they are being deceived, that the troops are not withdrawing, and the king must come." He summed up his position: "I reign in Paris. But it is over a furious people driven by abominable cabals."[5]

The numbers Lafayette mentions speak to one of the key differences between the American and French revolutions. When rebellious sentiments rose in Boston in the early 1770s, the total population of the city was perhaps fifteen thousand. The numbers involved in direct revolutionary agitation were a mere fraction of that number. In Paris in 1789, Lafayette reported facing five times as many people *as the entire population of Boston*, gathered in one place at one time. These immense numbers meant if the crowd became agitated, they could not be contained. To compare Boston and Paris is to compare a minnow to a whale. Controlling Boston was never an easy task. Controlling Paris proved nearly impossible.

To quell the immediate disturbances, Lafayette concluded the king must come to Paris. Despite the announcement of concessions, the people feared it was a trick. When this request was transmitted to Versailles, Marie Antoinette begged Louis not to go. But the king insisted and said—to convince himself as much as his wife—he would be safe among his people. So on July 17, three days after the fall of the Bastille, King Louis XVI climbed into a carriage bound for Paris. In truth, he did not know whether he would be embraced or torn to pieces.

At the gates of Paris, a delegation led by Bailly and Lafayette greeted him. Bailly presented the king with the keys to the city, saying, "I bring Your Majesty the keys to the good city of Paris." Bailly then alluded to King Henry IV, the wise and flexible founder of the Bourbon dynasty, who famously entered a hostile Paris in 1593 and skillfully turned potential enemies into loving subjects. "These are the same keys presented to Henry IV," Bailly told Louis. "He regained his people; here it is the people who have regained their king."[6]

As Louis entered the city, a company of Lafayette's militia surrounded his carriage. The king's life was now in Lafayette's hands. Gouverneur Morris, watching from the crowd, later reported to George Washington, "He had his Sovereign, during the late procession to Paris, completely within his power. He marched him where he pleased; measured out the degree of applause he should receive as he pleased; and if he pleased could have detained him prisoner."[7] But Lafayette meant the king no harm. They had known each other for twenty years. Despite their recent political estrangement, Lafayette did not want anything to happen to Louis. In fact, Lafayette said, "the day he surrendered to me, I became more devoted to his service than if he had promised me half his kingdom."[8] But Lafayette also swore not to compromise his principles. He once did that to secure election to the Estates-General and considered it a huge mistake. "If the king refuses the constitution, I will fight him," he said. "If he accepts it, I will defend him."[9]

As they rode through Paris, crowds mobbed every street. The Parisians themselves seemed unsure whether to embrace Louis or tear him to pieces. Jefferson observed, "About 60,000 citizens, of all forms and colors, [were] armed with the muskets of the Bastille and Invalides as far as they would go, the rest with pistols, swords, pikes, pruning hooks, scythes."[10] At the Hôtel de Ville, Bailly ushered the king up the steps, through an honor guard of Parisian leaders. Inside, Louis sat on a throne in front of a packed hall. Bailly handed the king a cockade—the decorative red-and-blue emblem already becoming the visual symbol of the Revolution. Louis pinned the cockade to his breast—an action speaking louder than any words. The king was *not* here to fight or resist; he was here to embrace and accept. The crowd applauded and shouted "Vive le roi!" and "Vive la nation!" The king affirmed Bailly as mayor and later reconnected with Lafayette, telling the marquis, "I have been looking for you, to let you know I confirm your nomination to the post of commander-general of the National Guard."[11] These confirmations indicated the king was ready to go along with the Revolution. Hopes now ran high tempers would subside. With peace restored, the National Assembly would draft a constitution and the king would accept it. The Revolution would be over by fall . . . winter at the latest.

⚞⚟

BUT WITHIN DAYS of the reconciliation between Paris and the king, tempers flared again. Angry mobs tracked down and captured two particularly hated royal officials: Joseph-François Foullon de Doué and Louis Bertier de Sauvigny. Foullon was a seventy-four-year-old arch-conservative who replaced the beloved Necker as minister of finance. The accepted anecdote in the street was that during a discussion of the famine conditions in Paris, Foullon casually remarked, "The people will be happy if we give them hay to eat."[12] It is not clear whether he said this with malice, concern, or whether he said it at all. But it didn't matter—the story spread. Bertier, meanwhile, was both Foullon's son-in-law and the *Intendant* of Paris—leader of the royal authorities in the city. People widely suspected Bertier of making a fortune in grain speculation during the long hungry winter—exploiting his office to get rich off their empty bellies.

During the recent riots, both men judiciously slipped into hiding and attempted to flee Paris. Foullon went so far as to fake his own death, but was betrayed by an angry tenant on the outskirts of Paris. The old man was arrested and transferred to the Hôtel de Ville, where an angry mob congregated, calling for Foullon's head. Alerted to the emergency, Lafayette arrived and chastised the crowd. "You want to kill this man without judgment!" Lafayette shouted. "That is an injustice which dishonors you and tarnishes all my efforts for liberty . . . I demand respect for the law, without which there is no liberty, without which I would not have supported the revolution in the new world, and without which I will not support the revolution here."[13] Summary execution without evidence, testimony, or appeal—whether inflicted by a single despot or an angry mob—was exactly the kind of tyranny Lafayette believed the Revolution needed to abolish. "I am not saying I will save him if he is guilty," Lafayette promised, but first there *must* be a trial.[14]

For the first time, the crowd ignored Lafayette's lecture. Unsatisfied with the pace of justice, they forced their way into the Hôtel de Ville, seized Foullon, and dragged him back outside. Without further delay or formality, they strung the old man up from a lamppost to hang. When the first attempts failed because the rope was too weak, a small group in front simply set upon Foullon, stabbed him to death, cut off his head, and mounted it on a pike. Someone brought out a handful of straw and shoved it into the dead man's mouth—to see who was happy to eat hay *now*.

The lynching of Foullon was only half the story. By sheer coincidence, a tumbrel bearing his son-in-law Bertier happened to roll past. He too had been apprehended and was being transferred to prison to stand trial. When the crowd spotted him, they swarmed the cart. They waved the pike with his father-in-law's head in his face. After a few minutes of emotional torture, Bertier too was dragged from the cart, lynched, and his head mounted on a pike. The jubilant crowd triumphantly paraded both heads through the streets. One man ran into the Hôtel de Ville waving a bloody piece of meat and shouting, "Here is Bertier's heart!"[15]

Lafayette was distraught. Only a week into the job, he already lost control of the city. He did not mourn the deaths of Foullon and Bertier so much as the death of the rule of law. He swore to restore order to Paris, and failed. Lafayette did not, in fact, reign in Paris. In his mind, there was only one thing to do: he submitted his resignation. "The people did not heed my advice," he told the leaders of Paris, "and the day I lose their confidence, as I said beforehand, I must leave a post where I can no longer be of use."[16] They were shocked and not a little frightened. Who else could do the job?

Later that day, Lafayette drafted an anguished letter to Simiane. "My embarrassments only increase," he wrote. "You cannot picture the dismay my resignation has caused. All the districts beg me to stay; they threw themselves on their knees, cried, swore to obey me in everything. What to do? I am in despair . . . if I stay I am in the terrible situation of seeing evil without being able to remedy it."[17] The leaders of Paris begged him to reconsider. They swore, "We, the electors of all the districts of Paris, reflecting the unanimous acclimation of all the citizens of Paris and our entire confidence in the virtues, talents, and patriotism of Monsieur de Lafayette, again proclaim him general of the National Guard . . . so that his zeal, seconded by all patriotic citizens, may lead to the perfection of the great work of public liberty."[18] Then they offered a salary of 120,000 *livres* for a year, and a 100,000 livre expense account if he would stay.

Lafayette retracted his resignation. But when he returned to his post, he followed Washington's example and refused to accept the salary. "When so many citizens suffer and so many expenditures are necessary," he said, "it is repugnant to me to augment them unnecessarily. My fortune is sufficient for the state in which I live, and my time does not permit official entertaining."[19] It was a strong show of civic generosity and self-abnegation. His financial managers gritted their teeth as their master's fortune dwindled further. Adrienne, meanwhile, returned to a state of constant worry. Her husband was no longer across an ocean fighting a war, yet the danger seemed greater than ever. Virginie wrote, "Not once in those days did she see him leave the house without feeling that she might be saying her adieu for the last time."[20]

⊰⊱

LAFAYETTE SPENT THE following weeks bringing order to the Paris militias, which now adopted their permanent historical name: the National Guard. In the chaotic atmosphere of mid-July, anyone with a gun was called to arms, but now they must become a regularized force. Lafayette recruited friends and fellow veterans of the American war to form a reliable officer corps. He drafted rules and regulations to properly organize just over thirty thousand men into six divisions. Lafayette's regulations stipulated the uniforms, flags, equipment, and other *accoutrement* necessary for each guardsman and every company. He also expected them to follow his example of civic virtue. Though a few members of the National Guard earned salaries, the vast majority were expected to voluntarily provide their own weapons, uniforms, and equipment. This effectively purged from the ranks anyone too poor to pay their own way. The National Guard, true to its original name, "*Garde bourgeoise*," would be a militia drawn principally from the prosperous middle classes. Even as he imposed these rules, Lafayette understood how delicate the situation was. "I may seem to be their chief," he wrote, "but I am very far from being their master."[21]

In designing the uniforms of the National Guard, Lafayette made perhaps his most lasting contribution not just to the Revolution, but to the history of France. In the riots of July, militiamen needed a way to identify themselves in the streets. At first, they donned green sprigs, cockades, or strips of cloth—as green was the color of liberty. But after someone pointed out green was also the color of the despised comte d'Artois, they switched to red and blue, the colors of the city of Paris.

When Lafayette formalized the uniforms of the National Guard in late July 1789, he added the white of the Bourbons to signal the new unity of the king and the nation. National Guard regulations henceforth stipulated all hats must bear, "a cockade of white dimity piped with blue and red."[22] Keenly aware of the power of symbolism, Lafayette understood the momentous work they were doing creating the visual symbols of liberty and equality: "I place before you a cockade which will go around the world; and an institution, civil and military at the same time, which is bound to triumph over the old tactics of Europe and which will reduce arbitrary governments to the alternative of being conquered unless they imitate it."[23] Thus the blue, white, and red tricolor cockade was born, which became the symbol not just of the National Guard specifically, but the French Revolution generally, and remains the national colors of France to this very day.

As Lafayette worked to win the loyalty and obedience of the National Guard, Adrienne helped as much as she could. Their home became a *de facto* headquarters with men and officers constantly coming and going. "My mother did the honors of her home to charm her numerous guests," Virginie recalled. "All through that time she was sustained by my father's principles, and was so wholly convinced of his power to do good and prevent evil that she endured with unbelievable strength of character the constant dangers to which he was exposed."[24] It was often said the National Guardsmen were more loyal to Adrienne than her husband. But her faith was not blind. She probably apprehended better than her husband the dangers lying ahead. "What she suffered in the depths of her heart can only be judged by those who listened to her," Virginie recalled. "She saw my father at the head of a revolution whose end it was impossible to predict. . . . No one was more terrified by the perils of those she loved."[25]

⚜

As THE LAFAYETTES toiled in Paris, the Revolution raced forward all around them. Cities throughout France copied the example of Paris. Third Estate electoral assemblies reconvened and declared themselves to be the legitimate municipal authorities. They organized their own local militia companies, which would soon be folded into the larger

National Guard structure created by Lafayette. In some places, royal authorities acquiesced peacefully; in others, they fought and resisted. But within a matter of weeks, most of the cities of France were under new leadership.

Meanwhile, even greater revolutionary energy burst out of the rural countryside. Carried away by rumors that the collapse of political authority meant they would soon fall prey either to criminal brigands or reactionary local lords, villagers armed themselves in self-defense. Later dubbed the Great Fear, the peasants' dread of chaotic lawlessness ironically *provoked* a wave of chaotic lawlessness. Having spent nearly two years on the brink of starvation, armed villagers descended on local châteaux to raid livestock, grain, bread, cheese, and wine. They also located registries of feudal obligations and debts and burned them in great heaping bonfires. If the people found noble families and their agents on the premises, they told them to simply stand aside and not get in the way. The main target of peasant wrath was paper and ink, not flesh and bone.

As the Great Fear spread, the delegates of the National Assembly did not know how to respond. It seemed as if the whole kingdom was crashing down and going up in flames. A clique of radicals, however, saw an opportunity to simultaneously quell the unrest *and* advance the Revolution. On the night of August 4, 1789, vicomte de Noailles, Lafayette's oldest friend, stepped to the tribunal of the National Assembly and proposed the complete abolition of noble privilege. The hope was a dramatic, sweeping gesture would pacify the raging countryside. But "noble privilege" was not, in and of itself, a legal category. It was a phrase used to describe a disjointed bundle of laws, customs, rules, and regulations built up over centuries. Tax exemptions, religious tithes, poaching laws, travel restrictions, and market fees all needed to be struck down individually. So Noailles's broad proposal kicked off a delirious all-night session of delegates rising, proposing, seconding, and affirming the elimination of each individual privilege in turn. One conservative delegate who watched in astonished horror wrote home, "It would have been useless, even dangerous, to oppose the general will of the nation. It would have designated you and your possessions to be victims of the fury of the multitude; it would have been safe to set your house on fire."[26] In just a few hours' work, the National Assembly effectively declared the entire legal apparatus of medieval feudalism null and void. When it was all over, the assembly was left to pick through the practical implementation of their antifeudal bender, but the implications of the Night of August 4 were clear: whatever new constitution emerged from the National Assembly, it would not be a few tweaks to the existing system, but an entirely new political, legal, and social order.

To help define the terms of the new order, a committee under the editorial direction of Abbé Sieyès and Mirabeau compiled a final version of a declaration of rights. Lafayette was so busy in Paris he did not take part in the final drafting, but was gratified to find the final seventeen-point list included almost all of his original articles. On August 26, 1789, the National Assembly approved a final document titled "The Declaration of the Rights of Man and of the Citizen." It was meant to serve specifically as the preamble to the new constitution, but more broadly, it served as the guiding light of postrevolutionary France.

⫛

DESPITE THESE PROMISING developments, bitter controversies still divided the National Assembly. Conservatives suggested, as a part of the checks and balances of the new constitution, the king have the right to veto proposed legislation. This was a power granted to the newly created president of the United States, and many moderates considered it seemed eminently reasonable. But radicals leapt to their feet. They argued the king was no republican president elected by the people to serve a temporary and fixed term. If the king of France was given a blanket universal veto, he could simply prevent the National Assembly from passing any legislation he disapproved of. They would all be back at square one. In the streets, the term "veto" was little understood, and the radical presses encouraged the most frightening reading of the obscure term. "The king will say *veto*," one broadsheet declared, "and you will have no bread."[27]

Lafayette, concerned about the intensity of the battle, attempted to reconcile the two factions. On August 25, he wrote Thomas Jefferson, "I beg for liberty's sake you will break every engagement to give us a dinner tomorrow Wednesday . . . being the only means to prevent a total dissolution and a civil war. The difficulty between them is the king's veto. Some want it absolute, others will have no veto. . . . If they don't agree in a few days, we shall have no great majority in a favor of any plan, and it must end in a war. . . . These gentlemen wish to consult you and me, they will dine tomorrow at your house as mine is always full."[28] This was not exactly the sort of meeting a credentialed foreign ambassador should be hosting, but Jefferson agreed.

On August 26, the same evening the Declaration of the Rights of Man was finally ratified, eight delegates representing both sides in the veto fight met for dinner at Jefferson's house. In his autobiography, Jefferson recounted:

> These were leading patriots, of honest but differing opinions, sensible of the necessity of effecting a coalition by mutual sacrifices, knowing each other, and not afraid therefore to unbosom themselves mutually. . . . The marquis introduced the objects of the conference by summarily reminding them of the state of things in the assembly, the course which the principles of the constitution was taking, and the inevitable result, unless checked by more concord among the patriots themselves. . . . [Lafayette] observed that although he also had his opinion, he was ready to sacrifice it to that of his brethren of the same cause: but that a common opinion must now be formed.[29]

They proceeded to debate each other for the next six hours. "During which time," Jefferson said, "I was a silent witness to a coolness and candor of argument unusual in the conflicts of political opinion; to a logical reasoning, and chaste eloquence, disfigured by no gaudy tinsel of rhetoric or declamation, and truly worthy of being placed in parallel with the finest dialogue of antiquity, as handed to us by Xenophon, by Plato, and Cicero."[30] In the end, they hammered out a hopeful compromise. The king would be granted a *suspensive* veto: the right to delay, but not ultimately stop legislation. Lafayette was relieved rational debate and a commitment to national unity prevailed.

With feudalism dismantled, the Declaration of Rights enshrined, and the king sporting a cockade on his breast, Lafayette believed all that was left to do was wrap up the revolution peacefully. It seemed reasonable to believe the French Revolution would be confined to one crazy, dangerous, but ultimately happy summer of 1789. Lafayette was already turning his attention to following the narrative arc established by George Washington. "I shall decline no burden, no danger," he said, "provided the moment calm is restored, I may rest."[31] Talleyrand found this posture forced and rubbing awkwardly against Lafayette's true nature: "His ambitions, and his efforts to distinguish himself, do not seem to be his own, but rather to have been taught to him. Whatever he does seems foreign to his nature. He always acts as though he follows someone else's advice."[32]

But even if he was following someone else's advice, Lafayette repeated the same wishes consistently in the early fall of 1789. Morris confirmed, "[Lafayette] tells me . . . he has had the utmost power his heart could wish that is grown tired of it . . . he wishes therefore, as soon as possible, to return to private life."[33] To Simiane, Lafayette wrote, "My situation is truly extraordinary. Here I am at the center of a great adventure and the only thing I really want is to get out of it, free from all reproach at having indulged any thoughts of personal ambition, and, having put everything to rights, to withdraw into obscurity at a quarter of my fortune which was mine when I came into the world." He in fact claimed, "I have only one ambition—to return to zero."[34]

As it turned out, Lafayette's hopes for the end of the Revolution and a peaceful retirement were ridiculously premature. He was nowhere near the end of his labors, nor could he fathom how far he would fall. Before this was all over, Lafayette *would* find himself returned to zero— penniless, nameless, and abandoned in the depths of a dungeon.

CHAPTER FOURTEEN

TO VERSAILLES OR
TO THE LAMPPOST

[1789]

HOSTING THE COMPROMISE DINNER WAS AMONG THE LAST things Thomas Jefferson did before returning home to the United States in September 1789. On the eve of his departure, he wrote a final assessment of the political situation in France to John Jay, then serving as secretary of state. Jefferson worried about division between the two patriotic factions he hosted because ultraroyalist defenders of the *ancien régime* and opportunistic agents of the duc d'Orléans both lurked in the tall grass. Jefferson hoped whatever their minor differences, the two patriotic factions would ultimately stick together to defend the Revolution. He believed Lafayette critical to this project: "His attachment to both is equal, and he labors incessantly to keep them together. . . . His command of the armed militia of Paris . . . and his influence with the municipality, would secure this city. . . . This turn of things is so probable that I do not think either section of the patriots will venture on any act which will place themselves in opposition to him."[1]

But it wasn't just scheming aristocrats who concerned Jefferson: "The patience of the people, who have less of that quality than any other nation in the world, is worn threadbare." This was understandable, because at the top of the list of things causing such talk was "the scarcity of bread which continues [to be] very great amidst a plenty of corn." Jefferson worried, "The want of bread, were it to produce a commencement of disorder, might ally itself to more permanent causes of discontent, and thus continue the effect beyond its first cause." On the whole though, Jefferson left Paris hopeful: "I do not see it as yet probable that any actual commotion will take place. And if it does take place I have strong confidence that the patriotic party will hold together, and their party in the nation be what I have described it."[2]

His countryman Gouverneur Morris agreed with much of this, though he was more pessimistic. The ever-cynical Morris saw attempts to keep Parisians fed subordinated to self-interest of greedy officials. The leaders of Paris spent their days "casting about for ways to make money on the present distress."[3] Morris also detected the machinations of Orléans to keep hearts inflamed, observing the duc was "plunging himself into debts and difficulties to support the present factious temper."[4] The situation was bad, and being badly managed, but agitators actively pushed toward the most explosive possible conclusion.

With the benefit of hindsight, Lafayette looked back on the fall of 1789 and mostly concurred with his American friends: "Three intrigues were going on at the same time. The court, the Orléans party, and that which later took the name Jacobin. The last two often acted together . . . the Jacobins wanted to make themselves feared; the Orléanists to keep undercover; the court helped them both by their mistakes."[5] All three men described the combination of elements that previously exploded in July 1789. Thomas Jefferson left France believing no further explosions would take place. Then he sailed home on the eve of one of the greatest commotions of the whole revolution: the Women's March on Versailles.

⁕

DESPITE HIS PUBLIC gestures, King Louis was not happy about the cockade pinned to his breast. In public, he played the part of citizen king. In private, he seethed with humiliated resentment. In the months following the fall of the Bastille, conservative friends, family members, and advisers encouraged him to nurse his resentments rather than transcend them. Some in the royal circle were so opposed to the course of the Revolution they quit the kingdom in protest. Just days after the fall of the Bastille, the comte d'Artois packed up his family and left the country, becoming the first of the *émigrés*—nobles who fled the Revolution out of fear, anger, or disgust. From self-imposed exile, Artois lobbied the other crowned heads of Europe to rescue the king of France from the people of France.

Louis himself refused to consider leaving. But that did not mean he was done fighting for his divine rights. In the autumn of 1789, Louis settled into a game of provocative foot-dragging over the Night of August 4 and the Declaration of the Rights of Man. The National Assembly may have voted for a pile of great reforms to rapturous applause, but those reforms did not take legal effect until the king affixed his signature. Rather than sign, Louis lobbed complaints and protests back at the National Assembly. He said their grandiose proclamations conflicted with fundamental laws of the realm and ignored ancient property rights. Until the assembly addressed his concerns, he would not sign.

The more radical presses of Paris warned the king was stalling until another counterrevolutionary coup could be staged. Among those raising the alarm was Jacques-Pierre Brissot, who returned from his sojourn in the United States and restarted his career in journalism. He founded a newspaper called *Le Patriote français* to push France in a democratic and egalitarian direction. His paper published contributions from the same group of liberal reformers who joined the abolition movement like the marquis de Condorcet, Étienne Clavière, and Abbé Grégoire.

But Brissot's rhetoric was tame in comparison with the work coming out of the Cordeliers district. The slim, dashing, long-haired Camille Desmoulins—who harangued the crowd from a table on the night of July 12—abandoned his legal career to devote himself full-time to political commentary. He had had already written a pamphlet called *La France libre* that was too incendiary for any publisher to touch before the Bastille fell. Then, in the wake of the lynching of Foullon and Bertier, Desmoulins wrote *Discours de la lanterne aux Parisiens*, which celebrated and justified the political violence accompanying the Revolution. He would soon publish a weekly journal called *Les Révolutions de France et de*

Brabant, full of the signature verve, passion, and explosive energy making Desmoulins one of the most radical and revered political writers of his generation.

But the most infamous of the new radical journalists was a diminutive forty-six-year-old with a degenerative skin condition named Jean-Paul Marat. Before the Revolution, Marat was an ambitious doctor frustrated by his failure to turn heads as an inventor or natural philosopher. In 1789 he reimagined himself as a journalist. Fellow doctor-turned-radical René Levasseur, who had no objection to Marat's politics, nonetheless said, "This energetic fanatic inspired a sort of repugnance and astonishment. I considered him with the restless curiosity one experiences contemplating certain hideous insects. His messy clothes, his livid face, his haggard eyes, had something terrible that upset the soul. All the colleagues I befriended judged him as I did."[6] And this was one of his allies talking. Marat began a daily newspaper originally called *Le Publiciste parisien*, but soon changed it to *L'Ami du peuple*—"The Friend of the People." It started as a rather milquetoast daily journal, offering praise for liberal nobles like Lafayette. But Marat found his voice, popularity, and purpose in life writing uncompromising populist screeds. Levasseur said Marat was "possessed by some fixed ideas . . . he was not afraid to proclaim that his principles could only triumph by making rivers of blood."[7] It was soon impossible to distinguish Marat's rhetorical exaggerations from deadly serious promises.

Working out of the Cordeliers district, both Desmoulins and Marat were protected and encouraged by the emerging leader of the neighborhood, Georges Danton. A barrel-chested and fun-loving glutton, Danton was an autodidact with a photographic memory who skyrocketed up the ranks of the legal profession through sheer force of talent rather than social or family connections. Danton was already a great legal orator when the Revolution provided an even greater stage. Danton's house became the headquarters of the most radically populist faction of the Revolution.

Lafayette believed the rhetoric coming out of the radical presses a major cause of ongoing disorders in Paris. But he was equally frustrated with the royal family for making the most exaggerated accusations of Brissot, Desmoulins, Marat appear true. One example would be when the king transferred the notoriously royalist Flanders Regiment from their garrison on the frontier to the palace of Versailles. This very fact of the transfer was troubling enough—they now formed a ruthlessly loyal guard around the royal family. But even worse were stories emerging from a welcome banquet held in their honor. It was said the soldiers threw tricolor cockades on the ground and trampled them. The press embellished and exaggerated these stories, but set against the backdrop of the king's resistance to the will of the National Assembly, the rumor mill easily produced a very sinister narrative. Having failed in July, the forces of reactionary conservatism prepared once again to crush the Revolution.

As with the insurrectionary riots of July, no amount of journalistic excess would have mattered absent ongoing food shortages and fear of starvation. Without this powder keg, everything else was simply sparks flying harmlessly through the air. In late September and early October 1789, prices once again spiked as food supplies dwindled. Lafayette and the National Guard spent these weeks protecting grain shipments and preventing those accused of hoarding or price gauging from being lynched. Already drifting away from his wistful hopes at retirement, Lafayette concluded wearily: "All hell has conspired against us."[8]

⚜

ON THE MORNING of October 5, 1789, the wives and mothers of Paris congregated at the market of Les Halles to shop for their families. This daily ritual preceded another distressingly daily ritual: the announcement there was not enough bread for all. The more politically active women had been arguing, planning, and strategizing for several days, and decided this was the last straw. A group made their way to the Hôtel de Ville, pushed their way through the door, marched up the stairs, and rang the bells, sounding the tocsin of citywide emergency. Crowds flocked to the scene. Morris said Danton "roared his denunciations, and Marat, equally condemnatory, made as much noise as the four trumpets on the Day of Judgment."[9] By eight o'clock in the morning, tens of thousands of women milled about in place de Grève, the open public square in front of the Hôtel de Ville.

Alerted of the gathering, Lafayette rushed to the scene—his role as preserver of order now took up far more time than his role as defender of liberty. Lafayette arrived around nine o'clock and found himself taking charge of a tense standoff. The women managed to lay hands on a couple of cannons, and the assembled National Guard companies did not want to use force to reclaim them. In fact, the guardsmen clearly sympathized with the women. If a person cannot be considered free in a world without a constitution or bill of rights, they certainly could not be considered free in a world where they lacked the basic necessities of life. There is no liberty on an empty stomach.

Lafayette took command of his troops and conferred with the political leaders inside the Hôtel de Ville. While they talked, some of the women decided enough was enough. Lafayette could hear the cries: "Bread!" and "To Versailles!"[10] Soon enough, a large group turned their backs on the Hôtel de Ville and walked in the direction of Versailles. No one stood in their way. As they marched off, pulling the cannons behind them, they announced their intention to bring back "the baker, the baker's wife's, and the bakers boy!"[11]

Lafayette could not stop this angry group of women from departing, but he now faced a standoff with his own men. The guardsmen let their commander-general know they wanted to follow the women to Versailles. They did not like the idea of the reactionary Flanders Regiment guarding the sovereign. They wanted the National Guard to take over the job themselves. Lafayette later described "the impatience of the national guard, indignant at the insults against the patriotic cockade."[12] They wanted to go to Versailles, and Lafayette spent the whole rest of the day attempting to persuade his men not to go. He issued orders for them to fan out across the countryside to gather as much grain, bread, and food as they could lay their hands on, hoping to undo the root causes of the disorder.

Much to Lafayette's embarrassing frustration, his men mostly remained rooted in place. According to Lafayette, a certain Lieutenant Mercier said to him, "General, we must go to Versailles, all the people want us to." He begged the commander-general to see reality: "The King has fooled us all! You and everyone else: he must be deposed . . . we must remove him. His son will be King. You will be Regent. All will be well."[13] This was the last thing Lafayette wanted. He did not want to depose the king. He absolutely did not want to be regent. Though the accusation would follow Lafayette for the rest of his life, he never aspired to be supreme executive of France. Any time the possibility presented itself he summarily rejected the idea.

By the afternoon, a cold heavy rain descended, and Lafayette's men became restless. Why was the commander-general standing against the will of the people? Then things became more overtly sinister. From the ranks there were shouts: "To Versailles or to the Lamppost!"[14] Lafayette realized if he did not take his men where they wanted to go, they would lynch him and go where they wanted to go anyway. To keep up the appearance he was still their chief, even as he was clearly far from their master, Lafayette induced the leaders of Paris to draft a statement saying they "authorized the Commander General, and indeed ordered him, to go to Versailles."[15] Lafayette went back outside and ordered his men to march.

Morris recorded in his diary, "Lafayette has marched by compulsion, guarded by his own troops who suspect and threatened him. Dreadful situation, obliged to do what he abhors or suffer an ignominious death, with the certainty that the sacrifice of his life will not prevent the mischief."[16] As Lafayette led his men out of Paris, there was no way to know what lay ahead. It was possible the Flanders Regiment was preparing armed resistance. It was possible he was about to lead his men into a battle he did not want to fight. When his forces got to pont de Sèvres on the extreme southwest periphery of Paris, they saw the road to Versailles clear and crossed the Seine. Lafayette later said that in this moment they "crossed a Rubicon."[17]

—※—

LAFAYETTE AND THE National Guard arrived in Versailles at eleven o'clock that night. On the outskirts of the village, Lafayette demanded his men renew their oath to defend "the nation, the law, and the king."[18] The National Guardsmen swore the oath. Having forced Lafayette to lead them here, they now agreed to actually obey his commands. Satisfied, but still nervous, Lafayette proceeded.

He soon learned what took place after the arrival of the first wave of angry Parisian women. The women first pushed their way into the National Assembly, presided over by the still obscure but radically inclined lawyer, Maximilien Robespierre. They camped out in the benches, heckled conservatives who questioned their presence, and cheered radical delegates who welcomed them. Others attempted to breach the gates of the palace but were pushed back. The king issued explicit orders not to fire on the women, so the guards used rifle butts to push the women back from the fence line. The king then invited a small delegation of women inside the palace, and upon hearing their grievances, ordered the royal bakeries to work continuously through the night to make and distribute bread.

As Lafayette approached Versailles, he received a messenger from Louis who said the king was "regarding his approach with pleasure and just accepted [Lafayette's] declaration of rights."[19] This was a surprisingly abrupt concession. The king's message was so nonchalant, it sounded as if his acceptance of the Declaration of Rights was always a foregone conclusion, and its occurrence just as an angry mob of Parisian women arrived was pure coincidence. But in reality, the king had been dragging his feet for months. Would he have signed off on the Declaration of Rights if his subjects remained docile and passive? Here again, certainly not. Just as happened in July, direct insurrectionary action secured what months of speeches, negotiations, and polite remonstrances could not. The uncouth revolutionaries of the street once again made it possible for the polite salon revolutionaries to achieve their ends.

Louis's outwardly generous welcoming of Lafayette also masked real fear of the marquis's intentions. Lafayette marched at the head of more than ten thousand armed men. Had he come to save the monarchy or overthrow it? Aware of this dangerous ambiguity, Lafayette dismounted his horse and entered the palace grounds alone to prove his fidelity. His men did not want him to go, believing he would be instantly clapped in irons. Meanwhile, those inside the palace believed it was the other way around—Lafayette came to clap irons on the king. As Lafayette entered the inner courtyard somebody said, "Here comes Cromwell." To which Lafayette retorted, "Monsieur, Cromwell would not have come here alone."[20]

An exhausted Lafayette entered the king's apartments around mid-night, and according to a witness was "covered in mud from head to foot."[21] Lafayette informed the king there was nothing to fear. Lafayette had come to *prevent* a riot and *protect* the royal family. But he also hinted the other rumors—that he lost control of the situation in Paris—were true. He said to Louis, "Sire, I thought it better to come here to die at the feet of Your Majesty than to die uselessly on the Place de Grève."[22]

After reassuring the king and queen he was not there to depose them, Lafayette went back outside and spent the night keeping the peace. The Parisian women settled into makeshift lodgings, but sporadic confrontations and unrest continued all night. Luckily, the National Guard honored their oath to obey orders. They set up patrols and posted guards throughout Versailles. Lafayette spent the night racing between houses of National Assembly delegates, the royal palace, and temporary National Guard headquarters. By the time dawn approached, Lafayette had been working, riding, and negotiating non-stop for twenty hours. Around four o'clock in the morning, he finally decided things were calm, safe, and secure enough to get some rest. He went to the Hôtel Noailles—the home he first moved into as the sixteen-year-old secret fiancé of Adrienne—and told an attending servant, "Good morning! I am falling asleep."[23]

⊹≡⊱

LAFAYETTE IS SOMETIMES chastised for being asleep at the switch—his incompetence, naïveté, and simplemindedness leaving him unable to control events. The fact he was *literally* asleep on the cataclysmic morning of October 6, 1789, is the centerpiece of this criticism. But though it is true Lafayette was asleep, one wonders what else he was supposed to do? In moments of popular unrest and protest, peaceful days often give way to violent nights. Knowing this, Lafayette maintained an all-night vigil and did not retire to bed until the safety of dawn approached. By that point, he had been awake for nearly a full day. It was not unreasonable to think the worst moment of danger was past and it was safe to shut his eyes for a few hours.

But the dawn of October 6, 1789, turned out to be one of the most infamous dawns in French history. Either by luck, accident, or design, a group of women awoke to discover a side gate to the inner courtyard of the palace was unlocked. It remains a mystery how and why the gate opened. Rumors quickly established it must have been a deliberate action of someone inside the palace—someone hostile to the royal family and sympathetic to the people. But it may have just as easily been palace attendants commencing their daily rounds without considering the implications of the routine unlocking of these gates. Whichever it was, the gate was unlocked. Within minutes, thousands poured inside.

Having endured a long, cold, hungry night and still full of deep rage at the injustices inflicted upon them and their families, they were not in the mood to bargain or negotiate. Palace guards tried to hold them back, but they were still under orders not to fire. So scuffling, shoving, and fighting broke out. Two guards soon lay dead and the crowd raged near the inner sanctum of the royal family. Marie Antoinette fled her bedchamber through a secret passage and spent a harrowing ten minutes locked out of the king's apartments listening to an angry mob shout for her head. Before the mob found her, however, the door was unlocked, and she passed out of immediate danger. But it was only a brief respite. In the king's apartments, the whole royal family gathered for what they genuinely feared might be their last moments together.

Lafayette had only slept a few hours when frantic messengers woke him to say the women breached the gates of the palace. He mounted a horse and raced to the palace, issuing orders on the fly for the National Guard to mobilize and get between the angry mob and the royal family. When Lafayette reached the palace he found the National Guard, the king's regular bodyguards, and the angry women in a tense standoff throughout several courtyards and passages. "In this cruel uncertainty," one of the royal guards later recalled, "M. de Lafayette happily arrived. He saved us."[24] Lafayette pushed on to the inner apartments and found a company of his National Guard surrounding the royal family, protecting them, not threatening them with death. They may yet get out of this alive.

Though the guards pushed the angry mob back into the courtyards, the emergency was hardly over. The royal family could hear loud cries from outside: "The king to the balcony!" and "The king to Paris!" Lafayette told Louis and Marie Antoinette the only thing that would *actually* resolve the crisis was a royal promise to leave Versailles and relocate to Paris. The king and queen balked at this suggestion. Not only was Versailles their home, but the whole reason the monarchy moved to Versailles nearly a century earlier was to escape the clutches of the Parisians. Lafayette implored them to reconsider. He said he could not guarantee their safety if they attempted to remain in Versailles. Finally, reluctantly, they agreed.

Lafayette led the royal family and a small coterie of ministers out onto the balcony. The king announced he and his family would listen "to the love of my good and faithful subjects" and return with them to Paris.[25] Happy cheers replaced angry shouting. In an effort to protect the king's bodyguard from further harm, Lafayette brought out a corporal and pinned a tricolor cockade on his uniform to signal the guard stood *with* the people not *against* them. There was no more cause for fear, alarm, or violence. More cheers erupted and Lafayette led the royal family and attendants back inside the royal apartments.

But it was not over yet. Though somewhat mollified, the crowd demanded the queen come to the balcony. With the crowd calling her name, Lafayette asked, "Madame, what do you intend to do?" The queen said, "I know the fate that awaits me. I am ready to die at the feet of my king in the arms of my children." But Lafayette believed this fate could be averted. "Come with me," Lafayette said to the queen. "What?" she replied. "Alone on the balcony?" "Yes, madam," he said. "Let us go."[26]

Lafayette led the queen out onto the balcony, to a roar of insults, shouts, and menacing anger. Neither Lafayette nor the queen could make themselves heard. So Lafayette improvised an unspoken gesture—he bowed theatrically and kissed the queen's hand. The sight of the popular Lafayette visibly displaying loyalty and fidelity to the queen, and the queen in turn accepting the gesture, changed the mood. Now the crowd cheered and shouted a cry not heard in many years: "Vive la reine!" The danger passed.

Lafayette spent the rest of the day overseeing preparations for a massive caravan of coaches, carriages, carts, women, and National Guard—tens of thousands of people—to return to Paris. For all the ways the Women's March on Versailles could have turned out, the total number of casualties was minor. There were injuries on all sides, and a few palace guards lay dead, but Lafayette and the National Guard managed to guide the crisis to a mostly peaceful resolution. In the midst of the crisis, Gouverneur Morris observed, "[Lafayette] is very much below the business he has undertaken, and if the sea runs high he will be unable to hold the helm."[27] And while it was true his men compelled Lafayette to go to Versailles against his better judgment, once there, he restored order, defended the royal family from mortal danger, and, hopefully, inspired the final union of the king and the nation. The king's aunt, who had known Lafayette since he was a teenager, said to him, "I owe you more than my life monsieur, I owe you the life of my poor nephew the king."[28] Later, it was said Lafayette "acquired for him from all parties the appellation of guardian angel on that day."[29] Lafayette himself wrote Simiane, "Things turned out better than we dared hope. The solidarity of the troops prevented what I feared from happening. Our army took an oath of loyalty to the king, in spite of scheming and plotting. The king and queen behaved very well."[30] As he oversaw preparations for everyone to return to Paris, Lafayette had every reason to believe while the seas ran very high indeed, he firmly steadied the helm.

Everyone departed for Paris on the afternoon of October 6. Lafayette rode alongside the royal carriage, serving as their personal escort and protector. The French monarchy never returned to Versailles. The great home of the Bourbon monarchy—*the* symbol of royal absolutism—was left behind forever. Its gates locked. Its galleries, theaters, chapels, and gardens abandoned. The center of an opulent and oppressive universe was left deserted and derelict. The fate of the monarchy and revolution now lay in Paris, where Louis would either reign as the people's king or he would no longer reign at all.

CHAPTER FIFTEEN

THE ZENITH OF HIS INFLUENCE

[1790]

Lafayette miraculously threaded the needle of the Women's March on Versailles. He deposited the royal family safely in the Tuileries Palace and watched with relief as tens of thousands of protestors returned home peacefully. The government remained intact. The body count was minimal. Neither Paris nor Versailles were in flames. Lafayette rightly counted it among his finest hours.

With the immediate emergency passed, Lafayette reflected on what caused the tumultuous incident in the first place. The gossip and rumors he heard all told the same story: the duc d'Orléans orchestrated the march on Versailles. The whole thing was meant to be the climax of Orléans's effort to force his cousin's abdication. Some of the rumors took on an imaginative life of their own. A lady in waiting to the queen went so far as to say, "Many people claimed they recognized the duc d'Orléans at 4:30 in the morning . . . at the top of the marble staircase pointing the way to the guardroom leading to the Queen's bedchamber."[1] The story was pure fantasy, but the underlying suspicion was plausible. Everyone knew Orléans funded the newspapers and street orators keeping the temperature of Paris running high. Lafayette received reports Orléans's agents planted and encouraged the idea of marching on Versailles. Lafayette, himself nearly lynched in front of the Hôtel de Ville, took the allegations against Orléans both seriously and personally.

In the days following, Lafayette conducted several personal interviews with Orléans. The duc swore innocence and claimed the rumors were baseless. Lafayette remained skeptical and later said he was absolutely ready to arrest Orléans, and if any hard evidence appeared, "I would have denounced him."[2] Despite the absence of hard proof, Lafayette suggested it might be prudent for Orléans to take a long vacation to England. The king seconded the suggestion. Eager to prove his loyalty, Orléans complied and, within a week of the Women's March on Versailles, packed his bags and departed France. If the duc d'Orléans *had* been attempting to replace Louis, he was only comfortable doing it from the shadows. To ensure Orléans did not come back, Lafayette sent an aid to England with a warning: "If you arrive in Paris, [Lafayette's] intention is to fight you the next morning, then justify himself in the National Assembly."[3] Lafayette's readiness to expel Orléans from the country was partly personal, but it was also proof of his loyalty to Louis and Marie Antoinette. Despite their complicated personal history, Lafayette still believed the Bourbons were the legitimate sovereigns of France. As commander-general of the National Guard, his job was to protect them. After coming to Paris, Lafayette repeatedly swore his fealty. The king appeared willing to believe it, but the queen remained harder to convince. While pleased Orléans was gone, she harbored suspicions about Lafayette's ultimate agenda. Marie Antoinette did not believe the story he was "forced" to march on Versailles. "She thought his whole army was devoted to him," her lady-in-waiting recalled, "and that everything he said about the violence they had done to him to make him march on Versailles was only a feint."[4] Responding to Lafayette's professions of loyalty and devotion, the queen famously quipped, "Monsieur Lafayette wishes to save us . . . but who is going to save us from Monsieur Lafayette?"[5]

❦

THE MOVE TO Paris fundamentally altered the course of the French Revolution. Both the king and the National Assembly now lived under the careful scrutiny of the Parisians. The royal family took up residence in the Tuileries Palace, a wing of the Louvre complex unused ever since Louis XIV turned a hunting lodge in Versailles into the new residence of the kings of France. The official story was the royal family relocated to Paris of their own free will. It was not clear what would happen if this official story was ever directly challenged.

The National Assembly, meanwhile, followed the sovereign and installed itself in the Salle du Manège, an indoor riding facility adjacent to the Tuileries Palace. The building was a long narrow rectangle with high ceilings and terrible acoustics, but it was the best option available. Workers transformed the great empty hall by constructing risers, benches, and a tribune to house the delegates and audience. The assembly held the first session in their new home on November 9, and from the start, conservative royalists congregated on the right side of the hall while radical democrats grouped on the left, introducing the left/right political spectrum persisting to this very day.

Of even greater consequence than affinity grouping *inside* the hall was affinity grouping *outside* the hall. When the Estates-General delegates first arrived in Versailles, regional delegations often found shared lodgings. But after the relocation to Paris, the delegates typically found accommodations with new ideological compatriots rather than old geographic neighbors. These affinity groupings cemented further as they joined the active social and political life of Paris. Like-minded men and women found each other at salons, dinners, parties, and performances, where they spent long evenings forging personal bonds and political alliances. Each morning, newspapers and journals flooded the streets trumpeting news and commentary from every imaginable perspective, giving everyone the opportunity to choose their own preferred version of the events. The Revolution was polarizing.

Further aiding growing polarization was a new force in French politics: political clubs. The most famous of new political clubs was officially called the Society of the Friends of the Constitution, founded shortly after the move to Paris. As the marquis de Lafayette considered himself a firm friend of the Constitution, he was among the founding members of the society, as was nearly every political leader pushing liberal political reform for the past several years. But though it began life as a large tent, the most spirited and committed members of the club came from the far left—both radical National Assembly delegates and their allies among the activists of Paris. They were not there to put the Revolution to bed, but keep it marching onward. The speeches, debates, and agenda of the club raced ahead of the more cautious stances of Lafayette and his liberal noble brethren. As the Society of the Friends of the Constitution became a hotbed of radical sentiment, their detractors began dismissively referring to them after the name of the Dominican monastery where they held their daily sessions: the Jacobins.

But though the Jacobins would go down in history as the largest and most influential of all the political clubs, in 1789 they were just one among many. Other clubs organized themselves under a variety of banners spanning the ideological spectrum. Some gathered under a broad umbrella like the Friends of the Monarchist Constitution, a group dedicated to drawing back from the most radical advances of 1789. Others narrowly focused on a single issue, like the Club Massiac, formed to lobby on behalf of the special colonial estate owners and who would spend the next four years blocking all attempts to end the institution of slavery. What they all shared in common was a growing understanding that political objectives were best achieved by strategic organization and planning. After the move to Paris, haphazard political amateurism gave way to hard-nosed professional discipline.

The greatest of the transformative factors, however, was the fact that all of this now unfolded in the laps of the Parisians. With not unjustified pride, the people of Paris considered themselves the saviors of the Revolution. In both July and October 1789, it appeared the royal family was preparing to stage a reactionary coup—in July when troops surrounded the city, and in October when the king refused to recognize the Declaration of Rights while transferring hyper-loyal military regiments to Versailles. On both occasions the National Assembly proved unable, on its own, to stand up to the threat of ultraroyalist conspirators. It was only after the people rose up that the king backed down. Henceforth, no political leader of any stripe, in any palace, salon, or assembly hall, could consider a course of action without taking into account the potential effect on the revolutionaries in the street. The Revolution had come to Paris.

AFTER THE MOVE to Paris, the marquis de Lafayette personally found himself at a unique political intersection. He now combined the roles of chief of police, royal adviser, National Assembly delegate, quasi–military general, and popular political symbol. He was neither of the far right nor the far left. He was both an advocate of liberty and defender of order. For the next year, this unique position made Lafayette one of the most influential leaders in France. His home became the headquarters of both National Guard operations as well as an informal shadow cabinet directing and guiding government policy. Gouverneur Morris worried Lafayette was doing too much, saying the marquis "cannot possibly act both as minister and soldier, still less minister of every department."[6]

Lafayette agreed with Morris, not just because he was overworked and stretched thin, but because he opposed such concentrations of power. Lafayette abhorred the idea of a single person combining political and military authority—even if that person was himself. So one of his top priorities in late 1789 was ensuring these powers did not become entangled. When offered the presidency of the National Assembly he declined, saying, "My present job is to ensure public tranquility, and, in my role as a member of the national assembly, to help strengthen our liberties and to protect the king and queen from all the conspiracies against them."[7] Though he did not resign his seat, it would be terrible precedent for the commander-general of the National Guard to simultaneously preside over the National Assembly. Lafayette also planned to decline any invitation from the king to make Lafayette prime minister, though with wry humor he acknowledged he would probably never have to decline such an offer. "Just between ourselves," he wrote Simiane, "I think ingratitude will save me from the embarrassment of being rewarded."[8]

As Lafayette distanced himself from political power, the comte de Mirabeau approached him about forming a powerful alliance. Mirabeau originally positioned himself as an Orléanist, but when his patron meekly accepted banishment in early October 1789, Mirabeau needed a new angle—and partnership with Lafayette seemed promising. The match made sense on paper. Both men were at the height of their popularity and Mirabeau was happy to assume the powers Lafayette declined. With Mirabeau's political skills and Lafayette's unassailable leadership of the National Guard, they would be unstoppable. So Mirabeau pitched himself. "You have a number of friends (though fewer than you think)," he wrote Lafayette, "not one of them but has value and virtue of a certain kind . . . but they are one and all completely ignorant of human nature and of the real feelings of the country . . . I am a great deal more necessary to you than all them put together."[9] Mirabeau pursued a political alliance with Lafayette for the better part of a year, but always found the commander-general of the National Guard frustratingly aloof. "I overcame the might of the King of England and the authority of the King of France, the unleashed fury of the people," Lafayette said, "I shall certainly not surrender to Monsieur de Mirabeau."[10]

Lafayette successfully dodged Mirabeau's attempted courtship, but this was not necessarily to his credit. Though the most withering portrayals of Lafayette's political naïveté are unjust, they are not entirely without merit. Modeling himself after Washington and his other American friends, Lafayette embraced their belief that in a virtuous republic, enlightened leaders must come together as free and independent individuals. They must form their own judgments about the best course of action free of dirty words like "faction" and "party." But while Lafayette credulously adopted this posture, he did not realize his more clever American friends said one thing while doing another. As Jefferson, Madison, and Hamilton decried organized factions, they worked tirelessly behind the scenes constructing alliances and organizations to advance their competing agendas. They understood that to achieve one's hopes and dreams in a dangerous political world, one needs partners and allies working together on a shared course of action. Lafayette credulously believed aloof independence was a virtuous asset. But it turned out to be a crippling liability.

Lafayette's more cynical friends worried his naïveté was already catching up with him. Gouverneur Morris wrote Washington, "Our friend Lafayette has given into measures as to the constitution which he does not heartily approve, and he heartily approves many things which experience will demonstrate should be injurious. He left America, you know, when his education was but half finished. What he learnt there he knows well, but he did not learn to be a government maker."[11] More damning, Morris said despite Lafayette's vain ambitions, "he must be used by others because he has not talents enough to make use of them."[12] Meanwhile, Talleyrand bluntly told Morris, "Lafayette has no fixed plan."[13] The marquis was simply adrift and alone, treading water each day, without knowing what to do.

Lafayette remained optimistic about the prospects for both himself and France. He believed the worst was behind them and the only thing left to do was guide the Revolution to a calm and peaceful conclusion. He wrote to Washington, "Our internal troubles and anarchy are much exaggerated . . . we have made more changes in ten months than the most sanguine patriot could have imagined . . . and that upon the whole, this Revolution, in which nothing will be wanting but energy of government, just as it was in America, will propagate [and] implant liberty and make it flourish throughout the world."[14]

※

AS LAFAYETTE ENCOURAGED his colleagues in the National Assembly to steer toward a final constitution, Lafayette understood his duty as head of the National Guard was to ensure public tranquility so they could finish the job. This remained a difficult task, as the cupboards of Paris remained distressingly bare. The harvest of 1789 was better, and the winter milder, but hunger and deprivation still lingered. One morning, a baker announced to a hungry crowd he was out of bread. Accused of hoarding, he was seized and lynched before anybody could arrive to save him. "There has been hanged a baker this morning by the populace, and all Paris is under arms," Morris wrote. "The poor baker was beheaded according to custom, and carried in triumph through the streets. He had been all night at work for the purpose of supplying the greatest possible quantity of bread this morning. His wife is said to have died of horror when they presented her husband's head stuck on a pole."[15]

Lafayette was upset about the summary lynching of a random baker, and furious when he found out members of the National Guard were present but made no effort to intervene. Afterward he addressed a meeting of his officers. "We are lost if the service continues to perform with such great sloppiness," he told them. "We are the only soldiers of the revolution; we alone must defend the royal family from any attack; we alone must establish the freedom of the representatives of the nation; we are the only guardians of the public treasury. The eyes of France and all of Europe are fixed on Paris."[16] For Lafayette this was not just about upholding the rule of law, it was about proving the rule of law *could* be upheld by self-governing citizens. With so many enemies of the Revolution eager to exploit any slipups, Lafayette wanted to give them as few opportunities as possible.

Unfortunately, the National Assembly was not going to make Lafayette's job easier. In the slack days before Christmas 1789, the assembly announced new rules for electoral participation. They divided the population of France into two groups: "active citizens" and "passive citizens." The former could participate fully in political decision making, while the latter would enjoy legal rights, but *not* political rights. The distinction between these two groups was not a measure of civic commitment or public engagement, but wealth. Those who paid a certain amount of taxes per year could vote and run for office. Those who did not, could not. The delegates of the assembly took it for granted political power must be left to the educated and responsible members of society—which to them meant men of property. It is one of the great ironies of the French Revolution they used the descriptors "active" and "passive" in making this distinction, when the very people they so casually wrote off as "passive" were the very group who provided the active energy necessary to make the revolution the men of property now claimed as their sole preserve.

The announcement gave the radical activists, journalists, and pamphleteers in Paris good reason to demand their followers remain vigilant. The Revolution must not abandon those who made the Revolution possible in the first place. The drumbeat in the popular presses was not simply agitation for agitation's sake; nor the people of Paris merely bloodthirsty zombies marching mindlessly to that beat. They knew they were being written out of the political process and planned to fight for their threatened rights. This was, after all, a revolution.

But some pushed well beyond the bounds of truth and justifiable outrage. Really coming into his own as a popular agitator, Marat believed centuries of oppression meant "everything is permitted to shake the people out of its deadly lethargy, recall to it the sense of its rights, inspire it with the courage to defend them; one cannot be a trouble-maker, when one cries out only for the nations' interest."[17] Marat would not feel bound by anything. All means justified the end, which was a free and liberated people. So he mixed exaggeration, fantasy, truth, slander, facts, accusations, and vitriol into a potent blend electrifying readers on a daily basis. Marat now laid the groundwork for the Reign of Terror by arguing that murdering the enemies of the Revolution was the surest path to permanent salvation. "Five or six hundred heads cut off at the time of the capture of the Bastille would have given you enduring peace, liberty, and happiness," Marat infamously wrote. "Today ten thousand heads will hardly suffice to save the country. In a few months perhaps you will perform a wonder, and cut off a hundred thousand."[18] Some took this to be mere rhetorical excess. But events would soon prove Marat was deadly serious.

Marat posed a difficult challenge for Lafayette—a difficult challenge for any free society. Lafayette was committed to the principle of freedom of speech and freedom of the press, but here was a journalist using fanatical lies and scurrilous accusations to incite the population to mass murder. Lafayette turned to the relevant parts of the Declaration of the Rights of Man and of the Citizen for guidance. Article 10 stated, "No one may be disquieted for his opinions, even religious ones, provided their manifestation does not trouble the public order established by the law."[19] And article 11 said, "The free communication of thoughts and of opinions is one of the most precious rights of man: any citizen thus may speak, write, print freely, except to respond to the abuse of this liberty, in the cases determined by the law."[20] Eventually Lafayette decided Marat *was* troubling public order and abusing his liberty. In January 1790, Lafayette ordered his arrest.

But Lafayette discovered the uncomfortable limits of his power. Helped by supportive neighbors in the Cordeliers district, Marat slipped into hiding, one step ahead of the National Guard, and leaders in the district like Georges Danton refused to give him up. Danton was no great friend of Marat's, but decided to make a public stand against Lafayette's attempt to censor free expression. Not wanting to provoke a major clash, Lafayette backed down. He endured a stinging rebuke from Marat in the next issue of the *L'Ami du peuple*. Marat offered sarcastic praise of Lafayette as the great defender of liberty, and offered the presumption the National Guard must not have been obeying his order. "If this tribunal can make soldiers oppress the people with impunity and without your consent, who will stop them from using the nation's forces against the public? What will happen to your functions as Commander General? What will the nation, which regards you as its avenger, think of you?" Marat demanded Lafayette "justify in the eyes of the nation the sincerity of the patriotic sentiments you possess."[21]

As Lafayette pondered this, he also dealt with ultraroyalists on the other end of the political spectrum who painted him as a crooked villain. A royalist paper pinned Paris's social problems on the corrupt incompetence of the revolutionaries: "Why, Citizens! Are Lafayette, Bailly, and the leaders of Paris leaving you short of bread? It is to grow fat at the expense of your substance!...You want them to report to the Nation, but you throw yourself into the arms of Lafayette; you give him a despotic empire, you make him master of everything. Your life is therefore even more outraged in the hands of the traitor Lafayette, this scoundrel, this vampire, than in that of your good king?"[22]

Lafayette's unique position at the center of the action meant, as Paris polarized, his attempt to hold the center offended everyone. Newspapers, politicians, and street orators accused him of being too harsh or too lenient; for doing too much or too little; for grasping at power or relinquishing it too easily; for being both a radical republican and a crypto-royalist; for embracing the Revolution and betraying it. One thing they all shared was a desire to fit Lafayette with a black hat.

Lafayette tried to take these attacks in stride. He wrote Washington an optimistic letter: "We have come this far in the Revolution without breaking the ship either on the shoal of aristocracy, or that of faction, and amidst the ever reviving efforts of the mourners and the ambitious, we are stirring towards a tolerable conclusion—now that everything that was is no more, a new building is erected, not perfect by far, but sufficient to ensure freedom, and prepare the nation for a convention in about ten years, where the defects may be mended . . . liberty is sprouting about in the other parts of Europe, and I am encouraging it by all the means in my power."[23]

⊞

IN THE SPRING of 1790, Lafayette's optimism did not seem implausible. A mild winter and better harvests calmed tempers in Paris. Lafayette went into full celebration and commemoration mode. In March, he sent Washington the main door key to the Bastille, which the people of Paris presented to him shortly after they stormed the fortress. "Give me leave, my dear General," he wrote, "to present you . . . with the main key of that fortress of despotism—it is a tribute which I owe as a son to my adoptive father, as an aid de camp to my general, as a missionary of liberty to its patriarch."[24]

On June 19, Paris celebrated the legal abolition of noble titles. Lafayette happily toasted the demise of the unearned privileges of the feudal aristocracy. For Lafayette, all that mattered was *what you did*, not *who you were*. "We will suppress these words: made noble," he said, "and say instead: such a person saved the state on such a day. It seems to me these words have something of that American character, the precious fruit of the new world which was to serve a great deal in the rejuvenation of the old."[25]

Elsewhere in France, municipalities settled into the new political order. Local city councils accepted new laws, regulations, and administrative hierarchies devised by the National Assembly. France transitioned from being a collection of feudal provinces to eighty-three rationally designed departments, each of equal size and power. They established their own National Guard companies, which became known as the *fédérés*. To celebrate what appeared to be the peaceful beginning of a new era, many towns and cities held festivals celebrating national unity and the successful triumph of the Revolution of 1789.

As the first anniversary of the fall of the Bastille approached, the leaders of Paris decided that, as capital of France and epicenter of the Revolution, they should host the largest and most spectacular unity festival of all. Mayor Bailly addressed leaders of Paris: "Gentlemen, a new order of things is rising and will regenerate all parts of the kingdom," he said. "Our union is our strength. . . . The zeal, courage, and patriotism of the National Guard are everywhere admired; we can judge here by the Guard of Paris; we see that it is civic virtue that made him take up arms . . . we recognize a citizen general who commands an army of citizens." This last bit referring to Lafayette. Bailly said Paris planned to invite delegates to represent National Guard companies from each of the eighty-three new departments to Paris for a celebration they dubbed the *Fête de la Fédération*. "We propose to our brothers to come," he said, "as representatives of the districts and departments, to meet within our walls, in our presence, and to add to the civic oath already taken by all French from one end of the kingdom to the other; we will all regard this ceremony as the beginning of the epoch of liberty."[26]

The realm responded. In the week before the planned celebration, National Guard delegates streamed into Paris. On the Champ de Mars thousands of previously unemployed workers happily toiled, digging and piling huge earthworks to serve as grandstands for three hundred thousand spectators. Where the Eiffel Tower now stands, they erected a temporary arch of triumph, modeled after the Roman examples of old. At the other end of the field, they built a platform and throne for the king. In the middle, they constructed an altar to the nation, where, on the afternoon of July 14, 1790, the marquis de Lafayette would stand and swear everyone to a great oath of loyalty to the king, the constitution, and the nation.

Even the royal family joined the spirit of the festival. Despite months of unhappy confinement in the Tuileries Palace, they made a show of coming down to Champ de Mars to performatively work and picnic among the people. But though their outward embrace of the new order alleviated concerns the Bourbons were implacably hostile to the Revolution . . . it was all an act. They could not wait for the Revolution to collapse and for things to go back to normal. In the week before the fête, Marie Antoinette said to a confidant, "Everything goes from bad to worse . . . the ministers and M. de Lafayette take missteps every day. We go along with them, and instead of being satisfied, these monsters become more insolent by the moment."[27]

A few days before, on July 10, 1790, about fourteen thousand National Guardsmen from around the kingdom assembled in front of the Hôtel de Ville and declared themselves the "Assembly of the Federation." They elected Lafayette to be their president. The next day, Lafayette led a group of fédérés to the National Assembly bearing a petition asking the assembly to finish the constitution. They swore the Tennis Court Oath more than a year ago—they really ought to be wrapping things up by now. "The nation, wanting to be free at last, asked you to give it a constitution," their statement read. "But in vain have we waited for it. . . . Complete your work gentlemen, by determining from the number of your decrees those which will form the French Constitution. Hurry up and reward our just impatience for this code."[28]

Then Lafayette led the delegation over to an audience with Louis and Marie Antoinette. "We present Your Majesty," they said, "with the most beautiful of all titles . . . 'king of a free people.' Rejoice, sire, in the prize of your virtue; let this expression of genuine homage, which despotism could never elicit, be the glory and compensation of the citizen king."[29] The king told the delegation to relay his best wishes to their fellows: "Tell them their king is their father, their brother, and their friend, that he can only be happy when they are happy."[30]

Many saw Lafayette as less benign and patriotic than he appeared. All educated Frenchmen knew their Roman history—they knew the names Marius, Sulla, and Caesar. Lafayette looked like he was attempting to join them. In *L'Ami de peuple* Marat pointed out to his readers the danger of a legislator who commanded a personal army: "Do you not understand that a citizen who has thirty-six thousand armed men under his orders must put a furious weight in the balance of the legislator?"[31] Mirabeau, spurred to excessive criticism by Lafayette's refusal to form a political alliance with him, warned the king Lafayette's double role as military commander and political leader was dangerous: "Master of the National Guard, and by that army, able to dispose of the executive power . . . if the ministers, devoted to [Lafayette's] ambition, do not refuse his influence, will he not be the most absolute, the most formidable dictator?"[32] A few days later Mirabeau told the king Lafayette might be planning to use the fête to seize power: "He is going to become generalissimo, have himself proposed supreme general, which is to say to receive the dictatorship of the nation."[33] The king read these warnings with trepidation, fear, and resentment.

❧

JULY 14, 1790, dawned cold and rainy, soaking thousands who camped out all night on the Champ de Mars to get the best seats for the festivities. Despite the weather, the celebration continued without delay or interruption. The morning was spent with a massive procession of representatives from every corner of public life: the fédérés, of course, but also notable dignitaries, soldiers from the army, and sailors from the navy. They all filed through the triumphal arch to fill the great empty field. The delegates of the National Assembly took up a position at one end. The royal family sat on the other, pointedly eschewing great trappings of royalty like robes, scepters, and crowns. When everyone settled into place, Talleyrand climbed to the altar of the nation to conduct a Mass. Still technically a bishop, Talleyrand was the only high-ranking ecclesiastic who agreed to consecrate this moment of triumphant revolutionary unity. Having never taken his religious duties very seriously, Talleyrand fumbled through the Mass with self-conscious chagrin, allegedly whispering to one of his attendants, "Don't do anything to make me laugh."[34]

When Mass was over, Lafayette made his grand entrance. Riding in on his great white horse, he reached the altar just as the rain stopped, the heavens parted, and the sun shone through. No event planner in history could have orchestrated a more dramatic entrance. Lafayette asked the fédérés to raise their hand and swear the oath he believed would forever mark the *end* of the French Revolution: "We swear to be forever faithful to the nation, Law and King, to protect persons and property . . . to remain united with all Frenchmen by unbreakable bonds of fraternity."[35] The oath was repeated in turn for each major contingent. The National Assembly swore as one. The royal family rose and swore fidelity to the nation to massive applause. Even the crowds on the grandstand raised their hands, rapturously crying, "We swear it!"

Newspaper reports and eyewitnesses agreed Lafayette was the star of the show. One exaggerated account said as Lafayette departed, he was mobbed by ten thousand people, "some kissing his face, others his hands, the less fortunate his clothes."[36] Getting carried away with this description, the story moved into gleeful satire, reporting the people even kissed Lafayette's horse: "If there had been an election, popular folly might have lavished on M. de Lafayette's horse . . . the honors [Caligula] bestowed upon his own in a fit of despotic frenzy."[37] This was overblown to the point of ridiculousness, but there was no denying Lafayette was the center of attention. One witness said, "You are witnessing Monsieur de Lafayette galloping into the centuries of history!"[38] Another marveled, "He seemed to command the whole of France. Mounted on a white horse, I can still see him, master of that vast space."[39] William Short, the new American minister to France, wrote, "The Marquis de Lafayette seems to have taken full possession of the *fédérés*—his popular manners please them beyond all measure and of course they approved his principles. When I left Paris he was adored by them—that moment may be regarded as the zenith of his influence."[40]

Not everyone was impressed or falling over in rapturous delight. Some watched suspiciously as Lafayette put the National Assembly off to one side and the king off to the other side, while he stood in the middle commanding a personal army. This looked like a man who planned to make himself a dictator. Mirabeau worried about Lafayette's private army returning to their homes across France, ready to follow *his* orders, not the king's. "It is useless to point out what degree the king compromised himself without profit," Mirabeau wrote the king on July 17, "and to what extent we have made [Lafayette] the man of the Federation, the unique man, the man of the provinces."[41]

But this was not Lafayette's intention. For a week after the Fête de la Fédération, Paris hosted an almost nonstop party. In the midst of it, Lafayette was offered overall command of the entire National Guard—not just leadership of the forces in Paris, but all of France. He rejected the offer. He did not believe that much power should concentrate in the hands of one man. Though an admirable gesture, William Short chided Lafayette for his defiant desire *not* to do what his enemies presumed he was planning to do.

The time will come perhaps when he will repent having not seized that opportunity of giving such a complexion to the revolution as every good citizen ought to desire. It would have been easy for him to have engaged the Assembly to have fixed the époque of the elections for the next legislature. I fear now that nothing but some crisis which I do not foresee will engage them to do it. It is natural enough to suppose that any body of men whatever who concentrate in themselves all sorts of power—who suppose themselves authorized to prolong their existence indefinitely—and who are exempt from all punishment for crimes unless caught in *flagrant délit* will not be readily disposed to descend from such a height.[42]

William Short was probably right. Though writing a contemporaneous analysis, he pegged the historical truth of Lafayette's life story. The Fête de la Fédération *was* the zenith of Lafayette's influence. He would never be as high as he was right then. Up until this point, everything always worked out for him. Every decision, risk, and gamble paid off. In July 1790, Lafayette was, as Mirabeau said, the unique man of the moment. Thirteen years of daring, luck, talent, and hard work carried Lafayette to his peak. But after the rise comes the fall.

CHAPTER SIXTEEN

AN OCEAN OF FACTIONS
AND COMMOTIONS

[1791]

A S THE HOPEFUL SUMMER OF 1790 DREW TO A CLOSE, LAFA-
yette received a letter from George Washington thanking him
for the key to the Bastille, which Washington called "the token
of victory gained by liberty over despotism." Washington also expressed
relief Lafayette weathered so many storms. "Happy am I, my good
friend," he wrote, "that amidst all the tremendous benefits which have
assailed your political ship, you have had address and fortitude enough
to steer her hitherto safely through the quick-sands and rocks, which
threatened instant destruction on every side; and your young King in
all things seems so well disposed to conform to the wishes of the Nation. In such an important, such a hazardous voyage, when everything
dear and sacred is embarked, you know full well my best wishes have
never left you for a moment."[1] This would be the last optimistic exchange between the two old friends.

Confident that arch-conservative royalists no longer possessed the
strength to turn back the clock on the Revolution, Lafayette's principal
concern became left-wing radicals. Though Lafayette helped inaugu-
rate the Jacobins in late-1789, he found the tenor of the meetings incompatible with his own beliefs and ceased attending. But despite the

stridency of their voices, he believed the radicals a minority. "All honest folk from the least comfortably off sections of the people, to those who were not out and out aristocrats, are for me," he wrote. "Except for a few Jacobins of bad reputation . . . the decent Jacobins are on my side in spite of my obstinate refusal to go near their club."[2] As an alternative, Lafayette and his liberal noble friends broke away and founded their own club, the Society of 1789. Their goal was to bring the Revolution to a close and return France to regular political life under the newly established constitutional monarchy.

But those left-wing activists did not plan to sit idly by and let Lafayette stop the Revolution. In April 1790, the leaders of the Left Bank Cordeliers neighborhood founded their own club: the Society of the Friends of the Rights of Man and of the Citizen, a mouthful of a name always referred to as simply the Cordeliers Club. Led by Danton, Desmoulins, and their friends, the Cordeliers Club was more open and egalitarian than even the Jacobins. Membership dues were a fraction of any other club, allowing people from all economic stations to join. And unlike the Jacobins, which allowed women to watch but not participate, the Cordeliers Club welcomed their full and equal participation. Their base was a monastery down the street from the cafés where they met for dinner, wine, food, and coffee, and to plot how to prevent aristocrats like Lafayette from stopping the Revolution too soon. The marquis became a favorite target and they eagerly crashed him into the very reefs he sought to avoid.

❦

THE FIRST GREAT crash came less than six weeks after Lafayette's zenith of the Fête de la Fédération. In August 1790, soldiers at Nancy, a garrison town near the main army headquarters in Metz, accused their officers of mistreatment and corruption. A local chapter of the Jacobin Club encouraged the men to speak out, as it was their patriotic duty to advance the spirit of liberty, equality, and democracy to all facets of society—including the army. When the soldiers felt their complaints unjustly ignored, they arrested their commanding officer, took possession of regimental pay chests, and refused to return to regular duty until certain demands were met. Three regiments of the French army were suddenly in open mutiny.

The commander of the Metz garrison, the marquis de Bouillé, personally led 4,500 loyal troops to Nancy to restore order. Bouillé just so happened to be one of Lafayette's cousins, and the two men exchanged letters about how to handle the situation. Lafayette's experience as a senior military officer led him to the straightforward conclusion the mutiny must be suppressed. He personally witnessed mutinies in the Continental Army and believed they simply could not be tolerated. However righteous and truthful the complaints, obedience must come first. When a debate opened in the National Assembly about the crisis, Lafayette made a point of personally addressing his colleagues. He said they must stand firmly on the side of military discipline. He said, "M. Bouillé needs the testimony of our approval and we must give it to him. I claim this for him, for the obedient troops, and for the national guards, who were created by liberty and will die for it."[3] When the assembly voted to grant Bouillé a free hand, Lafayette wrote his cousin, "The decree concerning Nancy is good: its execution must be complete and spirited."[4]

Meanwhile back in Nancy, the situation exploded. Bouillé issued a final ultimatum to the mutineers on August 31, but before they could respond, a skirmish broke out between the lines. A full-blown firefight commenced, leaving hundreds of soldiers killed and wounded on both sides. When the mutineers were ultimately defeated, Bouillé took his mandate from the National Assembly to act with decisive vigor. He ordered two dozen ringleaders immediately shot. Another forty conspirators received thirty-year sentences as galley slaves. Close to a hundred others were remanded to their home regiments for further individual punishment.

When news of these events reached Paris on September 2, Lafayette committed a political blunder. Focused on the narrow issue of military discipline, Lafayette congratulated Bouillé as "the savior of public affairs . . . I enjoy it doubly, as a citizen, and as your friend."[5] But the left-wing press turned the mutineers into sympathetic popular heroes. The news of the violent suppression and subsequent executions made Bouillé a villain and a butcher. Lafayette did not help his cause when he oversaw a ceremonial procession on the Champ de Mars on September 22 honoring the soldiers who fought and died *suppressing* the mutiny.

The verdict of the radical presses was merciless and unrelenting. Marat denounced Lafayette. "It was necessary to love the homeland," he wrote on September 15, "but what have you done for her? Far from espousing her cause, we always see you among her mortal enemies. With your soul of mud, fortune did everything for you, the Gods were jealous of your destinies, but to the happiness of being the savior of France you preferred the dishonorable role of ambitious greedy little courtier, treacherous trickster and, to heighten horror, a vile henchman of despotism." Marat promised all-out war on Lafayette: "Remember it was the *L'Ami du peuple* who first undermined your altars, and be assured we will not let go until you are overthrown."[6]

Desmoulins meanwhile went so far as to blame heartbreak over Lafayette's betrayal of the Revolution for the completely unrelated death of a patriotic editor. "He is dead with the name Lafayette on his lips," Desmoulins wrote, "looking at him like an ambitious officer who never had a soul large enough to play the role of Washington. . . . Yes, it is you, Lafayette, who killed him, not by the assassin's dagger or the legal knife of the judge, but by the pain of seeing only the most dangerous enemy of liberty in you, in whom we placed all our confidence, and who should be the firmest support of freedom."[7]

This wave of attacks in the press merged in the gossipy scandal rags. Anonymous tracts claimed Lafayette was not just in league with evil aristocrats, but was the queen's slavish lover. One pamphlet, titled *Evenings in Love with General Motier and the Beautiful Antoinette, by the Little Austrian Spaniel*, told lurid tales from the perspective of the queen's dog. This gossipy spaniel told its readers Marie Antoinette said, "Having everything to fear from Lafayette, it was necessary to use with him all the cunning of which a woman, and especially a German woman, is capable. Prayers, promises, tears, I spared nothing. It was in a moment of tenderness a pretty woman knows how to inspire that I captured my little bird. . . . Becoming my lover, he never ceases to give me constant attention, and he kisses me night and morning, which binds him to me even more."[8] Satirical cartoons circulated depicting Lafayette and the queen in all manner of acrobatic coitus. It was all preposterous—Marie Antoinette hated Lafayette's guts more than every radical in Paris put together—but the tracts pouring off the presses created a new impression of Lafayette. The Hero of Two Worlds was not an angel of liberty but a reactionary pig.

⁂

LAFAYETTE NEXT CRASHED into the contentious issue of religion. To finally solve the financial crisis, the National Assembly made the controversial decision in late 1789 to nationalize land owned by the Catholic Church. The land would be used to back paper bonds, called *assignats*, the government could use to pay its bills. As if this was not controversial enough, the assembly subsequently enacted a series of reforms collectively called the Civil Constitution of the Clergy. They abolished monasteries and convents; the people would elect bishops and other ecclesiastical offices; and the church's authority would be subordinated to the secular constitutional order. In July 1790, the National Assembly capped this project by directing all clergy in France to swear an oath of loyalty to the nation above any other authority. These reforms reflected a justifiable fear the church, as a bastion of traditional conservatism, would actively undermine the new enlightened revolutionary order. But when the pope condemned the Civil Constitution of the Clergy as heresy, he forced pious patriots to make a choice: save the Revolution or save their souls.

The national religious schism ran straight through the Lafayette household. As a devout Catholic, Adrienne refused to accept the Civil Constitution. As an advocate of freedom of religion, she refused to accept the National Assembly's right to punish priests who refused to swear the new civic oath. Virginie said her mother "encouraged them to exercise their functions and claim freedom of worship."[9] Adrienne's own pastor was among those who refused the oath, and she continued to attend his services, take Communion, and make her confession, even after it became a violation of the law. Virginie said Adrienne "went assiduously to the churches, and to the oratories where the persecuted clergy took refuge. She continually received nuns who complained and asked for protection."[10]

Adrienne's complicity with the *refusé* or *non-juring* priests soon became public and leant credibility to charges the family was in league with the Bourbons. The king was known to oppose the Civil Constitution. Marat wrote in *L'Ami du peuple*, "On the pretext of respecting religious opinions, Louis XVI authorized the rebel priests of Saint-Sulpice to preach revolt. [Lafayette's] wife is their abettor."[11] When Lafayette hosted a dinner for the newly installed constitutional bishop of Paris, a newspaper reported Adrienne "stayed in her own room, though she was in perfect health."[12] No less than the most ardent revolutionary, Adrienne refused to yield on principles she held dear.

Adrienne's religious scruples put Lafayette in a difficult position. He personally did not care about religion one way or the other, but as commander-general of the National Guard, he was obliged to uphold the Civil Constitution as the law of the land. It caused tension in the Lafayette household they both regretted. "My father was far from bothering her," Virginie recalled, "but you can imagine how painful it was for my mother to think she was doing him a real wrong by her conduct, and diminishing a popularity important to maintain."[13] Above all, however, both of them believed in freedom of worship as a core pillar of liberty, so Lafayette did nothing to force Adrienne to act against her conscience. Even as it tarnished his popular image.

⁂

By the beginning of 1791, Lafayette's vessel was clearly taking on water. He was no longer praised by everyone, but attacked by everyone. His next crash came from both sides at once. In February 1791, the king requested passports for his aging aunts to visit Rome for Holy Week. The radical presses in Paris exploded at the suggestion. It seemed both an insult to the new national church, and a flimsy excuse to sneak some more members of the royal family out of the country—to continue the process of emigration Artois kicked off after the fall of the Bastille.

When the National Assembly took the issue up, the Bourbons found an unlikely ally in the comte de Mirabeau. Mirabeau argued forcefully the two old women were entitled to freedom of movement. It would be unjust for the assembly to withhold permission to travel. Mirabeau's

speech surprised his colleagues, and convinced them to grant the passports. But Mirabeau's support was only surprising because no one knew
Mirabeau secretly entered the king's employ as an adviser and public
advocate. Believing the National Assembly now ran too far ahead of the
rest of the kingdom, Mirabeau foresaw a future where they fatally isolated themselves and France re-rallied to the king. Mirabeau wanted to
make sure he was on safe ground when the crash inevitably came. None
of this, however, would become public until after his death. Though
people did notice he was suddenly able to pay off his debts.

The looming departure of the royal aunts did not sit well with the
radical activists in Paris. On February 24, a crowd of demonstrators
marched to the Tuileries Palace to protest the decision. They demanded
to see the king, but Lafayette and the National Guard refused to let
them pass. He would not change his mind, even after Mayor Bailly personally requested a small delegation be allowed inside. The demonstration dissolved, but it only fueled rumors the Bourbons were preparing to
escape. A wild story spread there was a secret underground tunnel con-
necting the Tuileries Palace in the center of Paris to Château Vincennes
well beyond the eastern limits of the city. The belief took hold the royal
family was getting ready to fly the coop. The brewing anger and fear
soon bubbled over into what was later called the Day of Daggers.

On February 28, 1791, a rogue National Guard captain led about a
thousand workers out to Château Vincennes. Their plan was to raze the
enormous fortress complex, free any political prisoners found inside,
and seal the alleged secret passage before the king could escape. Alerted
to this plan, Lafayette mounted his white horse and led National Guard
companies out to stop them. He spent the rest of the day out on the
eastern perimeter of the Paris environs, dodging insults, projectiles, and
a few outright attempts to assassinate him.

Meanwhile, back in the heart of the city, word raced through what
was left of the conservative nobility that with Lafayette and the majority of National Guardsmen so far out of town, the king was physically
unprotected. About four hundred noblemen quickly armed themselves,
followed in the footsteps of their ancestors, and rallied to defend the
sovereign with their lives. If their armed defense of the king sparked
an ultraroyalist coup that ended the Revolution, so much the better.

When they arrived at the Tuileries Palace, a sympathetic chamberlain let them inside. They occupied the palace, surrounded the king, and waited. Alerted to this new danger, Lafayette raced back to the palace. Barging in, he demanded the nobles disarm themselves and leave, but they ignored him. Only after Louis, as caught in the middle as Lafayette, told his would-be protectors to disarm, did they sheath their blades and depart.

On the Day of Daggers, Lafayette successfully averted both a mob uprising and a reactionary coup. But Lafayette did not return home brimming with self-confidence. Left-wing radicals called him the king's stooge; ultraroyalist nobles called him the king's jailor. These factions shared nothing in common but the dream of seeing Lafayette's head on a pike. "My dear General," he wrote Washington a few weeks later, "Whatever expectations I conceived of a speedy termination to our revolutionary troubles, I am still tossed about in the ocean of factions and commotions of every kind—for it is my fate to be attacked, with equal animosity, from every side."[14] For once, Gouverneur Morris gave Lafayette some credit. "I am inclined to think," he wrote in his diary on March 3, "Lafayette will hold a good tug, being as cunning as anybody."[15] It was an ironically timed change of heart, as Morris dropped his skeptical pessimism just as Lafayette was about to lose control of the helm, crash into the reefs, and drown in the ocean of faction and commotion. Mirabeau, on the other hand, predicted Lafayette's fate with almost laser precision: "To speak only of an event easy to foresee . . . one day M. de La Fayette will open fire on the people. By that alone he will mortally wound himself."[16]

But Mirabeau would not live to see his prediction come true. A lifetime of hard living took its toll and Mirabeau's health flagged in the early spring of 1791. In April, he took to his bed and, after lingering dramatically for a few days to suck every last ounce of sympathy from his adoring public, died on April 2, 1791. Mirabeau was the first great leader of the Revolution to die, and his death set off a wave of public mourning. Having taken possession of an unfinished neoclassical church near the Luxembourg Palace, the National Assembly converted the building into a shrine to the nation dubbed the Pantheon, and voted Mirabeau the honor of being the first to be buried inside. Mirabeau's incriminating correspondence with the king would not be discovered for another two years. Including the damning advice the king get out of Paris as soon as possible.

⚏

EVER SINCE THE Revolution began, the possibility of King Louis fleeing France hung over the nation. Advisers and supporters begged for him to run. Enemies and detractors believed the king already had one foot out the door. But for the first two years of the French Revolution, Louis showed no intention of leaving. Despite almost daily suggestions from family and friends, Louis believed his place was with his subjects. Until the events of Easter 1791 changed everything.

As Easter approached, the king alerted the National Assembly of his intention to spend Holy Week at the royal château in Saint-Cloud. This did not seem like a controversial request, as the royal family did the same thing the year before. Besides, Saint-Cloud was just a few miles outside Paris—not even halfway to Versailles—it's not like he was requesting permission to go to Metz. But with rumors flying about the royal family making a run for it, the assembly greeted the request with suspicion. But for Louis, going to Saint-Cloud for Easter was not about getting away from France, but staying close to God. Louis was a pious Catholic. He hated the Civil Constitution of the Clergy, and considered it blasphemy. He could not stand the thought of spending Easter trapped in the Tuileries Palace with the heretical clergymen assigned to him by the National Assembly. This was not about his life, or his crown, but his soul.

On April 18, the royal family loaded their carriages for a trip. When word spread the family was leaving, a crowd gathered at the palace to physically block the gates. Lafayette, as was his lot in life, once again mounted his horse and rode off to confront an angry mob. Lafayette believed the royal family had every right to leave and ordered the crowd to let them pass. The crowd refused. As the king, queen, and their children sat in carriages, they watched Lafayette's helpless inability to control, direct, or disperse the crowd. After hours of futile haranguing, Lafayette gave up. He told the royal family they would have to go back inside. The crowd was not going to let them pass.

Ever since the king came to Paris from Versailles, everyone maintained the pretense he was there of his own free will. He was not a prisoner, but a happy, benevolent, and willing citizen king. The standoff over the holiday to Saint-Cloud exposed this myth to the harsh light of reality. Nobody's illusions were shattered harder than the king's. The mob at the gates could not have been clearer: the king was a captive, the Tuileries was his prison. Up until Easter 1791, the king steadfastly refused to consider leaving France. Now he turned to his wife and told her to activate whatever plans she may have laid. The time had come to stage a jailbreak.

The events of April 18 were as personally devastating for Lafayette as for the king. The disobedient crowd exposed his dwindling moral authority. A newspaper editorial said it best: "Monsieur de Lafayette is treading the path between two abysses, when sooner or later he will be the victim of one party or the other. Retirement alone can save him. The solution may not be the most heroic one, but it is at least the safest."[17] That night, he resigned as commander-general of the National Guard for the second time. Adrienne was not-so-secretly thrilled. Virginie said her mother was "overflowing with joy at the thought of my father's returning to private life."[18] Every day for the past two years Adrienne watched her husband ride off to confront mobs, assassins, and armed agitators. The fact he was still alive was something of a minor miracle.

But just as happened when Lafayette resigned the first time back in July 1789, the leaders of Paris begged him to stay. Who else could possibly do the job? A newspaper reported, "The municipality, headed by M. Bailly called upon M. de Lafayette at 11 o'clock at night. It conferred with him behind locked doors. The rooms of the house, the courtyard, and part of the street were swarming with members of the National Guard. It was raining torrents. Madame de Lafayette appeared and, addressing those who were outside, expressed her regret at not being able to provide shelter for them all, and made it clear how deeply touched she was by their zeal."[19] Lafayette resisted all entreaties for several days. Only after they agreed to restructure the Guard to purge disobedient malcontents did the commander-general agree to return to his post.

Adrienne bit her tongue and retied her knot of daily stress. "My mother's joy lasted only four days," Virginie said. Her mother "resumed her painful pursuit of worrying about my father's safety."[20] From across the Atlantic, Washington echoed these sentiments. "I assure you I have often contemplated with great anxiety," he wrote, "the danger to which you are personally exposed by your peculiar and delicate situation in the tumult of the times, and your letters are far from quieting that friendly concern."[21] And it was only going to get worse.

⊰⊱

QUEEN MARIE ANTOINETTE had been lobbying her husband to flee France for years. After the events of April 18, he finally allowed her to put her plans in motion. She had two principal accomplices on the outside. First, the devoutly loyal Swedish count Axel von Fersen, who was almost certainly the queen's lover in younger and happier days. The other was the marquis de Bouillé, convinced more than ever the Revolution must be crushed. Fersen arranged the logistics of the escape from Paris, while Bouillé ensured safe harbor for the royal family in a fortress near the garrison in Metz.[22]

Lafayette did not suspect a thing, even though rumors of a royal escape flew around Paris throughout May and June 1791. But rumors of this sort had been omnipresent background noise for years. In Lafayette's experience, they usually traced back to scurrilous rabble-rousers who did not know what they were talking about. The king continued to assure Lafayette he had no intention of leaving. On previous occasions, Louis honestly meant these assurances, but now he intentionally lied. As soon as Lafayette turned his back, the royal family plotted their escape.

After weeks of conspiracy, planning, and unforeseen delays, the operation was finally scheduled for the night of June 20. But on that fateful night, Lafayette nearly uncovered the plot without even realizing it. The members of the family slipped out of their apartments one by one in the midst of a bustling shift change of the palace servants. As the queen made her way through the courtyard, Lafayette's carriage suddenly appeared. For a split second, Marie Antoinette was lit up by the lanterns. But disguised as a lowly governess, she went unnoticed. Lafayette and Mayor Bailly had both come to discuss urgent business with the king. Had they arrived an hour later, Louis would have already snuck away and the escape would have been discovered instantly. But instead, Lafayette and Bailly found the king in his chambers. They met for an hour before departing at midnight, little realizing when the king said he was going to bed, he instead donned the uniform of a coachman and raced to meet his family, waiting nervously in a carriage for him.

Despite Lafayette nearly ruining everything at the last minute, the royal family got away. Their governess was dressed as an aristocrat and given false papers saying she was a Russian countess on her way home. They traveled undetected all through the night. The children's governess later recalled that the king kept one eye on his watch. When it ticked to eight o'clock in the morning the king said, "Lafayette must be feeling quite embarrassed." The governess said, "It was difficult to share [Lafayette's] anxiety, and to experience any other feeling than the joy of having shaken off his dependence."[23]

The king, however, turned out to be incorrect. At that moment Lafayette was not embarrassed, he was alarmed and panicked. Frantic guards woke him up to say the royal family were missing and no one knew where they were. Had they fled? Been abducted? If so, by whom? Ultraroyalists? Radical republicans? Lafayette rushed to the Tuileries but found no answers. Mayor Bailly and the president of the National Assembly, Alexandre de Beauharnais, joined him. They all agreed whatever the truth, and whoever was to blame, the king *must* be found and brought back. "Do you think," Lafayette asked them, "the arrest of the king and his family is necessary for public salvation and can alone avert civil war?" They said yes. "Well then, I take the responsibility upon myself." Lafayette wrote an order saying, "Enemies of the nation, having kidnapped the king and his family, all the national guards and all citizens are ordered to arrest them."[24] This was to be a national manhunt to solve the national crisis.

Then Lafayette faced the unenviable task of briefing the nation's political leaders. After consulting with the Paris leadership at the Hôtel de Ville, he pushed through hostile crowds toward the National Assembly. Once inside he announced the disappearance to his thunderstruck audience: "The National Assembly is informed of the attack which public enemies, in the abusive hope of compromising French liberty, executed last night on the king and part of his family."[25] Lafayette's public story was that enemies of the Revolution abducted the king. It was the only story he could afford to believe. If the king ran away of his own accord, the results would be disastrous.

But the king already destroyed Lafayette's thin hope it was an abduction, not an escape. Attendants discovered a document on the king's desk titled *Declaration of the King, Addressed to All the French, Upon His Departure from Paris*. The National Assembly received the document, where it was read aloud to ominous silence. The king made it plain he ran away, and blamed his departure on the unconscionable conduct of his subjects. "As long as the King hoped to see the order and happiness of the kingdom reborn by the means employed by the National Assembly," the address began, "no personal sacrifice was too much. . . . But today the only reward for so many sacrifices is to see the destruction of royalty, its powers unrecognized, properties violated, the safety of the people everywhere in danger, crimes going unpunished, and a complete anarchy establishing itself above the law."[26]

Louis proceeded to pour out two years' worth of pent up resentment over nearly six thousand carefully crafted words, complaining of problems high and low, from political and constitutional violations to perceived personal insults like the state of the Tuileries upon his return to Paris in 1789 where "nothing was ready to receive the King, and the layout of the old apartments was far from providing the conveniences to which His Majesty was accustomed in the other royal houses, and which any private individual might enjoy." Louis expected this all to be read by his people once he was safely away. But he wanted them to know he hoped they came to their senses. "Beware of the suggestions and lies of your false friends," he finished, "return to your King, he will always be your father, your best friend."[27] The king's address stunned the National Assembly. It was nothing less than a royal betrayal of the Revolution.

Lafayette's reputation, already badly bruised, was mercilessly pummeled. At best he was an incompetent idiot. At worst, in league with the royal family. Danton attacked him in the Jacobins and through the newspaper *Révolutions de Paris*: "The most honest man of his kingdom, that's what you called Louis XVI, the most honest man of his kingdom, this father of French, following the example of the Hero of Two

Worlds, has left his post." The paper denounced Lafayette's incompetence, saying, "The general of an army of thirty thousand men, who lets a whole family escape, warned eight days in advance of the plot, is a criminal or an imbecile."[28] Elsewhere, Danton issued a dire threat: "The commander-general promised on his head the king would not leave; we need the person of the king or the head of the commander-general."[29]

Luckily for Lafayette, they got the person of the king. When the fugitives briefly stopped in the little town of Sainte-Menehould, the postmaster recognized the distinctive profile of the king: big nose and bullfrog throat. The postmaster raced onto the next town, Varennes, and rousted the mayor and local National Guard. When the coach of the alleged Russian countess appeared, the leaders of Varennes detained the party and inspected the papers. The incredible discovery confirmed: the king and queen of France were in their custody. The incident is now called the Flight to Varennes—but really it should be called the Flight *As Far As* Varennes. They never reached their intended destination.

When Paris got news on the morning of June 22, the National Assembly dispatched three delegates to formally escort the royal family back to Paris. The quick secret escape turned into a slow public return. Observers, gawkers, and crowds packed the roads and towns. Local National Guard companies joined an ever-growing procession taking the family back to the capital. When they finally reached Paris on June 25, Lafayette met them at the edge of the city and escorted them through the huge gathered crowds. But these crowds neither cheered their sovereign nor brayed for his blood. Chilling silence prevailed. A notice had been posted everywhere: "ANYONE WHO CHEERS THE KING WILL BE BEATEN; ANYONE WHO INSULTS HIM WILL BE HANGED."[30]

By order of the National Assembly, Lafayette placed the family under arrest until they made a final determination about what *really* happened. Lafayette said to the king, "Sire, Your Majesty knows my loyalty to the crown, but I must tell you if the Crown separates itself from the people I will remain on the side of the people." The king replied, "That is true. You have acted in accordance with your principles. It is all a matter of party. . . . And now here I am." Lafayette asked, "Does your Majesty have any orders for me?" The king shook his head: "It seems that I am more subject to your orders than you are to mine."[31]

The Flight to Varennes delivered another savage blow to Lafayette's reputation and morale. He promised the king would never run. Then the king ran. He did not know what might happen next. He wrote Washington wistfully about the far more encouraging news he read about the young United States: "I rejoice and glory in the happy situation of American affairs. I bless the restoration of your health, and wish I could congratulate you on your side of the Atlantic, but we are not in a state of tranquility which may admit of my absence."[32] It would be a long time before Lafayette enjoyed anything resembling peace.

❦

THE FLIGHT TO Varennes set up Lafayette's final fall from grace. A panic-stricken National Assembly, betrayed by their king, could neither pretend nothing happened nor admit the truth. The logical consequences of the truth would be to depose the king, which none of them wanted to do. So instead they concocted a great big lie. After weeks of discussion, the committee investigating the incident announced enemies of the nations abducted the king. His "escape" was really a kidnapping. They declared the letter he left behind to be a forgery. No one believed these lies, not even the delegates themselves, but they believed they needed an official cover story to save the constitution.

The people of Paris disagreed. Almost as soon as the king was returned to the Tuileries Palace, radical activists in the Jacobins and Cordeliers Club organized a demonstration on the Champ de Mars. The conservative marquis de Ferrières reported to his wife, "All the firebrands of the capital were released that same evening in the clubs, and the cafes, howling horrors against Louis XVI and against the Assembly . . . a large group from the Palais-Royal and the lair of the Cordeliers, went to the Jacobins, and began to cry out they did not want a king . . . a petition was proposed, to carry it to the Champ de Mars, to the altar of the fatherland, to have it signed by all the citizens."[33] At the very altar of the nation where they all swore an oath to king, nation, and constitution, they planned to post a petition demanding the abdication of Louis XVI.

On the morning of July 17, 1791, organizers of the demonstration arrived at the Champ de Mars. As they prepared for the event, they discovered two men hiding inside the altar of the nation. These two were almost certainly a harmless pair of vagabonds, but in the tense atmosphere they were accused of being spies, saboteurs, or assassins. They were rousted, dragged off, and summarily lynched. Though there was no violence after this initial incident, it made it difficult to argue the protestors harbored entirely peaceful intentions.

Across town in the Hôtel de Ville, the leaders of Paris determined they could not let this demonstration on the Champ de Mars turn into another July 14 or October 5. With two people already dead at the hands of the mob, they acted decisively to prevent further violent chaos. In consultation with Lafayette and Bailly, they authorized a declaration of martial law, giving the mayor and the commander-general of the National Guard *carte blanche* to do whatever they believed necessary to disperse the crowd.

As the forces of order mustered, the protest on the Champ de Mars grew into the tens of thousands. The initial violence was forgotten. Families, peddlers, and entertainers all congregated for a long Sunday picnic in the park. They ate, played, chatted, and listened to speeches. Those so inclined came up and signed their names on the final copy of the petition. The document itself is often described as a "republican" petition calling for the overthrow of the monarchy, but it merely demanded the removal of Louis from power: "His betrayal, his desertion, protestation . . . entail a formal abdication of the constitutional crown entrusted to him." They specifically cited the statement the king left behind as galling proof of his perfidious infidelity: "Louis XVI, after having accepted the duties of kingship and sworn to defend the constitution, has deserted the post entrusted to him, has protested against this constitution by a declaration written and signed by his own hand, has sought to paralyze the executive power by his flight and orders." In light of these betrayals, their sole concrete demand was "the National Assembly accept, in the nation's name, Louis XVI's abdication on June 21st of the crown delegated to him, and provide for his replacement by all constitutional means."[34] It is estimated about six thousand people signed their names over the course of the day.

It is impossible to know what would have happened had Lafayette and Bailly not intervened. By all accounts, the demonstration was calm.

But peaceful protest during the day often turns violent when night falls. We will never know what would have happened because Lafayette and Bailly *did* intervene. And their arrival precipitated a tragedy. The order of events is incredibly confused thanks to conflicting accounts. Lafayette and some National Guard companies arrived in the afternoon and ordered the crowd to disperse. When they were ignored, Lafayette and his men regrouped and waited for reinforcements. At around seven o'clock in the evening, Bailly appeared with more men, waving the red flag of martial law and repeating the order to disperse. Then accounts get *very* confused.

Lafayette later recorded the National Guard "presented themselves at the entrance to Champ-de-Mars and were greeted by a hail of stones." This much is probably true. He went on to say, "There were also firearms and a pistol fired on the mayor." Lafayette and Bailly both claim someone in the crowd fired at the mayor. This claim is disputed but it's certainly not implausible a few people in the crowd were armed. Lafayette then said, "In the midst of this attack, the National Guard fired into the air to avoid injuring anyone; but the assailants, emboldened by this moderation, redoubled the attack against the municipal officers and the national guards, some of whom were attacked . . . then the National Guard fired in earnest."[35]

One thing everyone agrees is the National Guard fired directly into the crowd. It is not clear whether Lafayette gave an explicit order to fire, whether a threat from the crowd triggered retaliation, whether it was an unprovoked attack, or simply an undisciplined accident. Whatever the explanation, the National Guard *did* fire into the crowd, sparking mass panic. People ran in every direction as shots rang out. It was all over in a few bloody, noisy, confusing minutes. Lafayette and Bailly returned their companies to disciplined order. They succeeded in dispersing the crowd, but at what cost? The only way to know was to count the bodies.

As Lafayette remained on the Champ de Mars, he did not realize his own family was in danger. Part of the furious and aggrieved crowd marched in the direction of his house on rue de Bourbon. Virginie, nine years old at the time, later recalled the approach of a mob "screaming that my mother should be murdered and her head carried to meet her husband."[36] Virginie said, "I remember the dreadful cries we heard, the terror of everyone in the house, but above all the great joy of my mother at the thought the brigands who were arriving were no longer at the Champ de Mars. She embraced us, weeping for joy and, in this pressing danger, took the necessary precautions with great calm and so much relief."[37] Virginie said the mob came very near breaking into the house: "The guard was doubled, and they lined up in front of the house; the brigands were just about to enter the house, by the garden which looked out on the Place du Palais-Bourbon and whose small wall they were scaling, when a body of cavalry passing through, dispersed them."[38]

Lafayette and his family lived, but too many others died that day. The total number of dead is disputed, with estimates ranging from as low as a dozen to an exaggerated accusation of more than four hundred, with modern historians reasonably estimating fifty.[39] But for Lafayette, the specific number was hardly the point. Mirabeau's prediction came true: Lafayette fired on the people and dealt himself a mortal wound. The Massacre of the Champ de Mars was the last and greatest reef he crashed his vessel into.

The next issue of the *Révolutions de Paris* minced no words: "Blood has just flowed in the field of the federation; the altar of the nation is stained with it; men and women have been slaughtered; the citizens are appalled."[40] Lafayette could protest his innocence and argue the body count was exaggerated—he insisted to his dying day "the loss which took place on the side of the assailants has been madly exaggerated"— but his reputation as a popular hero was now as dead as the men and women who lay on the Champ de Mars.[41] He did not intend to preside over a massacre. That was not his nature. Lafayette was not a reactionary monster sadistically relishing the murder of his fellow citizens. But he could not undo what happened, nor simply wave away his own culpability. He was in charge that day. He was to blame. Almost exactly one year earlier he stood on that very spot in the middle of the Champ de Mars, basking in the triumphant cheers of adoring crowds. From that great peak he tumbled off a cliff, and drowned in the ocean of faction and commotion.

CHAPTER SEVENTEEN

HIS CIRCLE IS COMPLETED

[1791–1792]

THE SHOCKING EVENTS OF THE SUMMER OF 1791 CONVINCED the delegates of the National Assembly to complete their work and go home. The king called them to Versailles in May 1789 to resolve a financial crisis, and they unilaterally declared themselves a constitutional convention. Over the past two years, they approved a series of wide-ranging reforms that, taken together, formed the foundation of a postrevolutionary constitutional monarchy. But they never actually wrote the final draft of the constitution. The Flight to Varennes exposed how shaky that foundation really was—the monarch at the center of the constitutional monarchy turned out to be a completely unreliable partner. But rather than scrap everything and start over, the National Assembly forged ahead under the official cover story that reactionary villains kidnapped Louis against his will. They spent August and September ironing out the final language of what came to be called the Constitution of 1791. Once promulgated, they hoped both king and nation would accept the new order and move forward together.

Buried in the pile of decrees, laws, and statutes the delegates now cobbled together was an innocuous ordinance approved back in May 1791. Maximilien Robespierre, rising leader of the left-wing Jacobins, proposed he and his fellow National Assembly delegates forbid themselves from serving in the coming Legislative Assembly, the body that would succeed the National Assembly as soon as the constitution was finished. Robespierre's colleagues loved the idea. Some jumped at the chance to show their selfless virtue; others were exhausted and eager for retirement; radicals spied an opportunity to neutralize moderates and advance the Revolution; conservatives spied the same opportunity, but believed the result would help crash the Revolution. The upshot of Robespierre's self-denying ordinance was *none* of the people who crafted the Constitution of 1791—who understood how and why it came to be—were allowed the opportunity make it work. A rueful National Assembly delegate, Baron Malouet, later reflected, "There was only one final blunder left for us to make and sure enough we made it."[1]

After a few final rounds of negotiation, the king signed the final draft of the constitution on September 13. The National Assembly's job was complete. The delegates swore in June 1789 to continue meeting until they drafted a new constitution for France. It took more than two years, but they finally fulfilled that oath. They dissolved permanently on September 30, 1791. It was time to pass the reins.

The next day, a newly elected Legislative Assembly took over the Salle du Manège. The Legislative Assembly was meant to compose merely the legislative branch of the new constitutional government, sitting alongside an executive and judicial branch. But the delegates elected to the Legislative Assembly had new objectives. Many of the incoming delegates rose to prominence over the past two years criticizing the National Assembly's work. They were not satisfied with the power-sharing arrangement of the Constitution of 1791. Most prominent among the incoming representatives was Jacques-Pierre Brissot, elected to office on the strength of two years of radically democratic journalism. Brissot and his fellow representatives had no personal stake in the success of the Constitution of 1791 and believed the Legislative Assembly embodied the totality of national sovereignty. It was time for the next phase of the French Revolution to begin.

THE MARQUIS DE Lafayette did not see a role for himself in this new phase. The string of demoralizing setbacks over the past year left him exhausted and eager to lay his burdens down. So as his former colleagues in the National Assembly departed Paris, Lafayette followed them out the door. On October 8, 1791, Lafayette resigned as commander-general of the National Guard for the third and final time. No one tried to stop him this time.

In a farewell address to his men, Lafayette said, "At the moment when the National Assembly has deposited its powers, when the functions of its members have ceased, I also reach the end of the engagements which I contracted."[2] He thanked the men profusely for their service through twenty-seven months of Revolution. "I would like to recall, Gentlemen, how, in the midst of so many hostile plots, ambitious intrigues, licentious mistakes, you opposed with indefatigable firmness all perverse combinations, the fury of the factions, seductions of all types, for the pure love of the homeland."[3] Then he bade them a final farewell. "Receive the eyes of the most tender friend for the common prosperity, for the particular happiness of each of you, and that his memory, often present in your thoughts, mingles with the feeling which unites us all, of 'live free or die.'"[4]

As a parting gift his men presented the outgoing commander-general with a sword forged from melted locks taken from the now destroyed Bastille. As Lafayette departed, Mayor Bailly announced, "We shall never forget the Hero of Two Worlds, who played so great a part in the Revolution."[5] It was an emotional and bittersweet day, but unlike Lafayette's first two resignations, no one dropped to their knees and begged him to stay.

Lafayette and Adrienne packed up fourteen-year-old Anastasie, eleven-year-old Georges, and nine-year-old Virginie and departed for Lafayette's ancestral home in Chavaniac. Though his popular standing in Paris was at an all-time low, the further Lafayette got from the capital, the more cheers and acclaim he received. "My journey has been a long one," he wrote Madame de Simiane, "but being obliged to stop at every place I come to, parade on foot through the towns big and small, and receive enough civic crowns to fill a carriage, I could not travel as quickly as I usually do."[6] After eleven days and four hundred miles, the

family pulled into Chavaniac on October 19, auspiciously the tenth anniversary of Cornwallis's surrender at Yorktown.

When Lafayette ran off to America in 1777, he was merely a private
individual without rank, position, or public responsibility. And though
his personality almost certainly precluded this being a *permanent* retirement, he took his withdrawal from public life seriously. Local provincial
leaders offered to make him president of their provincial assembly, but
he declined. When Bailly retired as mayor of Paris, Lafayette's friends
encouraged him to run for the office, but he told them he wasn't coming back. Undeterred, they placed his name on the ballot in absentia.
Lafayette didn't garner many votes in the subsequent election, but he
didn't mind. He did not want the job.

Lafayette's personal correspondence reveals a man ready to rest on
the sidelines. "After fifteen years of revolution," he wrote Washington, "I
am in an excellent disposition to take advantage of a new state, [a] quiet
and pleasant life in the mountains where I was born. . . . I find myself
happy amidst people who are no longer anyone's vassals."[7] His sister-in-
law Pauline, herself married to a neighboring Auvergne noble, reported
to the duc d'Ayen, now living as an émigré in Switzerland, "What will
surprise you is the kind of life he intends to live in retirement. Not one
single secretary has been brought with him to the country. Books, Swiss
cows, Spanish sheep, and the Maltese donkey, will provide him his sole
occupation. Those [occupations] in which he has been involved the last
twenty-seven months have really truly exhausted him."[8] Lafayette told
Simiane, "Those who believe that I am coming here for a revolution
are great fools. I put as much pleasure and perhaps self-indulgence in
absolute rest as I have given for fifteen years to action."[9]

Lafayette's principal fixations after returning to his childhood home
were agricultural, not political. He hired a landscape architect and professional agronomist to help him turn Chavaniac into a model farm
using modern techniques and practices. He boasted to Washington
about his "good house, formerly a feudal manor, changed into a large
farm and run by an English farmer whom I brought in for my education."[10] This cost a lot of money, and he directed his financial managers
to sell more property from his portfolio to pay the bills. An accounting
of his finances show Lafayette's income now stood at about 57,000

livres annually, not too far off from the "quarter of my fortune" he once professed to be all he needed or wanted.[11]

Adrienne was content for the first time in years. "We live here in a world of profound peace," she wrote. "Monsieur de Lafayette revels in its delights as though he has never known a more active existence. His land, his house, mademoiselle his aunt, his children, his writings of a few letters now fill his life completely."[12] But she closed these happy reflections with a prophecy that would come true far faster than she would have imagined: "Only war against the *émigrés* could tear him away now and I hope nothing of that sort will happen."[13] She could not have imagined how specifically and immediately this prophesy would come true, ruining her family's chance at peace and happiness.

⚞⚟

AFTER THE FLIGHT to Varennes, aristocratic emigration accelerated. Noble families streamed out of France despite a law stating anyone who departed without a passport risked having lands, estates, and property confiscated. Lafayette's cousin, the marquis de Bouillé (who himself prudently quit France after being implicated in the Flight to Varennes), observed with satisfaction, "Emigration, which had been small until then, became almost general among the members of the first orders of the state . . . the roads in France were covered with men, women, and children who feared being buried under the ruins of the crumbling monarchy."[14]

Those who just wanted to get away resettled in England, Switzerland, Italy, Spain, or the Netherlands. Those more actively hostile to the Revolution flocked to the banner of the comte d'Artois, who made his base in Coblentz, a city in the Holy Roman Empire situated on the border with France. Bouillé said, "In the space of the few months following my exit from France, almost all the officers of the army left their flag, and came to join the French princes who had retired to Coblentz."[15] From this base, Artois lobbied the courts of Europe, most especially Austria and Prussia, to give him the money, guns, and soldiers necessary to rescue his brother from the clutches of the despicable revolutionaries. For the rest of his life, Lafayette used the term

Coblentz as an epithet for anything he thought backward, conservative, or reactionary.

Artois and his growing legion of *émigrés* were a well-known threat. Lafayette told Washington: "The *émigrés* line our borders, intriguing with all despotic governments."[16] The fear of invasion was understandable at the time, but in the full light of history, the danger was grossly exaggerated. Wherever they arrived in Europe, local authorities treated the émigrés as a barely tolerated nuisance. For centuries, France was a powerful and menacing adversary. Far from sympathizing with the Bourbons, the other crowned heads of Europe positively delighted in their humiliating struggles. As France burned, the other European powers did not reach for a bucket of water; they sat back to warm themselves by the fire.

But a vocal minority faction in the newly installed Legislative Assembly believed the émigrés posed a dire existential threat to the nation and the Revolution. Jacques-Pierre Brissot was among the key leaders of this faction, but as many of the other members came from the region around Bordeaux, the whole group came to bear the name of the geographic area: the Girondins. What the loosely affiliated Girondins shared in common was a radically democratic ideology asserting the nation was not the partner of the king, but his superior in every way. They also believed it was France's destiny to export the Revolution—to liberate Europe from the clutches of anachronistic medieval dynasties. After arriving in Paris, Brissot and the Girondins took over the Jacobin Club, where one could hear a preview of the next day's agenda for the Legislative Assembly. Their principal agenda in the autumn of 1791 was declaring war on the émigrés—which they believed would be a catalyst for completing the Revolution at home and spreading its universal values abroad. Thus, long before the Girondins went down in history as martyrs to idealistic moderation, they were identified as the "war party," eagerly leading France toward armed conflict. If, like Saturn, the Revolution devoured her children, it was only after the Girondins sacrificed her to Mars, god of war.

As the Girondins called the nation to mobilize for war, they found the king surprisingly willing to go along. But where the Girondins conceived of war as a catalyst for advancing the Revolution, Louis believed the opposite. The king was well acquainted with the state of the French army: at least a third of its officers had already resigned and emigrated, while another third were about to follow. If France marched to war, her armies would surely disintegrate upon first contact with the enemy. Far from opposing an armed conflict, Louis believed it the perfect solution to his unhappy predicament. When the Legislative Assembly asked the king to issue an ultimatum to the German principalities on the Rhine demanding they expel the émigrés or face war, Louis happily obliged.

On December 19, 1791, the king signed orders forming three new armies, each consisting of fifty thousand men and headed by a patriotic and reliable general. The minister of war assigned one army to the sixty-seven-year-old comte de Rochambeau. The hero of the American war was one of the few senior generals left who had not yet emigrated. The second army went to General Nicolas Luckner, a German-born officer serving in the French army since 1763 and a vocal supporter of the Revolution. For the third army, the minister could think of no one who combined military experience with revolutionary ardor quite like the marquis de Lafayette. With a mix of delight and contempt, King Louis signed an order recalling the recently retired Lafayette to military service—quite sure it would lead straight to Lafayette's defeat and humiliation.

⊰⊱

LAFAYETTE CAME TO Chavaniac prepared for prolonged retirement. Now, less than three months later, he packed his bags. As Adrienne feared, her husband could not refuse the call to arms. His king and his nation needed him; he must go. Besides, returning to his roots in the regular army presented a welcome alternative to the messiness of politics. Military life was simple and easy—even a full-blown war would be less complicated than managing revolutionary Paris. As Lafayette prepared to leave, his family did not know when they would see him again. As it turned out, when Lafayette rode away in December 1791, Adrienne, Anastasie, and Virginie would not see him again for four long years. Lafayette would not lay eyes on Georges again until 1798. Much was about to happen.

When Lafayette arrived in Metz, he was not thrilled by what he found. It was the "irruption into Canada" all over again, but on a massive scale. Not half the forces assigned to him were actually present. Those who *were* present were mostly patriotic volunteers recruited from city streets and peasant villages. Not only did these new soldiers lack discipline, they made a positive virtue of their egalitarian disdain for military protocol. They came not just to fight France's foreign enemies, but to convert the old army of aristocratic tyranny into a national army of free citizens. Gouverneur Morris reported to George Washington, "Their army is undisciplined to a degree you can hardly conceive. . . . Volunteers are in many instances that corrupted scum of overgrown population of which large cities purge themselves [with] every vice and every disease which can render them the scourge of their friends and the scoff of their foes."[17]

Lafayette recognized the difficulties but put on a brave face: "The danger for us lies with our state of anarchy, owing to the ignorance of the people," he wrote Washington in March 1792, "which are worked up by designing men, or aristocrats in disguise; but both extremes tend to defeat our ideas of public order. Do not believe, however, my dear General, the exaggerated accounts you may receive, particularly from England. That liberty and equality will be preserved in France, there is no doubt."[18]

Upon taking up his command, however, Lafayette made one of the most glaring and inexplicable mistakes of his career. Perhaps the exhausting frustrations of his years in Paris soured his attitude, but when he took command of his army, Lafayette imposed a harsh and unforgiving code of discipline. He treated his men not as eager and patriotic volunteers, but as unruly rabble. He missed a golden opportunity not only to redeem himself, but to shine as the perfect general for a new national army of free citizens. What makes the mistake so inexplicable is Lafayette watched Baron von Steuben drill, train, and mold the Continental Army at Valley Forge. Lafayette personally helped translate von Steuben's improvised field manual, which emphasized a republican army required a different approach: simple maneuvers and formations, discipline matched by genuine concern for the well-being of the soldiers, and orders issued with patient explanation. If ever there was a time to break out Steuben's field manual, it was here and now. But instead, Lafayette reverted to the outdated mentality of an aristocratic officer—what these men needed was a sharp tongue and short leash. Rather than fostering loyalty, love, and support, Lafayette drove them into sullen resentment. It was one of Lafayette's greatest blunders.

Despite the Girondins' best efforts, war did not come with the new year. Terrified of invasion, the German principalities responded to France's ultimatum by expelling the émigrés from their territory. Having been denied their chance at a quick and easy campaign, the Girondins turned their attention to Austria. Despite years of desperate appeals from Artois, Austria remained steadfastly aloof and showed no interest in a war with France. Even as the French became determined to start a war with someone, *anyone*, over the winter of 1791–1792, Austria refused to take the bait. Everything changed on March 1, 1792, when Marie Antoinette's brother, Emperor Leopold II, suddenly died. Leopold's twenty-four-year-old son Francis ascended to the throne. Much more bellicose than his father, Francis was spoiling to put revolutionary France in her place. Having finally found a willing partner, the two sides exchanged ultimatums and counter-ultimatums in the spring of 1792.

War was now inevitable. From his position on the front line, Lafayette wrote Adrienne, "I cannot hide from you my opinion that war is becoming more and more probable. There's still hope, but I should be much more inclined now to put my money on a war."[19] He expressed concerns about the political fractures in Paris—especially as men like Robespierre, Danton, and Desmoulins, whom he called "the hard core of the Jacobin rabble," denounced him on a daily basis.[20] But, he said, "as I have already made clear, the French nation is my only party, and my friends and I are at the disposal of anyone who will act for the best, defend liberty and equality, uphold the Constitution, and reject everything that may tend to give it either an aristocratic or republican coloring. When the will of the nation, expressed by the elected representatives of the people and by the King, shall have declared that war is inevitable, I shall do everything in my power to bring it to a successful conclusion."[21]

On April 20, 1792, King Louis declared war on Austria amid a flurry of intoxicated and patriotic cheering in the Legislative Assembly. With war declared, Prussia joined Austria in an anti-French coalition, and the German powers issued their own retaliatory declarations of war. Both sides entered the conflict under the impression victory would be quick and easy. The Austrians and Prussians believed the French armies fatally weakened by the emigration of their best officers and lack of disciplined experience in the rank and file. The Girondins, meanwhile, convinced the people of France the ruling dynasties of Europe were as aged, decrepit, and feeble as the Bourbons—they would be easily swept aside by the might of the French nation under arms. Neither turned out to be right, and their mutual miscalculations in the spring of 1792 triggered a series of conflicts between the European powers lasting, almost uninterrupted, for the next twenty-three years.

⊰⊱

IT WOULD HAVE been difficult to believe in the opening weeks of the war the conflict was going to last for a generation. Lafayette and Rochambeau tentatively advanced their armies toward the Austrian Netherlands (modern Belgium), but the French soldiers repeatedly turned and fled even the lightest skirmishes. One division concluded their chaotic retreats must be due to treasonous betrayals of their general, so they tracked him down after the battle and summarily lynched him. General Rochambeau was so disgusted with the conduct of the men that he chose to take no further part in the ignoble farce and resigned his command. Lafayette's forces behaved little better, but probably only survived because the Austrian and Prussians concluded it would be a waste of blood and treasure to invade. Much cheaper and easier to simply wait for the inevitable disintegration of the French army—which they expected at any moment.

Back in Paris, the Girondins scrambled to explain the unexpected reverses. As defeat could not be the fault of French inexperience, incompetence, or cowardice, they blamed treachery, betrayal, and treason. The Legislative Assembly passed punitive decrees against suspicious foreigners and ordered any priest who refused to swear the civic oath be deported. The king refused to go along with these measures and used his suspensive veto to delay implementation of the decrees. Lafayette wrote the king a letter of support saying, "Persist, Sire, and use the authority which the national will delegated to you . . . to defend constitutional principles against all their enemies."[22]

Then the king went further. Feeling ignored and disrespected by his Girondin ministers, the king used his authority to dissolve his cabinet. But as he made these moves, Louis invoked constitutional powers his opponents did not even believe he should have. In their view, the nation—represented by the Legislative Assembly—must be the supreme and ultimate authority, especially when faced with a king suspected of rooting for his own armies to lose a war. The leaders of the Jacobins and the Cordeliers Club went to work whipping their members into a fury. The streets of Paris rose once again.

Lafayette was furious at the reports he received from Paris. He concluded the principal threat to the national war effort was not treasonous conservatives but radical insurrectionaries. He wrote a scathing letter to the Legislative Assembly demanding they take hold of the situation. "The constitution is the law governing the legislature," he wrote. "I blame you, gentlemen, for the powerful efforts to divert you from the course you have promised to follow . . . can you deny . . . the Jacobin faction is causing all the disorder? I accuse them openly. Organized like a separate empire in the city, with branches across the country; directed by a handful of leaders blinded by ambition, this sect has formed a separate nation amidst the French people, usurping their powers and subjugating their representatives." He openly denounced the Jacobins, saying, "They would overturn our laws; they rejoice in disorder; they rise up against public authority that the people have established . . . I implore the national assembly to arrest and punish the leaders of violence for high treason against the nation."[23]

The response to this letter in the Jacobin Club was swift and loud. Desmoulins said, "You know very well that I have been killing myself for two years screaming at the departments: M. de Lafayette is a great scoundrel. Today when I saw his letter I said first: he is a great imbecile . . . but no, of course, he is not."[24] Their new line was Lafayette was in league with other European powers to overthrow the Revolution. Danton thundered, "There is no doubt Lafayette is the leader of the nobility, allied with the tyrants of Europe, and if it is true freedom rose from heaven, it will come to help us exterminate *all* its enemies."[25] Robespierre did not need to call on heaven when he could call on the virtuous citizens of France. "Strike down Lafayette and the nation is saved," he said, "when the decree is passed, the whole nation will execute it."[26]

On June 20, 1792, an angry mob marched to the Tuileries Palace. They came to demand the king recall his Girondin ministers and withdraw his vetoes. The palace guards could not stop them as they pushed their way inside. The king put on a brave face. "I have received the sacraments," he said. "I fear nothing. I shall do what the constitution orders me to do."[27] But the mob did not come to kill the royal family, only to intimidate them into compliance. They forced Louis to put on a cockade and red cap of liberty, and raise toasts to the nation while demonstrators filed past, hurtling sarcastic jibes and crude insults. When they finally left, there were no injuries, but the demonstrators left behind piles of garbage, some broken furniture, and a badly shaken royal family. One of the satisfied participants said of June 20, "The people are standing up. The tree of liberty we plant will blossom in peace or blood will flow. Do the enemies of the fatherland imagine the men of July 14 are asleep? Their awakening is terrible."[28]

When Lafayette heard of the events of June 20, he mounted his horse and rode to Paris. Clearly, a strongly worded letter was not enough, so he entered the Legislative Assembly on June 28 to repeat his denunciation of the Jacobins in person.

"The violence committed in the Tuileries has excited the indignation and alarms of all citizens, and particularly of the army," he said.

Gentlemen, it is as a citizen that I have the honor to speak to you; but the opinion that I express is that of all the French who love their country, its freedom, its peace, the laws it has given itself, and I have no fear of being disowned by any of them. . . . I beg the Assembly to, first, order the instigators and leaders of the violence committed on June 20 in the Tuileries, be prosecuted and punished as criminals

of the nation; Second, destroy a sect which invades national sovereignty, tyrannizes its citizens, and whose public debates leave no
doubt about the atrocities of those who lead it; Third, I beg you, in
my name and in the name of all the honest people of the kingdom,
to take effective measures to ensure respect for all the constituted
authorities . . . and give the army assurances the constitution will
not receive any attack in the interior, while brave Frenchmen lavish
their blood to defend it at the borders.[29]

One thing that cannot be denied about Lafayette is his bravery.
From Brandywine to Yorktown, from the streets of Paris to the corridors of Versailles, he never displayed a scintilla of cowardice. His
speech on June 28 is further proof of his fearlessness. When Lafayette
attacked the Jacobins in the Legislative Assembly, he was well aware
practically everyone in the room was a Jacobin. But this did not stop
him from denouncing them to their faces. It took guts. But it also did
no good. Lafayette's enemies in the Legislative Assembly were neither
impressed nor intimidated by the marquis's bold words. The president
of the assembly demanded to know why Lafayette deserted his post in
the middle of a war. He had no legitimate business in the Legislative
Assembly. They never authorized him to come to Paris. He must return
to the front line at once.

Rebuked, Lafayette managed to attend one final reception at the Tuileries Palace. He ran into Gouverneur Morris, who told Lafayette he
"must determine to fight for a good constitution or that wretched piece
of paper which bears the name. That in six weeks it will be too late." Lafayette asked if Morris meant an aristocratic system that kept the people out of the process. Morris said yes, that Lafayette must now surely
see "popular government is good for nothing in France." But even at
this late hour, Lafayette defended his principles and the Revolution. He
told Morris what he wanted for France was "the American constitution
with a hereditary executive."[30] Morris departed, shaking his head.

Lafayette learned the king was scheduled to review the Paris National Guard the next day. He offered to go along and remind the
Guard of their duty to defend the constitution and the king. His troops
on the front line might not like him, but the National Guard were

practically family. They had been through a great deal together—and their shared bonds of loyalty remained strong. Lafayette went so far as to suggest the king depart for his château in Compiègne under the protection of the National Guard. From that secure position he could "issue a proclamation forbidding his brothers and the other émigrés to advance any further . . . and pronouncing his support of the Constitution in terms that will leave no doubt as to his true sentiments."[31] But this triggered an absurd conversation where the queen scotched the idea of running away under Lafayette's protection, because "it would be bad for us to owe him our lives twice. . . . We would be better off locking ourselves away in a tower."[32] She would soon have a chance to determine for herself whether it would have been better to live under Lafayette's protection or be locked away in a tower.

The scheduled review of the National Guard never happened. The leaders of Paris canceled the event when told Lafayette might reassert his authority of the Guard. Lafayette instead returned to his army on the front. When he departed, he left behind his last best chance to alter the coming course of events. The political battle was in Paris, not out on the frontier. The armed forces most loyal to him were in Paris, not out on the frontier. The future of the Revolution would be decided in Paris, not out on the frontier. But despite these incontrovertible facts, Lafayette returned to the frontier. He returned to soldiers and officers who did not really know him or like him—many of whom considered him a traitorous villain, not a storybook hero. It's entirely possible Lafayette did not stand a chance either way. Morris wrote to Jefferson, "I verily believe that if M. de Lafayette were to return to Paris unattended by his armies that he will be torn to pieces."[33]

Lafayette concurred, and opened a dialogue with General Luckner about the possibility of marching their armies on Paris if rebellious mobs threatened the king and constitution. Luckner not only declined, but the correspondence was leaked to Lafayette's enemies in the Jacobin Club. On July 21, the Legislative Assembly took up a motion charging Lafayette with treason and conspiracy—completing the darkly absurd trajectory of his political career. From being a leader on the progressive leading edge of the Revolution, to being accused of treason against the nation. All without ever changing his own beliefs.

The charges against Lafayette were pushed aside by a bombshell dropped on July 25. The anti-French coalition issued the Brunswick Manifesto, declaring their enemy was not France, but the insane radicals who seized control of the government, threatened the royal family, and disturbed the peace of Europe. The Manifesto ended with a stark threat to the Parisians: "If the chateau of the Tuileries is entered by force or attacked, if the least violence be offered to their Majesties the king, queen, and royal family, and if their safety and their liberty be not immediately assured, we will inflict an ever memorable vengeance by delivering over the city of Paris to military execution and complete destruction."[34] The Brunswick Manifesto was meant to secure the safety of the royal family—instead it sealed their doom.

⊶⊰⊱⊷

As soon as the Brunswick Manifesto landed, Georges Danton and other left-wing leaders coordinated an insurrection. With the war going badly, the national government paralyzed by potentially treasonous gridlock, and the Allies threatening to raze Paris to the ground, they concluded something drastic must be done. Through late July and early August radical Jacobins, members of the Cordeliers Club, men and women of the working-class districts, and patriotic National Guard companies laid plans for an uprising. Unlike previous revolutionary uprisings, which were all accidental, spontaneous, and improvised, this uprising was carefully plotted and arranged.

On the morning of August 10, 1792, the tocsin bells rang out and thousands of armed citizens burst from their homes and congregated at the Hôtel de Ville. Danton and his lieutenants dissolved the municipal council of Paris and declared themselves the new leaders of the city. At about nine o'clock in the morning, allied National Guard companies led tens of thousands of armed Parisians toward the Tuileries Palace. Alerted to the danger, the royal family fled from the palace and placed themselves under the protection of the Legislative Assembly. While they huddled under guard, the insurrectionaries stormed the Tuileries Palace, where Swiss guards mounted a brief and bloody defense. Overwhelmed, many of the guards attempted to surrender, but restraint among the insurrectionaries was nonexistent. They killed those who surrendered, then hunted down and executed those who tried to run. By the late afternoon, nine hundred bodies lay strewn throughout the palace, six hundred of them massacred Swiss guards. The royal family was located and arrested—their lives spared only so they could stand trial for their crimes against the nation.

Out on the front line, news came fast and confused from Paris. Lafayette heard a violent mob massacred the Swiss Guard and arrested the king and queen. Ambitious scoundrels whipped Paris into a revolt against the legal constitution. Lafayette believed his duty was clear. He ordered his men to prepare to march on the capital. But after years of denying he was a Caesar or a Cromwell, Lafayette's men proved him right in the most embarrassing way possible. He mustered his soldiers together and demanded they swear an oath of loyalty. Two battalions outright refused. When Lafayette ordered them arrested for disobedience, no one moved. At a moment when Lafayette needed unhesitating loyalty, he found insubordinate defiance. He simply never earned the devotion and loyalty Caesar and Cromwell earned through years of shared sacrifice with their men. *Their* armies would follow them to hell and back. Lafayette's army would not budge.

The insurrection of August 10 was the final stake through the heart of Lafayette's Revolution of 1789. The royal family was placed in the Temple prison on the northern outskirts of Paris. The Legislative Assembly voted to transfer power to an emergency government. This temporary executive would rule until the people elected a national convention to draft a *new* constitution for France. Georges Danton became minister of justice in the emergency government. He now wielded enormous power over those who previously crossed him. On August 17, Danton signed an arrest warrant for one of his oldest *bêtes noires*, the marquis de Lafayette. The warrant charged "Motier-Lafayette, heretofore general of the Army of the North, of rebellion against the law, of conspiracy against liberty and of treason against the nation."[35] Danton ordered Lafayette to return to Paris to face these charges. Two stark options stood before him: go back to Paris and face near certain execution, or run for it.

It was a hard moment of truth. Throughout his life, Lafayette took risks and gambles, and they always paid off. Setbacks were always temporary: victories delayed, but never denied. This had been true since he first boarded *La Victoire* in 1777. Even as late as July 1792, Lafayette believed he could pull it off. If he kept pushing and striving, he would eventually win. But now he faced an altogether novel sensation: defeat. It was over. He lost. In this instance he was *not* up to the challenge. He was not good enough, strong enough, or smart enough. In this moment of truth he wrote, "The best way to serve is to take my head far away, which all the enemies of liberty have proscribed, and which I will never let fall under any despotism. Penetrated with grief at not being able, at this moment, to be useful to my country, I will only wish the sacred cause of liberty and equality, desecrated by crimes of a faction, is not, at least, for a long time enslaved, and by renewing the oath . . . to be faithful to the principles which animated my whole life."[36] Then he prepared to depart camp with about fifty loyal officers. On the night of August 19, 1792, Lafayette and his party crossed the lines into the Austrian Netherlands.

When he learned of Lafayette's escape, a relieved but terminally dejected Gouverneur Morris wrote Thomas Jefferson. "Thus his circle is completed," Morris wrote. "He has spent his fortune on a Revolution, and is now crushed by the wheel which he put in motion."[37] For the marquis de Lafayette the French Revolution was over. It was time for a new ordeal to begin.

SECOND INTERLUDE

The Prisoners of Olmütz

[1792–1797]

THE MARQUIS DE LAFAYETTE EXPECTED TO GET AWAY WITH-
out difficulty. *Émigré* officers had been streaming across the front
lines for more than a year. Not only did the Allies let them pass,
they *celebrated* defecting officers for abandoning the Revolution. But
Lafayette was not just any émigré officer. When he and his entourage of
about fifty officers, aides, and servants entered Rochefort on the night
of August 19, 1792, an émigré French officer attached to the Allied
armies pointed him out to the Austrian authorities. Lafayette and his
party were intercepted and taken into custody.

Lafayette initially believed his detention a mere formality until he
could explain himself. He was not, after all, an enemy. He was *fleeing*
the enemy. After three days in custody, he wrote Adrienne a reassuring
letter defending his conduct. "I am making no apology at all," he said,
"either to my children or to you, for having ruined my family. Not a
single one of you would have wanted to benefit from my having acted
up against my conscience. Come join me in England; let us establish
ourselves in America; we will find there the liberty that no longer exists
in France, and my love will try to compensate you for all the joys you
have lost. Goodbye, my dear love."[1] Clearly, he believed he was about
to be released.

But he was not released. The Austrians offered Lafayette safe passage out of the country if he revealed everything he knew about the French armies. Lafayette refused. He might be on the run from the current French government, but he was still a patriot. Sensing his detention was not just a formality, Lafayette called on American friends for help. He wrote William Short, now American ambassador to the Netherlands, asking Short to claim him as "an American citizen, an American officer, no more French service."[2] Lafayette's request caused problems for the American diplomatic corps in Europe. The United States was neutral in the war between France and the Allies. Claiming Lafayette as a citizen risked triggering a diplomatic incident—the Austrians may ask why the neutral United States allowed one of its citizens to serve as a general in the French army. Gouverneur Morris summed up the conclusion of the American diplomats in a letter to his colleagues: "Although the private feelings of friendship or humanity might properly sway us as private men, we have in our public character higher duties to fulfill than those which may be dictated by sentiments or affection toward an individual."[3] They would not claim Lafayette.

Unfortunately for Lafayette, this regrettable sentiment stretched across the Atlantic to his closest friends. President George Washington concluded his government could do nothing. Washington directed Secretary of State Thomas Jefferson "to neglect no favorable opportunity of expressing, *informally*, the sentiments and wishes of this country respecting the Marquis de Lafayette."[4] But Washington set aside his personal feeling and tied his own hands. Lafayette was on his own.

And Lafayette was very much *on his own*. A rising young Austrian diplomat working in the Netherlands named Klemens von Metternich said Lafayette's role in the Revolution "demands that he be treated as a prisoner of state by all the governments into whose power he fell."[5] The Austrian Empire recognized "prisoner of state" as a different legal category than "prisoner of war," and applied the label to foreigners deemed politically dangerous. The designation placed Lafayette and three other unfortunate companions beyond the scope of international treaties on the treatment of captured soldiers. The three others were Alexandre Lameth, César de La Tour-Maubourg, and Jean Bureaux de

Pusy, all liberal noble officers who crossed the lines with Lafayette. The Austrians considered them guilty of the same crime: fomenting the very revolution they now fled.

After moving Lafayette and the other prisoners of state from Rochefort deeper into Austrian territory, their captors placed them in closely watched solitary confinement. Lafayette drafted a letter describing their treatment with righteous umbrage: "We are so confined that I have a sentry at my door, and cannot walk in a little garden at the end of my staircase. We only walk in the courtyard. This conduct towards us is as unjust as it is impolitic."[6] Lafayette wrote this letter to Princess Adélaïde d'Hénin, an old friend (and possibly former mistress) now living as an émigré in England. Hénin became the most frequent recipient of Lafayette's prison letters, because it was easier for mail from the German states to reach England than France.

In the first week of September 1792, a small tribunal determined Lafayette's ultimate fate. He later said, "After each member had sung my praises in the name of his government, it was decided that the existence of M. de Lafayette . . . was incompatible with the security of the governments of Europe."[7] On September 8, a senior Austrian magistrate delivered the final verdict: Lafayette would be held indefinitely as a prisoner of state. "It is with regret that I am determined not to grant you the liberty you have demanded," the verdict read, "because it is you who were the instigator of the revolution that overturned France; because it is you who put fetters on your king, after having stripped him of all his legitimate rights and powers, and held him captive; because it is you who were the principal instrument of all the disgraces that are overwhelming this unhappy monarch."[8] Lafayette was never going to make it to England, nor establish himself in America. Instead, he would be transferred to Prussian custody and buried deep in central Europe to rot in forgotten anonymity. On September 16, he wrote Princess Hénin another letter describing his status: "Double sentries at our doors and around the house." This letter concluded with a final desperate cry, underlined and in English: "I can't get out."[9]

⚜

LAFAYETTE'S IMPRISONMENT PROBABLY saved his life. Back in France, his departure caused an uproar. Jacobin deputies and journalists denounced him. "Lafayette has just escaped the law, but he cannot escape the hatred of the nation and the horror of posterity!" said one.[10] "Finally Lafayette has unmasked himself!" said another.[11] All they could do now was hurl angry words, but if Lafayette had stayed in France they would have done quite a bit more.

In the wake of the insurrection of August 10, the new emergency government arrested hundreds of counterrevolutionary suspects. The jails of Paris overflowed. With the Allied armies marching on the capital, the government called for every able-bodied man to enlist in the army and fight a great patriotic war of national defense. But potential recruits hesitated to leave the city, convinced if they did, the arrested suspects would break out of jail and launch a violent counterrevolution. Eager to mobilize the Parisians for war, the authorities hit on a bloody but effective solution. They created improvised tribunals in each jail to issue summary death sentences to prisoners one after the other. These kangaroo courts issued accusations and verdicts practically in the same breath. Condemned prisoners were unceremoniously pushed into an adjacent alleyway and stabbed to death by a waiting gang of executioners. Later dubbed the September Massacres, the sweep of executions lasted four days and claimed somewhere between 1,000 and 1,500 victims. Lafayette might be a prisoner of state, but it was better than being stabbed to death in an alleyway.

On September 19, the Austrians handed the still-alive Lafayette to the Prussians, who would supervise his captivity. The Prussians moved Lafayette and the three other state prisoners—Lameth, Bureaux de Pusy, and La Tour-Maubourg—to the fortress at Wesel. Also joining Lafayette in prison were two personal valets, Jean-Pierre Comte and a young man called simply Demanges, as well as a loyal sixteen-year-old secretary named Felix Pontonnier. But they never saw each other. Once dumped in their cells, they were forbidden to communicate with other prisoners or the outside world. Six months later, Lafayette was finally able to write another letter to Princess Hénin describing his imprisonment at Wesel. "It would require a very long account to inform you of all the precautions that were devised to cut off every communication between us and the rest of the world, to retain us in our prison, to watch us closely, and to multiply our privations." The prisoners were told "we could not see each other, even on the bed of death." Conditions at the fortress were barely fit for human survival, and Lafayette's health collapsed. "I suffered very much in my lungs and nerves, from fever and lack of sleep."[12] He and the others languished in a miserable condition somewhere between life and death.

The state prisoners did not remain in Wesel for long. The armies of France, now forming a wall of mass-mobilized volunteers, miraculously held their ground under intense shelling at the Battle of Valmy on September 22, 1792. Not expecting such resistance, the Allied invasion not only ground to a halt, but led to fears in the Allied high command the French might go on the offensive. Not wanting to risk the potential liberation of Lafayette and the others, the Prussians moved the state prisoners four hundred miles east to the fortress at Magdeburg.

After a difficult journey, the prisoners were deposited in Magdeburg on January 4, 1793. This would be their home for the next year. Lafayette described the prison in a letter to Hénin sent three months after their arrival. "Entering successively through four gates," he wrote, "each one of which is armed with chains, locks, and bars of iron, you may reach, not without difficulty and noise, my cell. This cell is three paces broad and five and a half long. . . . The wall next to the ditch is dripping with moisture and that opposite permits the light of day but not the rays of the sun to enter through a small but closely grated window."[13] To an old Prussian friend he wrote, "Here all the inventions of the inquisition and the dungeons multiply around us . . . the deprivation of air, of movement, and all the moral tortures have been preferred like a slow poison."[14] In his dark and stagnant cell, Lafayette's health deteriorated further. He continued to be racked by fevers and a chest infection. He lost weight. Once, catching a glimpse of the increasingly skeletal Bureaux de Pusy, Lafayette said, "His appearance has greatly changed."[15] Presumably Bureaux de Pusy could have said the same of Lafayette.

Though the Prussians attempted to bury Lafayette in an anonymous tomb, friends in France, England, and the United States lobbied on his behalf. In an unofficial capacity, Gouverneur Morris made 10,000 florins available to the imprisoned Lafayette via Dutch banks. Other friends wrote letters, protested, and made public speeches calling attention to his disgraceful mistreatment. In England, Hénin petitioned the British government on Lafayette's behalf. She successfully prodded sympathetic members of the British Parliament to speak up. These members included, surprisingly, Lord Cornwallis, who waged such a ferocious fight against the young marquis during the final Virginia campaign in 1781. The ironic twist of loyalties was completed when Edmund Burke, who supported the American Revolution, but loathed the French Revolution, accused Lafayette of being "the origin and author of all these calamities," and angrily said, "This extraordinary affection of sorrow for the lot of one culpable individual was misplaced, ridiculous, and preposterous."[16] The British government took no action.

Meanwhile, inside prison, Lafayette's condition improved slightly in the spring of 1793. He drew from the funds Morris provided to purchase better food. The more lenient commandant at Magdeburg also allowed the prisoners to purchase books. Lafayette also used his money to bribe guards to smuggle correspondence out of the fortress, and pass clandestine notes between the prisoners written with ash and a toothpick. He wrote Hénin, "I have books, but with the blank pages torn out; no news, no gazettes, no means of communication, neither ink, nor pens, nor paper, nor pencils. It is only by miracle I got hold of this piece of paper on which I'm writing to you with a toothpick."[17] He was also allowed to walk outside for the first time, finally ending his long uninterrupted dungeon confinement. He wrote Hénin in June 1793, "Finally, after more than five months, I felt, not without astonishment, the contact of the outside air, I saw the sun again, and I am very happy."[18]

During his imprisonment Lafayette had plenty of time to worry about the mess he left behind. He received no news of Adrienne or his children, and did not know the impact of his departure on his friends and family. He even spared a bit of his limited paper to wonder about his noble emancipation experiment. "I do not know what they have done to my house in Cayenne," he wrote, "but I hope my wife managed to arrange things so the blacks who work on the land there have retained their freedoms."[19] Lafayette did not know the French government had long since declared him a traitorous émigré and confiscated all his property. To raise money, the government sold the smaller Cayenne plantations, and the enslaved people who worked there, to land speculators. The largest, La Belle Gabrielle, remained a productive state-owned property. The slaves in Cayenne were not freed until the French government issued an emancipation proclamation in February 1794, abolishing slavery in all French territories. Lafayette purchased his slaves with the intention of freeing them, but they were only liberated after he lost ownership of them.

Reconnected to the outside world for the first time, Lafayette finally received small pieces of news about events back in France. Following the insurrection of August 10, a national convention was elected to draft a new constitution. They promptly abolished the monarchy and declared France a republic. To consecrate this great political revolution, the National Convention put the deposed King Louis XVI on trial for treason and executed him on January 21, 1793. Lafayette could not help but mourn the tragic end of Louis—who was the author of so many of his own misfortunes, but to whom Lafayette remained loyal ever since their days as teenagers together at Versailles twenty long years ago.

Despite these small bits of news, Lafayette was mostly kept literally and figuratively in the dark. He knew next to nothing of the massive conflagration engulfing Europe after the execution of the king. After the execution of Louis, nearly all the European powers declared war on France. Despite facing domestic uprisings and factional conflicts, the French republican government, under the direction of Jacobin leaders like Robespierre and Danton, organized a mass national effort to save the Revolution. By the end of 1793, French armies pushed the Allies back. The Prussians concluded the war with France was a pointless quagmire and opened negotiations to pull out of the conflict. Not wanting Lafayette and the other state prisoners freed as a part of the negotiations, the king of Prussia asked Austrian emperor Francis I to accept custody.

After exactly one year at Magdeburg, Lafayette's jailers roused him on January 4, 1794, and transferred the state prisoners to the fortress at Neisse, on the border between Prussian and Austrian territory. This was the third consecutive disgusting jail cell Lafayette endured. "My regimen, with the exception of a few new treatments for isolation, is the same as in Magdeburg," he wrote Hénin. "You will be told that Neisse's air is bad . . . and I guarantee as best I can of the unhealthiness particular to my situation."[20] He would remain in this new dungeon for the next five months as bureaucrats finalized the paperwork to officially transfer him back to Austrian custody. He learned Lameth was too sick to make the journey, so it was just Lafayette, La Tour-Maubourg, Bureaux de Pusy, and their servants moving on together.

While in prison at Neisse, Lafayette learned for the first time the grisly details of what happened back in France. To quell domestic insurrection and win the war, the National Convention created an executive Committee of Public Safety under Robespierre's increasingly influential leadership. In October 1793, the Committee of Public Safety ushered in the Reign of Terror, aimed at purging enemies of the republic and purifying the nation. Lafayette learned the Revolutionary Tribunal pushed many of his old friends, comrades, and rivals into the ravenous maw of Madame la Guillotine. Queen Marie Antoinette, with whom Lafayette always shared a difficult and complicated relationship, was guillotined October 16, 1793. Jacques-Pierre Brissot and the other Girondins, with whom Lafayette once shared idealistic visions of social reform in the 1780s, were executed in a batch on October 31. The duc d'Orléans, considered the people's hero in 1789, and who went so far as to restyle himself "Philippe Egalité," was executed on November 6. Former mayor of Paris Jean-Sylvain Bailly was beheaded on November 12, with his scaffold erected on the spot of the massacre of the Champ de Mars. Had Lafayette remained in France and, by some miracle, *not* yet been executed, this is probably when and where he would have died. "The frightful news has brought back my insomnia and has caused me more pain than all the efforts of my persecutors could approach," he wrote. "I have much more energy to resist any personal situation and to defy the vengeance directed at me, but I simply do not have the energy to sustain the dangers threatening those I love."[21]

More than anyone else, though, Lafayette worried about his family. He only received sporadic updates about the fates of Adrienne, Anastasie, Virginie, Georges, his old aunt Charlotte still living in Chavaniac, or any of his Noailles relatives. He only knew they were in mortal danger and he could do nothing about it. In late January 1794, he wrote hopefully, "Madame de Lafayette, if she remained in her house . . . will be free and peaceful there, and yet, when I think that all the affection of her neighbors may not defend her effectively against some henchmen of the tyranny . . . I feel the most painful anxiety."[22] He was right to be anxious. For at that very moment, Adrienne endured a grueling and dangerous ordeal of her own.

⧈

ADRIENNE AND THE children were at Chavaniac on August 24, 1792, when they first learned Lafayette fled the country. Aware he was charged with treason, the confirmation of his escape from France triggered joyful relief. A few days later, Adrienne received the letter from Lafayette saying she and the children should go to England, and they would all emigrate to America together. But things did not work out for either of them. A stalwart Jacobin commissioner arrived at Chavaniac on September 10 bearing an order stating, "The woman Lafayette is to be arrested, together with her children, if they are found with her, and confined to a house of detention."[23] Adrienne managed to hide Georges and Virginie, but Anastasie, now fifteen, refused to leave her mother's side. Elderly Aunt Charlotte made a similar defiant declaration. The commissioner arrested the three women and took them to Le Puy-en-Velay, the largest town in the district.

Held in custody in Le Puy, Adrienne wrote the authorities in Paris, asserting her husband was no traitor and demanding the government end the persecution of her family. She wrote a long letter to Brissot, who remained, for the moment, one of the most influential political leaders in France. They were personal friends and collaborators for years; surely this counted for something. She wrote,

> I cannot persuade myself that a zealous friend of the blacks can be a follower of tyranny. I am sure you esteem, I would even say respect, M. Lafayette as a courageous and staunch friend of liberty, even as you persecute him because of opinions contrary to your own. . . . What your answer will be I do not know. It is easy to see that if it is dictated by the spirit of justice, it will restore me an unconditional liberty. . . . If it is in accordance with my heart's desire, it will

permit me to join my husband in England, as he wishes, so soon as he may be released from captivity, in order that we may together settle in America when traveling to that country becomes once again practicable.[24]

But while in Le Puy, Adrienne learned her husband was *not* going to be freed. The short-lived dream of going first to England then America was dead.

Thanks to the intercession of Brissot, the local authorities reduced Adrienne's imprisonment to house arrest at Chavaniac. But that was the only good news. Her husband's enemies placed Lafayette's name on the list of émigrés and confiscated all his property. His lucrative estates in Brittany and elsewhere were seized, as were the plantations in Cayenne. Even Chavaniac was seized and sold at auction, though the family was allowed to live there as tenants. Adrienne wrote George Washington asking him to intervene, but Washington responded saying there was nothing he could do. All he *could* do was personally place 2,310 Dutch guilders at her disposal. "The sum is," he wrote, "the least I am indebted for services rendered me by M. de la Fayette, of which I have never yet received the account."[25] Gouverneur Morris also assured Adrienne the United States would never forget her husband and personally loaned her 100,000 *livres* to help float the family financially through these difficult times. These personal loans were vital lifelines, but their American friends could do nothing officially.

Then things got even worse. In September 1793, the Committee of Public Safety issued the Law of Suspects, allowing for the summary arrest of political prisoners and marking the beginning of the Reign of Terror. A local priest offered to take Georges and hide the boy under a fake name—as the only son of the traitor Lafayette, Georges was sure to be in danger. On November 13, a company of soldiers arrived at Chavaniac bearing another arrest warrant for *La Femme Lafayette*. After first ordering she produce all family debt and property records so they could be burned in a revolutionary bonfire, the soldiers arrested Adrienne and took her to an improvised jail in the small town of Brioude. There, she joined other aristocrats rounded up from the surrounding countryside. Adrienne spent the next six months imprisoned in Brioude.

While in confinement, she learned the authorities in Paris arrested her older sister Louise, her mother the duchesse d'Ayen, and grandmother the maréchale de Noailles, and confined them to the Luxembourg Palace. The apartments Lafayette lived in as a boy now served as a prison for suspicious aristocrats.

The spring of 1794 brought a small ray of hope. Public opinion turned against the Reign of Terror. Even old radicals like Danton and Desmoulins deployed their unimpeachable revolutionary credentials to denounce Robespierre and the Terror. But Robespierre hit back and ordered Danton, Desmoulins, and the other leaders of the Cordeliers Club arrested and guillotined in April 1794. The Terror would not be ending anytime soon.

On May 27, 1794, Adrienne received dreadful news. The Committee of Public Safety ordered the mass consolidation of political prisoners in Paris. The only reason to issue such an order was if they meant to kill them all. Adrienne's children managed to visit her one last time before she left, and they bid each other a tearful and heart-wrenching farewell. They all believed the summons to Paris meant Adrienne was marching to her death.

Adrienne arrived in Paris on June 10, 1794. The Luxembourg Palace was by now overcrowded, so she was not reunited with her family. Instead, Adrienne was confined to a new makeshift prison, which just so happened to be the Collège du Plessis, where her husband once went to school. Each morning, an official read a list of names of prisoners to be moved to the Conciergerie, the last stop before facing the Revolutionary Tribunal. The Revolutionary Tribunal was itself the last stop before the guillotine. They were not issuing acquittals anymore. Only sentences of death.

Adrienne nervously listened to the announcements each morning, but they never called her name. She did not know it, but Gouverneur Morris and newly arrived American ambassador James Monroe worked desperately on her behalf. Monroe was a young protégé of Thomas Jefferson, but also an old comrade of Lafayette's from their days serving together in the Continental Army. Though Monroe's hands remained officially tied, he and Morris both made it clear to his counterparts in the French government the United States would be very upset to learn of the execution of the wife of the beloved marquis de Lafayette—so upset they might drop their neutrality and declare war. Morris told French officials, "The family of Lafayette is beloved in America . . . and therefore the death of his wife might lessen the attachment of some among them to the French Republic; that it would furnish the partisans of England with means of misrepresenting what passes here; that I cannot but think her existence of very little consequence to this government."[26] Though the Americans could not secure Adrienne's release, the Revolutionary Tribunal hesitated to bring her to trial. This hesitation saved her life.

The rest of Adrienne's family were not so lucky. On July 21, 1794, Adrienne's sister, mother, and grandmother were ordered to face the Revolutionary Tribunal. Absurdly, the prosecutor accused them of plotting with other prisoners in the Luxembourg Palace to overthrow the government. The formal charge was "planning to dissolve the National Convention and to assassinate the members of the Committee of Public Safety."[27] When the prosecutor interrogated Adrienne's grandmother, she responded, "What is that you are saying? You must forgive me I am extremely deaf, I cannot hear you." The prosecutor retorted, "So you were a deaf conspirator!"[28] And the audience roared with laughter. The three women were sentenced to death.

That evening they were taken to place du Trône (now place de la Nation), in a group of forty-five unfortunate souls. The tumbrel stopped and each prisoner in turn was led to the guillotine. A young priest devoted to the Noailles family witnessed their deaths. "Madame d'Ayen was tenth," he wrote. "She looked at me as though she were pleased to know that she was to die before her daughter." After the duchesse d'Ayen was beheaded, "the loving and dignified daughter took her place. What are my feelings when I look at that young woman, dressed all in white and looking much younger than she was, like a sweet little lamb about to have its throat cut. What happened to her mother happened to her: what an abundance of bright red blood poured from her head and neck! Now she is in bliss, I said to myself."[29]

Within days of their execution the mounting fear, disgust, anger, dread, and outrage finally boiled over. The guillotine now claimed child pickpockets and harmless old women. What was the point? When would it end? The answer turned out to be . . . now. In the middle of the night of July 27, 1794, the Committee of Public Safety was overthrown in a coup. Over the span of thirty-six hours, Robespierre and his allies were arrested, tried, and convicted by their own Revolutionary Tribunal. On July 28 they were all guillotined. After their deaths, the new government suspended further executions. Adrienne was relieved to discover she was going to live after all—then grief-stricken to discover her family missed salvation by less than a week.

⁂

WHILE ADRIENNE LANGUISHED on the precipice of death in the spring of 1794, her husband was finally transferred to the Austrians. On the night of May 18, 1794, Lafayette and his fellow prisoners arrived at the garrison city of Olmütz (now Olomouc in the Czech Republic). After midnight they were processed into the prison, once the dormitory of a defunct Jesuit college. Upon arrival, the Austrians did their best to blot Lafayette out of existence. According to Austrian protocol the object was "to treat such a dangerous person as if he had been transferred completely out of the world while retaining only his life, as if he no longer existed and has been forgotten."[30] The prisoners were stripped of their possessions and identities. Lafayette was henceforth only referred to as "State Prisoner #2" and his presence in the prison of Olmütz was officially denied.

At Olmütz they were no longer housed in a basement dungeon, but conditions were still terrible. More than anything, the prison of Olmütz stank. Their rooms were located near the guardhouse latrine, saturating their cluster of rooms in noxious vapors. Compounding the grotesque stench, the section of the river abutting their wing of the prison was the stagnant repository for the city sewers. La Tour-Maubourg described how it was especially bad in the summer because "all the sewers taking away the filth of the city pass under our windows . . . always giving an unbearable smell . . . spreading really mephitic and pestilential emanations."[31]

Initially, the commandant of the prison did not allow the state prisoners to leave their cells nor possess writing instruments of any kind. But as the months passed, things got better. They were allowed books to read from a censored list of materials. Lafayette also learned he would be able to afford better food and treatment thanks to a law passed by the Congress of the United States in March 1794. Embarrassed and ashamed at their inability to petition for Lafayette's release, Congress passed "An Act Allowing To Maj. Gen. Lafayette His Pay and Emoluments."[32] The act awarded Lafayette full backpay for his years of service in the Continental Army—a way of helping Lafayette without causing a diplomatic breach with either France or Austria. Ironically, Lafayette's entrance into the Continental Army was premised on a pledge to pay his own way, and in the end, he wound up one of the only generals paid his full salary. The funds were placed into a Dutch bank for Lafayette to draw from throughout his years in Olmütz.

Though Congress helped ameliorate his condition, several of Lafayette's more adventurous friends wanted to do much more. Frustrated by the failure of diplomatic approaches, a small group of loyal friends in England under the auspices of Princess Hénin decided to organize a jailbreak. They entrusted the job to a young Hanoverian physician named Justus Bollmann. Fluent in English, French, and German, Bollmann already acted as a courier for Lafayette's clandestine correspondence under the guise of being an innocent young man touring the German countryside. Bollmann arrived in Olmütz for the first time in July 1794 and confirmed Lafayette was inside the prison. He then traveled to Vienna, where he found a willing accomplice: a twenty-one-year-old student from South Carolina named Francis Huger, son of the Major Huger who lodged Lafayette on his first night in America. The younger Huger was studying medicine in Vienna, but eager to drop everything and render an adventurous service to the famous French marquis his family long boasted their connection to.

Returning to Olmütz, Bollmann and Huger opened direct communication with Lafayette. Their go-between was the prison doctor, who agreed to carry seemingly innocent letters with the details of the conspiracy written in invisible lemon juice in English, which Lafayette could read by holding the parchment up to a flame. Believing the Austrians intended for him to die in prison, Lafayette eagerly encouraged the plot. He revealed his jailors now allowed weekly carriage rides through the countryside. As they were so deep in Austrian territory, the authorities believed these carriage rides a safe indulgence. Instead they provided the perfect opportunity to escape.

On Saturday, November 8, 1794, Bollmann and Huger shadowed Lafayette's carriage, which contained a civilian driver, a private, and a sergeant. At about three o'clock in the afternoon, the carriage stopped at the clearing. Lafayette and the sergeant got out, while the carriage continued to a nearby inn. Lafayette and the sergeant were supposed to walk to the inn so Lafayette could get some exercise, but as soon as the carriage was too far ahead to help, Bollmann and Huger struck. They charged in on their horses, Bollmann dismounted, pulled out a pistol, and yelled in German, "Give us this man!" Instead, the sergeant grabbed Lafayette by the collar, partially strangling the prisoner as Lafayette cried in English, "Kill him! Kill him!" The two young rescuers didn't want to murder anybody, so they rushed forward, pulled the sergeant off Lafayette, and disarmed him after a brief four-man struggle that left Lafayette injured and bleeding. Bollmann handed the reins of one of the horses to Lafayette and yelled, "Go to Hof!" the next town along the main highway. But Lafayette did not know the area, and instead simply heard Bollmann say, "Get off!" Which he did, riding away on the horse as fast as he could. Huger was left holding the map and purse of money he was supposed to hand Lafayette, but which he forgot in the excitement.[33]

Riding north, Lafayette missed the turn to Hof and wound up on a minor back road. He came upon a local tanner who later testified about his strange encounter with the suspiciously wounded and dirty rider who spoke "very harsh and corrupt German," with a heavy French accent.[34] The tanner took Lafayette to the next town and immediately alerted the mayor. The mayor brought the stranger in for questioning, and a local Italian acting as a translator recognized Lafayette from a previous encounter. As soon as he was fingered, Lafayette offered the mayor a bribe to look the other way while he escaped out of the window. But the mayor was not interested in risking his neck for a random French fugitive. Instead, he sent word to Olmütz saying Lafayette was in custody. A company of soldiers arrived to escort the fugitive marquis back to prison at four o'clock in the morning. Lafayette had been a free man for not quite twelve hours.

Huger and Bollmann were also soon arrested. Huger tried to flee on foot and was captured in less than an hour. Bollmann got away on horseback, but after taking the correct turn to Hof, immediately lost track of Lafayette. Bollmann spent a week riding around the border between Prussia and Austria, until he was identified and arrested on November 16. At the subsequent inquest, Lafayette insisted it was all his idea, and the two young men were just following orders. Their subsequent punishments turned out to be surprisingly light: both Bollmann and Huger spent a few months in prison and were then released under the condition they never again set foot in Austrian territory.

Meanwhile, Lafayette faced grave consequences for his attempted escape. In exchange for those few brief hours of freedom, he lost all his privileges. For almost a week, he was not even allowed to see a doctor as his wounds from the fight with the sergeant became infected and his health collapsed. This was just the beginning of a full year of nearly fatal solitary confinement.

<hr />

WHILE HER HUSBAND'S jailbreak failed in Olmütz, Adrienne remained confined to the Collège du Plessis in Paris. In September 1794, many of her fellow prisoners were released, but she was not. The commissioner in charge of processing claims bore a personal grudge against Lafayette and insisted on keeping *La Femme Lafayette* in custody. Monroe and Morris continued to lobby incessantly on her behalf. They finally found sympathetic contacts inside the Directory—the new government established after the fall of the Committee of Public Safety—who agreed to set her free as a gesture of goodwill to the United States. After fourteen months of imprisonment, at least half of which she spent believing each day would be her last, Adrienne walked out of prison on January 21, 1795. Half her family had been murdered and her husband was buried alive in an Austrian tomb, but she was free and alive.

Upon her release, Adrienne moved into the home of her aunt Antoinette. The youngest of her mother's sisters, Antoinette was only three years older than Adrienne, so despite the genealogical tables rendering them "aunt" and "niece," they treated each other like cousins. Antoinette lived through the Terror because she was married to the comte de Ségur, Lafayette's oldest friend, who blossomed into an adroit diplomat. Ségur managed to navigate the revolutionary turmoil better than his former compatriots, and now provided a safe refuge for former aristocratic victims of the Reign of Terror. While staying with the Ségurs, Adrienne struck up a friendship with her husband's former mistress, Madame de Simiane, who herself barely escaped the Reign of Terror. Though tension would always exist between the two women, in the aftermath of the Revolution, those who survived from the old days tended to stick together—the past now dead and buried along with so many friends and relatives.

To put the family back on firm legal footing, Ségur, James Monroe, and other contacts inside their respective governments secured legal passports for Adrienne and the children under the more anonymous family name "Motier." Adrienne insisted Georges leave Europe at once. He managed to survive the Reign of Terror, but if the political winds shifted again, he would be in danger. Adrienne demanded he depart for the relative safety of the United States and wrote personally to George Washington: "Monsieur, I send you my son. . . . Though I have not had the consolation of gaining your ear and getting from you the kind of help I thought necessary to free my husband from the hands of our enemies. . . . My confidence in you has been in no way diminished, and it is with that deep and sincere feeling I now place my dear son under the protection of the United States . . . and under the special care of their President, the nature of whose sentiments toward my husband I so well know."[35] Georges's arrival in the United States in the summer of 1795 caused diplomatic complications for President Washington, but his personal sentiments eventually got the better of him. He invited Georges to live at Mount Vernon, where the teenager remained for the next two years.

Adrienne herself returned to Chavaniac and reunited with Anastasie and Virginie in a joyful release of tension and trauma. They had all believed they would never see each other again. Monroe forwarded more money, which Adrienne used to buy back Chavaniac from the speculator who purchased it at auction. Monroe also sent the three women American passports listing them as "the Motiers," citizens of Hartford, Connecticut—the one municipality in the United States that saw fit to grant citizenship to Lafayette *and his entire family*. But Adrienne and her daughters would not follow Georges across the Atlantic. Instead, Adrienne and her daughters boarded an American ship bound for Hamburg in late September 1795. From Hamburg they traveled overland to Vienna, where Adrienne planned to personally beg clemency and mercy from the emperor himself.

"The Motiers" arrived in Vienna in the first week of October 1795 and made calls on family acquaintances. The Noailles family were well known and liked in Vienna—one of Adrienne's uncles was the resident French ambassador for more than a decade. Through these connections, she secured a personal audience with Emperor Francis I on October 10, 1795. When Adrienne was ushered into the imperial chamber, the emperor was shocked to discover he stood face-to-face with Lafayette's wife. He allowed Adrienne to make her plea, but when she was done said, "I agree to you, [but] as for his freedom, that would be impossible for me, my hands are tied."[36] Adrienne boldly retorted, "Nothing is less complicated than returning a husband to his wife and children."[37]

But it *was* a complicated matter. The emperor reaccepted custody of the state prisoners on condition he would never release them. Unable to secure her husband's freedom, Adrienne requested what she considered the next best thing: permission to join Lafayette in captivity. The emperor did not refuse the request and said, "I agree to it. You will find M. de Lafayette well fed and well treated. . . . Your presence will be a further pleasure. You will be happy with the prison commandant. In prisons, prisoners are only known by their numbers; but we all know your husband's name well."[38]

Armed with papers signed personally by the emperor, Adrienne, Anastasie, and Virginie arrived at the prison of Olmütz on October 15. When the three women walked through the door of his cell, Lafayette could not believe his eyes. It had been a full year since the botched escape attempt doomed him to a state of permanent isolation. The shock soon gave way to a tearful and happy reunion, but Virginie later recalled, "Three years of captivity, the last one spent in complete solitude . . . his sufferings of all kinds, profoundly affected his health; the change in his face was frightening."[39] Adrienne wrote a concerned friend, "I will tell you only that we found him in the most absolute solitude, not knowing our frightful misfortunes; that it had been expressly prohibited to tell him if we existed, his children and I, that his wasting away is frightful, his chest a source of the horrible suffering."[40] But she also said, "You know the force and sweetness of his soul, despite the moral and physical tortures . . . there is not the least alteration in his character, nor the least imbalance in his temper."[41]

The reunion was happy and full of love, but Virginie said Lafayette feared the news they might be bearing. She said, "My father, after the first moment of happiness at this sudden reunion, dared not ask a question. He knew there had been a terror in France; but he did not know the names of the victims. The day passed without his daring to deepen his fears and without my mother having the strength to explain herself. It was not until the evening when we were locked up, my sister and I, in the adjoining but separate room, that she told my father she lost on the scaffold her grandmother, mother and sister."[42]

The arrival of his family ended Lafayette's three years of nearly continuous isolation. Surviving these years with his mind intact is a testament to Lafayette's fortitude and endurance, but he emerged believing no one should inflict or endure such cruel torture. He later said, "Solitary confinement was a punishment which should be experienced to be rightly appreciated," and that he "regarded solitary confinement as leading to madness."[43] He offered his own incorrigibility as proof it had no rehabilitative effect. Lafayette said he "had not found it to be the means of reformation, since he was imprisoned for wishing to revolutionize the people against despotism and aristocracy, and passed his solitude in thinking upon it, without coming out corrected in that respect."[44] One thing Lafayette *had* learned: solitary confinement was a cruel and unusual punishment with no redeeming qualities whatsoever.

Adrienne soon discovered the emperor allowed himself to be extremely misinformed about the conditions of Lafayette's confinement. "Regardless of what the Emperor said," she wrote, "there is nothing here but insects, stench, and dirt."[45] After a few days witnessing firsthand how bad things were, Adrienne demanded changes. These demands eventually wound their way to Vienna. Months later, the Lafayettes received a response from the emperor: "Madame Lafayette and

her daughters are to submit themselves to everything in state arrest
that is prescribed and to be observed for her husband as well as for all
state prisoners."[46] If they didn't like it, they were free to leave anytime.
But if that was the choice, it was no choice at all. Adrienne responded:
"Our feelings are the same, and the three of us say with all our hearts
that we are much happier with M. de Lafayette, even in this prison, than
anywhere else without him."[47]

So the family settled in. Anastasie and Virginie slept in a separate room, but spent most of their waking hours in confinement with
their parents in Lafayette's room. One day passed to the next, then
weeks, then months, then years. The prison of Olmütz was hot and
stifling in the summer, hard and frozen in the winter. All four suffered
recurrent health problems. Lafayette's chest condition continued to
plague him and he was now thoroughly emaciated. In the spring of
1796, Adrienne became deathly ill, suffering rashes, migraines, ar-
thritis, and stomachaches, all compounding one on top of the other.
These symptoms would only get better or worse, but never go away.
At one point, near death, her family asked permission for Adrienne
to leave the prison to see a real physician. The commandant granted
permission, but with the stipulation she would not be allowed to return. Adrienne made her position clear: "They will not tear me away
from here except with M. Lafayette, unless, perhaps, they drag me
away dead."[48]

⚜

THERE WERE TIMES when the Lafayettes believed they would die in
prison. But thanks to their limited correspondence, they knew friends
on the outside worked on their behalf. The Lafayettes' cruel confinement by the treacherous despots of Europe made the family a famous
cause célèbre on both sides of the Atlantic. The plight of "the Prisoners
of Olmütz" inspired an array of songs, plays, poems, and drawings. Ger-
maine de Staël—daughter of Jacques Necker and now a popular writer
more famous than her father—turned her pen to Lafayette's cause and
demanded the French government remember their captured son.

Even George Washington finally made an attempt to intervene.
Washington said his agitation over Lafayette's continued imprison-

ment was "increased by the visible distress of his son, who is now with me, and grieving for the unhappy fate of his parents. This circumstance, giving a poignancy to my own feelings on this occasion, has induced me to go a step further."[49] Washington drafted a personal letter to Emperor Francis. Stressing to the emperor he did not write in his capacity as president of the United States, Washington said, "In common with the people of this country, I retain a strong and cordial sense of the services rendered to them by the marquis de Lafayette; and my friendship for him has been constant and sincere. It is natural, therefore, that I should sympathize with him and his family in their misfortunes, and endeavor to mitigate the calamities which they experience; among which his present confinement is not the least distressing. Allow me, sir . . . to entreat that he may be permitted to come to this country on such conditions and under such restrictions, as your Majesty may think it expedient to prescribe."[50]

But it was all for naught. The emperor was not going to give Lafayette up, and his fellow sovereigns put him under no official pressure to change his mind. When friends of Lafayette in Parliament petitioned King George III to say a word on Lafayette's behalf, the king retorted, "Besides the very objectionable conduct of that gentleman towards this country, which would be reason enough for not appearing in his favor, I cannot see any right this, or any other country, has to meddle with the executive administration of any foreign one."[51] That was that.

As is often the case when appeals to humanity fall on deaf ears, brute force is required to secure justice. And brute force eventually unlocked the prison of Olmütz. War had been raging in Europe for five long years. The French went from scrambling a desperate defense of the republic to building a mighty war machine. By now, mass conscription, merit-based promotion in the ranks, and an entire national economy geared toward winning the war paid off. Prussia dropped out of the fighting back in 1794. French armies now campaigned against the Austrians on the east side of the Rhine. For the Lafayettes, French victory on the battlefield was probably the only hope left. Adrienne wrote Hénin in July 1796, "The success of the French arms alone can force these people into peace, and give us hope of a general article, or even a decree . . . that can possibly pull us from here."[52]

The man who finally rescued the Lafayettes from prison was a young general named Napoleon Bonaparte. Bonaparte was the quintessential prodigy of the new age of modern warfare. Born in 1769 to minor Corsican nobles, young Bonaparte's intellectual talents earned him an education in mainland France then officer training at the prestigious École Militaire in Paris. When the Revolution broke out in 1789, young Bonaparte became an enthusiastic Jacobin. After the war began in 1792, he secured the patronage of Robespierre's brother, which was at first a boon to his fortunes then, after the fall of the Committee of Public Safety, a potentially fatal weight around his neck. But Bonaparte survived. Stationed in Paris in October 1795 when a royalist uprising threatened the Directory, General Bonaparte took charge of the defense of the government. After crushing the revolt by firing his famous "whiff of grapeshot"[53] on charging insurrectionaries, the Directory rewarded him with command of the campaign in northern Italy.

For the next year, the twenty-six-year-old Bonaparte orchestrated a brilliant series of maneuvers establishing his courage, daring, tactical ingenuity, strategic vision, and a ruthless willingness to absorb casualties as long as the battle was won. Pressing up into the Alps toward Austria, Bonaparte's army won the decisive Battle of Rivoli in January 1797. The Austrian government faced the alarming reality of French armies sitting on an open road to Vienna. Emperor Francis had no choice but to sue for peace.

Bonaparte's triumphs on the battlefield meant he could impose such terms as he pleased. He could, for example, insist on the release of French prisoners of war *and* French prisoners of state. Bonaparte had never met Lafayette, but people who were there told Lafayette, "from the first day of the negotiations . . . Bonaparte spoke of us."[54] The French government supported the demand, instructing Bonaparte "obtain provisionally, if possible, the liberty of Lafayette, Bureaux-Pusy, and Latour-Maubourg . . . it is a matter of national honor that they leave behind the dungeons where they are kept because they began the revolution."[55]

Emperor Francis had his own national honor to consider. As the negotiations dragged on through the summer of 1797, the emperor finally consented to release Lafayette and the others, but insisted he was doing so not because of French demands, but as a friendly gesture to the United States. The order freeing Lafayette explained "that as His Majesty did not contract any definite commitment with the French touching on the release of the prisoners named above, the motive of the particular interest the United States of America appear to attach to it contributed greatly to bring His Majesty to this act of charity; but for the rest, His Majesty will always be quite gratified, should opportunities arise, to give the United States of America genuine tokens of his friendship and benevolence."[56] But the prisoners all knew who their liberator was. Lafayette later wrote to Jefferson, "Had it not been for the glorious display of [France's] military institutions and uncommon exertions of the conquerors, we never should have left our prison but for the scaffold."[57]

On September 19, 1797, almost exactly five years after being taken into custody at Rochefort, the doors of the prison of Olmütz opened and the marquis de Lafayette walked out into the world as a free man. They tried to bury him in a tomb, but he survived. His life was far from over.

Part III

The Republican Kiss

CHAPTER EIGHTEEN

LA GRANGE

[1797–1814]

L AFAYETTE WAS NOW FREE, BUT IT WAS THE FREEDOM OF A
ghost. When he crossed the lines in August 1792, he was the
rich and powerful marquis de Lafayette. He emerged from
prison five years later penniless and homeless. The French government
still legally considered him an outlaw, a traitor, and an *émigré*. From the
Directory's perspective, national honor was restored when they secured
Lafayette's release from prison, but they forbid him to return to France.
Meanwhile, his release from Olmütz stipulated he depart Austrian territory and never return. The logical thing would be emigration to the
United States—the one country on Earth that actually wanted Lafayette. But prolonged confinement left the whole family with a variety
of health problems. Neither he nor Adrienne were in any shape for
transatlantic travel. Even without the health problems, Lafayette felt
himself the aggrieved victim of unjust persecution—his family pride
and personal honor needed to be restored.

From Olmütz, the freed prisoners and their families accepted an
invitation to stay with Madame de Tessé. She now owned a house in
the Danish province of Holstein, and offered everyone a safe place to
recuperate. Once settled in Holstein, Lafayette drafted a formal letter

of thanks to Napoleon Bonaparte. "Citizen General," he said, "the prisoners of Olmütz, happy in the knowledge that they owe their freedom to the irresistible might of your soldiers, found consolation while still in captivity in the realization that their lives and liberties were bound up with the triumphs of the Republic and with your own personal glory. They are no less happy today to pay homage to their liberator."[1] This was the beginning of a years-long relationship with Bonaparte that proved nearly as fraught and complicated as Lafayette's relations with the Bourbons.

The Lafayettes, La Tour-Maubourgs, and Bureaux de Pusys lived with Madame de Tessé briefly, then secured enough money to rent a nearby château of their own. The three families lived together in one giant household of husbands, wives, children, and extended family. They spent their confinement apart, and wanted to spend their freedom together. Among those moving into the house was La Tour-Maubourg's unmarried younger brother Charles. Charles quickly fell in love with now twenty-year-old Anastasie, and despite the acute lack of money or property on either side—usually a fatal roadblock of aristocratic marriages—the couple married in the spring of 1798. Georges returned from his two years in America, hopping on a ship and sailing for France as soon as he heard his family was going to be released. Lafayette last saw him as a twelve-year-old boy. When Georges strolled through the door in February 1798, Lafayette saw an eighteen-year-old young man.

Despite lingering health problems, Adrienne spearheaded efforts on behalf of the family. Her name was *not* on the list of émigrés, and she still held a valid American passport, so she could come and go from France as she wished. When the weather warmed up in the early summer of 1798, she returned to Paris with Virginie to begin the process of rehabilitating everyone's names. The family also wanted to move to the Netherlands—now a French-aligned entity called the Batavian Republic, lest the Austrians attempt to scoop them back up. Adrienne and Virginie received many polite official hearings, and while they said Lafayette's name would *not* be stricken from the émigré list, the government indicated they would tolerate his presence in the Netherlands.

Ultimately the plan was still to go to America. In August 1798 Lafayette wrote Washington, "Affection, duty and propriety point out the beloved shores of America as the natural place of my retirement."[2] But unfortunately, by that point, Talleyrand had almost single-handedly destroyed the American relationship with France. After being named the Directory's foreign minister, Talleyrand demanded a bribe from American diplomats in exchange for a favorable treaty. It is hard to tell who was more surprised by this demand—the Americans presented with the bribe or Talleyrand when they refused to pay it. This incident became known in the United States as the XYZ Affair—after the redacted names of three French officials implicated in the scandal—and sparked an undeclared quasi-war with France between 1798 and 1800.

Lafayette's American friends discouraged his plan to move to the United States, telling him anti-French sentiment was at a peak. In a letter written Christmas Day 1798, Washington warned, "The scenes you would meet with, and the part you would be stimulated to act in case of an open rupture, or even if matters should remain in status quo, would be such as to place you in a situation which no address, or human prudence, could free you from embarrassment."[3] Alexander Hamilton concurred in a letter written a few weeks later: "It is my opinion that it is best for you to stand aloof. . . . It would be very difficult for you here to steer a course which would not place you in a party and remove you from the broad ground which you now occupy in the hearts of all."[4]

As the dream of moving to America stalled, events in Europe made the Lafayettes' position in the Netherlands frightfully insecure. General Bonaparte led a great expedition to conquer Egypt in 1798, which turned into a disastrous fiasco. Not only did the British wipe out Bonaparte's navy, but the French presence in the Eastern Mediterranean brought both the Russian and Ottoman Empires into the anti-French coalition. The tide of the war turned, and by 1799, there was a real chance the Allies would invade the Netherlands and recapture the Lafayettes. In his final letter to Washington, Lafayette reiterated "how ardently, in spite of difficulties, I long to be in America." He also said he may be forced to board a ship bound for America with very little warning. "In the improbable case where I would suddenly pop upon you," he said, "be certain, my dear general, that my motives should be such as to convince you of their urgency."[5] As late as August 1799, William Murray, the American ambassador to the Netherlands, reported

Lafayette still believed his escape to the United States imminent. "I found him still much bent upon going," Murray wrote Washington. "His plan, if he go[es], is to settle for life. To buy a farm near Mount Vernon—to land in the Chesapeake and hasten to present himself to his paternal house . . . that he is sure that he can convince you that he could have no asylum elsewhere from the present and probable future state of Europe."[6]

But just as all doors seemed to be closing in Europe, a narrow window opened in Paris. In June 1799, the Abbé Sieyès became one of the five executive members of the Directory. Sieyès was an old friend and ally of Lafayette's from their days together in the Society of the Friends of the Blacks, the Society of Thirty, and the Estates-General in 1789. As soon as Sieyès entered into the government, he granted Adrienne a personal audience. Adrienne told Sieyès the family feared reimprisonment and asked permission to return to France. Sieyès warned her that, despite his personal sympathy, the consequences would be dire if Lafayette stepped foot in France. Though initially discouraging, events were about to become very fluid.

By mid-1799, rampant corruption and failures on the battlefield made the Directory fatally unpopular. Ambitious men like Sieyès plotted to overthrow it. In September 1799, General Bonaparte dramatically returned from Egypt and entered conspiratorial talks with Sieyès, Talleyrand, and others to stage a *coup d'état*. Adrienne just so happened to be in Paris on November 9, 1799, when the conspirators successfully staged the nearly bloodless "Coup of 18 Brumaire." The coup ushered in a new system of government called the Consulate, with Bonaparte taking the lead as First Consul. To ward off accusations the coup was a cynical power-grab, supporters of the new government sung the praises of liberty, equality, and 1789. Adrienne sensed a golden opportunity. She dispatched a letter to her husband imploring him to return to France immediately. Lafayette later recalled a trusted aid "came to give me an account of the 18 Brumaire, and, bringing me a passport under an assumed name, he told me, on behalf of my wife, that if I adopted the idea of leaving for France, I would have to decide in a few days."[7] Lafayette did not need a few days. "I didn't think for a second," he remembered, "and two hours later I was on my way."[8]

When Lafayette returned to Paris in November 1799, it was the first time he set foot in the city since denouncing the Jacobins back in the summer of 1792. Operating under the principle it was better to ask forgiveness than permission, Lafayette wrote a letter to Bonaparte announcing his return to France and then met privately with Talleyrand, who stayed on as foreign minister in the new government. Both of them grumpily told Lafayette to go back to the Netherlands. But after Adrienne made a further appeal to Bonaparte, and Sieyès supported the idea of letting the family remain, the Consulate yielded. Lafayette was told through unofficial channels he could live in France as long as he stayed out of Paris and out of politics. If Lafayette made no trouble for them, they would make no trouble for him. Lafayette happily accepted this bargain. He was not interested in making trouble, he just wanted to come home.

⸙

THE MOST OBVIOUS place for the family to move was Chavaniac, but Lafayette explained to aging Aunt Charlotte the terms of the tacit agreement with the Consulate meant he could not return to his ancestral homeland. "No sooner had I arrived than I wrote Bonaparte and Sieyès telling them it was my intention to pay an immediate visit to you," he wrote. But, he went on, "it would have been impossible for me to turn up in our department without causing the very sensation I so much wish to avoid."[9] Cheering crowds welcoming him home was the opposite of laying low and staying out of sight. Luckily, Adrienne managed to win clear possession of an estate inherited from her mother about fifty miles southeast of Paris called La Grange. Uninhabited for years, the château was presently in a state of complete disrepair, but the Lafayettes secured financing to replace the roofs, remodel the interior chambers, and then undertake a complete overhaul of the grounds.

The family took up residence at La Grange in January 1800. Lafayette installed himself in a circular library in one of the towers overlooking the grounds and planned to devote himself entirely to farming, breeding, and the agricultural sciences. His promise to the government to stay out of politics was sincere, but a promise he made to Adrienne was solemn. "Nothing in the world," he told her, "I swear it to you on my honor, my love, and on the dead souls we mourn, can persuade me to give up the retirement plan that I have formed and in which we will spend the rest of our lives quietly."[10] He meant to keep this promise. La Grange became Lafayette's first real permanent residence after many years of bouncing between estates, apartments, tents, hotels, barracks, and prison cells. More than any other place in the world, even Chavaniac, La Grange was Lafayette's home.

La Grange became a home for everyone. The Lafayettes' financial and legal status were still shaky, so Anastasie, Charles, and their new baby—the first grandchild in the family—moved in with them, as did Georges and Virginie. They also welcomed a stream of friends and relatives for prolonged stays. The burgeoning sense of peace and happiness was disturbed, however, by the devastating news George Washington died in December 1799. Lafayette always held out hope he would be able to see his beloved friend and surrogate father one last time. He regretted their final letters were tinged by political estrangements between France and the United States. He also regretted being unable to join the public mourning for his friend. News of Washington's death kicked off a wave of public eulogies and epistles, culminating with a huge national memorial celebration organized by Bonaparte in Paris. But the First Consul still feared Lafayette's potential power and did not invite Lafayette to attend. So Lafayette, the man who bore among his most cherished honorifics the title "Friend of Washington," stayed home while his country honored the man he knew better than all of them put together. Washington mentored Lafayette in the camps of the Continental Army, advised him in letters from across the Atlantic, but could now only guide him in spirit.

From this depressing low point, Lafayette's public position steadily improved. As the First Consul solidified power, he agreed to remove Lafayette's name from the émigré list on March 1, 1800, restoring his legal rights and French citizenship. This paved the way for Georges to secure a commission as a lieutenant in the French army on the eve of a renewed offensive against the Austrians. The First Consul led an army back into the Alps, subsequently scoring a major victory at Marengo in June 1800. Bonaparte's military victories permanently secured his political position at home and opened space to reconsider his treatment of Lafayette. Bonaparte no longer wished to push the Hero of Two Worlds into the shadows, but instead sought to bring him back out into the light. Lafayette was, after all, one of the heroes of 1789 and a martyr of the Reign of Terror. He could be extraordinarily useful in Bonaparte's plan to reconcile all political factions and end the Revolution once and for all. Bonaparte invited Lafayette to a reception at the Tuileries Palace to celebrate the victory at Marengo. It was the first time the two men actually met in person.

In October 1800, the First Consul called upon Lafayette again, this time to help celebrate the new peace treaty between the United States and France ending the Quasi-War. Lafayette recalled, "There were present the American commissioners, several of my French colleagues, many generals, the Bonaparte family, and the First Consul with whom for two days I had an opportunity of talking a great deal." He went on to describe one of those conversations. "One of the first things he said to me," Lafayette recalled, "was that I must have found the French looking very coldly upon liberty. 'Yes,' I replied, 'but they are in a condition to receive it.' 'They are thoroughly disgusted,' he said, 'your Parisians, for example. The shopkeepers want no more of it.'"[11] Lafayette walked away believing Bonaparte's commitment to liberty and equality extremely suspect. At this reception, Lafayette also met the First Consul's oldest brother, Joseph, with whom Lafayette would strike up a lasting friendly relationship—Joseph ever attempting to win Lafayette to the cause of the Bonapartes and Lafayette ever attempting to win the Bonapartes to the cause of liberty.

After the signing of the peace treaty with America, Talleyrand asked Lafayette if he was interested in serving as new French ambassador to the United States. Lafayette declined. He did not really approve of the increasingly authoritarian tendencies of the Consulate. Besides, he said, "I told them all that I was too American to be able to play a foreign role there."[12] Lafayette would stick to the original bargain—he would stay out of politics. He would not publicly criticize the regime, but he would not publicly support them, either. When Lafayette returned to retirement at La Grange this time, it was clearly *his* decision to remain in peaceful rustic obscurity.

Despite their political differences, Bonaparte and Lafayette maintained a cordial personal correspondence. Lafayette continued to urge Bonaparte to stick to the enlightened and liberal ideals of 1789, while Bonaparte implored Lafayette to be realistic and support Bonaparte's postrevolutionary program of prosperous order and national glory. Their frank exchanges meant when someone warned Bonaparte about Lafayette's political hostility, the First Consul said Lafayette "will never say more than what he says to my face."[13] Lafayette was always up-front and blunt about where he stood. Once, at dinner with Joseph Bonaparte and Lord Cornwallis, Lafayette lamented the state of political liberty in France. When Bonaparte found out, he said to Lafayette, "I warn you Lord Cornwallis claims you are not corrected yet." Lafayette retorted, "About what? A love of liberty? What should repulse me? The crimes and excesses of the terrorist tyranny? They only made me hate any arbitrary regime even further and commit myself more and more to my principles." Lafayette assured Bonaparte he was not involved in any sedition. "I live a retired existence in the country," he said, "I do my best to avoid talking politics." But he also refused to lie when asked his personal opinion about the Consulate. He told Bonaparte, "Whenever people come to ask me if your regime conforms to my ideas of liberty, I will answer no."[14]

To win over Lafayette, the First Consul was not above tacit bribery. Knowing the Lafayettes were deeply in debt, Bonaparte directed his government to recognize Lafayette's title to La Belle Gabrielle, the largest of his plantations in Cayenne. The state never sold the property after it was confiscated in 1792, and returning it to Lafayette was a simple matter of filling out a few forms. Bonaparte told Lafayette as soon as the title was transferred, the state would immediately buy it back for 140,000 *livres*. All of this paperwork could be done in an afternoon and Lafayette would walk away with a badly needed cash windfall. This purchase agreement was part of the dark conclusion to Lafayette's noble experiment in emancipation. The slaves he owned were all freed by the emancipation decree of 1794, but when Lafayette read the contract he discovered he was "made to cede 'the blacks' and consequently recognize a right of property 'over those found' on the plantation."[15] Lafayette said, "This is the first notion that I had plans to reestablish slavery." He tried to get this clause removed and wrote Adrienne, "I declared I would not cooperate in any kind of slave system." But lawyers told him the sale was contingent on renouncing any and all claims to the property. "In the long run," Lafayette told Adrienne, "it was agreed that I should renounce my rights and all property of whatever kind that belonged to me in Cayenne."[16] Lafayette needed the money so he took it. Within a matter of weeks, Bonaparte published an act reestablishing slavery in the French colonies. The slaves Lafayette purchased to set free were only emancipated after Lafayette no longer owned them; then, once he regained his claim, he sold them all back into slavery. It is an ignoble end to a once noble experiment.

If the purchase of La Belle Gabrielle was meant to be a bribe, it didn't work. After successfully concluding the Treaty of Amiens, which brought a general peace to Europe for the first time since 1792, Bonaparte advanced his increasingly authoritarian powers still further. In May 1802, he held a national referendum asking the question: "Should the term of the First Consul be for life?" The announced results, clearly manipulated, were 3,568,000 "yes" to just 8,374 "no." But on the tiny list of those who voted no were both Lafayette and his son, Georges. In the official register recording his vote, Lafayette added the explanation, "I cannot vote for such a magistracy until public liberty is sufficiently guaranteed. Only then will I give my support to Napoleon Bonaparte."[17] Lafayette drafted a further letter to the First Consul expressing his personal best wishes and patriotic support for France, but saying he could not go along with a clear turn to dictatorship. Publicly, Bonaparte was impassive. When asked whether only dead-end Jacobins opposed the measure, Bonaparte nonchalantly said, "No, there were also some enthusiasts for liberty, Lafayette for example."[18] But privately he was furious. The correspondence between Bonaparte and Lafayette ceased. From now on the two men would be tense adversaries.

⸻

LAFAYETTE'S OPPOSITION TO Bonaparte was sincere, but also realistic. Opposing the First Consul did not mean trying to overthrow him. Instead, he kept his promise to Adrienne: he stayed at La Grange and devoted himself to farming and his growing family. Georges met and fell in love with Émilie Destutt de Tracy, the daughter of a prominent liberal philosopher named Antoine Destutt de Tracy, who became a great family friend and political ally of the Lafayettes. The two liberal allies spent their years in the political wilderness together and were thrilled when their children married each another. The following year, Virginie married a young officer named Louis Lasteyrie and began a family of her own. Soon La Grange overflowed with grandchildren. Though his yearning to play a great role on the public stage never deserted him, Lafayette was thoroughly content with his life as a farmer, husband, father, and grandfather.

Lafayette's pleasantly untroubled life was briefly interrupted in February 1803. Walking out of the naval office in Paris, he slipped on a patch of ice and broke his femur. Rather than accept what appeared to be an unavoidable life as an invalid, Lafayette agreed to wear an experimental contraption to properly set the bone. The contraption caused forty days of constant pain and then, when it was finally removed, tore off a chunk of his thigh. But the procedure was mostly successful and he was able to walk. For the rest of his life, Lafayette walked with a limp and a cane, which rather suited his reputation as an old veteran of war and revolution. That the real cause of the limp was a patch of ice on a slippery street rather than an old wound from the life of a revolutionary warrior was neither here nor there.

Meanwhile, as Bonaparte permanently entrenched his power, he made a number of radical moves to impose his vision on France. In late 1801, he sent a massive invasion to attempt to retake the Caribbean colony of Saint-Domingue, which Toussaint Louverture and other former slaves successfully liberated during the Revolution. When the expedition resulted in the catastrophic loss of almost the entire army by the end of 1802, Bonaparte cut his losses in the Americas. In the spring of 1803, he sold France's claim to the Louisiana Territory to the United States.

President Thomas Jefferson promptly asked his old friend Lafayette if he was interested in becoming the first territorial governor. "I sincerely wish you were here on the spot," Jefferson wrote, "that we might avail ourselves of your service as Governor of Louisiana, the seat of which government, New Orleans, is now among the most interesting spots of our country, and constitutes the most important charge we can confer. I believe too you would have found it a pleasant residence."[19] Jefferson reiterated this offer in March 1804: "I [would] rather have your single person there than an army of ten thousand men for the purpose of securing the tranquility and preservation of the country . . . you would immediately attach all the ancient French inhabitants to yourself and the U.S."[20]

As he considered this offer, Lafayette watched the flickering candle of liberty in France grow dimmer. In April 1804, Bonaparte took the ultimate step on his road to power. First Consul Bonaparte declared himself Emperor Napoleon I. Lafayette watched the transformation of France into an authoritarian empire with bitter disgust. It seemed a final cruel blow against all the hopes and dreams set in motion by 1789—the final legacy of Lafayette's revolution was not liberty and equality but a ruthless military dictatorship hell-bent on global conquest.

Jefferson's offer to move to Louisiana thus seemed like a perfect answer, but Lafayette ultimately declined. "My presence in Louisiana, you seem to believe, could be useful," he wrote back. "I am . . . no less excited than thirty years ago by the thought of following American freedom as it progresses on the continent. Serving her as a magistrate, missionary, or soldier would make the last days of my life as happy as the beginning." But he could not take the job, both on account of Adrienne's consistently poor health, and because he did not want to leave his homeland behind. It would mean admitting the cause of liberty was lost in France. "To pronounce this sentence myself," he said, "to proclaim it, so to speak, by expatriation, is repugnant to my hopeful nature . . . I cannot understand how, without being compelled to do so by a material force, I would leave this land, however disadvantageous it may seem; still less, how I could abandon the smallest hope . . . I tell myself that I, promoter of the revolution, must not recognize the impossibility of seeing it reestablished on its true bases, those of a just and generous freedom, in short, American freedom."[21] Lafayette began his quest for liberty in the new world, but he would finish it in the old world.

As he re-committed himself to the quest he began as a teenager, those he set out with passed away. Lafayette was devastated to learn his oldest friend, his first *real* friend, vicomte de Noailles, was killed in action in January 1804. Noailles emigrated to Philadelphia after the execution of his wife Louise, and after living there for nearly a decade, returned to service in the French army. He was killed fighting the British in the Caribbean. Just a few months later, Lafayette learned his oldest friend in America, Alexander Hamilton, was killed in a duel with Aaron Burr. He wrote Jefferson, who had long since become Hamilton's political rival, "The deplorable death of my friend Hamilton hurt me deeply. I am sure that, regardless of the differences between your two parties, you always admired him and feel his loss as deeply as I do."[22] Most of Lafayette's old friends were now in the grave. He felt himself becoming a man of a different time.

⊰⊱

NAPOLEON'S NEARLY UNBROKEN run of military success in 1805, 1806, and 1807 ensured Lafayette remained in anachronistic obscurity. The emperor of France became, for all intents and purposes, the emperor of Europe. He made his siblings kings of newly created provinces and kingdoms throughout the continent. Joseph Bonaparte, for example, became the king of Spain. There was no place in this world for an old defender of liberty like Lafayette. Nor any of his relations. Georges and his brother-in-law Louis Lasteyrie continued to serve in the army out of patriotic duty, but Napoleon knew how to hold a grudge. Still angry over Lafayette's vote against him on the Life Consulate, the emperor denied every recommended promotion for Georges and Louis. After being passed over once again, even after Georges saved the life of a general at the Battle of Eylau in early 1807, the two young men admitted their careers were cursed by the emperor's wrath and resigned.

This meant, however, they were home for the greatest tragedy yet to befall the family. Adrienne never fully recovered from her time in Olmütz. The ailments she picked up while in captivity routinely flared up and drove her to bed. In late 1807, she took a turn for the worse. She grew progressively sicker and this time did not get better. Her children transferred their mother to Paris to be closer to doctors. Lafayette was in Chavaniac on business but raced north to her bedside. The family spent weeks caring for her through what they all suspected was her final illness. Near the end Adrienne said to Lafayette, "I am going to die. Have you any grudge against me?" He replied, "What grudge could

I have, my dear? You have always been so sweet, so good." She asked, "So I have been a pleasant companion to you?" "Indeed you have," he replied. "Then bless me," she requested. So he did.[23] In her final hours she whispered to him, "I am all yours."[24] Adrienne de Noailles, marquise de Lafayette, passed away on Christmas Eve 1807. She was only forty-eight years old.

Her death hit Lafayette hard. He wrote César de La Tour-Maubourg, their fellow prisoner of Olmütz:

> During the thirty-four years of a union in which her tenderness, her goodness, her elevation of mind, her delicacy and generosity charmed and embellished my life and made of it an honorable thing. I came to be so used to all she meant to me that I could not draw a line of distinction between her existence and my own. She was fourteen years old and I sixteen when her heart first became inextricably blended with everything that mattered to me. I felt quite certain that I loved her and needed her, but it is only now, when, having lost her, I have to unravel what remains of myself from that sweet entanglement so as to face what is left me of a life which I once thought filled with so many distractions, that I realize how impossible it is that I shall ever more know happiness or well-being.[25]

To Thomas Jefferson he wrote a similar sentiment: "In her, at every moment of a union of thirty-four years, I have found the greatest blessing my heart could wish for and more than a compensation for every public misfortune. . . . Before this blow I confess I did not know what it was to be unhappy. . . . Now I feel myself irresistibly overpowered."[26]

❦

LAFAYETTE, NOW A widower, continued to keep a low public profile. He was in his midfifties and focused on projects at La Grange, his children, and now more than a dozen grandchildren. "I have become a pretty good agriculturalist," he said, "and lame though I am, I husband my strength where walking is concerned, and manage to do and to oversee what is essential."[27] But despite leading a private life, his political views were well known. "My neighbors, and especially my fellow farmers, had become accustomed to looking at me only from the point of view of the landlord arguing . . . I have nevertheless, at all times, expressed my opinion on the famous system of the emperor and my ardent desire to see its end."[28]

Napoleon certainly remained convinced Lafayette was a snake waiting in the grass: "Gentlemen," he said one day to the Council of State, "I know your dedication to the power of the throne. All France is chastened. I know only one man who is not, that is Lafayette: He has never retreated a line. You see him quiet; well, I tell you, he is quite ready to start again."[29]

Napoleon's imperial fortunes peaked in 1808. After conquering both Prussia and Austria, the young Tsar Alexander I of Russia stood poised to become Napoleon's partner in an imperial alliance stretching from Madrid to Moscow. But from this peak Napoleon began a precipitous and inexorable decline. In Spain, recurrent revolts led to a bleeding ulcer that refused to heal. Then Tsar Alexander grew cold to Napoleon's advances and chafed under the demands of his alliance with France. These conflicts led the tsar to break with Napoleon, leading to Napoleon's fateful decision to invade Russia in 1812. On the eve of this latest campaign, Lafayette wrote Jefferson analyzing Alexander's chances of defeating Napoleon's army: "Will Alexander fight pitched battles? Will he ask for conferences? There is a risk, in either case, of being defeated or caught; but if he drags the war long, he may well embarrass his rival."[30]

This was a prescient observation. A brutal winter and the Russian army's scorched-earth policy ravaged Napoleon's great army. The invasion of Russia resulted in bodies piled on top of bodies. Anonymous corpses littered the fields and roads as Napoleon pulled back and the Russian armies advanced. In 1813, Austria and Prussia threw off the French yoke and redeclared war.

Napoleon's political legitimacy at home was always tied to his military victories abroad. The news of failure and defeat in Russia led to the first stirring of political opposition in years. Lafayette reconsidered his posture of steadfast aloofness and wondered if perhaps the time was finally right to throw Napoleon off the throne. "As for me," Lafayette said of this period, "I quarreled with Napoleon since my vote against the consulate for life, I could not exercise any action in a despotic government which I had, from its first steps, refused to associate with. It was a lot, I dare say it, to have stood for twelve years amid prostrations from within and without; thus showing, in my isolation, a signal of disapproval and hope."[31]

Lafayette remained patriotic enough to lament the defeat of the French army, even as he delighted in the fate of Napoleon, whose hubris finally met its nemesis. But he felt helpless to act. "Seeing the storm Napoleon brought down over France," he said, "I felt tormented by my inability to combat domestic tyranny and foreign invasion."[32] But as history moved Napoleon off the stage, Lafayette spied an opportunity to make a comeback. He kept his promise to Adrienne to live with her in retirement for the rest of their lives. But she was gone now. It was time to return to the great stage of history.

CHAPTER NINETEEN

RESTORATION

[1814–1815]

I N December 1813, Lafayette traveled to Paris on painful personal business. Madame de Tessé was dying. Both she and her husband died within a few weeks of each other and Lafayette remained in Paris to attend to their affairs—which included his personal inheritance of a townhouse on 8 rue d'Anjou, which subsequently became his primary residence in Paris.

Even after discharging his family duties, Lafayette lingered in the capital. Each day brought news of the Allied coalition pushing Napoleon's armies backward. For the first time in nearly twenty years, battles were fought inside French territory. Napoleon issued decrees calling for mass conscription and an all-out war of national defense, but by now people were sick of the emperor and his wars. Lafayette felt this shift in public opinion and stood ready. "In 1814," he wrote, "France was tired of Bonaparte's ambition, his despotism, and his interminable wars; he himself had employed all the resources of his genius to kill the public spirit . . . on the day of danger, he finds himself alone."[1]

Despite Napoleon's final flurry of military brilliance in the Six Days' Campaign in February 1814, his situation was hopeless. Lafayette said, "The Emperor Napoleon had for a long time taken it upon himself to weary the patience of the French, the submission of the powers of the

Continent, and the favors of fortune."[2] The favors of fortune now ran out. Allied armies under British general Wellington pushed up from Spain. A grand coalition army of Prussians, Austrians, and Russians advanced toward Paris from the east. As they approached, cunning political survivors like the old foreign minister Talleyrand and longtime minister of police Joseph Fouché set about organizing not a glorious last stand, but a welcome party. Through backchannels, they came to an understanding with the Allies that the rest of Europe was fighting a war against Napoleon, not the people of France. Despite his own animosity toward Napoleon, Lafayette was still shaken when the Allied armies entered Paris and marched down the Champs-Élysées on March 31, 1814.

Tsar Alexander I was the central figure of the Allied occupation of Paris. Russia and the tsar were the first to defeat Napoleon, and what began in Moscow in 1812 now ended in Paris in 1814. Alexander was the enlightened heir of his grandmother Catherine the Great and was determined to be merciful. He stuck to the story that Napoleon was the enemy, not France. In a declaration to the people of Paris, he announced: "I am the friend of the French people. It is right, it is wise, to endow France with strong and liberal institutions which are in keeping with the current light. Our allies and I come only to protect the freedom of your decisions."[3] They came as liberators, not conquerors.

As Paris turned its back on the emperor, so too did his marshals. They retreated with the last remnants of his army to the royal château at Fontainebleau, about fifty miles southeast of Paris. Napoleon wanted to keep fighting, but his officers refused to follow him anymore. Lafayette said, "The marshals, natural interpreters of the army, advised Bonaparte to submit to his fate."[4] Napoleon abdicated the throne on April 6, 1814. Tsar Alexander and the Allies offered extremely generous terms of peace to both France and Napoleon. The emperor would be exiled to the small Mediterranean island of Elba with a retinue of retainers and a generous pension. This was supposed to be a comfortable enough fate to dissuade Napoleon from coming back and risking more severe punishments.

After Napoleon's fall, the question was, what came next? There were plenty of options to choose from. Nobody of influence wanted to restore the republic, a name now synonymous with terror at home and war abroad. The Austrians favored a regency for Napoleon's Austrian wife, Marie Louise, on behalf of their three-year-old son, who would reign as Napoleon II. But neither the French nor the other Allies would have it. There was some talk of transferring the crown to the young Louis Philippe, duc d'Orléans, son of the duc d'Orléans who played such a huge role in launching the great revolution of 1789 and was beheaded for his trouble in 1793. Tsar Alexander personally favored Jean Bernadotte, one of Napoleon's former marshals who switched sides after becoming heir to the throne of Sweden and Norway. But Talleyrand joined the British in pushing what they believed the safest option: the return of the legitimate Bourbon dynasty. The restoration of the Bourbons meant recognizing the man formerly known as the comte de Provence as King Louis XVIII.

The comte de Provence had not set foot in Paris since the night of June 20, 1791, the night *he* managed to escape, while his brother Louis XVI, sister-in-law Marie Antoinette, and their children were all caught in Varennes. Provence claimed the title King Louis XVIII after the execution of his brother in 1793, and the death of ten-year-old "Louis XVII," who died of revolutionary neglect in 1795. For the past twenty years, his insistence on being addressed as Louis XVIII was something of a sad and pathetic joke. After bouncing around various European cities, he settled into permanent exile in England, where he grew obese and suffered gout, leaving him an invalid. For years, he seemed destined to live and die as an eccentric resident of Buckinghamshire claiming to be the king of France. But the great wheel of revolution finally turned full circle. After much cajoling and negotiation, the French and Allied leaders in Paris agreed to recall the Bourbons to the throne.

Talleyrand, ever the practical politician, understood too much had happened since 1789 for France to simply accept a complete restoration of the *ancien régime*. The French nation and its citizens had grown used to their rights. If the Bourbons came back, they needed to accept certain constitutional conditions. Lafayette himself hoped for the reestablishment of the Constitution of 1791. "It was shown that not only the best, but the only means of salvation was returning to the first principles of the revolution," he wrote. "We have been assured that the king and his family have decided to go the same direction, and in general, their conduct and speeches have been in keeping with this assertion. The arrival of the king will decide the acceptance, the formation, and the evolution of this constitutional order."[5]

There is an old witty cliché that when the Bourbons returned to power they had learned nothing and forgot nothing—that their sole object was rebuilding what the Revolution had torn down and avenging themselves on twenty-five years' worth of family enemies. But this is not actually the case. Louis XVIII was himself a practical man. He understood a great deal *had* happened. He understood his return to power required some kind of constitution. So on May 2, 1814, just as he was about to enter Paris, Louis issued a proclamation assuring his subjects he planned to draft something called a "Charter of Government." This charter was not immediately forthcoming, but the proclamation ensured there would be no trouble when Louis formally entered Paris the next day. In fact, far from causing trouble, huge crowds flocked to cheer the returning king. More than anything else the people wanted peace, and more than anything else, the return of Louis XVIII meant peace.

※

UPON HIS ENTRANCE into Paris, Louis XVIII returned to the Tuileries Palace for the first time since 1791. When the new king opened his court, Lafayette felt obliged to pay his respects. He reported Louis "received me with remarkable politeness."[6] Lafayette reported the same of his old classmate, the comte d'Artois, whom he had not seen since 1789. Given their long history of mutual antipathy, the conspicuous courtesy of the Bourbon brothers came as a pleasant surprise. But this would be Lafayette's one and only visit to court—they didn't really want him there and he didn't really want to be there.

It was at this same reception Lafayette first encountered Louis Philippe, the duc d'Orléans. A tall and stout forty-year-old, the younger Orléans fled France in the spring of 1793 and inherited the family title after the Reign of Terror claimed the head of his father. Following his escape from France, Orléans lived in Switzerland, England, and then finally two years in Philadelphia. While in the United States, he befriended young Georges Lafayette during a visit to Mount Vernon.

"The manner in which the duc d'Orleans asked news of my son," Lafayette said, "whom he had seen in the United States . . . made it my duty to visit him . . . he spoke of our times of proscription, of the similarity of our opinions, of his consideration for me, for my principles, for my character, and this was in terms superior to the prejudices of his family." Lafayette left the encounter very impressed, calling Orléans "the only Bourbon compatible with the free constitution."[7] This was a belief Lafayette would hold for many years to come.

Lafayette's wariness of the restored Bourbons and regard for Orléans increased when he met Tsar Alexander at the salon of his friend Madame de Staël. When Lafayette mentioned the Bourbons seemed to have corrected themselves, Alexander laughed. "Corrected!" he said. "They are uncorrected and incorrigible. There is only one, the duc d'Orleans, who has liberal ideas; but for the others, never expect anything from it." Lafayette replied, "If that's your opinion, sire, why did you bring them back?" Alexander said, "It's not my fault; at least I wanted to slow them so the nation would have time to impose a constitution on them. They won over me like a flood."[8]

Lafayette and the tsar also talked about their shared hopes for the coming Congress of Vienna, including the possibility of outlawing the slave trade. Napoleon may have shamefully reintroduced slavery to the French Empire in 1802, but the British declared the slave trade illegal in 1807, and there was a chance the rest of Europe would follow their lead. Lafayette said he and the tsar held "a discussion on the immediate abolition of the slave trade." Alexander spoke in favor of abolition but said ruefully, "I can guess what [the colonists] think, the head of a country which admits serfdom has no right to speak thus; but many lords are ready to abolish it."[9] Lafayette left his meeting with Alexander saying, "He really is a great, good, sensible, noble minded man . . . and a sincere friend of liberty."[10]

Between Alexander's influential benevolence and Talleyrand's artful negotiations, the Allies and France signed the Treaty of Paris on May 30, 1814. The terms of the treaty were extremely generous. France would be reduced to its frontiers as of 1792, but there would be no financial reparations, nor a prolonged military occupation, *and* they would be given a seat at the coming Congress of Vienna, where all post-

Napoleonic territorial and financial disputes would be settled. The Allies, and Alexander in particular, saw such leniency as the beginning of permanent peace after twenty years of plunging bayonets into each other's chests.

A few days later, Louis XVIII promulgated his seventy-nine-article Charter of Government. For liberals like Lafayette, it was a troubling document. For starters it dated the Charter to the *nineteenth* year of His Majesty's reign, effectively declaring all intervening French governments illegitimate. The preamble reinforced this framing: "In thus attempting to renew the chain of time, which disastrous errors have broken, we have banished from our recollection, as we could wish it were possible to blot out from history, all the evils which have afflicted the fatherland during our absence."[11] Lafayette was happy to see the Charter included a two-house legislative branch, with an elected Chamber of Deputies and appointed Chamber of Peers, and promises to recognize freedom of speech, religion, and the press. But the Charter did not speak of these concepts as "rights." Nor was the legislature allowed to propose laws of their own: they could only approve or reject what the sovereign submitted.

Most of all, Lafayette was vexed by the political philosophy underpinning the Charter. This was not a true constitution rooted in popular sovereignty. The Charter was treated as a free gift from Louis to his subjects, rather than a constitution the king himself was ultimately bound to obey. Lafayette expressed to Jefferson "the illegality of a charter where the sovereignty of the people was flatly denied."[12] With hindsight making it even clearer, Lafayette later said, "I saw the first words of several good sentences, but the form of 'grant' was the first step of the counter-revolution."[13] But Lafayette also hoped France could fight for their rights without once again descending into revolutionary terror: "If the resistance of the Bourbons and their party necessitated a new July 14, it could still be done under the auspices of civil authority and by the best-intentioned men of the revolution."[14]

The great crisis seemed peacefully resolved by the summer of 1814. Lafayette returned to La Grange, where he settled into privately critiquing the restored Bourbons while admitting it was better than most of the alternatives. As the months went by, however, the people of

France grew disenchanted with their restored monarch. Louis might be a practical man, but many at his court—most especially his brother, the comte d'Artois—were not. Where the king believed the family must bow to reality, Artois led an ultraroyalist faction who wanted their privileges restored and their enemies punished. They considered themselves victims of the greatest crime in history and demanded restitution and revenge.

Most especially, Artois and his friends wanted their old property back. But there was a problem. Various French governments had long since sold confiscated estates to new owners, and those owners would resist dispossession. King Louis struggled to balance the two sides. He acknowledged the just claims of the aggrieved nobility, but if he simply ordered re-confiscation, it might trigger a revolt the Bourbons would not survive. Lafayette said of the controversy: "We must return to the observation of Cicero after the proscriptions of Marius and Sulla . . . a late reparation would only be a new spoliation."[15] Any move to reclaim lost property would be a foolish, and possibly fatal, provocation.

The greatest problem, however, was not material but spiritual: wounded national pride. Looking back, Lafayette described this overarching problem in a long summation of the glorious accomplishments of the Revolution and Empire. The French Revolution did not just introduce new rights, it made France the strongest power in the world. The French people accomplished

> the overthrow of all the thrones, thirteen hundred thousand republicans rising against the coalition of Europe and dispersing it on all points; then a series of conquests . . . the sovereigns trembling before the little corporal of the army of Italy who became Emperor of the great nation . . . incredible victories no longer surprising anyone, the French decrees signed in all the capitals, prodigious constructions paid for with the tributes of the vanquished or protected peoples; masterpieces from all centuries, from all countries, coming to meet at the Paris museum, and at the same time, since the Gordian knot of privileges had been cut, an immense career open, to talents, to ambition, to the speculations of the entire population; agriculture, industry, the sciences, the arts, intellectual research, the effective well-being and the political ideas

of five-sixths of the nation, accrues in twenty-five years, in a proportion which one would not find of example at no time in history!

After all that success, Lafayette said, "Suddenly, the nation had to shrink, like on Procrustes's bed, to the level of the humiliating circumstances and the contemptible prejudices of the counter-revolution; it was too much at once."[16]

After France got a taste of the reactionary spite of the Bourbons, they longed for the glorious days of the Bonapartes. Napoleon felt this longing as he sat in exile just off the coast.

⁂

"IT TOOK ONLY ten months of the government of the Bourbons to restore popularity to this man whom France hated for a long time," Lafayette later wrote.[17] Well aware public opinion was turning against the Bourbons, the exiled emperor left Elba and landed near Cannes on March 1, 1815, determined to regain his throne. As Lafayette observed, Napoleon represented national greatness and victory while the Bourbons stood for national ignominy and defeat. When he arrived in France, Napoleon found plenty of old officers and soldiers ready to rejoin him. As he marched north toward Paris, every army detachment sent to intercept him switched sides and declared their loyalty to the old emperor.

Lafayette was at La Grange when the news came. "The cry of alarm was brought to me at La Grange," he wrote. "Since my first visit to the King and [Artois], I had no connection with the court. . . . But the current crisis, however unpleasant were its two alternatives, gave me the need to be at the center of the news and within reach, if it was still possible, to take advantage of it for the good cause."[18] Lafayette raced to Paris, still considering the Bourbons the lesser of two evils. Liberals in the city, anxious to block Napoleon's return, held meetings during these anxious days in March 1815. Lafayette proposed calling together an assembly of *every* deputy who served in *any* national assembly stretching all the way back to 1789 to form a kind of super-representative body speaking on behalf of the entire nation. But his suggestion was ignored as unrealistic. The deliberations of Lafayette and his friends didn't matter anyway. The last garrison defending Paris defected to Napoleon, clearing the road to the capital. King Louis concluded his position was hopeless and fled to the Belgian city of Ghent on March 19, 1815. Napoleon entered Paris the next day.

Two obvious choices presented themselves to Lafayette: prove his loyalty to the Bourbons and follow the king, or retire to La Grange. But with his political blood pumping for the first time in twenty years, Lafayette elected to play a dangerous game. He chose a third option: stay in Paris and fight Napoleon from the inside. Upon his return, the emperor pledged to institute a new constitution recognizing the political freedoms his previous regime denied. Lafayette warned fellow liberals to be skeptical of Napoleon's claims he was a changed man.

Lafayette was most concerned about his friend Benjamin Constant. Lafayette and Constant first met in the liberal salons of the late 1780s, but they did not become friends until much later. In the mid-1790s Constant fell into a complicated relationship with Madame de Staël and joined her lobbying effort to get Lafayette out of prison. Following the Coup of 18 Brumaire, Constant temporarily served the new Consulate, but was ejected in 1802 as Bonaparte solidified power. De Staël was one of Bonaparte's fiercest critics, so she and Constant departed France for an extended European tour as prominent exiles of Napoleonic despotism. After Napoleon's first abdication in 1814, Constant returned to France, where he and Lafayette became reacquainted and struck up a lasting friendship.

Like Lafayette, Constant remained in Paris when Napoleon returned. But unlike Lafayette, he accepted Napoleon's professed liberal rebirth. Lafayette was concerned over Constant's credulity and warned his friend: "One can only be the active leader of a free people in a republic where, either as a president, or as a director, one is subject to continual criticism and legal responsibility . . . there can be no freedom in a country, unless there is a freely elected representation, raising and disposing public funds, making all the laws, organizing and dissolving military forces, deliberating in debates published by the newspapers, complete freedom of press, [and] supported by all that guarantees freedom individual . . . I wish to be assured that the Emperor can resign himself to such institutions; so far I don't see him wanting it."[19] But Constant did not heed this warning. Instead he collaborated with Napoleon and authored the "Additional Act," which significantly liberalized the imperial constitution.

The day before the Additional Act was promulgated, Joseph Bonaparte reached out to Lafayette and offered to make him a Peer in the new regime. Lafayette declined. He said he was "a man of the people . . . it is by the choice of the people that I will emerge from my retirement."[20] Lafayette indicated he would not allow himself to be *appointed* to any political position, but if he were *elected*, he would serve. Joseph left the meeting satisfied Lafayette was on board. When elections for a new Chamber of Representatives were held on May 8, Lafayette received the most votes in his district. Then, when the Chamber of Representatives met for the first time on June 3, Lafayette was elected one of its four vice presidents.

Lafayette's collaboration with the Bonapartes shocked some of his old friends. But Lafayette fully expected Napoleon to falter upon his return to power and wanted to be there to push him off the cliff if an opportunity presented itself. His greatest concern at the moment was preventing the Allies from re-invading France. He wrote to his old friend Princess Hénin, who fled with the king to Ghent, that an Allied invasion played into Napoleon's hand. It would turn him into a "necessary defender, whereas, if they did not invade the frontier, leaving him to grapple with domestic problems," he might simply collapse.[21] Napoleon needed military power to secure political power. If he was denied a war, he would reveal himself to be an obnoxious tyrant claiming authority he did not deserve. But the Allies were not just going to let Napoleon return without a fight and remobilized for war.

On June 7, 1815, Napoleon arrived in the Chamber of Representatives to deliver an inaugural address. When he spotted Lafayette approaching, he said, "So there is Lafayette, who has already declared war on me."[22] The two men had not seen each other since Lafayette's decision to vote against the Life Consulate back in 1802. "It has been twelve years since I've had the pleasure of seeing you," Napoleon said. "Yes, sire," Lafayette replied, "it has been that long." The emperor said, "I find you rejuvenated, the country air has done you good." "It has done me a lot of good," Lafayette answered. While they made this small talk, they sized each other up. Lafayette said, "Since neither one of us wanted to lower his eyes, we read there what each was thinking, but I found the muscles on his face contracted and even moved in a quite extraordinary way."[23] As for the speech Napoleon delivered, full of bromides to freedom and promises to respect liberal civil rights, Lafayette described it as the performance of "an old tyrant mad at the role which his position forced him to play."[24]

Lafayette was not the only person in the Chamber of Representatives hostile to the return of the emperor. Even though the chamber served under his auspices, they determined to test how independent Napoleon would allow them to be. With war clearly inevitable, Lafayette and his colleagues expressed concern about protecting "a single man at the expense of the nation." Lafayette said, "One feels a great distress, that with him gone, one could avoid the war."[25] But avoiding war was impossible. Napoleon's marshals, officers, and soldiers were ready to fight. They gathered their cannons, bayonets, rifles, horses, and carts and marched north to block the juncture of the Allied armies scrambling to restart their war machines. They would all soon meet at Waterloo.

❦

ON JUNE 20, 1815, Paris received news the Allies defeated Napoleon. The emperor came tumbling back into Paris that very night, and a battle for control of France began immediately. Napoleon demanded the Chamber of Representatives and Chamber of Peers award him dictatorial powers until he expelled the invaders and ended the national emergency. But most of the representatives and peers concluded this was not a *national* emergency, but merely *Napoleon's* emergency. They refused to grant him the powers he demanded.

The next morning, Lafayette climbed to the tribunal of the Chamber of Representatives to start the process of pushing Napoleon off the cliff. "Now is the time to rally around the old tricolor banner," he said. "That of '89, that of liberty, equality and public order; it is this alone that we have to defend against foreign pretensions and against internal attempts."[26] He laid out a plan for how to handle the crisis, with the final point reading, "The ministers of war, foreign relations, the interior and the police are invited to come immediately to the bosom of the assembly."[27] Lafayette proposed to exclude Napoleon from power and recenter the national government in the chambers.

Lafayette's speech led Napoleon to dispatch his younger brother Lucien to bring the Chamber of Representatives to heel. Lucien accused them of cowardice, ingratitude, and betrayal. Lafayette stood and responded from his seat: "It is a slanderous assertion we have just heard from the tribune. By what right does the speaker dare to accuse the nation of having been fickle, of having lacked perseverance towards the Emperor Napoleon? It followed him in the sands of Egypt and the deserts of Russia, on fifty battlefields, in his reverses as in his successes . . . and it is for having followed him thus that we have to regret the blood of three million French people!"[28]

Later in the day, Lafayette joined a council of about thirty high-ranking officials and ministers to discuss the crisis. Lafayette said forthrightly, "I ask that we all go to the Emperor to tell him that, from all that has happened, his abdication has become necessary for the salvation of the country."[29] But for the moment, the others declined to go that far.

The next day, however, the Chamber of Representatives threw down a gauntlet, announcing, "It was necessary either they be dissolved, or Napoleon be dethroned."[30] They further resolved if the emperor did *not* voluntarily abdicate, the chamber would declare him disqualified and vacate the throne. Later that afternoon, Napoleon admitted defeat. On June 26, 1815, he transmitted his formal abdication. Lafayette was among a small delegation sent to thank Napoleon for his peaceful resignation. "We found him calm and serene—he received us with a faint but gracious smile," Lafayette later recalled, "neither affecting the pathetic dignity of fallen greatness nor evincing the uncontrollable dejection of disappointed ambition."[31] Napoleon packed his bags and headed for Rochefort, where he planned to board a frigate and sail to exile in the United States.

Napoleon technically abdicated in favor of his young son, but the chambers ignored the fallen emperor's attempt to save his dynasty. Instead, they created a five-man provisional government. Lafayette later said he believed he would be elected one of the five men on the provisional government. But from his position in the Chamber of Peers,

Joseph Fouché seized the initiative and blocked the potentially meddle-some Lafayette from being elected.

Lafayette then attempted to take control of the National Guard, and believed to his dying day if put to an open vote, "it is likely that a large number of votes would be brought, as in the past, to the first commander who directed and organized this great institution."[32] But before such a vote could be taken, Fouché successfully induced the chambers to award appointment power to his handpicked five-man provisional government. They promptly selected a far more reliable ally. Benjamin Constant observed in his diary, "They have excluded Lafayette."[33]

To complete Lafayette's exclusion, the provisional government appointed him to a delegation that would meet the approaching Allies and sound out their intentions. Lafayette said, "I had reason to be unhappy: many things displeased me and repelled me in my new situation; moreover, I would have much preferred to stay to throw forward good articles of constitution. . . . However, I accepted the mission of plenipotentiary after my friends convinced themselves I could be of use there."[34]

Lafayette and a small group of commissioners, with Benjamin Constant acting as the group's secretary, rode out to Allied headquarters. The commissioners had reason to believe the Allies would be lenient. "Had they not solemnly declared they only took up arms against Bonaparte," Lafayette said, "that if the nation ceased to recognize him, they would cease to be his enemies?"[35] But when the commissioners reached the Allies on June 30, they were disappointed. Despite his former generous benevolence and professions of personal friendship, Tsar Alexander refused to meet with Lafayette or his colleagues. In fact, none of the heads of state would meet them. They were instead directed to a conference with lower-level functionaries.

At this meeting, one of Lafayette's fellow commissioners argued, "The only object of the war no longer existed . . . Bonaparte has once again become a private individual under the supervision of the government, and only asks for a passport to either go to the United States or to England."[36] The British representative said, "I must warn you, sir, that there is no possible peace with the Allied Powers, unless you deliver Bonaparte to us." Lafayette replied, "I am very surprised, that in proposing such cowardice to the French people, you prefer to address yourself to a prisoner of Olmütz."[37] Lafayette was no friend of Bonaparte, but he was not about to let him be chucked in an Austrian prison—Lafayette knew what that was like.

Lafayette's commission was a failure. It neither slowed the approach of the Allies nor won any assurances. They were treated as a nuisance. Meanwhile, the remnants of the French army retreated south across the Loire river and there was talk of continuing a patriotic war of national defense. When Lafayette returned to Paris on July 5, he seemed to favor this idea, saying, if he was in the government, "I would have pronounced in favor of a battle before capitulation, and I would have followed our brave army to the banks of the Loire."[38] But he was not in the government, and there would be no war of national defense.

Lafayette also failed in his attempt to arrange a passport for Napoleon to relocate to the United States. Instead, the British took Napoleon into custody at Rochefort. They would transport him not to America, but to the tiny island of Saint Helena in the South Atlantic where the former emperor would die in bitter neglect in 1821.

As the chambers waited for the Allies to enter Paris, they drafted a new constitution in the vain hope it might be ratified. For his part, Lafayette understood they were writing for posterity. He used almost the same terms he used to describe his presentation of declaration of rights on July 11, 1789, when he thought reactionary counterrevolution might overthrow the Estates-General at any moment. Here in 1815, he urged his colleagues to write a visionary constitution: "If we are overturned, the people must know what it has lost and what it must regain."[39]

But this time they *were* overturned. The Allied armies entered Paris on July 7. When the Chamber of Representatives attempted to resume their work on July 8, they found the doors locked and guarded by soldiers. Lafayette asked loudly "if it was an order from the Prince Regent of England."[40] He then called on his fellow representatives to follow him to his house where they could continue their sessions. It was, in many ways, an attempt to re-create the Tennis Court Oath—at least Lafayette hoped it would be. But upon reconvening at Lafayette's house, all they did was vote to disband.

When Louis XVIII returned to Paris later that same day, it marked 112 days since he fled the city on March 19. History rounded this number down and dubbed the period "The Hundred Days." The Hundred Days divided the return of the Bourbons into parts: the very brief First Restoration and much longer Second Restoration. There would never be a Third Restoration. The next time the Bourbons were chased out of France, it would be for good.

CHAPTER TWENTY

THE CERTIFICATE OF ANTIQUITY

[1815–1820]

W HEN LOUIS XVIII RETURNED TO PARIS IN THE BAGGAGE of the Allies for a second time, Lafayette found himself in social and political limbo. On the one hand, his decision to stay in Paris when Louis fled to Ghent marked him as a collaborator with the Hundred Days regime. He could expect no favors, access, or kind words from the Bourbons. But it was also clear he spent the Hundred Days working to undermine Napoleon. So despite his participation in the Hundred Days, no one mistook him for a Bonapartist. Lafayette was not targeted for serious punishment.

Others were not so lucky. If a spirit of generous reconciliation marked the First Restoration, bitter vengeance marked the beginning of the Second Restoration. Partisans of the Bourbons were furious the French people so easily reembraced Napoleon. Ultraroyalists and arch-conservatives concluded, as one partisan put it, "to stop their criminal plots . . . we need irons, executioners, torture. Death, death alone can frighten their accomplices and put an end to their plots. . . . It will only be by throwing a salutary terror into the souls of the rebels that you will prevent their guilty projects. It will only be by dropping the heads of their leaders that you isolate the factions."[1]

In the first months of the Second Restoration, France endured a "White Terror"—an expression derived from the white flag of the Bourbons, and now used generally to describe royalist or reactionary violence. Individuals who participated in the conspiracy to bring back Napoleon were targeted. Spontaneous royal and Catholic lynch mobs summarily killed hundreds of people. The White Terror then expanded to settle further lingering scores. Anyone identified as a republican, Jacobin, or Bonapartist could be beaten up, their homes destroyed, and other property confiscated. In the south, arch-Catholics went after their Protestant neighbors. The government purged seventy thousand people from the civil service for political unreliability. At the highest rung of power, the king drew up a list of fifty-four names who would *never* receive amnesty under any condition.

The Bourbons were not alone in their fury. The Treaty of Paris of 1815 was significantly harsher than the Treaty of Paris of 1814. All the Allies earned for their previous leniency was the French rushing to reembrace Napoleon. They now believed all of France, not just Napoleon, needed to be chastised, punished, and watched carefully. The new treaty required France to pay 700 million *francs* in monetary reparations to the Allied powers, further reduced France's final borders, and stipulated 150,000 foreign troops would occupy the kingdom for the next five years.

Lafayette managed to avoid serious repercussions. He was not lynched, persecuted, dispossessed, or driven in exile. The Prussians had occupied La Grange during the recent campaign, but returned it to him when they left. The most serious and permanent consequence was the end of his thirty-year relationship with Madame de Simiane. Their affection always transcended politics; she had never been anything but a traditional conservative, he had never been anything but a revolutionary reformer. Their divergent views always caused problems, but Lafayette's decision to participate in the Hundred Days was too much. When Louis XVIII fled Paris, Simiane followed. When Lafayette did *not*, she never came back to him. They barely ever spoke again.

Lafayette even felt safe enough to vote in the first election for a new Chamber of Deputies in August 1815, even though, in the atmosphere of the White Terror, anyone to the left of the comte d'Artois feared showing their face in public. The new chamber was thus packed with men described as being "more royalist than the king." The king himself dubbed them the "*Chambre introuvable*," usually rendered in English as the "Incredible Chamber" or the "Unobtainable Chamber," but might be more literally called the "Irretrievable Chamber." They wanted to undo *everything* that had happened since 1789 and no one was going to stop them. After casting his meaningless vote, Lafayette retired to La Grange to resume his life as an agriculturalist, and wait for the revolutionary wheel of history to turn again.

⌖

IN THE SUMMER of 1816, Lady Sydney Morgan, an Irish novelist and travel writer, visited Lafayette at La Grange. She said she approached the home of the Hero of Two Worlds "with the same pleasure as the pilgrim begins his first unwearied steps to the shrine of sainted excellence." Welcomed into his home, she described her host: "On the person of Lafayette, time has left no impression; not a wrinkle froze the ample brow; and his unbent, and noble figure, is still as upright, bold, and vigorous as the mind that informs it. Grace, strength, and dignity still distinguish the fine person of this extraordinary man."[2] This is a poetic description, but not exactly true. Time *had* left an impression on Lafayette. He walked with a noticeable limp, wore a hairpiece to cover his bald head, and was much heavier set than in his younger days. But given Lafayette spent five years in prison living an emaciated existence on the edge of starvation, he earned his paunch.

Lafayette was happy to play host to friends and admirers who revered him as a living symbol of liberal principles the reactionary powers of post-Napoleonic Europe attempted to bury. The young aspiring historian Augustin Thierry was a regular visitor at La Grange and described Lafayette as a shining light from a forgotten age: "Faithful to the habits of liberty, he cultivated his fields like Washington, and practiced in silence the genuine civic virtues, simplicity and industry."[3] Much later in life, Thierry called Lafayette "the man whom I love so much and whose character I admire so much. It is at La Grange that I received my education in civic reality, and until my last breath, I will be faithful to the principles of that great and noble school which will not perish."[4]

Lafayette stayed away from Paris as much as possible, but was gratified to watch from afar as the ultraroyalist supermajority in the Chamber of Deputies outraged public opinion with their flagrant attempts to restore as much of the *ancien régime* as possible. King Louis XVIII remained far more pragmatic than his most ardent supporters. Believing that if they continued on a violently reactionary path the Bourbons would be chased out of France again, the king dissolved the chamber in September 1816 and called for new elections.

To prevent a repeat of the Irretrievable Chamber, Louis expanded the electorate. Slightly. Henceforth, any man over thirty years old who paid 300 francs in annual taxes could vote. Any man over forty who paid 1,000 francs annually could stand for election as a deputy. Lafayette cleared both requirements easily, but was in a tiny minority. In a country of around thirty million people, there were fewer than one hundred thousand voters. But in the general election of the fall of 1816, with the acute fever of the White Terror passing, more moderate and sensible men won election. Following the general election of 1816, the plan was to hold annual elections replacing one-fifth of the chamber. This would hopefully create stability and continuity in the government. And make elections easier to control.

As the king, his ministers, and the Chamber of Deputies tacked in a more moderate direction, they signaled the relaxation of censorship laws. This resulted in an array of new journals and newspapers sprouting up in Paris. Lafayette was not a great writer, philosopher, or polemicist, but he wanted to *promote* writers who expressed his ideals better than he did. With no other public role to play, he got into the journalism business. Lafayette provided financial backing for a semiannual journal called *Le Censeur Européen*, which released its first issue in the spring of 1817. The journal published articles advocating a liberal approach to politics and economics, publishing the work of the economist Jean-Baptiste Say, the liberal historian Augustin Thierry, and, under a pseudonym, a young Auguste Comte. *Le Censeur Européen*'s advocacy of free market economics and political liberty put them squarely in the middle of what would become conventional nineteenth-century liberalism.

The journal also forthrightly attacked the concept of hereditary aristocracy, which Lafayette had been doing for thirty years. Lafayette's own disdain for the concept of nobility meant he now bristled when people publicly referred to him as "the marquis de Lafayette." He now preferred, and would eventually come to forcibly insist, on being addressed in public as "General Lafayette." He also discarded the fashions of his fellow aristocrats, and adopted those of the bourgeois men of business. Subdued suits, trousers, and overcoats replaced extravagant silken finery. The marquis de Lafayette was a dashing, culottes-sporting eighteenth-century dandy. General Lafayette was a stolid portrait of nineteenth-century landed gentry.

In the autumn of 1817, General Lafayette heeded a call from his friends to stand for election to the Chamber of Deputies. But the government was not *that* interested in liberal toleration. The Bourbons still feared and detested the name *Lafayette*. When he submitted himself as a candidate for the Paris elections in September 1817, agents of the government bribed, threatened, and cajoled the electors to oppose Lafayette at all costs. "They said, without doubt to make me unpopular, that I was the tricolor flag itself," Lafayette said. "They added that my nomination would cause the failure of the negotiations for the removal of foreign troops, and they dared say if the liberal electors succeeded, the Allied armies would march on Paris, and these exaggerated remarks, so flattering to me, were being repeated not only in the salons and cafés but even out loud in the electoral meetings."[5] A few years later he lamented, "The words liberty, equality, fraternity, republic, nation, and citizenship, instead of electrifying the masses, awaken memories and fears that our opponents know how to make the most of."[6] Lafayette came in a dismal and somewhat humiliating last place.

⚞⚟

INSTEAD OF BEING discouraged, Lafayette's ambitions only increased after his defeat in 1817. He struck up talks with a small clique of liberals to better organize for future elections—some of them unreconstructed republicans, some Bonapartists, others former liberal nobles like himself from the old days of 1789. Among them were the banker Jacques Laffitte, a popular if somewhat conservative liberal who shared Lafayette's political and economic outlook; Marc-René de Voyer d'Argenson, Lafayette's aide-de-camp in 1792 and now his partner in *Le Censeur*

Européen; Jacques-Charles Dupont de l'Eure, who served a variety of official roles dating all the way back to the First Republic and one of the commissioner sent to the Allies with Lafayette in 1815; and finally, Victor, duc de Broglie, the great nephew of Charles-François de Broglie, who once imagined himself stadtholder of America, and who was so instrumental in Lafayette's departure for the New World.

Slightly to the right of the faction around Lafayette were the more pedantically legalistic liberals called the *doctrinaires*. The most impressive of their group was rising historian, journalist, and sometimes government minister François Guizot, whose father was guillotined in the Reign of Terror. Guizot rooted his liberalism in the idea that practical reforms would *prevent* the slide toward revolution, as opposed to Lafayette, who believed such reforms were simply the first step of a larger revolutionary journey. All of these people held disparate opinions, but collectively formed a loose left-wing opposition to the government.

In the run-up to the elections of 1818, Georges said life at La Grange ceased to be a scene of a pastoral retreat and now resembled a party headquarters. "For about two months now," Georges wrote a friend, "we have been leading at La Grange the life of Paris, and the quantity of people whom we have received, with the difference that we begin to be together from the morning on."[7] Joining this bustling crowd was twenty-one-year-old Charles de Rémusat, who recently married one of Lafayette's granddaughters. Rémusat was more cerebral, detached, and cynical than his grandfather-in-law. Rémusat said Lafayette "reigned a bit like a despot in the midst of this gathering, but a loving and loved despot."[8] Rémusat also said La Grange "lacked the diversity which results from the freedom of opinions and characters. These lofty and liberal ideas, which so fortunately prevailed there, had been stagnant for too long and needed to be renewed by contradiction. . . . One would hardly dare show a personal pretension and an original opinion . . . basically no independence under the empire of the Patriarch of Liberty."[9] Young Rémusat applauded the sentiments and character of his in-laws, even as he detected something stuffy and predictable about their beliefs. He said at La Grange, "It was quite possible to die of boredom."[10]

With new elections approaching, Lady Morgan described how "there is at this moment twenty times more liberality and public spirit in France than in Ireland, or even in England. Every shop is crowded with the pictures of La Fayette and other patriots."[11] Thierry, meanwhile, wrote a brief and glowing portrait of Lafayette—an early entry in the now common genre of campaign biography. Thierry waxed, "You are truly the man who has best understood and best served liberty. In my meditations on reason and virtue in politics, I have never been able to equal in conception what your conduct has been. I cried upon reading your recollections of the beautiful days of '89." And, as always, Lafayette was linked to Washington. The title page of the pamphlet read: "You will never persuade a people who love liberty that they should fear the citizen to whom Washington bequeathed his sword."[12]

The liberal *indépendants* were well situated to challenge the election of 1818, but the regime still considered Lafayette a worrisome threat. An alarmed King Louis XVIII said to his favorite minister, Élie Decazes, "Those fellows talk of the possibility of the election of that animal Lafayette with an assurance which would almost rattle my own."[13] The immediate concern was if French voters started electing old revolutionaries, the project of persuading the Allied armies to end their occupation of France would stall. In late 1818, the government was focused on a diplomatic summit in Aix-la-Chapelle of the five great powers: Britain, Prussia, Russia, Austria, and France. Lafayette's election might seriously upset careful negotiations to remove the foreign troops. When Lafayette submitted his name to the electors of Melun—a city close to La Grange—Georges said the government used "every means, threats, promises, politenesses, etc." to prevent the election of his father.[14] And it worked. Lafayette lost again.

But this time, Lafayette had a backup plan. The principal problem, Georges said, was "this department is too near Paris."[15] It was too easy for the government to bribe and threaten individual voters. But it was much harder to coerce voters out in the provinces. There were technically no rules forbidding voters from electing any candidate they wanted. It was, of course, customary for a candidate to stand for election in his home department, mostly because that is where one found the greatest concentration of friends, allies, and supporters. But it wasn't legally required.

Lafayette's backup plan lay in the Sarthe, a region situated on the Lower Loire Valley in northwestern France. Lafayette had never been there, but a liberal activist, lawyer, and journalist named Charles Goyet spent the summer of 1818 diligently organizing a bloc of liberal voters. While organizing, he contacted Lafayette, requesting permission to nominate him for election in the department. Lafayette naturally preferred the honor of representing his home district, but arranged things so if he lost, Goyet would enter his name as a candidate for the Sarthe. "As soon as the election in Melun is finished," Lafayette wrote an ally in the region, "a man on horseback will leave to announce the news to my son and to you. We must inform M. Goyet that in any case, success or not, you will send a reliable man carrying the news. We must not leave the good voters of the Sarthe in uncertainty."[16] After his defeat in Melun, Lafayette sent the express rider to activate Plan B. Goyet got his small but surprisingly functional party machine working.

Goyet was right to be confident. In the election on October 27, Goyet's chosen candidates were the top four vote getters. Three carried outright majorities, while the recently added Lafayette came in fourth with 48 percent of the vote. Though this total far exceeded any other candidate, Lafayette's failure to secure a majority necessitated a runoff. The conservative president of the electoral assembly attempted to jam up Lafayette's election by postponing the runoff, hoping Goyet's voting bloc would disperse back to their homes. But Goyet was ready and distributed pamphlets reading: "Citizen voter, stay, in order to take part in the elections, until Friday morning. If essential business calls you home, come back on Friday: until 3 o'clock, you will still be able to deposit your ballot. Voters! Don't let yourselves be defeated by intrigue."[17] The voters listened. On Friday, October 30, 1818, Lafayette received 596 of 1,055 votes and was officially elected a member of the Chamber of Deputies. It was a shocking turn around for a government that thought it buried Lafayette just a week earlier.

Down in Aix-la-Chapelle, the prime minister fretted about the impact Lafayette's election would have on his discussions with the Allies. "Lafayette . . . it's too much," he said. "The effect is dreadful here, and more than one of these gentlemen will show his regret having signed the evacuation."[18] The king was furious and afraid his kingdom might once again be going to the revolutionary dogs. The following year an observer said, "The election of M. de la Fayette had shaken all of France and almost Europe."[19]

But this was all overblown. The Allies recognized their continued occupation of France was deeply unpopular. If they stayed much longer they might face genuine revolt. The comte d'Artois recently caused a scandal when a memo he wrote begging the Allies to stay—as he considered them the sole guarantee of Bourbon rule—leaked to the press. His intemperate remarks offended national pride, and public opinion turned even more against the occupation. The fear of the Allies reconsidering their plans in light of Lafayette's election was dramatically overstated. As the Allies prepared to withdraw from France in the winter of 1818, Lafayette prepared for a five-year term in the Chamber of Deputies.

⁂

AT THE OPENING session of the Chamber of Deputies on December 10, 1818, Lafayette was the most notable figure. Lady Morgan said, "When Lafayette entered, every eye was turned on him, and every tongue pronounced his name as admiration, fear, or hope dictated."[20] Benjamin Constant, who would himself soon join Lafayette as a deputy of the Sarthe in an upcoming by-election, wrote glowingly of Lafayette's unimpeachable devotion to liberty. "Has he given either his service or his praise to the caprices of despotism?" Constant asked. "I do not think he has. In 1789 he wanted what he wants today: his opinion carries its certificate of antiquity, and the words 'sudden conversion' and 'zeal of novice' cannot be applied to him."[21]

Lafayette entered the chamber hopeful the election results represented a shift toward liberalism. This hope was buttressed when the king promoted his favorite courtier, Élie Decazes, to the post of prime minister. Decazes believed it sound policy to reach out to the liberal opposition rather than arch-conservatives for support. This meant 1819 would be a year of moderate liberalization—most especially in treatment of the press. Lafayette's own commitment to the freedom of the press was deep enough that when prosecutors indicted an ultraroyalist journalist for publishing scandalous lies about him, Lafayette opposed the prosecution. "During the 42 years that my life has been subject to public judgment," he said, "I have asked no writer to speak well of me, nor bothered anybody for speaking ill of me, and furthermore, although very sensitive to kindness, I have never answered calumny."[22] This was a bold commitment to principles coming from a man run out of the French Revolution by libelous enemies in the press in 1792.

Lafayette and his allies successfully carried a series of laws expanding freedom of the press in the late spring of 1819. But aside from the success with the press laws, their gains turned out to be distressingly minimal. Lafayette wrote Goyet in May 1819, "The roadblocks to progress that we experience are distressing. I am no more ministerial than anybody else, I believe in the fault of the prefects and other agents; nonetheless often things occur which are due only to their powerlessness."[23] Which is to say, even if the government *wanted* to be more liberal, they were having trouble implementing reform.

Watching the Bourbons, the government, and more conservative deputies insist on maintaining rigid conservative principles rather than embrace much-needed reform, Lafayette warned the chamber he believed intransigent opposition to reform was a major cause of the French Revolution. In a speech in June 1819, he said, "I saw Turgot and Malsherbes propose popular reforms. They were told: 'the French people were of their nature both taxable and willing to work for free' so these patriotic ministers were sacrificed." Next came Jacques Necker in the early 1780s "who put his glory in doing good and said, 'a thousand crowns given to a courtier was the size of a village.' The king's heart heard him; but the courtiers overthrew him." After Necker came Calonne, who "risked summoning the Notables; and they defended their privileges against the king, as the following year they defended them against the people." Even after Calonne was dismissed, his successor Brienne "experienced more insurrectional opposition." By the time the Estates-General was finally called, things had backlogged out of hand, and "the National Assembly found it impossible to reform anything without changing everything."[24] Decades of resistance meant that by 1789 it was revolution or nothing.

Lafayette attempted to reframe the prevailing depiction of the French Revolution as a terrible catastrophe. No one better knew the crimes of individual revolutionaries, but Lafayette did not believe "The Revolution" was a bad thing. "If this reconstruction of history was imperfect," he said, "the general principles are not in doubt . . . because, despite all that was subsequently lost by anarchy, terrorism . . . bankruptcy and civil war, despite a terrible fight against all of Europe, there remains an indisputable truth: it is that the agriculture, industry, the public education of France, the ease and independence of three-quarters of its population, and . . . public morals have improved to a degree of which there is no example in any equal period of history."[25] Lafayette's point was the indisputably positive outcomes of the Revolution might have been attained *without* anarchy, terrorism, and civil war. If only those with privilege and power had been less greedy and more enlightened.

But from the conservative perspective, the nods to liberalism and popular reform were the very things inviting the Revolution to return. In the election of 1819, they were horrified when electors in the department of Isère elected the aging Abbé Grégoire. Grégoire was another old ally of Lafayette's from the days of '89—a member of their Society of Thirty and Society of the Friends of the Blacks. But while Lafayette wound up expelled from the Revolution in 1792, Grégoire sat in the National Convention. Most explosively, he voted *for* the execution of King Louis XVI. King Louis XVIII was furious at the election of one of his brother's executioners. He demanded his ministers do everything in their power to deny Grégoire his seat. They successfully found a pretext to annul the election and block Grégoire from entering the Chamber of Deputies, but it was a close call.

The election of Grégoire only added to the king's growing disenchantment with liberal outreach. He rejected Lafayette's theory of revolutionary history and now believed opening the door to reform meant letting in the flood of revolution. Lafayette and his friends were subsequently dragged through a trial for violating rules about the number of people who could gather for a political meeting. When asked if he thought the law applied to the gatherings he attended, Lafayette plucked his never failing courage and said it never occurred to him, because "that article is so incompatible with any constitutional regime, that in applying it to these meetings, or to any other of this kind, I would have assumed I was contradicting the charter and ridiculing the government."[26]

⚜

IN THE WAKE of Grégoire's election, the government planned to introduce a revised election law to stop this sort of thing from happening in the future. Lafayette remained optimistic it would not be so bad, right up until February 13, 1820, the moment the country was rocked by the assassination of the duc de Berry, the eldest son of the comte d'Artois and third in line for the throne. Though the assassin appeared to be a lone madman, conservatives blamed rabid neo-Jacobin revolutionaries.

It was easy for reactionaries to connect Berry's assassination to the wider threat of liberal revolution thanks to explosive events in Spain. On New Year's Day 1820 the Spanish army mutinied in Cádiz. Liberal officers, fed up with the reactionary absolutism of King Ferdinand VII, marched on Madrid and forced him to accept a liberal constitution at gunpoint. It was simple to connect these events to the assassination of Berry, which followed just a few weeks later.

With the sudden threat of liberal revolution rising in Europe, King Louis XVIII broke off cooperation with the left. He dismissed Decazes and brought in a new right-leaning government. This new government promptly introduced the long-rumored election bill. It was worse than Lafayette could have imagined. Soon dubbed "the Law of the Double Vote," the law created 172 additional seats in the Chamber of Delegates. These new delegates would be elected by special electoral colleges in each department, consisting only of the top taxpayers. But participation in the new electoral colleges did not exclude those superwealthy voters from voting in the regular elections. Thus, they got to vote twice: once for candidates in the normal elections, and then again in the new departmental colleges to select a second batch of candidates reserved just for them. Hence, "the Law of the Double Vote." The new structure was guaranteed to produce overwhelmingly conservative majorities.

Lafayette railed against a threat to the liberties of the nation in the spring of 1820. He believed the reactionary manipulations violated the

Charter of Government. In a speech in March 1820, Lafayette said, "To violate the charter is to annul it, to dissolve the mutual guarantees of the nation and the throne." Such violations would "restore us to ourselves and all the primitive independence of our rights and duties."[27] Lafayette reminded his audience if the rulers of a country violated fundamental principles of national sovereignty, the people may avail themselves of any nonelectoral methods to restore them.

He followed this up in May 1820, calling for a "return to the national, constitutional, peaceful and generous paths . . . our contemporaries are tired of revolutions, glutted with glory; but they will not allow themselves to be robbed of dearly won rights and interests." He warned especially that young radicals would not stand for such assaults on their liberties. "Do not force them," Lafayette said, "by threatening them to lose all the useful results of the revolution, to seize themselves again the sacred fasces of the principles of eternal truth and sovereign justice, principles applicable to all free governments and to which all other personal or political combinations can only be secondary considerations for a people of good sense."[28]

This was not just empty rhetoric. Outside sessions of the chambers, large crowds of students who were barred from officially participating in politics, cheered and jeered and menaced and applauded. The government accused liberals like Lafayette of fomenting revolt. Liberals accused the government of ordering troops to attack and arrest anyone who cried *vive la charte* rather than *vive le roi*. But the government wasn't wrong: Lafayette *was* egging them on.

The Law of the Double Vote passed on June 12, 1820. Lafayette believed the government made a grave mistake. It might secure them a conservative majority in the Chamber of Deputies, but the blatant rigging of the elections outraged public opinion. Lafayette spent months telling anyone who would listen that brazenly ignoring the will of the people was sure to invite a reckoning. Now the reckoning was at hand.

CHAPTER TWENTY-ONE

THE CHARCOAL BURNERS

[1820–1824]

L AFAYETTE'S TRANSITION FROM LEGAL OPPOSITION TO ILLE-
gal conspiracy took place in a general wave of liberal revolutions
across Europe in the early 1820s. The successful liberal revolt in
Spain in January 1820 inspired similar rebellions in Italy later that same
summer. These uprisings, in turn, helped trigger what turned into the
biggest ongoing revolution of the decade: the Greek War of Independence. Lafayette and his liberal friends thrilled at news of these events,
and Lafayette encouraged revolutionaries in Spain, Portugal, Italy, Po-
land, and the German principalities whenever he could. They seemed
to prove the reactionary governments of Europe ruled from atop a very
narrow pole. Things like the Law of the Double Vote ensured a conservative majority of deputies, but those deputies hardly represented
the will of the whole nation. Lafayette noted how few revolutionary
partisans were required in Spain and Italy to overthrow their absolutist regimes. "Several regiments only were necessary for the restoration
of the Cortez," he said. "150 men managed the Naples business . . . it
took only three drunks in Berlin to stir up a crowd and make the king
remember a few things."[1]

Believing he and his allies represented the *true* will of the people,
Lafayette became embroiled in a conspiratorial movement to force the

Bourbons to accept a liberal constitution. Or, if they refused, overthrow them. His turn to conspiracy brought the aging Lafayette into contact with a younger set of political activists—men and women who had not even been born yet in 1789. Unlike typical old-timers who habitually criticize the failings of young people, Lafayette loved the rising crop of students and young officers. He even declared in the Chamber of Deputies, "I must say, it is not true that in my youth the moral state of society in France was better than today. I affirm, on the contrary, that public morals, marital union, the love of fathers for their children, of children for their parents, far from having deteriorated over thirty years, have undergone a very noticeable improvement."[2] He believed those born *after* the Revolution were better suited to provide the energy and commitment necessary to defend its principles, as they were untainted by ancient prejudices.

The links between Lafayette and the militant liberal insurrectionaries of the early 1820s have always been difficult to establish. This is understandable, as Lafayette and his comrades spoke to each other in guarded code and burned any scrap of even remotely incriminating correspondence. In Lafayette's six volumes of collected notes, manuscripts, and correspondence, only a handful of documents even obliquely hint at his activities as revolutionary conspirator in 1820, 1821, and 1822.[3] But there is more than enough circumstantial evidence from eyewitness testimony, police interrogations, and Lafayette's own words to establish not only his deep involvement, but his prominent leadership.

That said, Lafayette was likely *not* involved in the first flare-up of revolutionary liberalism after the passage of the Law of the Double Vote. In the summer of 1820, a collection of radical students and young military officers dared to re-create the Spanish Mutiny of Cádiz. On the morning of August 19, 1820, students massed in the Sorbonne district of Paris—the old heart of the Cordeliers—while their allies in the army gathered a force at Château Vincennes on the eastern outskirts of the city. The soldiers were supposed to march into Paris, merge with the mob of students, and together storm the Tuileries Palace. But unfortunately, the uprising fizzled before it could even begin. An informant revealed the plot on the eve of its launch. Instead of marching on the Tuileries, everyone scattered to avoid a sweep of arrests by the tipped-off authorities. Though Lafayette took no part in the planning or execution of the failed uprising, he did allow a few young suspects to hide in his house until they could make a clean getaway.

The aborted uprising of August 19 had two principal results. First, it backfired completely. Both the government and public opinion turned even harder to the right. Conservative allegations that superficially anodyne liberal reforms served as a cover for violent Jacobins appeared indisputably true. Even moderates now tolerated reactionary policies in the interest of keeping order.

The other principal result would become apparent the following year. A few of the August 19 conspirators fled across the border into Italy. There, they made contact with secret groups who were critical to the recent liberal revolutions in Italy, and which would become the backbone of the next revolutionary insurrection in France: the Carbonari.

⚎

THE ORIGINS OF the Carbonari are wrapped in self-serving mystery. The name refers to the "charcoal burners," people who inhabited the dense woods of medieval Europe. Outside the reach of regular law and order and threatened by both unscrupulous local lords and criminal bandits, the original Carbonari made pledges of mutual support, assistance, and defense. Somehow, over the centuries, these pledges—and the signs used to identify one another—became detached from the actual forest-dwelling occupants in much the same way Freemasonry detached from real masonry in the 1700s. In fact, the modern version of the Carbonari owed much to the influence of Freemasonry, and both were defined by mystical rituals, elaborate internal hierarchies, and vows of absolute secrecy.[4]

The revolutionary character of the Carbonari developed in response to the Napoleonic occupation of Italy in the early 1800s. Italian freedom fighters used Carbonari networks to organize anti-French resistance cells. Members were required to keep a gun and cartridges close at hand, follow orders from superiors without question, and never breathe a word of their activities. Not that they would have much to tell if they were captured. The Carbonari pioneered the use of loosely connected networks of cells—called *vendite*—to prevent infiltration and exposure. An individual Carbonarist could only name the handful of comrades in his own cell. Even the highest-ranking leaders at the top of the network did not know the full membership of the organization they led.

The Carbonari thrived and spread during the Napoleonic era and persisted even after the French Empire collapsed. The Italian Carbonari embraced liberal constitutional principles in opposition to the reactionary monarchs installed across the Italian peninsula by the Congress of Vienna. In July 1820, members of the Italian Carbonari successfully rose up and expelled the absolutist King Ferdinand from Naples. When a handful of French refugees landed in Italy following the failed insurrection of August 19, sympathetic Italian comrades inducted them into their organization and taught them Carbonarist methods, strategies, and tactics. When these French insurrectionaries snuck back into France in early 1821, they brought with them a new set of blueprints and set to work building a Carbonari organization in France—an organization big enough and disciplined enough to stage a full-blown revolution.

The French organization would be a bit different, however. The Italians built their networks organically from the ground up over a period of decades. But the French leaders worked in reverse—first setting up a central organizing committee *then* recruiting members from the top down. The first thing the newly inducted French Carbonari did upon returning to France was form a *vente supreme* to coordinate recruitment. About twenty core members formed the vente supreme, evenly split between young militants and older leaders capable of providing funds, legal cover, and logistical support. The latter group included seven liberal members of the Chamber of Deputies: Lafayette's close friends Voyer d'Argenson and Dupont de l'Eure, as well as liberal stalwarts Jacques Koechlin, Jacques-Antoine Manuel, Pierre-François Audry de Puyraveau, and Jacques-Claude de Corcelle. And, of course, the most famous liberal stalwart of them all: General Lafayette.

Lafayette and his friends' abandonment of electoral politics frustrated people like Charles Goyet, who had *not* given up on legal campaigning. After the failed uprising of August 19, Goyet groused to Benjamin Constant, "It is up to us who have never conspired, who will never conspire, to defend the charter by our writings . . . sooner or later enlightened public opinion will accomplish what conspiracies will never do."[5] Goyet personally faced ongoing harassment for his political activities. It was hard for police officials to look at a liberal organizer like Goyet, see his close connections to Lafayette and other suspicious liberals, and *not* believe he was a principal organizer of an underground conspiracy.

After the liberals got blown out in the election of 1820, the police arrested Goyet and searched his house. When he was brought to trial, prosecutors called Lafayette as a witness. Asked to explain some allegedly incriminating letters, Lafayette refused to comment on evidence he believed seized illegally. "I would be afraid, in explaining myself in more detail on these letters," he said, "to give sanction to an arbitrary act and a police intrigue which I leave to public contempt." But, he added helpfully, "if ever, in the general interest, these opinions need some clarification, the national tribune is where I will comment."[6] This is the last thing the authorities wanted as it would give Lafayette a chance to gin up sympathy for his cause. The judge took a dim view of Lafayette's attitude and said the letters in question "contained principles destructive to the public order." To which Lafayette said, "You have that opinion; I have another; Europe will judge us."[7]

In December 1820, the two dozen conspirators arrested in connection to the August 19 uprising stood trial before the Chamber of Peers. But in a surprising twist, the peers turned out to be hostile to the prosecutors. Influential peers worked to keep the scope of the trial narrowly circumscribed, lest it touch embarrassingly on prominent friends and relatives. The duc de Broglie worked particularly hard. Broglie ensured the only person who could link his friends like Lafayette to the plot was removed from the witness list at the last minute. The case subsequently fell apart for lack of evidence. Of the twenty-nine defendants in custody, twenty-three were acquitted. The prosecutors settled for assigning official guilt to those defendants who already fled the country.

Protected from prosecution and investigation, and enjoying certain legal immunities as a member of the Chamber of Deputies, Lafayette spent the whole of 1821 focused on building a successful revolutionary organization. He all but announced what he was up to in a speech in June 1821. Chastising his fellow citizens for forgetting how terrible the *ancien régime* was, Lafayette said he once hoped the Charter of Government would prevent the return of political absolutism, but "this hope is completely destroyed." He said, "I believe I must declare it, after having already pointed out the counter-revolution's invasion of all our rights and the new order of duties which, in my opinion, would result for us; after having fought within the established institutions the dogma of parliamentary omnipotence, today that the counterrevolution has grabbed them, and at the point to which we have arrived, I limit myself to recognizing the powerlessness of those powers to save the nation."[8] It was clear to all sides Lafayette was coming just short of openly calling for a revolution.

⚜

WHILE LAFAYETTE SOUNDED his call for nationwide liberal revolt, he met an important new friend: twenty-five-year-old Frances "Fanny" Wright. Fanny and her sister Camilla were the orphan children of a rich Scottish family. Their inherited wealth allowed them to live as they pleased. A precocious young idealist, Fanny became obsessed with the United States, which she believed represented the vanguard of human progress. She and Camilla took an extended tour of the United States in 1818, and upon their return, Fanny wrote a popular book on American society and manners. Beautiful, intelligent, and brash, she then entered the liberal salons of London and came into the orbit of Jeremy Bentham, who was a correspondent of Lafayette. Bentham recommended Wright and her book to Lafayette, who always liked anyone who liked the United States.

In the summer of 1821, Wright visited Paris, ostensibly to get her book translated into French, but more importantly to meet the legendary General Lafayette: Hero of Two Worlds and Friend of Washington. She wrote an account of their first meeting to Bentham. "Our meeting was scarcely without tears, (at least on my side)," she wrote. "And whether it was that this venerable friend of human liberty saw in me what recalled him some of the most pleasing recollections of his youth (I mean those connected with America), or whether it was only that he was touched by the sensibility which appeared at the moment in me, he evidently shared my emotion. He remained about an hour, and promised to return in the evening." After dinner they stayed up late talking: "We held in earnest tête-à-tête until after midnight. The main subject of our discourse was America, although we wandered into many episodes and digressions."[9] They agreed on many things, including the immorality of slavery and a shared commitment to abolitionism. This was the beginning of an intense friendship lasting for years.

The relationship between Wright and Lafayette has been the subject of a great deal of speculation. She was a young woman who clearly worshipped him, while he was an aging but still virile man. It's not hard to draw the conclusion they had an affair. But biographers of both Wright and Lafayette generally conclude the two entered into a surrogate father-daughter relationship, rather than a sexual relationship. Wright never knew her parents and Lafayette was an orphan himself who understood the feeling. Lafayette's letters are sprinkled with affectionate descriptions of her as "the tender daughter of my choice."[10] While she wrote back to him, "You know I am your child, the child of your affection, the child of your adoption. You have given me the title and I will never part with it. To possess the title was the highest of my wishes—to deserve it is my proudest ambition."[11] That said, the true nature of their relationship behind closed doors remains a mystery.

Fanny and Camilla spent the entire summer of 1821 living with the Lafayettes at La Grange. They moved into the big house and lived alongside Georges, Émilie, and their children, as well as Virginie, her husband, Louis Lasteyrie, and their children. Anastasie and her husband, Charles La Tour-Maubourg, lived not far away and their eldest daughter recently gave birth, making Lafayette a great-grandfather for the first time. Lafayette's real children at first welcomed Fanny and Camilla, but soon resented their presence and claims to Lafayette's affections.

Lafayette, meanwhile, paid no attention to the upcoming elections, which were only bound to bring more conservatives into the chambers. In fact, Lafayette hardly even regretted their victories anymore. He now embraced something of an accelerationist theory of revolution: believing the ascendant ultraroyalists would inevitably make themselves so hated their behavior would guarantee the success of Lafayette's plan to launch a national rebellion. While the election predictably played out in the fall of 1821, Lafayette and Georges were both deep into planning that rebellion, along with a small cabal of close friends and supporters. Wright was brought into the conspiracy and would soon act as a willing courier and go-between with liberal sympathizers in Britain. After months of planning, the insurrection was set to launch at the end of the year.

⹉⹊

FROM THE SMALL amount of available evidence, it is clear recruitment into the French Carbonari proceeded rapidly through 1821. Colonels, lieutenants, and sergeants in the French army eagerly joined—either because they were young and idealistic, or because they were holdovers from the glory days of the empire feeling embarrassed and stifled by the Bourbons. In the civilian population, willing recruits came from ex-military officers forced into retirement and idealistic students eager for glory. But though the French Carbonari spread wide, its roots were shallow. Plenty of members expressed interest without making a true commitment. The desire of the leaders to grow the organization as quickly as possible also meant revealing details and plans to people they should never have been speaking to. There were plenty of leaks in this revolutionary vessel, and when it started to sink, most of the newly recruited French Carbonari abandoned ship.

At the end of 1821, Lafayette and his Carbonari comrades believed they were ready to launch their uprising. Their staging point would be Belfort, a garrison town on the eastern border with Switzerland. The local population was well primed to support an insurrection. Two of the movement's principal leaders, Jacques Koechlin and Voyer d'Argenson, were major employers and influential power brokers in the region. In December, a local magistrate noted with concern that Koechlin returned from a trip to Switzerland bearing a large amount of hard cash. Meanwhile, the 29th Regiment—an army unit particularly loaded with Carbonarists—had recently been transferred to the Belfort garrison. All the pieces seemed to be falling into place. The final plan was relatively simple: Carbonarist officers in the 29th Regiment would stage a mutiny and the local population would join in. Then Lafayette would appear and present himself as the leader of a provisional government. Other Carbonarist cells were told to consider the Belfort uprising the signal to stage their own mutinies and uprisings. With luck, the whole country would be in rebellion before King Louis XVIII knew what hit him.

But though Belfort *seemed* like a perfect opportunity, planning on the ground was extremely half-baked. Then, events on the other side of the kingdom complicated everything. Authorities in the western city of

Saumur uncovered some kind of insurrectionary conspiracy at the local riding academy on December 23, 1821. Police and military authorities cast out a net the following day, disrupting whatever *might* have been brewing in Saumur. But with so many potential suspects getting away, the police and local magistrates struggled to decipher what they had stumbled upon. They did not know if it was one tentacle of a huge national organization, or a just a handful of malcontents operating on their own.

The busted plot in Saumur put the authorities on notice and hindered the uprising in Belfort. Those inside the city wanted to move quickly, but Lafayette was not ready to go. He spent Christmas at La Grange, which was always a melancholy affair with the memory of Adrienne's death on Christmas Eve hanging over the family. But even after Christmas, Lafayette worried the mutineers in Belfort overstated their control of the situation. Lafayette's concerns turned out to be justified, but he agreed to move forward with the uprising on January 1. Lafayette and Georges climbed in a carriage and rode east to Belfort. Just before they departed, Fanny Wright, who was initiated into the conspiracy, wrote Lafayette, "Time at present hangs heavy on my hands and on my heart . . . I mean not however to call your attention from important matters to my idle words . . . write to me my friend—my father. One word will suffice—but let me know that word soon and often."[12] It was entirely possible Lafayette was about to become president of France or be shot for treason.

In the end, it turned out to be neither. Lafayette was right to fret about the arrangements awaiting him in Belfort. Rank-and-file soldiers reported extremely suspicious conversations with officers in the 29th Regiment to their superiors. Then, just as companies of mutineers mustered on January 1, a loyal colonel stumbled onto them and ordered them to return to their barracks. Meanwhile, another loyal official confronted a suspicious group of armed civilians loitering at the gates of the city. When he tried to question them, he was shot and wounded, while everyone else ran away. The city went into lockdown and the Belfort plot collapsed before it even began. It turned out not to be the spark of a raging inferno, but an easily snuffed out candle.

With everything falling apart, a rider mounted a horse and rode as fast as he could along the main road west, successfully intercepting

Lafayette and Georges before they reached Belfort. The Lafayettes detoured to a nearby friend's house, in case anyone asked questions about what they were doing traveling in the direction of a now exposed secret insurrection in Belfort. But before they could relax, they sent a servant ahead to discreetly track down some baggage they sent in advance—including their military uniforms. The servant found the baggage and carried it across the border to Basel, where he burned it all. It was almost certainly upon Lafayette's subsequent safe return to La Grange every incriminating scrap of paper was thrown into the fire.

But that was not the end of it. As the trial for those implicated in the Saumur plot began in February 1822, an idealistic general named Jean-Baptiste Berton launched a quixotic rebellion to turn things around. Berton declared himself leader of a "National Army of the West" and called on patriots to rally to his banner. But no one came. Within days, Berton and his lieutenants scattered to the winds. Lafayette's involvement in the western plots is murky, but in March a noncommissioned officer was caught and incriminated four sergeants in the garrison at La Rochelle. His confession aligned with documents already in hand mentioning, among others, "General L." When the police finally snared the fugitive Berton in June, they did it by using a police agent posing as a trusted emissary of General Lafayette. Everywhere one looks in the French Carbonari conspiracies of 1821 and 1822, one finds the name Lafayette.

Despite their best efforts, the authorities never proved Lafayette's complicity. At the trial of General Berton, a witness testified he accessed the group "with the help of cards which the Carbonari communicated with each other . . . that the marquis de Lafayette paid him for his trip; that he received instructions from these gentlemen for a new operation against Saumur." He further described Lafayette as "one of the most important agents of the new conspiracy."[13] But the credibility of the witness collapsed when he described Lafayette as a short man in his fifties with long black whiskers. This ridiculously inaccurate description led the judge to instruct the jurors, "Witness has an interest in conveying the impression that he was not in contact with M. de Lafayette. This is why he changes his first description today, and why he wants to reveal only part of the truth."[14] Berton was convicted and executed for treason in October 1822, but Lafayette was never even indicted.

Berton's trial was followed by the trial of the four sergeants of La Rochelle. These young noncommissioned officers became sympathetic martyrs after revelations emerged the police tortured them to extract confessions. It was also widely believed the four sergeants had been drawn into the conspiracy by superior officers in the Carbonari organization who were *not* pursued or prosecuted with the same rigor—a recurring theme throughout all the Carbonari trials in 1821 and 1822. Despite this, the four sergeants were convicted and executed in September 1822, joining a list of eleven total executions of captured Carbonarists. A few dozen other suspects were sent to prison, while probably three times as many fled abroad into permanent exile.

The final results of these trials—mostly targeting the younger, lower-ranking members—led to accusations Lafayette hung people out to dry. That he lied about his own involvement, hiding behind his immunity as a deputy, while others paid the price. A left-wing writer named Émile Gigault later excoriated Lafayette. "Under the Restoration," he said, "the blood of the Carbonari, who he was one of the principal leaders, ran from the scaffold . . . in the many plots in which [Lafayette] took part . . . he always knew how to play this terrible game with the heads of others."[15] But a Carbonari plotter who was there at the time said Lafayette was earnest about his work, not a Machiavellian intriguer. "He conspired in all sincerity of conscience, accepted the necessities of this role, occupied solely with the goal he aimed for. He would have conspired in the public square." If anything, Lafayette's problem was "deluding himself about crazy and dangerous people whom he admitted into his inner circle."[16]

The popular banker Jacques Laffitte later recalled a conversation with the doctrinaire deputy Pierre Paul Royer-Collard. Laffitte said Lafayette was not only a leader in the conspiracies, but actually seemed to be *trying* to be accused publicly. "Is he crazy?" asked Royer-Collard. On the contrary, Laffitte said, Lafayette was "the wisest, the most reasonable, the sharpest man you will ever meet . . . insurrection according to him is the most sacred of duties." Royer-Collard replied, "I'm not sure. Lafayette is a monument wandering around in search of its pedestal. If on the way he should find a scaffold or the chair of president of the Republic, he would not give two cents for the choice between them." Laffitte later told Lafayette about this conversation and Lafayette laughed and said it was true.[17]

Another conspirator, Armand Carrel, also believed everyone knew what they were getting into and Lafayette did nothing wrong.

> All the young people who compromised themselves in the affairs of August [19], of Belfort, of Marseilles, of Saumur, joined on their own account, knowing what they were doing and why they were devoting themselves . . . if they allowed themselves to be discovered before they have matured enough in their affairs, they are victims only of their own inexperience. . . . Never did the leaders of the opposition, never the men to whom one seems to hear the allusion, never Manuel, Lafayette, nor any of their political friends, made a profession of hiring sergeants, young officers, students, to then abandon them to the guillotine of the restoration.[18]

But Carrel also said, upon reflection, they were all nuts: "Why did we have the foolish idea that we could overthrow, by the plots of students and second lieutenants, a government supported by the laws and inertial force of 30 million men?"[19]

⸙

As THE CARBONARI threat was exposed and destroyed, the government turned its attention to the election of 1822, determined to clear Lafayette out of the Chamber of Deputies. Lafayette and Benjamin Constant's five-year terms as deputies of the Sarthe were wrapping up and they faced a tough reelection campaign. The authorities continued to harass Goyet and any printer who did business with him. They indicted Constant on trumped up charges relating to his ambiguous marital status, which precluded his ability to stand as a candidate again. Still unable to pin anything concrete on Lafayette, his enemies in the government instead combed through his tax records and declared he did not qualify to be a candidate or a voter because the property he claimed was not legally in his name. Georges said Lafayette "faced all the little tricks of five or six administration employees who would like to prove that my father lives on air, and that he possesses nothing in the world not even any revenue."[20] This turned out to be just an annoying hassle requiring Lafayette to resubmit updated records.

The government's efforts succeeded. They broke Goyet's liberal voting bloc and conservative candidates ran the table in the Sarthe. Lafayette and Constant both lost their bids for reelection. But it was not that easy to get rid of Lafayette. Though defeated in the Sarthe, he was simultaneously elected by voters in Meaux. So though Lafayette now represented a different district, he was still a member of the Chamber of Deputies.

It was hard to celebrate the victory. For Lafayette, the political situation across Europe was becoming extremely depressing. Just a few years earlier, it seemed like a liberal wave was sweeping Europe. But then the Austrian army marched into Italy, crushed the revolutionaries, and restored the old absolutist rulers. Liberals in the myriad tiny city-states in Germany faced a heavy blanket of oppression carefully engineered by Austrian chancellor Metternich. The Carbonari movements in both France and Italy were in full retreat. But the cruelest blow of all came in 1823. The five great powers of Europe concluded the liberal government in Spain must be overthrown, and tasked France with the job. Lafayette and his comrades long assumed the French army would be the basis of their own liberal revolution. They were horrified when the officers and soldiers proceeded to follow orders, invaded Spain, and overthrew the Spanish liberal regime in April 1823. All Lafayette's hopes and expectations seemed to be empty mirages. Maybe he was *not* in sync with the spirit of the age, but a man living beyond his time.

Discouraged, Lafayette spent most of 1823 living a quiet life at La Grange surrounded by children, grandchildren, and great-grandchildren. Fanny and Camilla were often in residence, as were other beloved old friends like the comte de Ségur, one of Lafayette's oldest friends. They were among the few who survived everything while so many of their friends and relatives were dead. With everything going wrong and living under implied accusations of light treason, Lafayette started receiving friendly overtures imploring him to take some time off and come visit the United States. "Do not let your love of country force you to cling to her until everything noble, great, and useful shall be buried in the ruins of fanaticism and crime," one American correspondent wrote. "Here you will be received with open arms as the friend of Washington, the early defender of our rights and liberties and the proud chief and head of the liberal party of all countries."[21] But Lafayette replied he was still a deputy. "As long as duty and even honor point out the field of action, can an old herald of the charge now sound a retreat?"[22]

Lafayette didn't have to worry about sounding the retreat, because he was soon swept right off the battlefield. Riding high, the conservative government called a surprise general election in early 1824. The government once again targeted Lafayette for defeat. He suspected they added ineligible names to the voter rolls in Meaux, while purging the names of his supporters even though they were clearly eligible to vote. He blamed his poor showing on "the refusal by the prefect to give cards to over forty electors, register them, and even to return their documents to them, and then the eliminations of the last days with the introduction of newcomers."[23] It was unscrupulous, but it worked. The general election of 1824 was a general wipeout for the liberals thanks to censorship, manipulation of the voter rolls, threats, bribes, and outright fraud. Liberals won just thirty-four seats and now made up only 8 percent of the Chamber of Deputies. Lafayette was defeated. This time, there was no Plan B. He was no longer a deputy.

As the Old World rejected him, Lafayette opened a letter from President James Monroe dated February 24, 1824. "My dear General," Monroe wrote, "Congress has passed a resolution . . . in which the sincere attachment of the whole nation to you is expressed, whose ardent desire is once more to see you amongst them . . . whatever your decision, it will be sufficient that you should have the goodness to inform me of it, and immediate orders will be given for a government vessel to proceed to any port you will indicate, and convey you thence."[24] When he received this letter, Lafayette surveyed the climate in France, and concluded a long vacation in America was just what he needed. It was time to get out of the stifling conservative atmosphere and go back to where people loved him and celebrated his ideals. It was time for Lafayette to return to America.

CHAPTER TWENTY-TWO

THE NATION'S GUEST

[1824–1825]

AS SOON AS HE RECEIVED THE LETTER FROM PRESIDENT Monroe, Lafayette began arranging his return to America. Georges planned to accompany him, along with a faithful servant named Bastien. To serve as secretary, Lafayette approached an idealistic young officer named Auguste Levasseur. Levasseur eagerly accepted the offer to join Lafayette's party; he happened to be a Carbonarist officer from the infamous 29th Regiment and deeply implicated in the failed Belfort uprising. Levasseur would act as traveling secretary and record keeper of the trip. Upon their return to France, Levasseur turned his notes into a two-volume account of the tour called *Lafayette in America in 1824 and 1825: Or, Journal of a Voyage to the United States*, which was part travelogue, part economic report, part social commentary, and part political manifesto.[1]

Fanny Wright and her sister Camilla desperately wanted to accompany Lafayette, and his children fought over whether it was appropriate for young unmarried women to travel with their father. Wright suggested the possibility of marrying Lafayette so she could travel as his wife. But Lafayette swore he would not remarry after Adrienne's death. Wright then suggested adoption, but Anastasie and Virginie were dead set against the idea. Lafayette *did* want them to come, though, so eventually they reached a compromise. Fanny and Camilla would travel to the United States separately and only join Lafayette after he made his initial grand entrance.

In July 1824, Lafayette, Georges, and Levasseur traveled to Le Havre to meet their waiting ship. As if to remind them why they were leaving, the local authorities broke up an impromptu farewell celebration staged by supporters in the city. This would be the last time for eighteen months Lafayette entered a town where the local authorities did not trip over themselves to invite everyone in a five-hundred-mile radius to fête, toast, and cheer him. In France, local leaders couldn't wait for Lafayette to leave. In America, they couldn't wait for him to arrive.

After four easy weeks at sea, Lafayette and the party arrived in New York on August 15, 1824. Newspapers publicized the imminent arrival of the Hero of Two Worlds, so when he reached Manhattan, boats of every shape and size packed the harbor. On shore, tens of thousands of people lined the streets, docks, and wharfs. A New York newspaper said, "This distinguished friend of civil liberty is again on our shores after a long absence . . . he left us weak, unorganized and tottering with infancy; he returns to us, and finds our shores smiling with cultivation, our waters white with the sails of every nation, our cities enlarged, flourishing and wealthy, and our free government, for whose establishment he himself suffered, perfected in beauty, union, and experience."[2] When Lafayette disembarked in Manhattan, an honor guard of aging veterans of the American War of Independence saluted the last surviving major general of the Continental Army. Lafayette had not set foot on American soil for forty years and already he could tell he was going to enjoy himself. It was nice to be loved again.

The grand tour started with a memorable blowout in New York City. After Lafayette disembarked, a welcome committee thrust him into the center of a huge parade traveling up Broadway from the shore to city hall. Levasseur said, "All the streets [were] decorated with flags and drapery and from all the windows flowers and wreaths showered upon the general."[3] Lafayette's welcome parade up Broadway established a model repeated many times, until it became a fixture of public life in New York City, eventually evolving into the famous ticker-tape parade. When Lafayette arrived at city hall, he was greeted by a giant banner welcoming "The Nation's Guest."

Lafayette's stay in New York was a whirlwind of balls, receptions, and banquets. He made himself available every afternoon to greet long lines of well-wishers. Some were strangers wanting to meet him for the first time, others old friends and comrades he knew from previous sojourns in America. Lafayette was always quick to remember everyone, whether he remembered or not. He also enjoyed an unexpected reunion with Francis Huger, whom Lafayette only met once, thirty years earlier, for about five minutes, during the failed prison break from Olmütz. That he *did* remember. Lafayette and Huger finally got the chance to do more than yell a few garbled words at each other while wrestling with an Austrian prison guard. Lafayette also met and befriended James Fenimore Cooper, who helped arrange the festivities, and an aspiring artist named Samuel F. B. Morse eager to paint Lafayette's portrait.

Lafayette's arrival happened to land in the middle of one of the most contentious presidential elections in a generation—which made the collective embrace by the Americans even more remarkable. The "Era of Good Feelings," defined by de facto one-party rule of Thomas Jefferson's Democratic-Republicans, was drawing to a close. The election of 1824 was an acrimonious four-man race pitting North against South, East against West. The leading candidates were John Quincy Adams of Massachusetts, who first sat at Lafayette's table in Paris as a young man back in the 1780s; William Crawford, an old stalwart Democratic-Republican from Georgia, whom Lafayette knew as American ambassador to France during the heady days of the Bourbon Restoration and the Hundred Days; Henry Clay, the dynamic orator from Kentucky who essentially invented the job of Speaker of the House; and finally, the man who commanded the most attention, populist general Andrew Jackson of Tennessee. So dominant was Jackson's personality that party labels in the 1820s are often simply denoted "Jacksonian" or "Anti-Jacksonian."

But though the election of 1824 was a brutal exercise in scorched-earth hyperpartisanship, Lafayette was something all Americans shared in common. "When we landed in New York," Levasseur wrote, "the people of the United States were occupied by the choice of a new political chief. . . . The newspapers, which, the evening before, were furiously combating for their favorite candidate, now closed their long columns on all party disputes and only gave admission to the unanimous expression of public joy and national gratitude. At the public dinners, instead of caustic toasts, intended to throw ridicule and odium on some potent adversary, none were heard but [toasts] to the guest of the nation, around whom were amicably grouped the most violent of both parties."[4]

Lafayette inspired universal love among all parties in America—a marked contrast to France, where he exceled at unifying otherwise disparate groups in their shared *hatred* of him. In America, he was a living legend—a pristine icon of the most glorious days of the Revolution. Lafayette was eager to play the role the Americans assigned him in every town and city he passed. He found himself as celebrated in Philadelphia as New Orleans; Vermont as much as South Carolina; rural hamlets as well as big cities; Jacksonians as well as anti-Jacksonians. Lafayette belonged to everyone, and wherever he went he was described as *the Nation's Guest*. Whether Lafayette intended it or not, his very presence reminded local and state leaders they were a single nation with a shared past and collective future. Lafayette certainly never let them forget it.

⸙

FROM NEW YORK, the Lafayette party went to Boston. Every town they approached erected triumphal arches, festive decorations, and banners welcoming "The Nation's Guest," establishing a pattern that would prevail in every stop on the journey. They also heard countless speeches from local leaders that Lafayette endured with grace and fortitude. Georges and Levasseur eventually grew weary of the exhausting daily grind of the never-ending celebrations, but the old man who survived the winter at Valley Forge and the prison of Olmütz remained unfazed by the onslaught of American well-wishers, no matter how repetitive and tiresome they became.

In Boston, the Massachusetts governor greeted them, as would governors of every state they visited. Lafayette and company spent five days and nights in and around Boston reuniting with old comrades and meeting new friends. A newspaper reported of one morning reception, "Numerous incidents in this scene brought tears from many manly eyes. One decrepit veteran, on crutches, was recognized by the General as a companion in arms at the memorable onset at Yorktown; others were recalled to recollection by events at Monmouth, at Brandywine, at West-Point, at Saratoga, and other places. Others, as belonging to the Light Army which the Marquis commanded in 1780, 81, &c. The hands of all these he seized with the most affectionate cordiality, frequently repeating. 'O! my brave Light Infantry!' 'My gallant soldiers!' 'Excellent troops.'"[5]

On a visit to the battlefield of Bunker Hill, Lafayette found organizers preparing for a great fiftieth anniversary celebration the following year. The centerpiece of the celebration would be the laying of a cornerstone for a massive monument. The organizers asked Lafayette, the last living Continental Army general, to consider taking part in the ceremony. Originally, Lafayette only planned to stay in the United States for about four months and return to France before winter. Moved by the offer, and overcome with joy at the reception he received everywhere he went, Lafayette said "that if he should then be in the U[nited] States it would be his earnest desire to be present."[6] After this offer, Lafayette changed his plans so he *would* be present. Rather than spending a few months visiting the major cities of the Eastern seaboard, he would instead spend more than a year visiting every single one of the United States.

While in Boston, Lafayette received a letter from John Adams, now eighty-nine years old. "I would wait upon you in person," Adams wrote, "but the total decrepitude and imbecility of eighty-nine years has rendered it impossible for me to ride . . . I pray you to appoint a day when you will do me the honor to pass the day with me in my cottage in our lapidary town of Quincy, with a few of your friends."[7] Lafayette went to Quincy to pay a call on the old man. When they arrived, Adams's grandson Charles Francis recorded in his diary, "The Marquis met my Grandfather with pleasure and I thought with some surprise, because really, I do not think he expected to see him quite so feeble as he is . . . Grandfather exerted himself more than usual and, as to conversation, appeared exactly as he ever has."[8] Adams couldn't get up and members of his family fed him dinner, but Lafayette found his mind was sharp as ever.

⚏

THE PARTY LEFT New England and traveled back to New York City, where they met Fanny and Camilla, just arrived from England. As feared, the presence of the two young women was socially awkward. They could not stand with him on stage or accompany his official retinue, which so frequently stopped for greetings and speeches. In particular, the Wrights ran afoul of Eleanor Parke Custis Lewis, Washington's step-granddaughter, who also joined Lafayette's party in New York. Nelly Lewis did not take kindly to the unaccompanied young women following Lafayette around. But they would always be there wherever he went, and Lafayette was glad for their comforting presence whenever he could get away from the glad-handing.

Part of the reason for the tension with Nelly Lewis was Fanny Wright's staunch abolitionism, while the Washingtons remained committed slave-owners. Lafayette was caught in between his own abolitionist principles and the desire for social harmony. Though he never publicly embarrassed his slave-owning friends in America, Lafayette also never missed an opportunity to demonstrate his own commitment to emancipation. Believing the universal education of the African population of paramount importance to successful emancipation, Lafayette made a point of visiting the African Free School, an academy established by the New York Manumission Society to give equal education to hundreds of black pupils. Lafayette was greeted by an address from a bright eleven-year-old student named James McCune Smith: "Here, sir, you behold hundreds of the poor children of Africa sharing with those of a lighter hue in the blessings of education; and, while it will be our pleasure to remember the great deeds you have done for America, it will be our delight also to cherish the memory of General La Fayette as a friend to African emancipation, and as a member of this institution." Young James McCune Smith would grow up to become the first African American to hold a medical degree, a prominent antebellum abolitionist, and mentor of Frederick Douglass.[9]

Departing New York City, Lafayette and company made a quick run up the Hudson River to Albany. For this leg of the trip, Alexander Hamilton's widow, Eliza, and her son Alexander Jr. joined the party. When asked what Hamilton meant to Lafayette, he reflected on his friend, now dead twenty years, "Hamilton was to me more than a friend, he was a brother . . . our friendship forged in days of peril and glory suffered no diminution from time." He then added wistfully, "We were both very young."[10]

Upon their arrival in Albany, Lafayette marveled at the changes since his first encounter with a hell of blunders, madness, and deception in the winter of 1778. He was even more shocked when visiting nearby Troy, which had been a handful of buildings last time he saw it, and was now a bustling and industrious city of eight thousand. There, he visited the Troy Female Seminary—a school founded by progressive educator and women's rights activist Emma Willard. After a program of songs, speeches, and poems, Willard presented Lafayette with her "Plan for Female Education," which Lafayette accepted with great interest.[11] While in Troy, Levasseur also observed with satisfaction, "There are scarcely 30 slaves in the city." A dinner companion told him legal slavery in New York was scheduled to expire in three years. Levasseur noted with hopeful satisfaction, "After 1827, liberty will no longer have to blush in the presence of colored men."[12] This turned out to be an overly optimistic prediction.

Traveling south toward Philadelphia, Lafayette made a point to call on an old acquaintance: Joseph Bonaparte. The brother of the emperor successfully escaped to America after the Hundred Days and was now living the life of a gentleman farmer outside Trenton, New Jersey. Despite winding up on different sides of politics in France, Lafayette and Joseph always personally liked one another. The party stopped at his house on September 25, and Bonaparte opened his doors so his neighbors could join the party, as he often did on special occasions like the Fourth of July. They spent a few hours talking, then Joseph escorted Lafayette toward Philadelphia. When they reached the state line, Bonaparte said, "Permit me to halt upon my frontiers and restore you to the tenderness of the Americans."[13] Their usual roles were now reversed, with Joseph living in quiet rustic obscurity and Lafayette having the triumphant run of an entire continent.

In Philadelphia, a local paper described the local residents gathering on the morning of Lafayette's arrival: "The citizens preparing to gratify their curiosity, as early as possible, by taking possession of the fences and eminences, balconies, scaffolds, roofs of houses, and upon the road and streets from the field of parade, the whole prescribed course of the procession, to the State-House."[14] Levasseur reported when they arrived, "The whole population came out to meet him . . . stages have been erected on each side of the streets, as high as the eves of the houses for the accommodation of spectators."[15] Lafayette's imminent arrival also prodded the city leaders of Philadelphia to appropriate money to restore and rehabilitate the old State House. They spruced it up and turned the rechristened Independence Hall into a permanent fixture of the city, no longer used for anything but exhibiting the birthplace of American liberty—which, not unlike Lafayette himself, was a tangible link to an increasingly mythical past.

Fanny Wright caused a minor scandal in Philadelphia when she arranged a meeting for Lafayette with a black man named Jonathan Granville. Granville was a representative from the free Republic of Haiti, who came to the United States to encourage black families to relocate to Port-au-Prince. Granville was a refined and well-educated emissary who served for a number of years in the French army. Wright said Granville "was delighted with his interview with the General," even though, to avoid causing a stir, they met "in private in [Lafayette's] bedroom." Wright also noted with approval Lafayette intentionally ruffled social feathers: "The General afterward purposefully conducted [Granville] to the receiving room crowded with visitors and then took a second affectionate leave of him, conducting him to the head of the stair in sight of all."[16] Though Lafayette was pleased to demonstrate his aversion to racist social norms, from this point forward, Nelly Lewis did everything in her considerable social powers to ice the Wright sisters out as unwelcome disruptions.

They departed Philadelphia on October 5 and moved on to Baltimore. At a reception at Fort McHenry, Lafayette reunited with a now eighty-three-year-old former French soldier named François Dubois-Martin, one of the small band of officers who first traveled to America with Lafayette aboard *La Victoire* in 1777. They were also joined by Washington's step-grandson, George Washington Parke Custis, whom Georges lived with at Mount Vernon for two years.

While at Fort McHenry, they also linked up with John Quincy Adams, presently secretary of state and candidate for president. Accompanying them on the ferry down the Chesapeake toward Washington, DC, Levasseur was amazed to find Adams, a man on the brink of becoming president of United States and scion of one of the greatest families in the country, preparing to sleep "on the humble mattress" laid out on the floor of a crowded makeshift dormitory.[17] Only after Lafayette insisted Adams sleep on a bed in his chamber did Adams accept better accommodations. "If there be any aristocracy in American manners," Levasseur recorded, "it must be confessed, that the great officers of the government partake of no such privileges."[18] It frankly blew his European mind.

Upon entering Washington, DC, they were greeted by President James Monroe—now known to Lafayette and Georges most especially as the revered savior of Adrienne, but whom Lafayette also knew from their days together as young officers in the Continental Army. A few days later they attended a dinner hosted by John Quincy Adams, when the American secretary of state rose and revealed momentous news just arrived from France: old Louis XVIII died on September 16. When Lafayette and his companions returned to France, the comte d'Artois would be reigning as King Charles X—the third and last of the Bourbon brothers to be king of France.

⚌

WASHINGTON, DC, was only a temporary stopover as Lafayette was eager to move quickly to his most anticipated destination: Mount Vernon. Georges actually knew the plantation better than his father did, having lived there for two years. It was an emotional return for both of them. "Georges felt his heart sink," Levasseur said, "at no more finding him whose paternal care softened his misfortunes."[19] They were immediately taken on a private visit to Washington's tomb.

"As we approach, the door was open," Levasseur recorded. "Lafayette descended alone into the vault, and a few minutes after reappeared, with his eyes overflowing with tears. He took his son and me by the hand, and led us into the tomb, where, by a sign, he indicated the coffin of his paternal friend. . . . We knelt reverently near his coffin which we respectfully saluted with our lips; rising, we threw ourselves into the arms of Lafayette and mingled our tears with his."[20] Back inside the house, Lafayette found the key to the Bastille he sent Washington in 1790—which still sits in Mount Vernon to this day.

From Mount Vernon, they made a short trip to Yorktown for the annual commemoration of Lord Cornwallis's surrender on October 19. Organizers erected a triumphal arch on the spot of the critical redoubt Lafayette's comrades stormed in the daring night raid so many years ago. During the ceremony, organizers placed a wreath on Lafayette's head, which Lafayette passed to Nicholas Fish, one of the officers who fought that night. Lafayette finished the ceremony "by paying a tribute of gratitude to the officers who directed the attack upon the redoubt, and among them named Hamilton, Gimat, Laurens, Fish and added it was in *their* name . . . that he accepted the proffered wreath."[21]

As they moved deeper into the southern states, Lafayette's company confronted the unavoidable contradiction of American liberty and American slavery. Levasseur, as much an abolitionist as Lafayette and Wright, was not comfortable with the things he now saw. "When we have examined the truly great and liberal institutions of the United States with some attention," he wrote, "the soul feels suddenly chilled and the imagination alarmed, in learning that at many points of this vast republic the horrible principle of slavery still reigns with all its sad and monstrous consequences."[22] As Levasseur published his journals under Lafayette's general editorial direction, and whose political views the journal was meant to promote, we can take Levasseur's observations as bearing Lafayette's stamp of approval.

When they met a community of French *émigrés* in Norfolk, Levasseur described meeting "a great number of French families, immigrants from Saint-Domingue . . . these families first made the choice of asylum here because of its proximity, but were induced to fix themselves, because they had permission to retain and work the unfortunate slaves they brought with them." It appeared the families supported themselves by renting their slaves to others, which Levasseur called "a sad and revolting spectacle."[23]

Reflecting back on his travels, Levasseur remained hopeful emancipation was inevitable, partly because everyone agreed slavery was terrible. "For myself," he wrote, "who have traversed the 24 states of the union, and in the course of a year have had more than one opportunity of hearing long and keen discussions upon this subject, I declare that I never have found but a single person who seriously defended this principle. This was a young man whose head, sufficiently imperfect in its organization, was filled with confused and ridiculous notions relative to Roman history, and appeared to be completely ignorant of the history of his own country; it would be waste of time to repeat here his crude and ignorant tirade."[24] But Levasseur did acknowledge

> in this part of the United States, the prejudices against the blacks, it must be confessed, keep a great number of slave-owners blind-folded. . . . It is in vain that some individuals, blinded by their prejudices, exclaim that there is no hope of improving the African race, which is only intermediate to man and the brutes, in the scale of being. Numerous facts have long since refuted this absurd assertion; and moreover, may it not be asked of those who are so proud of the whiteness of their skin, and who judge the blacks only by what they are, not what they are capable of, if they know well what would be the condition of their descendants after several generations, were slavery suddenly transferred from the blacks to the whites?[25]

Lafayette and Levasseur shared a concern this racist ignorance threatened the standing of the United States in the world for its ongoing violations of fundamental human rights: "If slave owners do not endeavor to instruct the children of the blacks, to prepare them for liberty; if the legislatures of the southern states do not fix upon some period, near or remote, when slavery shall cease, that part of the union will be for a still longer time exposed to the merited reproach of outraging the sacred principle contained in the first article of the Declaration of Rights; *that all men are born free and equal.*"[26] And as Lafayette had written in his own declaration of rights, violation of this sacred principle always left open the right of the victims of tyranny to exercise another fundamental right: resistance to oppression.

The next stop on the official itinerary was a visit to Thomas Jefferson at his slave plantation, Monticello. Lafayette and Jefferson had not seen each other since 1789, during the hopeful days after the fall of the Bastille. Lafayette's party spent a week at Monticello, and Jefferson escorted them to Charlottesville to tour his pride and joy: the University of Virginia. James Madison made an appearance and then took them to visit his home in Montpelier for four days. They made plans for a final reunion the following year before Lafayette departed the continent for good.

Levasseur noted while Lafayette stayed with his Virginian friends—all of them members of the plantation slave aristocracy—Lafayette did not shy away from bringing up emancipation: "Lafayette, who though perfectly understanding the disagreeable situation of American slaveholders, and respecting generally the motives which prevent them from more rapidly advancing in the definitive emancipation of the blacks, never missed an opportunity to defend the right which *all men without exception have to liberty*, broached among the friends of Mr. Madison the question of slavery. It was approached and discussed by them frankly. . . . It appears to me, that slavery cannot exist a long time in Virginia, because all enlightened men condemn the principle of it, and when public opinion condemns a principle, its consequences cannot long continue to subsist."[27] Levasseur, however, was far too optimistic about the noble sentiments of the Virginians and the future prospects of slavery. Condemning something in principle has little bearing on whether it is allowed to persist in reality.

⁂

LAFAYETTE AND COMPANY spent the winter of 1824–1825 in Washington, DC, and thus witnessed the finale of the hotly contested presidential race. The November election produced no clear results. Andrew Jackson won the popular vote, but no candidate secured a majority of the Electoral College. For the second time in the nation's young history, the House of Representatives decided the presidential election. While Congress geared up to settle the matter, they hosted the Nation's Guest on December 9 and 10, which required all the candidates and their bitterly partisan supporters to come together in the same place at the same time.

Henry Clay took the opportunity to show off his oratory by delivering the keynote speech. "The people of the United States," he said, "have ever beheld you true to your old principles . . . ready to shed the last drop of that blood which, here, you freely and nobly spilt in the same holy cause." He went on to say it was a rare and special gift for someone so consequential to witness the fruits of his life's work: "You are in the midst of posterity!" Clay exclaimed. "Everywhere you must have been struck with the great changes, physical and moral, which have occurred since you left us." But, Clay said, "in one respect, you behold us unaltered, and that is in the sentiment of continued devotion to liberty."[28]

They remained in Washington as partisans on all sides wrangled to secure a majority of votes in the House of Representatives. Finally on February 9, 1824, Clay's electors pledged themselves to Adams, and he won the vote. This left Jacksonian partisans steaming over a "Corrupt Bargain" when Adams subsequently appointed Clay secretary of state.

Earlier in the trip, Levasseur met some hard-core Jacksonian partisans in the Pennsylvania militia who threatened to take up arms if their man lost. After Adams won, he ran into them again. "Well," Levasseur said, "the great question is decided, and in a manner contrary to your hopes, what do you intend to do? How soon do you lay siege to the capital?" They laughed. "You recollect our threats," one said, "we went, in truth, to great lengths, but our opponents disregarded it and acted properly. Now that it is settled all we have to do is obey. We will support Adams as zealously as if he were our candidate, but at the same time shall keep a close watch on his administration and according as it is good or bad we will defend or attack it. Four years is soon past, and the consequences of a bad election are easily obviated."[29]

⊰⊱

ON FEBRUARY 23, 1825, the party departed Washington, DC, and headed south, traveling first to Fayetteville, North Carolina, one of hundreds of cities, towns, counties, colleges, squares, townships, streets, and parks named after Lafayette in America. North Carolina's Fayetteville boasts the honor of being the first to take his name when it first incorporated in 1783. The most recent site to take his name was the open space across from the White House, which was renamed Lafayette Square in his honor. As Lafayette continued his tour of the United States the pattern followed. Wherever one travels in the United States, there is bound to be a Lafayette *something* close at hand.

Fanny and Camilla did not join them for this leg of the tour. As a committed abolitionist, Fanny found the endless soliloquies to liberty sung by a bunch of slave-owners a bit much. "The enthusiasm, triumphs and rejoices exhibited here before the countenance of the great and good Lafayette have no longer charms for me," she wrote. "They who sin against the liberty of their country, against those great principles for which their honored guest poured on their soil his treasure and his blood, are not worthy to rejoice in his presence. My soul sickens in the midst of gaiety, and turns almost with disgust from the fairest faces for the most amiable discourse."[30] Wright began to dream her own dreams. Over the winter, she attended a series of lectures by the progressive socialist Robert Owen, who arrived in America to launch his utopian project called New Harmony in Indiana. Wright disengaged from Lafayette's tour and headed west to meet and interview the Owenites. She now dreamed of creating her own utopian colony serving as a model for emancipation and racial equality in the American West.

Meanwhile, Lafayette and company moved deeper south. In Camden, South Carolina, local Freemasons invited Lafayette to lay the cornerstone for a monument to Baron de Kalb. Lafayette was honored, and when he laid the cornerstone on March 8, he said, "Even on unlucky days, actions have been performed which reflect the highest honor on the name of which we are so justly proud, the name of an American soldier. Such have been, sir, the able conduct as a commander, the noble fall as a patriot, of General de Kalb . . . I gratefully acknowledge your kindness in associating me to the tribute paid to the memory of a friend, who, as you observe, has been the early confidant and companion of my devotion to the American cause."[31] Plenty of communities asked for Lafayette to dedicate monuments and memorials to the

American War of Independence, but the monument to de Kalb was special. Were it not for the baron, Lafayette might have lived and died as an obscure and inconsequential son-in-law of the Noailles.

As Lafayette continued south into Georgia, the party encountered the other great original sin of the United States. Entering the territory of the Muscogee Nation they found the Native population living through their final days in their ancestral lands. The Muscogee recently reached the end of a long losing campaign to resist encroachment by white settlers. Just a few months earlier, tribal leaders admitted defeat and signed the Treaty of Indian Springs. They agreed to move their people to the far side of the Mississippi River in exchange for monetary payments and future guarantees of autonomy. "The year 1827 was scheduled for their eviction," Levasseur said, "and it was not without sorrow that the Indians find that it is drawing near."[32] But not everyone was willing to give up. When he returned to his people with the treaty in hand, Muscogee leader William McIntosh was promptly arrested and executed for treason.

On March 31, Lafayette and his party met the first large assemblage of Muscogee at the Chattahoochee River. They were greeted by a young leader of the group speaking perfect English who knew of Lafayette and praised him for "not distinguishing blood or color" in his defense of liberty.[33] This young man turned out to be the son of the recently executed McIntosh. He did not like the treaty his father signed either, but "appreciated the real situation of his nation, he saw it gradually becoming weaker, and foresaw its speedy destruction. . . . Their vicinity to civilization having been of no service."[34] The young McIntosh joined the party as a guide and translator as they moved toward Mobile, Alabama.

Before leaving his new Native American friends, Lafayette gave one of his perfunctory and overly sanguine speeches. Levasseur said, "He again counseled them to be prudent and temperate; recommended their living in harmony with the Americans, and to always consider them as their friends and brothers."[35] Levasseur could not help but disagree with Lafayette's appraisal as he personally witnessed mistreatment of the Native population by encroaching whites. They came across one recently established village "almost entirely inhabited by persons who, in the love of gain had assembled from all parts of the globe . . . to turn to their own profit the simplicity and above all the new wants of the unfortunate natives. These avaricious wretches, who without scruple poison the tribes with intoxicating liquors, and afterwards ruin them by duplicity and overreaching, are the most cruel and dangerous enemies of the Indian nations, whom, at the same time, they accuse of being robbers, idlers, and drunkards."[36]

THEY SAID GOODBYE to the younger McIntosh and continued to Mobile, Alabama, which marked the beginning of a new phase of their travels. They boarded the riverboat *Natchez*, which ferried them along the gulf coast to New Orleans. They stayed in the city for about a week, mingled with the large French community, and briefly reunited with Fanny and Camilla, who rejoined the company after their journey to New Harmony. During the various celebrations a company of black soldiers who served in the recent War of 1812 presented themselves, and Lafayette greeted them with "esteem and affection." He made a point of shaking each one of their hands, saying, "I have often during the War of Independence seen African blood shed with honor in our ranks for the cause of the United States."[37]

On April 15, they reboarded the *Natchez* and began a thousand-mile trip up the Mississippi River to St. Louis. For the next two weeks, they steamed through near total wildness, with Louisiana, Arkansas, and Missouri on their left and Mississippi, Tennessee, and Kentucky on their right. On April 29, they were welcomed to St. Louis by Governor William Clark, famous for his joint leadership of the Lewis and Clark expedition to explore the Louisiana Territory. Outside St. Louis, Lafayette's company toured the great mounds that were becoming the cause of scientific and ethnographic speculation. Levasseur was told residents around the Mississippi River often "meet with much more interesting traces of the greatest antiquity, indicating that this world which we call *new*, was the seat of civilization, perhaps long anterior to the continent of Europe."[38]

The party backtracked down the Mississippi to Kaskaskia, Illinois, formerly the seat of French colonial administration in the region. They were greeted by Illinois governor Edward Coles, who moved to Illinois from Virginia specifically to free his slaves. Levasseur reported, "His liberated negroes are perfectly successful, and afforded a conclusive argument against the adversaries of emancipation."[39] While in Kaskaskia they also met a young Oneida woman speaking fluent French who was eager to show Lafayette "a relic very dear to me," which turned out to be a letter written by Lafayette to her father in June 1778 thanking him for his service—her father almost certainly being one of the Oneida warriors who fought with Lafayette during his handsome retreat from Barren Hill.[40]

Departing Kaskaskia, Lafayette's party backtracked farther down the Mississippi, then turned left up the Ohio River before turning right on the Cumberland River toward Nashville. On May 5, they visited Andrew Jackson. Jackson hosted them for a reception and showed off a pair of pistols Lafayette once gave Washington, and which Washington subsequently gifted to Jackson. At the reception, they heard a toast saying, "The present age encourages the reign of liberal principles. Kings are forced to unite against liberty and despotism to act on the defensive. Lafayette—tyrants have oppressed him, but freemen honor him."[41] This toast would have been heard with a tinge of regret by Lafayette, Georges, and Levasseur, three recently defeated Carbonarist revolutionaries for whom these words were not just empty rhetoric.

After departing Nashville, they returned to the Ohio River and continued on toward Louisville, Kentucky. But suddenly, at around midnight on May 8, 1825, their ship lurched to a crashing halt. Lafayette and the others rushed out on deck and were told the boat ran aground. The situation was dire—water flooded the hull and the boat was probably going to sink. They must abandon ship. Georges and Levasseur put Lafayette on a lifeboat, then attempted to save what they could from his cabin. Levasseur carried the salvaged baggage to shore, while Georges remained onboard to help others get away. As passengers safely reassembled on the banks of the river, Lafayette realized he could find no trace of Georges. "He was filled with anxiety, and in a state of the most violent agitation," Levasseur said. "He began to call Georges! Georges! with all his strength but his voice was drawn by the cries which arose from the vessel, and by the terrible noise made by the steam escaping from the engine."[42] But happily, Georges scurried to an exposed part of the half-sunk ship and was finally retrieved along with the last remaining passengers. The whole party spent the night beside huge bonfires as they attempted to dry off and stay warm. In the morning, they flagged down a passing boat, which, by sheer coincidence happened to be owned by one of the stranded members of Lafayette's American escort. The owner ordered the vessel to abandon its scheduled itinerary and take General Lafayette and his companions to Louisville.

By now it was the end of May, and they were going to have to hurry if they wanted to be back in Boston in time for the fiftieth anniversary celebrations at Bunker Hill. They hustled through Kentucky and Ohio on their way to Buffalo, New York. In Lexington, they stopped at another school dedicated to the education of women, which renamed itself the Lafayette Female Academy in his honor. Lafayette was thrilled "by the association of my name with this so very interesting Academy."[43] In Buffalo, they beheld the uniquely American coexistence of natural and man-made wonders. They paid a visit to Niagara Falls, which they described as "a sublime spectacle."[44] But they turned their attention to the equally impressive Erie Canal, a feat of engineering under construction since 1818, now linking the Great Lakes to the Hudson River. The canal was not yet officially open, but Lafayette's party was allowed to take a canal boat to speed their journey east.

⁂

LAFAYETTE MADE IT back to Boston just in time for the Bunker Hill celebrations on June 17, 1825. After being escorted to the site in a carriage drawn by six white horses, he laid the cornerstone of the Bunker Hill monument. After a day of mutually admiring speechmaking, Lafayette requested a bag full of the dirt from the excavation site so he could take it home with him and always keep soil from the birthplace of American liberty.

After Boston, Lafayette ensured he completed his quest to visit all twenty-four American states by making a rapid-fire circuit through New Hampshire, Vermont, and Maine in the span of just a few days. Then he headed south, passing through New York City, where he celebrated the

Fourth of July. One young attendee later recalled, "I remember I was taken up by Lafayette in his arms and held a moment—I remember that he pressed my cheek with a kiss as he sat me down—the childish wonder and nonchalance during the whole affair at the time—contrasting with the indescribable preciousness of the reminiscence since."[45] The boy was Walt Whitman.

Lafayette's party departed New York for the last time and headed for Philadelphia. On July 25, an entourage of Continental veterans escorted Lafayette to the site of the Battle of Brandywine, where his own legendary career began. "On arriving at the field of battle," Levasseur recorded, "General Lafayette recognized successively, and pointed out to us himself, all the principal points on which the two armies had maneuvered and fought on the 11th of September 1777. . . . He arrived at the spot where the first attack was made, and where he had been wounded, he paused for a moment; his ancient companions pressed around . . . amid the loudest acclamations and the cry a thousand times reechoed, Long Live Lafayette!"[46]

Then they went back to Washington, DC, and used it as a base for the planned reunion at Monticello with Jefferson, Madison, and Monroe. They spent the week reminiscing about old times, knowing this would be the last time they ever saw each other. "I shall not attempt to depict the sadness which prevailed cruel separation," Levasseur said, "which had none of the alleviation which is usually left by youth, for in this instance, the individuals who bade farewell, had all passed through a long career, and the immensity of the ocean would still add to the difficulties of a reunion."[47]

Back in Washington, DC, President Adams prevailed on Lafayette to stick around at the White House to celebrate Lafayette's birthday on September 6, which involved the final toast to the Nation's Guest from the president of the United States: "When the contest of freedom, to which you had repaired as a voluntary champion, had closed, by the complete triumph of her cause in this country of your adoption, you returned to fulfill the duties of the philanthropist and patriot in the land of your nativity. There, in a consistent and undeviating career of forty years, you have maintained, through every vicissitude of alternate success and disappointment, the same glorious cause to which the first years of your active life had been devoted, the improvement of the moral and political condition of man." Adams said Lafayette's devotion to France would mark him as a great man in his country, "for if, in after days, a Frenchman shall be called to indicate the character of his nation by that of one individual, during the age in which we live, the blood of lofty patriotism shall mantle in his cheek, the fire of conscious virtue shall sparkle in his eye, and he shall pronounce the name of Lafayette." But he said America would never forget him: "We, too, and our children, in life and after death, shall claim you for our own."[48]

Before Lafayette departed once and for all, George Washington Parke Custis conceived of sending a present to another liberty-loving American: Simón Bolívar. Bolívar recently completed a series of campaigns ending Spanish rule in Venezuela and Colombia and now campaigned in Peru. Citizens of the United States cheered the exploits of the *Liberator*, and Lafayette agreed Bolívar was the Washington of South America. The gift package included a pair of Washington's pistols, a portrait of the late president, and a letter from Lafayette. Lafayette offered the President Liberator, "personal congratulations from a veteran of the common cause," and said of the enclosed gifts, "I am happy to think that of all the existing men, and even of all the men of history, General Bolívar is the one to whom my paternal friend would have preferred to offer them. What more can I say to the great citizen whom South America hailed by the name of Liberator, a name confirmed by both worlds, and who, endowed with an influence equal to his disinterestedness, carries in his heart the love of liberty without any exception and the republic without any alloy?"[49] Lafayette departed for home proud the great work of liberty continued its inexorable march through the Americas.

It took months for Bolívar to receive the package, but when he did, he replied: "How can I express how much, in my heart, I attach importance to such a testimony of esteem so glorious for me? The family of Mount Vernon honor me beyond my hopes, for the image of Washington, given by the hands of Lafayette, is the most sublime of the rewards that a man can aspire to. Washington was the courageous protector of social reform, you are the citizen hero, the athlete of freedom in America and in the old world."[50]

By the time he received Bolívar's reply, Lafayette was already back in France. On September 8, 1825, a new naval frigate recently christened the *Brandywine* in Lafayette's honor set sail for Europe with Lafayette aboard. He never returned to the United States. And while he sailed away content in the knowledge the legacy of his past glories would live forever in the New World, he hoped a few final *future* glories still lay ahead in the Old World.

CHAPTER TWENTY-THREE

THE JULY REVOLUTION

[1826–1830]

AS LAFAYETTE AND HIS COMPANIONS MADE THEIR WAY BACK to La Grange, they stopped in Rouen on the evening of October 5, 1825. Residents of the city learned Lafayette was back. "Towards the end of the dinner," Levasseur recounted, "someone came to announce to the General that a crowd of persons in the street, accompanied by a band of musicians, wished to salute him." As this was a routine part of their lives for the past eighteen months, Lafayette "eagerly went out on the balcony to reply to this mark of esteem from the population of Rouen. But scarcely were the first acclamations heard, when detachments of the royal guard and gendarmes appeared from the extremities of the street, who, without any previous notice, began to disperse the crowd . . . the gendarmerie, anxious to prove themselves the worthy instruments of the power that employed them, bravely charged on the unarmed citizens, and were not to be checked by the cries of the women and children overthrown by the horses."[1] Lafayette was not in the United States anymore.

As he resettled at La Grange, Lafayette learned things were worse than when he left. The death of Louis XVIII meant the comte d'Artois now reigned as King Charles X. While Louis attempted to rule from the middle, Charles tossed any pretense of moderation or compromise with liberals. In July 1789, he was the very first *émigré*. For thirty-five years he harbored dreams of undoing the Revolution. Now he finally had his chance.

The new king posed no personal danger to Lafayette. He and Charles knew each other practically their whole lives. Though polar opposites of the political spectrum, the king still held a sentimental attachment to his old classmate. Charles once inquired how Lafayette was doing, and when his entourage expressed surprise he cared, the king said, "Ah, but you see, I know him so well. He has rendered our family the kind of services one cannot forget. We were born in the same year, we learned to ride together at the Versailles academy."[2] Charles believed Lafayette was a man of principles—even if he believed those principles deluded. The king once said, "Since the Revolution there were only two men in France who never changed, M. de La Fayette and myself." Charles said he and Lafayette had "two brains made pretty much the same way. Only they lodged different ideas, that's all."[3] But despite the personal regard, their beliefs were fundamentally incompatible. Both men of honor, they now circled each other like aging duelists in an open field.

Materially, the elevation of Charles X was actually a boon to Lafayette's fortunes. One of the king's great obsessions was restoring property to victims of the Revolution. Though his advisers convinced Charles he could not literally repossess all the estates, in April 1825, the government passed a law dubbed the "Émigrés Billions." Under the new law, families dispossessed by the Revolution could submit paperwork outlining what they lost, and the state would compensate them with an equivalent value in state bonds. Lafayette's financial manager dutifully submitted all his claims netting 325,000 *francs*. The Émigrés Billions also served as the final unfortunate epilogue to the failed emancipation project in Cayenne. Lafayette's accountants submitted claims that included the approximate value of the slaves he still owned in 1789—claims subsequently approved and paid off by the state.

But despite his newfound riches, the reactionary political climate did not suit Lafayette. He spent his first year in France sticking close to La Grange. He kept up a lively correspondence with liberal allies in Britain like Jeremy Bentham and Thomas Clarkson. Fanny Wright remained in the United States, and Lafayette did his best to promote and raise funds for a utopian experiment in emancipation she founded in Tennessee. He also corresponded with heads of state in the Americas like John Quincy Adams, Simón Bolívar, and president of Haiti Jean-Pierre Boyer. Lafayette was a longtime advocate of positive relations with France's former slave colony, which broke away from France after their own war for liberty, equality, and independence. As part of his quest to compensate owners for lost property, Charles insisted Haiti pay France the value of lost property in the former colony—a final total that, like Lafayette's claim, included the value of slaves who freed themselves.

Lafayette also wrote supportive letters to every Greek, Polish, Italian, Spanish, or Russian revolutionary who sought advice and guidance from the old Hero of Two Worlds. He encouraged young idealists everywhere to pick up the cause of liberty and equality, knowing his generation was rapidly passing. In the fall of 1826 he mourned the simultaneous deaths of Jefferson and John Adams, who both died on July 4, 1826—the fiftieth anniversary of the Declaration of Independence.

Lafayette stayed out of domestic politics but watched with detached amusement as King Charles discovered being king did not mean he was all-powerful. The chambers approved the Émigrés Billions, but resisted other reactionary initiatives aimed at rebuilding the power of the old nobility. Charles reserved special fury for the hostile press, whom he believed abused the liberties so generously granted by the Crown. Aggressive young firebrands like Adolphe Thiers pulled no punches. Alphonse de Lamartine, a writer, historian, and politician who knew Thiers well, said, "There was enough gunpowder in his nature to explode six governments."[4] In early 1827, the king's prime minister introduced what became mockingly known as the "Justice and Love Bill," whose sole object was making it impossible to operate a newspaper critical of the regime. Charles's rage mounted when the chambers rejected the bill. What good was it to be king if no one did what they were told, and everyone criticized you all the time?

Then in the spring Charles committed a huge blunder. Every year on April 29, he celebrated the memory of his glorious return to Paris in 1814. This celebration always included a review of the Paris National

Guard, presently numbering about twenty thousand active duty members. But the king's recent behavior did not endear him to the guardsmen, and when the king reviewed them on *this* April 29, some refused to take off their caps while others shouted insults from the anonymity of the assembled ranks. Humiliated and angry, Charles massively overreacted. He issued a decree disbanding the National Guard. The abrupt demobilization of the guard over a few insults made them hate the king more than ever. Charles massively compounded this blunder by making no effort to disarm the now *former* members of the National Guard. All of whom still had their swords, guns, and ammunition close at hand in the summer of 1830.

After two years of continuous retirement at La Grange, Lafayette finally returned to politics at the end of 1827. In August, his former liberal colleague in the Chamber of Deputies, Jacques-Antoine Manuel, suddenly died. Manuel was serving as deputy representing Meaux—the constituency Lafayette himself represented in 1824. Local opposition leaders lobbied General Lafayette to run for the seat in the fall of 1827. He won easily. Even after the government called a general election a few months later, Lafayette ran again and retained his seat.

Sitting with the left opposition in the Chamber of Deputies, Lafayette joined the fray as political tensions between the king, his ministers, and the chambers steadily increased. If Charles had his way, there would be no Charter of Government, no political freedom, and certainly no free press—all of which he considered grotesque aberrations contrary to the natural order of things. Lafayette, of course, considered them sacred objects worth defending to the death.

Things started coming to a head in 1829. From their low ebb in the mid-1820s, the liberal opposition gained more seats in the chambers every year and now formed a powerful political force. When the deputies voted no confidence in the king's current prime minister in the summer of 1829, the king responded by firing the prime minister. But instead of elevating a new prime minister palatable to the liberals, Charles stubbornly insisted that, as king, he had the right to name the ministers *he* wanted—the opinion of the chambers be damned. So he promoted a close friend and intransigent ultraroyalist named Jules de Polignac. The choice of Polignac was recklessly provocative. Polignac possessed an incredible combination of distasteful attributes—arrogance, stubbornness, myopia—all amplified by fears the angry king promoted Polignac as a precursor to abolishing the Charter of Government entirely.

⁂

LAFAYETTE FELT THE political electricity charging after the elevation of Polignac. He toured Auvergne in 1829, drawing huge crowds, emboldening him to speak in terms not used since the days leading up to the Carbonari uprisings. At a banquet of supporters in Le Puy, he said, "The Chamber of Deputies has been reproached, I know, for slowness in securing liberal improvements, but be assured, as soon as it discovers a plot against public liberties, it will find, as will the nation as a whole, sufficient energy to crush it."[5] In Lyon, he said, "After a long succession of brilliant despotism, and of constitutional hopes, I find myself amongst you at a moment which I might call critical, had I not everywhere encountered on my journey . . . the calm and even scornful steadfastness of a great people who know their own rights and feel their own strength."[6] Lafayette still believed France wanted a constitution and declaration of rights, and if the king tried to deny them, the nation would know what to do.

The rumors King Charles was ready to chuck the Charter of Government only increased at the opening session of the chambers on February 20, 1830. The king's address was a provocative challenge. He said, "If criminal maneuvers rise up obstacles against my government, which I hope will not be the case, I will find the strength to overcome them in my resolution to maintain public order, in the just confidence of the French people, and in the love that they have always demonstrated for their kings."[7] Charles was as convinced as Lafayette the people of France were with *him*. As for what the king considered "criminal maneuvers," he seemed to mean anything he personally deemed objectionable.

The threat from the king prompted 221 deputies—including Lafayette—to sign a protest on March 15. Their address opened by reminding Charles that the Charter "consecrates, as a right, the participation of the country in the discussion of public affairs." The deputies expressed dismay the king and Polignac seemed hell-bent on ignoring the will of the duly elected representatives of the nation. They said, "Permanent accord between the political views of your government and the wishes of your people [are] the indispensable condition of the normal conduct of public affairs." Ignoring the chambers broke the necessary cooperation allowing the Charter of Government to function. They said, "Our loyalty, our devotion compel us to tell you this accord does not now exist . . . your people are distressed by this because it is an affront to them; they are worried by it because it is a threat to their liberties."[8] The king responded to the "Address of the 221" not by heeding their warning, but by announcing the dissolution of the chamber and calling for new elections in July 1830.

This announcement set off a wave of protests and political mobilization across France. Lafayette wrote that Polignac displayed "a counterrevolutionary and fanatic sympathy," and "the prime minister was frivolous, presumptuous, unenlightened, believing himself called to raise the throne and the altar . . . strutting in the great role that the congregation imposes on him."[9]

In an attempt to change the subject, Polignac and the king decided to invade Algiers. The point was to engineer a quick and victorious little war to give the voters something to cheer as they went to cast their ballots. The French government seized on an otherwise minor diplomatic incident with the Algerians as a pretext for war. The opposition press begged voters not to be deceived: "They have the insane hope of making a victory against Algiers a victory against our liberties."[10] On July 5, 1830, a French invasion force stormed the North African coast and seized control of the country, beginning a 130-year-long colonial occupation essentially as a campaign stunt.

The king also took the unheard of step of promoting his preferred candidates. A monarch was supposed to reign above everyone and everything, not serve as the head of a political party. But Charles didn't care. He published an address to the voters saying, "Frenchmen, your prosperity is the source of my glory; your happiness is mine. At the moment when the electoral colleges are about to meet throughout the kingdom, you will hearken to the advice of your king . . . do not permit yourselves to be misled by the insidious words of enemies of public tranquility. Reject the groundless suspicions and false fears that would shake public confidence and excite grave disorders . . . it is your king who asks this; it is a father who calls you."[11]

None of it worked. In the elections held between July 5–19, 1830, the liberals triumphed. They elected more deputies than ever and now commanded a clear majority in the chamber. The king was beside himself, but Polignac remained almost mystically unconcerned. Political opposition based on abstract appeals to liberty might motivate a few overeducated elites, but they were a tiny minority. "The masses are concerned solely with their material interests," he told the king.[12] Meanwhile, the king's cousin, the duc d'Orléans, watched the election from his château on the western edges of Paris with increasing alarm. "At least the fault is not mine," he said. "I won't blame myself for not opening the King's eyes; what do you want? They listen to nothing. God knows where they will be in six months!"[13]

After the election results came in, the opposition braced for a response. Charles tried to defeat his political opponents and instead they came back stronger than ever. Liberal fear the king was about to suspend the Charter reached such a fever pitch, one paper laughed at the hysterical predictions. "The prophets of coup d'état are no more discouraged than astronomers who announce the end of the world," they mocked. "The end of the Charter was initially fixed at the 22nd; they placed a bet on that date. Now it's for the 26th, now for next Monday. . . . The coups d'état are always for tomorrow. They have been postponed until tomorrow for a long time. They will be postponed forever, until we admit they are useless and impossible, forever!"[14] The king wasn't *actually* going to stage a coup. Everyone needed to calm down.

Lafayette himself did not think anything would happen immediately. The king and his ministers withdrew to the royal château at Saint-Cloud, so Lafayette returned to La Grange to wait for the new session beginning August 3. It was sure to be intense, as the new liberal majority would begin by demanding the king fire Polignac. On the fateful morning of July 26, 1830, Lafayette wrote a brief letter saying neither the king nor the opposition would likely make a move until then. "There were great discussions in the last councils on the coup d'état, about which the king speaks. . . . Nevertheless, it seems that we have given it up for the moment."[15] Little did he know, at that very moment, King Charles was launching his coup.

※

ON JULY 27, 1830, Lafayette received his daily mail from Paris. Included in the bundle was a copy of the previous day's edition of *Le Moniteur Universel*, the official paper of record. He also found a short note attached to the paper from his grandson-in-law, Charles de Rémusat. Rémusat was a staunch defender of the liberal opposition and currently had a job writing for the *Le Globe*, one of the papers the king found so offensive to his delicate sensibilities. The note told Lafayette to read the *Moniteur*, then come to Paris immediately. The coup was on.

On the front page of the July 26 edition of the *Moniteur*, Lafayette read four new ordinances the king decreed by arbitrary fiat: The first suspended freedom of the press. The second dissolved the recently elected Chamber of Deputies before they even met. The third completely reorganized elections—reducing the number of deputies, changing eligibility requirements to exclude all but the wealthiest voters, and summarily disenfranchising three-fourths of the electorate. The fourth called for elections under the new rules to be held in September.

What he read stunned Lafayette. An accompanying editorial explained the king was perfectly justified in issuing the ordinances. He was not *overthrowing* the Charter but *defending* it from seditious maniacs. The editorial cited as justification Article 14 of the Charter, which stated, "The king is the supreme head of the state . . . and makes the necessary regulations and ordinances for the execution of the laws and the security of the state." The king claimed he was simply issuing necessary laws to protect the security of France from insidious journalists and liberal politicians stirring up trouble where no trouble really existed. The editorial said, "It must be recognized . . . these agitations . . . are almost exclusively produced and excited by the freedom of the press . . . the periodical press has been, and it is in its nature to be, only an instrument of disorder and sedition . . . its destiny is, in a word, to begin anew the revolution, whose principles it boldly proclaims." The editorial concluded, "Article 14 invests [the king] with a sufficient power. . . . Commanding necessity no longer permits postponement of the exercise of this supreme power. The moment has come for recourse to measures that adhered to the spirit of the Charter, but are outside the legal order, all of whose resources have been fruitlessly exhausted."[16] This last argument could have been pulled from one of Lafayette's own speeches. But it was twisted and deployed in the service of a reactionary coup from above, rather than a popular revolution from below.

Lafayette wasted no time. He packed his bags and rushed to Paris. He arrived on the evening of July 27, roughly thirty-six hours after the infamous Four Ordinances were published in the capital. He found the city in complete chaos. "Arriving here," he wrote back to La Grange, "I found regiments loading their arms, artillery of the Royal Guard, and much movement among the citizens. The workers mingled with the young people; barricades were made; several gendarmes had been killed, but even more citizens, as most of them had only stones."[17]

Rémusat and other friends filled him in on what happened in the interim. When the *Moniteur* hit the streets on July 26, opposition leaders and journalists flew into a panicked and furious uproar. Rémusat himself was at the offices of the *Globe* when a colleague burst in and cried, "Don't you know? The coup d'état is in the *Moniteur!*"[18] Stunned, Rémusat raced out the door to a meeting of editors and journalists at the offices of the *National*, one of the fiercest critics of the regime and edited by liberal firebrand Adolphe Thiers. "However," he said, "I did not go out without making sure M. de Lafayette would be informed." He wrote a hasty note, attached it to a copy of the *Moniteur*, and dispatched it to La Grange. Then he raced out the door.

At the offices of the *National*, Adolphe Thiers argued all journalists should band together and fight. Rémusat was among those who read and approved a declaration of protest that opened, "It has often been said over the past six months that the laws will be broken, that a coup d'état will be struck. Common sense refused to believe it. The ministry dismissed this talk as slander. However, the *Moniteur* has finally published these memorable ordinances, which are the most glaring violation of the laws. The legal regime is therefore interrupted, that of force has begun. In this situation obedience ceases to be a duty."[19]

That night, demonstrators gathered in the Palais-Royal—just as they had in July 1789. Then they flooded into streets, tearing down streetlights and pelting state buildings with rocks, bricks, and paving stones. At one point, an angry crowd spotted Polignac and Minister of the Navy Baron d'Haussez, lobbing projectiles at them as they hustled toward police headquarters. When the two men got inside, Polignac told Haussez it might be time to put the Royal Guard in Paris on alert. Haussez was incredulous: "That hasn't been done already?" And Polignac replied, with his patented brand of myopic serenity, "You're always worrying."[20] As the night went on, however, the crowds *did* disperse, allowing the prefect of police to optimistically report, "The most perfect tranquility continues to reign in all parts of the capital. No event worthy of attention is recorded in the reports that have come to me."[21]

On the morning of July 27, as Lafayette read the Four Ordinances in La Grange, opposition deputies, city leaders, and journalists gathered in several offices and salons to plan a response. Most hesitated to plunge over the Rubicon into open revolt—especially when they found out the king dispatched General Auguste de Marmont to Paris with orders to use the regular army to restore order. Marmont, for his part, was a political moderate who thought the ordinances an insane escalation. When he read about them in the paper, he said, "Well! You see, the lunatics, as I foresaw, have pushed things to the extreme. I will perhaps be obliged to get myself killed for acts that I abhor."[22] But when ordered to take control of Paris, he obeyed.

That afternoon, Marmont discovered the government had done nothing to prepare for the possibility of mass protests. Officers and men were on leave. No one had been briefed in advance. Nothing was ready. As Marmont scrambled to organize the divisions under his command, real fighting broke out near the Palais-Royal. When cavalry charged through a mob of protestors, they inflicted the first casualties of the conflict. Demonstrators retrieved the bodies and paraded them through the streets as martyred proof of the murderous intent of the government. That night, Parisians erected barricades throughout the narrow streets of central Paris to defend their neighborhoods. This was the atmosphere Lafayette walked into on the evening of July 27.

Meanwhile, Rémusat attended another meeting of opposition leaders and found himself bored and unconvinced they meant business. "How many useless words are spoken in this kind of a meeting cannot be imagined by a person who has not attended one," he later wrote. "There are the earnest and the impetuous, who want to speak to satisfy their temperaments and soothe themselves by declaiming at random. There are the boobs, who want to tell what they have seen or heard, believing it very important because it is all they know. There are the vain, who, preoccupied with themselves, insist upon explaining their conduct."[23] The meeting broke up when they learned the police issued arrest warrants for most of the opposition journalists. Rémusat may have spent the meeting feeling smugly superior, but when news of the warrants arrived, he bolted for the door like everyone else.

Back in Saint-Cloud, King Charles was kept informed as fighting in the streets continued over the night of July 27. But he insisted on believing things were not that bad. To a worried member of the Chamber of Peers, who came to beg the king to rescind the ordinances, he said, "You are mad, my dear duc. I repeat to you for the hundredth time there is nothing to fear, nothing to do; it is a flash in the pan that will make only smoke."[24] The king went to bed that night believing everything was fine. He did not realize the Revolution of 1830 was already well underway.

⌁

AFTER A BAD night's sleep with gunfire crackling through the night, Lafayette went out on the morning of July 28 and joined a meeting of opposition leaders, including the banker Jacques Laffitte and doctrinaire liberal François Guizot. The meeting was held at the home of Audry de Puyraveau, one of Lafayette's former coconspirators from the Carbonari days. Lafayette told the assembled leaders, "I admit that I can ill reconcile legality with the *Moniteur* of the 26th and the fusillade of the last two days."[25] In his opinion, they needed to immediately appoint a provisional government, saying they must not shrink or hesitate. Lafayette's aide-de-camp, Bernard Sarrans, said the general told them, "It was a question of a revolution . . . that his name was already being placed by the confidence of the people at the head of the insurrection;

that he ardently desired to obtain the consent of his colleagues in this regard, but that, if they did not make a decision by the next morning, he would believe himself free to act on his own."[26]

Meanwhile, out in the streets, Parisian insurrectionaries fought their way into the Hôtel de Ville and hoisted the tricolor for the first time in fifteen years. General Marmont declared martial law and dispatched three columns to hold different parts of the city. But these columns discovered the Parisians built *hundreds* of street barricades all around central Paris. The columns were quickly isolated from one another and pinned down by street fighters using everything from rifles to chamber pots hurled off rooftops to attack the soldiers. One column managed to retake control of the Hôtel de Ville, but they were not supplied to withstand a siege. After heavy fighting, all three columns withdrew back to the safety of the Louvre. Paris remained in the hand of the Parisians.

That night, Lafayette went out with a small coterie of aides to inspect the barricades. As he hobbled toward one, an armed citizen cried, "Halt there! Tell us what business you have to be walking about at this hour?" "Captain," replied Lafayette, "you see me overwhelmed with heartfelt emotion by the spectacle you present to me; come, and embrace me, and you will know that I am one of your own comrades." The guard was still suspicious until someone else said, "It's General Lafayette!" Pleased to be recognized, Lafayette said, "To arms, gentlemen!" and proceeded to inspect them as if he were back in the Continental Army.[27]

At 11:00 a.m. on July 29—the third of what would become known as the Three Glorious Days—Lafayette attended another meeting at Laffitte's. Lafayette reported an offer from a delegation of Parisians asking him to take command of the National Guard. He said he wanted to accept because "an old name from '89 can be of some use in the present grave circumstances."[28] The other leaders agreed. They then elected a five-man commission to govern the city in the name of the people and directed them to claim possession of the Hôtel de Ville.

As they made their way through the crowd, Sarrans said they marched "partly triumphal, partly warlike." Around them people cried "Vive la nation!" and "Vive Lafayette!" He described "men, women, and children lining the streets, hanging from the windows, and crowding the roofs, their handkerchiefs waving in the air, and the city reverberating with the exclamations of hope and joy." He said if someone who wasn't there tried to imagine what it was like, they "shall still have but an imperfect idea of the popular delirium which saluted the passage of Lafayette."[29] When Lafayette reached the Hôtel de Ville, a helpful citizen pointed the way to a conference room. Lafayette chuckled and said, "I know every step," before ascending the great staircase he had climbed many times before.[30]

Taking command of the remobilized National Guard, Lafayette issued a proclamation: "My dear fellow citizens and brave comrades. . . . The confidence of the people of Paris once more calls me to the command of the popular force. I have accepted with devotion and joy the powers that have been confided in me, and, as in 1789, I feel myself strong in the approbation of my honorable colleagues, this day assembled in Paris. I shall make no profession of my faith, my sentiments are well known. . . . Liberty shall triumph. Or we will perish together!"[31] The National Guardsmen demobilized by the king in 1827 picked up their guns and headed to the Hôtel de Ville. But it was not all fun and games and glorious proclamations. Lafayette learned Levasseur was badly wounded in the fighting the night before. His traveling companion in America would ultimately live, but it was a reminder real people were fighting and dying out there. The quicker the violence stopped the better.

Lafayette next posted an open letter to the soldiers of the army calling on them to mutiny: "Brave soldiers, the inhabitants of Paris do not hold you responsible for the orders which have been given you; come over to us, and we will receive you as brothers. . . . Gen. Lafayette declares in the name of the whole population of Paris, that it cherishes no sentiment either of hatred or hostility against the French soldiers: it is ready to fraternize with all those who will return to the cause of the country and of liberty."[32] When a detachment of soldiers guarding a bridge asked what they were supposed to do, Lafayette sent them an answer: "All conciliation is impossible . . . the royal family has ceased to reign."[33]

Soldiers began to listen. Around the Louvre, an entire defensive line defected to the insurrectionaries. The rest of the king's soldiers, stricken with panic, retreated in disorder up the Champs-Élysées in the face of a wave of armed insurgents making for the Tuileries. From a vantage point at place de l'Étoile—where the Arc de Triomphe now sits—Marmont spied the tricolor flying above the royal palace. By the evening of July 29, 1830, the fighting was over. Paris had won.

⚜

BACK IN SAINT-CLOUD, King Charles belatedly realized he made a huge mistake. He tried to salvage the situation by announcing the dismissal of Polignac and the cancellation of the Four Ordinances. But it took time for news of his capitulation to spread, and by then people concluded the king's self-inflicted wound was fatal. Whatever else happened, he had ceased to reign.

If Charles ceased to reign, who was going to replace him? As commander of the National Guard, all potential claimants to power lobbied Lafayette. A supporter of the Bourbons begged Lafayette to support the claim of the king's nine-year-old grandson. An old Bonapartist turned up at the Hôtel de Ville to secure the vacated throne for Napoleon's son, currently living in comfortable exile in Austria. He was escorted to a room and told Lafayette would be with him in a moment. It took him a few minutes to realize they stuck him in a room with barred windows and locked the doors behind him. Many armed students and street fighters demanded this revolution—and it was now a revolution—mark the end of kings and emperors and the return of a republic. They pressed Lafayette himself to become president of France.

But Lafayette was unhappy with all these options. He refused to even consider supporting the Bourbons. They proved over and over again their fundamental inability to reign over a free people. Nor would he support the return of the Bonapartes because, as he later wrote Joseph Bonaparte, "the Napoleonic system was brilliant in glory, but stamped with despotism, aristocracy, and slavery."[34] Besides, the return of the Bonapartes would guarantee some kind of war with the other great powers of Europe. The same seemed true of a republic. In 1830, the word *République* was still synonymous with dictatorship, war, and terror. It evoked memories of the guillotine at home and abroad. Declaring a republic would provoke a war with the other European powers, and probably spark a civil war to boot.

So what did Lafayette want? He wanted the same thing he wanted since 1789, which he summarized with the formula: "a popular monarchy, in the name of the national sovereignty, surrounded by republican institutions." From his vantage point, this object "appeared to be within our attainment; this was the program of the barricades and of the Hôtel de Ville of which I undertook to be the interpreter." He added one of his additional reasons for not supporting the declaration of a republic was he did not think the majority of French actually wanted it. "The first condition of republican principles being to respect the general will," he wrote. "I prevented myself from proposing a purely American constitution—in my opinion the best of all. To do so would have been to disregard the wish of the majority, to risk civil troubles, and to kindle foreign war. If I was wrong, my mistake was at least at variance with the inclinations I have always cherished, and even, supposing me to have possessed a vulgar ambition, it was contrary to what might be termed my interest."[35]

Lafayette's analysis of the situation left him with only one real choice: the duc d'Orléans. He and the duc never spent much time together after their first meeting in 1814. But Lafayette still remembered how he and Tsar Alexander agreed Orléans was the only Bourbon compatible with the free constitution. Sarrans later said, "Though . . . not much acquainted with [Orléans], Lafayette esteemed his personal character, and the simplicity of his manners . . . he had seen him an ardent patriot in his youth; that he had never fought except under the tricolored flag."[36]

This was a conclusion many of Lafayette's allies in the liberal opposition already reached. Jacques Laffitte was already laser-focused on ensuring Orléans became the new king. Laffitte dispatched Adolphe Thiers to sound out the duc's intentions. When Thiers reached the Orléans house, he learned the duc was in hiding, so instead held a brief but intense conversation with the duc's sister Adelaide. Widely considered the brains of the family, anyway, she agreed to throw her family's support behind the revolutionaries in Paris.

On the morning of July 30, placards appeared all over the city written by Thiers touting the virtuous patriotism of Orléans: "Charles X can never again enter Paris; he has caused the blood of the people to be shed," it read. "The Republic would expose us to frightful divisions; it would embroil us with Europe." Meanwhile, "the Duc d'Orléans is a prince devoted to the cause of the Revolution. . . . The Duc d'Orléans carried the tricolor under fire. . . . The Duc d'Orléans has declared himself; he accepts the Charter as we have always wanted it. It is from the French people that he will hold his Crown."[37] When Rémusat came to the Hôtel de Ville to sound out Lafayette's intention, he said, "We're talking a lot about the duc d'Orleans, and by the way, if we change government, it's just you or him." To this Lafayette said immediately, "Me? No. If it were up to me the duc d'Orleans will be king, just as surely as I will not be."[38]

⚜

To MAKE ORLÉANS king, his supporters overcame a number of practical difficulties. First, they convened as many deputies as they could find to declare Orléans "Lieutenant-General of the Realm," an archaic position allowing the duc to legally wield sovereign power. Historically, this office was invoked when a king was too young to rule or incapacitated in some way. In this case, the king's "incapacitation" was blundering into a position where nobody wanted him to be king anymore.

Then there was the matter of the Parisians manning the barricades. Would they accept Orléans? Armed students and street fighters clustered around the Hôtel de Ville determined to make sure this revolution did not simply replace one Bourbon for another. So it was with some courageous trepidation that newly appointed Lieutenant-General of the Realm Orléans mounted his horse at the Palais-Royal on July 31, and led a procession to the Hôtel de Ville to have his authority confirmed. When he arrived, the whole square was packed with armed onlookers, plenty of whom yelled "Vive la République!" and "Vive Lafayette!" In this uncertain atmosphere, Lafayette personally greeted Orléans and escorted him into the building.

A few minutes later, they appeared on the balcony holding a tricolor flag between them, signaling Lafayette's endorsement of Orléans. The great writer, historian, and statesman Chateaubriand later described the scene he witnessed: "M. de la Fayette, seeing the growing uncertainty of the assembly . . . gave the duc d'Orléans a tricolor, advanced on the balcony of the Hôtel de Ville, and kissed the prince in the eyes of the dumbfounded crowd, as he waved the national flag. La Fayette's republican kiss made a king. Strange results for the life of the Hero of the Two Worlds!"[39]

The next morning, Lafayette visited Orléans at the Palais-Royal to assuage fears Orléans would reign like his ousted cousin, Charles. Lafayette said, "You know that I am a republican, and that I consider the Constitution of the United States as the most perfect system that has ever existed." Orléans replied, "I think so too. It is impossible to have lived two years in America without being of that opinion; but do you think, in the situation in which France stands, and in the present state of public opinion, we can venture to adopt it here?" Lafayette said, "No. What the French people want at the present juncture, is a popular throne, surrounded by republican institutions." Orléans said, "That is just what I think."[40]

With a new king being made in Paris, the old king gave up. On August 2, 1830, Charles X signed a letter of abdication. He waited more than thirty years for his chance to undo the Revolution, and when he finally had the chance to do it, all he did was provoke another revolution, ending his family's reign over France forever. Charles X was the last Bourbon king of France. Forty years after first departing France as a bitter émigré, he did so again. Charles commenced a slow procession to the northern coast, on his way to his second and final exile in England. He died six years later. He never changed.

During the first week of August, Lafayette focused on commanding the National Guard and maintaining order in Paris, repeatedly interceding whenever protestors tried to break up sessions of the chambers. Meanwhile, a small group of Orléanists led by François Guizot hammered out a liberalized revision of the Charter of Government. Lafayette personally wanted a new charter written by an assembly specifically elected for the purpose, not hasty edits by a self-assembled committee behind closed doors. But the process of ensuring the Revolution of 1830 did not become *too* radical was already well underway. Lafayette was satisfied to see things like the Law of the Double Vote abolished and Article 14 rewritten to prevent future abuses, but dismayed to find the revised Charter still clinging to the idea of hereditary privileges.

Out in the streets, students and workers who fought on the barricades became incensed at the perceived hijacking of the revolution. On August 3, the first full session of the deputies, "a tumultuous crowd appeared before the doors of the chamber, with the manifest intention of dissolving it by force."[41] As many of them were his own young supporters, Lafayette strode out to meet them. "My friends," he told them, "it is my duty to take measures for defending the chamber against every attack, which might be made upon its independence . . . I have no force to oppose you, but if the liberty of the chamber is violated, the disgrace will land upon me . . . I therefore leave my honor in your hands, and I count upon your friendship for me, as a security that you will depart peacefully."[42] They calmed down and did not storm their way into the chambers.

After all the details were worked out, the duc d'Orléans presented himself to a joint session of the chambers on August 9 to be formally enthroned as Louis Philippe I, King of France. After his later disillusionment with both Louis Philippe and the July Monarchy, Lafayette regretted many of his decisions. But in the summer of 1830 everything radiated with bright hopes. He was commander of the National Guard, believing he stood vigil over a popular monarchy surrounded by republican institutions. It took more than forty years, but it appeared the dream of 1789 would finally be fulfilled.

CHAPTER TWENTY-FOUR

A TOWER AMID THE WATERS

[1830–1834]

T HE SUMMER OF 1830 WAS GLORIOUS. LAFAYETTE WAS RIDING higher than he had since 1789, and people noticed. A young Alexandre Dumas wrote, "The unanimity of the cries of *Vive la Fayette* proved that the man of 1789 had not lost, in 1830, an atom of his popularity . . . the man whom liberty consecrated king of the people in 1789, finds himself king of the people in 1830."[1] The historian Stendhal said, "The admirable Lafayette is the anchor of our liberty."[2] And later called him "a hero out of Plutarch."[3] On August 29, Lafayette staged a well-orchestrated review of sixty thousand National Guardsmen on the Champ de Mars for the new citizen-king Louis Philippe. When it was over, the king wrote Lafayette a glowing letter: "They have not only surpassed my expectations, but that it is not possible to express all the joy and happiness they have afforded me. A witness to the Federation of 1790, on the same Champ de Mars . . . I am enabled to draw a comparison . . . what I have just witnessed, is infinitely superior to what I then considered so complete."[4] Lafayette beamed at the exaggerated praise.

The warm rush of the summer cooled with the onset of autumn. Promises made by the king while the barricades stood were not kept after they came down. Lafayette was slow to notice. Rémusat said his grandfather-in-law "continued to be very happy with the king and his family . . . the king, naturally demonstrative and banal in his protestations, gave himself over voluntarily to profusions which, if well analyzed, committed him to very little, but which lulled M. de Lafayette in the illusion of complete sympathy that he took for the conformity of views."[5]

Lafayette accepted expediencies and compromises in the chaos of July, but still expected the "Program of the Hôtel de Ville" to become a part of the new order. To him, this meant abolishing hereditary peerages, reforming the judicial system, and massively expanding the electorate. These were the practical elements of the "popular monarchy surrounded by republican institutions" Lafayette believed Orléans promised in exchange for his "republican kiss." The revised Charter of Government, approved in a rush in early August, included several necessary reforms—including the recognition of national sovereignty as the basis of the constitution—but it left much to be desired.

Lafayette blamed a clique of overly cautious deputies and advisers for the delays. "I like the King better than his ministers," he told Rémusat, "and I like the ministers, better than the Chamber."[6] Lafayette now realized many leaders supported the July Revolution to *halt* the reactionary slide to the right, rather than *advance* a revolutionary push to the left. By the fall of 1830, the victors of the July Revolution drifted into two factions: the Party of Movement and the Party of Resistance. The former believed the July Revolution marked the beginning of further liberal reform and the expansion of political liberty. The latter believed it marked the *end* of reform and the return to regular order. Lafayette, of course, aligned with the Movement Party.

As his frustration with the pace of reform mounted, Lafayette told the king if he didn't make significant gestures toward real reform, he would be courting disaster. It's not like the armed republicans Lafayette coaxed to the side of the Orléanists had gone anywhere. Lafayette successfully mollified them in July by swearing Orléans supported republican institutions, but Lafayette told the king, "Continue to disavow the principle of your origin and I will answer for it that the Republic, or may I perhaps say the demagogic system, can desire no better auxiliary than your majesty."[7] If Louis Philippe didn't wake up, radical neo-Jacobins were going to stage a second revolution.

Lafayette pushed the government on a number of fronts, including abolition of the slave trade and equal civil rights of free people of color in French colonies. Napoleon's crimes still needed to be corrected. In a speech in the Chamber of Deputies, Lafayette said Napoleon "sent our best troops to lose their lives in the disastrous expedition to Saint-Domingue, which committed the double crime of re-establishing both slavery and the slave trade." That was now almost thirty years ago. Lafayette asked the minister of the navy "to tell us positively the determination of the government on the question of the slave trade, and on the condition of free men of color in our colonies."[8] A minister said, "A law establishing the punishments of piracy would be presented against the crime of trafficking, and a legislative project would also immediately enshrine the rights of men of color, recognizing there can be no men free under different conditions."[9] Lafayette took this as a partial victory, but slavery itself would not be outlawed until after the overthrow of the July Monarchy in 1848.

By October, a confrontation with the angry young republicans loomed. When Charles X abdicated the throne, his ministers scattered. But four of them, including Jules de Polignac, the most odious of them all, had been captured. They were slated to stand trial for treason, but Louis Philippe did not want them put to death. This was deeply unpopular in the streets, as friends and relatives of those who died fighting the bloody-minded despotism of Polignac's ministry demanded blood for blood. All through October and November 1830 street clashes broke out during demonstrations over the fate of the captured ministers.

In this volatile atmosphere, the king put Lafayette in charge of all armed forces in the city—not just the National Guard, but the regular army. The king ordered Lafayette to ensure there was no rioting on December 21, the day the judges announced their verdict—a verdict already determined to be imprisonment, not execution. Louis Philippe did not want to spare them, just to see them lynched by an angry mob.

Lafayette understood this was a political moment requiring political orders. He told his men they could not allow lawless looting and lynch mobs. They must look out for "well-intentioned, although misled citizens who imagine they serve justice by committing against her the greatest of offenses, that of menacing judges, or executing, as it is called, justice with their own hands; who suppose they serve liberty by employing measures which liberty reprobates."[10] This was not just about a single day. In Lafayette's opinion, the lynching of Foullon and Bertier in 1789 turned out, in retrospect, to be a preview of the Terror. "I will remind [you] at a former period the French people plunged into the horrors of that anarchy and sanguinary terror which gave birth to a bankruptcy, famine, and afterward passed through despotism to an odious restoration imposed by foreigners."[11]

His orders went on, in the third person:

However, the confidence of the Commander-in-Chief in the Parisian population, in the brave and generous conquerors of July, in the energetic youth, in whom he prided himself on being the constant friend, in his dear brothers-in-arms of the National Guard has not been for a moment shaken. They will always find him what he was at nineteen years of age; what he was in 1789, and is in 1830, he will continue to be during a few years he has yet to live. The man of liberty and public order, loving popularity more than life, but determined to sacrifice both rather than fail in his duty.[12]

When the showdown came, the National Guard exhibited loyal discipline. It helped that the authorities snuck Polignac and the other defendants out a side door before the verdict was officially read. But even without this precaution, Lafayette's National Guard maintained order. Despite a few altercations and angry demonstrations, there were no riots or lynch mobs. No barricades went up. The king, the government, and Lafayette all breathed a sigh of relief.

⚏

WITH THIS CRISIS passed, members of the coalescing Resistance Party moved against Lafayette, whom, despite his loyal service, they considered a destabilizing fanatic. Lafayette was aware he had enemies. "I know I weigh like a nightmare on the Palais-Royale," he said, "not on the King and his family who love me, who are the best people in the world, and who I love tenderly, but on those around them."[13] Being the commander of the entire National Guard, enjoying a great personal relationship with the king, and having a demonstrated capacity for delivering as much order as liberty, Lafayette felt secure.

Because Lafayette's influence centered on his command of the National Guard, that is where his enemies struck. One of the articles of the revised Charter of Government stated nobody could command National Guard forces larger than a single commune. Lafayette, meanwhile, was still serving as commander of the National Guard *of the entire kingdom*—making him commander in chief of a force comprising some three million men. On December 24, 1830, Lafayette's opponents in the Chamber of Deputies pointed out the irregular nature of the command: "General Lafayette cannot remain all his life the living law, at least, unless the political law be defunct."[14] They voted to enforce the rules as written in the Charter and offered to make Lafayette "Honorary Commandant of the National Guard" as a compensatory gesture.

The Christmas Eve attack upset Lafayette, not least because it was a day reserved for the memory of Adrienne. Lafayette knew his command was irregular and did not intend to remain on the job indefinitely—he wasn't Bonaparte after all—but he believed he earned the right to stay until *he* chose to step down. Believing himself more indispensable than he really was, Lafayette sent a wounded letter to the king: "The president of the council has kindly proposed to confer upon me the title of 'honorary commandant' . . . such nominal decorations are not agreeable with the institutions of a free nation, nor to me."[15] If he was not allowed to stay in his present position, he threatened to resign from the National Guard entirely.

The king invited Lafayette to talk. When Lafayette repeated in person his threat to resign, the king asked for time to confer with his ministers and advisers—who clearly told him to let Lafayette walk away. They were confident the National Guard was not Lafayette's personal praetorian guard and would remain loyal to the regime. Lafayette's republican kiss was no longer needed. The king declined to get involved, calling Lafayette's bluff and compelling him to resign.

On December 26, the king issued a proclamation: "You will share my regret when you learn the Gen. Lafayette has considered it his duty to tender his resignation. . . . His retirement is the more sensibly felt by me, inasmuch as only a few days have elapsed since the worthy general took a glorious part in the maintenance of public order."[16]

The next day Lafayette gave a speech in the Chamber of Deputies defending his conduct. "I have always thought the office of commander in chief of the national guards of the kingdom was not compatible, on general principles, with the institution of a constitutional monarchy," he said. "Therefore, when three million of my fellow citizens in 1790 proposed to confer this command upon me, by the acclamations of their 14,000 deputies in the field of the Federation, I hastened to prevent the possibility of it by obtaining from the assembly a prohibitive decree."[17] But the situation in 1830 was entirely different: "It was not the same at the Hôtel de Ville, when the Lieutenant General of the Realm, and afterward the King, proposed for me to retain the command. I believed I must accept, with the intention of resigning it, sooner in peace, later in case of war, when I no longer saw the need for it."[18]

His defensive speech then veered into attacks on the king's conservative advisers who prized order at the expense of liberty:

I would not have tendered my resignation, which has been received by the King, with all the expressions of his wanted kindness for me, before the crisis which we have just passed through. My conscience of public order is now perfectly satisfied. It is *not* the same with my conscience of liberty. We all know the motto of the Hôtel de Ville—a popular throne surrounded by republican institutions— that motto has been accepted, but we do not all hear it the same; it is not heard by the King's councilors as by me, who is more impatient to realize it.[19]

He then issued orders to his beloved National Guard announcing his resignation, thanking them for their patriotic service, and making it clear he was unwillingly pushed out the door.

Bernard Sarrans, Lafayette's aide-de-camp during the Revolution of 1830, summed up Lafayette's great problem. "Accustomed to finding his advantages in crises," he said, "[Lafayette] was at all times guilty of the fault—and no slight one in a statesman—of disdaining intrigues and especially all those of which he could personally be the object. This disregard of the petty machinations of the palace became a capital fault, at the close of a revolution which has been directed at least as much against men as against things."[20] Even after all these years, Lafayette still could not help but see politics as theater, of virtuous actors playing their parts, rather than a war of armies waging coordinated battles. So he was systematically outmaneuvered by those who did not make the same mistake.

Lafayette was not alone in getting tossed out, though. François Guizot and other members of the Resistance Party also moved against Jacques Laffitte. Laffitte was instrumental in making the duc d'Orléans king, and was Louis Philippe's first de facto prime minister. But he was now a leader of the Party of Movement. When Laffitte threatened to resign in March 1831 if France didn't do more to help beleaguered liberal movements in Italy, the king accepted his resignation. Laffitte later ran into Lafayette, who said, "Admit you have been a great idiot." Laffitte retorted, "I do, but if I'm idiot the first, you're the idiot the second, so we're even."[21]

⊟⊟

THOUGH PUSHED INTO the opposition by Louis Philippe's embrace of conservatism, Lafayette remained active in the Chamber of Deputies. François Guizot and the Resistance Party now touted a policy of *juste milieu*—a deliberate strategy of targeting the middle ground on any issue. Lafayette thought this approach ridiculous. In a speech in the Chamber of Deputies, he said, "We hear much, gentlemen, of moderation and the *juste-milieu*. . . . What are we to understand by these words? Does moderation consist in maintaining the center between two variable points? Which, when we say four plus four make eight, and an exaggerated claim pretends they make ten, believes it is more reasonable to maintain four plus four makes nine?"[22] This was not moderation. This was madness.

Lafayette also fought to further expand the electorate. In a speech in support of lowering the annual tax requirements for voting from 250 *francs* to 200, he said, "The right of election does not come from above, it belongs to all citizens and the only ground of exception should be incapacity to exercise it." He added, "I do not need . . . to return home in order to ascertain whether my neighbors and friends who pay only 200 francs are capable of choosing a Deputy. I am certain that not only they, but a mass of citizens who pay much less, are as capable as we are of making a good choice . . . I feel myself placed in an embarrassed situation at having it in my power to vote only for so high a qualification as 200."[23]

Though he remained active in politics, life as a deputy was less demanding than life as commander of the National Guard, so Lafayette paid more attention to his family and social life. Splitting his time between Paris and La Grange, he kept up an exhausting schedule even though he was now over seventy years old. "It is two o'clock," he wrote one day to his daughter-in-law Émilie, "and since I woke up I haven't had time to shave. Some twenty friends have been here discussing with me the advantages of solitude and of silence. I still found time to send off thirty-two letters and to read about an equal number."[24] The historian Stendhal observed Lafayette reigned over his salon with aloof good nature: "M. de Lafayette is extremely polite and even affectionate to everyone, but polite like a king."[25] Stendhal noted, however, Lafayette came alive in the company of young women. Stendhal said Lafayette "despite his age . . . often squeezed the petticoats of pretty girls from behind and without too much embarrassment."[26]

Lafayette also continued to play his self-proclaimed role as patron of all Americans who traveled to Paris. Anyone with an American passport knew they could call on General Lafayette if they needed assistance, advice, or help getting settled. Lafayette hosted a weekly dinner open to all comers, including regular luminaries like James Fenimore Cooper, who moved to France in 1826. When Samuel F. B. Morse arrived in 1831 to commence art training at the Louvre, he called on Lafayette. "When I went in, he instantly recognized me," he said, "took me by both hands, said he was expecting to see me in France, having read in the American papers that I had embarked."[27]

When progressive schoolteacher Emma Willard arrived in Paris, she announced her arrival to Lafayette. Willard was the founder of the women's academy Lafayette toured in Troy, New York. She expected a perfunctory reply from the old general—who was, after all, an important and busy man. She was shocked when he showed up on her doorstep to welcome her to Paris the next morning. Willard only reported a delightfully energetic conversation about education and politics where "his heart seemed to expand as to a confidential sister."[28] But, of course, the fact Willard was a younger woman helped.

In the summer of 1831, Lafayette mixed politics and personal affection when he met a twenty-one-year-old Italian refugee named Cristina Belgiojoso. Though she was the daughter of minor nobility, Belgiojoso arrived in Paris penniless. She was an idealistic radical who had joined a Carbonari cell in Milan and been forced to skip town one step ahead of the law while the authorities seized her passport and property. Lafayette took a political and personal interest in her well-being. The status of liberal refugees from the reactionary powers of Europe was a hotly contested issue in the Chamber of Deputies. Lafayette naturally believed France ought to be a welcoming safe haven. If he couldn't get the government to agree, he would do the job himself.

Belgiojoso later said, "Little by little I gained all the tenderness of M. de Lafayette and he became for me the best of fathers."[29] Lafayette made regular calls to her apartment, and Belgiojoso recalled they once got into a friendly argument about the best way to cook. "A struggle of politeness followed from this during which we ended up arguing over the handle of the pan and the place at the stove. Protesting his lack of obedience, I complained about the serious inconvenience of having the Hero of Two Worlds as my scullion."[30]

As with Fanny Wright, Cristina Belgiojoso became Lafayette's ambiguously surrogate daughter, and a regular visitor at La Grange during his twilight years. But his new companion did not prevent ongoing contact with Wright, whose work he continued to admire, encourage, and promote. When Fanny Wright returned to Paris in 1831 to get married, Lafayette was there to give away the bride.

⁂

By 1832, LAFAYETTE and his friends ran a rear guard action against the emerging conservative streak of the July Monarchy. The Resistance Party was winning. This was not only annoying to liberal deputies like Lafayette, but also younger political activists—the ones radicalized on the barricades of 1830, who seethed at the conservative betrayal. These young radicals were not like the militant liberals Lafayette joined in the Carbonari. This new generation did not fear the memory of the First Republic; they revered it. For them, Robespierre and Danton were not villains, but heroes. In the heart of the old Cordeliers district they formed an underground party called the Society of the Friends of the People. If the July Monarchy was going to betray the Revolution of 1830, the Society of the Friends of the People was going to redeem it. On the barricades.

In 1832, a devastating cholera outbreak swept through Paris. By the end of May, the death toll in the capital approached twenty thousand. The outbreak left the population of Paris—especially the lower classes—scared, hurt, paranoid, and angry. In early June the epidemic claimed the popular General Jean Maximilien Lamarque. Lamarque promoted egalitarian, democratic, and republican principles throughout a career stretching back to 1792. He was easily the most popular general in the French army—at least among the common people. Now he was dead. The Society of the Friends of the People mourned his loss, but spied an opportunity.

On June 5, 1832, Lamarque's funeral procession moved through the streets of Paris, followed by huge crowds, armed members of the Society of the Friends of the People among them. When the procession reached pont d'Austerlitz it stopped. A stage had been erected and Lafayette was scheduled to deliver a eulogy. As soon as Lafayette began his speech, commotion broke out. People shouted, "To arms!" A group of dragoons waded into the crowd and shots rang out. Six soldiers dropped dead. This led to more shouts of "To arms!" and "To the barricades!" Someone shoved a red liberty cap in Lafayette's hand, but he threw it on the ground in disgust. It was a symbol he detested.

As happened in July 1830, armed street fighters spent the evening of June 5 erecting barricades, raiding for weapons, and digging in for a fight. Their demand was not a "monarchy surrounded by republican institutions," but a republic. A *real* republic. But June 1832 was not July 1830. The National Guard stayed loyal to the regime. The king rode out personally to bolster morale instead of hiding in a château like his deposed predecessor. And leaders of the liberal opposition didn't want to go to bat for kids who idolized Robespierre, Danton, and Marat. Certainly Lafayette did not. Deflecting a false charge he was spotted in the crowd wearing a red liberty cap, he said, "I have always been opposed, with sincerity and with the approval of my countrymen, to the criminal violence of which, in 1792 and 1793, this red cap became in France the bloody symbol; neither have I bowed before the counter revolutionary usurpations which have by turns retarded the liberation of '89."[31]

There was fighting all through the night of June 5 and sporadic gunfire until the evening of June 6, but the June Rebellion of 1832 was quickly crushed. It would be Lafayette's last encounter with anything resembling a revolution. But he did not take part. He only made revolutions for *his* principles. He had no interest in resurrecting the principles of the First Republic—which he frankly considered the *worst* of all republics.

⊹

LAFAYETTE REMAINED ACTIVE in politics through 1832 and 1833. He corresponded with admirers and allies throughout America and Europe. He became especially interested in the cause of Polish independence and lobbied the government to do more to help. He continued to push for liberal reforms and patronized an array of philanthropic and charitable causes.

But he also reflected on his life and career. In July 1832, he wrote a short autobiographical justification of the life of one man, who lived in two worlds, in the service of three great revolutions. "During the course of my long life," he wrote, "since I entered the world under the reign of Louis XV, my compatriots have gone through so many conditions, prejudices, and different opinions that, to deserve praise or blame of having always remained the same, I resigned myself to successive criticisms, contradictions, and sometimes to a kind of isolation which people later came in great waves to find me."[32] His unfailing commitment to a few basic principles left him open to attack from conservative royalists, radical Jacobins, and authoritarian Bonapartists, who all perceived Lafayette to be a threat for wildly disparate reasons.

He then walked through his life from the beginning: "Thus, after my devotion to the American cause aroused the keenest irritation of the government and my family, not two years elapsed before this cause became that of France, and the young fool became the object of exaggerated enthusiasm and boundless confidence."[33] He was still proud to recall that when he left for America, they laughed at his brilliant madness, but when he returned they cheered him as simply brilliant.

As the French Revolution unfolded, Lafayette watched his principal critics turn from traditional conservatives to radical republicans. "When my republican professions and designs," he went on, "carried out in '89, were first regarded in high society, in the courts of France and others . . . as quite pleasant utopias inapplicable to Europe . . . there were already many people who, before the revolution, had no idea of freedom, and yet proscribed me for wanting to stop, in my foresight, at the popular monarchy of '91."[34] Lafayette could not help but be frustrated at how quickly the world changed. For years people told him he was *going too far*; then, when he succeeded, a bunch of new people popped up and yelled at him for *not going far enough*.

After the Revolution expelled him and he wound up in Olmütz, Lafayette watched from afar as the radical idealism of the Jacobins gave way to the cynical instincts of the Directory after the fall of Robespierre. "In my prison, instead of going into ecstasies with all the other republicans of Europe about the fine coup d'état . . . I preferred to remain proscribed rather than approve the violation of civil and political rights that, under the pretext of saving the Constitution, dealt it a fatal blow."[35] But here, Lafayette is revising his own history to paint a cleaner picture. He never preferred to stay in exile. The Lafayettes spent the years 1797–1799 continuously lobbying to return to France.

This inconvenience smoothed over, Lafayette continued his version of history. "When the First Consul, whose genius I recognized and was obliged to, moved toward despotism and a gradual destruction of all the liberties of '89 by making use of the terrible memories of '93, and when my constitutional friends, my Jacobin adversaries, my aristocratic enemies in the salons, as well as the kings of Europe, all blamed my republican obstinacy, I remained firm and stood up alone to the colossus."[36] This is all true. Lafayette never let the actions of others govern *his* beliefs. Bonaparte successfully painted a picture of revolutionary chaos and terror to justify an authoritarian dictatorship. Lafayette refused to play along, even though he himself was a victim of "the dreadful memories of '93."

Lafayette was also unmoved by the overtures of the Bourbons, even as they represented the only alternative to Napoleonic despotism. He watched the collapse of Napoleon's empire "without, however, wanting to throw myself with the rest of France, into the hopes of the 'freely granted' charter and the new devotion of the legitimate monarchy; just as, during the Hundred Days, I joined Bonaparte to defend our independence, then fought him to resist dissolving the Chamber of Representatives."[37] Here, Lafayette is again telling a story smoothed of imperfections, but one capturing an essential truth: both Bonapartes and Bourbons opposed Lafayette's principles of 1789. To him, they were not polar opposites, but two sides of the same unfree coin.

When the Revolution of 1830 came around, every political faction attempted to seize control of France. From his position as commander of the National Guard in the Hôtel de Ville, Lafayette chose the option he thought represented the best chance to see the principles of '89 enshrined. "When, during our beautiful revolution of July 1830," he wrote,

the majority of the combatants who surrounded me would have preferred the proclamation of the Republic, when Bonapartists would have adopted the name under an imperial presidency, when very liberal proposals of Bourbon legitimists reached me, and when the Hôtel de Ville was stronger than the Chamber, I preferred to remain united with the Deputies in an Orléanist coalition while wishing that, the Lieutenant General, once chosen, the constitution be written by a truly national convention. I even sacrificed that wish to the will of my colleagues, to the need for internal union and foreign peace, but only after I placed beyond attack the principle of the people's sovereignty and the arming of the whole nation.[38]

For Lafayette the Orléanist solution was never the *best* solution. But he believed it was the *best possible* solution.

Writing from the vantage point of 1832, after being pushed out of the National Guard and watching the Resistance Party thwart Lafayette's principles, he said, "Louis-Philippe has no obligation to me. I had neither commitment to, nor friendship with, him."[39] Lafayette was clearly as adept at rewriting recent events as ancient history. He *had* been friends with Orléans. At first, he sang the praises of the citizen king and absolutely believed Orléans owed his crown to Lafayette's intervention. But Lafayette concluded his current ill-will well deserved in retrospect. "The friendship I have since felt for him and his family comes after my actions in July and August 1830 only because I saw in him the combination most favorable to the interests of liberty and the nation; but on the condition of carrying out what has since been called the program of the Hôtel-de-Ville."[40] Because that program was *not* carried out, Lafayette criticized the regime. Just as he once criticized the *ancien régime*, the Jacobin republic, the Consulate, the Empire, and the Restoration. It was the story of a lifelong commitment to the simple principles of liberty he picked up in America as a teenager, and still defended as an old man in France.

⧗

IN FEBRUARY 1834, the seventy-six-year-old Lafayette contracted a terrible chest cold after a long winter carriage ride. His condition drove him into bed at his townhouse on rue d'Anjou in Paris. For the next several months his health improved, then collapsed, then improved again. His normally busy social calendar was severely curtailed, but he was always eager to welcome friends into his home. He could not participate in sessions of the Chamber of Deputies but tried to keep up with his correspondence. Georges, Anastasie, Virginie, and his mob of grandchildren tended to him, as did Cristina Belgiojoso, who was a regular bedside companion. Lafayette's doctor said, "I often found the excellent lady by his bedside . . . the pleasure of her conversation turned away his troubles and made him forget his sufferings for a few moments."[41]

As late as early May 1834, there was no reason to believe his illness would be fatal. On May 1, Lafayette opened a letter by apologizing for his delayed response, blaming "a long illness which, for two and a half months, has prevented me from attending the sittings of the Chamber."[42] The letter was written to John Murray, president of the Glasgow Emancipation Society, congratulating him on the recent British decision to outlaw slavery in their colonies. Lafayette offered reflections on the early history of emancipation in the Americas, which Murray had solicited. These thoughts included the pleasantly self-serving recollection, "I believe that the first European experiences began in the French colony of Cayenne, three years before the revolution of '89." This referred to his own failed experiment, which he said was interrupted "by the proscriptions of 91 [*sic*]; the blacks were confiscated and sold by the triumphant party."[43] Lafayette forgot his own mistakes and culpability, as old men on their deathbeds are wont to do.

The letter to Murray is the final letter in the six volumes of Lafayette's posthumously collected correspondence, letters, and manuscripts. In mid-May his health collapsed. On May 20, 1834, General Marie-Joseph Paul Yves Roch Gilbert du Motier, marquis de Lafayette, died peacefully in his bed. The next item in Lafayette's collected papers is the death notice issued by his family: "General Lafayette was taken from his family and his country on May 20. In accordance with his last wishes, his coffin was placed in the cemetery of Picpus where the companion of his life already rested and where the same tomb unites them."[44]

When the government learned Lafayette was dead, they feared a repeat of the June Rebellion of 1832. The funeral procession of a popular general was now a potentially dangerous event. The government of Louis Philippe announced their deep sympathies and claimed General Lafayette deserved nothing less than a funeral with full military honors. When two hundred thousand people lined the streets to catch a glimpse of his coffin as it wound its way through Paris, they were kept at a distance by a heavily armed escort of infantry and cavalry.

Chateaubriand painted a romantic picture of Lafayette's funeral procession: "I was in the crowd . . . when M. de La Fayette's convoy passed: at the top of the boulevard, the hearse stopped; I saw him, all gilded with a fleeting ray of the sun, shining above the helmets and the weapons: then the shadow returned and he disappeared."[45] But American artist and author Nathaniel Parker Willis saw it differently. Witnessing an intimidating spectacle not at all in keeping with Lafayette's principles, he said, "They buried the old patriot like a criminal. Fixed bayonets before and behind his hearse. His own national guard disarmed, and troops enough to beleaguer a city, were the honors paid by the citizen king to the man who made him!"[46] Another American acquaintance agreed: "They have buried liberty and Lafayette together."[47]

After the procession ended, Lafayette was buried in the private Picpus Cemetery beside Adrienne. When he was laid to rest, the dirt brought back from Bunker Hill was poured over the coffin. After a lifetime of war and revolution, Lafayette now rests forever in Paris, beside Adrienne, under the sacred soil of American liberty.

—※—

As NEWS OF Lafayette's death spread, the Hero of Two Worlds was eulogized on both sides of the Atlantic. John Quincy Adams delivered the official memorial in the House of Representatives. "Pronounce him one of the first men of his age," Adams said, "and you have not yet done him justice . . . turn back your eyes upon the records of time; summon from the creation of the world to this day the mighty dead of every age and every clime—and where, among the race of merely mortal men, shall one be found, who, as the benefactor of his kind, shall claim to take precedence of Lafayette?"[48]

Adams went on.

Lafayette discovered no new principles of politics or of morals. He invented nothing in science. He disclosed no new phenomenon in the laws of nature. [But] born and educated in the highest order of feudal nobility, under the most absolute monarchy of Europe, in possession of an affluent fortune, and master of himself and of all his capabilities, at the moment of attaining manhood, the principle of republican justice and of social equality took possession of his heart and mind, as if inspired from above. He devoted himself, his life, his fortune, his hereditary honors, his towering ambition, his splendid hopes, all to the cause of liberty.[49]

In Britain, liberal philosopher and politician John Stuart Mill said,

Those who could find no other flaw in his character have accused him of vanity: would to Heaven there were more persons in the world whose vanity was of the same kind! Never, we should imagine, was a man whom two great nations worshipped almost as a god so little intoxicated by his elevation. He never hesitated to confess an error; was never ashamed to retrace a false step; he never failed, when occasion required, to immolate to his country's good, not only his ambition, his fortune, his liberty, and his personal safety, but what was far dearer to him, the ascendancy of his favorite opinions, and the love of that people whose honest sympathy had been the delight of his life.[50]

But not *everyone* worshipped Lafayette like a god. Far from it. During his long life he made lots of enemies. Back in the days of the French Revolution, Mirabeau called him "the man of indecision, an incapable and nefarious windbag."[51] Lafayette's old nemesis Marat said Lafayette had a "soul of mud and small ambitions."[52] Danton called him "the vile eunuch of the revolution."[53] The marquis de Bouillé, Lafayette's cousin and co-architect of the Flight to Varennes, said, "He had ambition without the character and genius necessary to direct it: he reduced himself to the desire to make noise in the world in order to make people talk about him."[54] Before he died in exile in Saint Helena, Napoleon said, "Lafayette was yet another fool, he was in no way cut out for the role he wanted to play. His political good nature make him constantly duped by many things."[55]

Chateaubriand leveled an incredulous postmortem: "M. de La Fayette had only one idea, and unfortunately for him it was the one of the century; the fixity of this idea has made its empire; it served as a blindfold, it prevented him from looking to the right and to the left; he walked steadily in one line; he advanced without falling between the precipices, not because he saw them, but because he did *not* see them; blindness took the place of genius: whatever is fixed is fatal, and what is fatal is powerful."[56]

Cristina Belgiojoso, who was so close to Lafayette at the end of his life, watched Lafayette's reputation tarnished by the hands of more cynical commentators like Chateaubriand. "When he is given his place in history," she said in 1850, "it will be recognized, I am sure of this, that his political mistakes were caused by too high opinion of the human species and of men; he judged the latter according to himself. One can understand the serious errors he made in attributing to others the integrity, the uprightness, and the sincerity that were only in him."[57]

But in America, Lafayette's reputation continued to shine. In 1861, antislavery senator Charles Sumner called Lafayette "one who early consecrated himself to human freedom, and throughout a long life became its knight-errant, its hero, its apostle, its martyr—who strove for it as no man in all history ever strove—who suffered for it as few have suffered, and whose protracted career, beginning at a period when others are still at school, and ending only at the tomb."[58]

The best summation of Lafayette's life was delivered in the summer of 1832, when Lafayette attended a Fourth of July banquet. The annual celebrations hosted by Americans in Paris were a highlight of the year for the aging Hero of Two Worlds. On this occasion, Samuel F. B. Morse proposed a toast to Lafayette. He expressed "the honor and pleasure of having at our board our venerable guest on my right hand, the hero whom two worlds claim as their own. Yes . . . he belongs to America as well as to Europe. He is our fellow citizen, and the universal voice of our country would cry out against us did we not manifest our nation's interest in his person and character."

"There are some men," Morse continued,

who would wish to direct public opinion who are like buoys upon tidewater. They float up and down as the current sets this way or that. If you ask in an emergency where they are, we cannot tell you; we must first consult the almanac, we must know the quarter of the moon, the way of the wind, the time of the tide, and then we may guess where you will find them.

But our guest is not of this fickle class. He is a tower amid the waters, his foundation is upon a rock, he moves not with the ebb and flow of the stream. The storm may gather, the waters may rise and even dash above his head, or they may subside at his feet . . . still he stands unmoved. We know his sight and his bearings, and with the fullest confidence we point to where he stood six and fifty years ago. He stands there now. The winds have swept by him, the waves have dashed around him, the snows of winter have lighted upon him, but still he is there. I ask you, therefore . . . to drink with me in honor of General Lafayette.[59]

Santé . . . et adieu.

ACKNOWLEDGMENTS

THIS BOOK WOULD NOT HAVE BEEN POSSIBLE WITHOUT THE UN-failing love and support of my wife, Brandi. Everything I have ever accomplished is thanks to her. I also depended on the courage, strength, and good humor of my children, Elliott and Olive, who found themselves dropped into France without warning and made me more proud than I would have thought possible. I love them dearly. My parents, whom the book is dedicated to, have only ever encouraged and supported everything I do, even when I announce I'm absconding with the grandchildren to Paris.

This book would also not have been possible without Rachel Vogel, the best agent in the world, and Colleen Lawrie, the best editor in the world. I am also blessed with a hugely supportive team at PublicAffairs: Lindsay Fradkoff, Jaime Leifer, Miguel Cervantes, Brooke Parsons, and Clive Priddle.

While working in Paris, I spent a great deal of time at Bibliothèque historique de la Ville de Paris. The librarians there were friendly, helpful, and eternally patient. My love and thanks also to the staff at the Bibliothèque Publique d'Information, my other home away from home. I must confess I used to see Centre Pompidou as a horrible monstrosity ruining an otherwise beautiful historical neighborhood, but after spending so many hours there I now love it dearly. Vive Centre Pompidou, you big weirdo.

I also could not have done this without deciding that this whole business of studying French history required me to learn French. The French House at the University of Wisconsin, Madison, provided excellent instruction and delicious weekly dinners. My instructors at Alliance Français in Paris crammed me with even more instruction upon arrival. Finally my two children, who became fluent within months, spent the rest of our time in France happily correcting their father for his mispronunciations and garbled syntax. If for no other reason than to save themselves mortal embarrassment in public.

During our three years in France we were well taken care of. Dana and Clement are the best landlords in Paris. Life was mostly routine, but there were some pretty spectacular explosions thrown in the mix we would not have been able to get through alone. While visiting Lafayette's childhood home in Auvergne, our car broke down in the middle of a freak snowstorm. We were stranded for three days in Mazat-St-Voy at the Auberge du soleil, a little hotel that took remarkably tender care of the refugee American family who turned up on their doorstep. Later, while staying in Bois-le-Rois to finish the manuscript, I was leveled by kidney stones that required multiple trips to the hospital and ultimately two surgical procedures. My hosts and their son Nicholas became my chauffeur, minder, and translator as I painfully navigated the French health care system. The French only pretend to be rude. But it's all an act. In reality they are wonderful, caring, and generous people.

I must also thank my expat community in Paris. Rhys provided daily wisdom, making me a stronger and better writer than I could have ever imagined. Jim, Loren, Beth, Andy, Monica, Frances, Emily, Laurent, and everyone else who comes together to chat on Friday nights. Their collective warmth, compassion, and humor were an invaluable lifeline.

In October 2019, I visited the Dean Collection at Cornell University. Many thanks to Laurent Ferri and all the archivists at the Division of Rare and Manuscript Collections for their help, conversations, and hard-working diligence. Archivists and librarians are the best. While in Ithaca, I was also well taken care of by Nate Sibinga at the Telluride House. Joseph Friedman was kind enough to introduce me. I enjoyed the company of the students and profited mightily from many conversations with them over lunch. Londell fed me every day and was himself a source of great wisdom, insight, and jokes. Many thanks also to Brittany Rubin and the staff at the Johnson Museum of Art who took me on a basement tour of paintings and other materials from the Lafayette family home at La Grange.

I also want to thank all the Lafayette biographers who preceded me: Louis Gottschalk and Margaret Maddox, Étienne Charavay, Charlemagne Tower, Brand Whitlock, Stewart Jackson, Maurice de La Fuye and Émile Albert Babeau, Constance Wright, André Maurois, Noel Gerson, Sabra Holbrook, Olivier Bernier, Paul Pialoux, Sylvia Neely, Lloyd Kramer, Harlow Giles Unger, James R. Gaines, David Clary, Paul Spalding, Laura Auricchio, and Sarah Vowell. I hope I am worthy of sharing their collective company.

Finally, to my entire podcast family and all the fans who listen every week and truly make this possible: Thank you so much. I love you guys.

NOTE ON DIRECT QUOTES

RENDERING DIRECT QUOTES FROM LETTERS, CORRESPONDENCE, AND dispatches from 200 years ago presents an author with a special problem. Rules of spelling, punctuation, and capitalization were far from regularized, often making them a jarring mess to the modern eye. This mess sometimes has the effect of making intelligent and thoughtful correspondents sound like barely literate children. This is bad enough for native English speakers, but is especially true for Lafayette, who corresponded with his American friends in English, and was in the habit of capitalizing nearly every word, especially when excited. To make reading their words easier, I present direct quotes adhering to modern rules of spelling and punctuation.

For example, on June 16, 1792, Lafayette wrote a letter to George Washington concerning a recent tumult in Paris. The literal manuscript text reads: "I Rejoice and Glory in the Happy Situation of American Affairs—I Bless the Restoration of Your Health, and wish I Could Congratulate You on Your Side of the Atlantick—But we are not in that State of tranquillity which may Admit of My absence."

I have rendered this quote: "I rejoice and glory in the happy situation of American affairs. I bless the restoration of your health, and wish I could congratulate you on your side of the Atlantic, but we are not in a state of tranquility which may admit of my absence."

Nothing about the quote changes. It is an aesthetic decision to clean up the spelling and punctuation to create a more readable quote. If that means capturing spelling and punctuation less accurately, we find balance by more accurately capturing how it would have been read by contemporaneous recipients—who would not have registered such prose as jarring, stilted, or strange.

NOTES

Endnotes focus on citations of direct quotes from primary sources. See Bibliographic Note for full details on the sources used to build the narrative.

ABBREVIATION KEY

[AP-AFC]	*The Adams Papers: Adams Family Correspondence.*
[AP-PJA]	*The Adams Papers: Papers of John Adams.*
[LAAR]	*Lafayette in the Age of the American Revolution: Selected Letters and Papers, 1776-1790.*
[MCM]	*Mémoires, correspondance et manuscrits du général Lafayette.*
[PAH]	*The Papers of Alexander Hamilton.*
[PBF]	*The Papers of Benjamin Franklin.*
[PGW-CS]	*The Papers of George Washington: Confederation Series.*
[PGW-PS]	*The Papers of George Washington: Presidential Series.*
[PGW-RS]	*The Papers of George Washington: Retirement Series.*
[PGW-RWS]	*The Papers of George Washington: Revolutionary War Series.*
[PTJ-OS]	*The Papers of Thomas Jefferson: Original Series.*
[SPJJ]	*The Selected Papers of John Jay.*

CHAPTER 1: THE ORPHAN MARQUIS [1757–1772]

1. Charavay, *Le général La Fayette*, 2.
2. Gilbert du Motier Père, marquis de La Fayette, à Madame et Madame la marquise de La Fayette, 25 Juillet 1759. Reprinted in Pialoux, *Lafayette: Trois Révolutions*, 25.
3. Charavay, *Le général La Fayette*, 532.
4. Talleyrand-Périgord, *Mémoires du prince de Talleyrand* 1:18.
5. Charavay, *Le général La Fayette*, 533.
6. Gilbert du Motier, marquis de Lafayette, "Memoir of 1779," in *LAAR* 1:6.
7. Bouillé, *Manoirs Abandonnes*, 43.
8. Charavay, *Le général La Fayette*, 534.
9. Mercier, *Tableau de Paris* 1:148. Pointed to this quote by Auricchio, *The Marquis*, 15.
10. Mercier, *Tableau de Paris* 1:148.
11. Desmoulins, *Œuvres de Camille Desmoulins* 1:4.
12. Desmoulins, *Œuvres de Camille Desmoulins* 1:5.

13. Charavay, *Le général La Fayette*, 531.
14. Charavay, *Le général La Fayette*, 536.
15. Charavay, *Le général La Fayette*, 535.
16. Adams, *Works of John Adams* 3:149.

CHAPTER 2: A BIRD IN A GILDED CAGE [1773–1776]

1. Bacourt, *Correspondance entre le comte de Mirabeau* 1:63.
2. Bacourt, *Correspondance*, 63.
3. Bacourt, *Correspondance*, 64.
4. Charavay, *Le général La Fayette*, 538.
5. Ségur, *Souvenirs et anecdotes* 1:72.
6. "Memoir of 1779," *LAAR* 1:3.
7. "Memoir of 1779," *LAAR* 1:3.
8. Ségur, *Souvenirs et anecdotes* 1:72.
9. "Memoir of 1779," *LAAR* 1:3.
10. Ségur, *Souvenirs et anecdotes* 1:72–73.
11. Quoted in Cloquet, *Souvenirs*, 105.
12. "Memoir of 1779," *LAAR* 1:7.
13. "Memoir of 1779," *LAAR* 1:6.
14. Thomas Jefferson to John Jay, July 19, 1789, in *PTJ-OS* 15:284–291.
15. "Memoir of 1779," *LAAR* 1:7.
16. Lafayette to Adrienne, June 19, 1777, *LAAR* 1:63–64.
17. Saint-Germain, *Mémoires de St. Germain*, 45–46.

CHAPTER 3: WHY NOT? [JULY 1776–APRIL 1777]

1. Voltaire, *Candide*, 131.
2. Secret Committee of Congress to Silas Deane, March 3, 1776, *Deane Papers* (New York: New York Historical Society, 1887), 1:124.
3. Deane to Secret Committee, November 28, 1776, *Deane Papers* 1:371.
4. Deane to Secret Committee, December 6, 1776, *Deane Papers* 1:404.
5. Deane to Secret Committee, December 6, 1776, *Deane Papers* 1:404.
6. Ségur, *Souvenirs et anecdotes* 1:69.
7. "Memoir of 1779," *LAAR* 1:3.
8. "Memoir of 1779," *LAAR* 1:7.
9. Lameth, *Mémoires*, 107.
10. Lameth, *Mémoires*, 107.
11. "Agreement with Deane," December 7, 1776, *LAAR* 1:17.
12. "Agreement with Deane," December 7, 1776, *LAAR* 1:17.
13. "Memoir of 1779," *LAAR* 1:8.
14. "Memoirs in My Hand Through the Year 1780," in *MCM* 1:10.
15. "Memoir of 1779," *LAAR* 1:8.
16. "Memoir of 1779," *LAAR* 1:9.
17. Lafayette to the duc d'Ayen, March 9, 1777, *LAAR* 1:28.
18. Lafayette to William Carmichael, February 11, 1777, *LAAR* 1:20.
19. Ségur, *Souvenirs et anecdotes* 1:73–74.

20. Baron de Kalb to Silas Deane, March 25, 1777, *LAAR* 1:28.
21. Lafayette to Carmichael, April 19, 1777, *LAAR* 1:51.
22. Doniol, *Histoire* 2:395.
23. Lafayette to Carmichael, April 19, 1777, *LAAR* 1:50.
24. Lafayette to Adrienne, April 19, 1777, *LAAR* 1:49.

CHAPTER 4: BRILLIANT MADNESS [1777]

1. Lafayette to Adrienne, May 20, 1777, *LAAR* 1:57.
2. Lafayette to Adrienne, May 20, 1777, *LAAR* 1:56.
3. "Memoir by the Vicomte de Mauroy," *LAAR* 1:55.
4. "Memoir by the Chavalier Dubysson," *LAAR* 1:73.
5. "Memoir by the Chavalier Dubysson," *LAAR* 1:75.
6. Lafayette to Adrienne, July 17, 1777, *LAAR* 1:66.
7. Lafayette to Adrienne, June 19, 1777, *LAAR* 1:61.
8. Lafayette to Adrienne, June 19, 1777, *LAAR* 1:61.
9. "Journal of a Campaign in America by Du Rousseau de Fayolle," *LAAR* 1:71.
10. "Journal of a Campaign in America by Du Rousseau de Fayolle," *LAAR* 1:71.
11. "Memoir by the Chavalier Dubysson," *LAAR* 1:77.
12. George Washington to John Hancock, February 20, 1777, *PGW-RWS* 8:381.
13. Washington to Hancock, February 11, 1777, *PGW-RWS* 8:306.
14. Washington to Major General Horatio Gates, February 20, 1777, *PGW-RWS* 8:378.
15. Washington to Major General William Heath, July 27, 1777, *PGW-RWS* 10:438.
16. James Lovell to William Whipple, July 29, 1777, Smith, *Letters of Delegates to Congress* 7:393.
17. Resolution of Congress, July 31, 1777, *LAAR* 1:88.
18. Henry Laurens to John Gervais, August 8, 1777, *LAAR* 1:88.
19. Lafayette to Jared Sparks, 1828, in Sparks, ed., *Writings of Washington* 5:454.
20. The receipt of the purchase is located in Brice-Jennings Papers, MS 1997, Maryland Historical Society.
21. "Memoir of 1779," *LAAR* 1:91.
22. Lord Stormont to Lord Weymouth, April 9, 1777, *LAAR* 1:44.
23. Washington to Hancock, September 11, 1777, *PGW-RWS* 8:201.

CHAPTER 5: A HELL OF BLUNDERS, MADNESS, AND DECEPTION [1777–1778]

1. Lafayette to Adrienne, October 1, 1777, *LAAR* 1:116.
2. Lafayette to Adrienne, October 1, 1777, *LAAR* 1:114.
3. "Memoirs in My Hand Through the Year 1780," *MCM* 1:28–29.
4. Lafayette to Duboismartin, October 23, 1777, *LAAR* 1:130.
5. Ségur, *Souvenirs et anecdotes* 1:76.
6. Vergennes to Montmorin, December 11, 1777, in Doniol, *Histoire* 2:632.

7. De Kalb to comte de Broglie, September 24, 1777, quoted in Kapp, *Life of John Kalb*, 127.

8. Nathanael Greene to Washington, November 26, 1777, *LAAR* 1:159.

9. Lafayette to d'Ayen, December 16, 1777, *LAAR* 1:192.

10. Lafayette to d'Ayen, December 16, 1777, *LAAR* 1:193.

11. Lafayette to Adrienne, October 29, 1777, *LAAR* 1:137.

12. "Memoir of 1779," *LAAR* 1:95.

13. "Memoir of 1779," *LAAR* 1:96.

14. See editorial note for Lafayette to Henry Laurens, January 26, 1778, *LAAR* 1:256.

15. Alexander Hamilton to William Jackson, August 26, 1800, *PAH* 25:88.

16. Samuel Johnson, "Taxation No Tyranny; An Answer to the Resolutions and Address of the American Congress," (London: T. Cadell, 1775), 89.

17. "Memoir of 1779," *LAAR* 1:245.

18. "Memoir of 1779," *LAAR* 1:245.

19. Lafayette to Henry Laurens, February 19, 1778, *LAAR* 1:295.

20. Washington to Lafayette, March 10, 1778, *LAAR* 1:342.

21. "Memoir of 1779," *LAAR* 1:247.

22. Flexner, *George Washington in the American Revolution*, 287.

23. Stacy Schiff, *A Great Improvisation*, 142–143.

CHAPTER 6: THE ALLIANCE [1778–1779]

1. "Memoir of 1779," *LAAR* 2:6.

2. Washington to Gouverneur Morris, May 29, 1778, *PGW-RWS* 15:260–262.

3. "Memoirs in My Hand Through the Year 1780," *MCM* 1:50.

4. Custis, *Recollections*, 218.

5. General Charles Scott, quoted in Custis, *Recollections*, 413–414.

6. Lafayette to Governor Tompkins, 1824, quoted in Custis, *Recollections*, 218.

7. Lafayette to Lazare-Jean Théveneau de Francy, May 14, 1778, *LAAR* 2:49.

8. Lafayette to comte d'Estaing, July 14, 1778, *LAAR* 2:105.

9. John Laurens to Henry Laurens, August 22, 1778, Laurens, *Army Correspondence*, 218.

10. Greene to Washington, August 28, 1778, *PGW-RWS* 16:396–400.

11. John Laurens to Henry Laurens, August 22, 1778, Laurens, *Army Correspondence*, 220.

12. General Sullivan and His Officers to Count d'Estaing, August 22, 1778, Sullivan, *Letters and Papers* 2:243–246.

13. Lafayette to d'Estaing, August 22, 1778, *LAAR* 2:139.

14. Lafayette to d'Estaing, August 24, 1778, *LAAR* 2:141.

15. Lafayette to d'Estaing, August 24, 1778, *LAAR* 2:144.

16. Sullivan to Congress, August 31, 1778, Sullivan, *Letters and Papers* 2:286.

17. *Pennsylvania Packet*, September 12, 1778, *LAAR* 2:182.

18. Lafayette to d'Estaing, September 13, 1778, *LAAR* 2:182.

19. Lafayette to Lord Carlisle, October 5, 1778, *LAAR* 2:187–188.

20. Lord Carlisle to Lafayette, October 11, 1778, *LAAR* 2:189.

21. Lafayette to d'Estaing, September 21, 1778, *LAAR* 2:177, 176.
22. Lafayette to d'Estaing, October 20, 1778, *LAAR* 2:191.
23. "Memoir of 1779," *LAAR* 2:17.
24. Lafayette to Daniel Morgan, November 28, 1778, *LAAR* 2:204.

CHAPTER 7: PURCHASING GLORY [1779–1780]

1. Moré, *French Volunteer of the War of Independence*, 72–73.
2. Adrienne to Mlle. du Motier and Mme. de Chavaniac, February 16, 1779, *LAAR* 2:230, 231.
3. C. F. Adams, *Works of John Adams*, 3:149.
4. "Memoir of 1779," *LAAR* 2:226.
5. Hunolstein to Shuvalov, March 20, 1779, quoted in Gottschalk, *Lady-in-Waiting*, 54, 120.
6. Maurois, *Adrienne*, 78.
7. Maurois, *Adrienne*, 82.
8. Benjamin Franklin to Washington, March 5, 1780, *PGW-RWS* 24:626.
9. Lafayette to Franklin, May 19, 1779, *LAAR* 2:265.
10. Lafayette to Franklin, November 2, 1779, *LAAR* 2:335.
11. Lafayette to Vergennes, [May 17], 1779, quoted in Gottschalk, *Lafayette and the Close*, 17.
12. Lafayette to Franklin, October 14, 1779, *LAAR* 2:330.
13. Kapp, *Life of John Kalb*, 183.
14. Adrienne to Lafayette, December 24, 1779, *LAAR* 2:340.
15. Jacques-Philippe Morizot to Mlle. du Motier, March 25, 1780, in Gottschalk, *Lafayette and the Close*, 73.

CHAPTER 8: RED AND BLACK FEATHERS [1780–1781]

1. Lafayette to Washington, April 27, 1780, *LAAR* 3:3.
2. Martin, *Narrative of a Revolutionary Soldier*, 148.
3. Kapp, *Life of John Kalb*, 182.
4. Greene to Furman, January 4, 1780, quoted in Gottschalk, *Lafayette and the Close*, 57.
5. Ebenezer Huntington to Andrew Huntington, July 7, 1780, Huntington, *Letters*, 87. See also Gaines, *For Liberty and Glory*, 133–134.
6. Alexander Hamilton to John Laurens, January 8, 1780, *PAH* 2:255.
7. Lafayette to La Luzerne, September 10, 1780, *LAAR* 3:169.
8. Las Cases, *Memorial de Sainte Helene* 1:200.
9. Lafayette to Comte de Rochambeau and Chevalier de Ternay, August 9, 1780, *LAAR* 3:136.
10. Rochambeau to Lafayette, August 12, 1780, *LAAR* 3:140.
11. Rochambeau to La Luzerne, August 14, 1780, *LAAR* 3:141.
12. Rochambeau to Lafayette, August 27, 1780, *LAAR* 3:155.
13. Lafayette to Vicomte de Noailles, September 2, 1780, *LAAR* 3:156.
14. Thacher, *Military Journal*, 286–287.
15. Kapp, *Life of John Kalb*, 225.

16. Kapp, *Life of John Kalb*, 236.

17. Hamilton to James Duane, September 6, 1780, *PAH* 2:420–421.

18. Kapp, *Life of John Kalb*, 196–197.

19. Gottschalk, *Lafayette and the Close*, 131.

20. Flexner, *Traitor and the Spy*, 371, 372.

21. Flexner, *Traitor and the Spy*, 371.

22. Lafayette to Adrienne, October 8, 1780, *LAAR* 3:195.

23. Washington to Heath, September 26, 1780, quoted in Gottschalk, *Lafayette and the Close*, 141.

24. Lafayette to Rochambeau, October 4, 1780, *LAAR* 3:191.

25. Lafayette to Madame de Tessé, October 4, 1780, *MCM* 1:370.

26. Chernow, *Washington*, 389.

27. Lafayette to Adrienne, February 2, 1781, *LAAR* 3:309.

28. Hamilton to Philip Schuyler, February 18, 1781, *PAH* 2:564.

29. Lafayette to Hamilton, December 9, 1780, *LAAR* 3:253.

30. Instructions from Washington, February 20, 1780, *LAAR* 3:334.

CHAPTER 9: THE PLAY IS OVER [1781]

1. Clausewitz, *On War*, 123.

2. Clausewitz, *On War*, 123.

3. Plutarch, "Life of Pyrrhus," *Parallel Lives* 9:417.

4. Steuben to Washington, January 11, 1781, Sparks, ed., *Correspondence of the American Revolution* 3:205.

5. Lafayette to Washington, March 8, 1781, *LAAR* 3:386.

6. Lafayette to Thomas Sims, March 8, 1781, *LAAR* 3:385.

7. Thomas Jefferson to Lafayette, March 10, 1781, *LAAR* 3:390.

8. Bonsal, *When the French Were Here*, 78.

9. Vergennes to Lafayette May 11, 1781, *LAAR* 4:92.

10. Lafayette to Hamilton, April 10, 1781, *LAAR* 4:17.

11. Lafayette to La Luzerne, April 10, 1781, *LAAR* 4:23.

12. Lafayette to Greene, May 3, 1781, *LAAR* 4:79.

13. Lafayette to Washington, May 4, 1781, *LAAR* 4:82.

14. Lafayette to La Luzerne, May 9, 1781, *LAAR* 4:89.

15. Lafayette to Washington, May 24, 1781, *LAAR* 4:131.

16. Lafayette to Vicomte de Noailles, May 22, 1781, *LAAR* 1:123.

17. Steuben to Lafayette, June 3, 1781, *LAAR* 4:166–167.

18. "Historical Memoirs on the Years 1779, 1780, and 1781," *MCM* 1:272.

19. Lafayette to Greene, May 18, 1781, *LAAR* 4:111.

20. Greene to Lafayette, May 1, 1781, *LAAR* 4:74.

21. "Historical Memoirs on the Years 1779, 1780, and 1781," *MCM* 1:271.

22. Lafayette to La Luzerne, June 16, 1781, *LAAR* 4:185.

23. Lafayette to Greene, June 21, 1781, *LAAR* 4:203.

24. James McHenry to T. S. Lee, July 11, 1781, quoted in Gottschalk, *Lafayette and the Close*, 271.

25. Robert Andrews to George Weedon, September 26, 1781, *LAAR* 4:315.

26. Lafayette to Thomas Nelson, August 12, 1781, *LAAR* 4:314.

27. Lafayette to Washington, September 1, 1781, *LAAR* 4:382. See also: Lafayette to Washington, April 23, 1781, *LAAR* 4:60–61; Lafayette to Greene, June 3, 1781, *LAAR* 4:165; Lafayette to Washington, July 31, 1781, *LAAR* 4:290; and Lafayette to Thomas Nelson, August 12, 1781, *LAAR* 4:314.

28. Lafayette to Noailles, July 9, 1781, *LAAR* 4:241.

29. Lafayette to La Luzerne, August 14, 1781, *LAAR* 4:322.

30. Lafayette to Henry Knox, August 18, 1781, *LAAR* 4:333.

31. Nelson, *Anthony Wayne*, 137.

32. Washington to Noah Webster, July 31, 1788, *PGW-CS* 6:413–416.

33. Benjamin Rush to John Adams, April 22, 1812, quoted in Schutz and Adair, eds., *Spur of Fame*, 212–213. See also: *PGW-CS* 6:415.

34. Chernow, *Washington*, 408–409.

35. Chernow, *Washington*, 409.

36. Chernow, *Washington*, 409.

37. St. George Tucker to Mrs. Tucker, September 15, 1781, quoted in Gottschalk, *Lafayette and the Close*, 305.

38. Flexner, *Traitor and the Spy*, 449.

39. Lafayette to La Luzerne, October 3, 1781, *LAAR* 4:415.

40. Lafayette to La Luzerne, October 12, 1781, *LAAR* 4:416.

41. Lafayette to La Luzerne, October 12, 1781, *LAAR* 4:416.

42. Lafayette to Adrienne, October 22, 1781, *LAAR* 4:426.

43. Chernow, *Washington*, 419.

44. Lafayette to Maurepas, October 20, 1781, *LAAR* 4:422.

45. De Kalb to St. Paul, November 7, 1777, quoted in Gottschalk, *Lafayette Joins*, 53.

46. Quoted in Hamilton, *Life of Alexander Hamilton* 1:230.

47. Martin, *Narrative of a Revolutionary Soldier*, 106.

48. Washington to Joseph Jones, July 10, 1781, quoted in Gottschalk, *Lafayette and the Close*, 270.

49. "Report of d'Estaing," quoted in Gottschalk, *Lafayette Joins*, 306.

50. Gérard to Vergennes, October 20, 1778, Meng, ed., *Despatches and Instructions of Conrad Alexandre Gérard*, 346.

51. Chastellux, *Travels in North-America*, 108.

FIRST INTERLUDE: THE LIBERTIES OF ALL MANKIND [1782–1786]

1. Lafayette to Washington, January 30, 1780, *LAAR* 5:9.

2. Franklin to Robert Livingston, March 4, 1782, *PBF* 36:643–649.

3. John Ledyard to Isaac Ledyard, Summer 1785, quoted in Gottschalk, *Lafayette Between*, 267.

4. Lafayette to Washington, January 30, 1782, *LAAR* 5:8.

5. Lasteyrie, *Vie de Madame de Lafayette*, 203.

6. Franklin to Lafayette, September 17, 1782, *LAAR* 5:57.

7. Washington to Lafayette, October 20, 1782, *LAAR* 5:62.

8. Comte de Ségur to Lafayette, July 7, 1782, *LAAR* 5:51.

9. "Resolutions of Congress," November 23, 1781, *LAAR* 4:440.

10. Adams to James Warren, April 16, 1783, *LAAR* 5:123.

11. John Jay to Robert Livingston, November 17, 1782, in *SPJJ* 3:225–255.

12. Lafayette to Washington, January 30, 1782, *LAAR* 5:9.

13. Lafayette to Livingston, March 20, 1782, *LAAR* 5:21.

14. "On the Years 1782, 1783, and 1784 and the Third Voyage to America," *MCM* 2:4.

15. Lafayette to Jay, April 28, 1782, *SPJJ* 2:777–779.

16. Lafayette to Livingston, March 20, 1782, *LAAR* 5:21.

17. Lafayette to Washington, February 5, 1783, *LAAR* 5:91–92.

18. Declaration of Independence, July 4, 1776.

19. Lafayette to Washington, February 5, 1783, *LAAR* 5:92.

20. Washington to Lafayette, April 5, 1783, *LAAR* 5:121.

21. Lafayette to Adrienne, March 27, 1782, *LAAR* 5:117.

22. Charavay, *Le général La Fayette*, 97.

23. Charavay, *Le général La Fayette*, 97.

24. Lafayette to Adrienne, March 27, 1782, *LAAR* 5:117.

25. Charavay, *Le général La Fayette*, 97.

26. Lafayette to Mme. Hunolstein, March 27, 1783, quoted in Maurois, *Adrienne*, 108.

27. Abigail Adams to Mary Smith Cranch, April 15, 1785, in *AP-AFC* 6:82–85.

28. Condorcet, *Mémoires de Condorcet* 2:157.

29. Lameth, *Mémoires*, 110.

30. Boigne, *Récits d'une tante*, 25–26.

31. Lafayette to Vergennes, March 19, 1783, *LAAR* 5:112.

32. *Observations on Commerce Between France and the United States*, December 13, 1783, *LAAR* 5:172.

33. Gottschalk, *Lafayette Between*, 93.

34. "Laws of Maryland, Made and Passed at a Session of Assembly," December 28, 1784, quoted in Gottschalk, *Lafayette Between*, 145–146.

35. Madison to Jefferson, October 17, 1784, *LAAR* 5:273–274.

36. Barbé-Marbois, *Our Revolutionary Forefathers*, 185.

37. Barbé-Marbois, *Our Revolutionary Forefathers*, 185–186.

38. Lafayette to Adrienne, October 4, 1784, *LAAR* 5:260.

39. Lafayette to Prince de Poix, October 12, 1784, *LAAR* 5:267.

40. Madison to Jefferson, October 17, 1784, *LAAR* 5:273.

41. Gottschalk, *Lafayette Between*, 102.

42. "Voyage to the United States in 1784," *MCM* 2:100.

43. There is a great deal of confusion whether Lafayette ultimately hosted one or two young Native Americans in the 1780s. I am choosing to follow the evidence as interpreted by Gottschalk there were two: the younger Kayenlaha and older Peter Otsiquette. See specifically, Lafayette to Jefferson, February 8, 1786, *PTJ-OS* 9:261–262, where Lafayette mentions both of them.

44. Madison to Jefferson, October 17, 1784, *LAAR* 5:274.

45. "Friday, November 19, 1784," *Journal of the House of Delegates of the Commonwealth of Virginia*, 30.

46. "Recommendation for James," November 21, 1784, *LAAR* 5:277–278.

47. Washington to Lafayette, December 8, 1784, *LAAR* 5:279.

48. Lafayette to Washington, December 21, 1784, *PGW-CS* 2:226–228.

49. Neuilly, *Dix années d'emigration*, 10–11.

50. Charavay, *Le général La Fayette*, 137.

51. Lafayette to Washington, May 11, 1784, *LAAR* 5:322.

52. Lasteyrie, *Vie de Madame de Lafayette*, 209–210.

53. F. A. Vanderkemp to A. G. Mappa, July 27, 1792, in Vanderkemp, "Extracts from the Vanderkemp Papers," 53. See also Auricchio, *The Marquis*, 139.

54. His death was reported in *Gazette of the United States*, March 28, 1792. See also Auricchio, *The Marquis*, 139.

55. Lasteyrie, *Vie de Madame de Lafayette*, 207–208.

56. Lafayette to Adams, January 9, 1785, *AP-PJA* 18:91–95.

57. Lafayette to Washington, February 6, 1786, *PGW-CS* 3:538–547.

58. Lafayette to Knox, June 12, 1785, *LAAR* 5:330.

59. Arthur H. and Mary Marden Dean Lafayette Collection, Cornell University, Box 2, Folder 18.

60. Washington to Lafayette, May 10, 1786, *PGW-CS* 4:41–45.

61. Lafayette to John Adams, February 22, 1786, C. F. Adams, *Works of John Adams* 8:376–377.

CHAPTER 10: THE NOT ABLES [1786–1787]

1. Lafayette to Washington, January 13, 1787, *PGW-CS* 4:515.

2. Lafayette to Washington, January 13, 1787, *PGW-CS* 4:515.

3. Jefferson to Edward Carrington, January 16, 1787, *PTJ-OS* 11:48–50.

4. Bachaumont, *Mémoires secrets*, 184–185. Directed to these quotes by Auricchio, *The Marquis*, 147.

5. Lafayette to Washington, February 7, 1787, *PGW-CS* 5:13–15.

6. Talleyrand-Périgord, *Mémoires du prince de Talleyrand* 1:105.

7. Schama, *Citizens*, 225–226.

8. Jefferson to Abigail Adams, February 22, 1787, *PTJ-OS* 11:174–175.

9. Lafayette to Washington, February 7, 1787, *PGW-CS* 5:13–15. Emphasis added.

10. *Procès-verbal de l'Assemblée de Notables*, 73.

11. *Procès-verbal de l'Assemblée de Notables*, 138.

12. Calonne, *De l'état de la France*, 439.

13. "Sur la lettre à M. d'Hennings," *MCM* 3:225.

14. Taillemite, *La Fayette*, 145.

15. Bachaumont, *Mémoires secrets* 34:301. See also Auricchio, *The Marquis*, 156.

16. Maurois, *Adrienne*, 139.

17. Lafayette to Washington, May 5, 1787, *PGW-CS* 5:168–170.

18. "Assembly of Notables of 1787," *MCM* 2:165–166.

19. "Assembly of Notables of 1787," *MCM* 2:168.

20. "Assembly of Notables of 1787," *MCM* 2:171.

21. Lafayette to Washington, May 5, 1787, *PGW-CS* 5:168–170.

22. "Assembly of Notables of 1787," *MCM* 2:171–177.

23. "Assembly of Notables of 1787," *MCM* 2:177.

24. "Assembly of Notables of 1787," *MCM* 2:177.

25. "Assembly of Notables of 1787," *MCM* 2:177.

26. Lafayette to duc d'Harcourt, recounted in *MCM* 2:183.

CHAPTER 11: A CONSPIRACY OF HONEST PEOPLE [1787–1789]

1. Lafayette to Washington, August 3, 1787, *PGW-CS* 5:280–282.

2. Lafayette to Washington, October 9, 1787, *PGW-CS* 5:358–365.

3. "On the Royal Democracy of 1789 and the Republicanism of True Constitutionalists," *MCM* 3:198.

4. "On Mirabeau," *MCM* 2:365.

5. "Thomas Jefferson: Autobiography, 6 Jan.–29 July 1821," January 6, 1821, Founders Online, National Archives, https://founders.archives.gov/documents/Jefferson/98-01-02-1756.

6. Lafayette to Washington, May 20, 1788, *PGW-CS* 6:292–295.

7. Lafayette to Washington, October 9, 1787, *PGW-CS* 5:358–365.

8. Maurois, *Adrienne*, 145.

9. Jefferson to Madison, January 30, 1787, *PTJ-OS* 9:247–252.

10. Lafayette to Washington, October 9, 1787, *PGW-CS* 5:358–365.

11. Schama, *Citizens*, 252–253.

12. Lafayette to Washington, October 9, 1787, *PGW-CS* 5:358–365.

13. Maurois, *Adrienne*, 147.

14. Lafayette to Washington, October 9, 1787, *PGW-CS* 5:358–365.

15. Lafayette to Washington, May 20, 1788, *PGW-CS* 6:292–295.

16. Lafayette to Washington, October 9, 1787, *PGW-CS* 5:358–365.

17. Lafayette to John Adams, October 12, 1787, C. F. Adams, *Works of John Adams* 8: 456.

18. Clarkson, *History of the Abolition of the African Slave-Trade* 1:466.

19. Brissot, *Mémoires* 2:77.

20. Clarkson, *History of the Abolition of the African Slave-Trade* 1:492.

21. "Lafayette," quoted in Perroud, *J.-P. Brissot mémoires* 2:76–77.

22. Lafayette to Hamilton, May 24, 1788, *PAH* 4:652–654.

23. Condorcet to Lafayette, quoted in Gottschalk, *Lafayette Between*, 424.

24. "Assembly of Notables of 1787," *MCM* 2:183.

25. Marquis de Condorcet to Filippo Mazzei, quoted in Gottschalk, *Lafayette Between*, 416.

26. "Thomas Jefferson: Autobiography, 6 Jan.–29 July 1821," January 6, 1821, Founders Online, National Archives.

27. Lafayette to Latour-Maubourg, August 12, 1788, quoted in Gottschalk, *Lafayette Between*, 395.

28. Lafayette to Carmichael, August 20, 1788, quoted in Gottschalk, *Lafayette Between*, 398.

29. Lafayette to Carmichael, August 20, 1788, quoted in Gottschalk, *Lafayette Between*, 398.

30. Jefferson to St. John de Crèvecoeur, August 9, 1788, *PTJ-OS* 13:485–487.

31. Jefferson to James Monroe, August 9, 1788, *PTJ-OS* 13:488–490.

32. Jefferson to Dr. Richard Price, January 8, 1789, *PTJ-OS* 14:420–424.

33. Comte de Mirabeau to Duc de Lauzun, November 10, 1788, in Mirabeau, *Mémoires biographiques* 5:199.
34. Lafayette to Mme. de Tessé, in Maurois, *Adrienne*, 145.
35. "Assembly of Notables of 1787," *MCM* 2:184.
36. Sieyès, *Qu'est-ce que le tiers état?*, 27.
37. Lafayette to [Mme. Diane de Simiane], March 8, 1789, *MCM* 2:240.
38. Jefferson to Lafayette, May 6, 1789, *PTJ-OS* 15:97–98.
39. Washington to Lafayette, June 18, 1788, *PGW-CS* 6:335–339.

CHAPTER 12: THE CATECHISM OF FRANCE [1789]

1. Lafayette to [Simiane], "Ce Vendredi," *MCM* 2:308. Many letters with the recipient's name omitted are actually letters to Mme. de Simiane. I am following the subsequent identification done by Gottschalk and Maddox. See Gottschalk, *Lafayette Between*, 393.
2. Jefferson to Lafayette, May 6, 1789, *PTJ-OS* 15:97–98.
3. Maurois, *Adrienne*, 158.
4. "Account of the Events of May 5 to July 16, 1789," *MCM* 2:250.
5. *Archives parlementaires de 1787 à 1860* 8:213.
6. Morris, *Diary and Letters* 1:118.
7. Lafayette to Jefferson, July 9, 1789, *PTJ-OS* 15:255.
8. Lafayette to [Simiane], July 11, 1789, *MCM* 2:313.
9. Lafayette to [Simiane], July 11, 1789, *MCM* 2:313.
10. Lafayette to [Simiane], "Ce Vendredi," *MCM* 2:309.
11. Lafayette to Jefferson, July 9, 1789, *PTJ-OS* 15:255.
12. The final draft presented on July 11, 1789, is printed as "First European Declaration of the Rights of Man and Citizens," in *MCM* 2:252–253.
13. "Account of the Events of May 5 to July 16, 1789," *MCM* 2:252.
14. "On the Letter to M. d'Hennings," *MCM* 3:227.
15. "On the Letter to M. d'Hennings," *MCM* 3:227.
16. Young, *Arthur Young's Travels in France*, 153–154.
17. Morris, *Diary and Letters* 1:120–121.
18. Morris, *Diary and Letters* 1:123.
19. Condorcet, *Mémoires de Condorcet*, 2:53.
20. *Archives parlementaires* 8:220, 224.
21. "Account of the Events of May 5 to July 16, 1789," *MCM* 2:255.
22. Gottschalk and Maddox, *Through the October Days*, 102.
23. Lafayette to [Simiane], July 14, 1789, *MCM* 2:316.
24. Dury, *Petite Histoire de France*, 137.

CHAPTER 13: I REIGN IN PARIS [1789]

1. "Account of the Events of May 5 to July 16, 1789," *MCM* 2:255.
2. Bailly and Duveyrier, *Procès-verbal des séances et délibérations* 1:460.
3. Bailly and Duveyrier, *Procès-verbal des séances et délibérations* 1:460.
4. Bailly and Duveyrier, *Procès-verbal des séances et délibérations* 1:422.
5. Lafayette to [Simiane], July 16, 1789, *MCM* 2:317.

6. Bailly, *Mémoires* 2:231.

7. Morris to Washington, July 31, 1789, *PGW-PS* 3:360–363.

8. Lafayette, [unsigned/undated note], *MCM* 2:322.

9. Lafayette, [unsigned/undated note], *MCM* 2:322.

10. Jefferson to Jay, July 19, 1789, *PTJ-OS* 15:284–291.

11. "Account of the Events of May 5 to July 16, 1789," *MCM* 2:266.

12. "Account of the Events of July 16 to October 5, 1789," *MCM* 2:273.

13. Bailly, *Mémoires* 2:290–291.

14. Bailly, *Mémoires* 2:290.

15. Bailly, *Mémoires* 2:303.

16. "Extract from the Minutes of the Electors, July 23, 1789," *MCM* 2:281.

17. Lafayette to [Simiane], July 24, 1789, *MCM* 2:320.

18. "Account of the Events of July 16 to October 5, 1789," *MCM* 2:282–283.

19. "Account of the Events of July 16 to October 5, 1789," *MCM* 2:293.

20. Lasteyrie, *Vie de Madame de Lafayette*, 216.

21. Gottschalk and Maddox, *Through the October Days*, 123.

22. Gottschalk and Maddox, *Through the October Days*, 176.

23. Gottschalk and Maddox, *Through the October Days*, 176.

24. Lasteyrie, *Vie de Madame de Lafayette*, 215–216.

25. Lasteyrie, *Vie de Madame de Lafayette*, 215–216.

26. Marquis de Ferrières to M. de Rabreul, August 7, 1789, quoted in Ferrières, *Correspondance inédite*, 116.

27. Maurois, *Adrienne*, 169.

28. Lafayette to Jefferson, August 25, 1789, *PTJ-OS* 15:354–355.

29. "Thomas Jefferson: Autobiography, 6 Jan.–29 July 1821," January 6, 1821, Founders Online, National Archives.

30. Jefferson, "Autobiography."

31. Lafayette to [Simiane], July 24 or 25, 1789, *MCM* 2:321.

32. Talleyrand-Périgord, *Mémoires du prince de Talleyrand* 1:52–53.

33. Morris, *Diary and Letters* 1:135–136.

34. Lafayette to [Simiane], July 24 or 25, 1789, *MCM* 2:321–322.

CHAPTER 14: TO VERSAILLES OR TO THE LAMPPOST [1789]

1. Thomas Jefferson to John Jay, September 19, 1789, *PTJ-OS* 15:454–461.

2. Thomas Jefferson to John Jay, September 19, 1789, *PTJ-OS* 15:454–461.

3. Morris, *Diary and Letters of Gouverneur Morris* 1:167.

4. Morris, *Diary and Letters* 1:161.

5. Gottschalk and Maddox, *Through the October Days*, 309.

6. Levasseur, *Mémoires* 1:65.

7. Levasseur, *Mémoires* 1:64–65.

8. Lafayette to [Simiane], July 24 or 25, 1789, *MCM* 2:322.

9. Morris, *Diary and Letters* 1:172.

10. "First Account of the Events of October 5 and 6," *MCM* 2:336.

11. Maurois, *Adrienne*, 170.

12. "Second Account of the Events of October 5 and 6," *MCM* 2:346.

13. "First Account of the Events of October 5 and 6," *MCM* 2:336.

14. Maurois, *Adrienne*, 170.

15. Gottschalk and Maddox, *Through the October Days*, 339.

16. Morris, *Diary and Letters* 1:173.

17. "First Account of the Events of October 5 and 6," *MCM* 2:338.

18. "Second Account of the Events of October 5 and 6," *MCM* 2:347.

19. "First Account of the Events of October 5 and 6," *MCM* 2:338.

20. "First Account of the Events of October 5 and 6," *MCM* 2:338.

21. Gottschalk and Maddox, *Through the October Days*, 356.

22. La Tour du Pin Gouvernet, *Journal d'une femme* 1:222. Pointed to this source by Auricchio, *The Marquis*, 202.

23. Gottschalk and Maddox, *Through the October Days*, 367.

24. Charavay, *Le général La Fayette*, 190.

25. Gottschalk and Maddox, *Through the October Days*, 375.

26. "First Account of the Events of October 5 and 6," *MCM* 2:341.

27. Morris, *Diary and Letters* 1:158.

28. "First Account of the Events of October 5 and 6," *MCM* 2:343–344.

29. William Short to John Jay, October 9, 1789, quoted in Gottschalk and Maddox, *Through the October Days*, 385.

30. Lafayette to [Simiane], October 6, 1789, *MCM* 411.

CHAPTER 15: THE ZENITH OF HIS INFLUENCE [1790]

1. Campan, *La vie privée de Marie Antoinette* 2:80.

2. Lafayette to Mounier, October 23, 1789, *MCM* 2:416.

3. "Instructions for M. de Boinville," *MCM* 2:430.

4. Campan, *La vie privée de Marie Antoinette* 2:75.

5. Maurois, *Adrienne*, 181.

6. Morris, *Diary and Letters* 2:181.

7. Taillemite, *La Fayette*, 220.

8. Lafayette to [Simiane], Undated, *MCM* 2:414.

9. Mirabeau to Lafayette, quoted in Maurois, *Adrienne*, 180.

10. Maurois, *Adrienne*, 181.

11. Morris to Washington, January 22, 1790, *PGW-PS* 5:37–40.

12. Morris, *Diary and Letters* 1:215.

13. Morris, *Diary and Letters* 1:215.

14. Lafayette to Washington, March 17, 1790, *PGW-PS* 5:241–243.

15. Morris, *Diary and Letters* 1:200.

16. "During the Month of March Until July 14, 1789," *MCM* 2:376–377.

17. *L'Ami du peuple*, August 6, 1790, quoted in Popkin, *Revolutionary News*, 146–147. Pointed to this source by Auricchio, *The Marquis*, 213–214.

18. Popkin, *Revolutionary News*, 147–148. See also Tulard, Fayard, and Fierro, *Histoire et Dictionnaire*, 970.

19. "Declaration of the Rights of Man and of the Citizen," Tulard, Fayard, and Fierro, *Histoire et Dictionnaire*, 771.

20. "Declaration of the Rights of Man and of the Citizen," Tulard, Fayard, and Fierro, *Histoire et Dictionnaire*, 771.

21. Auricchio, *The Marquis*, 214.

22. *Le Courrier de Versailles à Paris et de Paris à Versailles*, October 12, 1789. All issues digitized by Bibliothèque nationale de France and available at retronews.fr /titre-de-presse/courrier-de-versailles-paris-et-de-paris-versailles. See also Auricchio, *The Marquis*, 212.

23. Lafayette to Washington, January 12, 1790, *PGW-PS* 4:567.

24. Lafayette to Washington, March 17, 1790, *PGW-PS* 5:243.

25. "During the Month of March Until July 14, 1789," *MCM* 2:408.

26. *Archives parlementaires* 16:117–118.

27. Marie Antoinette to comte de Mercy, July 12, 1790, quoted in Auricchio, *The Marquis*, 229.

28. "Federation of July 1790," *MCM* 3:4–5.

29. "Federation of July 1790," *MCM* 3:6.

30. "Federation of July 1790," *MCM* 3:6.

31. Taillemite, *La Fayette*, 233.

32. Taillemite, *La Fayette*, 235.

33. Taillemite, *La Fayette*, 238.

34. Tulard, Fayard, and Fierro, *Histoire et Dictionnaire*, 1109.

35. Charavay, *Le général La Fayette*, 234.

36. Charavay, *Le général La Fayette*, 234.

37. Auricchio, *The Marquis*, 219. I am following Auricchio's conclusion these descriptions are satirical, not literal.

38. Charavay, *Le général La Fayette*, 235.

39. Charavay, *Le général La Fayette*, 235.

40. William Short to Morris, July 27, 1790, quoted in Morris, *Diary of the French Revolution* 1:565.

41. Mirabeau to King Louis XVI, July 17, 1790, quoted in Charavay, *Le général La Fayette*, 236.

42. William Short to Morris, July 27, 1790, quoted in Morris, *Diary of the French Revolution* 1:565.

CHAPTER 16: AN OCEAN OF FACTIONS AND COMMOTIONS [1791]

1. Washington to Lafayette, August 11, 1790, *PGW-PS* 6:233.

2. Lafayette to M. de Bouillé, February 17, 1791, *MCM* 3:160.

3. Charavay, *Le général La Fayette*, 243–244.

4. Lafayette to M. de Bouillé, August 18, 1790, Bouillé, *Mémoires du Marquis de Bouillé*, 136.

5. Lafayette to Bouillé, September 3, 1790, Bouillé, *Mémoires du Marquis de Bouillé*, 164.

6. *L'Ami du peuple*, September 15, 1790, quoted in Charavay, *Le général La Fayette*, 245.

7. Charavay, *Le général La Fayette*, 246.

8. Charavay, *Le général La Fayette*, 252.

9. Lasteyrie, *Vie de Madame de Lafayette*, 218.

10. Lasteyrie, *Vie de Madame de Lafayette*, 218.

11. *L'Ami du peuple*, April 21, 1791, quoted in Maurois, *Adrienne*, 185.

12. *Journal de la Cour et de la Ville*, April 13, 1791, quoted in Maurois, *Adrienne*, 186.

13. Lasteyrie, *Vie de Madame de Lafayette*, 218–219.

14. Lafayette to Washington, March 7, 1791, *MCM* 3:167.

15. Morris, *Diary and Letters* 1:390.

16. Mirabeau to La Marck, September 10, 1790, quoted in Charavay, *Le général La Fayette*, 247.

17. *Journal de la Cour et de la Ville*, April 25, 1791, quoted in Maurois, *Adrienne*, 189.

18. Lasteyrie, *Vie de Madame de Lafayette*, 223.

19. *Le Moniteur Universel*, April 21, 1791, quoted in Maurois, *Adrienne*, 189.

20. Lasteyrie, *Vie de Madame de Lafayette*, 223.

21. Washington to Lafayette, July 28, 1791, *PGW-PS* 8:377.

22. The best English language account of the Flight to Varennes is Tackett, *When the King Took Flight*. Tackett provides most of the guidance for this section.

23. Tourzel, *Mémoires*, 312.

24. "The Departure and Arrest of the King, June 21, 1791," *MCM* 3:79.

25. "The Departure and Arrest of the King, June 21, 1791," *MCM* 3:81.

26. "Déclaration du Roi adressée à tous les Français, à sa sortie de Paris," digitized by BnF and available at gallica.bnf.fr/ark:/12148/bpt6k9751 5443.texte Image#.

27. "Déclaration du Roi."

28. *Révolutions de Paris, dédiées à la Nation*, June 18–25, 1791, all issues digitized by BnF and available at retronews.fr/titre-de-presse/revolutions-de-paris -dediees-la-nation.

29. "The Departure and Arrest of the King, June 21, 1791," *MCM* 3:85.

30. Maurois, *Adrienne*, 191–192.

31. "The Departure and Arrest of the King, June 21, 1791," *MCM* 3:91–92.

32. Lafayette to Washington, June 6, 1791, *MCM* 3:179.

33. Ferrières, *Correspondance inédite*, 395.

34. "Champ de Mars: Petitions of the Cordelier and Jacobin Clubs," digitized by World History Commons, and available at worldhistorycommons.org /champ-de-mars-petitions-cordelier-and-jacobin-clubs.

35. "Proclamation of Martial Law on the Champ de Mars, July 17, 1791," *MCM* 3:106.

36. Lasteyrie, *Vie de Madame de Lafayette*, 225.

37. Lasteyrie, *Vie de Madame de Lafayette*, 225–226.

38. Lasteyrie, *Vie de Madame de Lafayette*, 226.

39. Tackett, *When the King Took Flight*, 150.

40. *Révolutions de Paris, dédiées à la Nation*, July 16–23, 1791.

41. "Proclamation of Martial Law on the Champ de Mars, July 17, 1791," *MCM* 3:106.

CHAPTER 17: HIS CIRCLE IS COMPLETED [1791–1792]

1. Maurois, *Adrienne*, 196.

2. "Revisions of the Constitution," *MCM* 3:120.

3. "Revisions of the Constitution," *MCM* 3:121.

4. "Revisions of the Constitution," *MCM* 3:123.

5. Maurois, *Adrienne*, 196.

6. Lafayette to [Simiane], October 20, 1791, *MCM* 3:188.

7. Lafayette to Washington, January 22, 1792, *MCM* 3:418.

8. Pauline de Montagu to duc d'Ayen, undated, quoted in Maurois, *Adrienne*, 198.

9. Lafayette to [Simiane], October 20, 1791, *MCM* 3:189.

10. Lafayette to Washington, January 22, 1792, *MCM* 3:418.

11. Lafayette to [Simiane], July 24 or 25, 1789, *MCM* 2:321–322.

12. Adrienne to M. Morizot, December 1791, quoted in Maurois, *Adrienne*, 199.

13. Adrienne to M. Morizot, December 1791, quoted in Maurois, *Adrienne*, 199.

14. Bouillé, *Mémoires*, 268–269.

15. Bouillé, *Mémoires*, 268.

16. Lafayette to Washington, June 6, 1791, *MCM* 3:179.

17. Morris to Washington, December 27–31, 1791, *PGW-PS* 9:333–338.

18. Lafayette to Washington, March 15, 1792, *PGW-PS* 10:115.

19. Lafayette to Adrienne, April 18, 1792, *MCM* 3:428.

20. Lafayette to Adrienne, April 18, 1792, *MCM* 3:428.

21. Lafayette to Adrienne, April 18, 1792, *MCM* 3:430.

22. Lafayette to Louis XVI, June 16, 1792, *MCM* 3:439.

23. Lafayette to the Legislative Assembly, June 16, 1792, *MCM* 3:325–331.

24. Charavay, *Le général La Fayette*, 304–305.

25. Charavay, *Le général La Fayette*, 304.

26. Charavay, *Le général La Fayette*, 304.

27. Maurois, *Adrienne*, 204.

28. Tulard, Fayard, and Fierro, *Histoire et Dictionnaire*, 95–96.

29. "War and Proscription," *MCM* 3:335.

30. Morris, *Diary of the French Revolution* 2:257.

31. "War and Proscription," *MCM* 3:345.

32. "War and Proscription," *MCM* 3:346–347.

33. Morris to Jefferson, August 1, 1792, *PTJ-OS* 24:274.

34. Tulard, Fayard, and Fierro, *Histoire et Dictionnaire*, 606.

35. Charavay, *Le général La Fayette*, 304.

36. Charavay, *Le général La Fayette*, 329.

37. Morris to Jefferson, August 22, 1792, *PTJ-OS* 24:313.

SECOND INTERLUDE: THE PRISONERS OF OLMÜTZ [1792–1797]

1. Lafayette to Adrienne, August 21, 1792, *MCM* 3:467.

2. Lafayette to William Short, August 28, 1792, quoted in Spalding, *Prisoner of State*, 32. Spalding wrote the definitive work on Lafayette's five years in prison. This chapter is largely guided by his exhaustive and authoritative research.

3. Morris, *Diary of the French Revolution* 2:558–559.

4. Washington to Jefferson, March 13, 1793, *PTJ-OS* 25:382.

5. Metternich to Teschen, August 22, 1792, quoted in Spalding, *Prisoner of State*, 5.

6. Lafayette to Hénin, August 27, 1792, *MCM* 3:480.

7. "War and Proscription," *MCM* 3:413.

8. Teschen to Lafayette, September 8, 1792, quoted in Spalding, *Prisoner of State*, 17.

9. Lafayette to Hénin, September 16, 1792, *MCM* 4:219.

10. Spalding, *Prisoner of State*, 3.

11. Spalding, *Prisoner of State*, 3–4.

12. Lafayette to Hénin, March 15, 1793, quoted in Sparks, ed., *Life of Gouverneur Morris* 1:406–407.

13. Lafayette to Hénin, March 15, 1793, quoted in Sparks, *Life of Gouverneur Morris* 1:407.

14. Lafayette to M. d'Archenoltz, March 27, 1793, *MCM* 3:229.

15. Lafayette to Hénin, March 15, 1793, quoted in Sparks, *Life of Gouverneur Morris* 1:408.

16. Edmund Burke, "Debate on Fitzpatrick's Motion, March 17, 1794," quoted in Spalding, *Prisoner of State*, 40.

17. Lafayette to Hénin, March 13, 1793, *MCM* 4:222.

18. Lafayette to Hénin, June 22, 1793, *MCM* 4:233.

19. Lafayette to Hénin, March 13, 1793, *MCM* 4:223–224.

20. Lafayette to Hénin, January 27, 1794, *MCM* 4:259.

21. Spalding, *Prisoner of State*, 28.

22. Lafayette to Hénin, January 27, 1794, *MCM* 4:260.

23. Maurois, *Adrienne*, 219.

24. Adrienne to Brissot, September 12, 1792, *MCM* 3:481–483.

25. Washington to Adrienne, January 31, 1793, *PGW-PS* 12:75–76.

26. Morris to Washington, July 25, 1794, *PGW-PS* 16:433–435.

27. Maurois, *Adrienne*, 253.

28. Maurois, *Adrienne*, 253.

29. Maurois, *Adrienne*, 254–255.

30. "Orders on State Prisoners," August, 8, 1793, quoted in Spalding, *Prisoner of State*, 73.

31. "Letter Written by Latour-Maubourg Written at Olmütz," quoted in Cloquet, *Souvenirs*, 77.

32. "Statutes At Large: 3rd Congress," digitized by the Library of Congress and available at loc.gov/law/help/statutes-at-large/3rd-congress.php.

33. For details of the incident, see editorial notes for Lafayette to Bollmann, October 10, 1794, *MCM* 4:267–270. See also Spalding, *Prisoner of State*, 106–107.

34. Spalding, *Prisoner of State*, 114.

35. Adrienne to Washington, April 18, 1795, *PGW-PS* 18:51–54.

36. Lasteyrie, *Vie de Madame de Lafayette*, 353.

37. Spalding, *Prisoner of State*, 143.

38. Lasteyrie, *Vie de Madame de Lafayette*, 354.

39. Lasteyrie, *Vie de Madame de Lafayette*, 360.

40. Adrienne to Thomas Pinckney, February 10, 1796, quoted in Spalding, *Prisoner of State*, 147.

41. Adrienne to Masson and Romeuf, November 30, 1795, quoted in Spalding, *Prisoner of State*, 147.

42. Lasteyrie, *Vie de Madame de Lafayette*, 360–361.

43. Levasseur, *Lafayette in America* 1:154.

44. Levasseur, *Lafayette in America* 1:154.

45. Adrienne to Hénin, September 15, 1796, quoted in Spalding, *Prisoner of State*, 148.

46. Emperor Francis I to Chancellor Thugot, October 25, 1795, quoted in Spalding, *Prisoner of State*, 149.

47. Adrienne to M. de Ferrais, January 1796, quoted in Lasteyrie, *Vie de Madame de Lafayette*, 360.

48. Spalding, *Prisoner of State*, 150.

49. Washington to Pinckney, May 22, 1796, *George Washington Papers*, Series 2, Letterbooks 1754 to 1799: Letterbook 19, digitized by the Library of Congress and available at loc.gov/item/mgw2.019/.

50. Washington to Emperor Francis I, May 15, 1799, *George Washington Papers*, Series 2, Letterbooks 1754–1799: Letterbook 24, digitized by the Library of Congress and available at loc.gov/item/mgw2.019/. loc.gov/resource/mgw2.024/.

51. King George III to William Pitt, December 17, 1796, quoted in Spalding, *Prisoner of State*, 183.

52. Adrienne to Hénin, July 26, 1796, *MCM* 4:291–292.

53. Carlyle, *French Revolution: A History* 3:372.

54. Lafayette to Hénin, October 24, 1796, quoted in Spalding, *Prisoner of State*, 193.

55. Lazare Carnot to Gen. Henri Clarke, May 5, 1797, quoted in Spalding, *Prisoner of State*, 195–196.

56. Thugot to Buol, September 13, 1797, quoted in Spalding, *Prisoner of State*, 220.

57. Lafayette to Jefferson, April 19, 1799, *PTJ-OS* 31:94–97.

CHAPTER 18: LA GRANGE [1797–1814]

1. Lafayette to Citizen General Bonaparte, October 6, 1797, *MCM* 4:369.

2. Lafayette to Washington, August 20, 1798, *PGW-RS* 2:539–545.

3. Washington to Lafayette, December 25, 1798, *PGW-RS* 3:280–285.

4. Hamilton to Lafayette, January 6, 1799, *PAH* 22:404–405.

5. Lafayette to Washington, May 19, 1799, *PGW-RS* 4:54–59.

6. William Murray to Washington, August 17, 1799, *PGW-RS* 4:258–263.

7. "My Relationship with the First Consul," *MCM* 5:154.

8. "My Relationship with the First Consul," *MCM* 5:154.

9. Maurois, *Adrienne*, 380.

10. Lafayette to Adrienne, October 30, 1799, *MCM* 5:145.

11. "My Relationship with the First Consul," *MCM* 5:167.

12. "My Relationship with the First Consul," *MCM* 5:173.

13. "My Relationship with the First Consul," *MCM* 5:194.

14. "My Relationship with the First Consul," *MCM* 5:195.

15. "My Relationship with the First Consul," *MCM* 5:180.

16. Lafayette to Adrienne, April 3, 1802, quoted in Maurois, *Adrienne*, 416.

17. "My Relationship with the First Consul," *MCM* 5:198–199.

18. "My Relationship with the First Consul," *MCM* 5:200.
19. Jefferson to Lafayette, November 4, 1803, *PTJ-OS* 41:665–666.
20. Jefferson to Lafayette, March 30, 1804, *PTJ-OS* 43:140–141.
21. Lafayette to Jefferson, October 8, 1804, *MCM* 5:260.
22. Lafayette to Jefferson, October 8, 1804, *MCM* 5:262.
23. Maurois, *Adrienne*, 450.
24. Maurois, *Adrienne*, 456.
25. Maurois, *Adrienne*, 443.
26. Lafayette to Jefferson, April 8, 1808, Chinard, *Letters of Lafayette and Jefferson*, 272.
27. Maurois, *Adrienne*, 464.
28. "Collection of Some Items and Memories Relating to the Years 1814–1815," Introduction, *MCM* 5:302. (Hereafter, "Memories of 1814–1815.")
29. "Memories of 1814–1815," Introduction, *MCM* 5:303.
30. Lafayette to Jefferson, July 4, 1812, Chinard, *Letters of Lafayette and Jefferson*, 336.
31. "Memories of 1814–1815," Introduction, *MCM* 5:302.
32. "Memories of 1814–1815," Introduction, *MCM* 5:303.

CHAPTER 19: RESTORATION [1814–1815]

1. "Memories of 1814–1815," Chapter 3, *MCM* 5:480–481.
2. "Memories of 1814–1815," Introduction, *MCM* 5:295.
3. "Memories of 1814–1815," Introduction, *MCM* 5:306.
4. "Memories of 1814–1815," Introduction, *MCM* 5:301.
5. Lafayette to Joseph Masclet, April 23, 1814, quoted in Neely, *Lafayette and the Liberal Ideal*, 11–12.
6. Lafayette to Jefferson, August 14, 1814, *MCM* 5:490.
7. "Memories of 1814–1815," Introduction, *MCM* 35:308–309.
8. "Memories of 1814–1815," Introduction, *MCM* 5:311.
9. "Memories of 1814–1815," Introduction, *MCM* 5:310.
10. Lafayette to William Crawford, May 26, 1814, quoted in Neely, *Lafayette and the Liberal Ideal*, 17.
11. "Constitutional Charter of 1814," reprinted in Anderson, *Constitutions and Other Select Documents*, 456.
12. Lafayette to Jefferson, August 14, 1814, *MCM* 5:488.
13. "Memories of 1814–1815," Introduction, *MCM* 5:313.
14. "Memories of 1814–1815," Introduction, *MCM* 5:353.
15. "Memories of 1814–1815," Introduction, *MCM* 5:325.
16. "Memories of 1814–1815," Introduction, *MCM* 5:350–351.
17. "Memories of 1814–1815," Introduction, *MCM* 5:325.
18. "Memories of 1814–1815," Introduction, *MCM* 5:356.
19. Lafayette to Benjamin Constant, April 9, 1815, *MCM* 5:407–408.
20. "Memories of 1814–1815," Chapter 2, *MCM* 5:418.
21. Lafayette to Mme. d'Hénin, May 15, 1818, quotes in Neely, *Lafayette and the Liberal Ideal*, 25.

22. "Memories of 1814–1815," Chapter 3, *MCM* 5:444.

23. Lafayette to "Family," June 8, 1815, *MCM* 5:505.

24. Lafayette to "Family," June 8, 1815, quoted in Neely, *Lafayette and the Liberal Ideal*, 27.

25. Lafayette to "Family," June 12, 1815, quoted in Neely, *Lafayette and the Liberal Ideal*, 27–28.

26. "Memories of 1814–1815," Chapter 3, *MCM* 5:452.

27. "Memories of 1814–1815," Chapter 3, *MCM* 5:452.

28. "Memories of 1814–1815," Chapter 3, *MCM* 5:453–454.

29. "Memories of 1814–1815," Chapter 3, *MCM* 5:455.

30. "Memories of 1814–1815," Chapter 3, *MCM* 5:455.

31. Morgan, *France* 2:311.

32. "Memories of 1814–1815," Chapter 3, *MCM* 5:462–463.

33. Benjamin Constant, *Journaux intimes*, June 22, 1815, quoted in Neely, *Lafayette and the Liberal Ideal*, 30.

34. "Memories of 1814–1815," Chapter 3, *MCM* 5:463.

35. "Memories of 1814–1815," Chapter 3, *MCM* 5:464.

36. "Memories of 1814–1815," Chapter 3, *MCM* 5:471–472.

37. "Memories of 1814–1815," Chapter 3, *MCM* 5:472–473.

38. Lafayette to Dupont de Nemours, October 30, 1815, quoted in Neely, *Lafayette and the Liberal Ideal*, 35.

39. "Memories of 1814–1815," Chapter 3, *MCM* 5:477.

40. "Memories of 1814–1815," Chapter 3, *MCM* 5:478.

CHAPTER 20: THE CERTIFICATE OF ANTIQUITY [1815–1820]

1. Duvergier de Hauranne, ed., *Histoire du gouvernement parlementaire en France* 3:309.

2. Morgan, *France* 2:301–303.

3. Neely, *Lafayette and the Liberal Ideal*, 60. Neely's work is the definitive account of Lafayette's political activities during this period and served as the principal guidebook for the following chapters.

4. Neely, *Lafayette and the Liberal Ideal*, 61.

5. Lafayette to Sir Charles Morgan, November 9, 1817, quoted in Neely, *Lafayette and the Liberal Ideal*, 66.

6. "Commentary on *History of the French Revolution* by M. Thiers," *MCM* 4:214. Pointed to this quote by Kramer, *Lafayette in Two Worlds*, 84.

7. Georges Washington Lafayette to Bonne Chevant, October 4, 1818, quoted in Neely, *Lafayette and the Liberal Ideal*, 78.

8. Rémusat, *Mémoires*, 61.

9. Rémusat, *Mémoires*, 60–61.

10. Rémusat, *Mémoires*, 61.

11. Morgan, *Passages from my Autobiography*, 102.

12. Augustin Thierry, *Notice biographique sur le Général La Fayette*, quoted in Neely, *Lafayette and the Liberal Ideal*, 79. Neely was the first to identify Thierry as the author.

13. Louis XVIII to Decazes, quote in Neely, *Lafayette and the Liberal Ideal*, 81.

14. Georges Washington Lafayette to Bonne Chevant, October 4, 1818, quoted in Neely, *Lafayette and the Liberal Ideal*, 83.

15. Georges Washington Lafayette to Charles Goyet, October 22, 1818, quoted in Neely, *Lafayette and the Liberal Ideal*, 85.

16. Lafayette to M. Marchand, October 17, 1818, quoted in Neely, *Lafayette and the Liberal Ideal*, 87.

17. Published in *Propagateur*, 1819, quoted in Neely, *Lafayette and the Liberal Ideal*, 88.

18. Richelieu to Decazes, quoted in Neely, *Lafayette and the Liberal Ideal*, 90.

19. Broglie, *Souvenirs* 2:90.

20. Morgan, *Passages from my Autobiography*, 244–245.

21. Benjamin Constant, "Aux Redacteurs de la Renommée," *La Renommée*, July 5, 1819, quoted in Kramer, *Lafayette in Two Worlds*, 69.

22. Lafayette to M. Bellart, April 27, 1819, *MCM* 6:38.

23. Lafayette to Goyet, May 14, 1819, quoted in Neely, *Lafayette and the Liberal Ideal*, 108.

24. "On the Budget of the Minister of War," June 4, 1819, *MCM* 6:50.

25. "On the Budget of the Minister of War," June 4, 1819, *MCM* 6:50.

26. Quoted in Neely, *Lafayette and the Liberal Ideal*, 129.

27. "On Press Censorship," March 23, 1820, *MCM* 6:74.

28. "On the Draft Law on Elections," May 27, 1820, *MCM* 6:84–85.

CHAPTER 21: THE CHARCOAL BURNERS [1820–1824]

1. Lafayette to "Unknown," July 27, 1820, quoted in Neely, *Lafayette and the Liberal Ideal*, 151.

2. "On Public Education Expenses," *MCM* 6:42.

3. "On Secret Societies," *MCM* 6:133–142.

4. The definitive account of the French Carbonari is Spitzer, *Old Hatreds and Young Hopes*. Spitzer provides most of the details of the conspiracies and trials in this chapter.

5. Goyet to Constant, August 25, 1820, quoted in Neely, *Lafayette and the Liberal Ideal*, 155.

6. "Trial of M.M. Sauquaire-Souligné and Goyet," March 14, 1821, *MCM* 6:100.

7. "Trial of M.M. Sauquaire-Souligné and Goyet," March 14, 1821, *MCM* 6:102.

8. "On the Budget," *MCM* 6:123.

9. Frances Wright to Jeremy Bentham, quoted in Eckhardt, *Fanny Wright*, 52.

10. Lafayette to Wright, April 25, 1824, quoted in Neely, *Lafayette and the Liberal Ideal*, 190.

11. Wright to Lafayette, December 29, 1821, quoted in Eckhardt, *Fanny Wright*, 59.

12. Wright to Lafayette, December 29, 1821, quoted in Neely, *Lafayette and the Liberal Ideal*, 198.

13. Duvergier de Hauranne, ed., *Histoire* 7:79.

14. *Conspiracy Trial of Thouars and Saumur*, quoted in Spitzer, *Old Hatreds and Young Hopes*, 180.

15. Gigault, *Vie politique*, 36–37.

16. Pasquier, *Mémoires* 4:393.

17. Jacques Laffitte, quoted in Neely, *Lafayette and the Liberal Ideal*, 224.

18. Carrel, *Oeuvres politiques et littéraires* 3:169–170.

19. Duvergier de Hauranne, *Histoire* 6:653.

20. Georges Lafayette to Audry de Puyraveau, October 15, 1822, quoted in Neely, *Lafayette and the Liberal Ideal*, 225.

21. William Lee to Lafayette, April 20, 1823, quoted in Neely, *Lafayette and the Liberal Ideal*, 242.

22. Lafayette to William Lee, December 20, 1823, quoted in Neely, *Lafayette and the Liberal Ideal*, 247.

23. Lafayette to Charles Petit, March 12, 1824, quoted in Neely, *Lafayette and the Liberal Ideal*, 250.

24. James Monroe to Lafayette, February 24, 1824, quoted in Levasseur, *Lafayette in America* 1:10.

CHAPTER 22: THE NATION'S GUEST [1824–1825]

1. Levasseur, *Lafayette in America*. As the closest witness to Lafayette's tour, Auguste Levasseur provides many of the details and direct quotes in this chapter.

2. *New York Commercial Advertiser*, August 16, 1824, quoted in Brandon, *Lafayette, Guest of the Nation* 1:36. Brandon is another principal repository of contemporaneous anecdotes, speeches, and news reports concerning Lafayette's tour.

3. Levasseur, *Lafayette in America* 1:16.

4. Levasseur, *Lafayette in America* 2:23–24.

5. *Columbian Centinel*, August 28, 1824, quoted in Brandon, *Guest of the Nation* 1:111.

6. *Columbian Centinel*, August 28, 1824, quoted in Brandon, *Guest of the Nation* 1:117.

7. John Adams to Lafayette, August 22, 1824, Founders Online, National Archives, https://founders.archives.gov/documents/Adams/99-02-02-7912. Early access document.

8. Charles Francis Adams, August 29, 1824, quoted in Amanda M. Norton, "A Revolutionary Reunion: Lafayette and John Adams," *Massachusetts Historical Society*, www.masshist.org/beehiveblog/2017/08/a-revolutionary-reunion-lafayette-and-john-adams/.

9. "The Education and Medical Practice of Dr. James McCune Smith (1813–1865), First Black American to Hold a Medical Degree," *Journal of the National Medical Association* 95, no. 7 (July 2003): 603–614.

10. Lafayette to George Washington Parke Custis, quoted in William Jones, "Rekindling the Spark of Liberty: Lafayette's Visit to the United States," *The Schiller Institute*, November 2007, https://archive.schillerinstitute.com/educ/hist/lafayette.html.

11. *Troy Sentinel*, September 21, 1824, quoted in Brandon, *Guest of the Nation* 1:250.

12. Levasseur, *Lafayette in America* 1:121.

13. Levasseur, *Lafayette in America* 1:139.

14. *The United States Gazette*, September 30, 1824, quoted in Brandon, *Guest of the Nation* 2:62.

15. Levasseur, *Lafayette in America* 1:141–142.

16. Wright to Julia Garnett Pertz, November 12, 1824, manuscript online at Harvard University Library, https://iiif.lib.harvard.edu/manifests/view/drs:434673879$2i.

17. Levasseur, *Lafayette in America* 1:162.

18. Levasseur, *Lafayette in America* 1:162.

19. Levasseur, *Lafayette in America* 1:181.

20. Levasseur, *Lafayette in America* 1:182.

21. Levasseur, *Lafayette in America* 1:185.

22. Levasseur, *Lafayette in America* 1:203.

23. Levasseur, *Lafayette in America* 1:195

24. Levasseur, *Lafayette in America* 1:204.

25. Levasseur, *Lafayette in America* 1:206.

26. Levasseur, *Lafayette in America* 1:208.

27. Levasseur, *Lafayette in America* 1:222.

28. Speech by Henry Clay printed in *Niles Register*, December 18, 1824, and reprinted in Brandon, *Guest of the Nation* 3:168–169.

29. Levasseur, *Lafayette in America* 2:25.

30. Wright to Julia Garnett Pertz, October 30, 1824, quoted in Kramer, *Lafayette in Two Worlds*, 162–163.

31. Kapp, *Life of John Kalb*, 250.

32. Levasseur, *Lafayette in America* 2:71.

33. Levasseur, *Lafayette in America* 2:75.

34. Levasseur, *Lafayette in America* 2:76.

35. Levasseur, *Lafayette in America* 2:80.

36. Levasseur, *Lafayette in America* 2:82.

37. *Courier de la Louisiane*, April 13, 1825, quoted in Kramer, *Lafayette in Two Worlds*, 218.

38. Levasseur, *Lafayette in America* 2:123.

39. Levasseur, *Lafayette in America* 2:148.

40. Levasseur, *Lafayette in America* 2:136.

41. Levasseur, *Lafayette in America* 2:153.

42. Levasseur, *Lafayette in America* 2:161.

43. *Kentucky Reporter*, May 23, 1825, quoted in Kramer, *Lafayette in Two Worlds*, 207.

44. Levasseur, *Lafayette in America* 2:188.

45. Whitman, *Lafayette in Brooklyn*, 4.

46. Levasseur, *Lafayette in America* 2:237.

47. Levasseur, *Lafayette in America* 2:246.

48. Levasseur, *Lafayette in America* 2:249–250.

49. Lafayette to General Bolívar, September 1, 1825, *MCM* 6:212–213.

50. Bolívar to Lafayette, undated, *MCM* 6:219–221.

CHAPTER 23: THE JULY REVOLUTION [1826–1830]

1. Levasseur, *Lafayette in America* 2:267–268.
2. Charles X, quoted in Bernier, *Lafayette*, 275.
3. Hugo, *Choses vues*, 76.
4. Castries, *Monsieur Thiers*, 57.
5. "Speech of General Lafayette to his Fellow Citizens of Le Puy," *MCM* 6:327.
6. "Speech to the Deputation of Lyon," *MCM* 6:333.
7. Guernon-Ranville, *Journal d'un ministre*, 35–36.
8. *Moniteur*, March 19, 1830. All issues of the *Moniteur*, 1789–1901, digitized by BnF and available at retronews.fr/titre-de-presse/gazette-nationale-ou-le-moniteur-universel.
9. Lafayette to "Unknown," May 4, 1830, *MCM* 6:361.
10. *Journal des débats*, May 17, 1830. All issues of *Journal des débats politiques et littéraires* 1814–1944, digitized by BnF and available at https://gallica.bnf.fr/ark:/12148/cb39294634r/date.
11. *Moniteur*, June 14, 1830.
12. Jules Polignac, "Projet de note au Roi," April 14, 1830, quoted in Pinkney, *The French Revolution of 1830*, 62.
13. Guizot, *Mémoires* 2:13.
14. *Le Temps*, July 25, 1830. All issues of *Le Temps*, 1829–1842, digitized by BnF and available at retronews.fr/titre-de-presse/temps-1829-1842.
15. Lafayette to "Unknown," July 26, 1830, *MCM* 6:380.
16. *Moniteur*, July 26, 1830.
17. Lafayette to "Unknown," July 28, 1830, *MCM* 6:383.
18. Rémusat, *Mémoires*, 74.
19. Duvergier de Hauranne, ed., *Histoire* 10:536–537.
20. Baron d'Haussez, *Mémoires*, vol. 2 (Paris: Michel Lévy Frères, 1897), 250–251.
21. "Bulletin de Paris," July 26, 1830, quoted in Pinkney, 93.
22. "Deposition d'Arago," October 30, 1830, quoted in Pinkney, 90.
23. Rémusat, *Mémoires*, quoted in Pinkney, 98.
24. Marquis de Semonville, "Mémoire sur la Révolution de 1830," *Revue de Paris*, No. 5, September 1, 1894, all issues of *Revue de Paris* digitized by BnF and available at gallica.bnf.fr/ark:/12148/cb34404247s/date.
25. Bernard Sarrans, *Memoirs of General Lafayette and of the French Revolution of 1830*, vol. 1 (London: Richard Bentley, 1832), 283.
26. Editorial explanation, Lafayette to "Unknown," July 29, 1830, *MCM* 6:384.
27. Sarrans, *Memoirs of General Lafayette* 1:290.
28. "Meeting of Thursday July 29 at Chez Lafitte," *MCM* 6:388.
29. Sarrans, *Memoirs of General Lafayette* 1:304.
30. Sarrans, *Memoirs of General Lafayette* 1:306.
31. "Order of the Day for July 29, 1830," *MCM* 6:391.
32. Sarrans, *Memoirs of General Lafayette* 1:309.
33. Sarrans, *Memoirs of General Lafayette* 1:317.

34. Lafayette to Comte de Survilliers (Joseph Bonaparte), November 26, 1830, *MCM* 6:470.

35. Lafayette to Comte de Survilliers (Joseph Bonaparte), November 26, 1830, *MCM* 6:469.

36. Sarrans, *Memoirs of General Lafayette* 1:331.

37. Duvergier de Hauranne, *Histoire* 10:590.

38. Rémusat, *Mémoires*, 94.

39. Chateaubriand, *Mémoires d'outre-tombe* 5:345–346.

40. "On the Reception of July 31 at the Hôtel de Ville," *MCM* 6:411.

41. Sarrans, *Memoirs of General Lafayette* 1:363.

42. Sarrans, *Memoirs of General Lafayette* 1:363–364.

CHAPTER 24: A TOWER AMID THE WATERS [1830–1834]

1. Dumas, *Mes Mémoires* 6:168.

2. Bernier, *Lafayette*, 287.

3. Stendhal, *Souvenirs d'égotism*, 51.

4. Louis-Philippe to Lafayette, August 29, 1830, *MCM* 6:431.

5. Charles de Rémusat, quoted in Kramer, *Lafayette in Two Worlds*, 245.

6. Rémusat, quoted in Kramer, *Lafayette in Two Worlds*, 245.

7. Sarrans, *Memoirs of General Lafayette* 2:2.

8. "On Slave Trafficking and the Rights of Men of Color," *MCM* 6:439.

9. "On Slave Trafficking and the Rights of Men of Color," *MCM* 6:440.

10. "Order of the Day for December 19, 1830," *MCM* 6:490–491.

11. "Order of the Day for December 19, 1830," *MCM* 6:491.

12. "Order of the Day for December 19, 1830," *MCM* 6:491.

13. General Philippe-Paul de Ségur, *Histoire et Mémoires*, quoted in Kramer, *Lafayette in Two Worlds*, 245.

14. Charles Dupin, quoted in Sarrans, *Memoirs of General Lafayette* 2:127.

15. Lafayette to Louis-Philippe, December 25, 1825, *MCM* 6:499.

16. "Proclamation of the King," December 26, 1830, *MCM* 6:503.

17. "Explanation Given to the Chamber of Deputies," December 27, 1830, *MCM* 6:504–505.

18. "Explanation Given to the Chamber of Deputies," December 27, 1830, *MCM* 6:505.

19. "Explanation Given to the Chamber of Deputies," December 27, 1830, *MCM* 6:505.

20. Sarrans, *Memoirs of General Lafayette* 1:389–390.

21. Mike Duncan, *Revolutions Podcast*, Episode 6.8e, "The June Rebellion."

22. "Speech in the Session of February 20, 1831," *MCM* 6:537.

23. Sarrans, *Memoirs of General Lafayette* 2:221.

24. Bernier, *Lafayette*, 294.

25. Stendhal, *Souvenirs d'égotism*, 52.

26. Stendhal, *Souvenirs d'égotism*, 52.

27. Morse, *Letters and Journals*, 1:316. Pointed to this anecdote by McCullough, *Greater Journey*.

28. Willard, *Journals and Letters*, 39. See also McCullough, *Greater Journey*, 29.

29. Cristina Belgiojoso, "Souvenirs," *Le National*, October 11, 1850, quoted in Kramer, *Lafayette in Two Worlds*, 178. Kramer highlighted the importance of Belgiojoso in Lafayette's twilight years.

30. Cristina Belgiojoso, "Souvenirs," *Le National*, October 11, 1850, quoted in Kramer, *Lafayette in Two Worlds*, 177.

31. Lafayette to M. Madier de Montjou, June 13, 1832, *MCM* 6:673.

32. Lafayette, La Grange, July 12, 1832, *MCM* 6:682.

33. Lafayette, La Grange, July 12, 1832, *MCM* 6:682.

34. Lafayette, La Grange, July 12, 1832, *MCM* 6:682.

35. Lafayette, La Grange, July 12, 1832, *MCM* 6:682–683.

36. Lafayette, La Grange, July 12, 1832, *MCM* 6:683.

37. Lafayette, La Grange, July 12, 1832, *MCM* 6:683.

38. Lafayette, La Grange, July 12, 1832, *MCM* 6:683.

39. Lafayette, La Grange, July 12, 1832, *MCM* 6:684.

40. Lafayette, La Grange, July 12, 1832, *MCM* 6:684–685.

41. Cloquet, *Souvenirs*, 290.

42. Lafayette to A. M. Murray, May 1, 1835, *MCM* 6:763.

43. Lafayette to A. M. Murray, May 1, 1835, *MCM* 6:766.

44. "Death Notice," *MCM* 6:767.

45. Chateaubriand, *Mémoires d'outre-tombe* 6:386.

46. Willis, *Pencillings by the Way*, 346.

47. McCullough, *Greater Journey*, 129.

48. J. Q. Adams, *Eulogy, on Lafayette*, 27–28.

49. J. Q. Adams, *Eulogy, on Lafayette*, 28.

50. "Death of Lafayette," *Examiner*, May 25, 1834, printed in Mill, *Collected Works* 23:329.

51. Comte de Mirabeau, *Admirateurs & Opposants*, Exhibit, Musée de Château de Chavaniac-Lafayette.

52. Jean-Paul Marat, *Admirateurs & Opposants*, Exhibit, Musée de Château de Chavaniac-Lafayette.

53. Spalding, *Prisoner of State*, 4.

54. Marquis de Bouillé, *Admirateurs & Opposants*, Exhibit, Musée de Château de Chavaniac-Lafayette.

55. Napoleon Bonaparte, *Admirateurs & Opposants*, Exhibit, Musée de Château de Chavaniac-Lafayette.

56. Chateaubriand, *Mémoires d'outre-tombe* 6:385.

57. Cristina Belgiojoso, "Souvenirs," *Le National*, October 11, 1850, quoted in Kramer, *Lafayette in Two Worlds*, 182.

58. Sumner, *Lafayette*, 1.

59. Morse, *Letters and Journals*, 1:424–425.

BIBLIOGRAPHIC NOTE

THE ALPHA AND OMEGA FOR ANYONE STUDYING LAFAYETTE IS twentieth-century American historian Louis R. Gottschalk. Gottschalk turned his attention to Lafayette in the 1930s and dedicated his life to documenting every scrap of paper related to Lafayette and using them to write a massive multivolume biography. Gottschalk's first book, *Lafayette Comes to America*, was published in 1935 and covers Lafayette's birth through his departure for America aboard *La Victoire*. Subsequent volumes were published at intervals over the next several years: *Lafayette Joins the American Army* (1937), covering Lafayette's first tour of duty in the Continental Army; *Lady-in-Waiting: The Romance of Lafayette and Aglaé de Hunolstein* (1939), which explores the often ambiguous details of their relationship; and *Lafayette and the Close of the American Revolution* (1942), covering Lafayette's activities through the victory at Yorktown in 1781.

In the 1950s, Margaret Maddox took over editorial direction of Gottschalk's project and was the principal author for the final books of this series: *Lafayette Between the American and the French Revolution* (1965), which takes Lafayette through his election to the Estates-General; *Lafayette in the French Revolution: Through the October Days* (1969), which focuses entirely on the momentous six-month period between May and October 1789; and finally *Lafayette in the French Revolution: From the October Days Through the Federation* (1973), covering the aftermath of the Women's March on Versailles through the *Fête de la Fédération* in July 1790.

Unfortunately, the project ended unfinished after the deaths of Maddox and Gottschalk in the 1970s. They had produced more than three thousand pages, but still only documented Lafayette's life through age thirty-three. The abrupt end of the exquisitely detailed Gottschalk and Maddox biographies in the summer of 1790 reminds one of Edward Gibbon's remark in the *Decline and Fall of the Roman Empire*, when Ammianus Marcellinus's history cuts off in 378 CE: "It is not without the most sincere regret that I must now take leave of an accurate and faithful guide."

The spiritual successor of Gottschalk's project is the five-volume collection *Lafayette in the Age of the American Revolution* (*LAAR*), which collects papers, letters, and correspondence to, from, and about Lafayette. The first entry of the first volume is Lafayette's agreement with Silas Deane to join the Continental Army in December 1776. The final entry of the final volume is a letter from Lafayette to the French naval secretary dated December 29, 1785, recommending the French government purchase American resources like timber, tar, and hemp. The volumes were compiled between 1977 and 1983 under the direction of Stanley Idzerda at Cornell University. Idzerda was assisted by editors Roger E. Smith, Linda J. Pike, Mary Ann Quinn, Lloyd Kramer, Robert Rhodes Grout, Carol Godschall, and Leslie Wharton. *Lafayette in the Age of the American Revolution* is the working bible of primary sources for Lafayette's early life.

For papers covering the rest of Lafayette's long life, one must turn to the six-volume *Mémoires, correspondance et manuscrits du général Lafayette* (1837). After his death, Lafayette's family collected, organized, and published his letters and papers, and though it is referred to as Lafayette's "Memoirs," Lafayette never wrote a proper memoir, only occasionally and somewhat reluctantly drafting autobiographical essays. The six volumes are instead a collection of correspondence covering his entire life. Volume 1 compiles material from the days of the American Revolution; volume 2 covers the French Revolution, including his activities around the Assembly of Notables, the Estates-General, fall of the Bastille, his leadership of the National Guard, the Women's March on Versailles through to the *Fête de la Fédération* in July 1790; volume 3 documents his fall from grace: the Day of Daggers, the Flight to Varennes, the Massacre of the Champ de Mars through to his imprisonment in September 1792; volume 4 includes Lafayette's prison correspondence and later reflections and commentary of the course of the French Revolution; volume 5 covers his retirement in La Grange and ends with an autobiographical essay concerning his participation in the First Restoration and the Hundred Days; finally, volume 6 compiles Lafayette's political speeches and letters while serving in the Chamber of Deputies, including the Revolution of 1830 and its aftermath. The final entry of the sixth and final volume is the public notice his family published upon his death in May 1834.

As Lafayette's family and friends assembled these volumes, they often edited, deleted, or omitted unflattering letters and statements. In the case of the many illuminating but embarrassing letters to his longtime mistress

Madame de Simiane, the name of the recipient is routinely left blank. Contemporary scholars have done invaluable work reconstructing and identifying the omissions, deflections, and strategic edits. Despite these flaws, the collection remains the most comprehensive source of published letters and correspondence to and from Lafayette.

The physical papers these collections are built from are now spread throughout numerous libraries and archives. The largest physical repository of Lafayette's papers is the Arthur H. and Mary Marden Dean Lafayette Collection at Cornell University. The collection houses eleven thousand original manuscripts, documents, and letters, most of which were discovered in a sealed attic of the northwest tower at La Grange in the winter of 1955. Arthur Dean, an American diplomat and Cornell alumnus, arranged for the papers to be transferred to Cornell in the 1960s. The earliest piece in the collection is a land title dated to 1245; the most recent pieces are political memorabilia bearing Lafayette's likeness used in an election in 1874. The Dean Collection includes the correspondence and records between Adrienne and on-site managers of the Cayenne plantations, and records related to Lafayette's ownership of slaves, most of which are unpublished and remain only physical manuscripts. I was fortunate to spend two weeks at Cornell going through the Dean Papers in the fall of 2019, with many thanks to director Laurent Ferri and the librarians and archivists who offered helpful, kind, and illuminating guidance.

To fill in necessary details and information not found in the Lafayette family papers, one turns to the collected papers of his numerous correspondents, friends, and political allies. Beginning in the nineteenth century, governments and universities in both the United States and France undertook the task of editing and publishing archival materials for researchers to work from—making available letters, manuscripts, newspapers, petitions, essays, and proclamations as a part of ongoing national historical projects. The twenty-first century has seen the digitization of many of these collected volumes. The National Archives' Founders Online, for example, has digitized and published over 185,000 documents from the collected papers of George Washington, John Adams, Thomas Jefferson, Benjamin Franklin, Alexander Hamilton, John Jay, and James Madison—all of whom were Lafayette's personal friends and regular correspondents. In France, the Gallica digital library operated by the *Bibliothèque nationale de France* has scanned, digitized, and uploaded over seven million documents related to French history, including comprehensive bundles of journals, newspapers, letters, and parliamentary records. The sheer tonnage of primary source material now instantly available to researchers living anywhere in the world is truly incredible.

Existing in the shadowy frontier between primary and secondary sources are autobiographical memoirs written by those who, like Lafayette, participated in the tumultuous times of the American Revolution, the French Revolution, and the Revolution of 1830. Everyone who lived through this period seemed to consider it their sacred duty to write sprawling accounts of their lives—to document their own participation, justify their conduct, and settle old scores. The memoir that sheds light furthest back on Lafayette's life is *Mémoires, souvenirs et anecdotes* (1829), written by his childhood friend, the comte de Ségur. The memoir that sheds the most light on Lafayette's twilight years is *Mémoires de ma vie* (1874), written by his grandson-in-law Charles de Rémusat. These are just two of the many memoirs offering observations, anecdotes, and judgments of Lafayette, from lowly continental private Joseph Plumb Martin to great statesmen like Talleyrand, Guizot, and Chateaubriand. All these must be examined critically as they are generally self-serving, contradictory, and occasionally full of outright fabrications. But they are historically valuable and often make for entertaining reading.

After these first-person memoirs, we turn to third-person accounts written by those who knew Lafayette best. These include Auguste Levasseur's *Lafayette en Amérique, en 1824 et 1825, ou Journal d'un voyage aux États-Unis* (1829), documenting their tour of America and including many biographical sketches of Lafayette's military and political career. A few years later, Lafayette's aide-de-camp Bernard Sarrans published a biographical defense of Lafayette's conduct during the Revolution of 1830, *Lafayette et la révolution de 1830: histoire des choses et des hommes de juillet* (1832). Just after Lafayette's death, the family physician Jules Cloquet wrote *Souvenirs sur la vie privée du Général Lafayette* (1835), which published for the first time many family letters and personal details. Also of tremendous importance is Virginie's recollections of her mother, *Vie de Madame de Lafayette* (1869), written under her married name, Madame Lasteyrie. All of these accounts were written by friends, admirers, and relatives and cast their subjects in the most glowing light possible.

After the passing of the generation who knew him personally, Lafayette becomes the property of historians, academics, and biographers. Some wrote excessively flattering portraits, others were dismissively critical. There are too many biographies of Lafayette to list in full, but a few are worth noting. Before the arrival of Gottschalk and Maddox in the twentieth century, the most authoritative and balanced Lafayette biography was Charlemagne

Tower's *The Marquis de La Fayette in the American Revolution* (1895). But as is often the case for American biographers, Tower focused entirely on Lafayette's activities in the United States. The best French biography is Étienne Charavay's *Le général La Fayette, 1757–1834* (1898). Charavay was a professional archivist and, unlike many biographers before and since, wrote about Lafayette's entire life, not just his youthful exploits. He also included a previously unpublished autobiographical account written by Lafayette reflecting on his early life that has become the basis for all future accounts of Lafayette's childhood.

The work of Louis Gottschalk and Margaret Maddox naturally dominates the twentieth century (and all work on Lafayette since), but there are a couple of invaluable exceptions. André Maurois's *Adrienne: The Life of the Marquise de La Fayette* (1961) is not only the single best book written about Madame de Lafayette, but Maurois was among the first to examine the cache of papers found at La Grange in 1955—*Adrienne* often unfolds as long excerpts of previously unknown and unpublished family letters tied together with light narration. Also extremely valuable is Paul Pialoux's *Lafayette: Trois Révolutions pour la Liberté* (1989), which was published to coincide with the two hundredth anniversary of the French Revolution and which reproduces otherwise difficult to locate letters and manuscripts.

To begin my own study of Lafayette, I first turned to the most recent biographies available. Lloyd Kramer's *Lafayette in Two Worlds: Public Cultures and Personal Identities in an Age of Revolutions* (1996) is an excellent analysis of Lafayette's life and his often changing symbolic roles in the cultural milieu of his times. The first biography of Lafayette I ever read was Harlow Giles Unger's *Lafayette* (2003), which I used to begin the process of unpacking and analyzing the source material used to write an account of Lafayette's life. David Clary's *Adopted Son: Washington, Lafayette, and the Friendship that Saved the Revolution* (2007) and James R. Gaines's *For Liberty and Glory: Washington, Lafayette, and their Revolutions* (2007) were nearly simultaneous takes on the same theme of the relationship between Lafayette and Washington. Clary is particularly good on details of their time together in the Continental Army. Gaines excels on the conspiratorial intricacies of French support for the American rebellion. The most recent Lafayette biography is Laura Auricchio's excellent *The Marquis: Lafayette Reconsidered* (2014), which covers Lafayette's life in detail through his return to France after being released from Olmütz, with a wonderful eye for aspects of material culture and Lafayette's own attention to image, art, and symbolism.

A running theme of work on Lafayette is the propensity of his biographers to ignore the whole second half of his life. A few works of particular importance guided me through these under-studied years. The definitive account of Lafayette's years in prison is Paul Spalding's *Lafayette: Prisoner of State* (2010), which draws extensively from archival sources in France, Germany, Austria, Hungary, England, and the United States. Sylvia Neely's *Lafayette and the Liberal Ideal 1814–1824* (1991) is the definitive account of Lafayette's political life between the First Restoration and his departure back to America. Her work is the solid foundation upon which my own narrative of that decade is built. The best account of the French Carbonari and Lafayette's participation in the movement is Alan B. Spitzer's *Old Hatreds and Young Hopes* (1971). The fascinating life of Fanny Wright is covered in detail by Celia Eckhardt in *Fanny Wright: Rebel in America* (1984). Auguste Levasseur's *Lafayette in America* (1829) guided me through his great tour of the United States. Bernard Sarrans's *Memoirs of General Lafayette and of the French Revolution of 1830*, through Lafayette's political activities 1829–1832. The best English-language account of the Revolution of 1830 remains David Pinkney's *French Revolution of 1830* (1971).

My debt to all the other secondary sources and previous biographers listed in the bibliography is infinite. Without their efforts, my own work would not have been possible. I can only hope this book will now take a small place in the ever-unfolding historiography of the marquis de Lafayette and the Age of Revolution.

SELECT BIBLIOGRAPHY

Adams, Charles Francis, ed. *The Works of John Adams.* 10 vols. Boston: Little Brown & Company, 1851.

Adams, John. *The Adams Papers: Adams Family Correspondence.* 13 vols. Edited by Lyman H. Butterfield et al. Cambridge, MA: Harvard University Press, 1963–.

———. *The Adams Papers: Papers of John Adams.* 18 vols. Edited by Robert J. Taylor et al. Cambridge, MA: Harvard University Press, 1977–.

Adams, John Quincy. *Eulogy, on Lafayette: Delivered Before Both Houses of Congress, on the 31st of December, 1834.* New York: Craighead & Allen, 1835.

Anderson, Frank Maloy. *The Constitutions and Other Select Documents Illustrative of the History of France, 1789–1901.* Minneapolis: The H.W. Wilson Company, 1904.

Andress, David. *The French Revolution and the People.* London: Hambledon and London, 2004.

———. *Massacre at the Champ de Mars: Popular Dissent and Political Culture in the French Revolution.* Woodbridge, UK: Boydell Press for the Royal Historical Society, 2000.

———. *The Terror: The Merciless War for Freedom in Revolutionary France.* New York: Farrar, Straus and Giroux, 2005.

Archives parlementaires de 1787 à 1860. 102 vols. Edited by M. J. Mavidal et al. Paris: Dupont, 1867–.

Arendt, Hannah. *On Revolution.* England: Penguin Books, 1963.

Aulard, François-Alphonse. *La Société des Jacobins: recueil de documents pour l'histoire du club des Jacobins de Paris.* Paris: Jouaust, Noblet, Quantin, 1889–1897.

Auricchio, Laura. *The Marquis: Lafayette Reconsidered.* New York: Vintage, 2014.

Bachaumont, Louis Petit de. *Mémoires secrets pour servir à l'histoire de la République des Lettres en France, depuis MDCCLXII.* London: John Adamson, 1783–1789.

Bacourt, Adolphe Fourier de. *Correspondance entre le comte de Mirabeau et le comte de La Marck pendant les années 1789, 1790 et 1791.* 3 vols. Paris: Vve Le Normant, 1851.

Bailly, Jean-Sylvain. *Mémoires d'un témoin de la Révolution.* 3 vols. Paris: Levrault, Schoell et Cie, 1804.

Bailly, Jean-Sylvain, and Honoré Duveyrier. *Procès-verbal des séances et délibérations de l'Assemblée générale des électeurs de Paris, réunis à l'Hôtel-de-Ville le 14 juillet 1789.* 3 vols. Paris: Baudoin, 1790.

Bailyn, Bernard. *The Ideological Origins of the American Revolution.* Enlarged ed. Cambridge: Belknap Press, 1992.

Barbé-Marbois, François, marquis de. *Our Revolutionary Forefathers: The Letters of François, Marquis Barbé de Marbois.* Edited by E. P. Chase. New York, 1929.

Barrot, Odilon. *Mémoires posthumes de Odilon Barrot.* Paris: Charpentier et Cie, 1875–1876.

Beaufort, Raphael Ledos, ed. *Personal Recollections of the Late Duc de Broglie, 1785–1820.* 2 vols. London: Ward and Downey, 1887.

Bernier, Olivier. *Lafayette: Hero of Two Worlds.* New York: Dutton, 1983.

Bertier de Sauvigny, Guillaume de. *La Restauration, 1815–1830.* Paris: Hachette, 1977.

Blanning, T. C. W. *The Origins of the French Revolutionary Wars.* New York: Longman, 1986.

Boigne, Éléonore-Adèle d'Osmond, comtesse de. *Récits d'une tante: mémoires de la comtesse de Boigne, née d'Osmond.* 3 vols. Paris: Émile-Paul Frères, 1921–1923.

Bonsal, Stephen. *When the French Were Here: A Narrative of the Sojourn of the French Forces in America and Their Contribution to the Yorktown Campaign.* Garden City, NY: Doubleday, Doran, and Company, 1945.

Bouillé, Antoine de. *Manoirs Abandonnes.* Paris: La Société FeniXX, 2020 (1950).

Bouillé, François-Claude-Amour, marquis de. *Mémoires du Marquis de Bouillé.* Paris: Baudouin Frères, 1821.

Boutaric, M. E. *Correspondance secrète inédite de Louis XV sur la politique étrangère avec le Comte de Broglie, Tercier, etc.* 2 vols. Paris: Henri Plon, 1866.

Boyd, Julien P., ed. *The Papers of Thomas Jefferson.* 40 vols. Princeton, NJ: Princeton University Press, 1950–.

Brandon, Edgar Ewing. *Lafayette, Guest of the Nation: A Contemporary Account of the Triumphal Tour of General Lafayette Through the United States in 1824–1825, As Reported by the Local Newspapers.* 3 vols. Oxford, OH: Oxford Historical Press, 1950–1957.

Brands, H. W. *The First American: The Life and Times of Benjamin Franklin.* New York: Anchor Books, 2000.

Brinton, Crane. *The Anatomy of Revolution.* New York: Random House, (1939) 1965.

Brissot, Jacques-Pierre. *Mémoires, 1754–1793.* 2 vols. Paris: Pergamon Press, 1989.

Broglie, Achille-Léon-Victor, duc de. *Souvenirs, du feu duc de Broglie, 1785–1870.* 4 vols. Paris: Calmann Lévy, 1886.

Bullock, Steven C. *Revolutionary Brotherhood: Freemasonry and the Transformation of the American Social Order, 1730–1840.* Chapel Hill: University of North Carolina Press, 1996.

Burke, Edmund. *Reflections on the Revolution in France.* New York: Oxford University Press, 2002.

Calonne, Charles Alexandre de. *De l'état de la France, présent et a venir.* London: Chez Laurent, 1790.

Campan, Jeanne-Louise-Henriette. *Mémoires sur la vie privée de Marie Antoinette.* 3 vols. Paris: Baudoin Frères, 1826.

Carlyle, Thomas. *The French Revolution: A History.* 3 vols. London: Bell, 1902.

Carrel, Armand. *Oeuvres politiques et littéraires.* 5 vols. Paris, 1857–1859.

Castries, René de la Croix de. *Monsieur Thiers.* Paris: Perrin, 1983.

Charavay, Étienne. *Le général La Fayette, 1757–1834.* Paris: Sociéte de l'histoire de la Révolution française, 1898.

Chastellux, François-Jean, Marquis de. *Travels in North-America, in the Years 1780–81–82.* New York, 1828.

Chateaubriand, François-René de. *Mémoires d'outre-tombe.* 6 vols. Paris: Garnier Frères, 1910.

Chernow, Ron. *Alexander Hamilton.* New York: Penguin Press, 2004.

———. *Washington: A Life.* New York: Penguin Books, 2010.

Chinard, Gilbert, ed. *George Washington as the French Knew Him.* New York: Greenwood Press, 1969.

———. *The Letters of Lafayette and Jefferson.* Baltimore: Johns Hopkins Press, 1929.

Clarkson, Thomas. *The History of the Rise, Progress, and Accomplishment of the Abolition of the African Slave-Trade by the British Parliament.* 2 vols. London: L. Taylor, 1808.

Clary, David A. *Adopted Son: Washington, Lafayette, and the Friendship That Saved the Revolution.* New York: Bantam Books, 2007.

Clausewitz, Carl von. *On War.* Translated by Michael Howard and Peter Paret. Princeton, NJ: Princeton University Press, 1989.

Cloquet, Jules. *Souvenirs sur la vie privée du Général Lafayette.* Paris: A. Et W. Galignani et Cie, 1836.

Cobban, Alfred. *The Social Interpretation of the French Revolution.* Great Britain: Cambridge University Press, (1964) 1999.

Coe, Alexis. *You Never Forget Your First: A Biography of George Washington.* New York: Viking, 2020.

Collingham, H. A. C. *The July Monarchy: A Political History of France 1830–1848.* London: Longman, 1988.

Condorcet, Jean-Antoine-Nicolas, Marquis de. *Idées sur le despotisme à, l'usage de ceux qui prononcent ce mot sans l'entendre.* A. Condorcet O'Connor et F. Arago, eds. Paris: Firmin Didot Frères, 1847.

———. *Mémoires de Condorcet, sur la Révolution française, extraits de sa correspondance et de celles de ses amis.* 2 vols. Paris: Ponthieu, 1824.

———. *Réflexions sur l'esclavage des Nègres.* Neufchâtel: La Société Typographique, 1781.

Constant, Benjamin. *Mélanges de littérature et de politique.* Paris: Pichon et Didier, 1829.

Cooper, Duff. *Talleyrand.* New York: Grove Press, (1932) 1997.

Crook, Malcolm. *Napoleon Comes to Power: Democracy and Dictatorship in Revolutionary France.* Cardiff: University of Wales Press, 1998.

Custis, George Washington Parke. *Recollections and Private Memoirs of Washington.* New York: Derby & Jackson, 1860.

The Deane Papers. 5 vols. New York: New York Historical Society, 1887–1880.

Desmoulins, Camille. *Œuvres de Camille Desmoulins.* Paris: Librarie de la Bibliotèque Nationale, 1871.

Doniol, Henri. *Histoire de la participation de la France à l'établissement des États-Unis d'Amérique: Correspondance diplomatique et documents.* 5 vols. Paris: Imprimerie Nationale, 1886–1892.

Doyle, William. *Oxford History of the French Revolution.* 3rd ed. Oxford: Oxford University Press, 1990.

Drury, Bob, and Tom Clavin. *Valley Forge.* New York: Simon & Schuster, 2018.

Dumas, Alexandre. *Mes Mémoires.* 10 vols. Paris: Michel Lévy Frères, 1863–1884.

Dury, Victor. *Petite Histoire de France.* Paris: Hachette, 1883.

Duvergier de Hauranne, Prosper, ed. *Histoire du gouvernement parlementaire en France, 1814–1848.* 10 vols. Paris: Michel Lévy Frères, 1857–1871.

Eckhardt, Celia. *Fanny Wright: Rebel in America.* Cambridge, MA: Harvard University Press, 1984.

Egret, Jean. *The French Pre-Revolution 1787–1788.* Translated by Wesley D. Camp. Chicago: University of Chicago Press, 1977.

Farmer, Lydia Hoyt. *The Life of Lafayette, The Knight of Liberty in Two Worlds and Two Centuries.* New York: Thomas Y. Crowell & Co., 1888.

Ferrières, Charles-Élie de. *Correspondance inédite: 1789, 1790, 1791.* Edited by Henri Carré. Paris: A. Colin, 1932.

Flexner, James Thomas. *George Washington.* 4 vols. Boston: Little Brown, 1965–1972.

———. *The Traitor and the Spy: Benedict Arnold and John André.* New edition. Boston: Little Brown, 1975.

Franklin, Benjamin. *The Papers of Benjamin Franklin.* 42 vols. Edited by Leonard W. Labaree et al. New Haven and London: Yale University Press, 1959–.

Furet, François. *Interpreting the French Revolution.* Translated by Elborg Forster. Cambridge: Cambridge University Press, 1981.

Furet, François, and Mona Ozouf, eds. *A Critical Dictionary of the French Revolution.* Translated by Arthur Goldhammer. Cambridge, MA: Harvard University Press, 1989.

Furstenberg, François. *When the United States Spoke French: Five Refugees Who Shaped a Nation.* New York: Penguin Press, 2014.

Gaines, James R. *For Liberty and Glory: Washington, Lafayette, and their Revolutions.* New York: W.W. Norton & Company, 2007.

Gerson, Noel B. *Statue in Search of a Pedestal: A Biography of the Marquis de Lafayette.* New York: Dodd, Mead, & Co., 1976.

Gigault, Émile, *Vie politique de Marie-Paul-Jean-Roch-Yves-Gilbert Motié, Marquis de Lafayette.* Paris, 1833.

Goldstone, Jack. *Revolution and Rebellion in the Early Modern World.* Berkeley: University of California Press, 1991.

Goldstone, Jack, ed. *The Encyclopedia of Political Revolutions.* Washington, DC: Congressional Quarterly, 1998.

Gottschalk, Louis. *Lady-in-Waiting: The Romance of Lafayette and Aglaé de Hunolstein.* Baltimore: Johns Hopkins Press, 1939.

———. *Lafayette and the Close of the American Revolution.* Chicago: University of Chicago Press, 1942, rpt. 1974.

———. *Lafayette Between the American and the French Revolution, 1783–1789.* Chicago: University of Chicago Press, 1965.

———. *Lafayette Comes to America.* Chicago: University of Chicago Press, 1935.

———. *Lafayette Joins the American Army.* Chicago: University of Chicago Press, 1937.

Gottschalk, Louis, and Margaret Maddox. *Lafayette in the French Revolution: From the October Days Through the Federation.* Chicago: University of Chicago Press, 1973.

―――. *Lafayette in the French Revolution: Through the October Days*. Chicago: University of Chicago Press, 1969.

Gottschalk, Louis, Phyllis S. Pestieau, and Linda J. Pike, eds. *Lafayette: A Guide to the Letters, Documents and Manuscripts in the United States*. Ithaca, NY: Cornell University Press, 1975.

Gough, Hugh. *The Terror in the French Revolution*. 2nd ed. Palgrave Macmillan, (1998) 2014.

Guernon-Ranville, Martial, comte de. *Journal d'un ministre: oeuvre posthume du comte de Guernon-Ranville, ancien membre de l'Académie des sciences, arts et belles-lettres*. 2ème édition. Caen, 1874.

Guizot, François. *Mémoires pour servir à l'histoire de mon temps*. 2ème édition. 8 vols. Paris: Michel Lévy Frères, 1864.

Hamilton, Alexander. *The Papers of Alexander Hamilton*. 25 vols. Edited by Harold C. Syrett. New York: Columbia University Press, 1961–1987.

Hamilton, John C. *The Life of Alexander Hamilton*. vol. 1. New York: Halsted and Voorhies, 1834.

Haussez, baron de. *Mémoires*. 2 vols. Paris: Michel Lévy Frères, 1897.

Hibbert, Christopher. *The Days of the French Revolution*. New York: Morrow Quill, 1980.

Hobsbawm, Eric. *The Age of Revolution*. London: Weidenfeld and Nicolson, 1962.

Holbrook, Sabra. *Lafayette, Man in the Middle*. New York: Atheneum, 1977.

Holton, Woody. *Forced Founders: Indians, Debtors, Slaves, and the Making of the American Revolution in Virginia*. Chapel Hill: University of North Carolina Press, 1999.

Horn, Gerald. *The Counter-Revolution of 1776: Slave Resistance and the Origins of the United States of America*. New York: New York University Press, 2014.

Hugo, Victor. *Choses vues*. Paris: J. Hetzel, 1887.

Hunt, Lynn. *The French Revolution and Human Rights: A Brief Documentary History*. New York: Bedford, 1996.

Huntington, Ebenezer. *Letters Written by Ebenezer Huntington During the American Revolution*. New York: C. F. Heartman, 1915.

Idzerda, Stanley J., ed. *Lafayette in the Age of the American Revolution: Selected Letters and Papers, 1776–1790*. 5 vols. Ithaca: Cornell University Press, 1977–1983.

Israel, Jonathan. *Revolutionary Ideas: An Intellectual History of the French Revolution from The Rights of Man to Robespierre*. Princeton, NJ: Princeton University Press, 2014.

Jacob, Margaret C. *Living the Enlightenment: Freemasonry and Politics in Eighteenth-Century Europe*. Oxford: Oxford University Press, 1991.

―――. *The Radical Enlightenment: Pantheists, Freemasons and Republicans*. 2nd rev. ed. Lafayette, LA: Cornerstone Books, 2006.

Jardin, André, and André-Jean Tudesq. *Restoration & Reaction 1815–1848*. New York: Cambridge University Press, 1988.

Jasanoff, Maya. *Liberty's Exiles: American Loyalists in the Revolutionary World*. New York: Vintage Books, 2011.

Jaurès, Jean. *A Socialist History of the French Revolution*. Translated by Mitchell Abidor. London: Pluto Press, 2015.

Jay, John. *The Selected Papers of John Jay.* 5 vols. Edited by Elizabeth M. Nuxoll. Charlottesville: University of Virginia Press, 2010–.

Jefferson, Thomas. *The Papers of Thomas Jefferson: Original Series.* 44 vols. Edited by Julian P. Boyd. Princeton, NJ: Princeton University Press, 1950–.

———. *The Papers of Thomas Jefferson: Retirement Series.* 14 vols. Edited by J. Jefferson Looney. Princeton, NJ: Princeton University Press, 2004–.

———. *The Papers of Thomas Jefferson: Second Series.* 2 vols. Edited by James A. Bear Jr. and Lucia C. Stanton. Princeton, NJ: Princeton University Press, 1997.

Johnson, Samuel. "Taxation No Tyranny; An Answer to the Resolutions and Address of the American Congress." London: T. Cadell, 1775.

Jones, Colin. *The Longman Companion to the French Revolution.* New York: Longman, 1990.

Jordan, David P. *The King's Trial: Louis XVI vs. The French Revolution.* 25th anniv. ed. Berkeley: University of California Press, (1979) 2004.

Journal of the House of Delegates of the Commonwealth of Virginia, Session Beginning October 18, 1784. Richmond, VA: Thomas White, 1828.

Kafker, Frank A., and James M. Laux, eds. *The French Revolution: Conflicting Interpretations.* New York: Random House, 1968.

Kapp, Friedrich. *Life of John Kalb, Major General in the Revolutionary Army.* New York: Henry Holt and Company, 1884.

Klooster, Wim. *Revolutions in the Atlantic World, New Edition: A Comparative History.* 2nd ed. New York: New York University Press, 2018.

Kramer, Lloyd S. *Lafayette in Two Worlds: Public Cultures and Personal Identities in an Age of Revolutions.* Chapel Hill: University of North Carolina Press, 1996.

Kropotkin, Peter. *The Great French Revolution 1789–1793.* Translated by N. F. Dryhurst. New York: Schocken, 1909.

Lacroix, Sigismond, ed. *Actes de la Commune de Paris pendant la Révolution.* 7 vols. Paris, 1894–1905.

Lafayette, Gilbert du Motier de. *Correspondance inédite de La Fayette, 1793–1801; lettres de prison—lettres d'exil.* Edited by Paris Jules Thomas: C. Delgrave, 1903.

———. *Mémoires, correspondance et manuscrits du général Lafayette.* 6 vols. Paris: H. Fournier Ainé, 1837–1838.

Laffitte, Jacques. *Mémoires de Laffitte.* Edited by Paul Duchon. Paris: Firmin-Didot, 1932.

Lameth, Théodore. *Mémoires.* Paris: Fontemoing, 1913.

Las Cases, Emmanuel-Auguste-Dieudonné, comte de. *Memorial de Sainte Helene: Journal of the Private Life and Conversations of the Emperor Napoleon at Saint Helena.* 4 vols. London: Henry Colburn, 1836.

Lasteyrie du Saillant, Marie Antoinette Virginie de Lafayette, Marquise de. *Vie de Madame de Lafayette.* Paris: Léon Techener Fils, 1869.

La Tour du Pin Gouvernet, Henriette Lucie, marquise de. *Journal d'une femme de 50 ans, 1778–1815.* 2 vols. Paris: Librarie Chapelot, 1920.

Laurens, John. *The Army Correspondence of Colonel John Laurens in the Years 1777–8.* New York: Bradford Club, 1867.

Lawday, David. *The Giant of the French Revolution.* Great Britain: Grove Press, 2009.

Lefebvre, Georges. *The Coming of the French Revolution.* Translated by R. R. Palmer. Princeton, NJ: Princeton University Press, (1947) 2005.

———. *The French Revolution.* Translated by Elizabeth Moss Evanson. New York: Columbia University Press, 1962.

———. *The Thermidorians and the Directory.* Translated by Robert Baldick. New York: Random House, 1964.

Levasseur, Auguste. *Lafayette in America in 1824 and 1825: Or, Journal of a Voyage to the United States.* 2 vols. Translated by John D. Goodman. Philadelphia: Carey and Lea, 1829.

Levasseur, René. *Mémoires de R. Levasseur, de la Sarthe.* 4 vols. Paris: Rapilly, 1829–1831.

Linebaugh, Peter, and Marcus Rediker. *The Many-Headed Hydra: Sailors, Slaves, Commoners, and the Hidden History of the Revolutionary Atlantic.* 2nd ed. Boston: Beacon Press, 2000.

Linton, Marisa. *The Politics of Virtue in Enlightenment France.* Hampshire, UK: Palgrave, 2001.

Lyons, Martyn. *France Under the Directory.* New York: Cambridge University Press, 1975.

Madison, James. *The Writings of James Madison, Comprising His Public Papers and His Private Correspondence, Including His Numerous Letters and Documents Now for the First Time Printed.* 9 vols. Edited by Gaillard Hunt. New York: G. P. Putnam's Sons, 1900.

Maier, Pauline. *American Scripture: Making the Declaration of Independence.* New York: Vintage Books, 1997.

Mansel, Philip. *Louis XVIII.* Rev. ed. Great Britain: Sutton, 1999.

———. *Paris Between Empires: Monarchy and Revolution 1814–1852.* New York: St. Martin's Press, 2001.

Martin, Joseph Plumb. *A Narrative of a Revolutionary Soldier: Some of the Adventures, Dangers, and Sufferings of Joseph Plumb Martin.* New York: Signet Classics, 2001.

Massey, Gregory D. *John Laurens and the American Revolution.* Columbia: University of South Carolina Press, 2000.

Matthews, Andrew. *Revolution and Reaction: Europe 1789–1849.* New York: Cambridge University Press, 2000.

Maurois, André. *Adrienne: The Life of the Marquise de La Fayette.* Translated by Gerard Hopkins. New York: McGraw-Hill, 1961.

McCabe, Linda. *Ardent Adrienne, the Life of Madame de Lafayette.* New York: D. Appleton & Company, 1930.

McCullough, David. *The Greater Journey: Americans in Paris.* New York: Simon & Schuster, 2011.

———. *John Adams.* New York: Simon & Schuster, 2001.

McMahon, Darrin M. *Enemies of Enlightenment: The French Counter-Revolution and the Making of Modernity.* New York: Oxford University Press, 2001.

McPhee, Peter. *Robespierre: A Revolutionary Life.* New Haven, CT: Yale University Press, 2012.

———. *A Social History of France.* New York: Routledge, 1992.

Mellon, Stanley. *The Political Uses of History: A Study of Historians in the French Restoration.* Stanford, CA: Stanford University Press, 1958.

Meng, John J., ed. *Despatches and Instructions of Conrad Alexandre Gérard, 1778–1780; Correspondence of the First French Minister to the United States with the Comte de Vergennes.* Baltimore: Johns Hopkins, 1939.

Mercier, Louis-Sébastien. *Paris pendant la Révolution (1789–1798); ou, Le nouveau Paris.* 2 vols. Paris: Poulet-Malassis, 1862.

———. *Tableau de Paris.* 12 vols. Amsterdam, 1783.

Middlekauff, Robert. *The Glorious Cause: The American Revolution, 1763–1789.* Rev. ed. New York: Oxford University Press, 2005.

Mill, John Stuart. *Collected Works of John Stuart Mill.* 33 vols. Edited by J. M. Robson. London: Routledge and Kegan Paul, 1963–1991.

Mirabeau, Honoré-Gabriel Riquetti, comte de. *Mémoires biographiques, littéraires et politiques de Mirabeau.* 8 vols. Paris: Adolphe Guyot, 1834–1835.

Monroe, James. *The Writings of James Monroe, 1778–1831.* 7 vols. Edited by Stanislaus Murray Hamilton. Washington: United States Congress, 1849.

Moore, Lucy. *Liberty: The Lives and Times of Six Women in Revolutionary France.* New York: Harper Press, 2007.

Moré, Charles-Albert, comte de. *A French Volunteer of the War of Independence.* Translated by Robert B. Douglas. New York: J.W. Bouton, 1897.

Morgan, Edmund. *American Slavery, American Freedom.* New York: W.W. Norton and Co., 1975.

———. *The Birth of the Republic 1763–89.* 4th ed. Chicago: University of Chicago Press, 2013.

Morgan, Lady Sydney. *France.* 2 vols. London: Henry Colburn, 1817.

———. *Passages from my Autobiography.* New York: Appleton, 1859.

Morris, Gouverneur. *The Diary and Letters of Gouverneur Morris.* 2 vols. Edited by Anne Cary Morris. New York: Charles Scribner's Sons, 1888.

———. *Diary of the French Revolution.* 2 vols. Edited by Beatrix Cary Davenport. Boston: Houghton Mifflin, 1939.

Morse, Samuel F. B. *Samuel F.B. Morse: His Letters and Journals.* 2 vols. Boston: Houghton Mifflin Company, 1914.

Mousnier, Roland. *The Institutions of France Under the Absolute Monarchy, 1598–1789.* 2 vols. Translated by Brian Pearce and Arthur Goldhammer. Chicago: Chicago University Press, 1979.

Nash, Gary. *The Unknown American Revolution: The Unruly Birth of Democracy and the Struggle to Create America.* New York: Penguin Books, 2005.

Necker, Jacques. *Compte rendu au roi, par M. Necker, directeur général des finances, au mois de janvier 1781.* Paris: Imprimerie Royale, 1781.

Neely, Sylvia. *Lafayette and the Liberal Ideal, 1814–1824: Politics and Conspiracy in an Age of Reaction.* Carbondale: Southern Illinois University Press, 1991.

Nelson, Paul David. *Anthony Wayne, Soldier of the Early Republic.* Bloomington: Indiana University Press, 1985.

Neuilly, Ange Achille Charles, comte de. *Dix années d'emigration: souvenirs et correspondance du comte de Neuilly.* Paris: Douniol, 1865.

Palmer, R. R. *The Age of Democratic Revolution.* Princeton: Princeton University Press, (1959, 1964) 2014.

———. *Twelve Who Ruled: The Year of the Terror in the French Revolution*. Princeton, NJ, 1941. Reprint, Princeton, NJ: Princeton University Press, 2005.

Pasquier, Étienne-Denis, *Mémoires du chancelier Pasquier*. 6 vols. Paris: 1893–1895.

Paul, Joel Richard. *Unlikely Allies: How a Merchant, a Playwright, and a Spy Saved the American Revolution*. New York: Riverhead Books, 2010.

Perroud, Claude Marie. *J.-P. Brissot mémoires; correspondance et papiers*. 3 vols. Paris, 1912.

Pialoux, Paul. *Lafayette: Trois Révolutions pour la Liberté*. Brioude: Editions Watel, 1989.

Pinkney, David. *French Revolution of 1830*. Princeton, NJ: Princeton University Press, 1971.

Plutarch. *The Parallel Lives*. Vol. 9. Loeb Classical Library: Cambridge and London, 1920.

Popkin, Jeremy. *A New World Begins: The History of the French Revolution*. New York: Basic Books, 2019.

———. *Revolutionary News: The Press in France, 1789–1799*. Durham, NC: Duke University Press, 1990.

Price, Munro. *The Perilous Crown: France Between Revolutions*. Basingstoke, UK: Pan Books, 2007.

Procès-verbal de l'Assemblée de Notables tenue à Versailles en l'année MDCCLXXXVII. Paris, 1788.

Raynal, Abbé Guillaume. *Histoire philosophique et politique des établissements du Commerce des Européens dans les deux Indes*. 10 vols. Geneva: Pellet, 1783.

Rémusat, Charles de. *Mémoires de ma vie*. Paris: Perrin, 2017.

Ross, Stew. *Where Did They Put The Guillotine?* 2 vols. Yooper Publications, 2014.

Rudé, George. *The Crowd in the French Revolution*. Oxford: Oxford University Press, 1967.

Ryan, Alan. *On Politics: A History of Political Thought: From Herodotus to the Present*. New York: Liveright, 2012.

Saint-Germain, Claude-Louis, comte de. *Mémoires de M. le comte de St. Germain*. Amsterdam: M.M. Ray, 1779.

Sarrans, Bernard. *Memoirs of General Lafayette and of the French Revolution of 1830*. 2 vols. London: Richard Bentley, 1832.

Savas, Theodore, and J. David Dameron. *A Guide to the Battles of the American Revolution*. New York: Savas Beatie, 2010.

Schama, Simon. *Citizens: A Chronicle of the French Revolution*. New York: Vintage, 1989.

Schiff, Stacy. *A Great Improvisation: Franklin, France, and the Birth of America*. New York: Henry Holt, 2005.

Schutz, John A., and Douglass Adair, eds. *The Spur of Fame: Dialogues of John Adams and Benjamin Rush, 1805–1813*. San Marino, CA: Huntington Library, 1966.

Scurr, Ruth. *Fatal Purity: Robespierre and the French Revolution*. New York: Owl Books, 2006.

Ségur, Louis-Philippe, comte de. *Mémoires, souvenirs et anecdotes*. 3 vols. Paris: Firmin Didot, Fréres, Fils, et Cie, 1859.

Sieyès, Emmanuel, *Qu'est-ce que le tiers état?* Paris: Au siège de la Société de l'Histoire de la Révolution Française, 1888.

Skocpol, Theda. *States and Social Revolutions*. New York: Cambridge University Press, 1979.

Smith, Paul H., et al., eds. *Letters of Delegates to Congress, 1774–1789*. 26 vols. Washington, DC: Library of Congress, 1976–2000.

Soboul, Albert. *The Sans-Culottes*. Translated by Remy Inglis Hall. Princeton, NJ: Princeton University Press, (1968) 1980.

Spalding, Paul S. *Lafayette: Prisoner of State*. Columbia: University of South Carolina Press, 2010.

Sparks, Jared, ed. *Correspondence of the American Revolution; Being Letters of Eminent Men to George Washington, from the Time of His Taking Command of the Army to the End of His Presidency*. 4 vols. Boston: Little Brown & Company, 1853.

———. *The Life of Gouverneur Morris: With Selections from His Correspondence and Miscellaneous Papers; Detailing Events in the American Revolution, the French Revolution, and in the Political History of the United States*. 2 vols. Boston: Gray & Bowen, 1832.

———. *Writings of Washington*. 12 vols. Boston: Tappan and Dennet, 1834–1837.

Spitzer, Alan B. *Old Hatreds and Young Hopes*. Cambridge: Harvard University Press, 1971.

Stendhal. *Souvenirs d'égotism*. Paris: Gaillimard, 1927.

Sullivan, John. *Letters and Papers of Major-General John Sullivan*. 3 vols. Edited by Otis G. Hammond. Concord: New Hampshire Historical Society, 1930–1939.

Sumner, Charles. *Lafayette: An Oration*. New York: H. H. Lloyd, 1861.

Sydenham, M. J. *The Girondins*. Westport, CT: Greenwood Press, 1961.

Tackett, Timothy. *Becoming a Revolutionary: The Deputies of the French National Assembly and the Emergence of a Revolutionary Culture (1789–1790)*. University Park: Pennsylvania State University Press, 2006.

———. *The Coming of the Terror in the French Revolution*. Cambridge, MA: Harvard University Press, 2015.

———. *When the King Took Flight*. Cambridge, MA: Harvard University Press, 2004.

Taillemite, Etienne. *La Fayette*. Paris: Fayard, 1989.

Talleyrand-Périgord, Charles-Maurice de. *Mémoires du prince de Talleyrand*. 5 vols. Paris, 1891–1892.

Thacher, James. *A Military Journal During the American Revolutionary War, From 1775 to 1783*. Boston: Richardson and Lord, 1823.

Tocqueville, Alexis de. *The Ancien Régime and the French Revolution*. New York: Anchor, 1955.

Tourtier-Bonazzi, Chantal de. *Lafayette: Documents conservés en France*. Paris: Archives Nationales, 1976.

Tourzel, Louise Elisabeth de Croÿ d'Havré, duchesse de. *Mémoires de madame la duchesse de Tourzel: gouvernante des enfants de France pendant les années 1789, 1790, 1791, 1792, 1793, 1795*. Paris: E. Plan, 1883.

Tower, Charlemagne, Jr. *The Marquis de La Fayette in the American Revolution*. 2 vols. Philadelphia: J. B. Lippincott, 1901.

Traugott, Mark. *The Insurgent Barricade*. Berkeley: University of California Press, 2010.

Tulard, Jean, Jean François Fayard, and Alfred Fierro. *Histoire et Dictionnaire de la Révolution Française 1789–1799*. Paris: Robert Laffont, 1998.

Unger, Harlow Giles. *Lafayette*. Hoboken, NJ: Wiley, 2002.

Vanderkemp, F. A. "Extracts from the Vanderkemp Papers." *Buffalo Historical Society Publications*, vol 2. Buffalo: Bigelow Brothers, 1880.

Voltaire. *Candide ou l'optimisme*. Holland, 1761.

Vowell, Sarah. *Lafayette in the Somewhat United States*. New York: Roverhead Books, 2015.

Washington, George. *The Papers of George Washington: Confederation Series*. 6 vols. Edited by W. W. Abbot. Charlottesville: University Press of Virginia, 1992–1997.

———. *The Papers of George Washington: Presidential Series*. 19 vols. Edited by David R. Hoth. Charlottesville: University of Virginia Press, 1987–2016.

———. *The Papers of George Washington: Retirement Series*. 4 vols. Edited by W. W. Abbot and Edward G. Lengel. Charlottesville: University Press of Virginia, 1998–1999.

———. *The Papers of George Washington: Revolutionary War Series*. 26 vols. Edited by Philander D. Chase and Frank E. Grizzard Jr. Charlottesville: University Press of Virginia, 1985–.

Wharton, Francis. *The Revolutionary Diplomatic Correspondence of the United States*. 6 vols. Washington, DC: Government Printing Office, 1889.

Whitlock, Brand. *La Fayette*. 2 vols. New York: Appleton, 1929.

Whitman, Walt. *Lafayette in Brooklyn*. New York: George D. Smith, 1905.

Willard, Emma. *Journals and Letters from France and Great Britain*. Troy, NY: N. Tuttle, 1833.

Willis, Nathaniel Parker. *Pencillings by the Way*. London: H. G. Bohn, 1846.

Wood, Gordon S. *The Radicalism of the American Revolution*. New York: Vintage Books, 1992.

Wright, Constance. *Madame de Lafayette*. Borodino Books, (1959) 2017.

Young, Arthur. *Arthur Young's Travels in France during the Years 1787, 1788, 1789*. London: George Bell and Sons, 1909.

INDEX

Headnote: MdL stands for marquis de Lafayette

Credit: Brandi Duncan

Mike Duncan is one of the most popular history podcasters in the world and author of the *New York Times*–bestselling book, *The Storm Before the Storm: The Beginning of the End of the Roman Republic*. His award-winning series, *The History of Rome*, remains a legendary landmark in the history of podcasting. Duncan's ongoing series, *Revolutions*, explores the great political revolutions that have driven the course of modern history.

PublicAffairs is a publishing house founded in 1997. It is a tribute to the standards, values, and flair of three persons who have served as mentors to countless reporters, writers, editors, and book people of all kinds, including me.

I. F. STONE, proprietor of *I. F. Stone's Weekly*, combined a commitment to the First Amendment with entrepreneurial zeal and reporting skill and became one of the great independent journalists in American history. At the age of eighty, Izzy published *The Trial of Socrates*, which was a national bestseller. He wrote the book after he taught himself ancient Greek.

BENJAMIN C. BRADLEE was for nearly thirty years the charismatic editorial leader of *The Washington Post*. It was Ben who gave the *Post* the range and courage to pursue such historic issues as Watergate. He supported his reporters with a tenacity that made them fearless and it is no accident that so many became authors of influential, best-selling books.

ROBERT L. BERNSTEIN, the chief executive of Random House for more than a quarter century, guided one of the nation's premier publishing houses. Bob was personally responsible for many books of political dissent and argument that challenged tyranny around the globe. He is also the founder and longtime chair of Human Rights Watch, one of the most respected human rights organizations in the world.

· · ·

For fifty years, the banner of Public Affairs Press was carried by its owner Morris B. Schnapper, who published Gandhi, Nasser, Toynbee, Truman, and about 1,500 other authors. In 1983, Schnapper was described by *The Washington Post* as "a redoubtable gadfly." His legacy will endure in the books to come.

Peter Osnos, *Founder*